Cracking the GRE® Chemistry Subject Test

THE STAFF OF THE PRINCETON REVIEW

THIRD EDITION

Penguin
Random
House

PrincetonReview.com

The Princeton Review
24 Prime Parkway, Suite 201
Natick, MA 01760
E-mail: editorialsupport@review.com

Published in the United States by Penguin Random House, LLC, New York, and in
Canada by Random House of Canada, a division of Penguin Random House Ltd.,
Toronto.

ISBN: 978-0-375-76489-9

Printed in the United States of America on partially recycled paper.

10

Third Edition

Editorial

Rob Franek, Senior VP, Publisher
Casey Cornelius, VP Content Development
Mary Beth Garrick, Director of Production
Selena Coppock, Managing Editor
Meave Shelton, Senior Editor
Colleen Day, Editor
Sarah Litt, Editor
Aaron Riccio, Editor
Orion McBean, Editorial Assistant

Random House Publishing Team

Tom Russell, Publisher
Alison Stoltzfus, Publishing Manager
Melinda Ackell, Associate Managing Editor
Ellen Reed, Production Manager
Andrea Lau, Designer

ACKNOWLEDGMENTS

A special thanks to Adam Robinson, who conceived of and perfected the Joe Bloggs approach to standardized tests and many of the other successful techniques used by The Princeton Review.

Also, thanks to Allegra Burton, Stephen White, Maria Dente, Brian Gibney, Dawn Yarne, and Jerry Abrams for their invaluable contributions.

CONTENTS

1

About the GRE
Chemistry Subject Test

ABOUT THE GRE CHEMISTRY SUBJECT TEST

The General and Subject Graduate Record Examinations (GRE) are created and administered by the Educational Testing Service Inc. (ETS), a private, for-profit corporation located in Princeton, New Jersey. Official ETS information about the General GRE and Chemistry GRE can be found online at **www.gre.org**. Here's additional contact information for ETS:

Address: GRE-ETS
            P.O. Box 6000
            Princeton, NJ 08541-6000

Phone: 1-609-771-7670
            1-866-473-4373
            Monday–Friday 8:00 A.M. – 7:45 P.M. EST (except for U.S. holidays)

Fax: 1-609-771-7906

E-mail: Use form provided at www.gre.org

GRE CHEMISTRY TOPICS

The GRE Chemistry Subject Test consists of: *Inorganic/General Chemistry* (25%), *Organic Chemistry* (30%), *Physical Chemistry* (30%), and *Analytical Chemistry* (15%). However, the fractional weight on Physical Chemistry is a bit misleading; ETS has grouped topics under Physical Chemistry that are traditionally considered General Chemistry topics, such as *equilibrium, colligative properties, electron configuration*, and *rate laws*. So actually only about 15–20% of the exam is really the hard-core stuff learned in a Physical Chemistry course.

TEST DATES

Currently, the Chemistry GRE is offered on just three Saturdays throughout the year: in April, November, and December. So it is important to plan to take the test well in advance of any graduate school application to allow yourself the option, if necessary, of retaking the exam.

Note that students claiming special circumstances may request to take the test on the Monday following each Saturday testing date. Monday testers always receive a different exam since ETS is always concerned about minimizing any chance of cheating.

TESTING FEE

As of press time, the fee is $130 if you are taking the exam on U.S. soil and $150 everywhere else in the world. But don't be surprised if it goes up $5 or $10 in the next year or so.

TEST FORMAT

Unlike the General GRE, all GRE Subject Tests are conventional paper and pencil exams. The Chemistry GRE consists of about 136 independent multiple choice questions of equal weight. Each question has five answer choices—(A) through (E)—which you select by bubbling in the proper oval on the answer sheet.

TESTING TIME

The permitted testing time for the GRE Chemistry Subject Test is 2 hours and 50 minutes. Considering that there are about 136 questions, testers have, on average, 1.25 minutes (one minute, fifteen seconds) per question. Even though each question counts equally, some questions take more time than others. Therefore, it is essential that testers who endemically run long when taking exams skip the long questions in order to peg a greater number of the short ones.

SCORING

Testers receive their scores by mail six weeks after the test date. ETS counts up how many questions the tester answered correctly and then subtracts $\frac{1}{4}$ point for each question answered incorrectly. Questions left blank do not count for or against the score.

The calculated number is the *raw score*. Then the raw score is converted into a *scaled score* in the range of 200–990, where 200 is the lowest possible score and 990 is the highest possible score (although sometimes the highest possible score for a particular test administration can be less than 990, due to statistical weirdness). Also included will be a percentile score, which indicates what percentage of the testing population scored below that tester. For example, here's the raw/scaled score conversion key that applies to the practice test in the back of this book:

TOTAL SCORE					
Raw Score	Scaled Score	%	Raw Score	Scaled Score	%
141	950	99	76–78	690	62
139–140	940	99	73–75	680	60
137–138	930	98	71–72	670	58
135–136	920	97	68–70	660	54
133–134	910	96	65–67	650	52
131–132	900	95	63–64	640	49
			60–62	630	46
129–130	890	94	57–59	620	43
127–128	880	93	54–56	610	40
124–126	870	92	52–53	600	38
121–123	860	90			
119–120	850	89	49–51	590	34
116–118	840	88	46–48	580	31
113–115	830	86	44–45	570	28
111–112	820	85	41–43	560	25
108–110	810	84	38–40	550	22
105–107	800	82	36–37	540	19
			33–35	530	17
103–104	790	80	30–32	520	14
100–102	780	79	28–29	510	12
97–99	770	78	25–27	500	9
95–96	760	76			
92–94	750	74	22–24	490	7
89–91	740	73	20–21	480	6
87–88	730	71	17–19	470	4
84–86	720	69	14–16	460	3
81–83	710	67	12–13	450	2
79–80	700	64	9–11	440	1
			6–8	430	1
			4–5	420	1
			1–3	410	1
			0	400	1

To Guess or Not to Guess

Although you are penalized for incorrect answers, statistically it DOESN'T matter whether you leave questions blank or not. Here's why: Say that the test is almost over and you haven't gotten to the last 10 questions. If you leave them blank, you get no credit, because blank questions equal 0 points according to ETS's scoring method. Now, if, instead, you guess on all of them and randomly choose one of the five answer choices for each, probability says that you'd likely get 2 out of the 10 correct. Considering the way the exam is scored, this means that you would get $2(+1) + 8\left(-\dfrac{1}{4}\right) = 0$ points, the same as if you left them blank.

ALWAYS GUESS ANYWAY. First of all, leaving blanks on a bubble answer sheet can increase the risk of misplacing subsequent bubbled answer choices, and a seriously messed-up answer sheet is the surest reason for having to take the test again. Secondly, the minute you can rule out one or more of the answer choices in a question, guessing works to your advantage. Practice *Process of Elimination*, because even if it doesn't always lead to just one answer choice, eliminating some choices in those questions that you are uncertain about will always earn you a better score.

On the Day of the Test

According to ETS, you should be at the testing center no later than 8:30 A.M., or else you risk being turned away. Plan on being at the testing center for a total of $\pm\dfrac{1}{2}$ hours because of extra time required for administrative paperwork associated with the exam. When you're done, go bowling.

Required/Restricted Items on Test Day

You need a bunch of No. 2 pencils and a big eraser. As far as documentation, once you register for the exam, ETS will remind you of the required documentation that you need on test day. Basically, you'll need the registration card that they send you in advance as well as a photo ID with your signature on it, such as a passport, driver's license, military ID, or national ID. If you don't have one of these, pay extra attention to ETS's fine print when you register for the exam to see what you will need to bring instead; otherwise, they will have no problem delaying you outside the testing center.

The list of forbidden items is long and glorious and can be found in the GRE registration materials or on the GRE website. But the most important items to mention at this point are: *no calculators*, *no timers that make noise*, and *no headsets*!

Sending Off Scores

When you register for the Chemistry GRE (and again on the day of the exam), you can list up to four schools to which you want ETS to send your scores for no fee. Having your scores sent to additional schools will cost you $13 per school.

Note that GRE scores are good for five years.

Canceling Scores

You can void the exam at any point during the morning of the test. Voiding essentially results in your answer key getting tossed in the trash, and no record of that day ever appears on any future GRE report. Honestly, you should only consider doing this if you're convinced that things have gone seriously wrong (for example, if you have a 104° F fever and have drooled all over the answer sheet).

TAKING THE TEST MORE THAN ONCE

ETS will let you take the GRE Chemistry Subject Test as many times as you want—after all, they make at least $130 a pop.

However, since all previous scores show up on the report sent to schools (only voided tests are left off), make every attempt to take the GRE just once. Don't take the test without preparing. Each additional GRE score on your report makes you look more like a professional test taker and less like a potential graduate student.

ETS PRACTICE GRE CHEMISTRY SUBJECT TEST

Once you register for the exam, ETS will send you a full-length Chemistry GRE practice test. It's a very good resource, especially to take as a warm-up a couple of days before the exam to get into the swing of things.

2

Inorganic Chemistry

GENERAL CHEMISTRY

There are more than 105 elements, and all matter consists of these elements or compounds composed of them. Chemistry is the study of how these elements form compounds and, in turn, how they react with each other. We will cover eight topics under this heading: *Atomic Structure, Periodic Trends, Bonding, Chemical Equilibrium, Acid-Base Chemistry, Chemical Properties of the Elements, Metal Coordination Complexes,* and *Special Topics.*

ATOMIC STRUCTURE

THE FUNDAMENTAL PARTICLES

The fundamental particles that constitute all matter are protons, neutrons, and electrons—as far as the Chemistry GRE is concerned. In reality, protons and neutrons may be made of even more fundamental particles, such as quarks. Furthermore, there are other mass-bearing particles that are not associated with atoms, such as neutrinos, humming around the universe. But the Chemstry GRE says all atoms are made of protons, neutrons, and electrons, so let's leave it at that.

The basic properties of the fundamental particles:

	Mass (in g)	Mass (in *amu*)	Charge Unit	Magnetic Spin
Proton	1.673×10^{-24}	1.007	+1	$\pm\dfrac{1}{2}$
Neutron	1.675×10^{-24}	1.008	0	$\pm\dfrac{1}{2}$
Electron	9.110×10^{-28}	0.0001	–1	$\pm\dfrac{1}{2}$

The conversion factor between grams (g) and atomic mass units (amu) is 6.02×10^{23} amu/g. In case you were wondering, that's where *Avogadro's number* (6.02×10^{23}) comes from.

ATOMIC SYMBOLS

The nuclei of atoms are made of protons and neutrons. For that reason, protons and neutrons are sometimes collectively called **nucleons**. The number and type of nucleons in a particular nucleus are what give an atom its identity.

The **mass number** is the total number of protons and neutrons in the nucleus. It is called the mass number because it is the approximate mass, in amu, of the nucleus since each proton and neutron has a mass of about one amu. Mass number is represented with the letter A.

The **atomic number** is the total number of protons in the nucleus. It is called the atomic number because the chemical identity of an atom (i.e., what element that atom is) is entirely determined by the number of protons. Atomic number is represented with the letter Z.

Each atomic symbol consists of a one- or two-letter elemental identifier, E, preceded with the mass number as a superscript and the atomic number as a subscript.

$$^A_Z E$$

For example, the atomic symbols for nuclei with the following compositions are:

$$9 \text{ Protons} + 10 \text{ Neutrons} = {}^{19}_{9}\text{F}, \text{ or simply } {}^{19}\text{F}$$

$$18 \text{ Protons} + 22 \text{ Neutrons} = {}^{40}_{18}\text{Ar}, \text{ or simply } {}^{40}\text{Ar}$$

Very often, the atomic number is left out because the atomic number and elemental identifier are redundant.

Some final comments about neutrons. Although the number of neutrons (N) is not explicitly given in the atomic symbol, it can be calculated as $N = A - Z$. Nuclei that have the same number of protons (Z) but different numbers of neutrons (N), called **isotopes**, have nearly exact chemical and physical properties. Among the many versions of definitions for isotopes, here's one that seems to be the most useful for getting the correct answer on a multiple-choice test:

> **DEFINITION:** Isotopes are two or more nuclei of the same element that have different mass numbers.

BINDING ENERGY

An atom of a stable isotope weighs *less* than the sum of the masses of its constituents. For instance, the total mass of the particles in a ${}^{200}_{80}\text{Hg}$ atom is 201.66588 amu, but the observed atomic mass of ${}^{200}_{80}\text{Hg}$ is only 199.9683 amu. The missing 1.6975 amu of matter has been converted to the energy that's required to overcome proton-proton repulsion and hold the nucleus together. In the case of ${}^{200}_{80}\text{Hg}$, the **binding energy** is E_{bind} = 931 MeV or 7.90 MeV/nucl. The binding energy of elements 1–8 (including ${}^{16}_{8}\text{O}$) is low and proportional to the number of protons and neutrons (nucleons). For the elements from ${}^{16}_{8}\text{O}$ to ${}^{238}_{92}\text{U}$, the binding energy of the stable isotopes is almost constant, at about 8 MeV per nucleon. The energies involved in nuclear reactions far exceed those involved in chemical reactions. For the former, the interconversion of mass and energy is normal. For the latter, it is negligible. In nuclear reactions, the *total mass and energy* of the reacting species does not change during the course of the reaction.

BALANCING NUCLEAR REACTIONS

Balancing nuclear reactions requires conservation of 1) mass, 2) charge, 3) energy, and 4) spin.

Conserving mass and charge means that the sum of the mass numbers (superscripts) and atomic numbers (subscripts) on either side of a nuclear reaction arrow must be equal. For example, look at the following:

$$\ {}^{3}_{1}\text{H} + {}^{6}_{3}\text{Li} \rightarrow ?$$

$$\ {}^{222}_{86}\text{Rn} \rightarrow {}^{218}_{84}\text{Po} + ?$$

The missing nuclei are ${}^{9}_{4}\text{Be}$ and ${}^{4}_{2}\text{He}$, respectively.

For the Chemistry GRE, don't worry about using neutrinos and antineutrinos to conserve magnetic spin.

Nuclear Decay, A.K.A. Radioactivity

Some nuclei have endemic deficiencies and instabilities that cause them to undergo nuclear decay in an attempt to correct their problems.

DEFINITION: The nucleus prior to nuclear decay is called the parent, and the nucleus formed as a result of nuclear decay is called the daughter nucleus.

There are three main modes of nuclear decay: α, β, and γ, where β decay is actually a category of three subtypes.

Type of Decay	Nuclear Transformation	Emitted Nuclear Particle	Example
Alpha, α	Loss of 2p's and 2n's	High velocity ^4_2He, also called an **alpha particle**	$^{238}\text{U} \rightarrow {}^{234}\text{Th} + {}^4\text{He}$
Beta Family			
Normal Beta, β^-	$^1_0\text{n} \rightarrow {}^1_{+1}\text{p} + {}^0_{-1}\text{e}$	High velocity $^0_{-1}\text{e}$, also called a **beta particle**	$^{32}\text{P} \rightarrow {}^{32}\text{S} + {}^0_{-1}\text{e}$
Electron Capture	$^1_{+1}\text{p} + {}^0_{-1}\text{e} \rightarrow {}^1_0\text{n}$	None	$^{50}\text{V} + {}^0_{-1}\text{e} \rightarrow {}^{50}\text{Ti}$
Positron Emission, β^+	$^1_{+1}\text{p} \rightarrow {}^1_0\text{n} + {}^0_{+1}\text{e}$	High velocity $^0_{+1}\text{e}$, called a **positron**	$^{54}\text{Co} \rightarrow {}^{54}\text{Fe} + {}^0_{+1}\text{e}$
Gamma, γ	Loss of energy	Gamma ray photon	$^{99m}\text{Tc} \rightarrow {}^{99}\text{Tc} + {}^0_0\gamma$

proton $\left({}^1_+\text{p}\right)$; neutron $\left({}^1_0\text{n}\right)$; electron $\left({}^0_{-1}\text{e}\right)$; positron $\left({}^0_{+1}\text{e}\right)$

Some things to keep in mind:

1. The electron configurations of atoms are always ignored during nuclear transformations because the energy released is so large; electrons around the nuclei are completely scrambled.

2. High velocity ^4_2He, also called **alpha particles**, are just helium nuclei with lots of energy and no electrons. Once emitted in alpha decay, they smash into nearby atoms, slow down, steal two electrons from someone else, and then settle into life as ordinary, inert He atoms.

3. Positron emission and electron capture result in the same overall nuclear transformation; only the mechanism is different.

4. The mass number of nuclei that undergo gamma decay is tagged with the letter *m*, which stands for **metastable**, so that the higher energy parent nucleus can be distinguished from the lower energy daughter nucleus.

5. Finally, some find it useful to sum up things this way:

   - **Alpha:** Daughter has mass number 4 less than parent, atomic number 2 less than parent.

- **Beta:** Daughter will always be a different element but will have the same mass number as parent.
- **Gamma:** Daughter is identical to parent, except it has less energy.

STABILITY AND HALF-LIFE

The total number of nuclei that decay in a given time is proportional to the total number of nuclei present.

- The probability that a nucleus will decay in a given time is constant and independent of the surrounding of the nucleus. This is called a **first-order decay**. The expression that relates the number of nuclei n that remain at time t to the number originally present, n_0, at time $t = 0$ is $n = n_0 e^{-kt}$, where k is a first-order rate constant. In a first-order decay, the time required for any amount of material to decay by half is constant and independent of the amount originally present. From the previous equation, we can derive: $t_{\frac{1}{2}} = \dfrac{\ln 2}{k} = \dfrac{0.693}{k}$. If the half-life of a radioactive substance is one day, then this means that one day is required for 1 mg, 1 g, 1 kg or 1 ton of that substance to decay to half of its original mass.

- While all elements with $z > 82$ are radioactively decaying toward $^{206}_{82}\text{Pb}$, they are observed because these nuclear reactions can have long half-lives, e.g., $^{234}_{92}\text{U} \rightarrow {}^{230}_{90}\text{Th} + {}^{4}_{2}\text{He}$ has a half-life of 245,000 years.

Transmutation

Artificial transmutation is the process by which one element is transformed into another. The first artificial transmutation was carried out in 1919 by Sir E. Rutherford, and it looked like this: $^{14}_{7}\text{N} + {}^{4}_{2}\text{He} \rightarrow {}^{17}_{8}\text{O} + {}^{1}_{1}\text{H}$. High energies are necessary to bring positively charged nuclei close enough together for a fusion to take place. One method of fusing two nuclei is to use a **particle accelerator**.

- When an accelerated particle such as a neutron strikes a target nuclei, the nucleus can split into two or more fragments, in a process called **nuclear fission**.
- When an accelerated particle is captured by a target nucleus to produce a larger nucleus, this process is called **nuclear fusion**.
- When $^{235}_{92}\text{U}$ is bombarded by slow neutrons, fission occurs, resulting in several fission products: $^{235}_{92}\text{U} + {}^{1}_{0}\text{n} \rightarrow {}^{139}_{56}\text{Ba} + {}^{94}_{36}\text{Kr} + 3{}^{1}_{0}\text{n}$. The ^{235}U fission is a potential **chain reaction** because it produces three neutrons for every one that's used to initiate the fission of one nucleus. Each fission of a nucleus liberates neutrons that will cause the fission of more than one nucleus.

SIZE AND SHAPE OF THE NUCLEUS

Neutron-scattering experiments have shown that the radius of a nucleus is proportional to the cubic root of its mass number:

$$r = \left(1.33 \times 10^{-13}\right) \bullet \sqrt[3]{A} \text{ cm}$$

The entire atomic radii, including the electron clouds, are about twenty thousand times these figures. Many nuclei are spherical, and many are elongated like footballs.

ELECTRON CONFIGURATION

The energy and distance from the nucleus of an electron is quantized, meaning that it can only have certain values. A more rigorous treatment of this follows later in the Physical Chemistry portion of this manual. For now, the goal is to come up with the electron configuration of a particular atom or ion; thus we will use conclusions obtained from the Bohr model of an atom to get started.

> **DEFINITION:** A Bohr atom is an atom with only one electron. Therefore H, He⁺, Li²⁺ all qualify as Bohr atoms.

PRINCIPLE QUANTUM NUMBER, n

In a Bohr atom, the electron orbit around the nucleus can be thought of as simply a spherical path. Only paths that are certain energies (distances) away from the nucleus are permitted. These certain distances, called **energy levels** or **shells**, are numbered, starting with the innermost one and counting away from the nucleus. They are labeled just as they're counted: $n = 1$, $n = 2$, $n = 3$, etc. (so there is no such thing as an $n = 0$ energy level). Once we begin counting, we could continue forever, because there is an infinite number of energy levels.

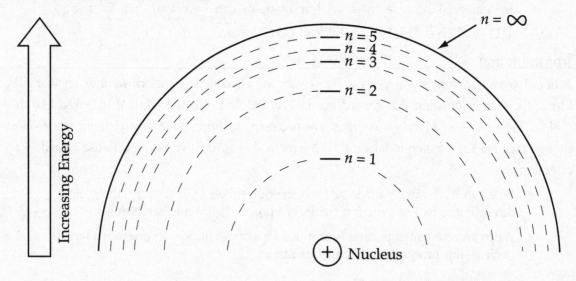

Bohr Model

Bohr Model

The last energy level of an atom is defined as $n = \infty$. Infinity has no practical consequence here, though, since the spacing between energy levels decreases with increasing n's. By the time one counts up to $n = 100$ or so, the distance from the nucleus doesn't change anymore, and thus the atom has an outer boundary.

One last thought: Each successive n is bigger, allowing it to accommodate more electrons. The Bohr model shows that the number of electrons that can fit in a given energy level, n, is related by

$$\text{number of electrons} = 2n^2$$

So for the first four energy levels, an atom can accommodate 2 ($n = 1$), 8 ($n = 2$), 18 ($n = 3$), and 32 ($n = 4$) electrons per shell, respectively.

In sum, here's what to remember for the Chemistry GRE regarding the principle quantum number, n.

1. **Energy** and **distance** (from the nucleus) are synonymous terms when talking about atomic electrons.

2. **Energy levels** (also called *shells*) go from $n = 1$ to $n = \infty$.

3. The spacing between energy levels decreases with increasing distance from the nucleus (or with increasing n, or with increasing energy).

4. **Ground state** configuration is one in which the electrons are in the lowest available energy levels.

5. **Excited state** configuration is one in which the electron is NOT in the lowest available energy level.

6. The number of electrons that can fit in a given n equals $2n^2$.

7. **Valence electrons** are those electrons with the largest value of n.

SECONDARY QUANTUM NUMBER, ℓ

According to the previous section, the Bohr model indicates that $n = 2$ has room for 8 electrons. In an atom with only one electron (i.e., a Bohr atom), it really doesn't matter which of the 8 slots an electron occupies in $n = 2$ because they're all the same energetically—in other words, the electron slots are **degenerate**.

> **DEFINITION:** Quantum states or configurations that have identical energies are said to be degenerate.

But the moment an atom has a second electron, things change drastically. Phenomena that are only possible when an atom has two or more electrons, such as electron-electron repulsion, magnetic coupling, and nuclear shielding effects, suddenly complicate things. Sets of electron slots within the same energy level may become nondegenerate, where some creep up in energy and some creep down in energy (although the overall energy for any energy level must remain the same as before). In other words, the energy levels, or shells, are subdivided into **subshells**.

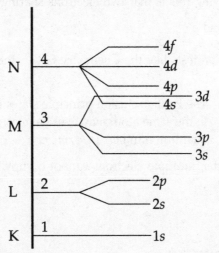

The difference in the energy of subshells is due to differences in the angular momentum created when the electron takes paths with different shapes. For this reason, each type of subshell has an associated angular momentum term, l, where l is labeled with a 0, 1, 2, 3, etc., depending on its shape. This label is also called the secondary quantum number, l.

Subshells are more commonly identified using letters as opposed to the numbers described above in order to avoid confusion with n's.

$\ell = 0$, use 's'
$\ell = 1$, use 'p'
$\ell = 2$, use 'd'
$\ell = 3$, use 'f'
$\ell = 4$ or higher; just use up letters in alphabet after 'f'

MAGNETIC QUANTUM NUMBER, m_ℓ

Subshells are further divided into electron *orbitals*. Each orbital can house two electrons, and each type of subshell has a corresponding number of orbitals:

Every s has 1 orbital.
Every p has 3 orbitals.
Every d has 5 orbitals.
Every f has 7 orbitals.

As with energy levels (n), and subshells (l), each orbital has its unique quantum number, m_ℓ. But instead of counting off integers starting from 1 (in the case of n) or 0 (in the case of l), the first orbital in a subshell is labeled $m_\ell = 0$, and then the rest are labeled by progressively counting off ± integers on either side of zero. In other words, the third type of quantum numbers, or **magnetic quantum numbers**, m_ℓ's, are:

For s subshells, 1 orbital labeled $m_l = 0$
For p subshells, 3 orbitals labeled $m_l = -1, 0, +1$
For d subshells, 5 orbitals labeled $m_l = -2, -1, 0, +1, +2$
For f subshells, 7 orbitals labeled $m_l = -3, -2, -1, 0, +1, +2, +3$

SPIN QUANTUM NUMBER, m_s

Each orbital, regardless of what subshell it belongs to, can potentially house up to two electrons. The only requirement is that the magnetic spin of the pair must be aligned in opposite directions and cancel out. Another way of saying this is that two electrons sharing an orbital must have the **spin quantum numbers**, $m_s = +\dfrac{1}{2}$ and $-\dfrac{1}{2}$.

This has little consequence on tests like the Chemistry GRE, other than its relation to the **Pauli exclusion principle**.

DEFINITION: The Pauli exclusion principle states that no two electrons in the same atom may ever have completely identical quantum numbers (n, ℓ, m_ℓ, m_s)

Like all other forms of matter, multiple electrons cannot occupy the same point in space at the same time.

Each quantum number is allowed only certain values. The principle quantum number (n) may only be an integer greater than or equal to one. The secondary quantum number (l) must be a positive integer value between 0 and n. Values of m_l are limited to any integer between $-l$ and $+l$, including zero. The spin quantum number can assume values of $+\frac{1}{2}$ and $-\frac{1}{2}$.

FILLING ORBITALS

Below is the orbital model for any multi-electron atom that takes into account n, ℓ, m_ℓ, m_s, where each box represents an orbital that can house up to two electrons with $m_s = +\frac{1}{2}$ and $-\frac{1}{2}$.

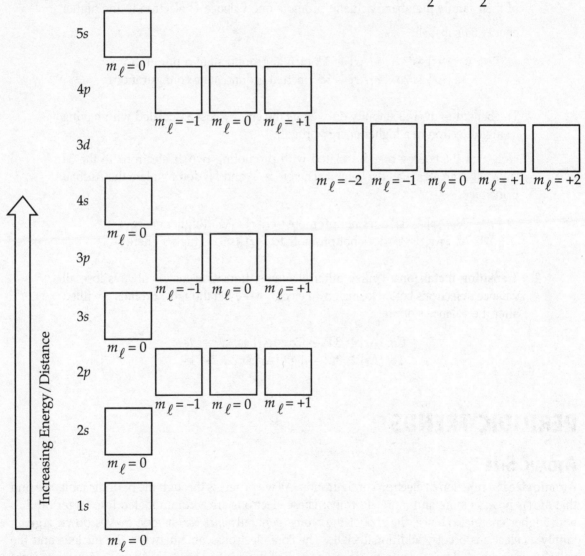

The Rules:

1. **Aufbau principle:** To find the correct ground-state electron configuration of an atom, always completely fill all lower-energy orbitals before filling any higher-energy orbitals.

2. **Hund's rule:** When partially filling degenerate orbitals of p, d, and f subshells, always put one electron in each orbital before pairing them up. Also, orient unpaired electrons so that their magnetic spins are all aligned in the same direction.

3. **Ions:** The ground state electron configuration for a monoatomic ion is identical to that of the neutral element with the same number of electrons. In other words, O^{2-}, F^-, Na^+, and Mg^{2+} have identical electron configurations to Ne, $1s^22s^22p^6$.

The Exceptions:

1. **Violation of the Aufbau principle:** Extra stabilization is realized when an atom has a $\frac{1}{2}$ filled or completely filled d orbital. For this reason, Cr and Cu (and some of their family members) actually promote one valence $4s$ electron to the higher energy $3d$ subshell:

$$Cr: [Ar]\ 4s^23d^4 \rightarrow [Ar]\ 4s^13d^5 \text{ (actual ground state configuration)}$$
$$Cu: [Ar]\ 4s^23d^9 \rightarrow [Ar]\ 4s^13d^{10} \text{ (actual ground state configuration)}$$

The benefit to overall stability outweighs the energy cost associated with having a single electron in a higher energy orbital.

Note that the energy cost associated with promoting two $4s$ electrons to the $3d$ subshell is greater than the benefit. Therefore, V and Ni don't violate the Aufbau principle:

$$V: [Ar]\ 4s^23d^3 \text{ does not promote to } [Ar]\ 4s^03d^5 \text{ (higher energy)}$$
$$Ni: [Ar]\ 4s^23d^8 \text{ does not promote to } [Ar]\ 4s^03d^{10} \text{ (higher energy)}$$

2. **Transition metal ions:** Unlike other elements, transition metals always lose all valence s electrons before losing any d electrons—even though d orbitals are filled after the valence s orbitals.

$$Co: [Ar]\ 4s^23d^7 \rightarrow Co^{2+}\ [Ar]\ 4s^03d^7 + 2e\text{-}$$
$$Fe: [Ar]\ 4s^23d^6 \rightarrow Fe^{3+}\ [Ar]\ 4s^03d^5 + 3e\text{-}$$

PERIODIC TRENDS

ATOMIC SIZE

Atomic size is a function of electron configuration. As we progress through the periodic table, we find that atoms possess more and more electrons. These electrons are accommodated into larger orbitals with higher energies. Hence, the size of the atoms generally *increases* as one moves down a given family as electrons occupy additional shells. The core electrons come between the nucleus and the valence electrons, *shielding* them from the strong pull of the positive protons. As you move left to right across a periodic row, however, atomic size decreases. This is due to the fact that electrons that are added as one moves across a row are entering the same valence shell, yet the charge of the nucleus increases as more and more protons are added. Consequently, the valence electrons are pulled closer to the nucleus as one moves to the right within a periodic row.

To summarize the atomic size trend, *atomic size increases as one moves down or to the left in the periodic table.*

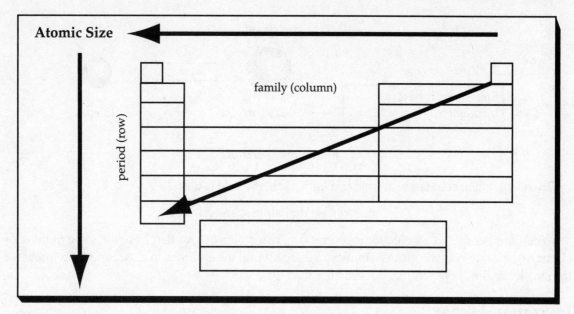

The largest atoms are the ones in the lower left of the periodic table, such as cesium and rubidium (radii ≈ 250 picometers), while the smallest are those in the upper right, such as helium and neon (radii ≈ 50 picometers). As you might expect, though, the smallest atom is hydrogen.

Adding or removing an electron from an atom has a dramatic effect on its size. In general, adding electrons to an atom—thereby forming an anion—increases its size, while removing electrons—forming a cation—reduces its size. For example, as an oxygen atom gains electrons to become an oxide ion, its size dramatically increases due to additional electron-electron repulsion in the $n = 2$ valence shell.

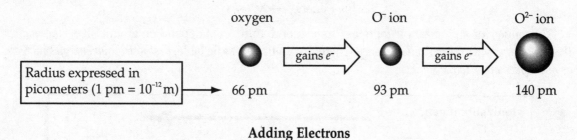

Adding Electrons

Alternatively, when a potassium atom loses an electron to form a potassium ion, its size dramatically decreases since there are no longer any occupants in the $n = 3$ shell.

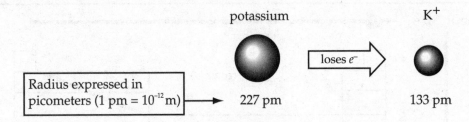

Removing Electrons

Therefore, when comparing atomic and ionic radii, the rule is this:

cation < neutral atom < anion

When comparing two **isoelectronic** species (i.e., two atoms or ions that have the same number of electrons), the one with the greater atomic number will pull the electrons in closer and therefore have the smaller radius. For example, F^- is smaller than O^{2-}.

IONIZATION ENERGY

The removal of an electron from a neutral atom is called **ionization**. This process always requires the input of energy (i.e., it is an **endergonic** process). The energy that is required to remove a single electron from an isolated gas-phase atom

$$X(g) + \text{energy} \rightarrow X^+(g) + e^-$$

is called the **first ionization energy**. We can, of course, remove additional electrons (provided the atom has them), and we label those energies accordingly. The **second ionization energy**, for example, is the energy required for the reaction:

$$X^+(g) + \text{energy} \rightarrow X^{2+}(g) + e^-$$

The values for all ionization energies (first, second, third, etc.) depend on atomic size—*the smaller the atom, the greater the ionization energy.* Therefore, in the periodic table, *first ionization energies increase as one moves up or to the right.*

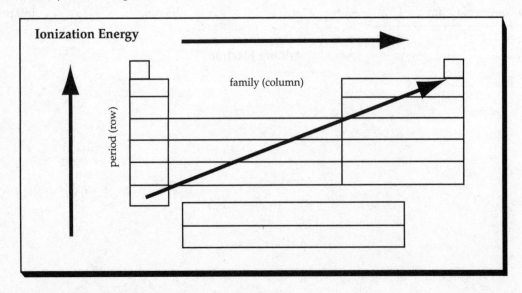

Elements like helium, fluorine, and oxygen have large first ionization energies since their electrons are tightly held by the nucleus, while cesium, francium, and rubidium have very low ones. In the following graph, we plot the first ionization energy (in kJ per mol) as a function of the atomic number for the first thirty elements. Note the energy peaks at the noble gases and the much lower ionization energies for the alkali metals.

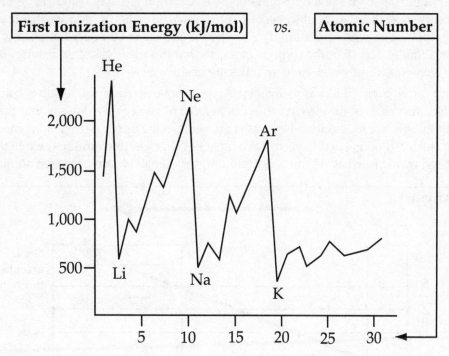

Although the second and third ionization energies do not follow a well-defined trend, it is a fact that *each subsequent ionization energy is always greater than the previous one.* That is, the second ionization energy is greater than the first, the third ionization energy is greater than the second, and so on.

ELECTRON AFFINITY

The **electron affinity** of an atom (or ion) is defined as the amount of energy involved in adding a single electron to an isolated gas-phase atom:

$$X(g) + e^- \rightarrow X^-(g)$$

For most elements, this process liberates energy (i.e., the process is **exergonic**). For example, energy is liberated when a fluorine atom acquires an electron:

$$F(g) + e^- \rightarrow F^-(g) + 322 \text{ kJ} \quad EA = -322 \text{ kJ/mol}$$

Since fluorine wants an electron to complete its $2p$ sublevel, energy is released in the favorable process of electron acquisition. By convention, we assign a *negative* value to energy that is *released* (as in the case with fluorine).

However, not all atoms will readily accept an additional electron. For example, a beryllium atom requires the input of energy to accept an additional electron:

$$Be(g) + e^- + 241 \text{ kJ} \rightarrow Be^-(g) \quad EA = +241 \text{ kJ/mol}$$

Since beryllium's path to stability requires *losing* electrons, it strongly objects to getting an extra one, and energy must therefore be absorbed. By convention, we assign a *positive* value to energy that is *absorbed* (as in the case with beryllium). This is why the elements of the beryllium family have positive electron affinities. Similarly, the addition of an electron to a noble gas atom requires the input of energy, and, consequently, their electron affinities are positive as well.

The trend for electron affinity is as follows: As you move across a row or up a column in the periodic table, the values of the electron affinities become more negative. We say that the element's electron affinity—its *love* for electrons—*increases*. Elements in the upper right-hand corner of the periodic table (such as fluorine and oxygen) have large negative electron affinities, while those in the lower left-hand corner (such as cesium and rubidium) have small negative electron affinities.

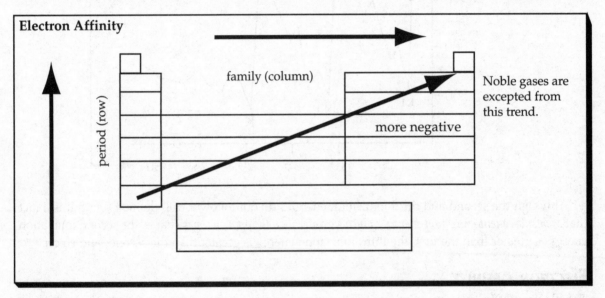

ELECTRONEGATIVITY

The ability of an atom *in a molecule* to polarize bonding electrons toward itself is called its **electronegativity**. Note that this property differs from electron affinity in that electronegativity deals exclusively with *bonded* atoms. Greedy, *highly* electronegative atoms want more electrons badly—and usually get them—while the elements with *low* electronegativities usually serve as the victims and lose some of their electron density. Electronegativity is a measure of the ability of an atom to attract electron density from other atoms to which it is bonded, and scales between 1 and 4. The scale is somewhat arbitrary and has no units, but the values can be compared to one another. The relative values of electronegativity play an important role in making qualitative predictions about atomic interactions and bonding.

You certainly will not be expected to remember the elements' exact electronegativity values. However, you should be familiar with the fact that electronegativity generally increases as one moves up or to the right within the periodic table.

Electronegativity Values

We will not assign electronegativity values to the noble gases.

H 2.1																	
Li 1.0	Be 1.5											B 2.0	C 2.5	N 3.1	O 3.5	F 4.1	
Na 1.0	Mg 1.3											Al 1.5	Si 1.8	P 2.1	S 2.4	Cl 2.9	
K 0.9	Ca 1.1	Sc 1.2	Ti 1.3	V 1.5	Cr 1.6	Mn 1.6	Fe 1.7	Co 1.7	Ni 1.8	Cu 1.8	Zn 1.7	Ga 1.8	Ge 2.0	As 2.2	Se 2.5	Br 2.8	
Rb 0.9	Sr 0.9	Y 1.1	Zr 1.2	Nb 1.3	Mo 1.3	Tc 1.4	Ru 1.4	Rh 1.5	Pd 1.4	Ag 1.4	Cd 1.5	In 1.5	Sn 1.7	Sb 1.8	Te 2.0	I 2.2	
Cs 0.9	Ba 0.9	*La 1.1	Hf 1.2	Ta 1.4	W 1.4	Re 1.5	Os 1.5	Ir 1.6	Pt 1.5	Au 1.4	Hg 1.5	Tl 1.5	Pb 1.6	Bi 1.7	Po 1.8	At 2.0	
Fr 0.9	Ra 0.9	Ac 1.0															

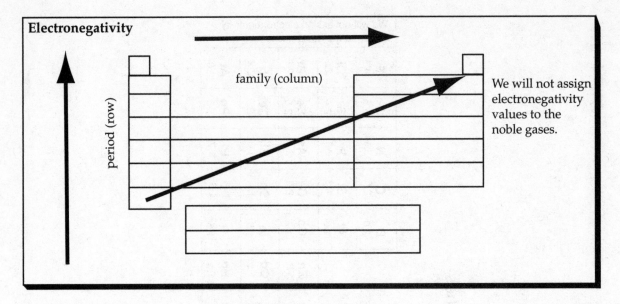

In addition to remembering the general trend, you may find it particularly useful to memorize the order of the six most electronegative atoms:

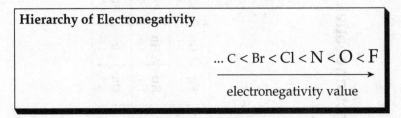

The fact that fluorine, oxygen, and nitrogen are the three most electronegative atoms has a profound influence on the type of intermolecular forces that exist between molecules that contain these atoms. The similar electronegativity values of C and H, 2.5 and 2.1, leads to relatively nonpolar C–H bonds in organic compounds.

ACIDITY–BASICITY

Acidity *increases as one moves down or to the right* in the periodic table.

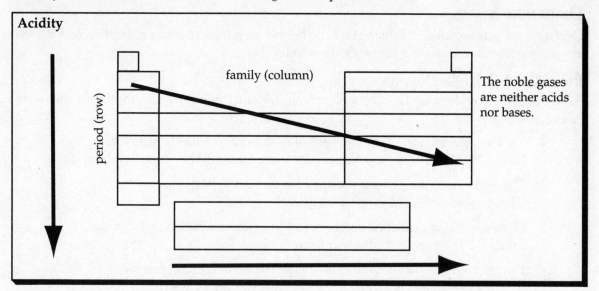

Basicity follows the *opposite* trend. The direction of this trend is different from the other four so don't confuse them. The most acidic elements (weakest bases) are those in the lower right-hand corner of the periodic table, such as iodine and bromine, and the weakest acids (strongest bases) are those in the upper left-hand corner, such as lithium and sodium.

The five periodic trends discussed here can be summarized pictorially as follows:

Summary of Periodic Trends

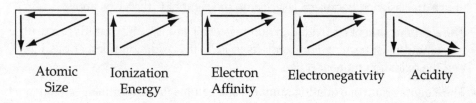

BONDING

OXIDATION STATES

Oxidation states (also called oxidation numbers) help to keep track of electron distribution between various reactants and products in a chemical reaction.

Rules About Oxidation Numbers

An element in any compound can be assigned an oxidation number according to the following rules:

1. The oxidation number of any free element or atom in its elemental state is zero. For Fe, Na, H_2, O_2, N_2, H, O, and N, all of the atoms have zero oxidation numbers.

2. The oxidation number of any one-atom ion is equal to its charge: Na^+ has an oxidation number of +1, Mg^{2+} of +2, Cl^- of –1.

3. Hydrogen has an oxidation number of +1 in all compounds except metallic hydrides (MH), where its oxidation number is –1.

4. Oxygen has an oxidation number of –2 in all compounds except peroxides, where its oxidation number is –1, and in OF_2 where it's +2 (and F is –1).

5. In combinations of nonmetals that don't involve H or O, the nonmetal that is either to the right of or above the other in the periodic table (so the least metallic, or most electronegative element) is assigned an oxidation number that has the same value as the charge of its most commonly encountered negative ion. For instance, in CCl_4, Cl would be –1 and C is +4. However, in CH_4, H is +1 and C is –4. In SF_6, F is –1 and S is +6, but in CS_2, S is –2 and C is +4. CS_2 is a borderline case. C is above S in the periodic table, but S is to the right of C. The oxidation numbers above are assigned because S is *farther* to the right of C than C is above S.

6. The algebraic sum of the oxidation numbers of all atoms in the formula of a neutral compound must be zero. For example, in PCl_5, the oxidation number of Cl is –1, and the oxidation number of P is +5.

7. The algebraic sum of oxidation numbers of all atoms in the formula of an ion must equal the charge of the ion. So in SO_4^{2-}, O is –2 and S must be +6 in order for the sum of all oxidation numbers to be equal to –2.

8. In chemical reactions, the *total oxidation number is conserved*.

*If the oxidation number of an element **becomes more positive** during a chemical reaction, the element is **oxidized**; if it becomes more negative, the element is **reduced**. This type of chemical reaction is called a reduction-oxidation or redox reaction.*

Note: Oxidation states are different from formal charges. For examples, the formal charge on carbon in CH_4 is zero, while the oxidation number is –4. In a balanced chemical equation, *oxidation and reduction must balance each other exactly*.

THE OCTET

An element's chemical properties are exclusively determined by the stability of its electronic configuration. Unstable configurations are characteristic of highly reactive atoms, while stable configurations result in chemical inactivity. Remember: All atoms work to become stable; thus, an element's chemical behavior is governed by its desire to maximize its stability. At this point, it is important to understand that chemical stability is greatest when: (1) all electrons are in the lowest energy orbitals available, a condition referred to as the **ground state**, and (2) all electrons are associated with a **closed shell** (a condition referred to as an **octet** when considering s and p valence electrons).

An atom has a complete octet when it has filled its valence s and p subshells with the required 2 + 6 = 8 electrons, thereby assuming the electronic configuration of one of the noble gases. After all, the noble gases are called "noble" because they are chemically inert, and they are chemically inert because of their octet stability. Other elements may attempt to emulate the noble gases through the acquisition or disposal of valence electrons. Atoms attain a noble gas configuration by the most direct means possible. This translates into the fact that within the periodic table, elements on the left and in the center typically lose their valence electrons to become positively-charged ions **(cations)**, while elements on the right tend to supplement the valence electrons they already possess to become negatively charged ions **(anions)**. This observed divergence in valence character is a fundamental cause for the chemical and physical dissimilarities between metal and nonmetal elements. Metals tend to lose electrons to become cations. Nonmetals, which occupy the upper-right portion of the table, tend to gain electrons to become anions (noble gases excepted).

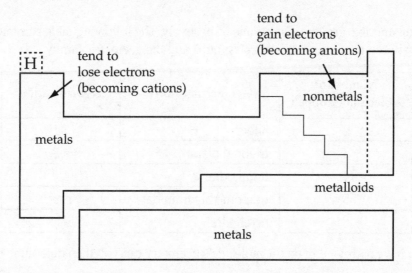

(H is considered a nonmetal since, for one thing, it's a gas at room temperature; metals—except mercury—are solids at room temperature. However, H undergoes reactions similar to those of the alkali metals.) **Metalloid** elements—elements that lie right along the delineation staircase line between metals and nonmetals—can possess properties characteristic of either metals or nonmetals.

VALENCE SHELL ELECTRON PAIR REPULSION (VSEPR) THEORY

The shape of simple molecules is predicted by Valence Shell Electron Pair Repulsion (VSEPR) Theory. Perhaps the most remarkable aspect of this theory is the fact that such an overwhelming title has been given to such a straightforward concept. VSEPR theory has only one rule: *Electron pairs, whether bonding or nonbonding, attempt to move as far apart as possible.*

For example, the bonding electrons in magnesium hydride, MgH_2, repel one another and attempt to move as far apart as possible. In this molecule, two pairs of electrons are most distant when they point in opposite directions. So MgH_2 looks like:

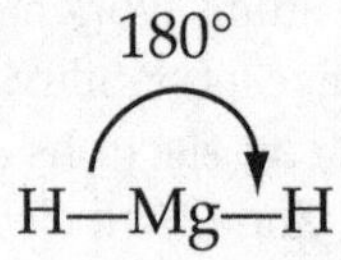

180°

H—Mg—H

where the angle between the bonds is 180°. A molecule with this shape is described as being **linear**. Molecular shape depends upon the geometric (symmetry) family to which the molecule belongs. An atom's geometric identity is based solely on its number of **electron groups**. While bonding and non-bonding pairs of electrons are counted as individual electron groups, double and triple bonds only count as one electron group even though they involve two and three pairs of electrons, respectively. For example, the **central atoms** in the molecules

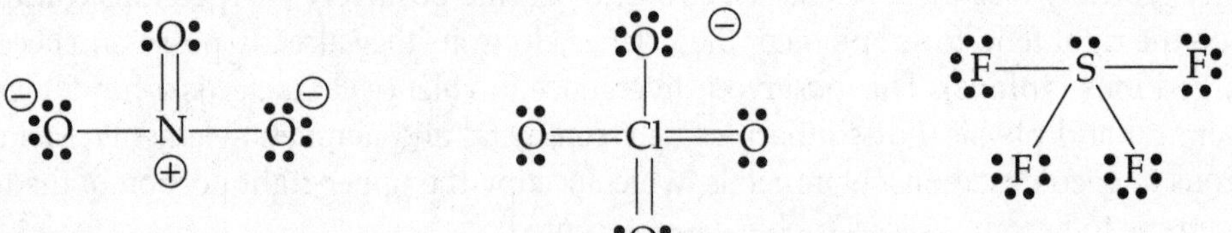

have three, four, and five groups of electrons, respectively. The following table summarizes this correspondence between the number of electron groups and the geometric family:

Number of Electron Groups	Geometric Family	Hybridization
2	linear	sp
3	trigonal planar	sp^2
4	tetrahedral	sp^3
5	triagonal bipyramidal	dsp^3
6	octahedral	d^2sp^3

Only after you have narrowed in on the molecule's geometry can you then determine the molecule's overall shape.

Determining Molecular Shapes:

1. Count the total number of **groups** of electrons, including both bonding and non-bonding electrons (double and triple bonds only get counted once), and then determine the molecule's **geometric family**. Keep in mind that the geometry of a molecule is not necessarily its shape.

2. Determine the **shape** of the molecule based upon the number of nonbonding pairs. The following table summarizes all of the common molecular shapes:

	Geometric Family				
	Linear	Trigonal Planar	Tetrahedral	Trigonal Bipyramid	Octahedral
0 nonbonding pairs of electrons					
Shape:	Linear	Trigonal Planar	Tetrahedral	Trigonal Bipyramidal	Octahedral
1 nonbonding pair of electrons					
Shape:		Bent	Trigonal Pyramid	See-saw	Square Pyramid
2 nonbonding pairs of electrons					
Shape:			Bent	T-Shaped	Square Planar

Note: The shape of a molecule is identical to its geometry when the central atom has *no* nonbonding electrons.

Determining Hybridization

Every pair of electrons must be housed in an electronic orbital (either an *s*, *p*, *d*, or *f*). The carbon atom in methane (CH_4) has *four* pairs of electrons surrounding it (four single covalent bonds + zero lone pairs), so it must provide four electronic orbitals to house these electrons. Orbitals always get used up in the following order:

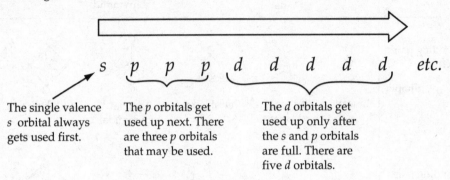

The single valence *s* orbital always gets used first.

The *p* orbitals get used up next. There are three *p* orbitals that may be used.

The *d* orbitals get used up only after the *s* and *p* orbitals are full. There are five *d* orbitals.

So in the case of the carbon atom in methane, we start using up orbitals from the left and work our way across:

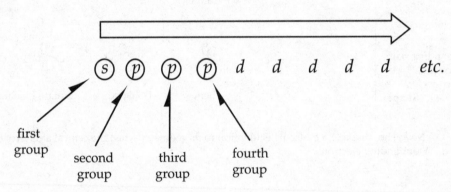

first group

second group

third group

fourth group

Therefore, the hybridization of the carbon atom in methane is $s + p + p + p$, which is abbreviated sp^3. The sum of the exponents in hybridization nomenclature tells how many orbitals of this type are used. For example, in methane, there are four hybrid orbitals (since $sp^3 = s^1p^3$, and $1 + 3 = 4$). Here's another example: The hybridization of the phosphorous atom in PO_4^{3-} (the phosphate ion) is sp^3 and the geometry of the phosphate molecule is tetrahedral. At first glance one might think that its structure should be very different from methane, but since the bonds are arranged into four groups, the geometry is tetrahedral.

group one

group four
(double bonds only count
as one group)

group two

group three

COVALENT BONDING

Ordinary Covalent Bonds

From an atom's point of view, covalent bonds are nothing more than a means to an end—**closed-shell stability**. Atoms with similar electronegativities cannot give and take electrons in order to meet their closed-shell requirements (unlike, say, the reaction of sodium metal and chlorine gas). In cases of two atoms with similar electronegativities, a compromise is made: a **covalent bond**. Typically, each atom contributes one electron (so that there are two electrons total) to form a covalent bond between them. If the electronegativities of the bonding atoms are identical or very nearly identical (i.e., the two values don't differ by more than about 0.4 electronegativity units), then the bonding electrons will be shared *equally*. Covalent bonds in which the electron pair spends the same amount of time around each atom are called **nonpolar bonds**. Most nonpolar bonds exist between atoms of the same elements; for example, C–C, H–H, F–F, and K–K. However, bonds between atoms with nearly identical electronegativities are also classified as nonpolar, such as C–H, B–Si, or P–I.

The electron distribution of a nonpolar, single covalent bond:

Polar Covalent Bonds

Alternatively, bonding electrons between atoms whose electronegativity difference is higher (0.5 to 1.5 units) will spend more time around the more electronegative atom. In this manner, the more electronegative atom will acquire a partial negative charge and the less electronegative atom will be left with a partial positive charge. A rule of thumb is that the greater the electronegativity difference between the bonding atoms, the greater the polarization (unevenness) of the bonding electrons. Covalent bonds that are fatter at one end than at the other are referred to as **polar bonds**. Polar covalent bonds may be thought of as the middle ground between pure covalent (nonpolar) bonds and the complete electron transfer observed in ionic compounds. Examples of polar covalent bonds include C–F, O–H, Li–C, and S–Cl.

The electron distribution of a polar, single covalent bond:

METALLIC COVALENT BONDING

The exceptionally high electrical conductivity of metals provides us with insight into the nature of metallic bonding. If we examine the electronic configuration of common metals, we see that they always have more valence orbitals than valence electrons to fill them. For example, Li ($1s^2 2s^1$) has only one valence electron for its $2s$ and $2p$ orbitals. Therefore this electron is relatively free to move through the crystal lattice structure. One model of metallic structure is that the lattice of positive metallic ions exists in a **sea of electrons** that holds the ions tightly together. The atoms in the crystal structure can easily be displaced in planes with respect to each other, which explains the **malleability** (ability to be hammered into shapes) and **ductility** (ability to be drawn into sheets/wires) of metals. The displacement in the sea of electrons provides a constant shield between the positive ions and does not allow the development of strong repulsive forces.

BAND THEORY

A more detailed model of metallic bonding is provided by the **band theory**, in which the metal is thought of as a giant molecule in which delocalized molecular orbitals cover the entire structure.

Example:

Sodium (Na): $(1s^2 2s^2 2p^6 3s^1 3p^0)$

When the $3s$ orbital of one Na atom overlaps the $3s$ orbital of its immediate neighbor, two molecular orbitals (MO), one bonding (with lower energy) and one antibonding (with higher energy) are formed. When a third atom joins the first two, a third molecular orbital is created: The central MO is nonbonding and is surrounded by a bonding and a nonbonding one, at lower and higher energy levels, respectively. When N atoms come together in a single line, N molecular orbitals are formed, with N distinct energy levels. These N molecular orbitals are very closely spaced in energy and form a virtually **continuous band** covering a range of energies, as shown below:

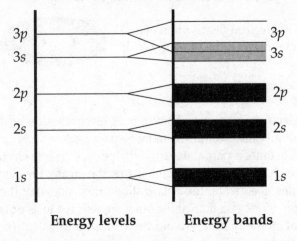

The gray band is the **valence band** ($3s$). It contains the freely moving valence electrons.

The empty band ($3p$) that overlaps the valence band is the **conduction band**; if electrons jump into it, the material will be able to conduct electricity.

This model leads us to the following points:

- When a valence band is not fully occupied, valence electrons can move in many energy states.

- Valence electrons can jump into the **conduction** band.

- The width of the band depends on the degree of overlap of the atomic orbitals between neighboring atoms: the greater the overlap, the wider the band.

- A band is thus a near-continuum of a finite number of energy levels.

- The band constructed from the overlap of s orbitals is called an **s band**. Similarly, **p bands** and **d bands** can be constructed.

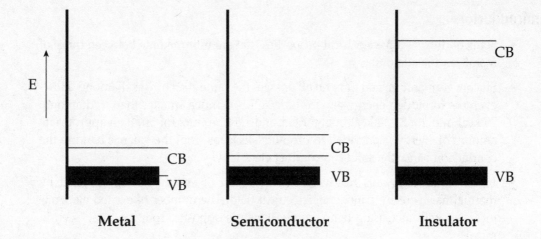

Metal	**Semiconductor**	**Insulator**

- A metal has overlapping valence and **conduction** bands (VB and CB).

- Insulators have a big gap between their VB and CB.

- A semiconductor has a small gap between the VB and CB; adding energy (heat, light) can then excite electrons that can jump from VB to CB.

PHYSICAL AND CHEMICAL CONSEQUENCES OF BAND THEORY

Insulators

- Partially filled bands of delocalized orbitals account for electrical conduction in solids.

- A solid in which electrons saturate a band and a considerable gap exists between the completely filled band and the next available one is called an **insulator**.

- Insulators do not conduct electricity under normal conditions.

- Boron and carbon (diamond) are insulators.

Example:

Carbon in diamond:

When the delocalized sp^3 orbitals interact with each other, two bands of delocalized orbitals are formed: one from bonding orbitals and one from antibonding orbitals. There are just precisely enough valence shell electrons to fill these bonding orbitals, and this makes the bonding in diamond incredibly strong. The valence band that contains electrons does not overlap the next band, which has completely unfilled orbitals, and there is a **forbidden energy gap** between the valence band and the conduction band. If a sufficiently large amount of energy is provided to promote electrons from the valence to the conduction band (across the forbidden energy gap), an insulator can be made to conduct electricity. In diamond, the gap between the top of the valence band and the bottom of the conduction band takes about 120 kcal/mol of energy to overcome.

Semiconductors

- Semiconductors have electrical properties that are intermediate between those of metals and insulators.

- Silicon, germanium, and gray tin all possess the same structure as diamond. However, the forbidden energy gap in these solids is much smaller than in diamond: 25 kcal/mol for Si, 14 kcal/mol for Ge, and 1.8 kcal/mol for Sn. If an appropriate amount of energy is provided to promote electrons from the valence band to the conduction band, the solid can conduct electricity.

- In semiconductors, this relatively small amount of energy can be supplied by thermal means or by a moderate electrical field. The number of excited electrons increases with increasing temperature, which is opposite from the trend seen in metals.

Unlike metals, semiconductors are substances with electrical conductivities that increase with increasing temperature.

- The main difference between a semiconductor and an insulator depends on the size of the band gap in the insulator.

Because insulators can be made to conduct electricity if sufficient energy is provided to send electrons across the forbidden energy gap, the distinction between insulators and semiconductors is considered artificial and is often ignored. Silicon is a good example of this. Because of its energy gap of 25 kcal/mol, it is sometimes considered an insulator in the pure state, and sometimes a semiconductor. But a silicon crystal is considered a semiconductor when it's mixed with certain impurity atoms.

Intrinsic Semiconductors

An intrinsic semiconductor is a solid in which the band gap is so small that some electrons from the valence band will occupy energy levels in the conduction band. This slight electron population in the conduction band will result in the introduction of **negative carriers** (electrons) into the upper level and **positive holes** into the lower. As a result, the solid is conducting: The electrons sent into the conduction band can move freely, and the positive holes left in the valence band move in one direction, as electrons jump to fill them from adjacent bonding pairs in the opposite direction. But at room temperature, a semiconductor has a much lower conductivity than a metal because of the small number of electrons and holes that can act as carriers.

Extrinsic Semiconductors

A substance that is normally an insulator can become semiconducting if small amounts of other atoms are introduced into the lattice, rendering it impure. The result of this is a substance called **an extrinsic semiconductor.**

Example:
Silicon (Si):

The structure of a silicon solid is similar to that in which carbon participates in diamond. But in silicon, the energy gap is much smaller: E_g = 25 kcal/mol. This gap can be narrowed if impurities such as boron or phosphorus (a few ppm) are substituted for some silicon atoms in the crystal lattice. The process of introducing the impurity is called **doping**. Phosphorus and astatine (Group V) possess five valence electrons, one more electron than silicon. After four of them have covalently bonded with neighboring silicon atoms, one extra electron is left and is available for each substituting dopant atom. If the donor atoms are far apart from each other, the donor band will be very narrow. In a silicon crystal doped with phosphorus atoms, the energy of the extra electron is close to that of the conduction band. The donor band is close to the conduction band, and the thermal excitation of electrons from the donor band to the empty conduction band enables a current to flow. Only 0.25 kcal/mol is required to free the donated electron of phosphorus and make silicon a semiconductor. This process is called **n-type conductivity** because the charge carriers are negative electrons. N-type semiconductors are formed when a doping atom possesses more external electrons than the parent atom. A similar effect can be achieved if boron or gallium (Group III) is introduced in the silicon lattice instead of phosphorus. Boron has one fewer electron than silicon. For each boron atom introduced in the crystal lattice, a vacancy is created in the valence band. The dopant atoms form a very narrow and empty **acceptor band** that lies close to and above the filled Si valence band. At a temperature of T = 0 K, this acceptor band is empty, but at higher temperatures, thermal excitation promotes Si electrons into it, effectively creating holes in the Si valence band. This process allows other electrons in the band to become mobile; an electron from a neighbor of a boron atom drops into its empty orbital, which creates a vacancy that can be filled by an electron from the next Si atom. This creates a cascade or domino effect, in which an electron from each of a row of atoms moves one place toward the neighboring atom. So electrons become mobile both in the valence and the acceptor bands. The process in the valence band can also be seen as a hole moving across a row of atoms, in the direction opposite to the flow of electrons. This is called **p-type conductivity** because the charge carriers are now positive holes.

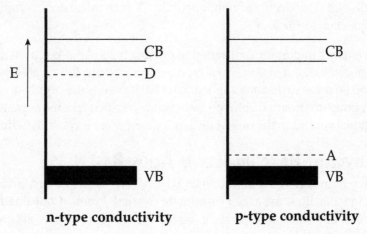

n-type conductivity   p-type conductivity

Semiconductor Applications

- The most important applications of band theory are based on **p-n junctions**.

- A p-n junction consists of a p-type semiconductor that's in close contact with an n-type semiconductor. In the p-type, the charge carriers are the holes, and in the n-type, the charge carriers are extra electrons.

- At the interface between both semiconductors, a few electrons of the n-zone migrate spontaneously toward the p-type zone. This migration confers a negative charge to the p-zone (because of gained electrons) and a positive charge to the n-zone (because of lost electrons and holes created in the low-energy MO).

- This accumulation of charge is called a **contact** or **junction potential**.

- If the p-zone is connected to the negative pole of a battery and the n-zone to the positive pole, the electrons are attracted to the (+) pole and the holes to the (−) pole, which is opposite to the normal direction of the displacement of electrons and holes at the junction. The junction offers a resistance to the current flow and is said to be **inversely polarized**. No current can flow through the system.

- If the p-zone is connected to the positive pole, and the n-zone to the negative pole of the battery, the flow of electrons takes place in the normal direction at the junction. The junction is then **directly polarized**. The current can flow freely.

- A p-n junction makes an excellent **rectifier**. When inserted in a circuit in which the electrical potential alternates continually, a p-n junction allows the current to flow only in the direction of direct polarization, so an alternative current (ac) can be transformed into a direct current (dc). Before p-n junction technology was available, vacuum tubes were used as rectifiers. They were large, fragile, and unreliable. Today, all solid state electronic components in TV sets, calculators, computers, etc., use p-n junction technology.

Transistors are another important application of p-n junctions. An n-p-n transistor is made by inserting a p-type semiconductor between two n-type semiconductors; this creates two interfaces—and attaching the (+) and (−) poles so that one applied potential increases the supply of carriers for another potential. An n-p-n transistor inserted between two circuits can then take the current in one circuit and produce a proportional current in the other one at a higher power level, thus acting as an amplifier.

COORDINATE COVALENT BONDING (LEWIS ACIDS-BASES)

Covalent bonds may form between a transition metal ion, such as Fe^{3+} or Cr^{3+}, and a polar molecule, such as water or ammonia; these are called **coordinate covalent bonds**. **Coordination complexes** are molecules that consist of a transition metal ion bonded to polar molecules via coordinate covalent bonds, like $H_3B - NH_3$.

A coordinate covalent bond is formed by the donation of a pair of electrons from a polar molecule. A molecule that *donates* a pair of electrons to form a covalent bond is called a **Lewis base**, while one that *accepts* such a pair is called a **Lewis acid**. The formation of a coordination complex constitutes a **Lewis acid-base** reaction. For example, a cobalt(III) ion will readily form an octahedrally symmetric coordination complex with ammonia:

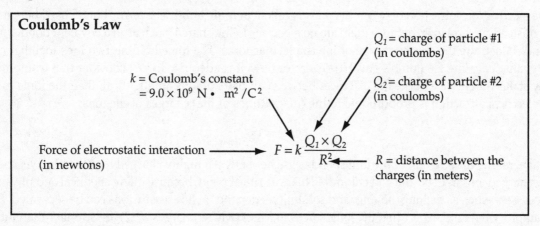

hexaammine cobalt(III) complex

Note that the resulting complex has a charge equal to the sum of its parts.

In coordination chemistry, the Lewis base is called a **ligand** (or **chelator**). Common examples of ligands include ammonia, water, alcohols, halide ions, cyanide ions, carbon monoxide, and most other nitrogenous molecules. The strengths of various coordinate covalent bonds are by no means equal. Some ligands, such as cyanide and carbon monoxide, form strong coordinate covalent bonds, while others, such as water and halide ions, form weakly bound complexes that can easily fall apart.

More details regarding the properties of coordination complexes are given under the Transition Metals section.

INTERMOLECULAR FORCES

Intermolecular forces are those that exist between two or more molecules; *inter* means *between*. This term should not be confused with *intra*molecular forces; these hold atoms together to form *a* molecule (e.g., covalent bonds); *intra* means *within*. All intermolecular forces are forms of the electromagnetic force and involve the interaction between charges. Since all molecules experience some degree of intermolecular forces, this implies that even neutral molecules have some sort of uneven charge distribution, because when we talk about the electromagnetic force, we're talking about charge interactions. A pair of charges may interact in only two ways: *Like charges repel* and *opposite charges attract*. Therefore, we expect intermolecular forces to come in two types: **cohesive** (attractive) and **repulsive**.

The strength of charge-charge interactions is embodied in the following equation, **Coulomb's law**, which quantifies the electrostatic force:

Coulomb's Law

Q_1 = charge of particle #1 (in coulombs)

k = Coulomb's constant $= 9.0 \times 10^9$ N $\cdot$ m^2/C^2

Q_2 = charge of particle #2 (in coulombs)

Force of electrostatic interaction (in newtons) $\longrightarrow$ $F = k \dfrac{Q_1 \times Q_2}{R^2}$ $\longleftarrow$ R = distance between the charges (in meters)

Coulomb's law tells us that like charges *repel* (*F* is positive) and opposite charges *attract* (*F* is negative). In addition to this, Coulomb's law reveals that the force, whether positive or negative, is *proportional* to the charges of the species and *inversely proportional* to the square of the distance between them. For example, if the space between two charges is doubled, the force between them drops to *one-fourth* its previous value.

Repulsive Forces

Electron cloud repulsion (the driving force behind VSEPR theory) prevents atoms, which are 99.99% empty space, from passing right through one another. You can stay suspended on the floor (against gravitational acceleration) because the electron clouds of the atoms on the bottom surface of your shoes strongly repel the electron clouds of the atoms on the surface of the floor. The consequences of electron cloud repulsion are commonly studied in organic chemistry and biochemistry; scientists in these fields call electron cloud repulsion **steric hindrance**. However, at this point, it is only important to remind yourself that electron clouds repel one another.

Cohesive Intermolecular Forces

A molecule must have some degree of charge in order to experience intermolecular forces, and according to experimentation, *all* molecules experience intermolecular forces. Therefore, all molecules, even neutral ones, must have some charge, or at least some charge separation, some of the time. In addition, molecules with greater charge or greater charge separation will experience greater intermolecular attraction, since, by Coulomb's law, force is proportional to charge (assuming that the internuclear distances are the same).

There is a vast diversity in the strength of attractive intermolecular forces. Hard, high-melting-point solids, like geological minerals (rocks), are a consequence of very strong intermolecular forces. Tenuous gases, such as molecular oxygen or nitrogen, are the product of very feeble ones. Since liquids are neither hard solids nor diffuse gases, we conclude that the intermolecular forces they experience lie somewhere in between those of granite and air. The wide range of intermolecular cohesive forces has led scientists to divide the broad category of intermolecular forces into *three* smaller domains. We categorize intermolecular attractions by potency: strong (**ionic**), intermediate (**dipole**), and very weak (**dispersion**).

Ionic Forces

The electrostatic attraction between two ions is called an **ionic bond**. The term "bond" used here may be misleading, however, because there are no electrons being shared, such as in a covalent bond. Ionic bonds constitute the strongest type of intermolecular force. The force holding two ions together can be evaluated using Coulomb's law. However, for now, it is adequate to just consider that Coulomb's law states that if we assume the distances between all pairs of ions are identical, then the ionic force of electrical attraction is proportional to the (magnitudes of the) charges of the ions:

$$\text{Force} \propto Q_1 Q_2$$

Therefore, the strength of the ionic bond is greater between highly charged ions than between singly charged ions like sodium and chloride. This is a critical point, because many chemical and physical processes—such as melting, boiling, and solubility—depend on how easily ions can be separated. For example, we would expect that the ionic forces in MgO (whose charges = ±2) are stronger than those in NaCl (whose charges = ±1).

Dipole Forces

Polar molecules—those with a **dipole moment**—have an asymmetric distribution of electron density. The result is that one end of the molecule has a negative charge and the other end has a positive charge (even though the *overall* charge of the molecule is *zero*).

Polar molecules arise from internal polar covalent bonds. A covalent bond between two elements with differing electronegativities, such as the bond between a carbon atom and an oxygen atom, will be uneven. This is because a covalent bond behaves as if it were a rope in a tug-of-war. The atom with the higher electronegativity will pull more strongly, since electronegativity is the measure of an element's ability to reel in electrons. Since our electron "rope" has a negative charge because it is made of two electrons, the more electronegative atom acquires a partial negative charge (denoted δ^-), leaving the more electropositive atom with a partial positive charge (denoted δ^+). Conceptually, polar bonds lie somewhere between the even sharing of electrons (nonpolar bond like H–H) and the complete polarization (like Na and Cl) that forms ions.

But just because a molecule has polar bonds does not necessarily make that molecule polar; the structure of the molecule must also be taken into consideration. In highly symmetric molecules such as carbon dioxide and BF_3, polar bonds may be oriented in such a way that the dipole moments (symbolized by an arrow, pointing from the atom with the partial positive charge to the atom with the partial negative charge) cancel out.

In these cases, the overall molecule is nonpolar. By contrast, the dipole moments of the polar N–H bonds in an ammonia molecule do not cancel, but instead add to give a net nonzero dipole moment.

dipoles cancel

dipoles cancel

net dipole

polar bonds
nonpolar molecule

polar bonds
nonpolar molecule

polar bonds
polar molecule

If a molecule is polar, it behaves like a very weak ion. In a fluid medium, electrostatic forces cause polar molecules to align their charged regions near the oppositely charged regions of their neighbors. For example, liquefied HCl molecules take on an orientation like this:

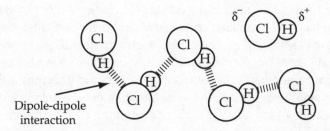

Dipole-dipole
interaction

The interactions between the charged portions of polar molecules are called **dipole forces**. Dipole forces are weaker than ionic forces but still may have a major effect on the physical properties of a compound. The strength of dipole-dipole interactions is about 1% the strength of ion-ion interactions. There is a notable exception to this, however.

Water, ammonia, hydrogen fluoride—in fact, any molecules that have an H–O, H–N, or H–F bond—experience unusually strong dipole-dipole attractions, ranging in strength from 3% to 5% of the magnitude of the ion-ion attraction in NaCl. Due to their unusually high strength, these types of dipole-dipole interactions are considered special and collectively called **hydrogen-bonding** interactions.

For the purpose of the GRE Chemistry Subject Test, the definition of a **hydrogen bond** is quite rigid: A *hydrogen bond is a strong dipole-dipole interaction involving a hydrogen atom covalently bonded to a fluorine, oxygen, or nitrogen atom that is attracted to the partial negative charge of another fluorine, oxygen, or nitrogen atom.*

London Dispersion Forces

London dispersion forces (or simply London forces or dispersion forces) may be considered the consolation prize of intermolecular forces, because any atom or ion that has at least one electron experiences them. Dispersion forces arise from a momentary non-homogeneous distribution of electrons in an atom. As the electrons fly around, even around the nuclei of a perfectly nonpolar molecule, it happens that sometimes more electrons are on one side of the nucleus than on the other. When this occurs, the atom has a slightly positive side and a slightly negative side: an **instantaneous dipole**. Such an instantaneous dipole in one molecule can induce an instantaneous dipole in another nearby molecule. The **dispersion force** is then *the attraction between two adjacent, instantaneous, oppositely charged dipoles that just happen to pop up at the same time.* Since instantaneous dipoles pop up randomly and are gone so quickly, dispersion forces are very short-ranged and very weak. Individual dispersion forces are much weaker than either ionic or dipole forces.

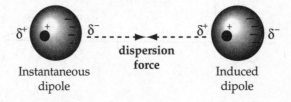

Chemists ignore the cohesive contribution of dispersion forces in ionic or polar molecules because they are insignificant when compared to ion-ion, ion-dipole, or dipole-dipole attractions. However, in nonpolar molecules, dispersion forces are the sole cohesive force. The strength of dispersion forces generally increases as the number of electrons increases, so the physical characteristics of large, non-polar molecules are significantly influenced by dispersion forces.

Covalent vs. Ionic Compounds

When the electronegativities of a compound's constituent elements differ by no more than about 1.5 electronegativity units (such as compounds made of all nonmetal elements), electrons will be shared, and the atoms will be covalently linked. For example, carbon dioxide is a covalent compound. However, if the electronegativity of two elements differs by more than 1.5 electronegativity units, such as that between a metal and a nonmetal, the compound will be ionic. This means that when atoms from the right of the periodic table (the highly electronegative ones) combine with atoms from the far the interaction is likely to be ionic. Just about everything else is covalent.

CRYSTAL LATTICES

- Ions in an ionic compound (also called salts) are arranged in a regular pattern called a **crystal lattice**.

- The term **crystal** refers to this type of solid. The array that constitutes the crystal lattice is regular—it repeats itself periodically.

- The smallest unit that repeats itself indefinitely in three dimensions is called the **unit cell**.

- The energy of these electrostatic interactions is called **lattice energy** (U).

- Crystallography is the branch of chemistry that studies the structure of **unit cells**.

Types of Crystal Lattices: The Crystal Systems

There are seven types of crystalline structures, each of which possesses a characteristic unit cell that repeats itself to give a solid structure without voids.

The size and geometry of a unit cell is denoted by the lengths (a, b, and c) of the three axes and the three angles (α, β, and γ) that occur between pairs of intersecting axes (b and c, a and c, a and b, respectively).

The seven crystal systems are:

1. **Cubic.** Cell edges: $a = b = c$; cell angles: $\alpha = \beta = \gamma = 90°$; example: NaCl.

2. **Tetragonal.** Cell edges: $a = b \neq c$; cell angles: $\alpha = \beta = \gamma = 90°$; example: $Hg(CN)_2$.

3. **Hexagonal.** Cell edges: $a = b = c \neq d$; cell angles: $\alpha = \beta = \gamma = 120°$, the edge d is perpendicular to the plane described by edges a, b, and c; example: PbI_2.

4. **Rhombohedral.** Cell edges: $a = b = c$; cell angles: $\alpha = \beta = \gamma \neq 90°$; example: $NaNO_3$.

5. **Orthorhombic.** Cell edges: $a \neq b \neq c$; cell angles: $\alpha = \beta = \gamma = 90°$; example: K_2CrO_4.

6. **Monoclinic.** Cell edges: $a \neq b \neq c$; cell angles: $\alpha = \gamma = 90°$, $\beta \neq 90°$; example: $K_3Fe(CN)_6$.

7. **Triclinic.** Cell edges: $a \neq b \neq c$; cell angles: $\alpha \neq \beta \neq \gamma$; example: $CuSO_4 \cdot 5H_2O$.

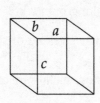 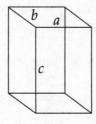 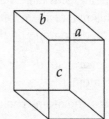

cubic: $a = b = c$ tetragonal: $a = b \neq c$ orthorhombic: $a \neq b \neq c$

Most of these basic systems may be divided further. For instance, there exists a simple cubic primitive unit cell (P) that contains atoms only at the corners, a body-centered unit cell (bcc or I) that contains atoms at the corners as well as at the center of the unit cell, and a face-centered unit cell (fcc or F) that contains atoms at its corners and in the center of each of the six faces.

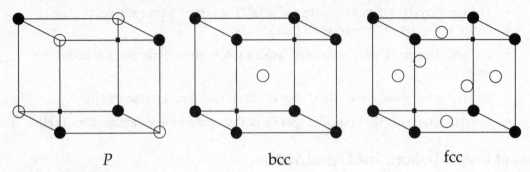

P   bcc   fcc

Close Packing of Spheres

There are four types of crystalline solids:

- **Ionic solids**, which are made of positive and negative ions arranged in regular arrays; each ion is surrounded by ions of the opposite charge (e.g., $NaCl$, CaF_2). The unit cells are held together by coulombic forces that act between the cations and anions. These solids are hard, brittle, and have high melting and boiling points. They are poor conductors of electricity and heat.

- **Covalent solids** are made of atoms that are held together by very strong covalent bonds (e.g., quartz, SiO_2). They are very hard and have high melting points. They are usually poor conductors of heat and electricity. Sometimes different forms of covalent crystals occur but are made up of the same element (e.g., graphite and diamond are two covalent solids that are made of carbon).

- **Molecular solids** are made of neutral molecules (like H_2O, sucrose, I_2, P_4); they are held together by dipole forces or London dispersion forces. They are soft and are poor conductors of electricity and heat.

- **Metallic solids** are made of one closely packed metal element. Each lattice point of the unit cell in metallic solids is occupied by a metal cation (the atom without its outershell electrons). The free valence electrons circulate around the metallic cations; this makes them very good electricity and heat conductors. They can be soft or hard, depending on the element, and have variable melting points.

The structures of many solids can be described in terms of the regular stacking of spheres that represent the ions or atoms.

In some substances, the atoms pack together as closely as possible; these metals are called **close-packed structures**.

This geometry allows for the least waste of space and the maximum number of neighbors.

Types of Close Packing

Spheres in a close-packed structure have several layers. In the first layer, a single sphere is surrounded by six neighbors:

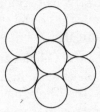

In the second layer, the spheres are not placed directly above those of the first layer, but rather occupy the voids between adjacent spheres:

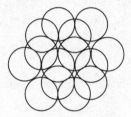

Four spheres (three in the first layer, in triangular formation, and one above) create a regular tetrahedron about a void, which is called a **tetrahedral hole** (or T-hole). A second kind of hole, bound by six spheres (three in the first layer, in triangular formation, and three in the second layer, above, also in triangular formation but offset by 60° with respect to the three spheres in the first row) is also generated. These are called **octahedral holes** (or O-holes) and they are illustrated below. The atoms of the first layer are labeled 1 and those of the second layer, 2:

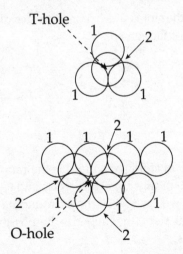

A third kind of hole is also defined, which is between three adjacent spheres in the same layer; this is called a **triangular hole**. For spheres of equal diameter, the size of the holes varies in the following order: triangular < tetrahedral < octahedral. The third layer can be arranged in either of two ways and can therefore lead to two possible structures. In one of the possible structures, the spheres of the third layer lie directly above the spheres of the first layer. This packing of layers gives a lattice with a **hexagonal unit cell** and is known as **hexagonal close packing (hcp)**. In the second of the two possible structures, the spheres of the third layer are placed directly above the holes of the second layer. In this arrangement, the third layer lies over neither of the previous two. The fourth layer would go directly above the first one, in an abc–abc… type of arrangement. This arrangement corresponds to a lattice with a **face-centered cubic unit cell**. The crystal structure is therefore a **cubic close packing (ccp)** or, more accurately, **face-centered cubic (fcc)**.

If there are N atoms in a crystal, there are N O-holes and $2N$ T-holes. The O-holes are the larger of the two and can each accommodate a sphere of radius up to 0.41 times that of the largest sphere without causing distortion of the structure. The T-holes are much smaller and can only accommodate spheres of radius up to 0.23 times those of the close-packed spheres.

CALCULATING UNIT CELL VOLUMES

For a simple cubic close packing cell, with its spheres in each of the eight corners touching their immediate neighbors, the length of one edge of the cubic cell is equal to twice the radius of the sphere:

$$L_{ccp} = 2r \text{ and } V_{ccp} = L^3 = 8r^3$$

The **body-centered cubic cell (bcc)** has one sphere in each corner and one in the middle of the cell.

The cell in the middle prevents those in the corners from touching each other. Instead, the spheres touch each other along the **body diagonal**. The length of this diagonal is equal to $4r$. The lengths of the edges of the cell are:

$$L_{bcc} = \frac{4}{\sqrt{3}}r \text{ and } V_{bcc} = \left(\frac{4}{\sqrt{3}}r\right)^3 = \frac{64}{3\sqrt{3}}r^3$$

For the face-centered (fcc) cell, the atoms touch along the **face diagonal**. The length of this diagonal is $4r$ and the lengths of the edges of the cell are:

$$L_{fcc} = \frac{4}{\sqrt{2}}r \text{ and } V_{fcc} = \left(\frac{4}{\sqrt{2}}r\right)^3 = \frac{32}{\sqrt{2}}r^3$$

COORDINATION NUMBER

The coordination number (CN) of an atom (or an ion) is the number of its closest neighbors within the lattice. Coordination numbers typically range between 1 and 6. The coordination number depends on the size of the central atom, as well as that of the surrounding atoms. The smaller the surrounding atom and the larger the central atom, the higher is the possible CN. Coordination numbers are associated with specific geometries:

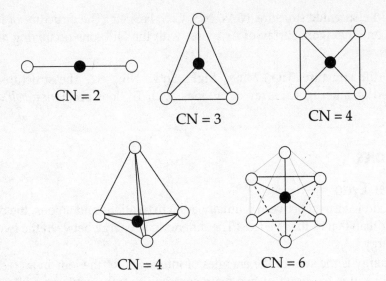

CN = 2

CN = 3

CN = 4

CN = 4

CN = 6

CN = 2 defines a linear geometry

CN = 3 defines a trigonal pyramidal or trigonal geometry

CN = 4 defines a tetrahedral or planar (rare) geometry

Ionic Solids and Close Packing of Spheres

The crystal structure of many ionic solids is usually described in terms of the systematic filling of O- and/or T-holes in a close-packed structure of ions (usually anions) by smaller ions (usually cations). Ionic substances tend to adopt a few basic structures. Most can be seen as lattices in which the anions (usually the largest ions) stack together in cubic patterns, with cations (usually the smallest ions) occupying the T- or O-holes.

The basic structures of ionic solids:

- **The rock-salt, or halite structure: NaCl**, AgCl, AgBr, KBr, LiCl, RbI, TiO, MgO, CaO, etc. In NaCl, the structure is based on a cubic array of bulky chloride ions, with the cations (Na^+) occupying *all of the O-holes*.

- **The zincblende, or sphalerite structure: ZnS**, CdS, HgS, CuCl, etc. In ZnS, the structure is based on a cubic array of Zn^{2+} ions, with S^{2-} ions occupying *half of the T-holes*.

- **The fluorite structure: CaF_2,** $BaCl_2$, PbO_2, HgF_2, etc. The structure of CaF_2 is based on a cubic array of F^- ions, with Ca^{2+} ions occupying *all of the T-holes*.

- **The anti-fluorite structure: K_2O,** K_2S, Li_2O, Na_2O, etc. This structure is the inverse of the fluorite structure; the positions of the cations and anions are reversed. The structure of K_2O is based on a cubic array of O^{2-} ions, with K^+ ions occupying *all of the T-holes*.

- **The wurzite structure: ZnS**, ZnO, MnS, BeO, etc. The structure of ZnS, another polymorph of zinc sulfide, is based on a hexagonal array of Zn^{2+} ions, with the S^{2-} ions occupying *half of the T-holes*.

- **The nickel-arsenide structure: NiAs,** NiS, CoS, FeS, etc. The structure of NiAs is based on a hexagonal array of As^{3-} ions, with the Ni^{3+} ions occupying *all of the O-holes*.

- **The rutile structure: TiO_2,** MnO_2, MgF_2, SnO_2, NiF_2, etc. The structure of TiO_2 is based on a hexagonal array of O^{2-} ions, with Ti^{4+} ions occupying *half of the O-holes*.

LATTICE ENERGIES

The Born-Haber Cycle

When an ionic solid is formed between mutually attractive cations and anions, the overall energy of the solid is lower than that of the free ions. The difference in energy between the two forms is called the **cohesive energy**.

The **lattice energy** is the sum of the energies of interaction of the ions in a crystal. It cannot be measured directly and is the result of two main contributions: the coulombic interactions between ions and the van der Waals repulsive energy.

The coulombic interaction can be evaluated theoretically using compressibility data, and it is called the **Madelung constant**. To get around the impossibility of measuring the lattice energy directly, experimental thermochemical data can be used in conjunction with a **Born-Haber cycle**. The Born-Haber cycle is a calculation of the total energy of a crystal determined by considering all of its formation steps and including a lattice energy contribution.

As an example of a Born-Haber cycle, we will discuss the formation of sodium fluoride from its constituting elements.

The reaction is:

$$Na(s) + \frac{1}{2} F_2(g) \rightarrow NaF(s)$$

The energetic factors associated with each step are obtained by breaking down the reaction into different steps.

Step 1: Sublimation of solid sodium

$Na(s) \rightarrow Na(g)$ $\qquad \Delta H_{sublimation} = +109 \text{ kJ/mol}$

Step 2: Ionization of gaseous sodium atoms

$Na(g) \rightarrow Na^+(g) + e^-$ $\qquad \Delta H_{ionization} = +496 \text{ kJ/mol}$

Step 3: Dissociation of fluoride molecules

$F_2(g) \rightarrow 2F(g)$ $\qquad \Delta H_{dissociation} = +154 \text{ kJ/mol}$

For one mole of F atoms, the enthalpy is +77 kJ/mol.

Step 4: Formation of fluoride ions (electron affinity)

$F(g) + e^- \rightarrow F^-(g)$ $\qquad \Delta H_{ionization} = -328 \text{ kJ/mol}$

Step 5: Formation of sodium fluoride from gaseous sodium and fluoride ions

$Na^+(g) + F^-(g) \rightarrow NaF(s)$ $\qquad \Delta H_{lattice} = -923 \text{ kJ/mol}$

The sum of the five processes represents the global reaction, and the sum of the five individual enthalpy values is equal to the total energy value.

$$Na(s) + \frac{1}{2}F_2(g) \rightarrow NaF(s) \qquad \Delta H_{total} = -569 \text{ kJ/mol}$$

Coulombic Contributions to Lattice Energies

To calculate the lattice energy of an ionic solid, we need to take into account the attractions and repulsions between ions. The **lattice energy**, also defined as the energy released when one mole of the free gaseous ions come together from infinite interionic separation to make up the crystal, can be calculated from the **Born-Landé equation**:

$$U = \frac{N_A \cdot z_+ z_- \cdot e^2}{4\pi\varepsilon_0 (r_+ + r_-)} \bullet \left(1 - \frac{1}{n}\right) \bullet M$$

where N_A is Avogadro's number (6.022×10^{23} mol^{-1}), z_+ and z_- are the charges of the positive and negative ions, e is the charge of the electron (1.602×10^{-19} C), ε_0 is the vacuum permittivity constant (9.95×10^{-12} C^{2}J^{-1}m^{-1}), $(r_+ + r_-)$ is the equilibrium distance between the ions, M is the Madelung constant, and n is Born's exponent.

The value of n generally lies between 7 and 10, and is related to the size of the ions. The Madelung constant, M, is the sum of an infinite series, and it represents the effect on the ion of its neighboring ions. It reflects the relative positions of ions within the crystal, and is therefore dependent on the geometry of the crystal. For the structural types described in the previous section, the values of M are cesium chloride (1.763), fluorite (2.519), rock salt (1.748), rutile (2.4008), sphalerite (1.638), and wurtzite (1.641). The Born-Landé equation only takes into account the attractive component of the total potential energy of the solid. The **Born-Mayer** equation, however, takes both the attractive and repulsive components into account:

$$U = \frac{N_A \cdot z_+ z_- \cdot e^2}{4\pi\varepsilon_0 (r_+ + r_-)} \bullet \left(1 - \frac{d^*}{d}\right) \bullet M$$

where d^* is a constant estimated from measurements of compressibility, usually set at 0.345 Å.

Consequences of Lattice Energies

The two equations shown above tell us that for a given crystal type (or for a given value of M), the lattice enthalpy increases with increasing ionic charge and decreasing ionic radii.

The effects of lattice energies and ionic charges and radii on three physical properties of ionic solids are listed below.

- **Thermal stability**: In general, large anions are stabilized by large cations, and large cations by large anions. For example, let us consider the decomposition temperature of thermally unstable carbonate compounds. Magnesium carbonate decomposes at 300°C, whereas barium carbonate does not decompose until a temperature of 800°C is reached.

- **High oxidation numbers and small ions**: Cations with high oxidation numbers are stabilized by small anions. For example, the only known halides of Ag(II), Co(II), and Mn(IV) are fluorides. The heavier halides of heavy metals with high oxidation numbers, such as copper(II) iodide and iron(III) iodide, decompose at room temperature. To explain this, let's examine the redox reaction $MX + \frac{1}{2}X_2 \rightarrow MX_2$, where X is a halogen. The conversion of $\frac{1}{2}X_2$ to X^- is more exothermic for F_2 than for the heavier Cl_2, and the lattice energy plays a major role in this. In the conversion of MX to MX_2, the charge of M goes from +1 to +2, so the lattice enthalpy increases according to the Born-Mayer equation. As the radius of the anion increases, the difference in the two lattice energies diminishes. So to have an *increase* in thermodynamic stability, the radius of the anion must decrease.

- **Solubility**: In general, compounds that contain ions with widely different radii are generally soluble in water. Consider the sulfate of the alkaline earth elements: the sulfate ion is large, and the solubilities of the alkaline earth metal sulfates decrease, from magnesium to barium sulfate. As a matter of fact, the barium ion is used in the gravimetric determination of sulfate ions. In contrast, the solubilities of alkaline earth metal hydroxides increase, from magnesium to barium hydroxide.

CHEMICAL EQUILIBRIUM

DYNAMIC EQUILIBRIUM

Many chemical reactions are reversible. One hundred percent conversion of reactants to products does not occur for reversible reactions because competing reactions revert products to reactants. Eventually, the rates of the forward and reverse reactions become equal, and the overall amounts of reactants and products remain constant, even though individual molecules continue to react. At this point, the system is said to be in **dynamic equilibrium.**

> **DEFINITION:** In a dynamic equilibrium, individual molecules continue to react; however, there is no net change in the amount of reactants and products.

Furthermore, chemical systems in dynamic equilibrium will remain in equilibrium indefinitely until acted upon by an outside influence.

EQUILIBRIUM CONSTANTS

There's no way of determining, simply by looking at a balanced chemical equation, whether or not it is at equilibrium and whether the system will be mostly reactants, mostly products, or somewhere in between. Instead, the relative amounts of reactants and products at equilibrium are encoded in an **equilibrium constant**, K. Numerical values of K's are determined by plugging in equilibrium concentrations into the correct equilibrium expression. Equilibrium expressions are devised by the following method:

Step 1: Write "K = [product C][product D].../[reactant A][reactant B]...."

Step 2: Substitute the number "1" for any molecule that is a solid (s), liquid (l), or the solvent.

Step 3: All coefficients in the balanced chemical equation become corresponding exponents in the equilibrium expression.

So, for example, the equilibrium expressions for the following equilibria are:

$$PbI_2(s) \Leftrightarrow Pb^{2+}(aq) + 2I^-(aq) \qquad K = [Pb^{2+}][I^-]^2$$

$$NO(g) + \frac{1}{2}O_2(g) \Leftrightarrow NO_2(g) \qquad K = [NO_2]/[NO][O_2]^{\frac{1}{2}}$$

$$HCOOH(toluene) + CH_3OH(toluene) \Leftrightarrow HCOOCH_3(toluene) + H_2O(toluene)$$

$$K = [H_2O][HCOOCH_3] / [HCOOH][CH_3OH]$$

For the last example, H_2O appears in the equilibrium because it is NOT the solvent; toluene is. H_2O is also not a liquid (l) here; it is dissolved in toluene, therefore it counts in the equilibrium expression just like any other molecule.

Finally, equilibrium constants are almost always followed by a subscript. The subscript is simply included for tracking purposes—i.e., it indicates what sort of chemical process is occurring. For example:

K_{eq} is a generic equilibrium constant.

K_p is used for gaseous equilibrium.

K_a is used for acid equilibrium.

K_b is used for base equilibrium.

K_{sp} is used for dissolution equilibrium of ionic substances.

The subscript does NOT change the binding rules and regulations inherent to all equilibrium constants. So never let the subscript of a K confuse you—if it does, simply scratch it out and treat it like any other K you've encountered.

LE CHÂTELIER'S PRINCIPLE

Chemical systems in dynamic equilibrium will remain in equilibrium indefinitely until acted upon by an outside influence. Le Châtelier discovered that there are three perturbations that, in principle, can disturb a chemical equilibrium. They are:

1. Δ CONCENTRATION—Changing the concentration of a reactant or product *that appears in the equilibrium expression* temporarily knocks the system out of equilibrium. In an attempt to reestablish the original position of equilibrium, the system responds by increasing the rate of either the forward or reverse reaction:

   • Increasing [reactant] or decreasing [product] shifts the system to the right.

   • Decreasing [reactant] or increasing [product] shifts the system to the left.

Again, in both cases, the system will eventually return to the original position of equilibrium as dictated by that system's K_{eq}.

2. Δ **PRESSURE**—Changing the external pressure, P, on a system at equilibrium by changing the volume of the reaction container temporarily knocks the system out of equilibrium *only if the balanced reaction has different numbers of gas molecules on the reactant and product sides*. In these cases, in an attempt to reestablish the original position of equilibrium, the system will increase the rate of either either the forward or reverse reaction such that:

    *   Increasing external P shifts the system toward the side with fewer gas molecules.

    *   Decreasing external P shifts the system toward the side with more gas molecules.

Again, in both cases, the system will eventually return to the original position of equilibrium as dictated by that system's K_p.

3. Δ **TEMPERATURE**—Changing the temperature, T, of a system at equilibrium *always changes the position of equilibrium*. Unlike changes to concentration and pressure, change in temperature does not simply knock the system out of equilibrium, but rather *moves the actual position of equilibrium because all K's are temperature dependent*. The direction of the shift can be predicted by the following method:

    Write "HEAT" into the reaction (as a reactant for endothermic reactions or as a product for exothermic reactions). Then, since temperature is "HEAT," use the same procedure in the Δ CONCENTRATION rule to predict how increasing or decreasing T moves the position of equilibrium either to the left or right.

So changing T always changes the value of *K*. That's one of the most important concepts in chemistry, so let's say it one more time.

> *The only way of changing the value of an equilibrium constant (K) is to change T.*

REACTION QUOTIENT, Q

We've already said that plugging in equilibrium concentrations into an equilibrium expression gives the value of the equilibrium constant, K_{eq}. However, if nonequilibrium numbers are plugged into an equilibrium expression, a value different from K_{eq} is obtained. That different value is called the reaction quotient, Q. Sometimes Qs are used to figure out the direction a nonequilibriated system must shift in order to reach equilibrium. Here's how:

*   Keeping in mind that equilibrium expressions always have the form [products]/[reactants], when Q > K the system has too much product and must therefore shift to the left to reach equilibrium.

*   Likewise, when Q < K, the system has too much reactant and must shift to the right to reach equilibrium.

*   If Q = K, then the system is already at equilibrium and we shouldn't really be talking about a Q in the first place.

ACID-BASE CHEMISTRY

THE AUTOIONIZATION OF H_2O

There is no such thing as pure water. Even the most carefully filtered water has trace impurities. That's because small amounts of $H^+(aq)$ and $OH^-(aq)$ are ever present, formed during the spontaneous dissociation of water, a process called **autoionization**:

$$H_2O \ (aq) \Leftrightarrow H^+(aq) \ + \ OH^-(aq)$$

Autoionization is reversible, and equilibrium is quickly established where $[H^+]$ and $[OH^-]$ are equal as long as there is nothing else in solution.

This equilibrium is upset by the addition of compounds that directly change $[H^+]$ or $[OH^-]$, as predicted by Le Châtelier's principle. In fact, aqueous acid-base chemistry is nothing new, it is simply the study of how other compounds in solution disturb the autoionization equilibrium of water via Le Châtelier's principle.

DISSOCIATION CONSTANT FOR WATER, K_w

The equilibrium expression for the autoionization of water is:

$$K_w = [H^+][OH^-]$$

(Recall that H_2O doesn't appear in the equilibrium expression because it is the solvent.)

For pure water at 25°C, $[H^+]$ and $[OH^-]$ have been measured to be 10^{-7} M. Therefore, in pure water,

$$K_w = [H^+][OH^-]$$
$$= (10^{-7} \ M)(10^{-7} \ M)$$
$$= 10^{-14} \ M^2 \text{ at } 25°C$$

Furthermore, regardless of whether more $[H^+]$ or more $[OH^-]$ is added later, K_w or $[H^+] \times [OH^-]$ of any aqueous solution must equal 10^{-14} M^2 at 25°C. That's because *the only way to change the value of an equilibrium constant is to change temperature.*

Why pH?

The $[H^+]$ of pure water at 25°C is 10^{-7} M. Many people find working with an exponential, especially a negative exponential, difficult. For example, try these simple problems:

$$10^{-3} + 10^{-5} = ?$$

$$10^{-7} \div 2 = ?$$

The answers are 1.01×10^{-3} and 5×10^{-8}, respectively. Get them correct? If not, you're not alone because it's often tough to have mathematical intuition when it comes to an exponential. To aid in this, the concept of pH was developed to compare the acidity or basicity of solutions.

Given $[H^+] = 10^{-7}\ M$

$$pH = -\log(10^{-7})$$

$$= 7$$

p is the abbreviation for the numerical operation of $-log$, where the negative log is taken of whatever number follows the p. For example, given that

$$K_w = [H^+][OH^-] = 10^{-14}\ M^2$$

taking the p of every term gives:

$$pK_w = p[H^+] + p[OH^-] = 14$$

Note that we don't care about the units here, so after taking the $-log$ of something, the resulting number has no units.

Doing $\log_{10}$ in Your Head

For some, having to perform a base ten logarithm ($\log_{10}$) is just as daunting as working with the original exponential. If so, try doing logs this way:

> Realize that *log* is a question; it is asking the number that follows: "Hey, number, what's your exponent when you are written as a base ten number (in other words, 10 to some power)?"

$$\log 10^4 = ?$$

("Hey, 10^4, what's your exponent when you're written as $10^?$?")

Answer: 4

Try these:

$$\log 10^{-8} =$$

$$\log 1{,}000 =$$

$$\log 0.01 =$$

$$\log 1 =$$

The answers are -8, 3, -2, and 0, respectively.

Now, taking a logarithm of a number that isn't an even factor of 10 can seem tough. For example:

$$\log 58 = ?$$

Well, on the Chemistry GRE, you can just interpolate and make a guess.

> 58 is between 10 and 100. Since log 10 = 1 and log 100 = 2, log 58 has to be between 1 and 2.

And that's good enough, because the Chemistry GRE is a multiple-choice test, and there will be only one answer choice between 1 and 2.

By the way, you can solve **natural logs**, *ln*, the same way. Just change the question to: "Hey, number, what's your exponent when you are written as a base *e* number (in other words, e^x)?"

Definitions of Acids and Bases

Over the years, several different definitions for acids and bases have been thrown around. For example:

Arrhenius: Acids produce $H^+(aq)$; bases produce $OH^-(aq)$.

Lewis: Acids accept a pair of electrons to form a covalent bond; bases donate a pair of electrons to form a covalent bond.

Lowry-Bronsted: Acids are proton donors; bases are proton acceptors.

The Lowry-Bronsted definition is the one most widely used today, although, it is commonplace for chemists to flip between Lowry-Bronsted and Arrhenius definitions without realizing it.

Lowry-Bronsted Definition

According to the most common way of defining acids and bases, the Lowry-Bronsted definition, *acids are proton donors and bases are proton acceptors*. Keep in mind that the term "proton" is used to mean $H^+(aq)$, and that $H^+(aq)$ is the same as $H_3O^+(aq)$:

An Acid: HA(*aq*) can also be written as

$$HA(aq) + H_2O(l) \rightarrow H_3O^+(aq) + A^-(aq)$$

A Base: $A^-(aq) + H^+(aq) \rightarrow$ HA(*aq*) can also be written as

$$A^-(aq) + H_2O(l) \rightarrow HA(aq) + OH^-(aq)$$

Most compounds behave as either just acids or just bases no matter what other chemical species are in solution. However, a handful of molecules/ions can't seem to make up their minds about what they are and elect either to donate or to accept $H^+(aq)$ in response to whatever else is in solution; these are called **amphoteric** molecules/ions.

DEFINITION: Amphoteric molecules/ions can either donate or accept a proton.

An example is the bicarbonate ion, $HCO_3^-(aq)$:

In acidic solutions: $\quad HCO_3^-(aq) + H^+(aq) \rightarrow H_2CO_3(aq)$

In basic solutions: $\quad HCO_3^-(aq) + OH^-(aq) \rightarrow CO_3^{2-}(aq) + H_2O(l)$

Strong Acids and Bases

Acids and bases that completely dissociate, and stay dissociated, are referred to as *strong*. The term *strong* is NOT used as a common adjective in acid-base chemistry; it has a very specific meaning: It means **complete dissociation**. For example, HCl is a strong acid and NaOH is a strong base:

$$HCl(aq) \rightarrow H^+(aq) + Cl^-(aq)$$

$$NaOH(aq) \rightarrow Na^+(aq) + OH^-(aq)$$

Dissociation here is considered 100% and irreversible, so a one-way reaction arrow is used with strong acids and bases. Keep this in mind when you're asked to calculate the pH of strong acid-base solutions; it makes the mathematics simpler.

Knowing the list of strong acids and bases is a must.

<u>Strong Acids</u>

HCl	hydrochloric acid
HBr	hydrobromic acid
HI	hydroiodic acid
HNO_3	nitric acid
H_2SO_4	sulfuric acid (only the first H is strong)
$HClO_4$	perchloric acid (the one that's usually forgotten)

<u>Strong Bases</u>

Group I hydroxides such as LiOH, NaOH, KOH, etc.

Calculating pH for Strong Acid-Base Solutions

Strong acids and bases completely dissociate. Therefore, for strong acids, [H$^+$] equals the [STRONG ACID] given, and for strong bases, [OH$^-$] equals the [STRONG BASE] given.

Example:

What is the pH of 1.0 M $HNO_3(aq)$?

Solution:

First, write the balanced chemical equation:

$$HNO_3(aq) \rightarrow H^+(aq) + NO_3^-(aq)$$

Second, realize that there is really no HNO_3(aq) in solution. It's all dissociated. Therefore, what we really have is:

$$HNO_3(aq) \rightarrow H^+(aq) + NO_3^-(aq)$$

$$\cancel{1.0\,M} \qquad 1.0\,M \quad 1.0\,M$$

Third, since pH is the $-log$[H$^+$], we get:

$$pH = -log[H^+]$$
$$= -log(1.0\ M) = -log(10^0\ M)$$
$$= 0$$

It's a good idea to remember that for 1.0 M strong acid, pH = 0 because these solutions are commonly used in the Chemistry GRE laboratory questions. Plus, when they're hurried, some test takers have been known to think $-log(1) = 1$.

Example:

What is the pH of 1.0 M KOH(aq)?

Solution:

First, write the balanced chemical equation:

$$KOH(aq) \rightarrow K^+(aq) + OH^-(aq)$$

Second, realize that there is really no KOH(aq) in solution. It's all dissociated. Therefore, what we really have is:

$$KOH(aq) \rightarrow K^+(aq) + OH^-(aq)$$
$$\cancel{1.0\,M} \qquad 1.0\,M \quad 1.0\,M$$

Third, take the pOH since that's what we have:

$$pOH = -log[OH^-]$$
$$= -log(1.0\ M) = -log(10^0\ M)$$
$$= 0$$

Fourth, recall that pH + pOH = 14 (at 25°C), and solve for pH:

$$pH = 14 - pOH$$
$$= 14 - 0 = 14$$

It is also a good idea to remember that for 1.0 M strong base, pH = 14 because these solutions are commonly used in the Chemistry GRE laboratory questions.

Weak Acids and Bases

Acids and bases that partially, reversibly dissociate are referred to as *weak*. Again, the term *weak* is NOT used as a common adjective in acid-base chemistry; it has a very specific meaning: it means *partial, reversible dissociation*. For example, HF is a weak acid and NH_3 is a weak base:

$$HF(aq) \rightleftharpoons H^+(aq) + F^-(aq)$$

$$NH_3(aq) + H_2O(l) \rightleftharpoons NH_4^+(aq) + OH^-(aq)$$

The reversible double-reaction arrow is used in weak acid-base dissociation reactions.

No one memorizes the list of weak acids and weak bases because each has tens of thousands of entries. Instead, the way to identify a weak acid and weak base is first to recognize whether a compound is acidic or basic, and then know that if it's not one of the strong acids and strong bases, it must be weak.

> **Weak Acids**: An acid that isn't one of the six strong acids.
>
> **Weak Bases**: A base that isn't one of the strong bases.

Calculating pH for Weak Acid or Weak Base Solutions

Weak acids and bases partially, reversibly dissociate. As such, a dissociation constant, K_a for acids or K_b for bases, must be used to calculate the pH of a solution of weak acid or base.

Example:

Given that $K_{aHF} = 7 \times 10^{-4}$, what is the pH of 1.5 M HF(aq)?

Solution:

First, write the balanced chemical equation:

$$HF(aq) \rightleftharpoons H^+(aq) + F^-(aq)$$

Second, write the equilibrium expression so we can use K_{aHF}:

$$K_{aHF} = \frac{\left[H^+\right]\left[F^-\right]}{\left[HF\right]}$$

Third, write the algebraic expression (plug in numbers where you have them, plug in letters where you don't):

$$(7 \times 10^{-4}) = \frac{(x)(x)}{(1.5M - x)}$$

A couple of things about this last step: First of all, the stoichiometry of the reaction indicates that for every *one* HF that dissociates, *one* H^+ and *one* F^- are produced. That's how we get to use just x's in the algebraic expression instead of having to use three unrelated variables, which of course would render this problem indeterminate. Second of all, the equation above is actually a quadratic equation. So it can be solved using:

$$\frac{-b \pm \left(b^2 - 4ac\right)^{\frac{1}{2}}}{2a} \quad \text{(quadratic equation)}$$

However, in cases where [HA] is AT LEAST 3 orders of magnitude (10^3) larger than K_a, the fraction of HA lost due to dissociation is tiny and is completely ignored by chemists (this same rule applies for weak bases). So, for this problem, we can now write:

$$(7 \times 10^{-4}) = \frac{(x)(x)}{(1.5M)}$$

Fourth, solve the algebraic expression:

$$(7 \times 10^{-4}) = (x)(x) / (1.5\ M)$$
$$x^2 = (7 \times 10^{-4}) \times (1.5\ M) = 1 \times 10^{-3}$$
$$x = 1 \times 10^{-1.5}$$

Fifth, don't sweat the fractional exponent because it's about to disappear when calculating pH:

$$pH = -log[H^+]$$
$$= -log(1 \times 10^{-1.5}\ M)$$
$$= 1.5$$

Here's another example to make sure you've got it:

Example:

Given that $K_{bNH_3} = 1.8 \times 10^{-5}$, what is the pH of 0.5 M $NH_3(aq)$?

Solution:

First, write the balanced chemical equation:

$$NH_3(aq) + H_2O(l) \rightleftharpoons NH_4^+(aq) + OH^-(aq)$$

Second, write the equilibrium expression so we can use K_{bNH_3}:

$$K_{bNH_3} = \frac{\left[NH_4^+\right]\left[OH^-\right]}{\left[NH_3\right]}$$

Third, write the algebraic expression (plug in numbers where you have them, plug in letters where you don't):

$$(1.8 \times 10^{-5}) = \frac{(x)(x)}{(0.5M - x)*}$$

*Since $[NH_3]$ is AT LEAST 3 orders of magnitude larger than K_{bNH_3}, we can now write:

$$(1.8 \times 10^{-5}) = \frac{(x)(x)}{(0.5M)}$$

Fourth, solve the algebraic expression:

$$(1.8 \times 10^{-5}) = \frac{(x)(x)}{(0.5M)}$$

$$x^2 = (1.8 \times 10^{-5}) \times (0.5\ M) \cong 1 \times 10^{-5}$$

$$x = 1 \times 10^{-2.5}$$

Fifth, don't sweat the fractional exponent because it's about to disappear when calculating pOH:

$$pOH = -log[OH^-]$$
$$= -log(1 \times 10^{-2.5}\ M)$$
$$= 2.5$$

Sixth, recall that pH + pOH = 14 (at 25°C), and solve for pH:

$$pH = 14 - pOH$$
$$= 14 - 2.5 = 11.5$$

Conjugate Acid-Base Pairs

Conjugate pair is a common term used to note a special relationship between two ions/molecules. Specifically:

DEFINITION: A conjugate pair is made up of two molecules that have identical molecular formulas, except that one of them has an additional H^+.

Some examples of conjugate pairs:

$$HCl/Cl^- \qquad H_2O/OH^- \qquad H_2PO_4^-/HPO_4^{2-} \qquad Na^+/NaOH^*$$

*Note that $Na^+(aq)$ can also be thought of as $Na(H_2O)^+$, which makes the last example a bit more obvious (or simply memorize that aqueous metal ions are the conjugates of their metal hydroxides).

Some molecules/ions that are often MISTAKEN for conjugate pairs are:

$$H_3O^+/OH^- \qquad H_2SO_4/SO_4^{2-} \qquad H_2CO_3/CO_3^{2-}$$

Since all of these differ by more than one H^+, they do NOT qualify as conjugate pairs.

Now, the member of a conjugate pair having an extra H^+ is called the **conjugate acid**, and the member with one fewer H^+ is the **conjugate base**.

A word of caution: Just because a molecule is called a conjugate acid or base doesn't mean it's actually acidic or basic in solution.

For example, take the following conjugate pair:

$$OH^-/ O^{2-}$$

By definition, hydroxide is the conjugate acid of the pair, but of course, OH^- is actually a base in solution.

Conjugate Pairs of Weak Acids/Bases and Their *K*'s

Here's a derivation that is pretty important to see again before taking the Chemistry GRE. Take any conjugate pair of a weak acid and weak base, such as NH_4^+ and NH_3. Writing out the balanced dissociation reactions in water for each gives:

For $NH_4^+(aq)$: $\qquad NH_4^+(aq) \rightleftharpoons H^+(aq) + NH_3(aq)$

For $NH_3(aq)$: $\qquad NH_3(aq) + H_2O(l) \rightleftharpoons NH_4^+(aq) + OH^-(aq)$

Then, writing out the equilibrium expressions for each gives:

For $NH_4^+(aq)$: $\quad K_{aNH_4^+} = \dfrac{\left[NH_3\right]\left[H^+\right]}{\left[NH_4^+\right]}$

For $NH_3(aq)$: $\quad K_{bNH_3} = \dfrac{\left[NH_4^+\right]\left[OH^-\right]}{\left[NH_3\right]}$

Rearranging each so that $[NH_4^+]$ is by itself on the left yields:

$$\text{For } NH_4^+(aq): \quad [NH_4^+] = \frac{[NH_3][H^+]}{[K_{aNH_{4+}}]}$$

$$\text{For } NH_3(aq): \quad [NH_4^+] = \frac{K_{bNH_3}[NH_3]}{[OH^-]}$$

Now these can be set equal to one another:

$$\frac{[NH_3][H^+]}{K_{aNH_4^+}} = \frac{K_{bNH_3}[NH_3]}{[OH^-]}$$

The $[NH_3]$'s cancel out, and then grouping the K's and concentration respectively leaves:

$$(K_{aNH_4^+})(K_{bNH_3}) = [OH^-][H^+]$$

Since we've already seen that $[OH^-] \times [H^+] = K_w = 10^{-14}\ M^2$ at 25°C for any aqueous solution, then:

$$(K_{aNH_4^+})(K_{bNH_3}) = [OH^-][H^+] = K_w = 10^{-14}\ M^2, \text{ or}$$

$$pK_{aNH_4^+} + pK_{bNH_3} = 14$$

In other words, *the sum of the pK_a and pK_b of a conjugate pair of a weak acid and weak base must always be equal to 14 at 25°C.* That's a handy bit of info to keep in mind.

The Conjugate Rules

Whether a molecule/ion is actually acidic or basic in solution has nothing to do with the terms **conjugate acid** or **conjugate base**. However, if the acid-base properties of one member of a conjugate pair is already known, then the acid-base properties of the other can be inferred using the *conjugate rules* (as determined in the previous section). There are four conjugate rules covering all of the possible combinations of strong/weak acids/bases:

The Conjugate Rules:

1. *The conjugate acid of a strong base is neutral.*

    Example: Na^+ (the conjugate acid of NaOH) is neutral.

2. *The conjugate base of a strong acid is neutral.*

    Example: Cl^- (the conjugate base of HCl) is neutral.

3. *The conjugate acid of a weak base is an acid.*

    Example: NH_4^+ (the conjugate acid of NH_3) is acidic.

4. *The conjugate base of a weak acid is a base.*

    Example: F^- (the conjugate base of HF) is basic.

Memorize these conjugate rules. They are required in order to make sense of acid-base titration experiments.

BUFFERS

Buffers are just Le Châtelier's principle applied to acid-base equilibrium. They minimize (not prevent) a change in pH when additional acid or base is introduced into solution. Since Le Châtelier's principle requires equilibrium in the first place—i.e., reversible reaction arrows—it's pretty clear that a buffer must be made out of weak acids and bases as opposed to strong ones. Furthermore, the weak acid and weak base must be conjugates, because if they're not, they immediately react, neutralize one another, and fail to establish a reversible reaction.

DEFINITION: A buffer must consist of a conjugate pair of a weak acid and weak base.

Calculating pH of Buffers

Thanks to the algebraic skills of Henderson and Hasselbalch, calculating the pH of a buffer solution has been reduced to an exercise in plug and chug. The most common version of the Henderson-Hasselbalch equation is:

$$pH = pK_a + \log \frac{\left[A^-\right]}{\left[HA\right]}$$

Unfortunately, people often remember this equation incorrectly, either due to the habit of taking –*logs* in acid-base chemistry, or due to confusion about whether [A⁻] or [HA] is in the numerator. So here is a "conceptual test" to check any version of the Henderson-Hasselbalch equation:

Conceptual test: *The addition of a base to any solution, whether buffered or not, will cause the pH to increase—that's a fact. The only difference between a buffered and normal solution is the magnitude of the pH change. So look at any version of the Henderson-Hasselbalch equation and see what happens as [A⁻] increases. If pH doesn't increase, then something's amiss. So,*

$$pH = pK_a + \log \left(\frac{\left[A^-\right]}{\left[HA\right]} \right)$$

Increasing [A⁻] makes the numerator of the fraction $\left(\frac{\left[A^-\right]}{\left[HA\right]} \right)$ bigger, which makes $\left(\frac{\left[A^-\right]}{\left[HA\right]} \right)$ bigger. Now, the logarithm of a bigger number is also bigger (proof: 100 is bigger than 10; log 100 = 2 and log 10 = 1; therefore logs of bigger numbers are still bigger, just not by as much). Therefore, if the $+ \log \left(\frac{\left[A^-\right]}{\left[HA\right]} \right)$ is bigger, then adding it to pK_a gives a bigger pH. So this version checks out.

Of course, the Henderson-Hasselbalch equation can be worked out for pOH. Feel free to go through the derivation, but here is what you would get:

$$pOH = pK_b + \log \left(\frac{\left[HA\right]}{\left[A^-\right]} \right)$$

This passes the "conceptual test" because increasing the amount of acid [HA] should always increase the pOH of any solution.

Example:

Given the $K_{a(\text{Acetic acid})} = 1.8 \times 10^{-5}$, what is the pH of a solution of 0.1 M acetic acid and 0.01 M sodium acetate?

Solution:

First, write the balanced chemical equation that establishes the equilibrium:

$$HC_2H_3O_2(aq) \rightleftharpoons H^+(aq) + C_2H_3O_2^-(aq)$$

Of course, Na^+ is ignored because the conjugate rules indicate it doesn't affect pH in any way.

Second, write the relevant version of the Henderson-Hasselbalch equation:

$$pH = pK_{a(\text{Acetic acid})} + \log \left(\frac{\left[C_2H_3O_2^- \right]}{\left[HC_2H_3O_2 \right]} \right)$$

Third, convert the K_a to pK_a, and write the algebraic expression:

$$pH = 4.7 + \log \left(\frac{0.01\,M}{0.1\,M} \right)$$

Fourth, solve it:

$$pH = 4.7 + \log \left(\frac{0.01\,M}{0.1\,M} \right)$$

$$= 4.7 + \log 10^{-1}$$
$$= 4.7 + (-1)$$
$$= 3.7$$

Some Final Facts About Buffers

Here's another look at the Henderson-Hasselbalch equation, but this time, the concentration terms, M, are expanded into the equivalent $\left(\dfrac{\text{moles}}{V} \right)$.

$$pH = pK_a + \log \left\{ \frac{\left[\left(\dfrac{\text{moles}}{V_{(A-)}} \right) \right]}{\left[\left(\dfrac{\text{moles}}{V_{(HA)}} \right) \right]} \right\}$$

Since HA(aq) and A$^-(aq)$ are in the same solution, the volumes of both $V_{(HA)}$ and $V_{(A-)}$ must be equal. Therefore, volume cancels out, leaving:

$$pH = pK_a + \log \left\{ \frac{\left[\left(\text{moles}_{(A-)} \right) \right]}{\left[\left(\text{moles}_{(HA)} \right) \right]} \right\}$$

Examining this version of the Henderson-Hasselbalch reveals some additional properties of buffers:

- If you're given the number of moles of HA and A⁻ in a Chemistry GRE problem, don't waste time converting to molarity just to plug into the Henderson-Hasselbalch equation. Just put in the moles.

- If the number of moles of HA and A⁻ are equal, then the Henderson-Hasselbalch equation can be simplified to $pH = pK_a$ (or $pOH = pK_b$).

- The pH of a buffer solution doesn't change with changing volume, since volume no longer appears in the equation. Therefore, diluting or concentrating (through evaporation or osmosis) a buffer does not change its pH.

The third point is arguably the most important chemical property of a buffer. Therefore, worth restating:

Diluting or concentrating a buffered solution DOES NOT change its pH.

ACID-BASE TITRATIONS

An acid-base titration is an experimental technique used to acquire information about a solution containing an acid or base. Specifically, an acid-base titration can be used to figure out:

1. The concentration of an acid or base

2. Whether an unknown acid or base is *strong* or *weak*

3. The pK_a of an unknown acid, or pK_b of unknown base

Regardless of the specific objective, the titration experiment is carried out the same way. The procedure consists of adding a strong acid or base of known identity and concentration, called the **titrant**, to the unknown acid or base solution. Titrant is carefully added step-wise and changes in pH are monitored and recorded. With each aliquot of titrant, a fraction of the unknown base or acid molecules are neutralized and converted into their conjugates.

This procedure continues until either the pH of the solution starts to level off after passing through pH 7, or a color change is observed if using a chemical pH indicator.

Analyzing a titration curve, a curve obtained by plotting solution pH as a function of the volume of added titrant, provides all required information.

The Equivalence Point

The key location on any titration curve is the **equivalence point** (also called the **inflection** and the **end point**). It is the point during the experiment where just enough titrant (in moles) has been added to completely neutralize the subject acid or base. At the equivalence point, no unreacted titrant or unknown base/acid remain in solution—only their conjugates do. Keep in mind that conjugate acids and bases need not be neutral (recall the conjugate rules); therefore, do not make the mistake of automatically associating the equivalence point with pH 7.

The equivalence point is located by eyeballing the titration curve: The equivalence point is the point at which the curve is the steepest (line is most vertical).

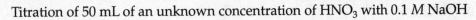

Titration of 50 mL of an unknown concentration of HNO₃ with 0.1 M NaOH

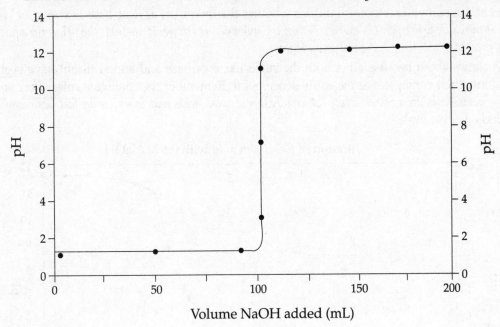

Volume NaOH added (mL)

Determining Concentration

As defined earlier, the equivalence point is that point in the experiment where just the right amount of titrant has been added to completely neutralize the unknown acid or base. Therefore, since the number of moles added of each is equal at the equivalence point, an adaptation of the dilution equation, $M_i V_i = M_f V_f$, can be applied:

$$\text{Molarity}_{(subject)} \times \text{Volume}_{(subject)} = \text{Molarity}_{(titrant)} \times \text{Volume}_{(titrant)}$$

Rearranging this to solve for Molarity$_{(subject)}$ gives:

$$\text{Molarity}_{(subject)} = \frac{\left(\text{Molarity}_{(titrant)} \times \text{Volume}_{(titrant)}\right)}{\text{Volume}_{(subject)}}$$

Therefore, for the prior titration curve:

$$\text{Molarity}_{(HNO_3)}$$

$$= \frac{\left(0.1\,M \times 100\,\text{mL}\right)}{50\,\text{mL}}$$

$$= 0.2$$

The concentration of HNO₃ was 0.2 M.

Strong or Weak

The pH at the equivalence point indicates whether the unknown acid or base is strong or weak. *If the pH at the equivalence point is exactly 7, then the unknown is strong. If, instead, the pH at the equivalence point is greater or less than 7, the unknown is weak.*

This comes about because all of both the subject acid or base and added titrant have been neutralized into their conjugates at the equivalence point. Remember the conjugate rules: *The conjugates of strong acids/bases are neutral, while the conjugates of weak acids and bases are in fact basic and acidic, respectively.* For example:

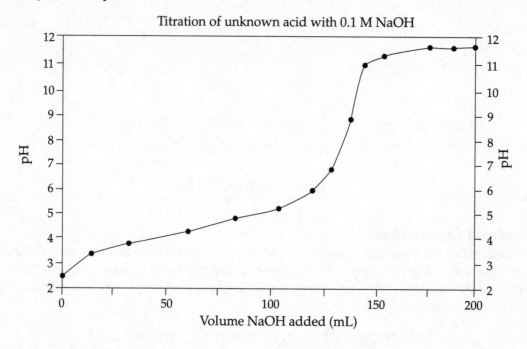

Titration of unknown acid with 0.1 M NaOH

Since the equivalence point for this titration curve lies above pH = 7 (around pH = 9), original subject acid or base is *weak*.

Determining pK_a (pK_b)

Foremost, a warning: Never try to figure out the pK_a or pK_b of a *strong* subject acid or base—you could go through the motions, but your resulting answer would be incorrect.

Figuring out the pK_a of a *weak* unknown acid (or pK_b for a *weak* unknown base) requires finding a second location on the titration curve, the **half-equivalence point**. The half-equivalence point, as its name suggests, is the point at which enough titrant had been added to neutralize exactly one-half of the original unknown acid or base. One can identify this point by locating the equivalence point and then backtracking halfway to zero along the *x*-axis.

The half-equivalence point is an important location on the titration curve because it is the point at which equal amounts of the unknown acid or base and its conjugate exist in the solution. That means the solution is a buffer, so the Henderson-Hasselbalch equation applies:

- For titration of weak acid with strong base: $\quad \mathrm{pH} = \mathrm{p}K_a + \log\left(\dfrac{\left[\mathrm{A}^-\right]}{\left[\mathrm{HA}\right]}\right)$

- For titration of weak base with strong acid: $\quad \mathrm{pOH} = \mathrm{p}K_b + \log\left(\dfrac{\left[\mathrm{HA}\right]}{\left[\mathrm{A}^-\right]}\right)$

Furthermore, since $[A^-] = [HA]$ at the half-equivalence point, the Henderson-Hasselbalch equations simplifies to:

- For titration of weak acid with strong base: $pH_{(at\ the\ half\text{-}eq\ point)} = pK_a$
- For titration of weak base with strong acid: $pOH_{(at\ the\ half\text{-}eq\ point)} = pK_b$

Therefore, the solution's pH at the half-equivalence point is actually the pK_a of the unknown weak acid. For a weak base, the pK_b is quickly calculated by:

$$pK_b = pOH_{(at\ the\ half\text{-}eq\ point)} = 14 - pH_{(at\ the\ half\text{-}eq\ point)}$$

- For the prior titration curve, the unknown weak acid has a $pK_a = 4.5$.

Acid-Base Indicators

An acid-base indicator is just the conjugate pair of a weak acid or base where each conjugate is a different color. For example:

$$H\text{–}Indicator(aq) \;\rightleftharpoons\; H^+(aq)\ +\ Indicator^-(aq)$$
$$(Red) \hspace{5.5cm} (Yellow)$$

Since only a trace amount of acid-base indicators are used in titrations, their acid-base dissociation doesn't impact the solution's overall pH. Instead, the indicator's dissociation equilibrium is shifted one way or another depending upon solution's pH according to Le Châtelier's principle. So as with the example above, in acidic solutions this indicator will be driven to the conjugate acid form (red), and in basic solutions this indicator will be driven to the conjugate base form (yellow).

That's great, but practically speaking, you'll be fine on the Chemistry GRE if you just know that *indicators change color at a pH ± 1 of their* pK_a.

> **DEFINITION:** Chemical acid-base indicators are substances that change color in a pH range ± 1 of their pK_a.

So, for example, Thymol Blue, which has a $pK_a = 2$, undergoes a red-to-blue color change in the pH range 1 to 3. Keep this in mind when selecting an appropriate chemical indicator.

CHEMICAL PROPERTIES OF THE ELEMENTS

GROUP CHEMISTRIES

The elements of the s and p blocks of the periodic table are collectively referred to as **main group elements**. All of the elements in the s block (Groups I and II) are metals, and seven of the p-block elements are usually considered metals. This section outlines the occurrence and recovery, as well as the physical and chemical properties, of main group elements. We will discuss the groups in the following order: Groups I and II, Groups III and IV, Groups V and VI, and Groups VII and VIII.

Group I (Alkali Metals) and Group II (Alkaline Earths)

Occurrence and Recovery

- **Sodium (Na) and potassium (K)** are the sixth and eighth most abundant elements, respectively, in the Earth's crust.

- Because the alkali are all highly reducing, their recovery requires expensive technology; for instance, the electrolysis of molten salts: **Lithium (Li)** is found in the mineral spodumene, $LiAl(SiO_3)_2$, and is recovered by electrolysis of molten LiCl and KCl.

- **Sodium** is found in rock salt (NaCl) and seawater and is recovered by electrolysis of molten NaCl.

- **Calcium (Ca) and magnesium (Mg)** are, respectively, the fifth and seventh most abundant elements found in the Earth's crust. These metals are mostly recovered by the electrolysis of molten salts.

- **Beryllium (Be)** is found in beryl, $Be_3AlSi_6O_{18}$, and is recovered by the electrolysis of molten $BeCl_2$.

- **Magnesium** is also found in dolomite, $CaMg(CO_3)_2$, and it is recovered by the reaction, at 1200°C, of $MgCaO_2$ with FeSi.

- **Calcium** is also recovered from limestone, $CaCO_3$, by the electrolysis of molten $CaCl_2$.

Physical Properties

- The properties of lithium and its compounds differ markedly from those of the other members of its group.

- The alkali metals are all soft and silvery-white.

- The melting and boiling points of compounds formed from alkali metals decrease down the group, varying from 180°C and 1,340°C for Li, to 40°C and 680°C for Cs, respectively.

- They crystallize in the body-centered cubic crystal structure.

- As can be expected from their electronic configuration, the first ionization energy of alkali metals is very low, the product is an ion that has the much more stable rare-gas structure, and the second ionization energy is much higher than the first. Consequently, the chemistry of these elements is dominated by their low electronegativities (1.0 for Li, to 0.7 for Cs), the ease with which they form ions, and the structure of the ions formed.

- Nearly all compounds of these elements are ionic.

- The ionization energies of the alkali elements decrease with increasing atomic radius.

- Alkaline-earth elements are all metallic in appearance.

- Their melting and boiling points are higher than those of the alkali metals. These values also decrease down the group, varying from 1,280°C and 2,700°C for compounds of Be, to 960°C and 1,140°C for compounds of Ra, respectively.

- The first four elements crystallize in close-packed structures. Be and Mg crystallize in the hexagonal close-packed structure, Ca is hexagonal and face-centered, and Sr is face-centered. Ba exhibits a body-centered structure.

- The first two ionization energies of the alkaline-earth elements, meaning the removal of the ns^2 electrons, are rather low, and there is a considerable gap between the second and the third. As is the case in the alkali metals, the IEs decrease with increasing atomic radius.

- Their electronegativities vary from 1.5 for Be, to 0.9 for Ba, which indicates that they will form compounds that have strong ionic character.

Chemical Properties

- The standard potentials of alkali metals are very uniform and only vary from –3.04 V (for Li) to –2.92 V (for Cs). This tells us that they are all capable of being oxidized by water (–0.83 V): $M (s) + H_2O (l) \rightarrow M^+(aq) + OH^- (aq) + \frac{1}{2} H_2 (g)$. This reaction is very rapid and exothermic for sodium and the heavier alkali, and the hydrogen generated is combustible.

- All alkali form binary compounds with halogens. Most of the alkali halides have a (6,6)-coordination rock-salt structure, except CsCl, CsBr, and CsI, which have the more closely packed (8,8)-structure. At high pressures the halides of Na, K, and Rb undergo a transition from a (6,6) to an (8,8)-structure.

- All alkali salts are soluble in water.

- The complexes formed with the alkali ions arise from the coulombic attraction created by small donors possessing O or N atoms. For the s group elements, the smaller the ion and the greater its charge, the greater the stability of the complex formed.

- The most common stable complexes of Group I cations are formed with polydentate ligands such as 18-crown–6 ether or bicyclic 2.2.1 and 2.2.2 cryptate ligands.

- The standard potentials of alkaline-earth metals vary a little more than those of the alkali metals: from –1.98 V for Be to –2.93 V for Ba. They are also capable of being oxidized by water: $M (s) + 2H_2O (l) \rightarrow M^{2+} (aq) + 2OH^- (aq) + H_2 (g)$. This reaction is less rapid for the alkaline earths than for the alkali metals.

Example:

Which forms the most stable carbonate, a magnesium or a barium ion? Is there a trend in solubility?

Solution:

$MgCO_3$ is more soluble than $BaCO_3$. Compare the relative size of the two cations with that of a carbonate ion. Large anions are generally stabilized by large cations. The radius of the carbonate ion is of the same order of magnitude as that of the barium element. The solubility of carbonates should decrease from the smaller to the larger elements in a group.

GROUP III AND IV ELEMENTS

Occurrence and Recovery

- **Boron (B)** is a rare element (~9 ppm). It is found in hydrated sodium borates, such as borax, $Na_2B_4O_5(OH)_4 \cdot 8H_2O$.

- **Aluminium (Al)** is much more abundant (~80,000 ppm). It is primarily found in bauxite, which consists of various hydrates of aluminum oxide, $Al_2O_3 \cdot H_2O$.

- **Carbon (C)** and **silicon (Si)** are also very abundant (~180 ppm and 270,000 ppm, respectively). Carbon is recovered as diamond graphite, or geologic hydrocarbons. Silicon is recovered from the reduction of silica (SiO_2), with carbon, at very high temperatures.

- **Germanium (Ge)** is not very abundant and is recovered in the treatment of zinc ores.

- **Tin (Sn)** is recovered from the reduction of cassiterite (SnO_2) with carbon in a furnace, and **lead (Pb)** is recovered from lead sulfides, which are converted to oxides and reduced with carbon.

Physical Properties

- The lightest members of Group III and IV are nonmetals, and the heaviest are metals.

- Boron and silicon have very similar physical properties. In compounds, they are both chemically hard (there is a big difference between their ionization energies and their electron affinities). In their elemental form, they are hard, semiconducting solids.

- Carbon and boron, like most of the elements in the p block, are polymorphous. All of the carbon atoms in diamond are covalently bonded to four neighbors and form a tightly bonded three-dimensional structure. Because of this, diamond is very hard and is a very poor electrical conductor. Graphite, however, consists of layers of planar sheets made up of the overlap of sp^2 hybrids of carbon atoms. The overlap of the remaining p orbitals forms a p conduction band, which makes graphite a good electrical conductor. Because of the weak London dispersion forces between sheets of carbon atoms, graphite is slippery and is often used as a lubricant.

- Thallium and lead, the last elements of Groups III and IV, respectively, crystallize into a close-packed structure and can therefore be considered metals. There is wide structural diversity within the boron group. In solid boron, the icosahedral B_{12} units are the basis of its chemistry.

Chemical Properties

- The majority of the compounds of most elements of the two groups contain the elements in the +3 oxidation state for Group III and +4 for Group IV.

- Thallium and lead are exceptions; +1 for thallium and +2 for lead.

- The chemical properties of boron, carbon, silicon, and germanium are typical of those of nonmetals.

- The first two elements of each group easily form compounds with oxygen and fluorine, as evidenced by the large number of oxanions they form: borates, aluminates, carbonates, and silicates.

- Boron forms simple trihalides BX_3, which are Lewis acids. These halides undergo nucleophilic displacement reactions to form BR_3 compounds (R = alkyl groups). In boron nitrogen compounds, BN is isoelectronic with C–C. One form of BN resembles diamond, and the other resembles graphite. Molecular compounds including the BN bond include Lewis acid-base complexes and aminoboranes.

- Boranes are a very large group of compounds that fall into three different classes: closoboranes, $[B_nH_n]^-$; nidoboranes, B_nH_{n+4}; and arachnoboranes, B_nH_{n+6}.

- Carbon plays a central role in organic chemistry and is also a member of a great number of inorganic and organometallic compounds.

- Carbon compounds include hydrocarbons and halogenated hydrocarbons, as well as oxygen and nitrogen compounds.

- Saline carbides are largely ionic solids, and are formed by the elements of Groups I and II and by aluminum. Metallic carbides are formed by d- and f- block elements. They are electric conductors.

- Metalloid carbides are formed by boron and silicon and are covalent solids. Halides of silicon and germanium are mild Lewis acids due to hypervalence of their central atoms.

- Silicates are compounds that contain metals and the tetrahedral SiO_4^{2-} structure. In silicates, the SiO_4^{2-} building block may share one or two oxygen atoms with an adjacent SiO_4^{2-}.

- Aluminosilicates are similar to silicates except that aluminum atoms replace some of the silicon atoms.

Example:

Is $B_{10}H_{14}$ a closo-, nido-, or arachnoborane?

Solution:

It is a nido borane because it conforms to the general nido borane formula (B_nH_{n+4}).

Group V and VI Elements

Occurrence and Recovery

- **Nitrogen (N)** and **oxygen (O)** are obtained by the distillation of liquid air at very low temperatures.

- Nitrogen is converted into **ammonia** by the Haber process, which occurs at high temperatures and pressures: $N_2(g) + 3H_2(g) \rightarrow 2NH_3(g)$

- **Phosphorus (P)** is extracted from fluorapatite, $Ca_5(PO_4)_3F$, and hydroxyapatite, $Ca_5(PO_4)_3OH$. White phosphorus exists as a tetrahedral P_4 molecule. Red phosphorus exists as an amorphous solid. Phosphoric acid is obtained by the reaction of these phosphate rocks with sulfuric acid.

- **Arsenic (As)**, **antimony (Sb)**, and **bismuth (Bi)** are usually found in sulfide ores. These elements exist in several different elemental forms, or allotropes.

- **Sulfur (S)** is found in its native form in an S_8 ring and in metal sulfides.

- **Selenium (Se)**, **tellurium (Te)**, and **polonium (Po)** are found in metal sulfide ores.

Physical Properties

- Nitrogen and oxygen are the only members of their groups that exist in gaseous form and as diatomic molecules under normal conditions.

- All of the other elements of Groups V and VI are solids.

- Metallic character increases down these groups.

- Oxygen has two allotropes: O_2, which possesses a double bond and a triplet ground state, and ozone, O_3, which is a highly unstable and strongly oxidizing agent.

Chemical Properties

- Nitrogen and oxygen are among the most electronegative elements in the periodic table (3.04 and 3.44 respectively).

- Their chemical properties are markedly different from those of the other group elements. Oxygen never achieves the rest of the group's maximum oxidation state (+6), but nitrogen does (+5), under strong oxidizing conditions.

- Because of their small radii, nitrogen and oxygen rarely have oxidation numbers greater than 4, but the heavier members of Groups V and VI can reach +5 and +6 (PCl_5 and SeF_6 for example).

- Because of its triple bond, N_2 is highly unreactive. Under extreme conditions, strong reducing agents can transfer electrons to the molecule and break the bond. For example, the slow reaction of lithium with N_2 at room temperature yields Li_3N.

- The halides of nitrogen and oxygen are few due to their resistance to oxidation.

- The halides of the heavier elements are more numerous. For Group V, formulas are generally of the type EX_3 and EX_5, and for Group VI, they're EX_2, EX_4 and EX_6, where X is a halide.

- The two most important oxanions of nitrogen are NO_3^- (oxidation number = +5) and NO_2^- (+3). N(V) is found in nitric acid, HNO_3, N(III) is found in nitrous acid (HNO_2), and N(IV) is found in a gaseous equilibrium mixture: N_2O_4 (g) $\leftrightarrow$ $2NO_2$ (g).

- The oxides of phosphorus include P_4O_4 and P_4O_{10}, which are both cage compounds.

- The important oxanions are $H_2PO_2^-$ (oxidation number = +1), HPO_3^{2-} (+3), and PO_4^{3-} (+5).

- There are many known compounds that contain a PN bond (isoelectronic with SiO). For example, phosphazenes are rings or chains that contain R_2PN units.

- The oxanions of sulfur include the unreactive sulfate ion, SO_4^{2-} (S = +6), the reducing sulfite ion, SO_3^{2-} (+4), and the oxidizing peroxosulfate ions:

  $S_2O_8^{2-}$ (O_3S-OO-SO_3^{2-}).

Example:

What is the probable structure of $AsCl_5$?

Solution:

Trigonal bipyramid.

Group VII (Halogens) and VIII Elements (Noble Gases)

Occurrence and Recovery

- Because of their high reactivity, halogens are found only as halides in nature.

- **Iodine (I)**, the most easily oxidized, is also found as the iodate (IO_3^-) ion.

- The primary sources of **fluorine (F)** are insoluble deposits of calcium fluoride.

- Chlorides, bromides, and iodides are soluble and found primarily in ocean water. The elements are recovered by the oxidation of the halides.

- Most of the **helium (He)** on Earth is produced by alpha emission and is found in gas wells.

- **Argon (Ar)** and **neon (Ne)** are the most abundant rare gases in the atmosphere and, like **krypton (Kr)** and **xenon (Xe)**, are obtained by the distillation of liquid air.

Example:

Helium is the second most abundant element in the universe—why is there so little of it on Earth?

Solution:

Because helium is the lightest of the noble gases, it can escape into space. Only H_2 (g) and He (g) have molecular velocities sufficient to escape the Earth's atmosphere.

Physical Properties

- The structures of the elements of each of these groups display a remarkable uniformity.

- The halogens are all nonmetals and diatomic molecules except A+. The rare gases are all atomic gases with very low reactivity.

- The halogens show a displacement of the maximum absorption toward the longer wavelengths of the light spectrum from fluorine to iodine: Fluorine is colorless, chlorine is green, bromine is red, and iodine is purple.

Example:

Which of the following two species is the most stable: $NaI(s)$ or $CsI(s)$?

Solution:

CsI is more stable. I^- is a large ion and will be stabilized by an ion of similar size. Remember the rule: Large anions are stabilized by large cations.

Chemical Properties

- The halogens are among the most reactive of the nonmetallic elements, and the rare gases (their neighbors) are the least reactive.

- Fluorine is the most reactive, the most electronegative, and the strongest oxidant of all of the halogens.

- Fluorine stabilizes metal ions in their highest oxidation state; AgF_4^- (Ag = +3), BiF_5 (Bi = +5), PtF_6 (Pt = +6). Therefore, metal fluorides, as well as fluorocarbon polymers, are usually used to contain and handle fluorine and reactive fluorine compounds.

- The fluorine atom is very small; its electrons are strongly held by the nucleus. This gives fluorine compounds a very low polarizability and a weak dispersion interaction.

- Because of its high electronegativity (3.98), the fluorine atom tends to attract the electrons of neighboring atoms very strongly in covalent compounds. This effect gives rise to the enhanced acidity of fluorine-containing acids.

- Iodine can form aggregates described by the formula I_n^-. I_3^-, for instance, can be seen as an aggregate of I_2 and I^-.

- There are several known interhalogens (compounds containing a halogen-halogen bond). These compounds are in the forms XY, XY_3, XY_5, and XY_7, where X is generally Cl, Br, or I and Y is F.

- Most halogen oxides are unstable (OF_2, Cl_2O). The halogen oxyanions and oxyacids, however, are numerous and stable.

- The strength of oxacids grows along with the number of oxygen atoms: $HClO$ is less acidic than perchloric acid, $HClO_4$.

- The halogen oxyanions form metal complexes, particularly metal perchlorates and periodates. Halogen oxyanions and oxides are very powerful oxidizing agents.

- The most important compounds of noble gases are the xenon fluorides: XeF_2, XeF_4, and XeF_6. Compounds that contain bonds between xenon and oxygen, carbon, and nitrogen are also known. The compounds of the other noble gases are much less common.

CHEMISTRY OF THE TRANSITION ELEMENTS

The elements found between Groups II and III on the periodic table are called transition metals. They are characterized by special properties that arise from their *d*- and *f*- electron configurations.

Properties of Transition Metals

- Important elements in this group include **iron (Fe)**, **copper (Cu)**, and **nickel (Ni)**.

- They are recovered as ores, and the pure elements are extracted and purified by various metallurgical means (crushing, flotation, smelting, etc); they also occur as salts.

- The metals in the 4th row (Sc to Cu) have electrons in their 4th shell but incomplete 3rd shells (vacancies in the $3d$ orbitals).

- The metals in the 5th row (Y to Cd) have electrons in their 5th shell but incomplete 4th shells (vacancies in the $4d$ orbitals).

- Transition metals have different oxidation states. This allows them to form different compounds with the same element (for example, FeO formed from Fe^{2+}, and Fe_2O_3 formed from Fe^{3+}).

- These different oxidation state are made possible by the fact that electrons can be lost from two different valence shells; in the 4th period, these are $4s$ and $3d$.

- The electronegativity increases from left to right across the periodic table; transition metals with higher electronegativity are less reactive than alkali metals.

- Transition metals form both covalent and ionic compounds.

Chromium (Cr) is recovered from minerals such as chromite (FeO $\cdot$ Cr_2O_3) and krokoite ($PbCrO_4$).

- The pure metal is obtained from:

$$Cr_2O_3 + 2Al \rightarrow Al_2O_3 + 2Cr$$

- It has oxidation states of +2, +3, +4, and +6.

- Cr(II) forms chlorides ($CrCl_2$), and Cr(III) forms oxides (Cr_2O_3) and oxyhydrates ($Cr_2O_3 \cdot xH_2O$), as well as chlorides ($CrCl_3$) and sulfates [$Cr_2(SO_4)_3$]

- Cr(IV) and Cr(VI) both form oxides, CrO_2 and CrO_3, respectively.

Manganese (Mn) has oxidation numbers +2 and +7 in acidic media and +4 and +6 in basic media.

- Manganese is recovered from minerals such as manganite [MnO(OH)], pyrolusite (MnO_2), and hausmannite (Mn_3O_4).

- It is purified in the following way: $3MnO_4 + 8Al \rightarrow 9Mn + 4Al_2O_3$.

- It is used in the production of alloys and manganese steel, which contain about 10–15% Mn.

- Mn(II) forms sulfates ($MnSO_4$), chlorides ($MnCl_2$), oxides (MnO), and sulfides (MnS).

- Mn(III) forms oxyhydrates ($Mn_2O_3 \cdot xH_2O$) and oxides (Mn_2O_3).
- Mn(IV) also forms oxides (MnO_2), and Mn(V) forms another oxide, Mn_2O_7.
- MnO_4^- is a strong oxidant.

Iron (Fe) is recovered from minerals such as magnetite (Fe_3O_4), hematite (Fe_2O_3), pyrite (FeS_2), and siderite ($FeCO_3$).

- Iron is the 4th most abundant element (4.7%).
- Iron's most common oxidation states are +2 (Ferrous) and +3 (Ferric).
- The pure metal is produced from the reduction of iron oxide:

$$Fe_2O_3 + 2Al \rightarrow 2Fe + Al_2O_3$$

- Elemental iron is a silvery-white metal, somewhat soft, with a high melting point, 1,535°C.
- It is used in several alloys, the most famous being **steel**, which has a carbon content that varies between 0.02 to 2.06%.

Nickel (Ni) is recovered from minerals such as chloanthite, (Ni, Co, Fe)As_3, and NiAs.

- Nickel has the oxidation states +2, +3, and +4.
- The metal is obtained by aluminothermal methods:

$$3NiO + 2Al \rightarrow 3Ni + Al_2O_3$$

- Ni(II) forms oxides (NiO), chlorides ($NiCl_2$), sulfates ($NiSO_4$), carbonates ($NiCO_3$),

  and hydroxides [Ni $(OH)_2$]; Ni(III) forms oxyhydrates ($Ni_2O_3 \cdot xH_2O$).

Copper (Cu) is recovered from minerals such as chalcopyrite ($CuFeS_2$), bornite (Cu_5FeS_4), cuprite (Cu_2O), and azurite ($2\,CuCO_3 \cdot Cu(OH)_2$). It is a reddish, soft metal that can be hardened by hammering; it has a high melting point, 1,083°C.

- Next to silver, copper is the best conductor of electricity and heat.
- Its common oxidation states are +2 and +1.
- Copper is resistant to H^+. Only oxidizing acids, such as HNO_3, react with copper.
- Copper is present in the following alloys: bronze (Cu + another metal, i.e., 10% Sn), new silver (45 to 67% Cu + 12 to 45% Zn + 10 to 26% Ni).

Zinc (Zn) is recovered from minerals such as zincblende (ZnS) and smithsonite ($ZnCO_3$).

- Zinc has one oxidation state, +2.
- The metal is purified by electrolysis of the oxide, obtained from

$$2ZnS + 3O_2 \rightarrow 2\,ZnO + 2SO_2$$

and then reduced with coal:

$$ZnO + C \rightarrow Zn + CO$$

- It is a bluish-white, soft metal. Its compounds are zinc oxides (ZnO), hydroxides [$Zn(OH)_2$], chlorides ($ZnCl_2$), and sulfides (ZnS).

LANTHANIDES AND ACTINIDES

- Together with **scandium (Sc)**, **yttrium (Y)**, and **lutetium (Lu)**, the lanthanides are called **rare metals** and their oxides, **rare earths**.

Z	Symbol	Name
57	La	lanthanum
58	Ce	cerium
59	Pr	praseodymium
60	Nd	neodymium
61	Pm	promethium
62	Sm	samarium
63	Eu	europium
64	Gd	gadolinium
65	Tb	terbium
66	Dy	dysprosium
67	Ho	holmium
68	Er	erbium
69	Tm	thulium
70	Yb	ytterbium
71	Lu	lutetium

- They are recovered from various minerals such as gadolinite, cerite, and monazite.

- The oxidation state of lanthanides is generally +3. Ce and Tb also occur as +4; and Eu, Sm, and Yb occur as +2.

- Their properties are the result of partially filled f subshells.

- All **actinides** are radioactive elements, and all have Z > 82.

Z	Symbol	Name
89	Ac	actinium
90	Th	thorium
91	Pa	protactinium
92	U	uranium
93	Np	neptunium
94	Pu	plutonium
95	Am	americium
96	Cm	curium
97	Bk	berkelium
98	Cf	californium
99	Es	einsteinium
100	Fm	fermium
101	Md	mendelevium
102	No	nobelium
103	Lr	lawrencium

- The actinides up to $Z = 94$ are naturally occurring; others are produced in nuclear reactors.
- **Uranium (U)** is recovered from minerals like uranium pitchblende ($mUO_2 \cdot nUO_3$).
- The ^{235}U isotope can undergo nuclear fission.
- U has oxidation states +4 and +6; uranium hexafluoride, $UF_6(g)$, is used to separate U-isotopes.
- **Thorium (Th)** has an oxidation state of +4 and forms ThO_2 (which has a very high melting point of 3,390°C) as well as complex thorates ($Na_6[Th(CO_3)_5]$).

METAL COORDINATION COMPLEXES

Most transition metals/ions readily form coordination complexes with good Lewis bases, or **ligands**. Ligands that form a single coordination covalent bond are called monodentate, while multidentate ligands that form more than one bond are called **chelates** or **chelating ligands**. Many stable coordination complexes are formed from chelates that form five- and six-membered rings. Metals commonly accommodate two to six coordinate covalent bonds in the metal's partially occupied d-orbitals. The number of coordinate covalent bonds to the metal center determines the coordination number of the metal complex.

The nomenclature of inorganic complexes is based on the number and type of ligands bound to the metal center. Ligands are listed in alphabetical order, regardless of number, prior to the name of the metal ion with the oxidation state in roman numerals in parentheses. In cases where the coordination complex is part of an ionic compound, the cation is named first, followed by the cation.

$[Co(NH_3)_6]^{2+}$ hexamine cobalt (II)
(point group = O_h)

$PtCl_2(NH_3)_2$ *trans*-diamino-dichloro-platinum (II)
(point group = D_{2h})

Octahedral complexes of the type MA_3B_3, like $Co(III)(NH_3)_3Cl_3$ have two possible stereoisomers, one where the ligands bind in coplanar fashion (meridonal or *mer-*) and one where they bind in a cofacial fashion (facial or *fac-*).

mer-triamminetrichlorocobalt (III)
(point group = C_{2v})

fac-triamminetrichlorocobalt (III)
(point group = C_{3v})

Basic familiarity with three aspects of coordination complexes is required on the Chemistry GRE: 1) some familiarity with the nomenclature used to describe the geometry/symmetry of coordination complexes, called **molecular point groups**, 2) a rudimentary understanding of the model explaining how the presence of ligands can affect the electron configuration of the metal atom, called **crystal field theory**, and 3) a way of gauging the relative stability of a complex, called the **18 electron rule**.

MOLECULAR POINT GROUPS

The planar molecule X_2Y_4 can be represented using its symmetry elements in this way:

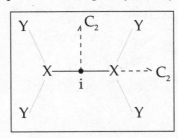

Identity (*E*):	All molecules have identity, i.e., they can rotate about 360° and yield the same, indistinguishable configuration.
Center of symmetry (*i*):	A line that divides a molecule into two identical parts, such that every atom through *i* meets equivalent atoms at a distance equidistant from *i*.
Rotation axis (*C_n*):	Rotation about 360°/*n* yields the same configuration; above, there are two axes of rotation about 360°/2 = 180°. The molecule above has two C_2 axes. This is expressed as $2C_2$.
Mirror plane (σ):	Reflection through a mirror plane yields the same configuration. The molecule above has two mirror planes: the one shown above and another perpendicular to it along the vertical C_2 rotation axis. This is expressed as $2\sigma_v$, where the subscript *v* stands for "vertical." The molecule above also has a third mirror plane, called a σ_h, where the *h* stands for horizontal. This plane is perpendicular to the plane of the paper and to the σ_v shown, and includes the horizontal C_2 rotation axis.
Rotation-reflection axis (*S_n*):	Some molecules exist such that rotation about an axis, followed by a reflection through a plane perpendicular to the axis, yields the same configuration.

When these reflections are applied to a molecule and result in a representation that's indistinguishable from the starting configuration, they are called **symmetry operations**.

The group of all possible symmetry operations that can be performed on molecules of a given configuration is called a **molecular point group**. All molecules and ions can be assigned to a specific point group. A few examples are given in the following table. When a molecule has no symmetry at all—besides *E*—it is assigned to the C_1 point group.

Pt. Group	Elements	Examples
C_1	E	CHFClBr
C_2	E, C_2	H_2O_2
C_{2v}	$E, C_2, 2\sigma$	CH_2Cl_2, NO_2, H_2O
D_{2h}	$E, 3C_2, 3\sigma, i$	C_2H_4
D_{3h}	$E, 2C_3, 3C_2, 4\sigma, 2S_3$	BF_3, cyclopropane
D_{4h}	$E, 2C_4, 5C_2, i, 2S_4, 5\sigma$	*trans*-SCl_2F_4, $[Cu(NH_3)_4]^{2+}$
T_d	$E, 3C_4, 8C_3, 6\sigma, 6S_4$	CH_4, $NiCl_4^{2-}$
O_h	$E, 8C_3, 6C_2, 6C_4, 3C_2,$	$P+Cl_6^{2-}$, SF_6
	$i, 6S_4, 8S_6, 9\sigma$	

CRYSTAL FIELDS

- Normally d orbitals are degenerate orbitals; they lie at the same energy. However, under the influence of an approaching **crystal** or **ligand field**, consisting of charged ligands, the energy of these orbitals will be split by the electric field into two or more groups groups that will have different designations, depending on the symmetry of the resulting orbitals:

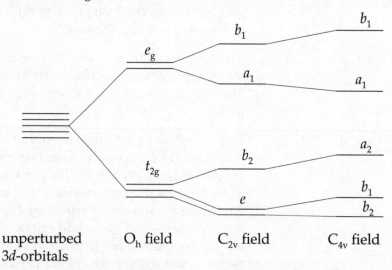

- Some of the common point groups to which transition metal complexes belong are the octahedral (O_h), tetrahedral (T_d), and square planar (C_{4v}).

- In the case of octahedral symmetry, there are two ways to fill the d orbitals; designated **high spin** (HS) and **low spin** (LS), respectively. Whether a complex will be HS or LS depends on the strength of the crystal field interactive energy; i.e., whether the approaching ligands are strong or weak. When the strength of the crystal field interaction energy is less than the energy required to pair up the electrons (the **pairing energy**), the complex is high spin, and when the crystal field interaction energy is greater than the pairing energy, the complex is low spin. When the ligands are strong, they interact strongly with the *d* orbitals, and this results in a larger energy separation between the e_g and t_{2g} orbitals. In this case, electrons will then fill only the lower t_{2g} orbitals first, as dictated by the Aufbau principle (completely fill lower energy levels first). For weak crystal fields the splitting is smaller and the electrons will then occupy the orbitals following Hund's rule (spread e⁻ first before pairing them up): The five orbitals all take one electron before any of them accepts a second one.

Example:

Filling of *d*-orbitals by the six electrons of the Fe^{2+} ion under octahedral symmetry:

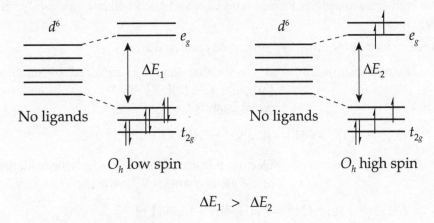

$$\Delta E_1 > \Delta E_2$$

CONSEQUENCES OF E$_G$/T$_{2G}$ SPLITTING

- Transition metal complexes are often highly colored due to charge transfer and ligand field or d-d transitions in the UV-vis (UV-visible) region. Due to selection rules, charge transfer absorptions are more intense than d-d band absorptions. The energy of d-d bands is related to the crystal field interaction energy.

- Transition metal complexes often have different degrees of paramagnetism depending on crystal field strength. The spin-only effective magnetic moment (μ_{eff}) of a metal complex is a function of the number of unpaired electrons *n* and is given by: $(\mu_{eff}) = \sqrt{n(n+2)}$ in units of Bohr magnetons (B. M.). High-spin Fe(III) complexes have five unpaired electrons and have μ_{eff} values near 5.9 B. M., while low-spin complexes have only one unpaired electron and have μ_{eff} values near 1.73 B. M.

- Octahedral d¹[Ti(III)], d⁹Cu[(II)], and high-spin d⁴[Mn(III)] transition metal complexes often distort to lower symmetry to remove the electronic degeneracy. This kind of distortion is a result of the Jahn-Teller effect.

The formation of a complex can be expressed as follows:

$$M^{n+} + L \rightarrow ML^{n+} \qquad K_{eq} = \frac{\left[ML^{n+}\right]}{\left[M^{n+}\right]\left[L\right]}$$

The stability of the complexes formed with divalent ions follows the **Irving-Williams series**, in which K_{eq} increases from left to right:

$$Ba^{2+} > Sr^{2+} > Ca^{2+} > Mg^{2+} > Mn^{2+} > Fe^{2+} > Co^{2+} > Ni^{2+} > Cu^{2+} < Zn^{2+}$$

The **spectrochemical series** provides an estimate of the ability of incoming ligands to cause the splitting of d orbitals:

$$Br^- < Cl^- < SCN^- < F^- < OH^- < oxalate < H_2O < NH_3 < pyridine < NO_2^- < CN^- < CO$$

So in octahedral symmetry, complexes formed with Br^- ions will have a smaller splitting of d-orbitals and will be high spin; complexes formed with CO as a ligand will have a large d-orbital splitting and will be low spin.

The main reactions that coordination compounds undergo are:

- Ligand substitution: A coordinated ligand is replaced by another one: $[ML_nX] + Y \rightarrow [ML_nY] + X$, where L, X, and Y are different ligands

Example: $[Co(NH_3)_5Cl]^{2+} + OH^- \rightarrow [Co(NH_3)_5OH]^{2+} + Cl^-$

- Redox reactions: Electron transfer processes in which the oxidation state of the metal changes: $V^{2+} + Ru^{3+} \rightarrow V^{3+} + Ru^{2+}$

Example: $V(H_2O)_6^{2+} + Ru(NH_3)_6^{3+} \rightarrow V(H_2O)_6^{2+} + Ru(NH_3)_6^{2+}$

The TRANS Effect

Ligand substitution in square planar Pt complexes can yield either *cis* or *trans* products. This depends on the nature of the ligand *trans* to the incoming ligand. Ligands can be arranged in a series of increasing *trans* effect: $H_2O < OH^- < NH_3 < Cl^- < Br^- < I^- < NO_2^- < CO < CN^-$.

THE 18 ELECTRON RULE

The first thing to bear in mind is that this rule is a rule of thumb and that it does not necessarily reflect the actual distribution of electrons in the complex. It is used to predict reactivity or stability, and it works as follows:

1) Assign to the metal its number of valence s and outermost d electrons.

2) For the ligands, assign electrons as per the following table:

Ligand	Electrons Donated to M
H, CH_3, CH_2CH_3, CN, OH, CI, NO	1
PR_3, NH_2, NH_3, CO, RCN, ROOR'	2
Cyclopentadienyl, indenyl	5
Benzene	6
Cyclooctatetraene	8

3) Add up both contributions.

4) When the organometallic complex has a charge, consider a positive charge as an electron deficiency and subtract it from the total; similarly, consider a negative charge as an excess of electrons and add the corresponding number to the total.

Finally, complexes that have 18 electrons counted this way tend to be more stable than ones that don't.

Examples:

Co:	9 electrons	$(4s^23d^7)$
2 Cp:	10 electrons	
	19 electrons	(not very stable)

W:	6 electrons	$(6s^25d^4)$
6 CO:	12 electrons	
	18 electrons	(very stable)

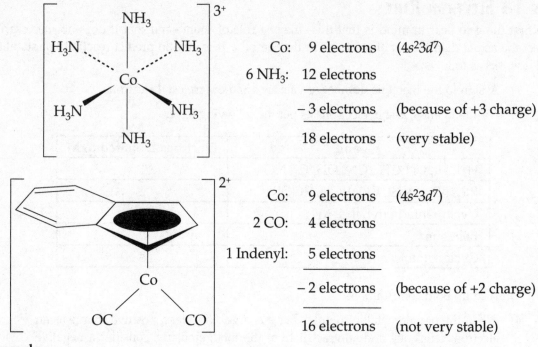

Co: 9 electrons $(4s^2 3d^7)$

6 NH$_3$: 12 electrons

$-$ 3 electrons (because of +3 charge)

18 electrons (very stable)

Co: 9 electrons $(4s^2 3d^7)$

2 CO: 4 electrons

1 Indenyl: 5 electrons

$-$ 2 electrons (because of +2 charge)

16 electrons (not very stable)

Example:

Do (a) Ni(CO)$_4$, (b) [Fe(CO)$_4$]$^{2-}$, and (c) [Fe(η^5–C$_5$H$_5$)$_2$]$^+$ obey the rule above?

Solution:

(a) yes, (b) yes, (c) no. In each case, consider the number of valence electrons around the metal atom, the number of electrons donated by the ligand, and the charge of the ion, if applicable. Ex. (c) 8 + 5 + 5 − 1 = 17, and not 18.

SPECIAL TOPICS

Five special inorganic chemistry topics are covered under this heading: *organometallic chemistry, environmental chemistry, catalysis, applied solid-state chemistry,* and *bioinorganic chemistry.*

ORGANOMETALLIC CHEMISTRY

- An **organometallic** compound is a substance that contains at least one metal-carbon bond. The suffix "metallic" includes main group metals, metals of the *d*- and *f*-blocks, as well as metalloids such as boron, silicon, and arsenic.

- Any one of four possible M–C forming reactions can be used to obtain most organometallic compounds:

    1. Metal + organohalide: 2M + RX → MR + MX, where R is an alkyl group and X is halogen.

Example:

The synthesis of a **Grignard** reagent, which is an organometallic compound:

$$Mg + CH_3Br \rightarrow CH_3MgBr$$

2. Transmetallation: M + M'R → MR + M', where M is a metal that is more electropositive than M';

3. Double displacement: MR + EX → MX + ER, where E is a *p*-block metalloid and M is more electropositive than E.

Example:

The synthesis of tetramethyl silicon:

$$Li_4(CH_3)_4 + SiCl_4 \rightarrow 4LiCl + Si(CH_3)_4$$

4. Hydrometallation: MH + H$_2$C = CH$_2$ → MH$_2$C-CH$_3$. In the case of unsymmetrical alkenes, the M group attaches to the less hindered carbon atom, and the smaller H attaches to the most hindered C.

Example:

Predict the products of the reaction of gallium with dimethylmercury. What kind of reaction is this reaction? Write the balanced equation.

Solution:

Gallium is a Group III element; it's more electropositive than mercury. It's likely to undergo a transmetallation reaction with dimethylmercury, yielding a trivalent covalent compound:

$$2Ga + 3Hg(CH_3)_2 \rightarrow 2Ga(CH_3)_3 + 3Hg$$

- The *s*-block elements form organometallic compounds that have highly polar M$^+$–C$^-$ bonds. The ionic character of these bonds increases for the heavier elements.

- The organometallic compounds of group III (B to Tl) are more polar in nature than are those of the *s*-block elements.

- BR$_3$ and GaR$_3$ compounds are unassociated planar trigonal molecules. The trend in their nucleophilic character is as follows: AlR$_3$ > GaR$_3$ > BR$_3$.

- The organometallic compounds of the Group IV metals (Si to Pb) are electron-poor. The bonds in these organometallic compounds are not very polar. These elements form MR$_4$ compounds with tetrahedral geometry. The low polarity of their bonds and the steric hindrance around the central atom accounts for the resistance of these compounds to hydrolysis.

- The organometallic compounds of Group V (As to Bi) are electron-rich. This Lewis basicity arises due to the presence of a lone pair of electrons on the central atom. AsR$_3$, :SbR$_3$, and :BiR$_3$ are all trigonal pyramidal. The central atom may exist in oxidation states of +3 and +5, as in AsR$_5$, although ER$_5$ compounds are much less common. The AsR$_3$ compounds and some SbR$_3$ compounds may form complexes with some *d*-block metals.

- The term **hapticity** is often used to describe organometallic compounds in the *d*- and *f* groups. The hapticity (η) is the number of atoms of a ligand that are attached to a metal atom. Hapticity ranges from η^1 to η^8.

- Organometallic compounds of the *d*-block elements in Groups VI, VII, and VIII generally have 18 valence electrons around their central metal atom. For Groups 9 and 10, valence electrons number 16 or 18. Complexes that obey these rules are generally stable.

Environmental Chemistry

Over the past 20 years, the commercial use of organometallic compounds has increased to the point where their interaction with the natural environment has become inevitable. For example, fuel additives (methyllead), polymers (organosilicons), and pesticides (organomercury and organotin) now all affect our environment.

- The major classes of **toxic organometallic** compounds found in the environment include organomercury, organotin, organolead, organoarsenic, and organosilicon compounds, as well as some organometallic compounds of the metals and metalloids of the p block (antimony, germanium, thallium, etc.). The presence of toxic compounds of cobalt, manganese, and cadmium has also been reported.

- Organometallic compounds are usually more toxic than their parent inorganic metal compounds. Mercury, lead, and tin are prime examples. (Arsenic is an exception.)

- Many natural, aromatic, coordinating ligands exist in soil water and in sediments and can bind very strongly to metals and organometallic substances. This binding increases the stability of the coordinated organometallics.

- Radicals are often present in the air, and many airborne particulate species can act as catalysts for the decomposition of the organometallic species.

- Toxic effects are maximum for the monopositive species (obtained from the neutral saturated organometallics that have lost one organic group). Examples of these include R_3Pb^+, R_3Sn^+, and CH_3Hg^+.

- The toxicity of neutral organometallics (i.e., R_4Sn) comes from their conversion to monocations by the organism that absorbs them. One of the most striking toxic effects of this in higher animals is the reduction of the myelin coating of nerve fiber, which leads to damage of the central nervous system.

- Some organometallic compounds may be created in the environment starting from inorganic precursors, often through the process of **biomethylation**. Methylation of mercury and arsenic in the environment is well known. Methyltin has been found in ocean water and rivers. Biomethylation usually takes place as a result of the reaction of methyl carbanions CH_3^-, from naturally occurring biological agents such as cobalamin, CH_3CoB_{12}. The methylation of mercury from CH_3CoB_{12} is as follows: $CH_3CoB_{12} + Hg^{2+} \rightarrow CH_3Hg^+ + H_2OCoB_{12}^+$. Bacteria found in sediments can also cause the methylation of mercury, and species such as $Hg(CH_3)_2$ and $[Hg(CH_3)]^+$ can easily penetrate cell walls, thus entering the food chain.

Catalysis

Catalysis is a **cyclic process**. A catalyst introduces new reaction mechanisms (pathways), which causes the catalyzed reaction to possess a lower Gibbs free energy of activation than a noncatalyzed reaction. However, the Gibbs free energy of the overall reaction (being a state function) is not affected by a catalyst. A catalyst also does not influence the position of a chemical equilibrium.

A catalyst is a substance that increases the rate of a chemical reaction without being consumed. Catalysts act by lowering the activation energy of reactions.

Catalysis can be classified as either **homogeneous** or **heterogeneous.**

- In **homogeneous catalysis**, the catalyst and the reagents are present in the same phase. One example of a homogenous catalyst is the catalytic hydrogenation of alkenes by an organometallic compound, chloro(tristriphenylphosphine)rhodium (I) or Wilkinson's catalyst, shown below:

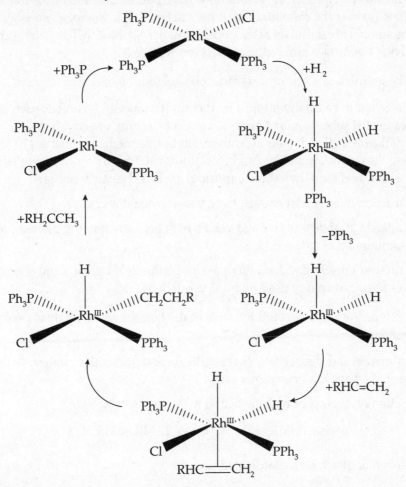

Clockwise from the top structure, the catalytic cycle includes the basic organometallic reactions of (1) oxidative addition of H_2, (2) ligand dissociation of PPh_3, (3) coordination of $RHC=CH_2$, (4) alkyl migration, (5) ligand dissociation of alkane, and (6) coordination of PPh_3.

- In **heterogeneous catalysis**, the catalyst is present in a phase different from that of the reactants. Most heterogeneous catalysts are solids and are easily separated from the products of the reaction. This makes them more attractive than homogeneous catalysts from an economic point of view.

Example:

Determine if the following processes are examples of homogeneous or heterogeneous catalysis: (a) the hydrogenation reaction of vegetable oil by powdered nickel; (b) the oxidation of SO_2 by oxygen, in the presence of nitrous oxide (NO).

Solution:

(a) Heterogeneous; (b) Homogeneous.

Homogeneous catalysts have the same phase as that of the reactants, whereas heterogeneous catalysts do not.

- The **turnover frequency**, N, of a catalyst is defined as the ratio of the rate of the reaction (v) over the concentration of the catalyst ([C] in homogeneous catalysis) or the amount of catalyst (in heterogeneous catalysis): $N = v/[C]$. In heterogeneous catalysis, the surface area of the catalyst can replace [C].

In order to be useful, a catalytic process must possess four distinct characteristics:

1. The reaction to be catalyzed must be thermodynamically favorable; each step of the catalyzed process must have a lower Gibbs energy of activation $(\Delta G^{\dagger\dagger})$ than that of the uncatalyzed reaction. Stable catalytic intermediates must not be formed during the process. Impurities may slow down catalysis by coordinating with the active sites of the catalyst; these impurities are called catalyst poisons.

2. The reaction must be fast enough to be useful when it is catalyzed.

3. The catalyst must be selective and yield a high proportion of the desired product and a minimum of side products.

4. The catalyst must have a long lifetime and go through a great number of cycles without being altered or used up by side reactions.

Five reaction types, or steps, account for most of the homogeneous catalytic processes of hydrocarbon transformation.

1. Coordination and dissociation of reactants (ligands) with the catalyst. Both processes must have low activation energy.

2. Migration of an alkyl or hydride ligand to an unsaturated ligand:

$$L + H\text{--}MR_2\text{--}(CH_2\text{=}CH_2) \rightarrow L\text{--}MR_2\text{--}CH_2CH_3$$

3. Nucleophilic attack on a coordinated ligand:

$$L_5M\text{--}CO + OH^- \rightarrow (L_5M\text{--}(CO)\text{--}OH)^- \rightarrow (L_5M\text{--}H)^- + CO_2$$

4. Oxidation and reduction. The metal ion of metal complexes used in the catalytic oxidation of organic substances may alternate between two different oxidation states.

5. Oxidative addition: $L_4M + AX \rightarrow A\text{--}(L_4M)\text{--}X$ and reductive elimination, the reverse process. One of the best known catalytic systems is the Wilkinson's catalyst, $RhCl(PPh_3)_3$, which is used for the hydrogenation of alkenes. This process involves some of the steps mentioned above.

APPLIED SOLID-STATE CHEMISTRY

- **Solid-state chemistry** is sometimes also called **materials chemistry**. It is concerned with the synthesis, structure, properties, and applications of solid materials.

- The materials involved are usually, but not exclusively, inorganic. Areas of interest include metals, crystal defects, solid solutions, phase transition, and phase diagrams.

- The majority of inorganic solids are nonmolecular. Their structure and properties are based on how the atoms or ions are situated in three dimensions. In contrast, the structure and properties of molecular substances are attributed to the individual molecules. Because minerals are naturally occurring, they are included in the scope of solid-state chemistry. The materials of interest are usually crystalline, but the study of glass is also an important part of this science.

- The **defect structure** of solids constitutes an important field of solid-state chemistry. All solids contain defects of some sort that greatly influence such properties as electrical conductivity, mechanical strength, corrosion, and chemical reactivity.

- **Point defects** occur at single sites, whereas **extended defects** occur in one, two, or three dimensions. These defects can be intrinsic or extrinsic.

- **Intrinsic defects** are present for strictly thermodynamic reasons: the presence of defects in a solid introduces disorder in a perfect structure, increasing the entropy of the system. The formation of defects is an endothermic process, which raises the enthalpy (H), of the system. The Gibbs free energy, $G = H - TS$, is usually lowered by the presence of defects, as long as $T > 0$.

- Two types of intrinsic point defects have been recognized: the **Schottky defect** and the **Frenkel defect**. The former corresponds to a vacancy; a point defect in which an atom or ion is missing from its usual site. This does not change the overall stoichiometry of the solid. The latter corresponds to a point defect in which an atom or ion has been displaced to an interstitial site in the lattice. This also does not alter the stoichiometry of the solid. Frankel defects are more common in open structures, in which the coordination numbers are low. The presence of Schottky or Frenkel defects can be determined by density measurements.

Example:

The theoretical density of titanium monoxide, TiO, is $d = 5.7$ g/cm^3. Its measured density is $d = 4.9$ g/cm^3. Does the solid contain defects? If so, of which type?

Solution:

The solid contains vacancies on the cation and the anion sites in equal numbers. A defect caused by vacancies should lower the measured density of the solid from that predicted, whereas a defect caused by the displacement of an atom should not.

- **Extrinsic defects** are not determined by thermodynamics and can be controlled by synthetic conditions and purification of the solid. An example of this is that electron-rich atoms are introduced into silica to increase its electrical conductivity.

- Introducing defects into solids has provided chemists with a way to change the **optical properties** of solids. For example, adding Cr(III) to colorless Al_2O_3 yields red ruby; the color is a result of splitting the d orbitals of Cr(III). Ruby absorbs light in the UV region and emits a strong red radiation that can be used in **laser technology**.

- Nonstoichiometric compounds are substances that have variable composition but constant basic structure. Their formulae deviate from whole-number ratios. They are encountered among the halides of the early d-block metals and among the oxides of metals that can have more than one oxidation number. For instance, the composition of wüstite (FeO) can vary from $Fe_{0.90}O$ to $F_{0.95}O$ at 1,000°C.

- In solid electrolytes, one or several types of ions can diffuse across the lattice, for instance, Ag_2HgI_4, in which the Ag^+ ion can diffuse at an appreciable rate. Applications of this phenomenon include electrochemical cells such as batteries, fuel cells, and electrochemical sensors.

- **Superconductors** are another important class of solids; they possess the ability to conduct electricity without resistance. Until recently, substances such as mercury had to be cooled to below 20°K to become superconducting. Since 1986, high-temperature superconductors (HTSC) such as $YBa_2Cu_3O_7$, which becomes superconducting at a temperature above the boiling point of current refrigerants such as liquid nitrogen, have been used. The superconductors have structures that are related to that of perovskite.

BIOINORGANIC CHEMISTRY

Bioinorganic chemistry studies the function of metals and nonmetals in biological processes. It can also be defined as the biochemistry of the function of the elements traditionally studied by inorganic chemists.

The following is a list of some metals that are important for biological functions:

Metal	Biological Role
Na^+, K^+	Charge carriers in essential body electrolytes required to maintain homeostasis; required for nerve synapses Na^+ is main cation of extracellular fluids; K^+ is main cation of intracellular fluids.
Mg^+, Ca^{2+}	Ca is main component of bone and teeth. Critical for blood coagulation and transmission of nerve impulses, Mg^{2+} is an enzyme activator; Ca^{2+} acts as a trigger in nerve signal transduction.
$Fe^{3+/2+}$	Present in heme proteins such as myoglobin (O_2 storage in muscle), hemoglobin (O_2 carrier in blood), and the cytochromes (electron transfer in mitochondrial respiratory chain).
Zn^{2+}	pH control, liver function, synthesis of DNA.
Co^{2+}	Essential component of vitamin B_{12}.
Mn, Cr, Ni, Mo	Other essential trace elements.

Cell Membranes

Cells are surrounded by a membrane barrier that separates their interior and exterior. Some substances are produced inside the cell and need to be exported through the cell wall. These can be substances that are required for body biochemistry or unwanted byproducts. Alkali cations function as **carriers** of molecules across the cell membrane.

Calcium Binding Proteins

8, 7, and 6-coordinate calcium is found in many so-called calcium binding proteins, such as parvalbumin, troponin, staphylococcal nuclease, thermolysin, and concavallin. They have various functions, including acting as receptors for intracellular calcium and structural intermediates for enzyme catalysis.

Metalloenzymes

Enzymes are **biological catalysts**. Metalloenzymes are an important class of enzymes characterized by the presence of a metal ion that is an essential participant in catalyzed reactions. Examples are:

Carboxypeptidase A: catalyzes the hydrolysis of the C-terminal residues in peptide chains with participation of Zn^{2+}.

Carbonic anhydrase: zinc metalloenzyme found in plants, animals, and micro-organisms. It catalyzes the reversible hydration of CO_2.

Heme Proteins

Heme proteins have several biological functions. They are involved in electron transfer reactions (cytochrome *c*, cytochrome *c* oxidase, cytochrome P450), they act as oxygen carriers (myoglobin, hemoglobin), and many heme proteins catalyze a variety of biochemical reactions (peroxidases). All are characterized by an active group, the **heme**, which is embedded in a protein matrix that consists of folded, linked amino acid chains. The heme is a macrocyclic porphyrin ring that contains iron as its central metal and whose chemistry is influenced by ring substituents that differ from one type of heme protein to another. The iron can be 4, 5, or 6-coordinate and is always coordinated to four nitrogens in the porphyrin ring. There are two additional coordination sites, above and below the plane of the ring. In hemoglobin, the 5th ligand coordination occurs with the nitrogen of the sidechain of a histidine residue, and the 6th ligand can be oxygen or carbon monoxide.

Blue Copper Proteins

Blue copper proteins (azurin, plastocyanin, and stellacyanin are involved in electron transport and copper strorage functions. Their active group consists of a copper ion coordinated to amino acid residues in a distorted tetrahedral geometry.

PRACTICE PROBLEMS

1. What is the oxidation number of Si in SiF_6^{2-}?

    (A) +2

    (B) +4

    (C) +6

    (D) –6

    (E) –4

2. What is the oxidation number of Co in $[Co(NO_3)_5]^+$?

    (A) +2

    (B) +3

    (C) +4

    (D) +5

    (E) +6

3. $CsXeF_7$ is one of the ionic substances formed with xenon. What are the coordination number and the oxidation number of xenon in this compound?

    (A) CN = 6, ON = +7

    (B) CN = 7, ON = +6

    (C) CN = 6, ON = +4

    (D) CN = 8, ON = +6

    (E) CN = 8, ON = +3

4. What change of oxidation number do nitrogen and oxygen undergo in the following reaction?

$$2\,NH_3 + \frac{5}{2}O_2 \rightarrow 2\,NO + 3\,H_2O$$

    (A) N (–3 → –1), O (–2 → 0)

    (B) N (+3 → –2), O (–2 → 0)

    (C) N (0 → +2), O (–2 → 0)

    (D) N (–3 → +2), O (0 → –2)

    (E) N (+3 → +2), O (0 → +2)

5. Which of the following statements is the most accurate about the first ionization energies of atoms?

   (A) IEs decrease regularly from left to right across a period.

   (B) IEs remain constant moving from left to right across a period.

   (C) IEs decrease from left to right across a period except for irregularities in atoms with three and six valence electrons.

   (D) IEs increase from left to right across a period except for irregularities in atoms with three and six valence electrons.

   (E) IEs increase with increasing atomic number (Z) in a group.

6. Which of the following statements is the most accurate about the trends in atomic radii?

   (A) Atomic radii decrease with increasing atomic number (Z) from left to right across a period, but increase with increasing Z down a group.

   (B) Atomic radii increase with increasing Z across a period, but do not change in a column.

   (C) Atomic radii decrease with increasing Z across a period, but decrease with increasing Z down a group.

   (D) Atomic radii decrease with increasing Z across a period, but do not change in a group.

   (E) Atomic radii increase with increasing Z across a period and also increase with increasing Z in a group.

7. Which of the following species has the largest ionic radius?

   (A) Ga^{3+}

   (B) Tl^{3+}

   (C) B^{3+}

   (D) Al^{3+}

   (E) In^{3+}

8. Which elements are more likely to form strong bases?

  (A) *s*-block metals
  (B) *p*-block metals
  (C) *p*-block nonmetals
  (D) *d*-block metals
  (E) *f*-block metals

9. What is the most reactive nonmetal in period 2?

  (A) C
  (B) N
  (C) O
  (D) F
  (E) Ne

10. Which of the following atoms has the greatest tendency to capture an additional electron?

  (A) F
  (B) Na
  (C) Cl
  (D) S
  (E) Ne

11. ^{214}Po and ^{210}Po differ by four

  (A) isotopes
  (B) protons
  (C) valence electrons
  (D) neutrons
  (E) electrons

12. When an element decays by β^- emission, the atomic number of the resulting element

  (A) decreases by 1
  (B) increases by 1
  (C) decreases by 2
  (D) increases by 2
  (E) does not change

13. Which of the following particles are essential to sustain a nuclear fission chain reaction?

    (A) neutrons
    (B) alpha particles
    (C) electrons
    (D) protons
    (E) beta particles

14. Which of the following statements is false?

    (A) Among protons, neutrons, alpha particles, and beta particles, the beta particle has the smallest mass.
    (B) An applied electrical field does not affect gamma rays.
    (C) Nuclear fusion in the sun converts hydrogen to helium, with a release of energy.
    (D) During nuclear decay, mass is converted to energy.
    (E) ^{14}C is an isotope of ^{14}N.

15. Brass is an alloy of copper and zinc. It has a face-centered cubic (fcc) cell with the copper at the faces of each unit cell and the zinc at the corners. How many atoms of each element does each unit cell contain?

    (A) 3 Zn and 1 Cu
    (B) 1 Zn and 3 Cu
    (C) 1 Zn and 1 Cu
    (D) 3 Zn and 3 Cu
    (E) 2 Zn and 2 Cu

16. Which of the following factors contributes to increased electrical conductivity in semi-conductors?

    I. An increase of temperature
    II. Exposition to light
    III. Addition on an impurity (doping)

    (A) I only
    (B) II only
    (C) III only
    (D) I and III only
    (E) I, II, and III

17. What is the correct expression for the heat of formation (Q) of sodium fluoride if the following thermochemical values are available?

S = heat of sublimation of sodium
I = ionization energy of sodium
D = energy of dissociation of fluorine
E = electron affinity of fluorine
U = lattice energy

(A) $Q = S + I + \dfrac{1}{2}D - E - U$

(B) $Q = S + I + D - E - U$

(C) $Q = S + I + \dfrac{1}{2}D + E - U$

(D) $Q = S + I - \dfrac{1}{2}D - E - U$

(E) $Q = S + I - D - E - U$

18. A compound has the formula XF_4. The element X cannot be

(A) Sn
(B) Si
(C) Sc
(D) C
(E) Ge

19. An element has the electronic structure $1s^2 2s^2 2p^6 3s^2$. To which group does this element belong?

(A) Group I
(B) Group II
(C) Group III
(D) Group VI
(E) Group VIII

20. An atom in Group IIIA of the periodic table of the elements is most likely to

(A) form a 3+ ion
(B) form a 3– ion
(C) be a poor conductor of heat and electricity
(D) be a nonmetal
(E) have an oxide of the general formula RO

21. Which of the following must happen to form cations from neutral atoms?

 (A) Protons must be gained

 (B) Protons must be lost

 (C) Electrons must be gained

 (D) Electrons must be lost

 (E) Neutrons must change

22. Which of the following elements is a metal that does not react with acids?

 (A) Uranium

 (B) Helium

 (C) Sodium

 (D) Iron

 (E) Gold

23. Select one of the following answers for questions (a) to (e):

 (A) Group I

 (B) Group II

 (C) Group VI

 (D) Group V

 (E) Group VIII

 (a) The elements of this group react with water to form hydrogen gas.

 (b) The elements of this group are characterized by atoms that are gaseous at STP.

 (c) The elements of this group are characterized by half-filled p orbitals.

 (d) The elements of this group are characterized by the start of pairing p electrons.

 (e) The elements of this group are characterized by very reactive metals.

 Select one of the following answers for questions (f) to (i):

 (A) Amorphous compound

 (B) Nonpolar covalent compound

 (C) Polar covalent compound

 (D) Metal

 (E) Ionic substance

 (f) Solid lithium is a(n)

 (g) Methane is a(n)

 (h) Gaseous hydrochloric acid is a(n)

 (i) Lithium chloride is a(n)

24. Which of the following bonds are ionic?

        I. H–Cl

        II. Rb–Cl

        III. S–Cl

    (A) I only

    (B) II only

    (C) III only

    (D) I and II only

    (E) None of the above

25. Which of the following statements is true?

    (A) A catalyst modifies the enthalpy of a system.

    (B) A catalyst modifies the nature of the product of a reaction.

    (C) A catalyst modifies the entropy of a system.

    (D) A catalyst modifies the activation energy of a system.

    (E) A catalyst modifies the equilibrium position of a system.

26. Rank boron, strontium, chlorine, and lithium in order of increasing electronegativity.

27. Why don't we assign electronegativity values to the noble gases?

28. Identify the smaller species in each of the following pairs:

    (A) S and O

    (B) Ar and K

    (C) Ca^{2+} and K^+

    (D) I^- and Br^-

29. Rank barium, calcium, argon, sulfur, and copper in order of increasing first ionization energy.

30. Rank the elements carbon, calcium, fluorine, aluminum, and oxygen in order of least-negative to most-negative electron affinity.

31. Identify the stronger base in each of the following pairs:

    (A) H_2O and H_2Se

    (B) H_2O and NH_3

    (C) H_2O and HF

32. Which one of the following chemical species has an octet configuration?

    (A) K

    (B) Cl^-

    (C) O^-

    (D) Fe^{2+}

    (E) Ar^+

33. Write the complete Lewis structure for sulfur dioxide, SO_2. Include any formal charges and specify the shape of this molecule.

34. For each of the following, identify the shape of the molecule and the hybridization of the central atom: BrF_3, CO_2, PO_3^{3-}, and $XeOF_4$.

35. Which of the following compounds are covalent and which are ionic?

    (A) Na_2CO_3

    (B) H_2CO

    (C) NH_2OH

    (D) NH_4Br

    (E) PbO_2

    [*Note:* Multi-atom (polyatomic) ions, such as NH_4^+ and CO_3^{2-}, are also called *complex ions*.]

36. Identify which of the salts in each of the following pairs of ionic compounds has the greater ionic attraction:

    (A) NaI or CaS

    (B) Li_2O or LiF

37. Which of the following dipole-dipole interactions are hydrogen bonding interactions?

    (A) water ↔ glass (= SiO_2)

    (B) ammonia ↔ water

    (C) hydrogen sulfide ↔ hydrogen fluoride

    (D) ammonia ↔ hydrogen chloride

38. Which of the following acids is the weakest?

    (A) CH_3COOH $K_a = 1.75 \times 10^{-5}$

    (B) C_6H_5COOH $K_a = 6.30 \times 10^{-5}$

    (C) HCOOH $K_a = 1.76 \times 10^{-4}$

    (D) HNO_2 $K_a = 5.10 \times 10^{-4}$

    (E) HF $K_a = 6.70 \times 10^{-4}$

39. What is the volume of 0.5 M NaOH required to prepare 100 mL of 0.1 M NaOH?

    (A) 5 mL

    (B) 10 mL

    (C) 15 mL

    (D) 20 mL

    (E) 25 mL

40. What is the pH of a 10^{-4} M solution of HCl?

    (A) 2

    (B) 4

    (C) 7

    (D) 9

    (E) 11

41. The following titration curve is representative of which of the following titrations?

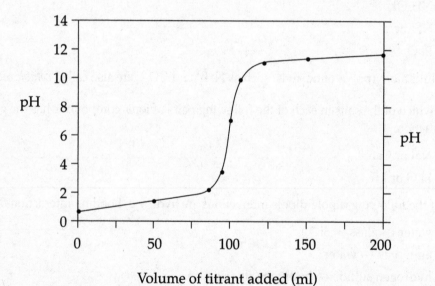

Volume of titrant added (ml)

    (A) HCl with NaOH

    (B) CH_3COOH with NaOH

    (C) HCl with NH_3

    (D) NaOH with HF

    (E) KCl with HNO_3

42. Which of the following acids is polyprotic?

   (A) CH_3COOH
   (B) H_2CO_3
   (C) HOCl
   (D) HNO_3
   (E) All of them

43. During a redox reaction, the oxidizing agent will

   (A) lose electrons
   (B) be oxidized
   (C) gain electrons
   (D) all of the above
   (E) none of the above

ANSWERS TO PRACTICE PROBLEMS

1. **B**   To answer this question you have to remember that the oxidation number of halogens is –1 and that the algebraic sum of *all the oxidation numbers* is equal to zero in a neutral atom or to the charge of the ion, as is the case here. Therefore: oxidation number (Si) = –2 – 6(–1) = +4.

2. **E**   The nitrate ion has an oxidation number of –1. According to the rule stated above, oxidation number (Co) = +1 – 5(–1) = +6.

3. **B**   First recognize that Cs is an alkaline metal and the charge of its ion is +1; therefore the anion is XeF_7^-. Then determine the oxidation number of Xe: –1 – 7(–1) = +6, and count the number of atoms bonded to the Xe (7 fluorine atoms).

4. **D**   Determine the oxidation number of N and O in both the reactants and the products. Rule 1: The oxidation number of a free element or atom in its elemental state is zero.

5. **D**   In a period, all the valence electrons possess the same principal quantum number (*n*). As the number of electrons increases, so does the nuclear charge that binds them more strongly to the nucleus. There is also greater stability associated with half-filled orbitals (np^3 and a resulting decrease of IE from np^3 to np^4 configurations) and filled orbitals (ns^2 and np^6 and a resulting decrease from $(n + 1)s^2$ and ns^2np^1 configurations).

6. **A**   Across a period, all of the valence electrons are at the same energy level, which is pulled together more strongly as the atomic number increases. In a group, the addition of successive energy levels causes the valence electrons to be farther from the nucleus as *n* increases.

7. **B**   All of these ions are formed from group (III) elements. Down a group, atomic and ionic radii increase.

8. **A**   An indication of the metallic character of an element is the strength of the base formed from the reaction of its oxide with water. For instance, $Li + \frac{1}{2}O_2 \rightarrow Li_2O$ and $Li_2O + H_2O \rightarrow 2\,Li^+ + 2OH^-$. Oxides of the elements at the upper right of the periodic table react with water to form acids: $SO_3 + 3H_2O \rightarrow 2H_3O^+ + SO_4^{2-}$.

9. **D**   Fluorine is the most electronegative element and can react violently with elements having very low electronegativities, such as Cs.

10. **A**   The elements in the upper right corner of the periodic table possess the highest electron affinities of all elements. By capturing an additional electron, fluorine completes its valence shell and thus acquires the structure and stability of a noble gas.

11. **D**   These are the isotopes of polonium. They have the same atomic number, 84, (thus 84 protons and electrons) but differ by their **mass number**, which is the number in the upper left corner of the atomic symbol. The mass number *A* is the sum of the number of protons and neutrons in the nucleus: $A = n + p$.

12. **B**   During beta decay, or electron emission, one neutron decays into a proton, which stays in the nucleus, and a fast electron is ejected from the nucleus (the beta particle). The mass number A of the new element is the same, but the atomic number has increased by one.

13. **A**   During a nuclear fission reaction, one *slow* neutron is required to initiate the reaction and three fast neutrons are produced; this perpetuates the chain reaction.

14. **E**   Isotopes are atoms of *the same element* that have the same Z but different values of A.

15. **B**   In a face-centered cubic cell, the atoms that occupy each of the eight corners belong to eight adjacent cubic cells. Or, each corner of one cubic cell contains one-eighth of an atom. The atoms at each of the six faces belong to only two unit cells, or each face has half of an atom. Summing up, we have $8 \times \dfrac{1}{8} = 1$ atom (Zn), and $6 \times \dfrac{1}{2} = 3$ atoms (Cu).

16. **E**   An increase in temperature makes the electrons more mobile. They can also absorb light and "jump" into a conduction band. The addition of impurities to a semiconductor can either increase the number of negative carriers (like the electron-rich phosphorus atoms introduced into a silicon crystal) or the number of positive holes (like the electron-deficient boron introduced into a silicon crystal).

17. **A** Q is the sum of the heat produced in every step of the formation of NaF from solid sodium and gaseous fluorine atoms. The processes corresponding to S, I, and D are endothermic and are assigned a positive sign in the sum. Because only one fluorine atom is required, the value of D must be divided by two. Fluorine is the element with the highest electron affinity and taking an electron is an exothermic process. U is the energy released when a gaseous sodium ion binds a gaseous fluorine ion. E and U are exothermic processes and are assigned negative signs.

18. **C**   Sn, Si, C, and Ge all belong to Group IV and have four valence electrons (ns^2np^2), thus allowing them to form four covalent bonds with fluorine atoms. Sc belongs to Group IIIB and has the electronic configuration $[Ar]4s^23d^1$.

19. **B**   This element only has two electrons in its highest electron shell ($n = 3$). Therefore it is an alkaline-earth.

20. **A**   Elements in this group have the electronic configuration ns^2np^1 and are more likely to form cations by losing their valence electrons (metals) than anions. All Group IIIA elements are metals, with the exception of boron, and they're all good conductors.

21. **D**   A cation is a species with a number of electrons inferior to the nuclear charge. The formation of cations involves the loss of valence electrons, usually through transfer to atoms with high electron affinities, such as fluorine.

22. **E**   Gold offers a very good resistance to acid and is known as a noble metal.

23.

   (a)   **(A)** This behavior is characteristic of the reactive alkali metals, which readily react with water to form hydroxides and hydrogen. For example,
   $$2Na(s) + 2H_2O(l) \rightarrow 2NaOH(aq) + H_2(g)$$

   (b)   **(E)** Noble gases have completely filled outer energy levels and are nonreactive under normal conditions. Under STP conditions, very weak interactive forces exist between individual atoms.

   (c)   **(D)** The elements of Group V are characterized by the electronic configuration ns^2np^3. In accordance with Hund's rule, which states that pairing can only occur after all individual orbitals of a given subshell have received one electron, the np^3 configuration corresponds to the half-filling of these orbitals.

(d) **(C)** Pairing of electrons in orbitals only starts after each orbital has received one electron (ns^2np^4).

(e) **(A)** With their ns^1 electronic configuration, alkali metals have the lowest ionization energy and react very rapidly with nonmetals possessing high electron affinities.

(f) **(D)** Elemental lithium is an alkali metal.

(g) **(B)** Examine the symmetry and structure of the CH_4 molecule. Although each of the four C–H bonds is slightly polar, their respective orientation is such that the resultant dipole moment of the molecule is zero.

(h) **(C)** The difference in electronegativity between the H and Cl atoms is about 0.5. Therefore the diatomic HCl molecule is polar. HCl in aqueous solution is considered a strong acid and dissociates completely.

(i) **(E)** LiCl consists of an active metal and an active nonmetal; the difference in their respective electronegativities is 2.5, characteristic of ionic substances.

24. **B** Examine the difference of electronegativity between the atoms. Rb and Cl also belong to opposite ends of the periodic table.

25. **D** A catalyst increases the rate of chemical reaction by lowering the activation energy.

26. Based upon the fact that electronegativity increases as one moves up or to the right of the periodic table, the correct order of increasing electronegativity is: strontium < lithium < boron < chlorine.

27. Electronegativity is the measure of an atom's ability to attract bonding electrons in a molecule. Since noble gases generally do not form molecules, we don't assign them electronegativities.

28. The smaller species in pair (A) is O, in pair (B) it's Ar, in pair (C) it's Ca^{2+}, and in pair (D) it's Br^-.

29. The correct answer is Ba < Ca < Cu < S < Ar.

30. Calcium is a member of the beryllium family and actually has a positive electron affinity. Since electron affinity becomes more negative (in general) as we move across a row or up a column, we expect the other four elements to have electron affinities that become more negative in the order Al, C, O, F. Thus, electron affinity becomes more negative in the order Ca, Al, C, O, F.

31. The more basic species in pair (A) is water, in pair (B) it's NH_3, and in pair (C) it's water.

32. **B** The electronic configurations for these species are

(A) K: [Ar] $4s^1$ — no octet

(B) Cl^-: [Ne] $3s^23p^6$ — octet configuration

(C) O^-: [He] $2s^22p^5$ — no octet

(D) Fe^{2+}: [Ar] $3d^6$ — no octet

(E) Ar^+: [Ne] $3s^23p^5$ — no octet

33.

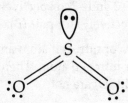

—All atoms are neutral.
—SO_2 has a *trigonal planar* geometry; however, its shape is *bent*.

34.

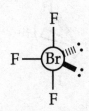

T- shaped and sp^3d hybridized

$$O = C = O$$

Linear and *sp* hybridized

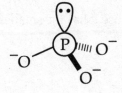

Trigonal pyramid and sp^3 hybridized

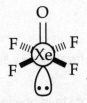

Square pyramid and sp^2d^3 hybridized

35.   **(A):** Ionic between the sodium and carbonate $CO_3{}^{2-}$, although the carbonate ion is covalently bonded internally.

(B) and **(C):** Formaldehyde, H_2CO, and hydroxyamine, NH_2OH, are pure covalent compounds.

(D) and **(E):** Ammonium bromide, NH_4Br, and lead(IV) oxide, PbO_2, are both ionic compounds, although the ammonium ion (like $CO_3{}^{2-}$) is also covalently bonded internally.

[Note: Multi-atom (polyatomic) ions, such as $NH_4{}^+$ and $CO_3{}^{2-}$, are also called *complex ions*.]

36.   Since the ionic force between two ions is proportional to the charges of the ions, the correct answers are CaS (charges of Ca and S are +2 and –2, respectively) for pair (A), and Li_2O (charges of Li and O are +1 and –2, respectively) for pair (B).

37.   Hydrogen bonds exist between a fluorine, oxygen, or nitrogen atom and a hydrogen covalently bonded to another fluorine, oxygen, or nitrogen atom. Therefore, (A) and (B) are examples of hydrogen bonding, but (C) and (D) are not:

hydrogen bonding   hydrogen bonding

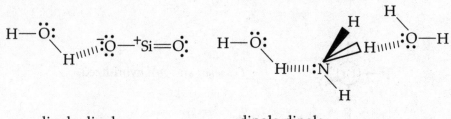

dipole-dipole   dipole-dipole

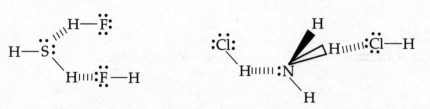

38. **A**   Acetic acid (CH_3COOH) is the weakest acid because it has the smallest K_a. This is indicative of less dissociation in solution.

39. **D** $V_i = \dfrac{V_f \times M_f}{M_i} = 100 \text{ mL} \times \dfrac{0.1M \text{ NaOH}}{0.5M} = 20 \text{ mL}$

40. **B**   Since HCl is a strong acid, we can assume that 100% of the HCl is dissociated and therefore the $[H^+] = 10^{-4}M$, pH = $-log[H^+]$

$$= -log\,[10^{-4}M]$$

$$= 4$$

41. **A**   Since the equivalence point occurs at pH7, this is a titration of a strong acid with strong base.

42. **B**   Carbonic acid is a polyprotic acid because it has more than one ionizable proton. Polyprotic acids dissociate according to the following equilibria:

$$H_xA \leftrightarrow XH^+ + A^{x-} \qquad K_a = K_{a1} + K_{a2} + \ldots + K_{ax}$$

where x is the number of ionizable protons. When $x = 2$, a polyprotic acid can be called diprotic.

H_2CO_3 has $x = 2$ and dissociates as follow:

1. $H_2CO_3 \leftrightarrow H^+ + HCO_3^-$ $K_{a1} = 4.3 \times 10^{-7}$

2. $HCO_3^- \leftrightarrow H^+ + CO_3^{2-}$ $K_{a2} = 4.8 \times 10^{-11}$

43. **C**   An oxidizing agent is reduced and therefore gains electrons.

3

Organic Chemistry

ORGANIC CHEMISTRY

Organic chemistry is the study of carbon, its compounds, and the reactions that they undergo. We will cover six topics under this heading: *IUPAC Nomenclature, Isomers, Reaction Mechanisms, Functional Groups, Reactive Intermediates,* and *Special Topics.*

IUPAC NOMENCLATURE

The International Union of Pure and Applied Chemistry (IUPAC) regulates the systematic nomenclature of all compounds. In this section, we will review the basic principles of hydrocarbon nomenclature. We will describe the nomenclature of functional groups in a later section, as specific compounds are introduced. Hydrocarbons are classified as follows:

Hydrocarbon	Characteristic	Example
Saturated:		
acyclic, unbranched	C–C, linear chain	CH_4 ethane
univalent radicals	C–C, one H lost	CH_3 ethyl
acyclic, branched	C–C, nonlinear chain	3-methylhexane
cyclic	C–C in ring structures	cyclopropane
Unsaturated:		
alkenes	C=C, linear chain	ethene
dienes, trienes	two or more C=C, linear	hexadiene
alkynes	C≡C, linear chain	pentyne
cyclic	C=C in ring structures	cyclopropene
Aromatic:		
benzene and derivatives	six-membered ring structure with conjugated C=C bonds	toluene
fused benzene system	six-membered ring structures with conjugated C=C bonds, fused	naphthalene
other		porphyrin

SATURATED HYDROCARBONS

- **Acyclic, unbranched alkanes**

Acyclic hydrocarbons have their carbons arranged in chains. They have only single C–C bonds, which is why they are designated "saturated"; the carbons bind the maximum number of hydrogens possible. They are also called **alkanes**. Their names consist of a numerical prefix with the ending *-ane*.

n	Name	Formula
1	Methane	CH_4
2	Ethane	C_2H_6
3	Propane	C_3H_8
4	Butane	C_4H_{10}
5	Pentane	C_5H_{12}
6	Hexane	C_6H_{14}
7	Heptane	C_7H_{16}
8	Octane	C_8H_{18}
9	Nonane	C_9H_{20}
10	Decane	$C_{10}H_{22}$

- **Univalent radicals**

Univalent radicals are obtained by removing one hydrogen from an alkane. They are called **alkyls** and they are named by replacing the *-ane* ending of the alkane by *-yl*. The carbon atom with the free valence is assigned the number 1.

Examples:

$$\underset{4}{CH_3}\!-\!\underset{3}{CH_2}\!-\!\underset{2}{CH_2}\!-\!\underset{1}{CH_2}\bullet \qquad \underset{10}{CH_3}\!-\!\underset{9\text{-}2}{[CH_2]_8}\!-\!\underset{1}{CH_2}\bullet$$

butyl   **decyl**

- **Branched alkanes**

These compounds are named after the longest carbon chain in the molecule. The name is prefixed by a term describing the side chain and the number of the carbon it's attached to.

Examples:

2-methylpentane

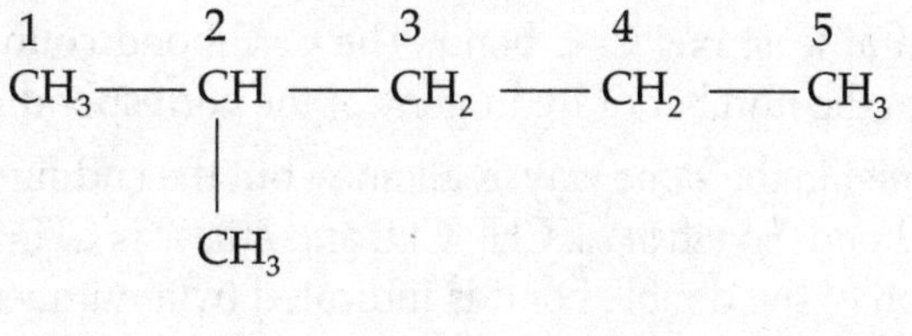

$$\underset{1}{CH_3}\!-\!\underset{2}{CH}\!-\!\underset{3}{CH_2}\!-\!\underset{4}{CH_2}\!-\!\underset{5}{CH_3}$$
$$|$$
$$CH_3$$

2, 3, 5-trimethylhexane

$$\underset{6}{CH_3}\!-\!\underset{5}{CH}\!-\!\underset{4}{CH_2}\!-\!\underset{3}{CH}\!-\!\underset{2}{CH}\!-\!\underset{1}{CH_3}$$
$$\qquad\;\; |\qquad\qquad\quad |\qquad |$$
$$\quad\; CH_3\qquad\qquad CH_3\;\; CH_3$$

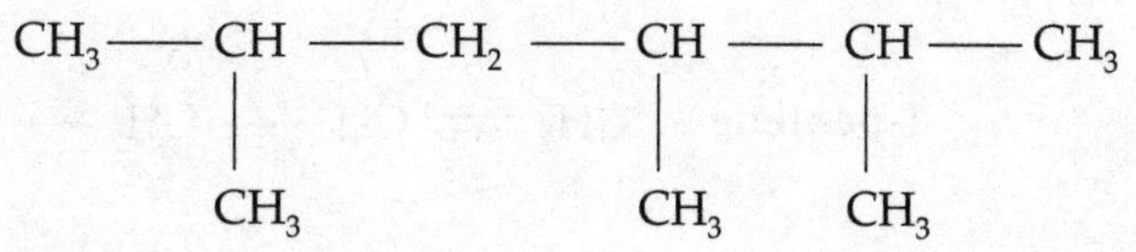

Naming alkanes:

—use the longest C-chain to name the alkane
—assign numbers to the carbons starting with the end nearest a branch
—the substituent groups (-yl) prefix the name of the alkane
—and they are prefixed by the number of the carbon to which they are attached
—if they are different, they are listed in alphabetical order
—if they are the same, they are prefixed di-, tri-, tetra-, etc.

- **Cycloalkanes**

Alkanes closed in a ring structure are called **cycloalkanes**. They are named like the acyclic alkanes and prefixed with *cyclo-*. In cycloalkanes, the carbons are listed alphabetically and numbered in the direction that gives the lowest possible number to the other substituents:

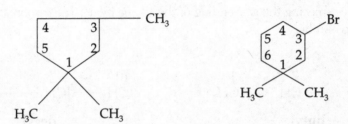

1, 1, 3-trimethylcyclopentane   **3-bromo-1, 1-dimethylcyclohexane**

Unsaturated Hydrocarbons

- **Alkenes**

Alkenes contain at least one C=C bond. The C=C bond counts as one **element of unsaturation** because it decreases the number of hydrogens of the corresponding unsaturated alkane by two.

Alkenes are named in the same way as alkanes, but the ending *-ene* is used to indicate the presence of the double C=C bond. So eth*ane* is CH_3–CH_3 and eth*ene* is CH_2=CH_2. With chains that exceed three carbons, the location of the double bond is indicated by a number.

Examples:

$$\overset{1}{CH_2} = \overset{2}{CH} - \overset{3}{CH_2} - \overset{4}{CH_2} - \overset{5}{CH_3}$$

1-pentene

$$\overset{1}{CH_3} - \overset{2}{CH} = \overset{3}{CH} - \overset{4}{CH_2} - \overset{5}{CH_3}$$

2-pentene

- **Dienes, trienes, tetraenes**

Alkenes with two double bonds are called **dienes**, alkenes with three are called **trienes,** and four, **tetraenes**. Numbers are used to show the locations of the double bonds and the substituents:

$$\underset{1}{CH_2} = \underset{2}{CH} - \underset{3}{CH} = \underset{4}{CH} - \underset{5}{CH_3}$$

1, 3-pentadiene

2-methyl-1, 4-pentadiene

$$\underset{1}{CH_2} = \underset{2}{C} - \underset{3}{CH_2} - \underset{4}{CH} = \underset{5}{CH_2}$$
$$|$$
$$CH_3$$

- **Alkynes**

Alkynes contain a triple $C \equiv C$ bond. They are named after their parent alkane, but have the ending *-yne*. They are named following the same rules as for alkenes:

1-propyne

$$\underset{3}{CH_3} - \underset{2}{C} \equiv \underset{1}{C} - H$$

2-methyl-1-penten-3-yne

$$\underset{1}{CH_2} = \underset{2}{C} - \underset{3}{C} \equiv \underset{4}{C} - \underset{5}{CH_3}$$
$$|$$
$$CH_3$$

- **Cyclic unsaturated hydrocarbons**

Alkenes also form ring structures, called **cycloalkenes**. Likewise, dienes form **cyclodienes**. In the nomenenclature, the position of the double bonds and ring substituents are noted:

1, 3-cyclohexadiene

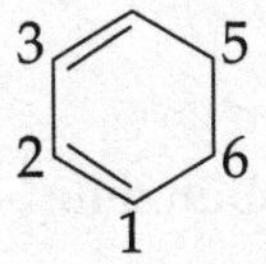

3-nitro-1-cyclohexene

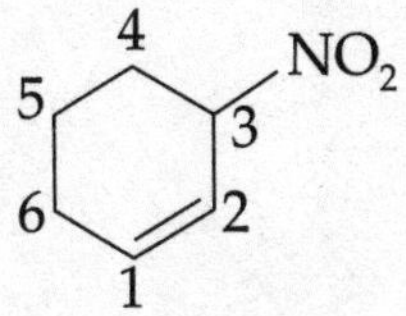

1, 3, 5, 7-cyclooctatetraene

1-ethylcyclopentene

AROMATIC HYDROCARBONS

- **Benzene and derivatives**

Benzene derivatives are named using the following convention for two substituents:

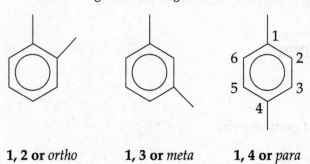

1, 2 or *ortho* **1, 3 or** *meta* **1, 4 or** *para*

The benzene derivatives are often referred to by their common names, which are as follows (the second name given is the systematic name; these are rarely used):

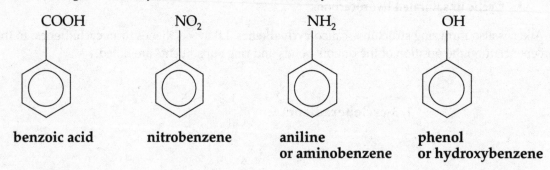

benzoic acid   nitrobenzene   aniline
or aminobenzene   phenol
or hydroxybenzene

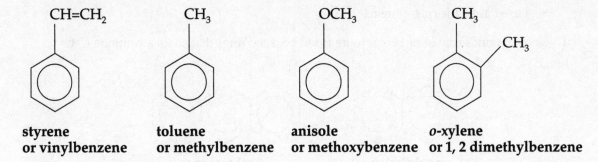

styrene
or vinylbenzene

toluene
or methylbenzene

anisole
or methoxybenzene

o-**xylene**
or 1, 2 dimethylbenzene

Numbers are used when there are more than two substituents, and substituents are listed in numerical order:

2-iodo-3-nitro-5-hydroxybenzoic acid

1, 3, 5-trinitrobenzene

3, 4-dinitrophenol

2, 4, 6-trichloroaniline

- **Fused aromatic ring systems**

These compounds consist of two or more fused benzene rings that share a common C–C bond:

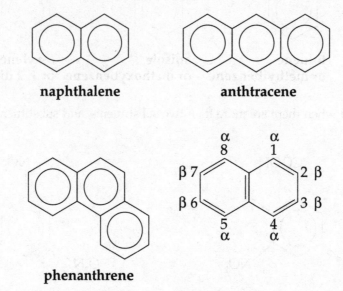

naphthalene　　　　　　　**anthtracene**

phenanthrene

Their substituent compounds are named using the above convention, either with numbers or Greek letters.

- **Larger aromatic ring systems**

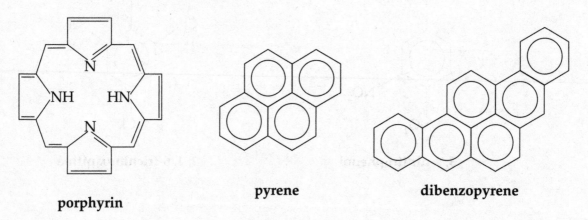

porphyrin　　　　**pyrene**　　　　**dibenzopyrene**

ISOMERS

There are three main classes of isomers that are important in organic chemistry: constitutional, conformational, and stereoisomers.

CONSTITUTIONAL ISOMERS

Constitutional (also called structural) isomers differ in the positions of their constituent atoms. For example:

n-butane   vs.   iso-butane

1-bromobutane   2-bromobutane

The chemical and physical properties of constitutional isomers are different.

CONFORMATIONAL ISOMERS

Atoms around a single (sigma) bond may rotate relative to one another; this gives rise to different orientations, called conformations. For example, ethane has two conformations.

- **Conformations of ethane**

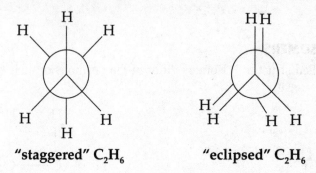

"staggered" C_2H_6 "eclipsed" C_2H_6

The "eclipsed" conformation has a higher energy (3 kcal/mol) than the "staggered" conformation ("*E*" and "*S*," respectively, in the following diagram).

Energy profile for the C–C bond rotation in ethane

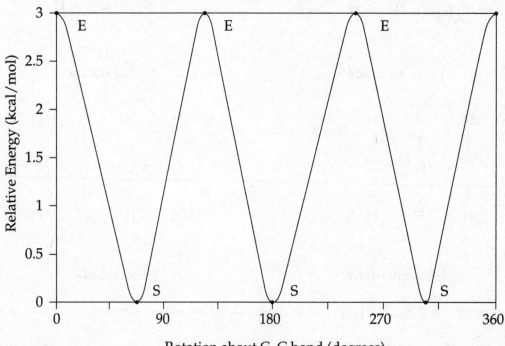

The relative populations of eclipsed *(E)* and staggered *(S)* ethane conformations at room temperature can be estimated by using:

$$K = e^{-\Delta G/RT}$$

where $\Delta G = 3$ kcal/mol, $T = 300$ K, and $R = 1.987$ cal/ K/mol.

$K = \dfrac{1}{159} = \left[\dfrac{E}{S}\right]$, and 99.375% of the ethane molecules are in the staggered form at 25°C.

- **Conformations of butane**

There are more conformational isomers of butane than of ethane, and they are shown below with their respective rotation energies.

"syn" butane
5 kcal/mol

"gauche" butane
0.8 kcal/mol

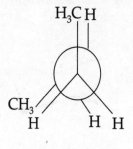

"eclipsed" butane
3.5 kcal/mol

"anti" butane
0 kcal/mol

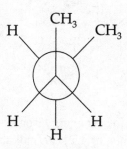

"eclipsed" butane
3.5 kcal/mol

"gauche" butane
0.8 kcal/mol

The relative populations distribute as follows at room temperature:

	syn	eclipsed	gauche	anti
Energy (kcal/mol):	5	3.5	0.8	0
Rel. population:	1	13×2	$1,203 \times 2$	4,644
Percent:	0.01	0.37	34.00	65.62

The relative populations of conformational isomers are temperature-dependent.

- **Conformations of cyclohexane**

Atoms in rings cannot rotate. However, ring systems of five or more sp^3 hybridized atoms can flop around to give different conformations. For example, planar cyclohexane is not very stable because of the ring strain associated with maintaining planarity. To relieve ring strain, cyclohexane undergoes eclipsing effects, which yield three main nonplanar conformers with almost no ring strain. They are called:

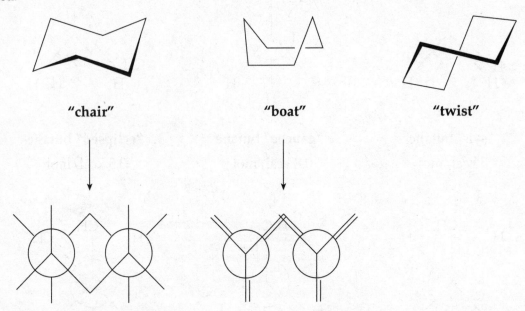

The lowest energy isomer—and the most stable—is the chair configuration, followed by the twist conformer, at 5.5 kcal/mol above the chair conformer, and the boat at 6.4 kcal/mol above the chair conformer. The twist conformation is not detectable at room temperature.

STEREOISOMERS

Stereoisomers differ in their spatial, 3-D arrangements. The different types of stereoisomers are:

- **Geometrical isomers,** which arise when rotation about a bond—or bonds—is not possible. This is because of either ring systems or π bonds:

cis-2-butene   *trans*-2-butene

- **Enantiomers,** which are nonsuperimposable, chiral mirror images (chiral centers are sp^3-hybridized atoms with four different substituent groups).

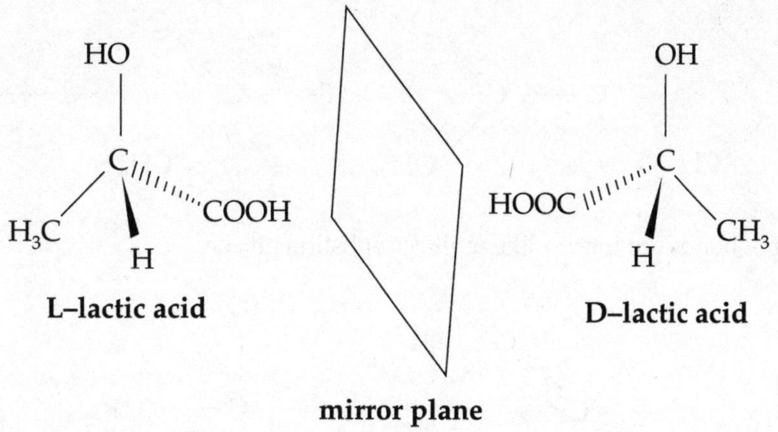

L–lactic acid   mirror plane   D–lactic acid

- **Diastereomers,** which are stereoisomers that are not mirror images of each other.

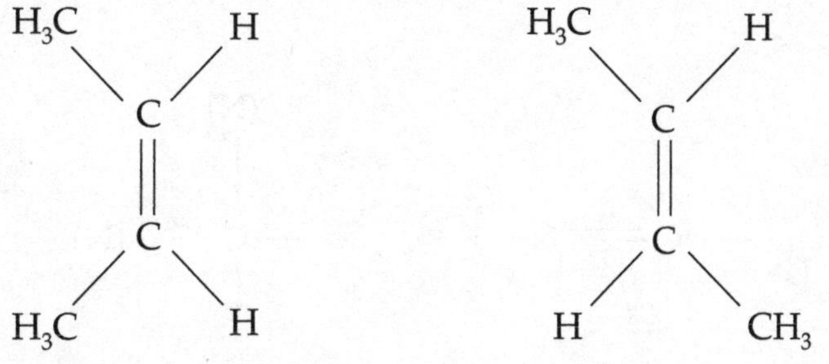

Geometrical isomers are also diastereomers.

> **Enantiomers** *have identical physical and chemical properties; they are not easy to separate.* **Diastereomers** *have different physical and chemical properties; they are easy to separate by conventional means (distillation, chromatography, and crystallization).*

Racemic Mixtures

A 50-50 mixture of a pair of enantiomers is called a racemic mixture. Conversion of one pure enantiomer to an equal mixture of the two is called **racemization**.

The *R* and *S* Convention to Identify Enantiomers

The actual 3-D arrangement of atoms about a chiral center (C*, N*, S*, P*,...) is called the **absolute configuration**. This convention involves a set of rules used to describe the absolute configuration of each chiral center in a molecule in terms of (*R*) and (*S*) prefixes, which stand for "right" and "left," respectively. The rules are:

Step 1a: Substituent groups of chiral center are given a priority based on *increasing* mass number; thus: I > Br > Cl > S > P > Si > F > O > N > C > D (Deuterium) > H.

Step 1b: If two or more substituents have the same type of atom directly bonded to the center, the priority is decided by comparing the next atom of greatest mass on those substituents. For example:

Step 1c: Multiple bonds are treated like multiple substituents, i.e.,

Step 2: Visualize the chiral center with the substituent with the lowest priority pointing away from you. If there is a hydrogen substituent, it will have the lowest priority.

Step 3: Rotate the chiral center from groups with priority 1, 2, and 3 (like a wagon wheel). If rotating counterclockwise, then it's (S); if rotating to the right, then (R).

Example:

Enantiomers of glyceraldelhyde

MESO AND OPTICAL ACTIVITY

Meso

Although rare, molecules do exist that have chiral centers but are not chiral overall. Molecules with this special property are called meso molecules. For example, in spite of the fact that meso molecules possess chiral centers, the mirror image of a meso molecule is identical in every way to the original.

mirror plane

Meso molecules are special because they have an internal mirror plane—i.e., one side of the molecule is the exact mirror image of the other side of the molecule.

Meso:

Meso:

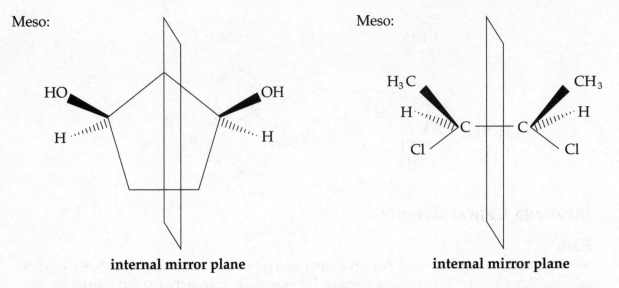

internal mirror plane

internal mirror plane

On the Chemistry GRE, the name of the game is identifying whether a molecule is meso. *If it has chiral centers and an internal mirror plane, then it's meso.* Furthermore, since one side of the molecule has to be the mirror image of the other side, meso molecules always have an even number of chiral centers and equal numbers of R's and S's.

Optical Rotation

There are five things about this to know for the Chemistry GRE:

1. *Plane-polarized light (PPL) is a group of photons that are all moving in the same direction AND have electromagnetic fields oscillating in the same plane.*

2. *Chiral centers have optical activity and rotate plane-polarized light.* Chiral centers that rotate PPL to the left are assigned an "ℓ" or "negative degrees of rotation," while chiral centers that rotate PPL to the right are assigned a "*d*" or "positive degrees of rotation."

   Note that there is no direct relationship between R and S and ℓ and *d*. For example, a chiral center with absolute configuration R can be either ℓ or *d*.

3. *Enantiomers rotate PPL equal magnitudes, but in opposite directions.* For example, if chiral molecule A has optical activity of +28°, then its enantiomer (mirror image) will rotate PPL –28°.

4. *Racemic mixtures are optically inactive; they do not rotate PPL.* Since racemic mixtures are 50-50 mixtures of enantiomers, the optical activities of enantiomers cancel out and no net rotation is observed.

5. *Meso molecules are optically inactive; they do not rotate PPL.* Since a meso molecule can be thought of as a racemic mixture built into each molecule, the optical activity of the chiral center cancels out and no net rotation is observed.

REACTION MECHANISMS

Organic reactions can be classified according to mechanisms that describe the steps and types of intermediates involved in product formation. There are four basic organic reaction mechanisms: substitution (S_N1, S_N2), elimination (E1, E2), addition, and rearrangement. They are covered in this order: Nucleophilic displacements and addition, nucleophilic aromatic substitution, electrophilic addition, electrophilic aromatic substitution, Elimination reactions (E2 and E1), the Diels-Alder reaction, and other cycloadditions.

SUBSTITUTION (ALSO KNOWN AS NUCLEOPHILIC DISPLACEMENT)

In a substitution reaction, one atom or group of atoms is substituted for another. The **nucleophile** (Nu), which is a species that has an unshared pair of electrons, becomes attached to an alkyl group.

$$Nu:^- \ + \ R\ddot{X}: \longrightarrow NuR \ + \ :\ddot{X}:^-$$

A fragment, called the **leaving group** (X), is displaced from the alkyl group, taking with it the electrons that bonded it to the carbon atom. This type of bond breakage is called **heterolytic cleavage** because the leaving group retains both electrons from the broken bond.

$$HO^- \ + \ CH_2 \!-\! Br \longrightarrow HO\!-\!CH_2 \ + \ Br^-$$

nucleophile   leaving group   CH₃   CH₃

Nucleophilic substitution can occur by one of two possible mechanisms:

1. Simultaneous Nu–C bond formation and C–X bond cleavage:

$$Nu^- + R \!-\! X \longrightarrow \left[\overset{\delta^-}{Nu} \text{----} \overset{\delta^+}{R} \text{----} \overset{\delta^-}{X} \right]^- \longrightarrow Nu \!-\! R + X^-$$

In this case, the rate of the reaction would depend on the concentration of both Nu⁻ and RX, because they are both involved in the transition state.

$$rate_{SN2} = k[Nu][RX]$$

This mechanism is called **S_N2**, in which S_N stands for nucleophilic substitution and the 2 indicates that the rate-determining step is bimolecular.

2. Heterolytic cleavage of the C–X bond, followed by the formation of a Nu–C bond:

$$RX \longrightarrow X^- + \left[R^+ \right] \xrightarrow{Nu^-} NuR$$

This is a two-step process that involves the formation of a **carbocation**. The rate of the reaction depends only on the rate of ionization of RX and is independent of the concentration of Nu⁻.

$$\text{rate}_{SN1} = k[RX]$$

This process is called an S_N1 reaction, and the 1 indicates that the rate-determining step is unimolecular.

Example:

What is the product of the reaction of ethyl bromide with potassium cyanide? Write a mechanism and clearly identify the nucleophile, the substrate, the product, and the leaving group.

Solution:

In potassium cyanide, the nucleophile is the negatively charged cyanide ion, CN^-. A nucleophilic substitution of bromide by cyanide occurs, and the product is ethyl cyanide.

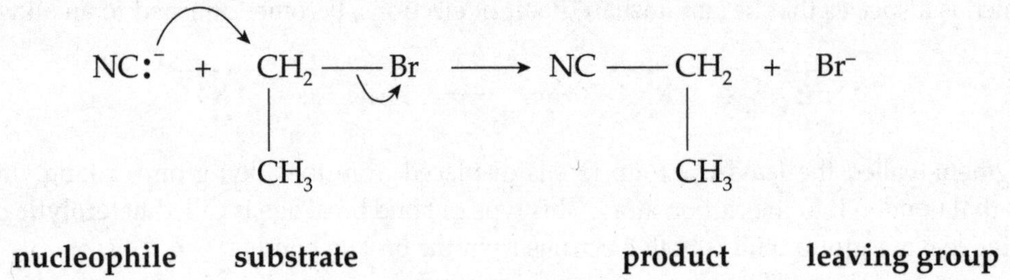

nucleophile   substrate   product   leaving group

In an S_N2 reaction, the nucleophile collides with the substrate on the side opposite the bond between the carbon atom and the leaving group. This back-side displacement occurs with inversion of configuration around the carbon atom (called a Walden inversion).

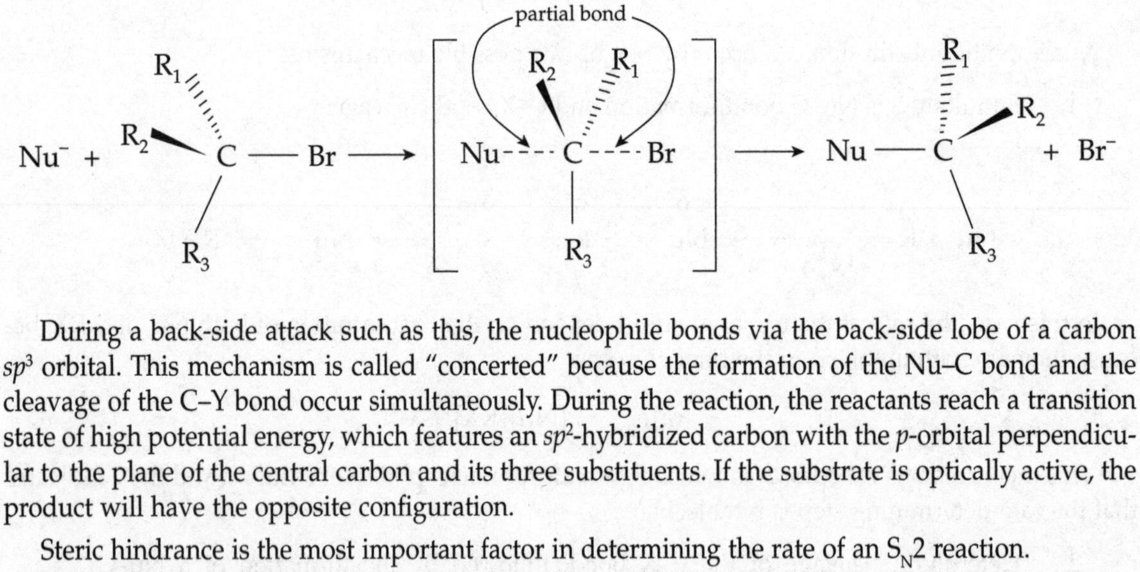

During a back-side attack such as this, the nucleophile bonds via the back-side lobe of a carbon sp^3 orbital. This mechanism is called "concerted" because the formation of the Nu–C bond and the cleavage of the C–Y bond occur simultaneously. During the reaction, the reactants reach a transition state of high potential energy, which features an sp^2-hybridized carbon with the p-orbital perpendicular to the plane of the central carbon and its three substituents. If the substrate is optically active, the product will have the opposite configuration.

Steric hindrance is the most important factor in determining the rate of an S_N2 reaction.

The potential energy needed to form a crowded transition state is much higher than that for a transition state with less spatial crowding. The relative rates of S_N2 reactions are as follows:

methyl > primary > secondary > tertiary

(These terms refer to zero, one, two, and three alkyl substituents on the carbon atom, respectively.)

Methyl, primary, and secondary halides almost always undergo S_N2 reactions, while bulkier tertiary halides react exclusively according to the S_N1 mechanism.

Example:

Which of the following compounds would undergo the fastest S_N2 reaction? Explain.

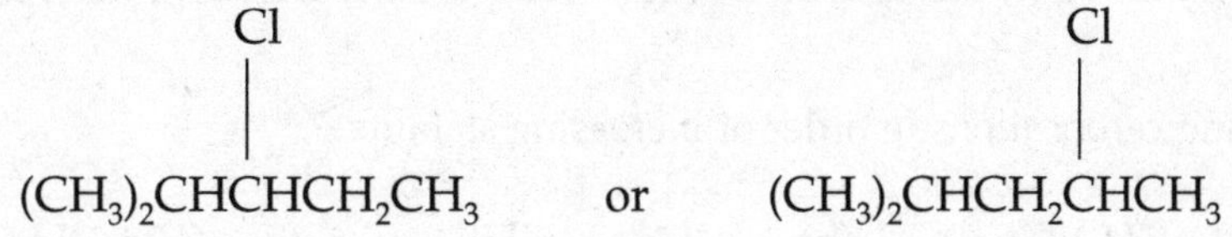

Cl
Cl
(CH3)2CHCHCH2CH3
or
(CH3)2CHCH2CHCH3

Solution:

To answer this question, you must examine the space around the carbon atom bearing the leaving group. In the second compound, the substituents of the carbon atom are smaller than those of the first compound. There is less steric hindrance, and this compound will therefore undergo the faster S_N2 reaction.

Because of steric hindrance, tertiary alkyl halides undergo S_N1 reactions. This process first involves a slow ionization step to form a **carbocation**, followed by bonding of the carbocation to a nucleophile with an unshared pair of electrons:

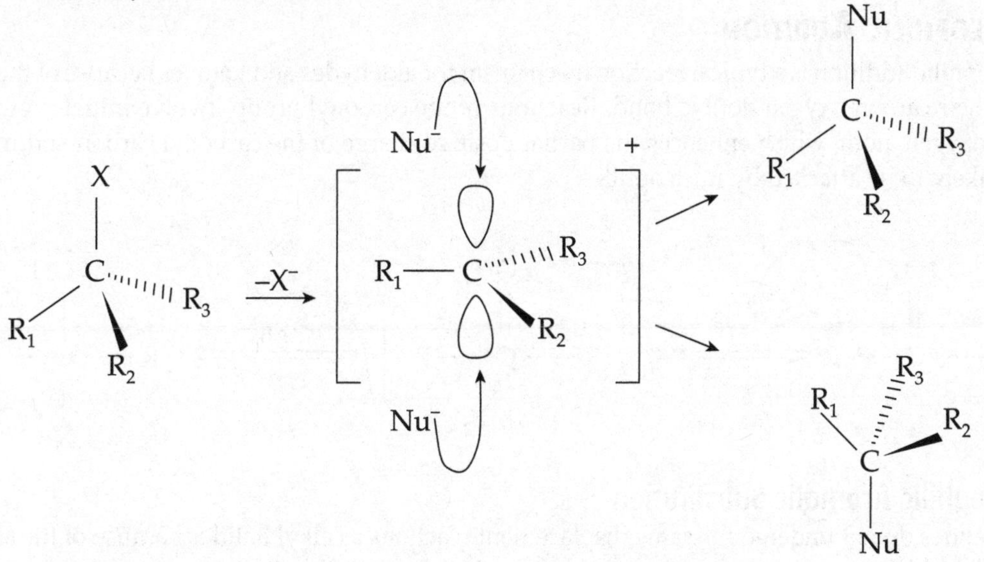

X
C
R1
R2
R3
–X⁻
Nu⁻
R1
C
R3
R2
Nu⁻
+
Nu
C
R1
R2
R3
R1
R3
R2
C
Nu

The *sp*²-hybridized carbocation has a plane of symmetry, and nucleophilic attack is equally likely to happen on both sides. If the reactant contains a chiral C–X bond, the product of the reaction will be racemic (50% R and 50% S), and without universal inversion (unlike in S_N2 reactions).

Carbocations are a very reactive species, but they do, however, have a certain degree of stability due to factors that contribute to the dispersion of their positive charge, due to inductive effects. For instance, the alkyl groups of tertiary alkyl halides are electron donors and inductively stabilize carbocation intermediates:

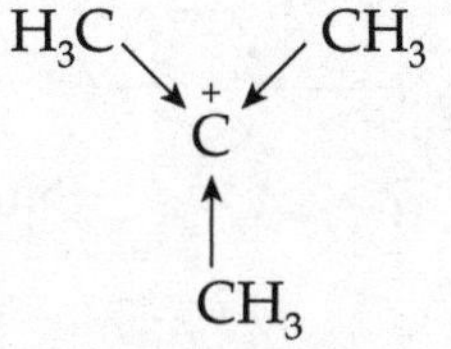

H3C
CH3
+
C
CH3

Furthermore, as the leaving group departs, the bond angles of the sp^2-hybridized intermediate expand from ~ 109° to 120°, which relieves strain during the reaction with the substrate. This lowers the activation energy of highly substituted halides—compared to unsubstituted halides.

Example:

List the following carbocations in order of increasing stability:

(a) $(CH_3CH_2CH_2)_3C^+$ (b) 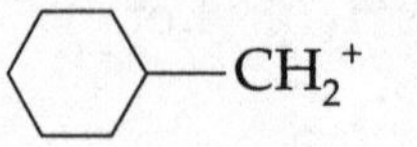 ⬡—CH_2^+ (c) $(CH_3CH_2CH_2)_2CH^+$

Solution:

The answer is b < c < a.

The greater the number of alkyl substituents, the greater the inductive effect and steric assistance, and the greater the stability of the carbocation. The order of reactivity of alkyl halides is:

$$tertiary > secondary > primary$$

NUCLEOPHILIC ADDITION

Nucleophilic addition is a typical reaction mechanism for aldehydes and ketones because of the polarity of their carbon-oxygen double bond. Reactions of the carbonyl group involve initial protonation of the oxygen atom, which enhances the partial positive charge of the carbonyl carbon and makes it more likely to be attacked by nucleophiles.

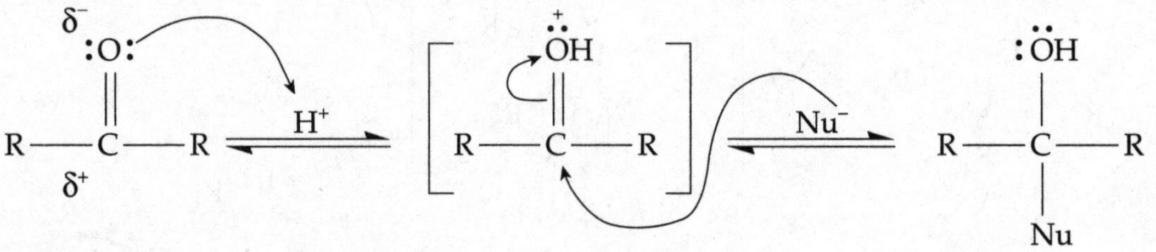

Nucleophilic Aromatic Substitution

Aryl halides do not undergo the same displacement reactions as alkyl halides because of the strength of the bond between their sp^2 carbon and halide. However, aryl halides can undergo nucleophilic aromatic substitution reactions in the presence of an electron-withdrawing substituent on the ring. This is because an electron-withdrawing substituent will make the ring less electron-rich and more susceptible to nucleophilic attack.

There are two major mechanisms for nucleophilic aromatic substitution:

1. Addition of a nucleophile and formation of a carbanion intermediate, followed by the loss of the halide ion:

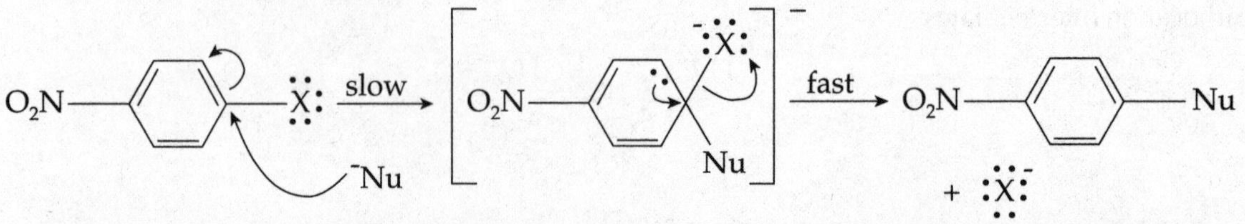

The carbanion is stabilized by resonance and the removal of negative charge by the electron-withdrawing group. Electron-withdrawing *ortho-* and *para-*substituents stabilize the carbanion intermediate more than *meta-*substituents.

2. In the absence of electron-withdrawing substituents, nucleophilic aromatic substitution is very rare and proceeds through a benzyne intermediate:

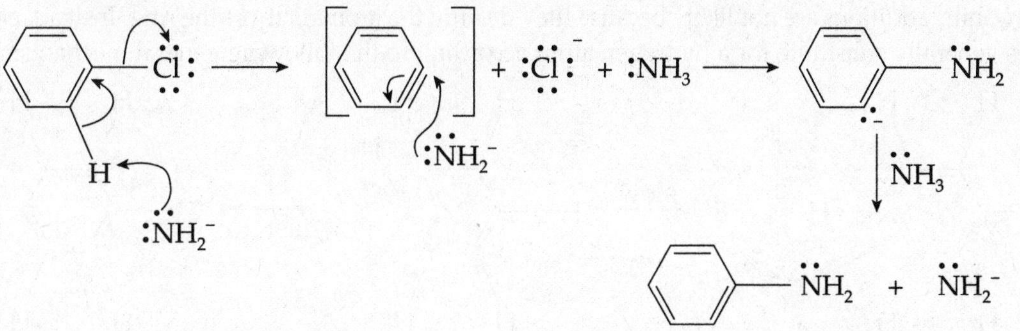

The benzyne triple bond is made of an *sp-sp* sigma bond, and top-bottom and side-to-side overlap of the two sets of *p-p* orbitals.

ELECTROPHILIC ADDITION

Addition reactions are characteristic of compounds with pi bonds. The pi-electron cloud represents a far more reactive electron system than a σ bond, so the electrons of multiple bonds behave as do Lewis bases toward Lewis acids. During addition reactions, the substrate does not lose any atoms. For instance, the reaction of an alkene with the highly polarized HCl molecule proceeds in two steps: initial attack by the **electrophile** (electron-deficient species such as H^+, CH_3^+, Br^+, NO_2^+ or HSO_3^+) to form a carbocation, followed by reaction with the negative halide ion.

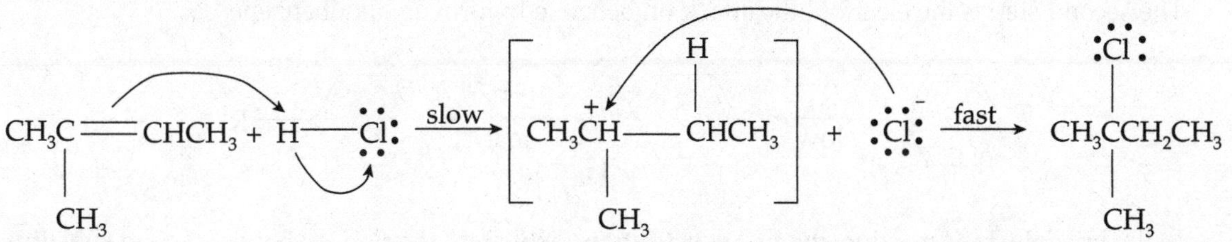

The reaction is called an **electrophilic addition** reaction because the initial attack i.e., is by an electrophile. If the alkene is unsymmetrical, the addition follows Markovnikov's rule, i.e., in additions of HX to unsymmetrical alkenes, the H^+ of HX goes on the C=C carbon with the greatest number of hydrogens.

Example:

What is the product of the reaction between 1-methylcyclohexene and HI?

Solution:

1-iodo-1-methylcyclohexane.

The sp^2 carbon that bears the methyl group does not have an attached hydrogen atom. The sp^2 carbon at position 2 has one hydrogen atom. Therefore, the H^+ is added at position 2 and I^- at position 1.

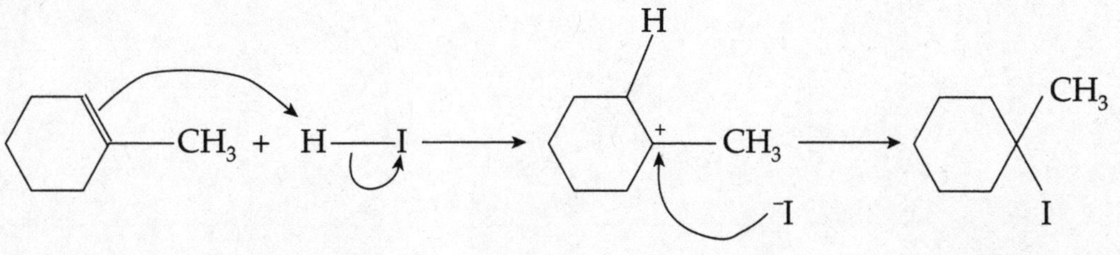

Electrophilic Aromatic Substitution

Aromatic rings, with their electron-rich pi-electron clouds, are easily attacked by electrophiles, but electrophilic additions are not likely because they destroy the aromaticity of the ring. Instead, electrophiles generally substitute for a hydrogen atom according to the following general mechanism:

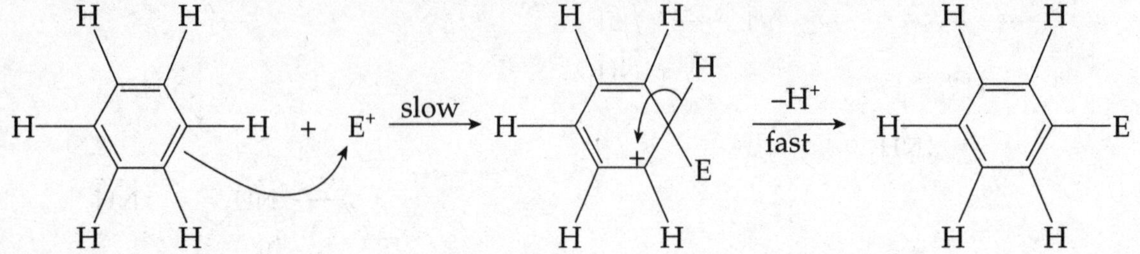

(The required electrophile is generated by a specific reaction, prior to the electrophilic substitution step; it's obtained through the reaction between a Lewis acid and a reagent.)

Example:

The alkylation of benzene (a Friedel-Crafts reaction):

The first step is the generation of a carbocation:

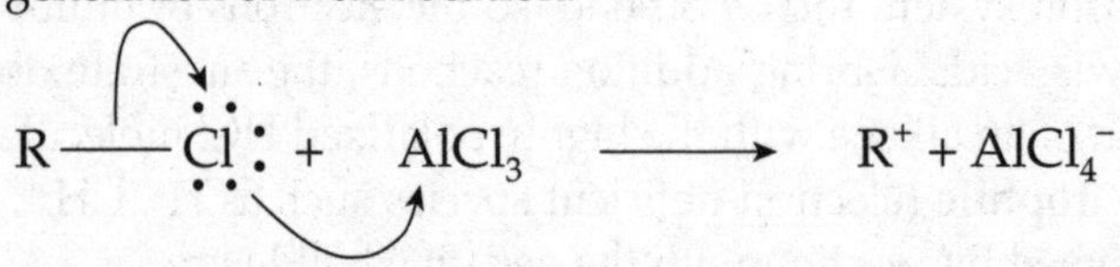

$$R - \ddot{Cl} : + \quad AlCl_3 \longrightarrow R^+ + AlCl_4^-$$

The second step is the electrophilic attack on benzene to form an alkylbenzene:

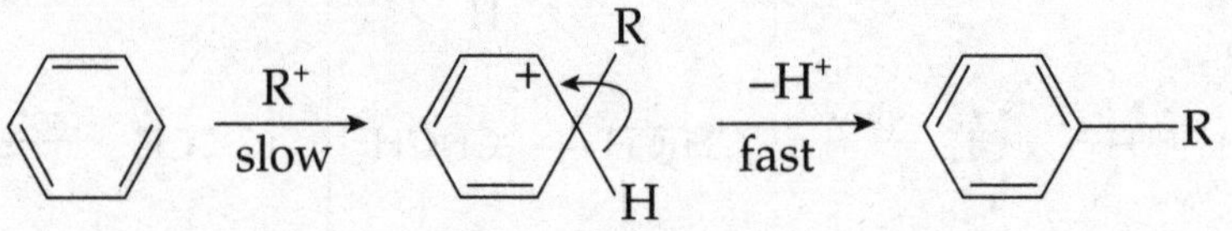

In the Friedel-Crafts reaction, the first substitution "activates" the ring so that the second substitution may occur.

In aromatic electrophilic substitutions, electrophiles can be generated via the following reactions:

1. For the halogenation of benzene:

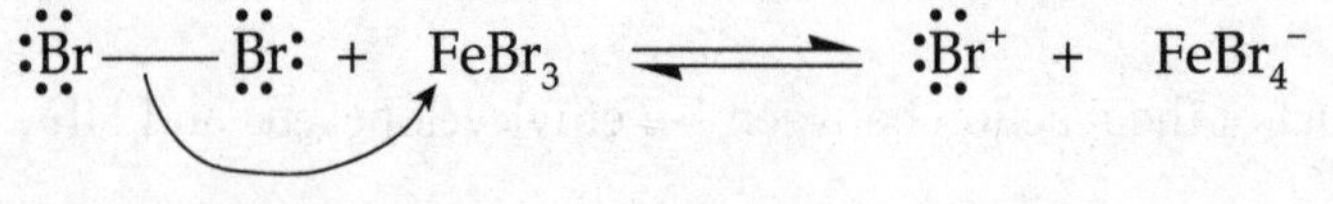

$$:\ddot{Br} - \ddot{Br}: + \quad FeBr_3 \quad \rightleftharpoons \quad :\ddot{Br}^+ + \quad FeBr_4^-$$

2. For the nitration of benzene:

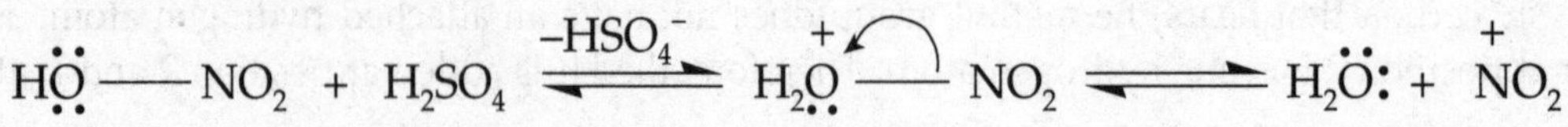

$$H\ddot{O} - NO_2 + H_2SO_4 \quad \overset{-HSO_4^-}{\rightleftharpoons} \quad H_2\overset{+}{\ddot{O}} - NO_2 \quad \rightleftharpoons \quad H_2\ddot{O}: + \quad \overset{+}{N}O_2$$

3. For the acylation of benzene (note the resonance structures of the acylium ion):

$$RC(=O)-\ddot{\underset{..}{C}}l: + AlCl_3 \longrightarrow RC(=O)----Cl----AlCl_3 \xrightarrow{-AlCl_4^-} \left[R----\overset{+}{C}=\ddot{\underset{..}{O}} \longleftrightarrow R-C\equiv\overset{+}{O}: \right]$$

4. For the sulfonation of benzene:

$$H_2SO_4 + SO_3 \longrightarrow \overset{+}{H}SO_3 + HSO_4^-$$

ELIMINATION

An elimination reaction occurs when a molecule loses atoms or ions. When an alkyl halide reacts with a strong base, the elements H and X are lost from the substrate, and the product is an alkene.

$$CH_3CH-CH_2 + :\ddot{O}H \longrightarrow CH_3CH=CH_2 + H_2O + :\ddot{\underset{..}{Br}}:^-$$

The carbon that bears the halogen is referred to as the α-carbon and the carbon adjacent to it is the β-carbon. This reaction is also called **dehydrohalogenation**.

Two mechanisms are possible for elimination reactions: **E2 elimination** or **E1 elimination**.

E2 Elimination

In this mechanism, a base removes a hydrogen atom; the C–H bond cleaves heterolytically. The adjacent carbons form a carbon-carbon double bond by ejecting the leaving group. The reaction does not involve a carbocation intermediate: It is a concerted reaction, just like the S_N2 reaction.

In E2 reactions, the 2 refers to the two reactants involved in the transition state. The rate of reaction is proportional to the concentration of both base and substrate:

$$\text{rate}_{E2} = k[\text{base}][\text{substrate}]$$

E2 reactions generally obey **Saytzeff's rule**, which states that when more than one β-carbon bears hydrogen atoms, it is the most substituted carbon that undergoes elimination.

Another consideration in E2 reactions is **anti-elimination** or anti-positioning, which determines the stereochemistry of the alkene product. For example, 1-bromo-1,2-diphenylpropane has two chiral carbons (C1 and C2). The possible enantiomers are (1R, 2R), (1S, 2S), (1R, 2S), or (1S, 2R), but in only one of these possible conformations are the H and the Br in an *anti* position. If either the (1R, 2R) or

(1S, 2S) react, the *anti* alignment of H and Br places both phenyl groups on the same side of the molecule, and a (Z)-alkene is obtained (also called a *cis*-alkene). If the (1R, 2S) or (1S, 2R) react, (E)-alkenes are produced, i.e., with the phenyl groups on opposite sides (or *trans* to each other).

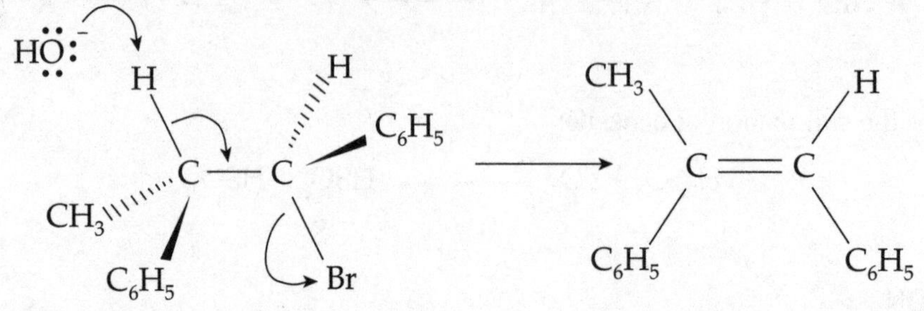

(1S, 2S)-1-bromo-1,2-diphenylpropane   (Z)-1,2-diphenyl-1-propene

This reaction is **stereospecific** because different stereoisomers of the substrate yield stereoisomerically different products.

Example:

What are the products of the reaction of 2-bromo-2-phenylpentane with KOH? Which alkene product should predominate?

Solution:

C1 and C3 are the two β-carbon atoms. Of these, C3 is the most substituted and so should lose a hydrogen atom.

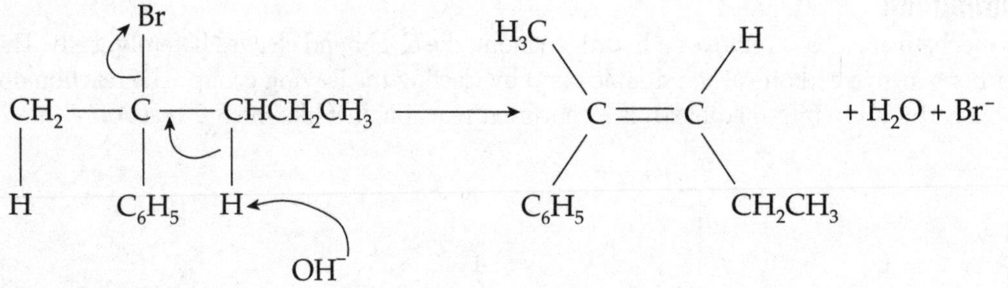

The major product formed is 2-phenyl-2-pentene, and the minor product is 2-phenyl-1-pentene.

Most dihydrohalogenations obey Saytzeff's rule. However, in certain circumstances, the less substituted alkene predominates, and this is called the **Hofmann product**. The most common factor leading to the Hofmann product is **steric hindrance**, which may be caused by:

(a)   The size of the attacking base

(b)   The size of the group surrounding the leaving group

Example:

Write the Saytzeff and Hofmann product of the E2 reaction of 2-bromo-2,4,4-trimethylpentane with potassium methoxide. Which product should predominate?

Solution:

According to Saytzeff's rule, C3 is the most substituted β-carbon. However, that side of the leaving group is bulkier than the other and does not facilitate the attack of the base. The Hofmann product should predominate.

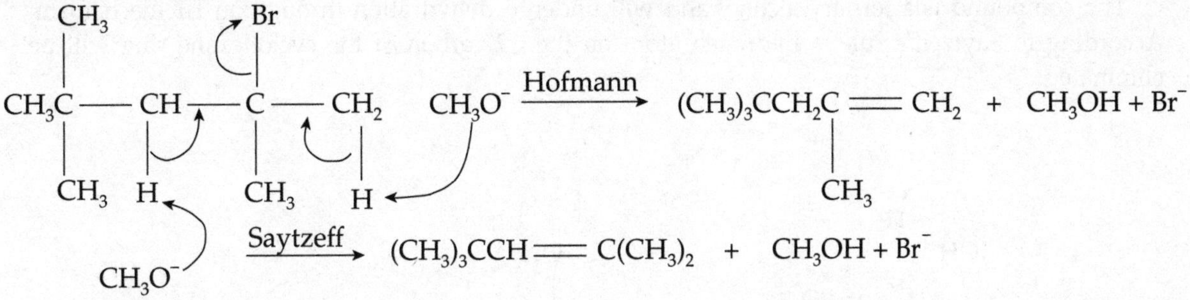

E1 Elimination

The second possible mechanism for elimination is called E1. The first step of an E1 reaction involves the formation of a carbocation through loss of X^-, without cleavage of the C–H bond. In the second step, a weak base removes an H^+ ion from the carbon atom adjacent to the positive carbon:

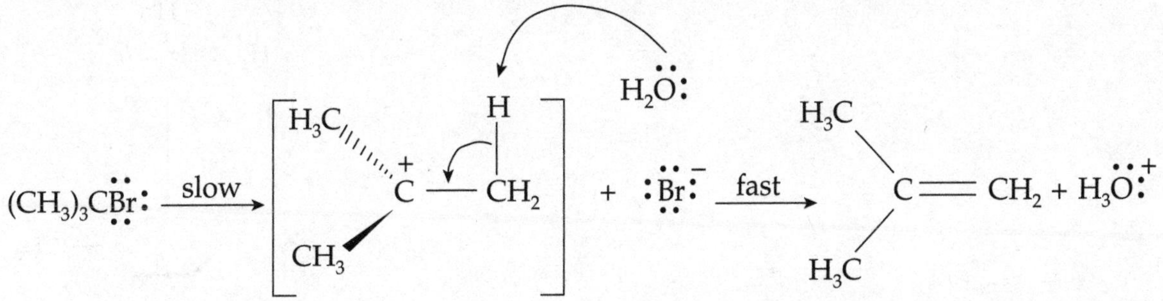

As is the case in S_N1 reactions, E reactions are first order reactions and their rate depends only on the concentration of the substrate:

$$rate_{E1} = k[\text{substrate}]$$

Tertiary halides undergo E1 elimination faster than the other alkyl halides. Saytzeff's rule is obeyed and the most stable alkene is produced.

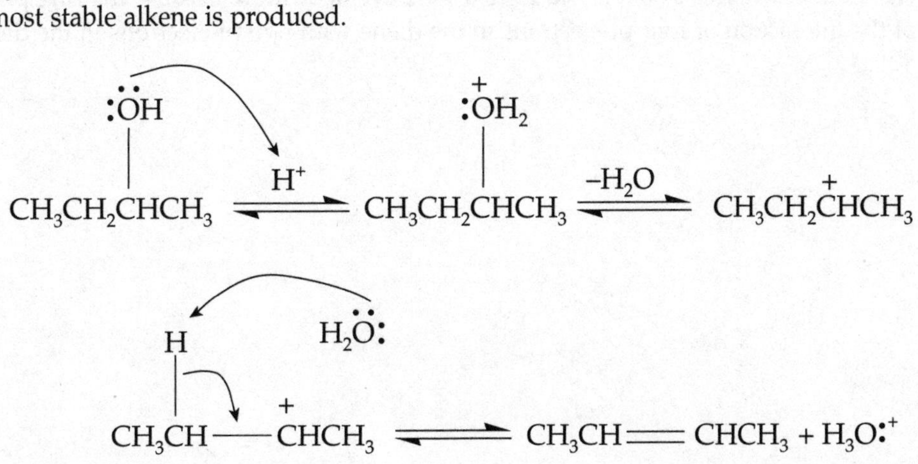

Example:

What is the product of the reaction of 1-methyl-1-cyclohexanol with H_3PO_4? Write one possible mechanism.

Solution:

The compound is a tertiary alcohol and will undergo dehydration through an E1 mechanism. According to Saytzeff's rule, a hydrogen atom on the C2 carbon of the cyclohexane ring will be eliminated:

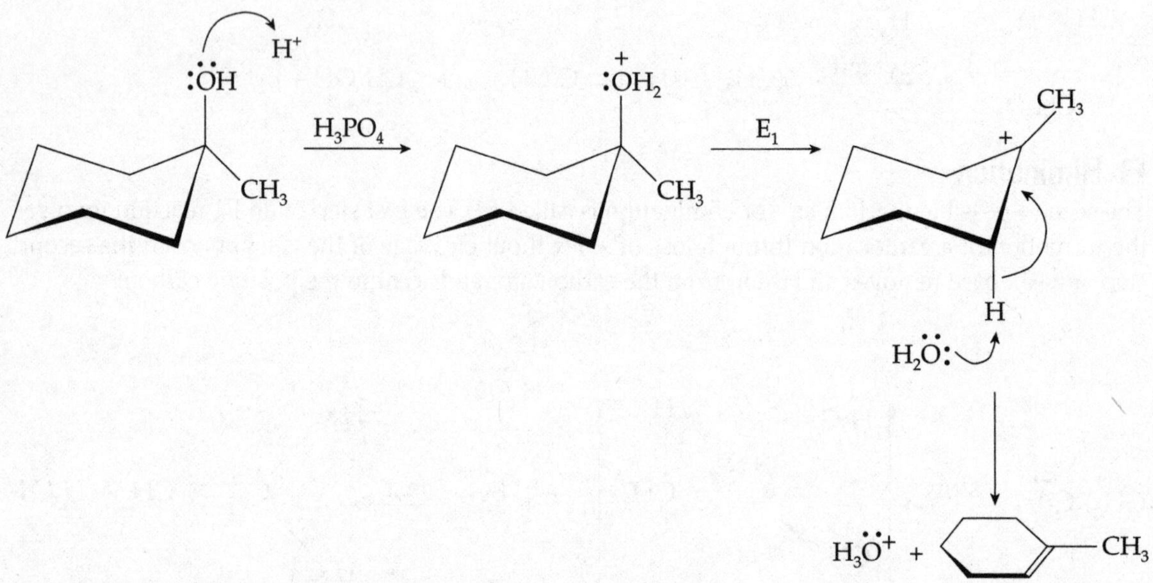

THE DIELS-ALDER REACTION AND CYCLOADDITIONS

The Diels-Alder reaction belongs to a class of reaction called **pericyclic reactions**, which are characterized by a cyclic transition state. In the Diels-Alder reaction, a conjugated diene is heated and reacted with an alkene or an alkyne, called **dienophiles** ("lover of dienes") to yield a six-membered ring.

The Diels-Alder reaction is also referred to as a **4 + 2 cycloaddition**, because the ring produced is the result of the interaction of four pi-electrons in the diene with two pi-electrons in the dienophile.

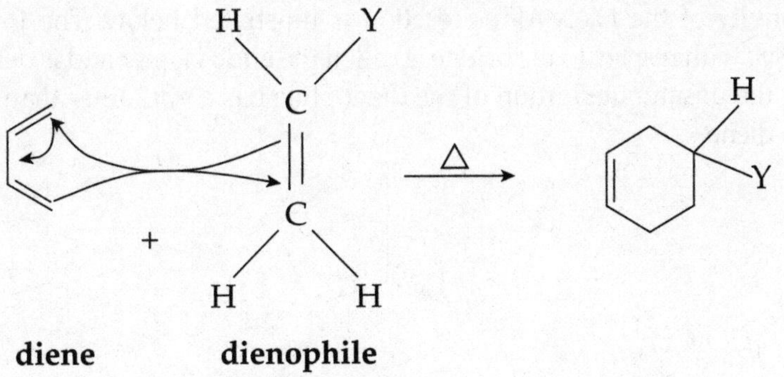

diene　　　　**dienophile**

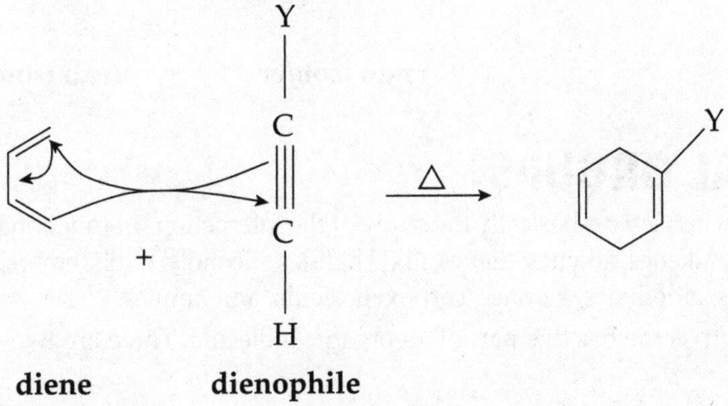

diene　　　　**dienophile**

Y is an electron-withdrawing group; usually a group that contains a C=O or a C≡N. The diene is an electron-rich species, and the dienophile is an electron-poor species. The reactivity of the diene is improved when it incorporates electron-donating groups such as alkyl or –OR groups. A good dienophile should have at least one electron-withdrawing group (designated Y, above), and preferably more than one to pull the electron density from the pi bond.

Two examples of substituted dienophiles and their possible reactions are:

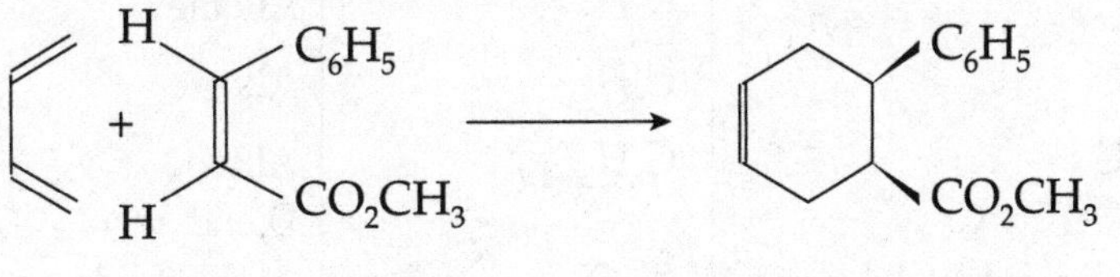

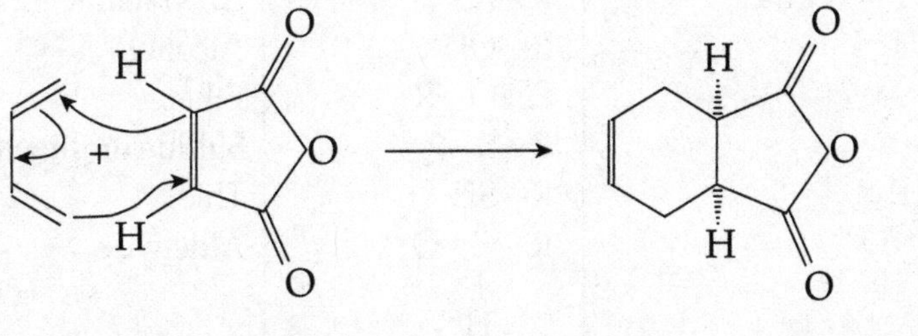

The diene must have a *cis* conformation in the transition state, so *cis*-substituted dienophiles are preferred. As shown above, the product of a Diels-Alder addition always contains one more ring than is present in the reactants.

The stereoselectivity of the Diels-Alder reaction is illustrated below. The isomer in which the –CO$_2$CH$_3$ group is *syn* with respect to the bridge is called the **endo** isomer and is derived from a transition state in which the unsaturated group of the dienophile has a *syn* rather than an *anti* orientation with respect to the diene.

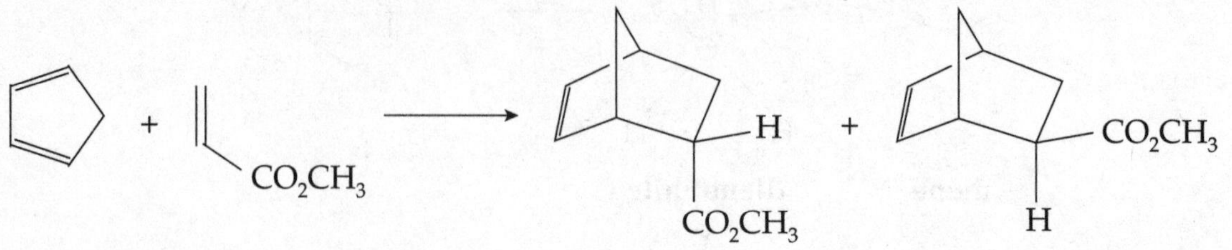

endo isomer   exo isomer

FUNCTIONAL GROUPS

The study of organic chemistry is basically the study of the interactions of functional groups of organic compounds: alkanes, alkenes, alkynes, dienes, alkyl halides, alcohols, thiols, ethers, epoxides, sulfides, aromatic compounds, aldehydes, ketones, carboxylic acids, and amines.

A **functional group** is the reactive part of an organic molecule. There are two types of functional groups:

(i) functional groups defined by the types of carbon-carbon bond they contain (C–C, C=C, or C≡C)

(ii) functional groups defined as specific atoms or groups of atoms that replace hydrogen in a hydrocarbon

Important Functional Groups in Organic Chemistry		
Functional Group	**Formula**	**Name**
C–C	C$_n$H$_{2n+2}$	Alkane
C=C	C$_n$H$_{2n}$	Alkene
C≡C	C$_n$H$_{2n-2}$	Alkyne
C=C–C=C		Diene
–X, X = F, Br, Cl, I	R–X	Alkyl halide
–OH	R–OH	Alcohol
–O–	R–O–R	Ether
–S–	R–S–R	Sulfide or thioether
–SH	R–SH	Thiol

–C=O
  |
  H
	R–C=O
	  |
	  H
		Aldehyde

–C=O
  |
	R–C=O
	  |
	  R
		Ketone

–C=O
  |
  OH
	R–C=O
	  |
	  OH
		Carboxylic acid

ALKANES

Alkanes are acyclic hydrocarbon chains with the general formula C_nH_{2n+2}. They are characterized by **single C–C** bonds and are called **saturated** because their carbons bind as many hydrogens as possible. **Alkyl groups** are symbolized as **R** in general formulas. Two prefixes are used to specify the geometry of alkyls: $n\text{-}C_nH_{2n+1}$, where *n* stands for a normal, linear C-atom chain; and $i\text{-}C_nH_{2n+1}$, where *i* stands for an "iso" arrangement of the carbons; i.e., where the second carbon in the chain has a branch. Alkyl groups occur in the following geometries:

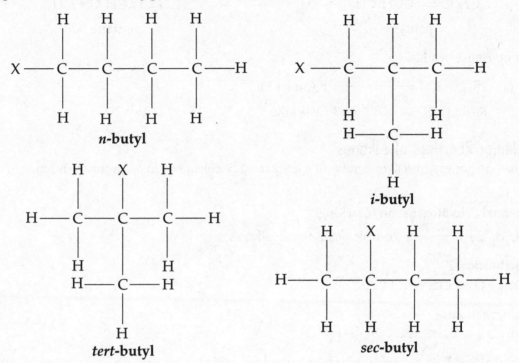

n-butyl

i-butyl

tert-butyl

sec-butyl

Synthesis of Alkanes

1. Reduction of alkyl halides (RX)

1.1 $2RX + Zn + 2H^+ \rightarrow RH + Zn^{2+} + X^-$

Example: $2CH_3Cl + Zn + 2H^+ \rightarrow 2CH_4 + Zn^{2+} + 2Cl^-$

1.2 $4RX + LiAlH_4 \rightarrow 4RH + LiX + AlX_3$

Example: $4CH_3Cl + LiAlH_4 \rightarrow 4CH_4 + LiCl + AlCl_3$

1.3 $RX + (n\text{-}C_4H_9)_3SnH \rightarrow RH + (n\text{-}C_4H_9)_3SnX$

Example: $CH_3Cl + (n\text{-}C_4H_9)_3SnH \rightarrow CH_4 + (n\text{-}C_4H_9)_3SnCl$

1.4 $RMgX + H_2O \rightarrow RH + Mg(OH)X$

Example: $CH_3MgBr + H_2O \rightarrow CH_4 + Mg(OH)Br$

Reaction 1.4 above involves an intermediate step, the formation of a **Grignard reagent**, R–MgX. These reduction reactions all feature the replacement of a halogen (X) by a hydrogen, and the number of carbon atoms in the products equals that of the reactants.

2. Catalyzed hydrogenation of alkenes and alkynes to produce alkanes

$$CH_3{-}\underset{\underset{\textstyle CH_3}{|}}{C}{=}CHCH_3 + H_2 \xrightarrow{\text{Pt or Ni}} CH_3{-}\underset{\underset{\textstyle CH_3}{|}}{CH}{-}CH_2CH_3$$

2-methyl-2-butene   **2-methylbutane**

$$CH_3C{\equiv}CCH_2CH_3 + 2H_2 \xrightarrow{\text{Pt or Ni}} CH_3CH_2CH_2CH_2CH_3$$

2-pentyne   **pentane**

3. Corey-House synthesis

(a) $2R{-}Li + CuI \xrightarrow{\text{under dry ether}} R_2CuLi + LiI$

(b) $R_2CuLi + R'{-}X \rightarrow R'{-}R + RCu + LiX$

The Major Reactions of Alkanes

Alkanes are not very reactive; significant energy must be consumed in order for the reaction to happen.

1. Thermal dehydrogenation (Cracking)

$$C_nH_{2n+2} + \xrightarrow{\text{heat}} \text{mixture of smaller chain alkanes}$$

2. Combustion

$$RH + O_2 \rightarrow CO_2 + 2H_2O$$

3. Halogenation

$$RH + X_2 + \xrightarrow{\text{heat or light}} RX + HX$$

This halogenation reaction proceeds by radical formation and is stepwise, in three major steps:

- The **initiation step**: In which a **reactive intermediate** is generated; in this case, a **free radical** of the halogen atom. The radicals are generated by the absorption of light and subsequent homogeneous bond dissociation. Radicals lack an octet of electrons and are extremely reactive, as well as **electrophilic**, because they are electron-deficient.

- The **propagation steps**: In the presence of an alkane, the radical formed will break one of the C–H bonds. One electron remains on the alkane, which becomes an alkyl radical since it loses a hydrogen and an electron, and the other electron forms the bond in the newly formed H–X molecule. In a second propagation step, the alkyl radical reacts with a halogen molecule to form the halogenated alkane.

- The **termination steps**: The reaction is over when the free radicals are used up and no new ones are formed. So a termination step produces fewer radicals than it uses up.

Example:
Bromination of methane: $CH_4 + Br_2 \rightarrow CH_3Br + HBr$

1. Initiation step:

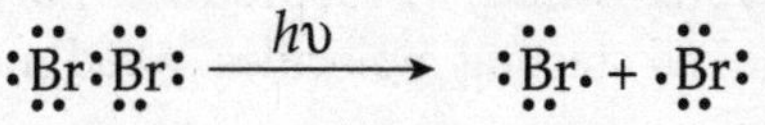

$$:\ddot{B}r:\ddot{B}r: \xrightarrow{h\upsilon} :\ddot{B}r\cdot + \cdot\ddot{B}r:$$

bromine molecule   two bromine radicals

2. Propagation steps:

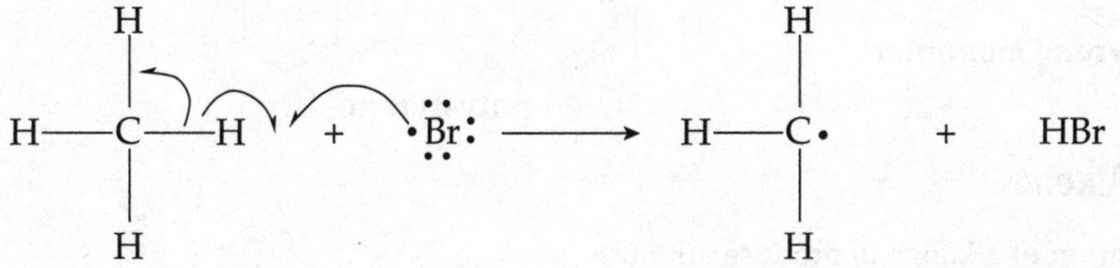

methane   bromine radical   methyl radical   hydrogen bromide

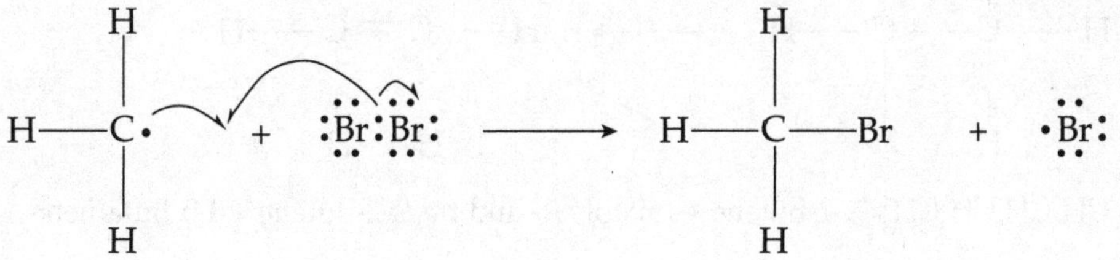

methyl radical   bromine   bromomethane   bromine radical

3. Termination steps:

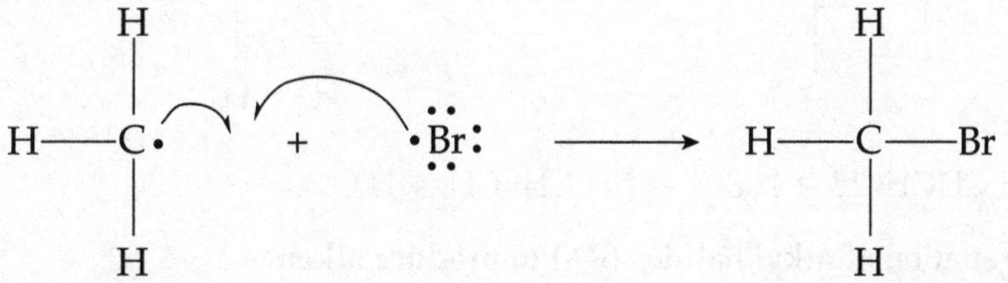

methyl radical   bromine radical   bromomethane

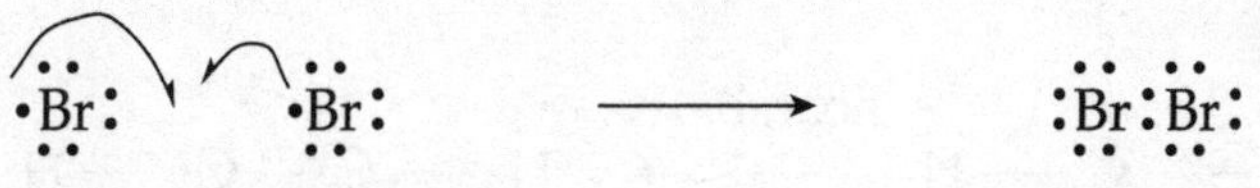

bromine radicals   bromine

ALKENES

Alkenes are acyclic hydrocarbon chains with the general formula C_nH_{2n}. They are characterized by **C=C** bonds and are said to be unsaturated because they react with hydrogen to produce saturated alkanes.

- Alkenes easily undergo **polymerization**, which produces **polymers**, which are large molecules made of chain-linked starting molecules called **monomers** or **mers**.

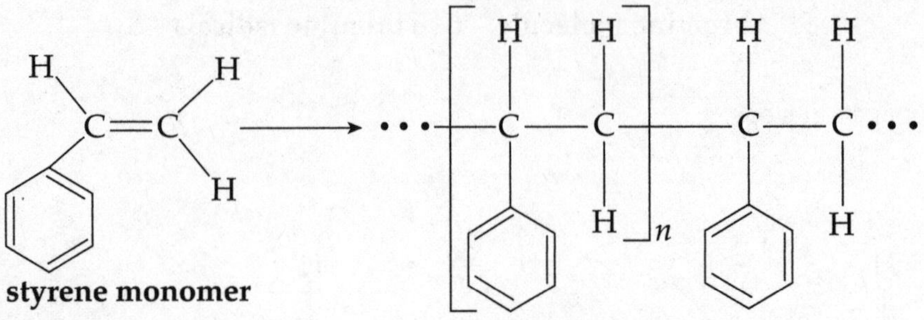

styrene monomer

polystyrene

Synthesis of Alkenes

1. Dehydrogenation of alkanes to produce alkenes

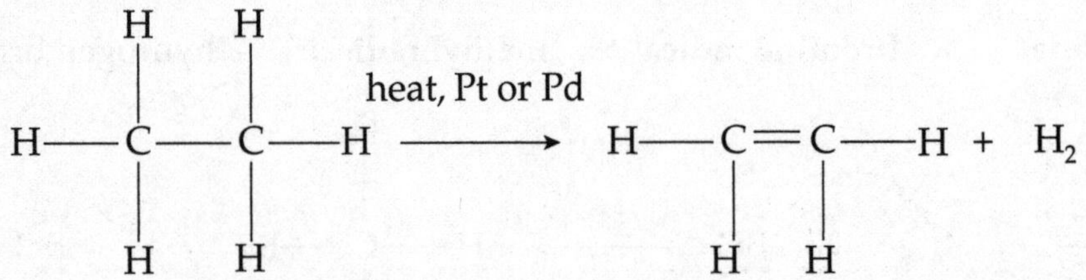

Example: $CH_3CH_2CH_2CH_3 \rightarrow$ 1-Butene + mix of *cis*- and *trans*-2-Butene + 1,3-Butadiene + H_2

2. Dehydration of alcohols (ROH) to produce alkenes

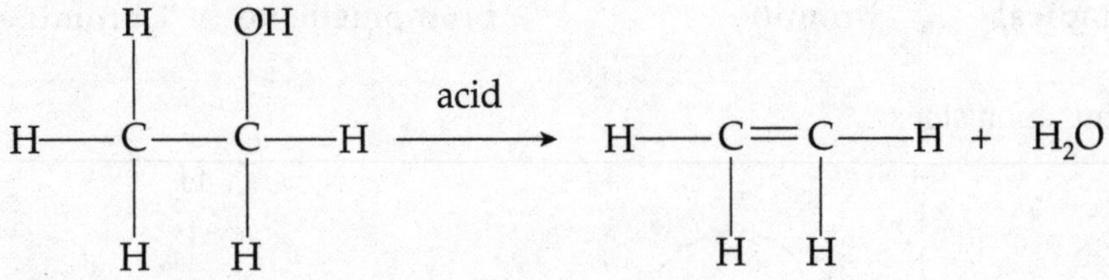

Example: $CH_3CHOHCH_3 + H_2SO_4 \rightarrow CH_3CH=CH_2 + H_2O$

3. Dehydrohalogenation of alkyl halides (RX) to produce alkenes

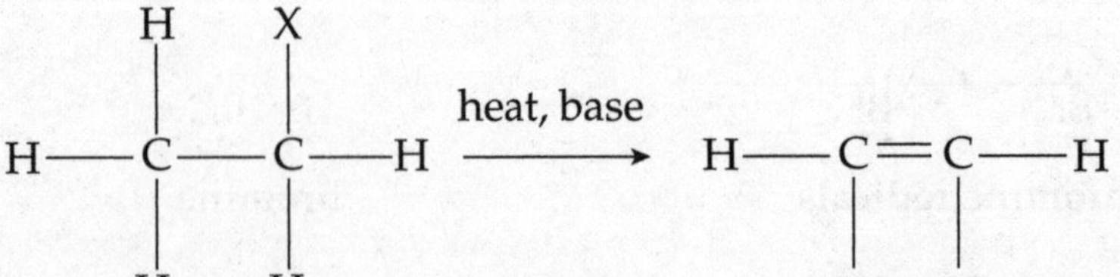

Example:

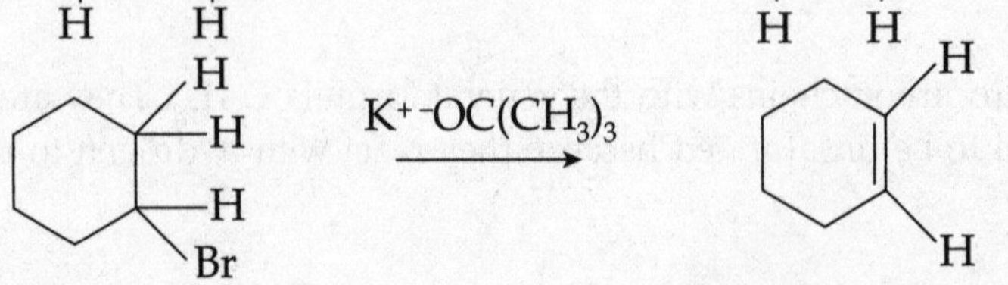

cyclohexyl bromide

cyclohexene

4. Dehalogenation of vicinal dihalides to produce alkenes

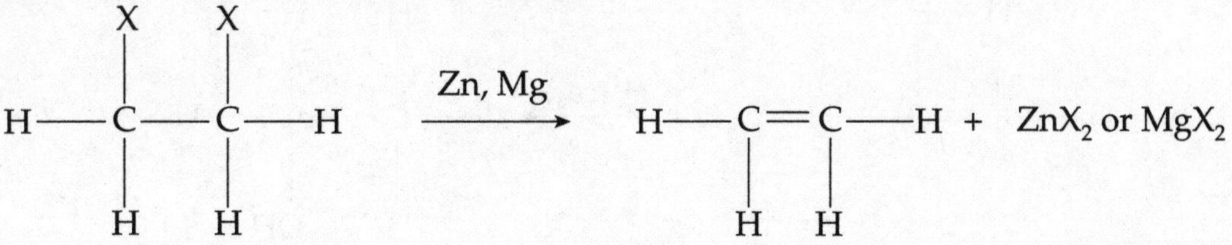

Example:

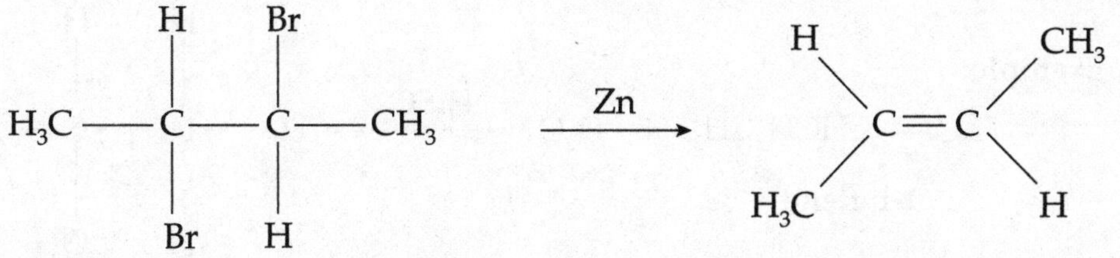

5. Reduction of alkynes (RC–CR) to produce alkenes

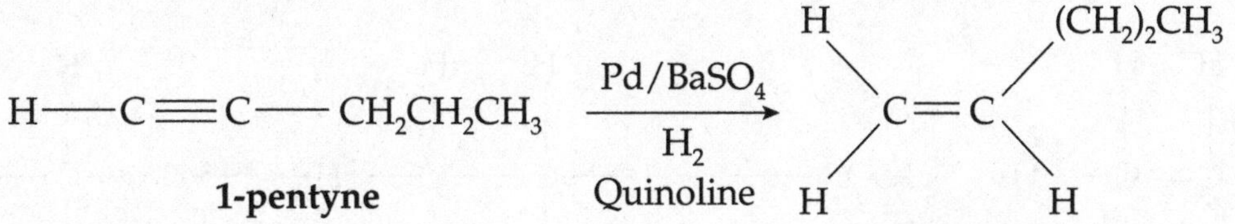

1-pentyne → **1-pentene**

Reactions of Alkenes

1. Addition of hydrogen halides (HX) across double bonds (Markovnikov addition)

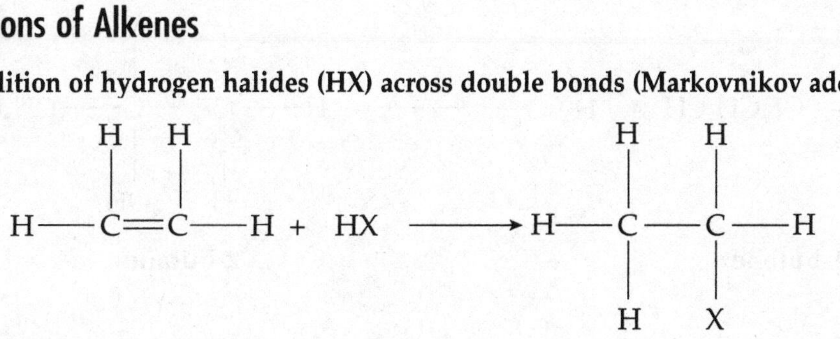

Example:

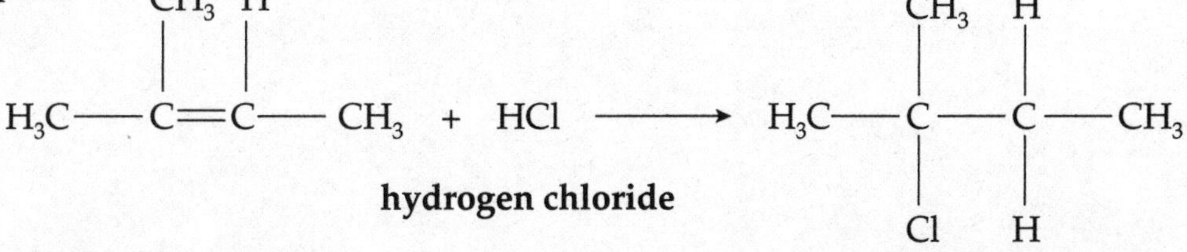

hydrogen chloride

2-methyl-2-butene → **2-methyl-2-chlorobutane**

Markovnikov's rule *states that addition of a proton to the double bond of an alkene yields a product in which the proton is bonded to the carbon atom that already bears the greater number of hydrogens.*

2. Hydration of alkenes to produce alcohols (Markovnikov addition)

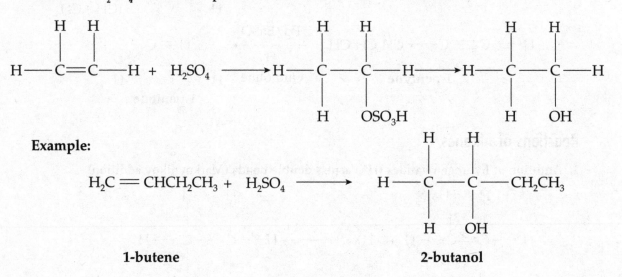

Example:

$$H_2C = CHCH_2CH_3 \; + \; H_2O \xrightarrow{H_2SO_4} H-\overset{\overset{\displaystyle H}{|}}{\underset{\underset{\displaystyle H}{|}}{C}}-\overset{\overset{\displaystyle H}{|}}{\underset{\underset{\displaystyle OH}{|}}{C}}-CH_2CH_3$$

1-butene   **2-butanol**

3. Addition of H_2SO_4 to alkenes to produce alcohols (Markovnikov addition)

Example:

$$H_2C = CHCH_2CH_3 \; + \; H_2SO_4 \longrightarrow H-\overset{\overset{\displaystyle H}{|}}{\underset{\underset{\displaystyle H}{|}}{C}}-\overset{\overset{\displaystyle H}{|}}{\underset{\underset{\displaystyle OH}{|}}{C}}-CH_2CH_3$$

1-butene   **2-butanol**

4. Oxymercuration-demercuration of alkenes to produce alcohols (Markovnikov addition)

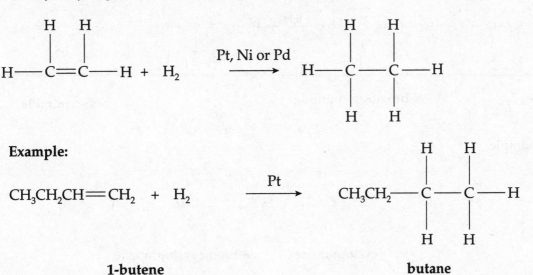

Example:

1-butene → 2-butanol

5. Catalytic hydrogenation of alkenes to produce alkanes

Example:

1-butene → butane

6. Cyclopropanation

Example:

cycloheptene   1,2-dichlorocycloheptene

X_1, X_2 = H, Cl, Br, or I

7. Allylic substitution

N-bromosuccinimide   succinimide

Example:

cyclopropene   3-bromocyclopropene

8. Ozonolysis of alkenes to produce carbonyl groups

$$R_1-C(H)=C(H)-R_2 + O_3 \longrightarrow \text{ozonide} \xrightarrow{H_2O/Zn} R_1-\overset{O}{\underset{\|}{C}}-H + R_2-\overset{O}{\underset{\|}{C}}-H$$

ozonide   **carbonyls**

ALKYNES

Alkynes are acyclic hydrocarbon chains with the general formula C_nH_{2n-2}. They are characterized by $C\equiv C$ bonds. The reactivity of alkynes is somewhat comparable to that of the alkenes. One of the most important alkynes is ethyne ($HC\equiv CH$), which is commonly called acetylene.

As is the case for alkenes, an alkane can yield several alkynes, depending on the location of the triple bond.

Example:

Possible alkynes from hexane:

1-hexyne
$HC\equiv CCH_2CH_2CH_2CH_3$

3-hexyne
$CH_3CH_2C\equiv CCH_2CH_3$

4-methyl-2-pentyne
$CH_3CHC\equiv CCH_3$
|
CH_3

2-hexyne
$CH_3C\equiv CCH_2CH_2CH_3$

4-methyl-1-pentyne
$CH_3CHCH_2C\equiv CH$
|
CH_3

Preparation of Alkynes

1. Dehydrohalogenation of dihalides (X = Cl, Br, I)

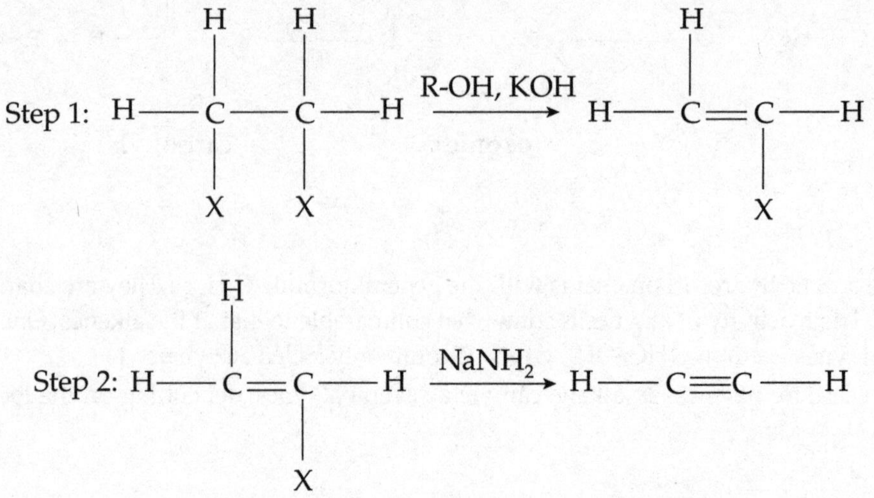

Step 1:
$$H-\underset{\underset{X}{|}}{\overset{\overset{H}{|}}{C}}-\underset{\underset{X}{|}}{\overset{\overset{H}{|}}{C}}-H \xrightarrow{\text{R-OH, KOH}} H-\overset{\overset{H}{|}}{C}=\underset{\underset{X}{|}}{C}-H$$

Step 2:
$$H-\underset{\underset{X}{|}}{C}=\overset{\overset{H}{|}}{C}-H \xrightarrow{\text{NaNH}_2} H-C\equiv C-H$$

The above reaction involves the dehydrohalogenation of a ***vic*-dihalide**. The prefix *vic-* stands for *vicinal* and it describes in this case halogens on adjacent carbons. If the halogen atoms (X) are bound to the same carbon, the dihalide is then called a *geminal* or ***gem*-dihalide**. Alkynes can also be prepared by the dehydrohalogenation of *gem*-dihalides.

2. Alkyl substitution

$$HC\equiv CH + NaNH_2 \rightarrow HC\equiv CNa$$
or

$$HC\equiv CH + RMgX \rightarrow HC\equiv CMgX$$

Reactions of Alkynes

Alkynes are nucleophilic just like alkenes; therefore, they undergo the same electrophilic addition reactions as alkenes do.

DIENES

Some alkenes have more than one carbon double bond (C=C) in their formulas—for instance, **dienes**, which have two C=C bonds, or trienes with three and tetraenes with four. Some important dienes are:

$$CH_2=CH-CH=CH_2$$
1,3-butadiene

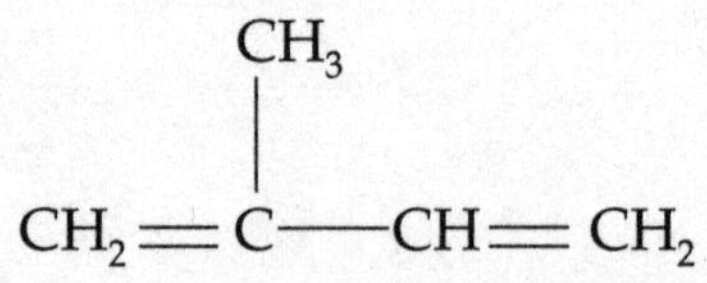

$$CH_2=\underset{\underset{}{}}{\overset{\overset{CH_3}{|}}{C}}-CH=CH_2$$
2-methyl-1,3-butadiene

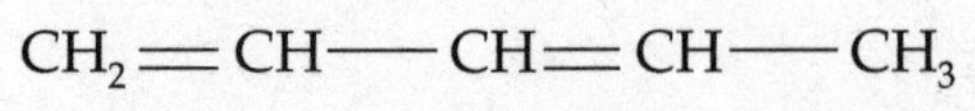

$$CH_2=CH-CH=CH-CH_3$$
1,3-pentadiene

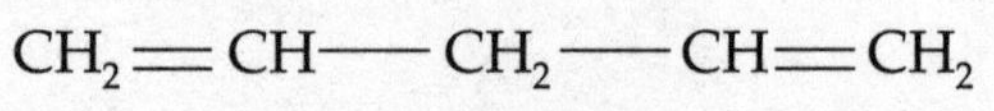

$$CH_2=CH-CH_2-CH=CH_2$$
1,4-pentadiene

When double bonds are separated by only one single bond, they are said to be **conjugated**. If they are separated by more than one C–C bond, they are **isolated**. In the above examples, 1,3-butadiene, 2-methyl-1,3-butadiene, and 1,3-pentadiene are all **conjugated dienes**. Compounds containing conjugated double bonds are more stable than ones that contain isolated bonds because the double bonds can interact with each other via resonance.

Synthesis of Dienes

1. Dehydration of diols

$$HOCH_2CH_2CH_2CH_2OH \xrightarrow{H_2SO_4} CH_2=CH-CH=CH_2$$

2. Dehydrogenation of alkenes

$$CH_2=CHCH_2CH_3 \xrightarrow{-H_2} CH_2=CH-CH=CH_2$$

3. Dehydrohalogenation of dihalides

$$CH_3CHXCH_2CH_2X \xrightarrow{\text{strong base, heat}} CH_2=CH-CH=CH_2$$

Reactions of Dienes

1. Addition of hydrogen

$$CH_2=CH-CH=CH_2 + 2H_2 \xrightarrow{\text{Pt, Pd, or Ni}} CH_3CH_2CH_2CH_3$$

2. Diels-Alder reaction

$$CH_2=CH-CH=CH_2 \quad + \quad CH_2=CH_2 \xrightarrow{\text{heat}}$$

1,3-butadiene   **ethylene**   **cyclohexene**

ALKYL HALIDES

When an alkane loses a hydrogen, the hydrogen can be replaced by a halogen atom (F, Cl, Br, I), so that a compound known as an **alkyl halide** is formed. Alkyl halides are usually abbreviated **RX**, with X = F, Cl, Br, or I.

Preparation of Alkyl Halides

1. Alcohol (ROH) + HX

$$R\text{-}OH + HX \rightarrow RX + H_2O$$

2. Alcohol + PX$_3$

$$3R\text{-}OH + PX_3 \rightarrow 3RX + H_3PO_3$$

3. Addition of HX to alkenes

$$R_1\text{-}CH=CH\text{-}R_2 + HX \rightarrow R_1\text{-}CH_2\text{-}CHX\text{-}R_2$$

4. Halogenation of alkanes with Cl$_2$ or Br$_2$

$$RH + X_2 \rightarrow RX + HX$$

Reactions of Alkyl Halides

1. Synthesis of higher alkanes

Step 1: $R\text{-}CH_2\text{-}X + 2Na \rightarrow R\text{-}CH_2\text{-}Na + NaX$

Step 2: $R\text{-}CH_2\text{-}Na + X\text{-}CH_2\text{-}R \rightarrow R\text{-}CH_2\text{-}CH_2\text{-}R + NaX$

2. Synthesis of R–OH using NaOH

$$R\text{-}CH_2\text{-}X + NaOH \rightarrow R\text{-}CH_2\text{-}OH + NaX$$

3. Elimination

$$R\text{-}CH_2CH_2X + KOH \xrightarrow{\text{ethanol}} RCH=CH_2$$

4. Synthesis of Grignard reagents (GR)

$$RX + Mg \xrightarrow{\text{ether}} RMgX$$

USE OF GRIGNARD REAGENTS

- Formaldehyde + GR → primary alcohol

$$H_2C=O + CH_3MgX \rightarrow CH_3\text{-}CH_2\text{-}(O^-MgX^+) + H_2O \rightarrow CH_3\text{-}CH_2OH + MgX(OH)$$

- Aldehyde + GR → secondary alcohol

$$RCHO + R'MgX \rightarrow RCH(O^-MgX^+)R' + H_2O \rightarrow RCH(OH)R' + MgX(OH)$$

- Ketone + GR → tertiary alcohol

$$RCOR' + R''MgX \rightarrow RR'R''C(O^-MgX^+) + H_2O \rightarrow RR'R''COH + MgX(OH)$$

- Nitrile + GR → ketone

$$RC\equiv N + R'MgX \rightarrow RC=N(MgX)R' + H_2O \rightarrow RCOR' + NH_3 + MgX(OH)$$

- Carbon dioxide + GR → carboxylic acid

$$CO_2 + RMgX \rightarrow RCOOMgX + HCl \rightarrow RCOOH + MgXCl$$

ALCOHOLS

An alcohol is defined as a compound that has an **–OH functional group** bound to a carbon. The alcohols of alkanes are saturated, acyclic compounds with general formula $C_nH_{2n+1}OH$ and are abbreviated **ROH**. If the –OH group is bound to an aromatic carbon, the compound is a **phenol**, abbreviated **ArOH**:

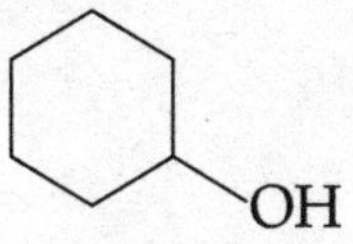

cyclohexanol 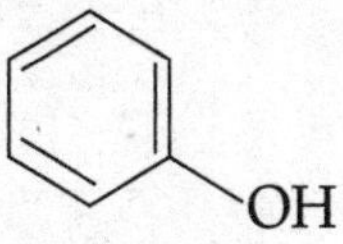   **phenol**

- Depending on the location of the –OH group, alcohols are called:

Primary	$R–CH_2(OH)$	*Ex*: CH_3CH_2OH (ethanol)
Secondary	$R_1 \longrightarrow C(OH) \longrightarrow R_2$	*Ex*: $CH_3CHOHCH_2CH_3$ (2-butanol)
	$\mid$	
	H	
Tertiary	$R_1 \longrightarrow C(OH) \longrightarrow R_2$	*Ex*: $(CH_3)_3COH$ (2-methyl-2-propanol)
	$\mid$	
	R_3	

- A primary alcohol has its –OH group bound to a primary carbon; i.e., a carbon that's directly bonded to only one other C atom.

- A secondary alcohol has its –OH group bound to a secondary carbon; i.e., a carbon that's directly bonded to only two other C atoms.

- A tertiary alcohol has its –OH group bound to a tertiary carbon; i.e., a carbon that's directly bonded to three other C atoms.

When alcohols have double and triple C–C bonds, they are named by adding the suffix –ol to the corresponding alkene/alkyne name so that the lowest carbon number is that to which the –OH group is attached:

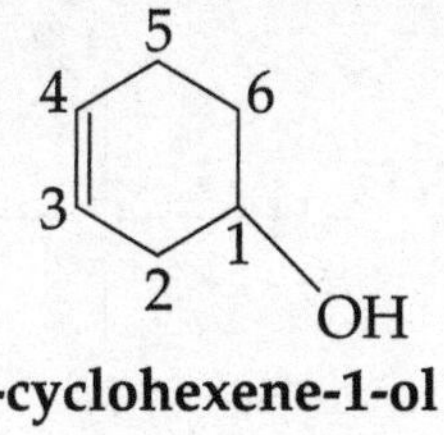

3-cyclohexene-1-ol 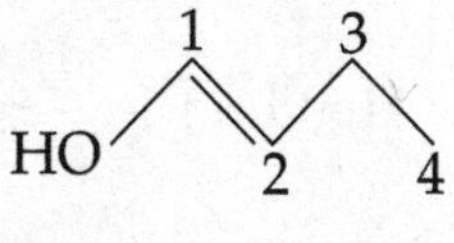   *trans*-**1-buten-1-ol**

- The proton of the –OH group of alcohols is weakly acidic and can be removed by a strong base to yield an **alkoxide ion**:

$$\text{H}-\overset{\cdot\cdot}{\underset{\cdot\cdot}{\text{O}}}-\text{H} + \text{B:}^- \rightleftharpoons \text{R}-\overset{\cdot\cdot}{\underset{\cdot\cdot}{\text{O}}}:^- + \text{HB}$$

  alcohol   **strong base**   **alkoxide ion**

Synthesis of Alcohols

1. Hydration of alkenes

$$\text{R–CH=CH}_2 + \text{H–OH} \xrightarrow{\text{H}^+_{(cat)}} \text{R–CH(OH)–CH}_3$$

2. Hydrolysis of alkyl halides

$$\text{RX} + \text{OH}^- \rightarrow \text{ROH} + \text{X}^-$$

3. Preparation from Grignard Reagents (GR)

- Formaldehyde + GR → primary alcohol

$$\text{H}_2\text{C=O} + \text{CH}_3\text{MgX} \rightarrow \text{CH}_3\text{–CH}_2\text{–(O}^-\text{MgX}^+) + \text{H}_2\text{O} \rightarrow \text{CH}_3\text{–CH}_2\text{OH} + \text{MgX(OH)}$$

- Aldehyde + GR → secondary alcohol

$$\text{RCHO} + \text{R'MgX} \rightarrow \text{RCH(O}^-\text{MgX)}^+\text{R'} + \text{H}_2\text{O} \rightarrow \text{RCH(OH)R'} + \text{MgX(OH)}$$

- Ketone + GR → tertiary alcohol

$$\text{RCOR'} + \text{R''MgX} \rightarrow \text{RR'R''C(O}^-\text{MgX)}^+ + \text{H}_2\text{O} \rightarrow \text{RR'R''COH} + \text{MgX(OH)}$$

4. Oxymercuration-demercuration of alkenes

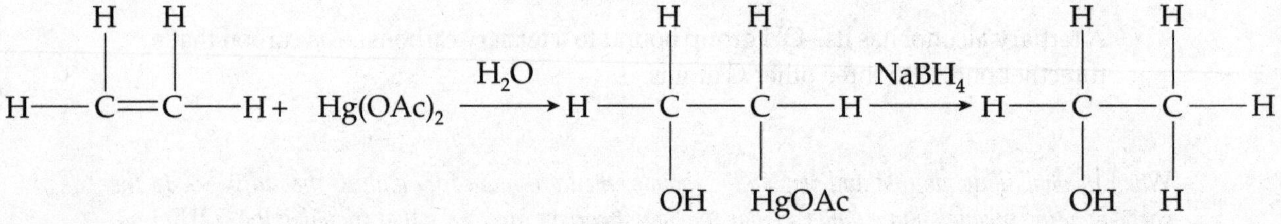

Example:

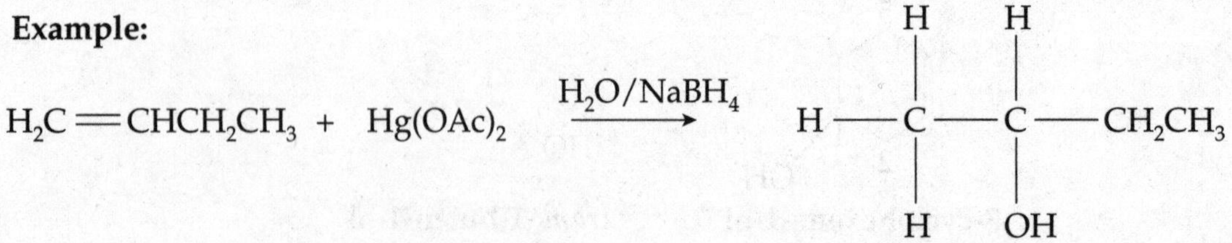

1-butene   **2-butanol**

5. Hydroboration-oxidation of alkenes

$$RCH{=}CH_2 + (BH_3)_2 \rightarrow (RCHCH_2)_3{-}B + H_2O_2/OH^- \rightarrow RCHCH_2$$

with:
- on the intermediate: H below the B-bearing carbon
- on the product: H and OH below the two carbons

Reactions of Alcohols

1. Oxidation of primary alcohols to carboxylic acids

$$R{-}CH_2{-}OH + \xrightarrow[H_2SO_4]{Na_2Cr_2O_7} RCOOH$$

2. Oxidation of primary alcohols to aldehydes

$$R{-}CH_2{-}OH \xrightarrow[pyridine\ (PCC)]{CrO_3} RCHO$$

3. Oxidation of secondary alcohols to ketones

$$R_1{-}C(OH){-}R_2 \xrightarrow[H_2SO_4]{Na_2Cr_2O_7} R_1{-}CO{-}R_2$$

with H below the central carbon

4. Reduction of alcohols to alkanes

$$R{-}OH \xrightarrow{LiAlH_4,\ TiCl_4} R{-}H$$

5. Synthesis of alkyl halides

$$R{-}OH + HX \rightarrow R{-}X$$

6. Dehydration to alkenes

$$H{-}\underset{\underset{H}{|}}{\overset{\overset{H}{|}}{C}}{-}\underset{\underset{OH}{|}}{\overset{\overset{H}{|}}{C}}{-}H \xrightarrow{H^+_{(cat)},\ heat} \overset{H}{\underset{H}{}}C{=}C\overset{H}{\underset{H}{}} + H_2O$$

7. Dehydration to ethers

$$2R{-}OH + H^+_{(cat)} \rightarrow R{-}O{-}R + H_2O$$

8. Tosylation

$$R{-}OH + O{=}\overset{\overset{Cl}{|}}{\underset{}{S}}{=}O \xrightarrow{pyridine} O{=}\overset{\overset{RO}{|}}{\underset{}{S}}{=}O$$

with benzene rings bearing CH_3

tosyl chloride   **alkyl tosylate**

9. Acylation

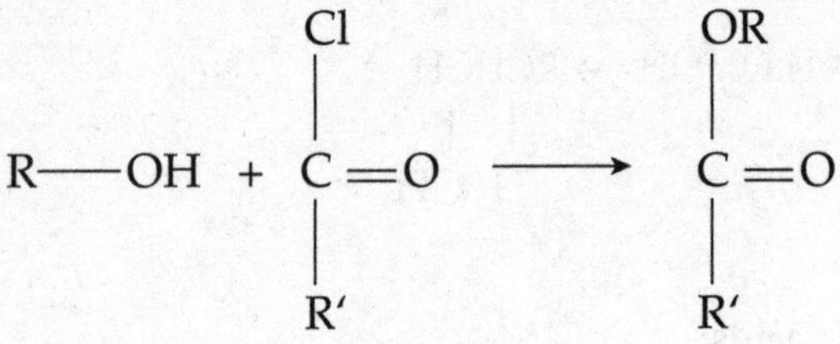

$$R\text{—}OH + \underset{\substack{| \\ R'}}{\overset{\substack{Cl \\ |}}{C}}=O \longrightarrow \underset{\substack{| \\ R'}}{\overset{\substack{OR \\ |}}{C}}=O$$

$$\qquad\qquad\quad \textbf{acyl chloride} \qquad\quad \textbf{ester}$$

10. Deprotonation to alkoxide

$R\text{–}OH + Na \rightarrow R\text{–}O^- \, {}^+Na$

$R\text{–}OH + K \rightarrow R\text{–}O^- \, {}^+K$

Example:

$CH_3CH_2\text{–}OH + K \rightarrow CH_3CH_2O^-K^+$ (potassium ethoxide)

THIOLS

Thiols or **mercaptans** have an **–SH (sulfhydryl) functional group** bound to a carbon. Their general formula is $C_nH_{2n+1}SH$, and they are abbreviated **RSH**.

Examples:

$CH_3CH(CH_3)CH_2CH_2SH$	3-methyl-1-butanethiol
$CH_3CH{=}CHCH_2CH_2SH$	3-pentene-1-thiol

Synthesis of Thiols

1. From alkyl halides and HS^-

$RX + HS^- \rightarrow X^- + RSH$

2. From disulfides

$R\text{–}S\text{–}S\text{–}R \; (+ \text{ Li and liquid } NH_3) \rightarrow RSH$

3. From alkenes

$R'CH{=}CH_2 + H_2S \, (+\, RO^-) \rightarrow RSH$

Reactions of Thiols

1. Synthesis of thioesters

$RSH + \; R'\text{–}COCl \rightarrow R'\text{–}COSR$

2. Synthesis of thioethers

$RSH + \; OH^- + R'X \rightarrow R\text{–}S\text{–}R'$

3. Synthesis of thioacetals

$2RSH + \; R'\text{–}CH{=}O \; \rightarrow R'\text{–}CH(SR_2)$

4. Synthesis of sulfonic acids

$RSH + KMnO_4 \rightarrow R\text{–}SO_3H$

ETHERS

Ethers can either be **simple** ethers, **R–O–R** or **Ar–O–Ar**, when the R or Ar groups are identical, or **mixed** ethers, **R–O–R'** or **Ar–O–Ar'** or **R–O–Ar**, when the groups bonded to the oxygen are not the same. For the most part, they are named by using the names of the R or Ar group to which is added "ether." The IUPAC nomenclature names ethers as substituted alkanes.

$$CH_3CH_2OCH_2CH_3$$

diethyl ether

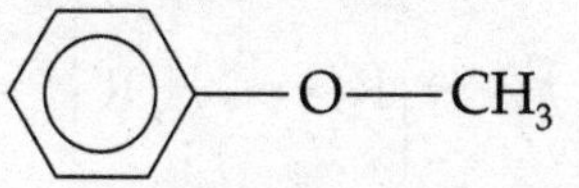

methyl phenyl ether

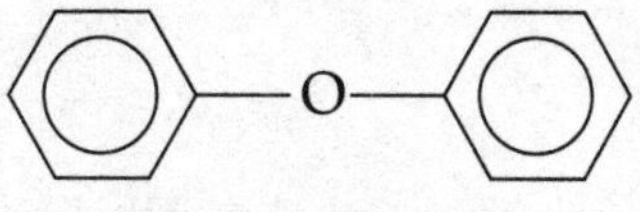

diphenyl ether

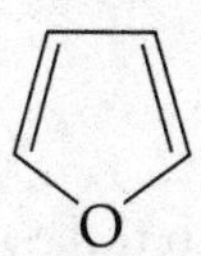

furan

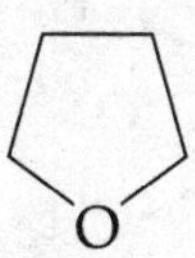

tetrahydrofuran

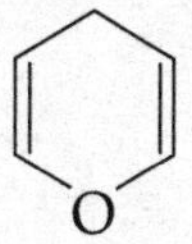

pyran

Synthesis of Ethers

1. Williamson synthesis

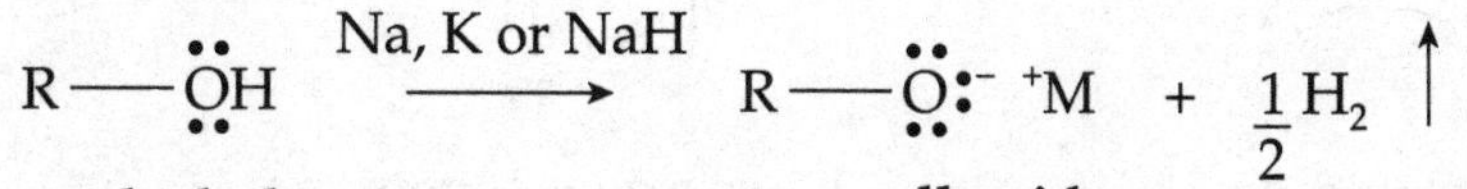

alcohol   **alkoxide**

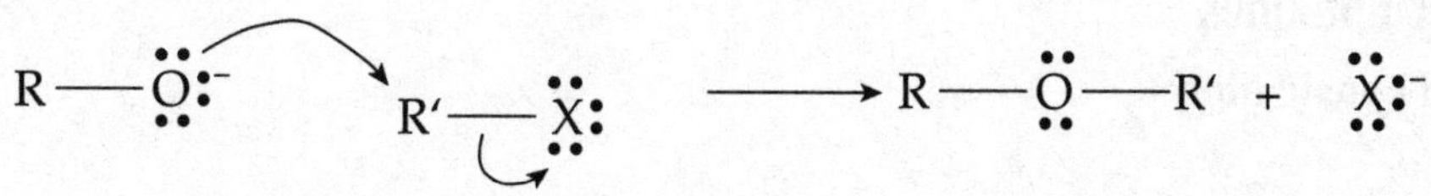

alkyl halide or tosylate   **ether**

Example:

$$(CH_3)_3C—OH \xrightarrow{K} (CH_3)_3C—O^- {}^+K \xrightarrow{CH_3CH_2CH_2Br} (CH_3)_3C—OCH_2CH_2CH_3$$

2. Intermolecular dehydration

$$2ROH + H_2SO_4 \rightarrow ROR + H_2O \quad \text{(R is primary)}$$

Reactions of Ethers

1. Cleavage by HBr or HI

$$ROR' + HX \rightarrow RX + R'X \qquad X = Br \text{ or } I$$

The reaction occurs in two steps:

Step 1: $ROR' + HX \rightarrow \left[R\!-\!\overset{\displaystyle H}{\underset{}{O}}\!-\!R' \right]^+ \rightarrow RX + R'OH$

Step 2: $R'OH + HX \rightarrow R'X + H_2O$

EPOXIDES

Epoxides are **cyclic ethers** with **three-membered rings**. They are also called **oxiranes**.
Examples:

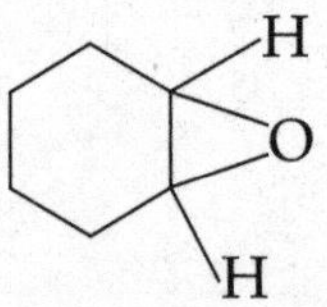

epoxycyclohexane 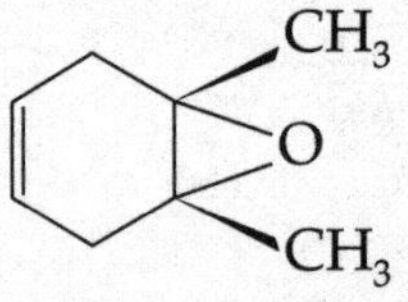   *cis*-**4,5-epoxy-4,5-dimethylcyclohexene**

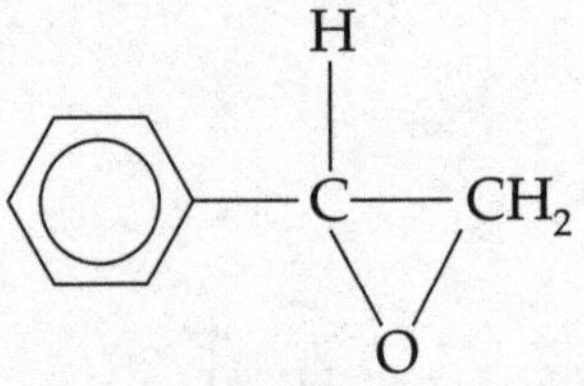

1-phenyloxirane 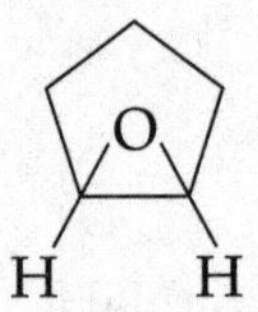   **1,2-epoxycyclopentane**

Synthesis of Epoxides

1. Peroxyacid epoxidation

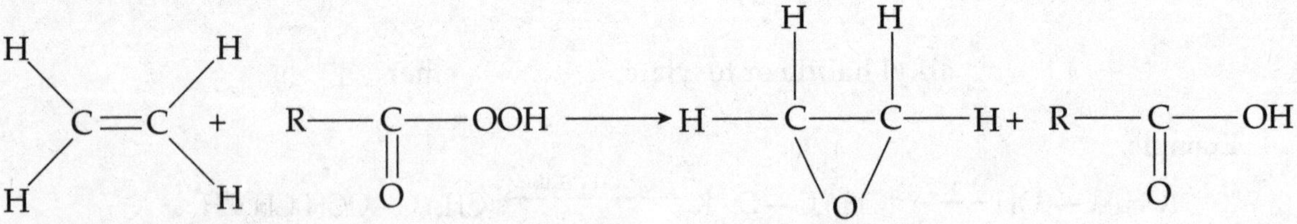

2. From halohydrins

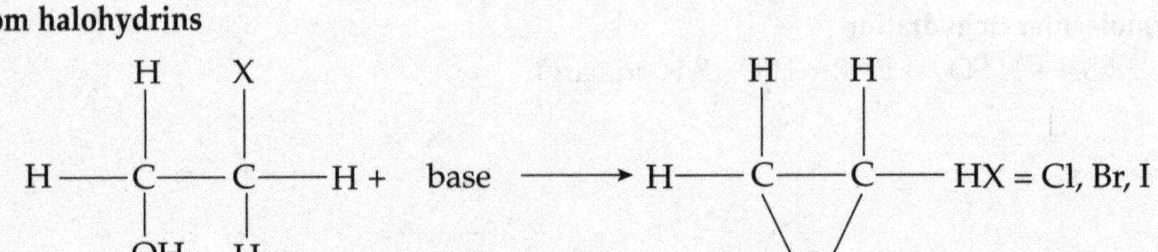

Reactions of Epoxides

1. Acid-catalyzed cleavage

With H_2O:

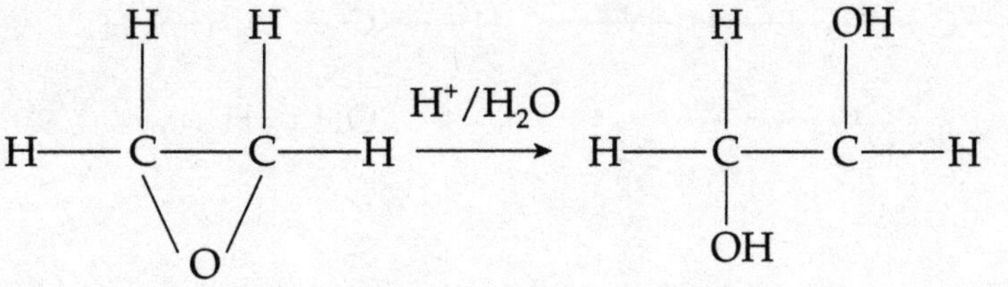

anti-diol

With ROH:

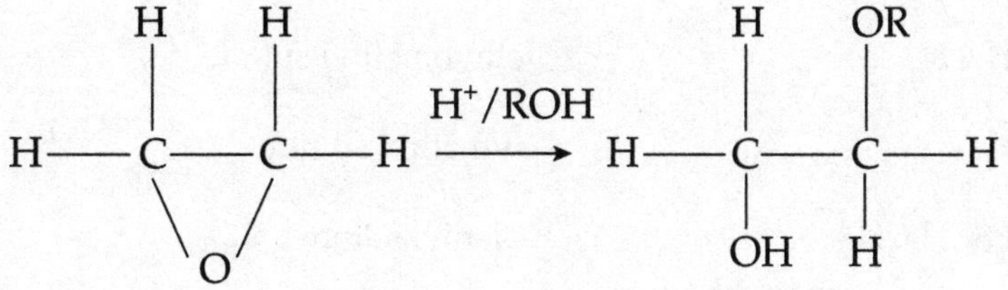

With hydrohalic acids:

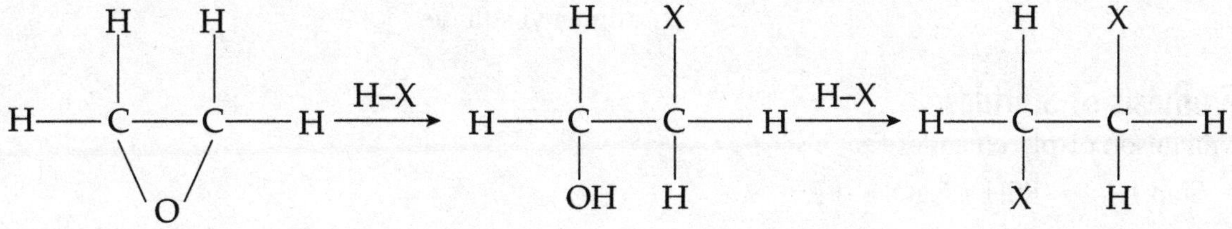

2. Base-catalyzed cleavage

With alkoxides:

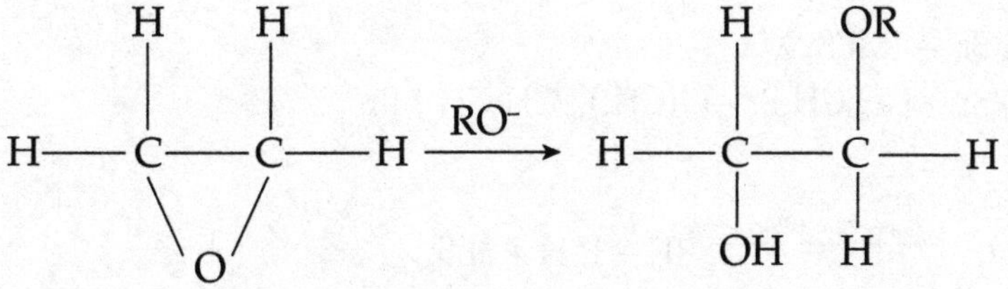

With organometallic compounds like Grignard reagents:

$$\underset{\substack{\text{H} \\ | \\ \text{H}-\text{C}-\text{C}-\text{H} \\ \diagdown\text{O}\diagup}}{\overset{\substack{\text{H} \quad\;\; \text{H}}}{}} \quad \xrightarrow{\text{R–M/H}_2\text{O}} \quad \underset{\substack{\text{OH} \;\;\; \text{H}}}{\overset{\substack{\text{H} \quad\;\; \text{R}}}{\text{H}-\text{C}-\text{C}-\text{H}}}$$

SULFIDES

Sulfides or **thioethers** contain a sulfur atom between R groups. They are abbreviated **R–S–R** and, like ethers, they can be simple or mixed, depending on whether the R groups are identical or not.
Examples:

$CH_3SCH_2CH_3$ ethyl methyl sulfide

CH_3SCH_3 dimethyl sulfide

$CH_3CH_2SCH_2CH_3$ diethyl sulfide

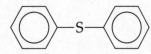   diphenyl sulfide

Synthesis of Sulfides
Williamson displacement of RS:

Step 1: $RSH + NaOH \rightarrow RS^-$

Step 2: $RS^- + R'X \rightarrow R\text{–}S\text{–}R' + NaX$

Reactions of Sulfides

1. Synthesis of sulfonium salts

$R\text{–}S\text{–}R + R'Br \rightarrow R_2R'S{:}^+X^-$

Example: $(CH_3)_2S{:} + CH_3CH_2Br \rightarrow [(CH_3)_2SCH_2CH_3]^+Br^-$

2. Hydrogenolysis

$R\text{–}S\text{–}R' + H_2 \xrightarrow{\text{Raney Ni catalyst}} RH + R'H + H_2S$

AROMATIC COMPOUNDS

Aromatic compounds are **cyclic, unsaturated** compounds that have **conjugated** double bonds. The archetypal aromatic compound is benzene (C_6H_6).

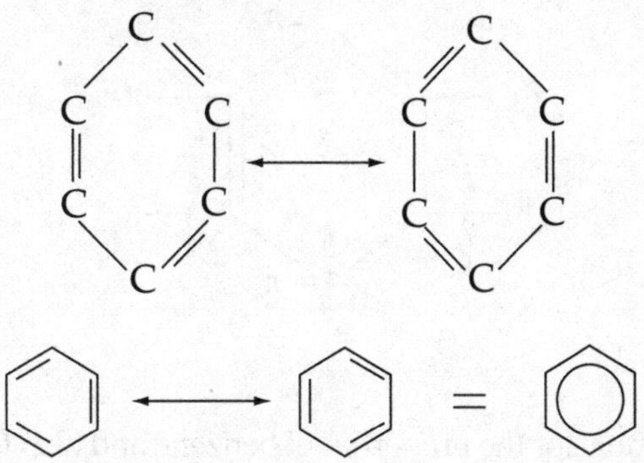

As shown previously, benzene, as was first proposed by Kekulé, consists of a cyclic structure with alternating double bonds. But double bonds are shorter than single bonds, so this picture was modified to account for the fact that the carbon bonds in benzene are all the same length (1.397 Å) by introducing the **resonance** representation, in which the π electrons are assumed to be delocalized over the whole ring. This also explained some of the unexpected properties of benzene and its derivatives, such as its low degree of reactivity and resistance to oxidation.

But the resonance model could not fully account for the unusual stability of the benzene ring. To understand further reasons for its stability requires **molecular orbital theory**, which includes a description of π-electron delocalization.

According to this view, benzene is a planar ring consisting of six sp^2 hybridized carbon atoms, each s-bonded to two carbon neighbors and one hydrogen. Each carbon also has an electron in a p orbital, perpendicular to the plane of the ring. These p orbitals overlap with adjacent p orbitals to form a π-bonding system above and below the plane of the ring:

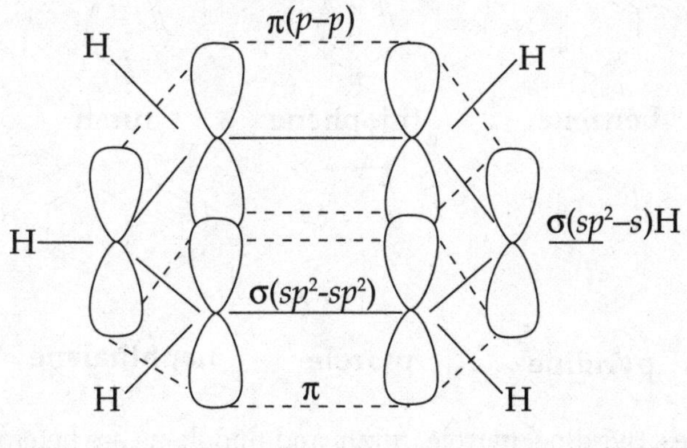

The six p orbitals form six π molecular orbitals. The lowest in energy are the bonding orbitals that contain the six π electrons.

The higher energy antibonding orbitals, π^* in the diagram below, are empty. The distribution of π electrons over the bonding p orbitals makes them **delocalized** over all six carbon atoms. This configuration of completely filled bonding orbitals is energetically very favorable and is what confers on benzene its stability and resulting chemical properties.

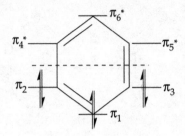

AROMATICITY

Molecular orbital theory accounts for the properties of benzene and also for the properties of any compound designated as having **aromatic character**. That term implies the following:

- A cyclic structure with conjugated π bonds containing unhybridized p orbitals that can overlap with other ring carbons to form the delocalized pi electron system

- A structure in which delocalization of the π-electron system lowers the total electronic energy

- The structure can be described by **Hückel's rule**:

> *A compound is aromatic if the number of its π electrons is equal to $2 + 4n$, where n is zero or an integer and represents filled electron shells. For n = 0, 1, or 2, aromatic systems have 2, 6, and 10 π electrons.*

Examples:

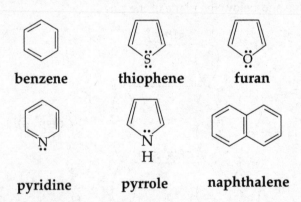

benzene   thiophene   furan

pyridine   pyrrole   naphthalene

In the above examples, pyridine, pyrrole, furan, and thiophene are heterocyclic compounds with aromatic character. Pyrrole has six π electrons and two unshared electrons on the N atom overlap in the π system. Likewise, furan also has six π electrons, and two electrons on the O atom overlap in the π system of the ring. In the case of pyridine, the electron pair of the N atom does not overlap with the π electron system.

When the π electron delocalization increases the electronic energy, the compound is called **antiaromatic**.

A compound is antiaromatic if the number of its π electrons is equal to 4n, where n is an integer. For n = 1, 2, or 3, antiaromatic systems have 4, 8, and 12 π electrons.

Example:

antiaromatic cyclobutadiene

The antiaromatic cyclobutadiene is less stable than its open chain analog.

Some Benzene Derivatives

toluene

chlorobenzene

ethylbenzene

aniline

styrene

1,2-dimethylbenzene (*o*-xylene)

_p_-aminobenzoic acid

_p_-nitrobenzenesulfonic acid

_p_-xylene

REACTIONS OF BENZENE AND ITS DERIVATIVES

1. Halogenation

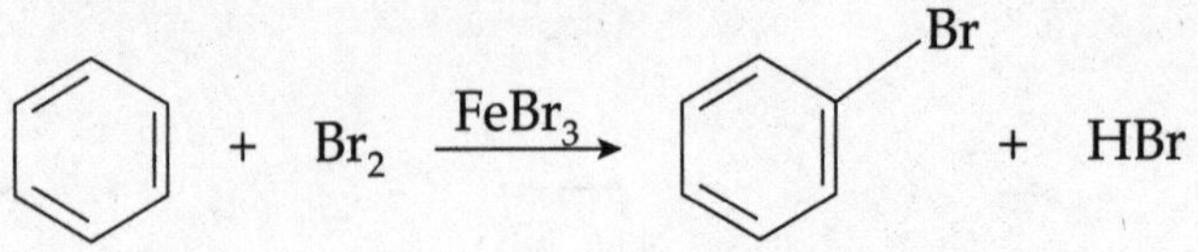

bromobenzene

2. Nitration

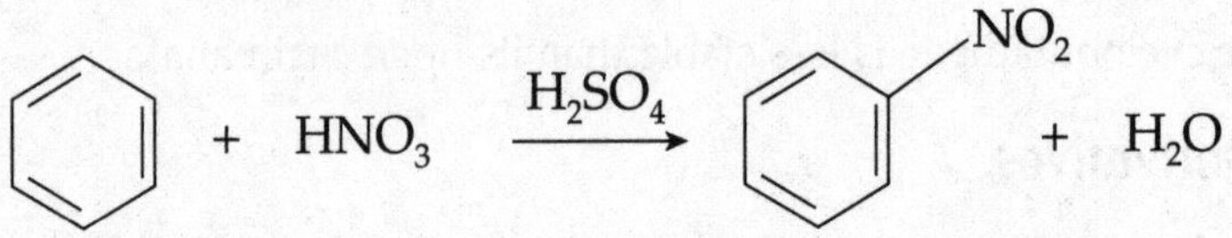

nitrobenzene

3. Sulfonation

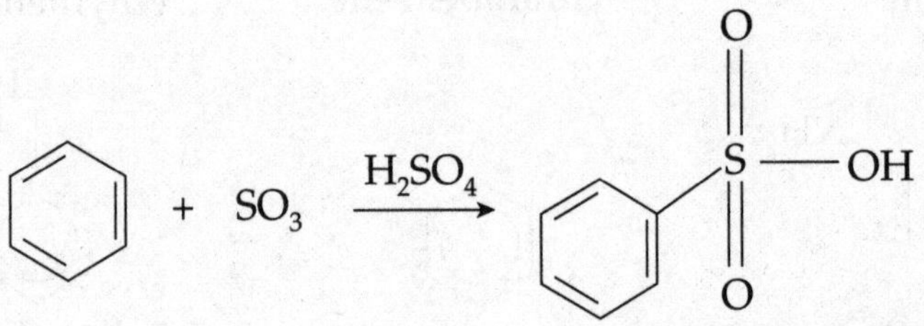

benzenesulfonic acid

4. Alkylation (Friedel-Crafts)

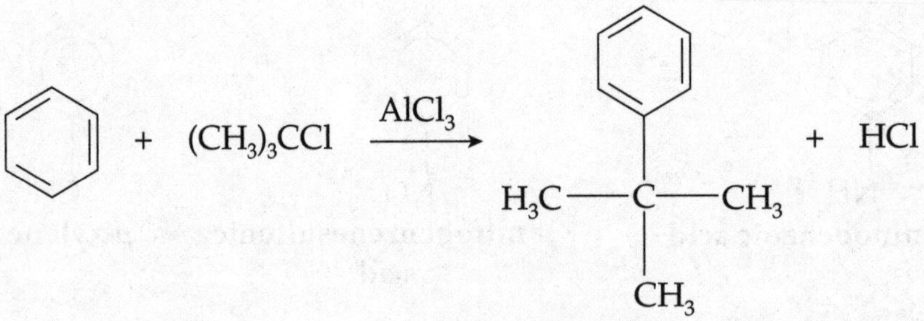

t-butylbenzene

5. Acylation (Friedel-Crafts)

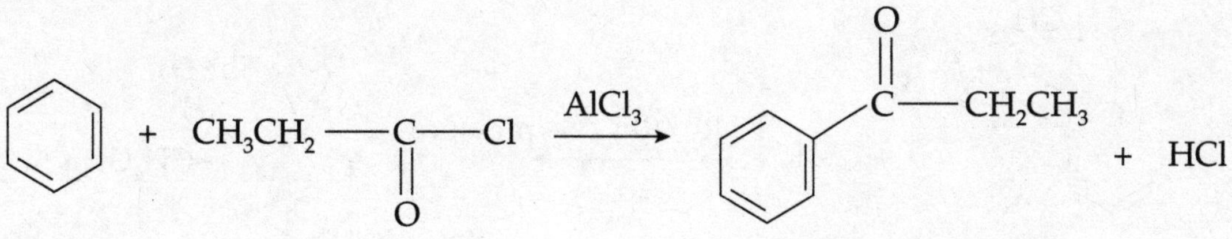

phenyl ethyl ketone

6. Gatterman-Koch synthesis

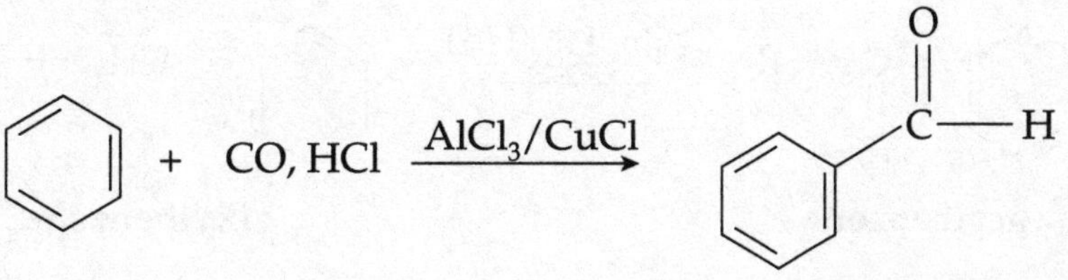

benzaldehyde

7. Chlorination

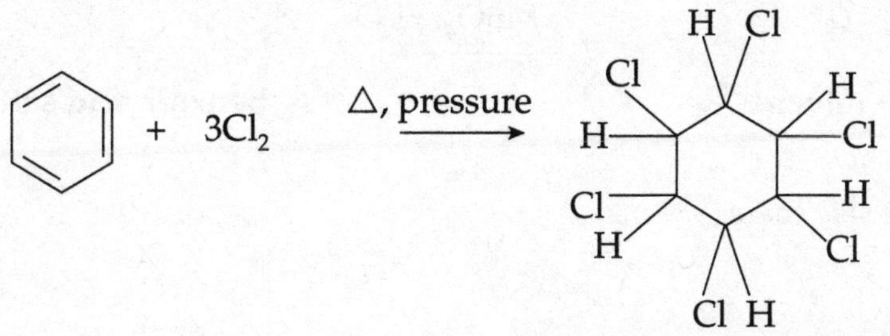

hexachlorocyclohexane

8. Birch reduction

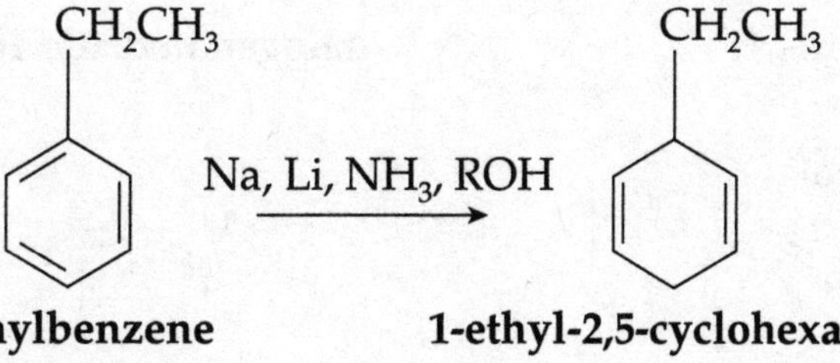

ethylbenzene   **1-ethyl-2,5-cyclohexadiene**

9. Catalyzed hydrogenation

CH₂CH₃

CH₂CH₃

+ 3H₂ →(Ru/Rh, △ + pressure)→ 1,2-diethylcyclohexane

o-diethylbenzene   **1,2-diethylcyclohexane**

10. Clemmensen reaction

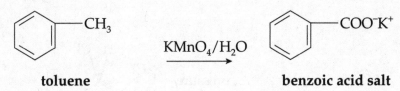

acylbenzene   **alkylbenzene**

11. Oxidation by KMnO₄

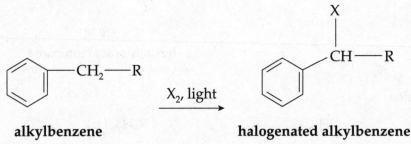

toluene   **benzoic acid salt**

12. Halogenation of side chain

alkylbenzene   **halogenated alkylbenzene**

13. Hydrogenolysis of alcohols

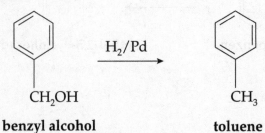

benzyl alcohol   **toluene**

14. Hydrogenolysis of ethers

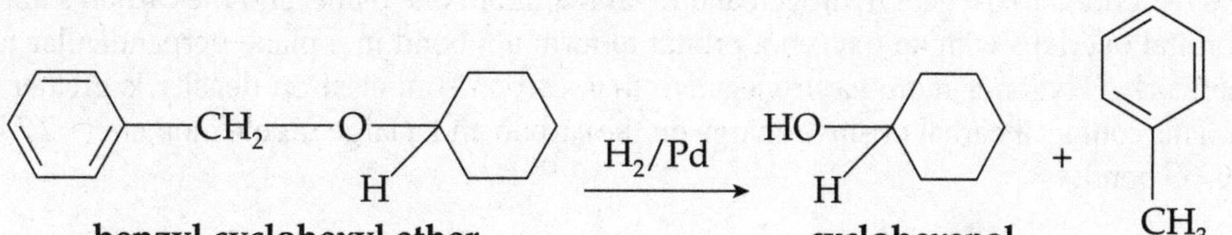

benzyl cyclohexyl ether → (H₂/Pd) → cyclohexanol + toluene

Aldehydes

Aldehydes, abbreviated **RCHO**, contain a **carbonyl (C=O)** functional group bonded to one hydrogen and to **one alkyl or aryl group**. The IUPAC names of aldehydes are obtained by replacing the final "e" in alkanes by the suffix *–al* (for one C=O group) or *–dial* (for two C=O groups). Carbons are numbered starting with the carbonyl C, which is assigned 1. Common names are derived from carboxylic acid IUPAC names, replacing the suffixes *–ic, –oic,* or *–oxylic acid* by *–aldehyde*. Greek letters are used to identify the carbons; the first after the C=O group is the α carbon, the second is the β carbon, etc.

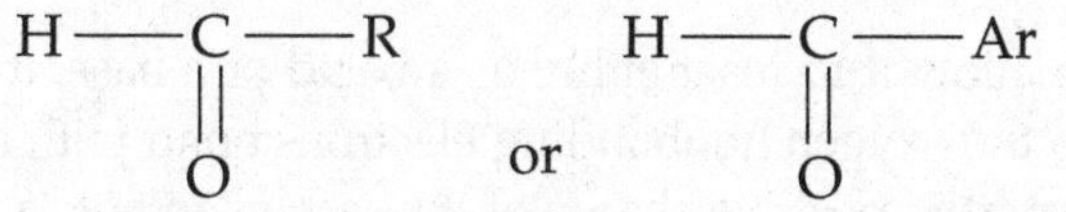

aldehyde

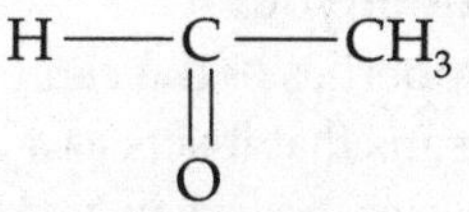

acetaldehyde
(ethanal)

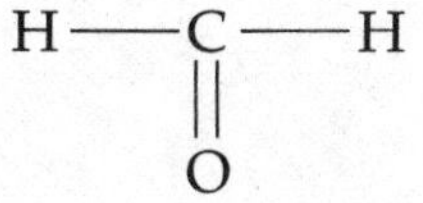

formaldehyde

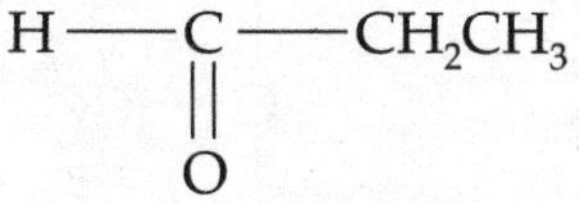

propionaldehyde
(propanal)

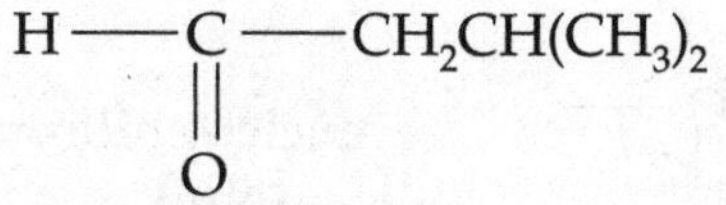

3-methylbutyraldehyde
(3-methylbutanal)

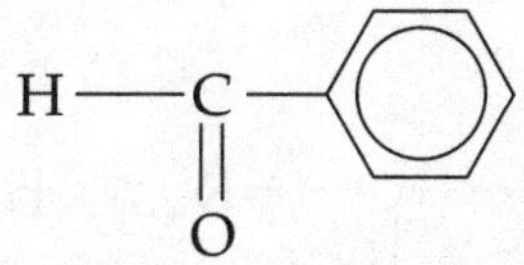

benzaldehyde

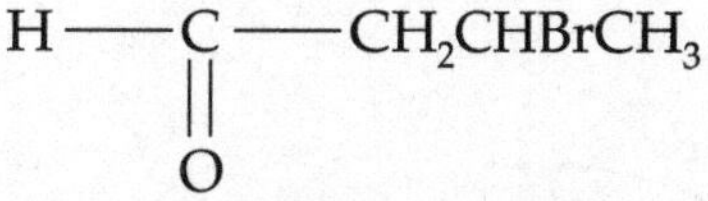

3-bromobutyraldehyde
(3-bromobutanal)

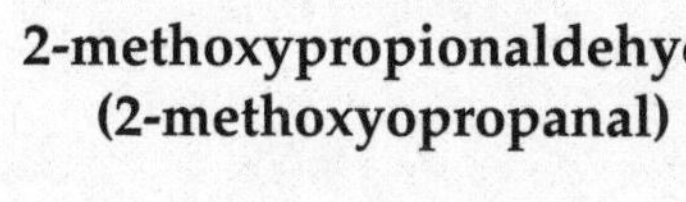

2-methoxypropionaldehyde
(2-methoxyopropanal)

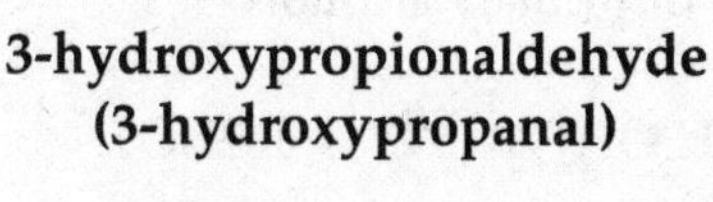

3-hydroxypropionaldehyde
(3-hydroxypropanal)

The chemistry of aldehydes is governed by the carbonyl group, in which the carbon is sp^2–hybridized. It is σ–bonded to oxygen, hydrogen and to an R atom in one plane, and the carbon's unhybridized p orbital overlaps with an oxygen π orbital to form a π bond in a plane perpendicular to the σ bond network. Oxygen is more electronegative than carbon so π electron density is greater on the oxygen. This confers a partial positive charge on the carbon and a large dipole moment (~ 2.7 Debye) on the C=O bond:

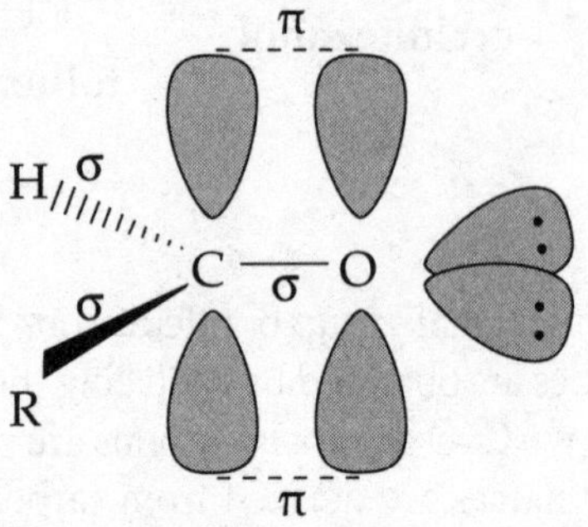

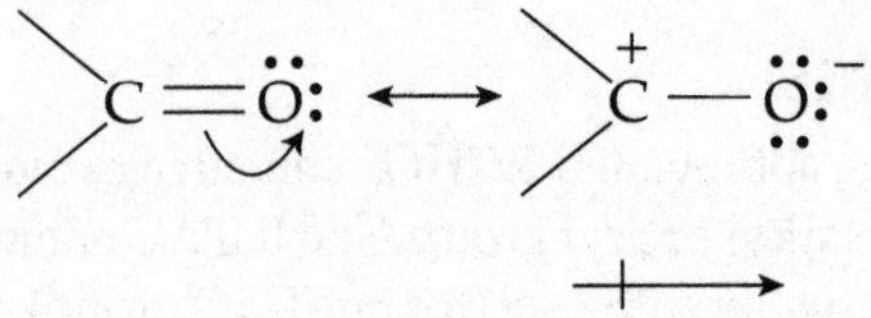

Not surprisingly, aldehydes are very reactive because carbon can act as an electrophile and the oxygen as a nucleophile.

Reactivity of Aldehydes

The electronic properties of the carbonyl group allow it to react either as an acid or a base; it is **amphoteric**. This means that it acts as a base when the oxygen nonbonding electrons bond with a H^+ or other positive species, and as an acid when the partial positive charge of the carbon accepts a pair of electrons from a nucleophile.

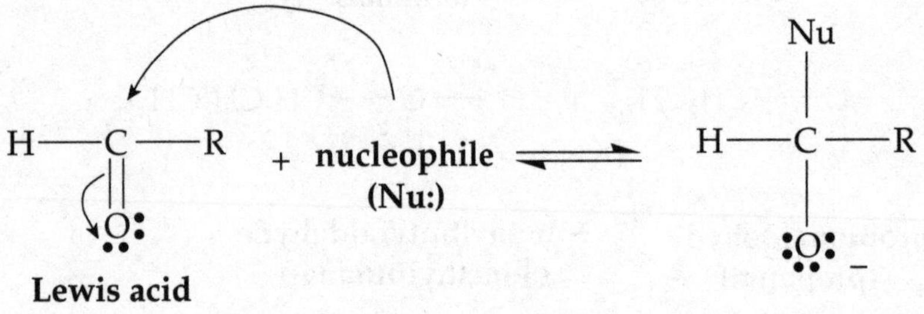

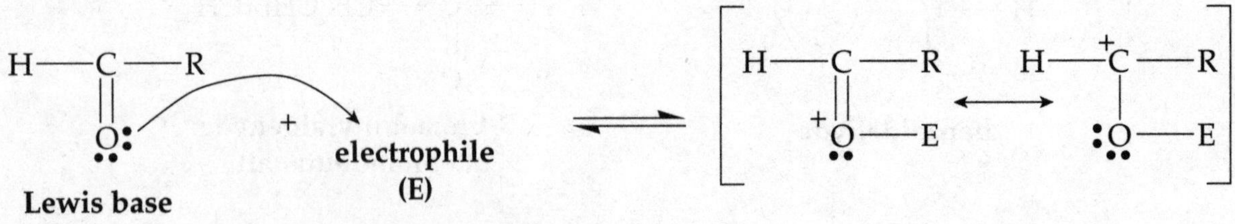

Synthesis of Aldehydes

1. Oxidation of primary alcohols

$$R\text{–}CH_2OH \xrightarrow[\text{H}_2\text{SO}_4]{\text{K}_2\text{Cr}_2\text{O}_7} RCHO$$

2. Ozonolysis of alkenes

$$RCH=CHR \xrightarrow[\text{(CH}_3)_2\text{S}]{O_3} RCHO + R'CHO$$

3. Gatterman–Koch formylation

$$HCl + CO + Ar–H \xrightarrow{AlCl_3} Ar–CHO$$

Example:

toluene   *p*-methylbenzaldehyde

4. Hydroboration–oxidation of alkynes

$$R–C{\equiv}CR \xrightarrow[\substack{\text{H}_2\text{O}_2 \\ \text{NaOH}}]{\substack{\text{(1) BH}_3 \\ \text{(2) THF}}} 2RCHO$$

5. Reduction of acyl chlorides

$$R–COCl \xrightarrow{\text{(H}_2\text{, Pd, BaSO}_4)} RCHO$$

Reactions of Aldehydes

1. Hydration

2. Addition of Grignard reagent

$$R - \overset{\overset{\displaystyle O}{\|}}{C} - H \ + \ R'MgX \ \longrightarrow \ R - \overset{\overset{\displaystyle OH}{|}}{\underset{\underset{\displaystyle R'}{|}}{C}} - H \qquad \text{(2° alcohol)}$$

3. Reduction

$$R - \overset{\overset{\displaystyle O}{\|}}{C} - H \ \xrightarrow[\text{H}^+]{\text{LiAlH}_4} \ R - \overset{\overset{\displaystyle OH}{|}}{CH_2} \qquad \text{(1° alcohol)}$$

4. Synthesis of cyanohydrins

$$R - \overset{\overset{\displaystyle O}{\|}}{C} - H \ \xrightarrow{\text{HCN}} \ R - \overset{\overset{\displaystyle OH}{|}}{\underset{\underset{\displaystyle CN}{|}}{C}} - H \qquad \text{(cyanohydrin)}$$

5. Synthesis of imines

$$R - \overset{\overset{\displaystyle O}{\|}}{C} - H \ \xrightarrow[-\text{H}_2\text{O}]{\text{H}_2\text{NR}'} \ R - \overset{\overset{\displaystyle NR'}{\|}}{C} - H \qquad \text{(imine or Schiff base)}$$

6. Synthesis of oximes

$$RCHO + H_2NOH \rightarrow R - \overset{\overset{\displaystyle OH}{\overset{\displaystyle |}{\underset{\displaystyle N}{\|}}}}{C} - H \qquad \text{(oxime)}$$

7. Synthesis of acetals

$$R - \overset{\overset{\displaystyle O}{\|}}{C} - H \ + \ 2R'OH \ \underset{}{\overset{\text{H}^+_{(cat)}}{\rightleftharpoons}} \ R - \overset{\overset{\displaystyle OR'}{|}}{\underset{\underset{\displaystyle OR'}{|}}{C}} - H \qquad \text{(acetal)}$$

8. Oxidation

$$RCHO \xrightarrow{\text{KMnO}_4} RCOOH \qquad \text{(carboxylic acid)}$$

9. Clemmensen reduction

$$RCHO \xrightarrow{\text{Zn(Hg), HCl}} RCH_3 \qquad \text{(alkane)}$$

KETONES

Ketones, abbreviated **RCOR**, contain a **carbonyl (C=O)** functional group bonded to **two alkyl or aryl groups**. The IUPAC names are obtained by replacing the final "e" in alkanes by the suffix *–one*. In open chain ketones, carbons are numbered starting with the carbon closest to the carbonyl C. Numbering in cyclic ketones starts with the carbonyl carbon. Common names are derived from carboxylic acid names; the suffixes *–ic*, *–oic*, or *–oxylic acid* are replaced by *–ketone*. Some systematic names are never used. For example, dimethyl ketone is called acetone. Ketones containing a phenyl group use the suffix *–phenone*.

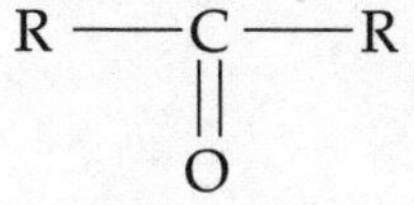

ketone

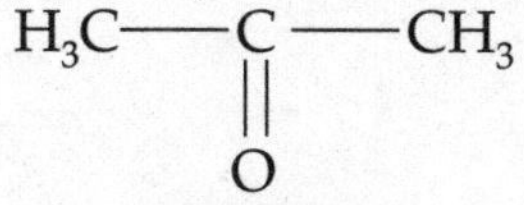

acetone (dimethylketone)

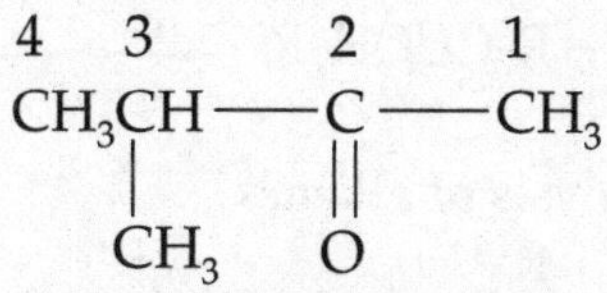

methyl isopropyl ketone (3-methyl-2-butanone)

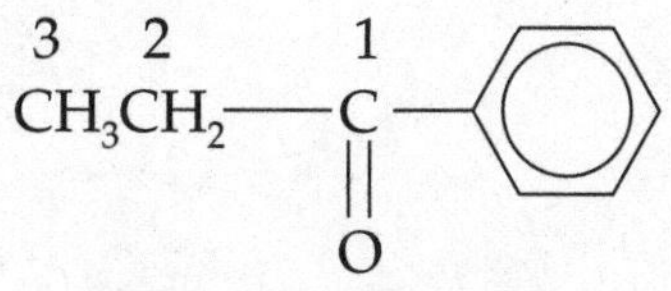

ethyl phenyl ketone (1-phenyl-1-propanone)

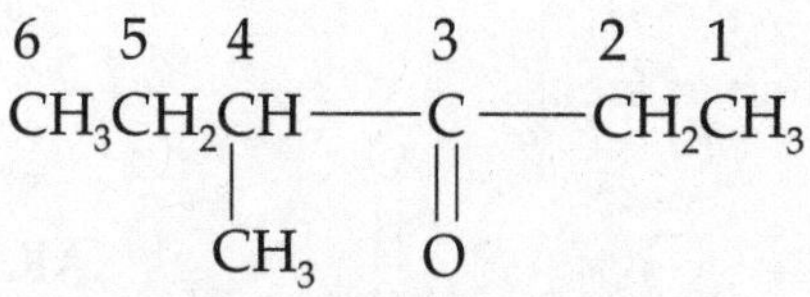

ethyl *sec*-butyl ketone (4-methyl-3-hexanone)

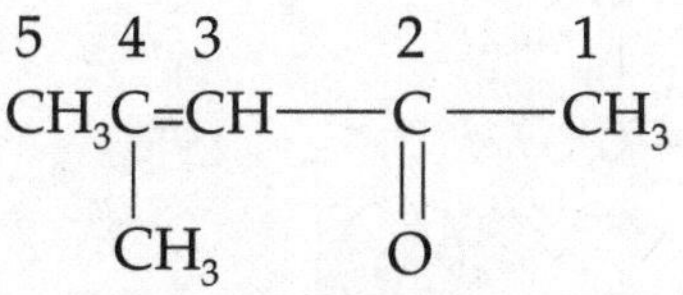

mesityl oxide (4-methyl-3-penten-2-one)

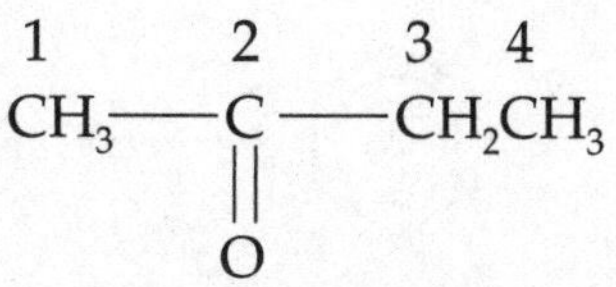

methyl ethyl ketone (2-butanone)

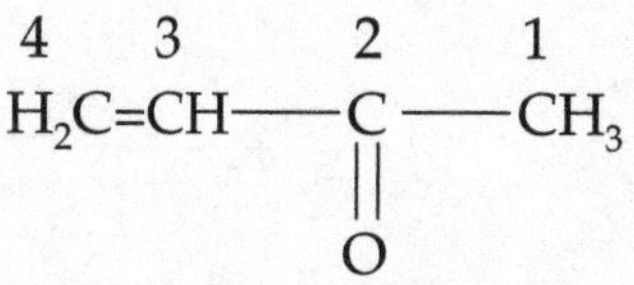

methyl vinyl ketone (3-buten-2-one)

benzophenone

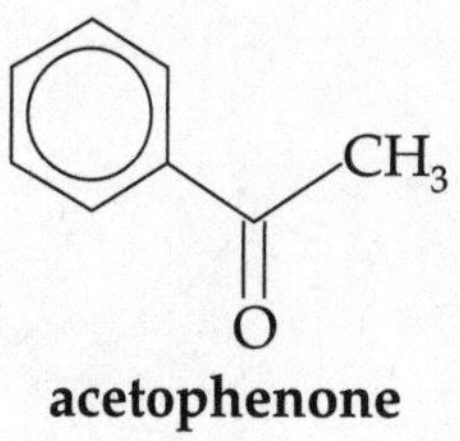

acetophenone

Like aldehydes, the properties of ketones are governed by their **carbonyl group**. Aldehydes and ketones have similar chemistries. For example, ketones tend to be good electrophiles, but the presence of two electron-donating R groups in ketones—instead of one—lowers the electrophilicity of the carbonyl carbon, so ketones are generally less reactive than their corresponding aldehydes because there is less partial positive charge on the C=O carbon.

Synthesis of Ketones

1. Oxidation of secondary alcohols

$$\text{R–CHOH–R}' \xrightarrow[\text{H}_2\text{SO}_4]{\text{K}_2\text{Cr}_2\text{O}_7} \text{RCOR}'$$

2. Ozonolysis of alkenes

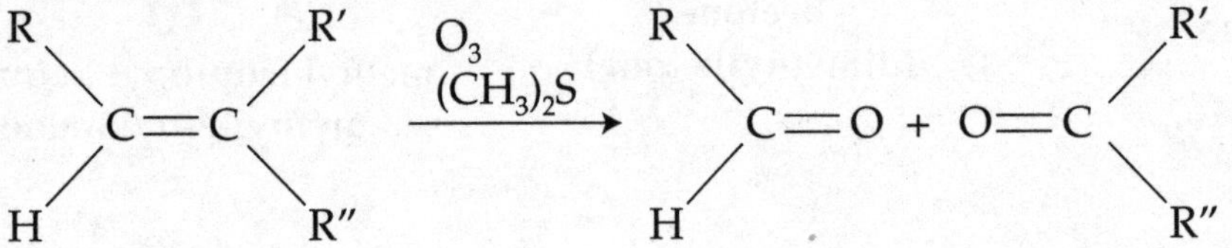

3. Acylation of arenes

a)

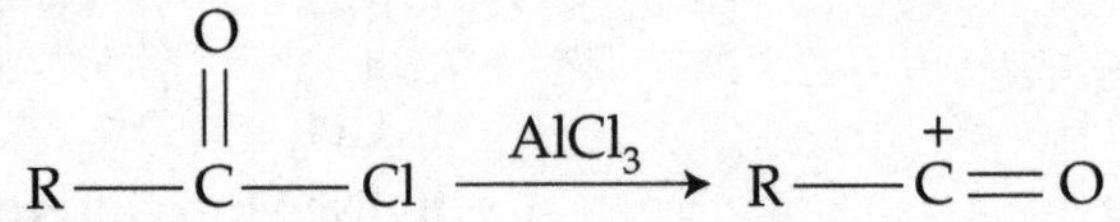

(acylonium ion)

b)

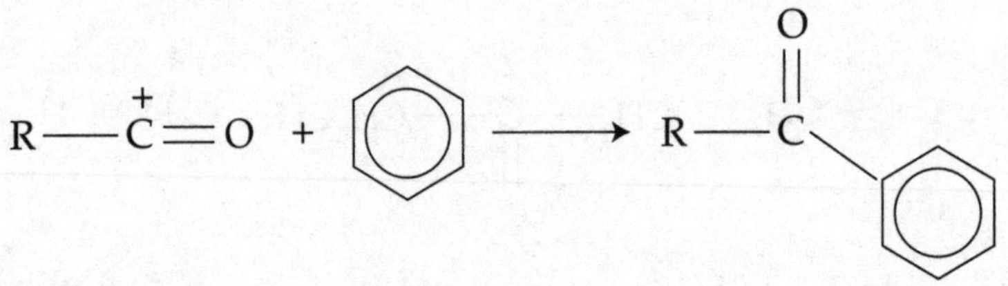

4. Alkylation of 1,3-dithianes

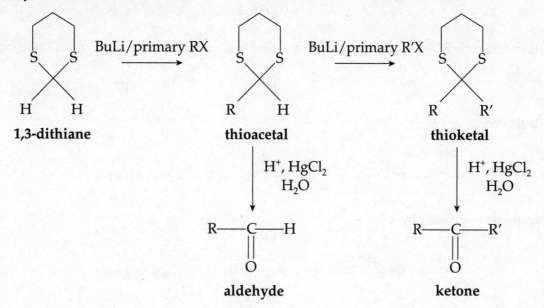

1,3-dithiane   →   thioacetal   →   thioketal

BuLi/primary RX

BuLi/primary R′X

H^+, $HgCl_2$
H_2O

H^+, $HgCl_2$
H_2O

aldehyde

ketone

5. Synthesis from organolithium and carboxylic acids

$$R-\overset{\overset{\displaystyle O}{\|}}{C}-OH \ + \ 2R'Li \longrightarrow R-\overset{\overset{\displaystyle OLi}{|}}{\underset{\underset{\displaystyle R'}{|}}{C}}-OLi \ \xrightarrow{H^+} \ R-\overset{\overset{\displaystyle O}{\|}}{C}-R'$$

6. Synthesis from nitriles

$$R-C\equiv N \ + \ R'MgX \longrightarrow R-\overset{\overset{\displaystyle NMgX}{\|}}{C}-R' \ \xrightarrow{H^+, H_2O} \ R-\overset{\overset{\displaystyle O}{\|}}{C}-R'$$

Reactions of Ketones

1. Hydration

$$R-\overset{\overset{\displaystyle O}{\|}}{C}-R' \ \underset{}{\overset{H_2O}{\rightleftharpoons}} \ R-\overset{\overset{\displaystyle OH_2}{|}}{\underset{\underset{\displaystyle OH_2}{|}}{C}}-R' \quad \text{(hydrate)}$$

2. Addition of Grignard reagent

$$R-\overset{\overset{\displaystyle O}{\|}}{C}-R' + R''MgX \longrightarrow R-\overset{\overset{\displaystyle OMgX}{|}}{\underset{\underset{\displaystyle R''}{|}}{C}}-R' \xrightarrow{H^+} R-\overset{\overset{\displaystyle OH}{|}}{\underset{\underset{\displaystyle R''}{|}}{C}}-R' \quad \text{(3° alcohol)}$$

3. Reduction

$$R-\overset{\overset{\displaystyle O}{\|}}{C}-R' \xrightarrow{LiAlH_4} R-\overset{\overset{\displaystyle OH}{|}}{CH}-R' \quad \text{(2° alcohol)}$$

4. Synthesis of cyanohydrins

$$R-\overset{\overset{\displaystyle O}{\|}}{C}-R' \xrightarrow{HCN} R-\overset{\overset{\displaystyle OH}{|}}{\underset{\underset{\displaystyle CN}{|}}{C}}-R' \quad \text{(cyanohydrin)}$$

5. Synthesis of imines

$$R-\overset{\overset{\displaystyle O}{\|}}{C}-R' \xrightarrow{H_2NR''} R-\overset{\overset{\displaystyle NR''}{\|}}{C}-R' \quad \text{(imine or Schiff base)}$$

6. Synthesis of oximes

$$RCOR' + H_2NOH \rightarrow R-\overset{\overset{\displaystyle N-OH}{\|}}{C}-R' \quad \text{(oxime)}$$

7. Synthesis of ketals

$$R-\overset{\overset{\displaystyle O}{\|}}{C}-R' + 2R''OH \underset{}{\overset{H^+_{(cat)}}{\rightleftharpoons}} R-\overset{\overset{\displaystyle OR''}{|}}{\underset{\underset{\displaystyle OR''}{|}}{C}}-R \quad \text{(ketal)}$$

8. Clemmensen reduction

$$RCOR' \xrightarrow{Zn(Hg),\ HCl} RCH_2R'$$

Carboxylic Acids

Carboxylic acids, abbreviated **RCOOH** or **ArCOOH**, contain a **carboxyl** functional group bonded to **one alkyl or aryl group**. The IUPAC names are obtained by replacing the final "e" in alkanes by the suffix –*oic acid*. Carbons are numbered starting with the carboxyl C, which is assigned 1. Common names use Greek letters to identify the carbons, the first after the COOH group being the α carbon, and the second, the β carbon. Aromatic carboxylic acids (ArCOOH) are named as derivatives of benzoic acid.

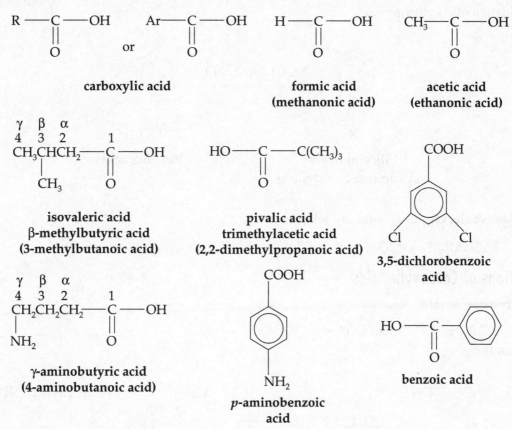

carboxylic acid

formic acid
(methanonic acid)

acetic acid
(ethanonic acid)

isovaleric acid
β-methylbutyric acid
(3-methylbutanoic acid)

pivalic acid
trimethylacetic acid
(2,2-dimethylpropanoic acid)

3,5-dichlorobenzoic
acid

γ-aminobutyric acid
(4-aminobutanoic acid)

p-aminobenzoic
acid

benzoic acid

Synthesis of Carboxylic Acids

1. Oxidation of primary alcohols and aldehydes

$$RCH_2OH \xrightarrow[\text{KMnO}_4]{\text{H}_2\text{CrO}_4} R-\overset{\displaystyle O}{\underset{\displaystyle }{C}}-OH$$

2. Carboxylation of Grignard reagents

$$RX \xrightarrow[\text{ether}]{\text{Mg}} RMgX \xrightarrow{CO_2} RCOO^- \, {}^+MgX \xrightarrow{H^+} RCOOH$$

3. Hydrolysis of nitriles

$$RCH_2X \xrightarrow[\text{acetone}]{\text{NaCN}} RCH_2C\equiv N \xrightarrow[H_2O]{H^+_{(cat)}} RCH_2COOH$$

4. Oxidation of alkylbenzenes

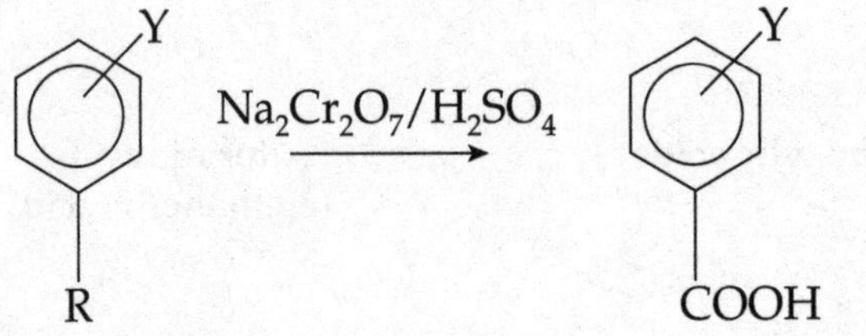

$$\xrightarrow{Na_2Cr_2O_7/H_2SO_4}$$

alkylbenzene
(Y can resist oxidation)

a benzoic acid

5. Oxidative cleavage of alkenes and alkynes

$$RCH=CR'R'' \rightarrow RCOOH + R'COR'' \qquad \text{(carboxylic acid + ketone)}$$

Reactions of Carboxylic Acids

1. Conversion to salts

$$RCOOH \xrightarrow{\text{base}} RCOO^-Y^+ + H_2O$$

Example:

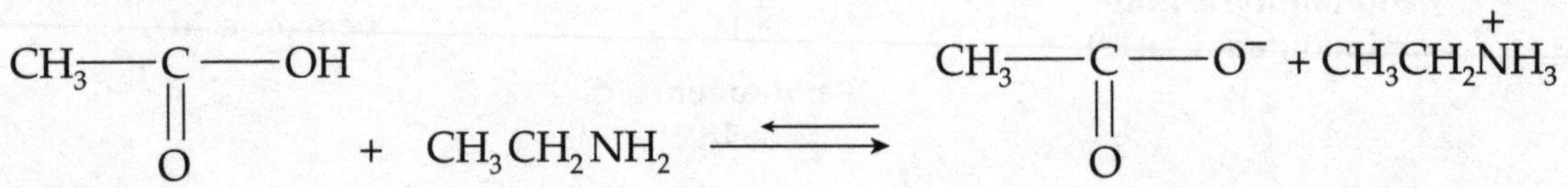

acetic acid   **ethylamine**   **ethylammonium acetate**

2. Synthesis of acid chlorides

$$RCOOH + SOCl_2 \rightarrow RCOCl + SO_2 + HCl$$

Example:

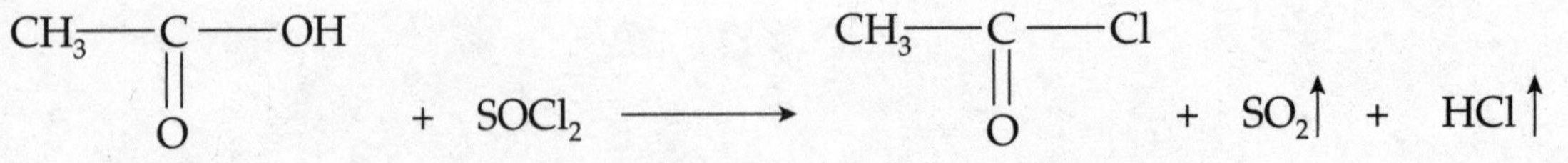

acetic acid   **thionyl chloride**   **ethanyl chloride**

3. Esterification

$$RCOOH + R'OH \underset{}{\overset{H^+_{(cat)}}{\rightleftharpoons}} RCOOR' + H_2O \qquad \text{(ester)}$$

$$RCOOH + CH_2N_2 \rightarrow RCOOCH_3 + N_2 \qquad \text{(methyl ester)}$$

4. Synthesis of amides

$$RCOCl + R'NH_2 \rightarrow RCONHR' + HCl$$

5. Synthesis of anhydrides

$$RCOCl + R'COOH \rightarrow R-\overset{\overset{\large O}{||}}{C}-O-\overset{\overset{\large O}{||}}{C}-R' + HCl$$

6. Synthesis of primary alcohols

$$RCOOH \xrightarrow[H_2O]{LiAlH_4} RCH_2OH \qquad \text{(primary alcohol)}$$

7. Synthesis of ketones (alkylation)

$$RCOOH \xrightarrow[H_2O]{2RLi} RCOR' \qquad \text{(ketone)}$$

Example:

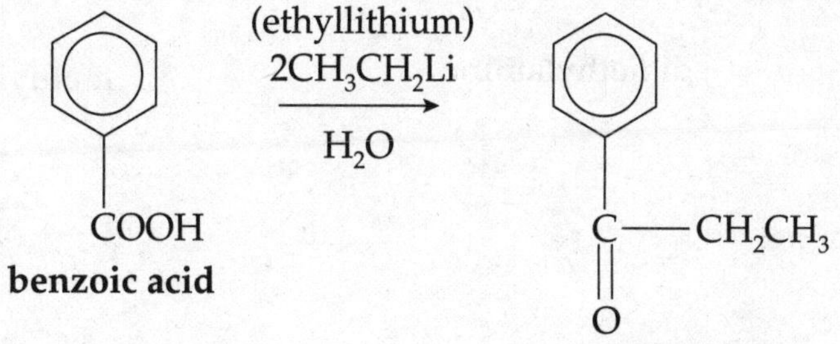

COOH
(ethyllithium)
2CH3CH2Li
H2O
C
CH2CH3
O

benzoic acid **propiophenone**

AMINES

Amines contain the **amine (NH$_2$)** functional group. Depending on how many alkyl or aryl groups are bonded to the nitrogen atom, they are classified as primary, secondary, tertiary, or quaternary:

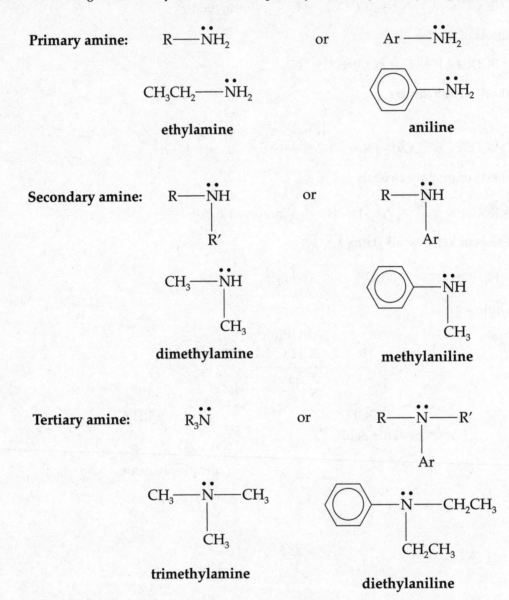

Primary amine: R——N̈H$_2$ or   Ar——N̈H$_2$

CH$_3$CH$_2$——N̈H$_2$

ethylamine

——N̈H$_2$

aniline

Secondary amine: R——N̈H   or   R——N̈H
                        | |
                        R′   Ar

CH$_3$——N̈H
        |
        CH$_3$

dimethylamine

——N̈H
    |
    CH$_3$

methylaniline

Tertiary amine: R$_3$N̈   or   R——N̈——R′
                                         |
                                         Ar

CH$_3$——N̈——CH$_3$
        |
        CH$_3$

trimethylamine

——N̈——CH$_2$CH$_3$
    |
    CH$_2$CH$_3$

diethylaniline

Quaternary amine: $\overset{+}{R_4N}$ or

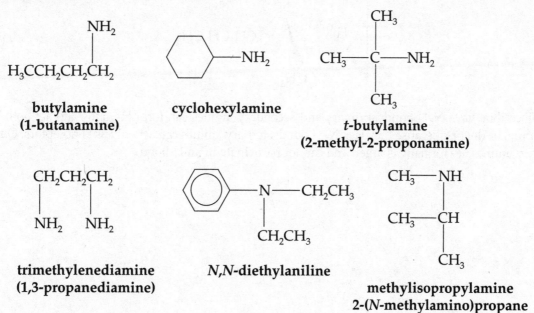

tetramethylammonium ion

The IUPAC names are obtained by replacing the final "e" in alkanes by the suffix –*amine*. The longest carbon chain provides the root name and a number indicates the location of the amine group in the chain. Substituents on the nitrogen atom are identified with the prefix *N*–. Common names use the name of the alkyl group bonded to nitrogen and followed by the suffix –*amine*. The prefixes *di, tri,* and *tetra* are used for identical substituents. Aromatic and heterocyclic amines have historical common names.

butylamine
(1-butanamine)

cyclohexylamine

t-butylamine
(2-methyl-2-proponamine)

trimethylenediamine
(1,3-propanediamine)

***N,N*-diethylaniline**

methylisopropylamine
2-(*N*-methylamino)propane

p-nitroanaline   pyrrolidine   pyridine   pyrimidine   imidazole

Polarity of Amines

Amines are derived from ammonia, which has a distorted tetrahedral geometry (trigonal pyramidal shape), resulting from the sp^3–hybridization of the nitrogen atom. A lone pair of electrons occupies one of the tetrahedral positions, and it adds to the dipole moments of the N–C and N–H bonds. Thus amines are polar molecules.

Since they have N–H bonds, primary and secondary amines can form H-bonds and act both as acceptors or donors. Because they lack N–H bonds, tertiary amines can act only as H-acceptors. Quaternary amines are formally charged and cannot participate in an H-bond.

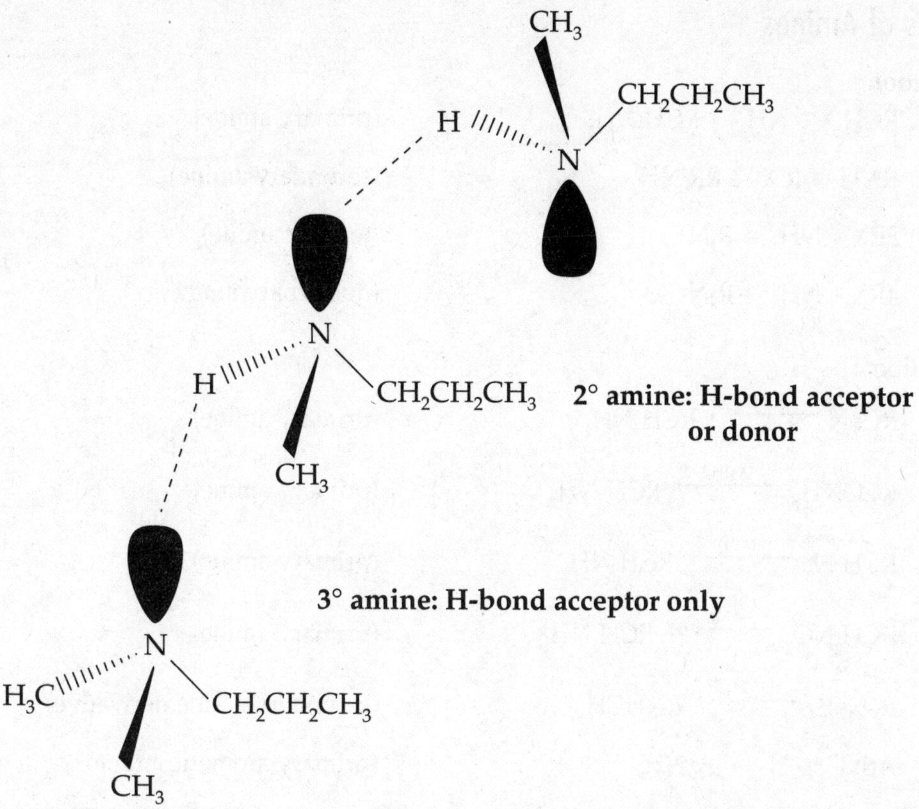

2° amine: H-bond acceptor or donor

3° amine: H-bond acceptor only

The lone pair of nonbonding electrons on the nitrogen of most amines allows them to act as Lewis bases (nucleophiles) and bind electrophiles. They can also act as proton bases by accepting an H^+ from an acid:

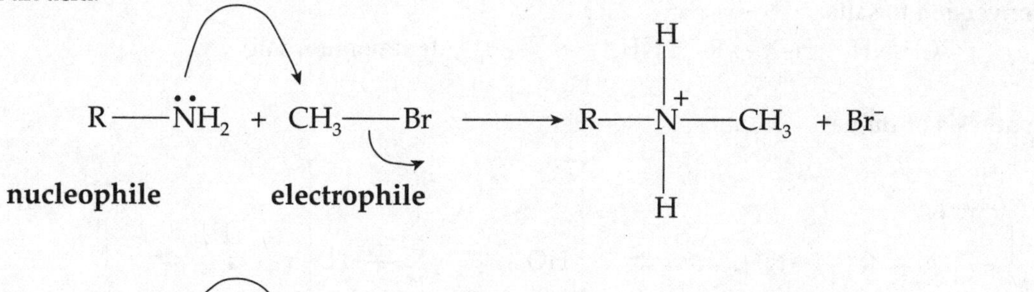

nucleophile   **electrophile**

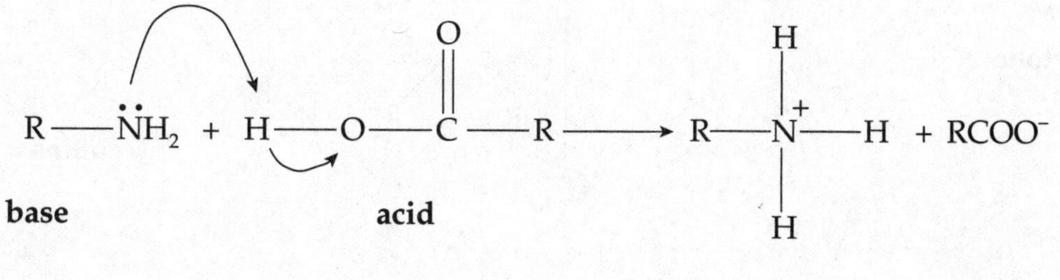

base   **acid**

Synthesis of Amines

1. Alkylation

$$RCH_2X + NH_3 \rightarrow RCH_2NH_2 \qquad \text{(primary amine)}$$

$$RNH_2 + R'X \rightarrow RR'NH \qquad \text{(secondary amine)}$$

$$3RX + NH_3 \rightarrow R_3N \qquad \text{(tertiary amine)}$$

$$4RX + NH_3 \rightarrow R_4N^+ \qquad \text{(quaternary amine)}$$

2. Reduction

$$RC\equiv N \xrightarrow{\text{LiAlH}_4} RCH_2NH_2 \qquad \text{(primary amine)}$$

$$RCONH_2 \xrightarrow{\text{LiAlH}_4} RCH_2NH_2 \qquad \text{(primary amine)}$$

$$RCH_2N_3 \xrightarrow{\text{LiAlH}_4} RCH_2NH_2 \qquad \text{(primary amine)}$$

$$RCH_2NO_2 \xrightarrow{\text{LiAlH}_4} RCH_2NH_2 \qquad \text{(primary amine)}$$

$$R-N\equiv C \xrightarrow{\text{LiAlH}_4} RNHCH_3 \qquad \text{(secondary amine derivative)}$$

$$ArNO_2 + H_2 \rightarrow ArNH_2 \qquad \text{(primary aromatic amine)}$$

$$ArNHOH + H_2 \rightarrow ArNH_2 \qquad \text{(primary aromatic amine)}$$

Reactions of Amines

1. Conversion to salts

$$RCH_2NH_2 + H-X \rightarrow RCH_2NH_3^+ + X^- \qquad \text{(ammonium salt)}$$

2. Synthesis of imines

imine = Schiff base

3. Synthesis of oximes

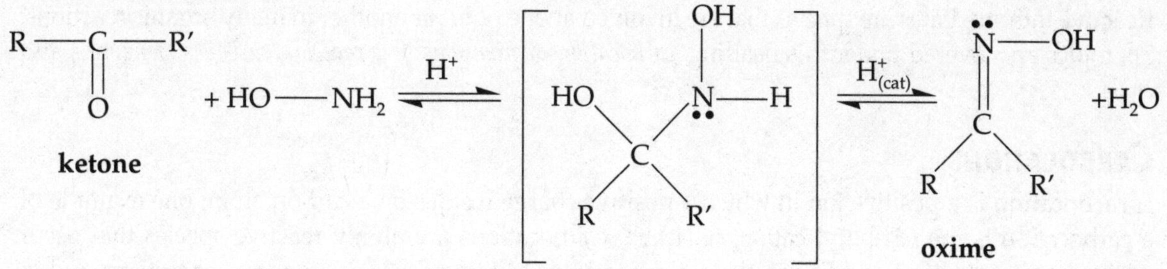

$$R-\underset{\underset{O}{\|}}{C}-R' \; + \; HO-NH_2 \; \underset{}{\overset{H^+}{\rightleftharpoons}} \; \left[HO-\underset{\underset{\underset{R'}{|}}{\underset{R}{|}}{C}}{\overset{OH}{\overset{|}{\underset{\cdot\cdot}{N}}}}-H \right] \; \underset{}{\overset{H^+_{(cat)}}{\rightleftharpoons}} \; \underset{\underset{R'}{}}{\underset{R}{}}C=\overset{\cdot\cdot}{N}-OH \; + H_2O$$

ketone   oxime

4. Alkylation

$$R–NH_2 + XCH_2R' \rightarrow \qquad RNHCH_2R' + HX \qquad \text{(salt of a 2° amine)}$$

5. Acylation

$$R-\underset{\underset{O}{\|}}{C}-Cl \; \xrightarrow{R'-NH_2} \; R-\underset{\underset{O}{\|}}{C}-NHR' \; + \; HCl \qquad \text{(amide)}$$

Example:

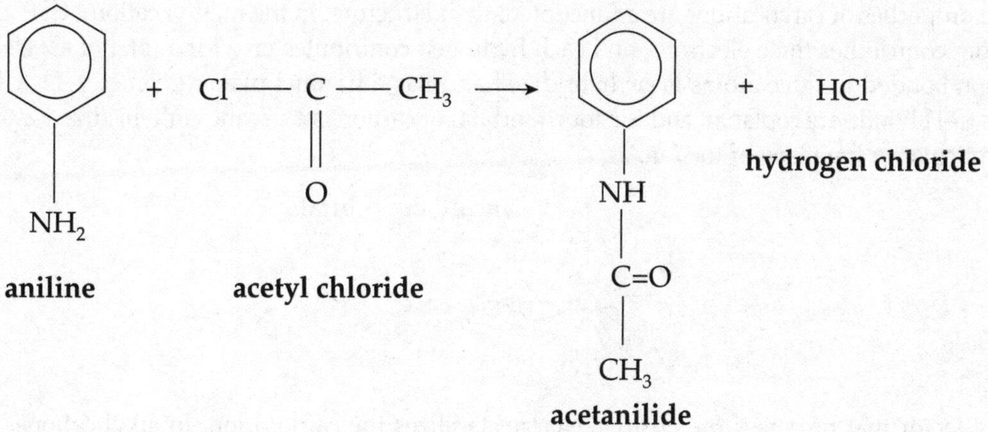

aniline   acetyl chloride   **hydrogen chloride**

acetanilide

6. Oxidation of 2° amines

$$RR'NH \; \xrightarrow{H_2O_2} \; RRNOH + H_2O \; \text{(secondary hydroxylamine)}$$

7. Oxidation of 3° amines

$$R_3N \; \xrightarrow{H_2O_2} \; R_3N^+–O^- + H_2O \; \text{(tertiary amine oxide)}$$

8. Diazotization

$$R–NH_2 \; \xrightarrow{NaNO_2/HCl} \; [R–N^+\equiv N]^+ \; Cl^- \; \text{(alkane diazonium salt)}$$

REACTIVE INTERMEDIATES

Reactive intermediates are species that are involved at one point or another in many organic reactions. Six topics are covered under this heading: *carbocations, carbanions, free radicals, carbenes, benzynes,* and *enols.*

CARBOCATIONS

A **carbocation** is a positive ion in which a positive charge resides on a carbon atom; one example of a carbocation is the *tert*-butyl cation, $(CH_3)_3C^+$. Carbocations are highly reactive species that occur as intermediates in S_N1 and E1 reactions. Carbocations can be primary, secondary, or tertiary, and in numbering their chains, the positive carbon is assigned as 1:

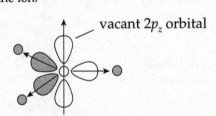

| propyl cation, primary | 1-methylpropyl cation, secondary | 1-ethylcyclohexyl cation, tertiary |

propyl cation, primary   **1-methylpropyl cation, secondary**   **1-ethylcyclohexyl cation, tertiary**

The properties of carbocations are a function of their structure. In the methyl cation, $^+CH_3$, the carbon atom contributes three electrons, and each hydrogen contributes one, for a total of six electrons. A carbon bonded to three atoms is sp^2 hybridized and has a trigonal planar geometry. In $^+CH_3$, the three σ C–H bonds are coplanar, and the fourth orbital of carbon is a vacant, unhybridized $2p$ orbital, perpendicular to the plane of the ion:

vacant $2p_z$ orbital

Any factor that disperses the positive charge stabilizes the carbocation. In alkyl cations, the inductive effect stabilizes them because the electron density of the C–C σ bonds is shifted toward the positive carbon:

This shift of electron density reduces the partial positive charge on the carbocation. Therefore, the more alkyl groups attached to the cation, the greater its stability:

$$\overset{+}{C}H_3 \ < \ CH_3\overset{+}{C}H_2 \ < \ (CH_3)_2\overset{+}{C}H \ < \ (CH_3)_3\overset{+}{C}$$

or

$$Me < 1° < 2° < 3°$$

Example:

What is the most stable carbocation that has the formula $C_5H_{11}^+$?

Solution:

Write down all possible isomeric $C_5H_{11}^+$ carbocations. There are two possible primary and three secondary isomers, as well as one tertiary isomer, $(CH_3)_2C^+CH_2CH_3$. The 3° carbocation is the most stable because it has the greater number of alkyl groups directly bonded to the carbocation.

Carbocations adjacent to π systems are also stabilized by resonance.

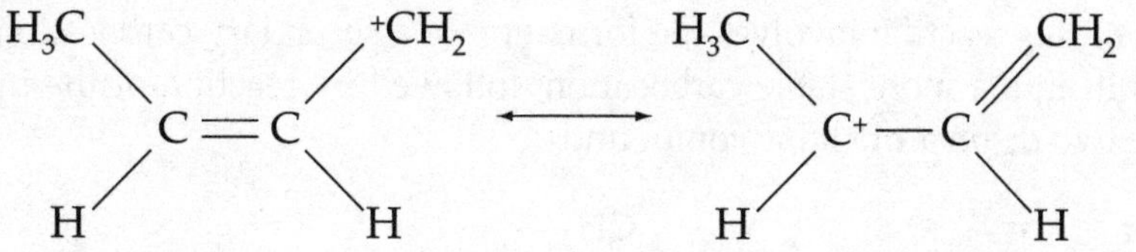

Furthermore, delocalization of the carbocation through resonance can lead to unexpected products during addition/substitution reactions.

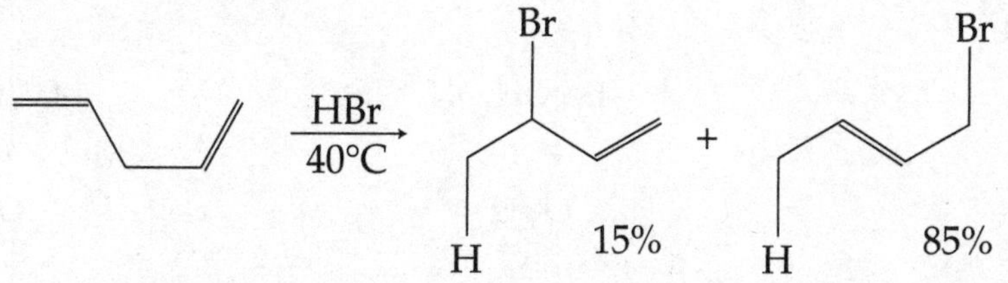

The positive charge of the carbon and the vacant p orbital combine to make carbocations very **electrophilic** (electron-loving). Electrophiles combine with nucleophiles (nucleus- or positive- charge-loving); an unshared pair of electrons on a nucleophile can interact with the vacant $2p$ orbital of a carbocation.

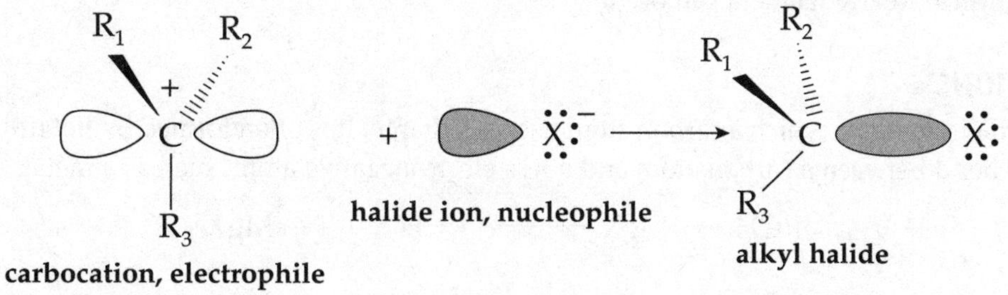

During the course of S_N1 and E1 reactions, carbocation rearrangement often occurs:

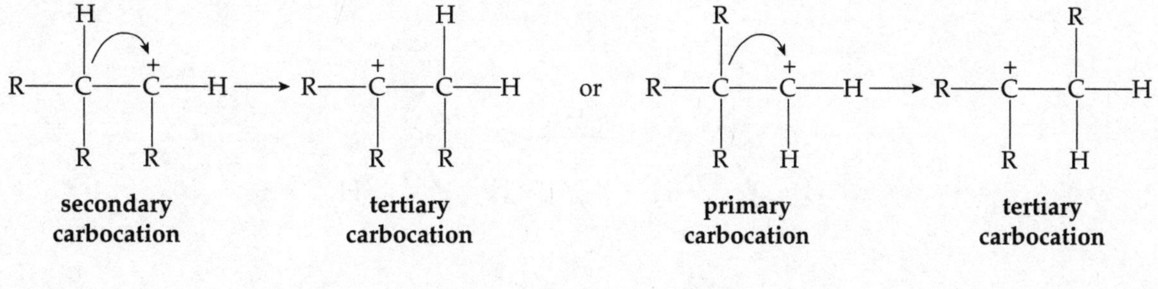

The energy of a secondary carbocation is higher than that of a tertiary carbocation, so this energy is lowered by the shift of an –H atom or a –CH_3 group with its bonding electrons from an adjacent carbon atom. This means that a secondary carbocation can rearrange into a more stable tertiary carbocation in a process called a **1,2-shift**, or a **Wagner-Meerwein transposition**.

Example:

What S_N1 products can be obtained by the reaction of 2-bromo-3,3-dimethylbutane with methanol? Show the structure of the carbocation intermediate involved.

Solution:

The first step of this reaction involves the formation of a secondary carbocation, which can rearrange by a 1,2-shift into a more stable carbocation, followed by reaction of the intermediates with methanol to give two distinct methoxy compounds:

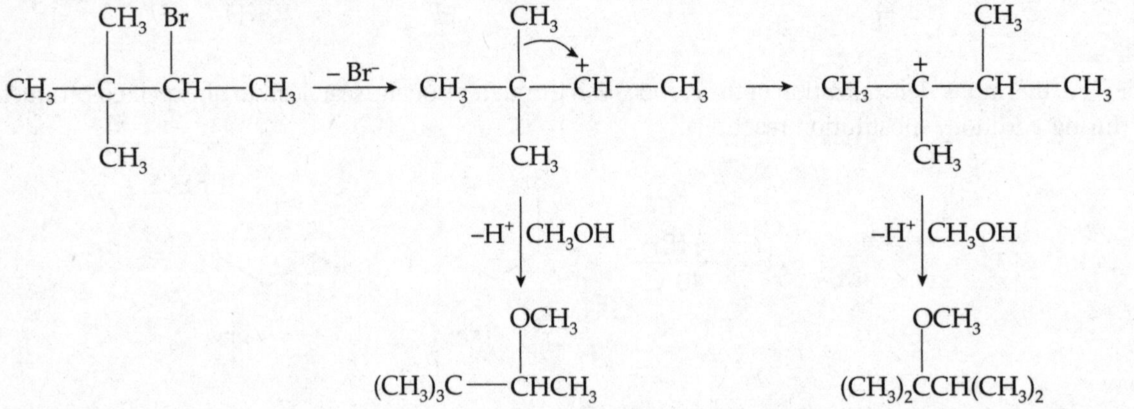

The secondary carbocation leads to the "normal" product and the tertiary carbocation leads to the rearrangement product. If a more stable carbocation or another carbocation with equal stability can be easily formed, rearrangement can occur.

CARBANIONS

A **carbanion** is an ion in which a carbon atom has a –1 charge. It is often formed by **heterolytic cleavage** of the bond between a carbon atom and a less electronegative atom, such as a metal:

$$RCH_2\text{---}MgX \longrightarrow RCH_2^- + {}^+MgX$$

The methyl anion is sp^3-hybridized and has a tetrahedral geometry with an electron pair in one of the sp^3 orbitals. The structure of the carbanion obtained from methane is:

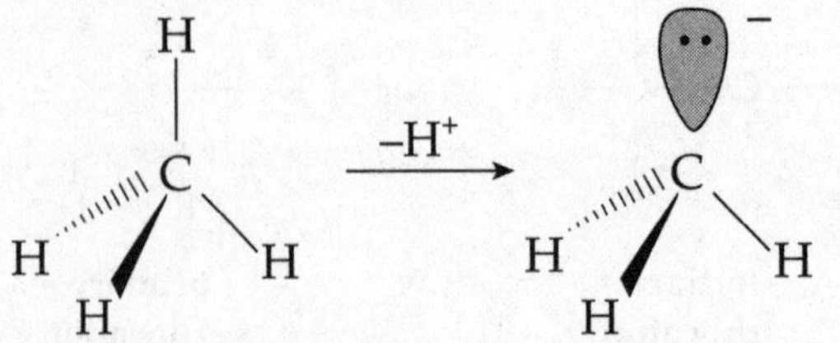

Carbanions are **conjugate bases** of hydrocarbons. The pK_a of methane is 60, so it is a very weak acid, and CH_3^- is a very strong base. Hydrocarbons display a great range of acidity; alkynes are far more likely to be deprotonated than alkenes, and alkenes are more likely than alkanes:

$$H_2O \quad > \quad HC\equiv CH \quad > \quad H_2C=CH_2 \quad > \quad CH_3CH_3$$

$$(pK_a = 15) \quad (pK_a = 25) \quad (pK_a = 36) \quad (pK_a = 50)$$

The acidity of a proton depends on the hybridization of the carbon atom. The nonbonding pair of a carbanion is more stable in an orbital with more s character. In an alkynyl anion, the electron pair occupies an sp orbital, which has 50% s character.

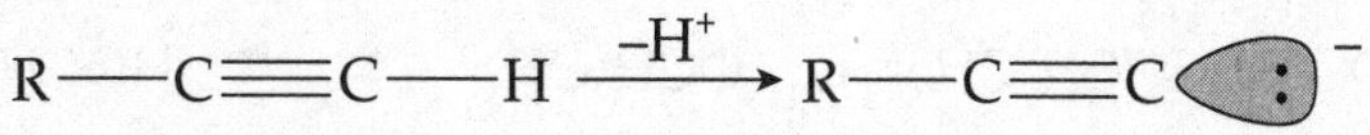

Alkynyl anions are therefore the most stable hydrocarbon ions. The electron pair of an alkenyl or aryl anion occupies an sp^2 orbital and has 33.3% s character:

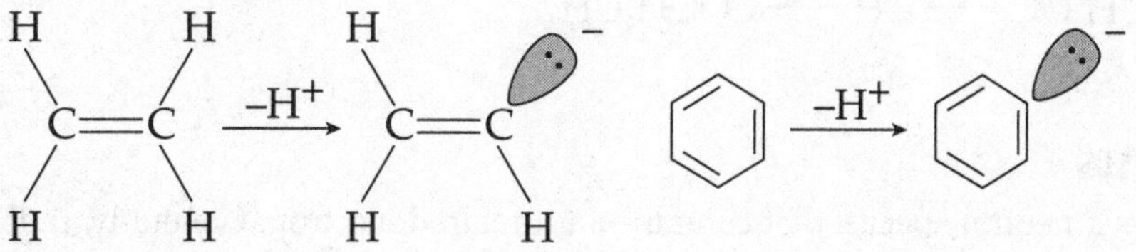

The electron pair of an alkyl anion occupies an sp^3 orbital and has 25% s character. They are the least stable of all hydrocarbon carbanions.

Electronegative substituents have a strong influence on the stability of carbanions. For example, nitromethane is acidic enough to react with base because the anion formed is stable:

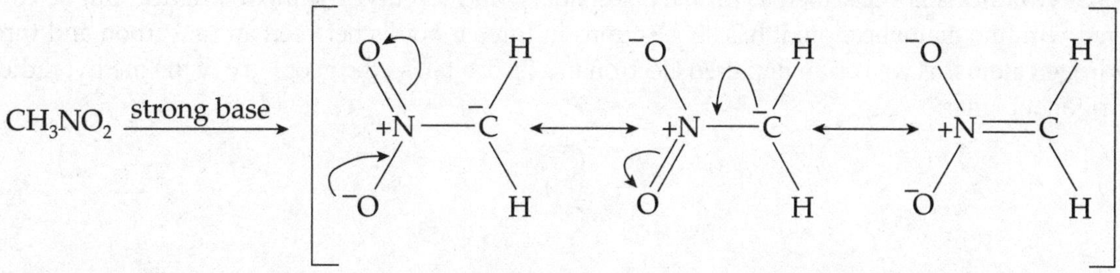

The stability of the ion is due to the electronegativity of the oxygen atoms. The inductive and resonance effects draw the negative charge from the carbon atom into the nitro group. In order of decreasing electron-withdrawing ability, the most common substituent groups are ordered in this way:

$$-NO_2 \ > \ -SO_2R \ > \ -CN \ > \ -C=O \ > \ -CO_2R \ > \ -Ph \ > \ C=C \ > \ -X \ > \ -H$$

A group located between $-SO_2R$ and $-CO_2R$ in that listing is not electronegative enough to yield a compound with a measurable acidity relative to water. However, two such groups attached to a carbon atom greatly enhance the acidity of a C–H bond.

For example, the α H in ethyl acetate is not abstracted by ethoxide:

$$CH_3-\overset{\overset{\displaystyle O}{\|}}{C}\overset{\displaystyle}{\underset{\displaystyle OCH_2CH_3}{}} \quad + \quad {}^-OCH_2CH_3 \quad \xcancel{\longrightarrow} \quad {}^-CH_2-\overset{\overset{\displaystyle O}{\|}}{C}\overset{\displaystyle}{\underset{\displaystyle OCH_2CH_3}{}}$$

However, an α H in maleic ester is readily abstracted:

$$CH_3CH_2O\overset{\overset{\displaystyle O}{\|}}{C}CH_2\overset{\overset{\displaystyle O}{\|}}{C}OCH_2CH_3 \quad + \quad {}^-OCH_2CH_3 \quad \rightleftharpoons \quad HOCH_2CH_3 \quad +$$

$$CH_3CH_2O\overset{\overset{\displaystyle O}{\|}}{C}\!-\!{}^-CH\!-\!\overset{\overset{\displaystyle O}{\|}}{C}OCH_2CH_3$$

FREE RADICALS

A **free radical** is a neutral species that contains an unpaired electron. Generally, radicals are formed by **homolytic bond cleaveage**; each fragment carries one electron from the broken bond.

$$RH_2C\!-\!\!H \longrightarrow RH_2C\bullet + \bullet H$$

Alkyl radicals are classified as primary, secondary, and tertiary. The methyl radical can be compared with the methyl cation; it has six electrons in three σ bonds between an sp^2 carbon and three hydrogen atoms, as well as an unpaired electron in a $2p$ orbital, so the geometry of the methyl radical is trigonal planar:

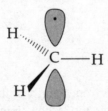

Free radicals have a half-filled $2p$ orbital and are stabilized by electron-donating substitutents, such as alkyl groups. Their order of increasing stability is:

$$\bullet CH_3 < \bullet CH_2R < \bullet CHR_2 < \bullet CR_3$$

$$\qquad\qquad\quad 1° \qquad 2° \qquad 3°$$

Example:

What is the most stable radical with the formula C_5H_{11}?

Solution:

Write down all possible isomers of C_5H_{11}. Of these, the radical with an unpaired electron on a tertiary carbon is the most stable:

$$CH_3CH_2\overset{\bullet}{C}(CH_3)_2$$

The stability of free radicals is related to their bond dissociation energies (BDE); the lower the BDE, the more stable the radical.

The chlorination of methane provides the classic example of free-radical involvement in a reaction. The net result is the substitution of one or more chlorine atoms for hydrogen atoms:

$$CH_4 + Cl_2 \xrightarrow{\text{hv}} CH_3Cl + CH_2Cl_2 + CHCl_3 + CCl_4 + HCl$$

This prototypical free-radical reaction proceeds in three steps:

1. **Initiation**—dissociation of the radical precursor molecule and the formation of two free radicals under light or high temperature:

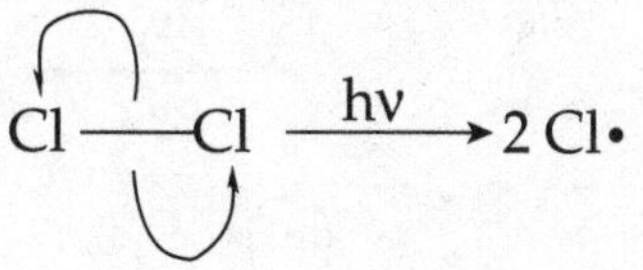

$$Cl\!-\!Cl \xrightarrow{\text{hv}} 2\,Cl\bullet$$

2. **Chain propagation**—the free radical abstracts a hydrogen atom from the alkane:

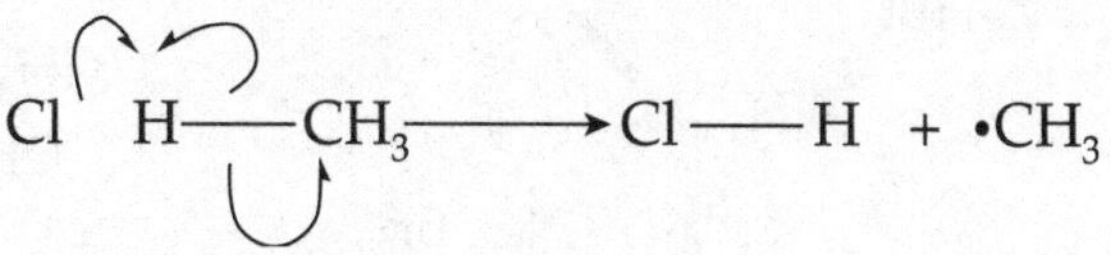

$$Cl \quad H\!-\!CH_3 \longrightarrow Cl\!-\!H + \bullet CH_3$$

Then the alkyl radical reacts with another precursor molecule:

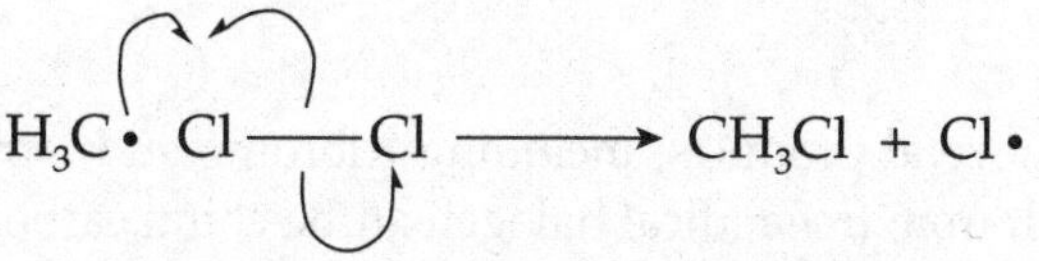

$$H_3C\bullet \quad Cl\!-\!Cl \longrightarrow CH_3Cl + Cl\bullet$$

This step yields one of the products of the reaction and generates a new free radical that can abstract a hydrogen atom from another alkane molecule. The reaction is self-perpetuating. The number of possible passes through the propagation step is called the **chain length** and depends partly on the energy of the free radicals generated. For the chlorination of hydrocarbons, the chain length is about 10,000.

3. **Termination of the propagation cycle**—occurs when free radicals combine with one another:

$$\bullet CH_3 \ + \ \bullet Cl \longrightarrow CH_3Cl \quad \text{or} \quad Cl\bullet + Cl\bullet \longrightarrow Cl_2 \quad \text{or}$$

$$\bullet CH_3 \ + \ \bullet CH_3 \longrightarrow CH_3CH_3$$

There can be many products in a free-radical reaction because the high-energy free radical is not particularly selective about which hydrogen it abstracts during propagation.

Example:

Write the propagation steps that lead to the formation of dichloromethane from chloromethane.

Solution:

Remember the two parts of the propagation step: formation of the chloromethane radical followed by its reaction with molecular chlorine:

$$Cl\bullet \; + \; CH_3Cl \; \longrightarrow \; \bullet CH_2Cl \; + \; HCl$$

$$\bullet CH_2Cl \; + \; Cl_2 \; \longrightarrow \; CH_2Cl_2 \; + \; Cl\bullet$$

If a hydrogen is abstracted from the chiral carbon of a pure enantiomer, **racemization** is observed:

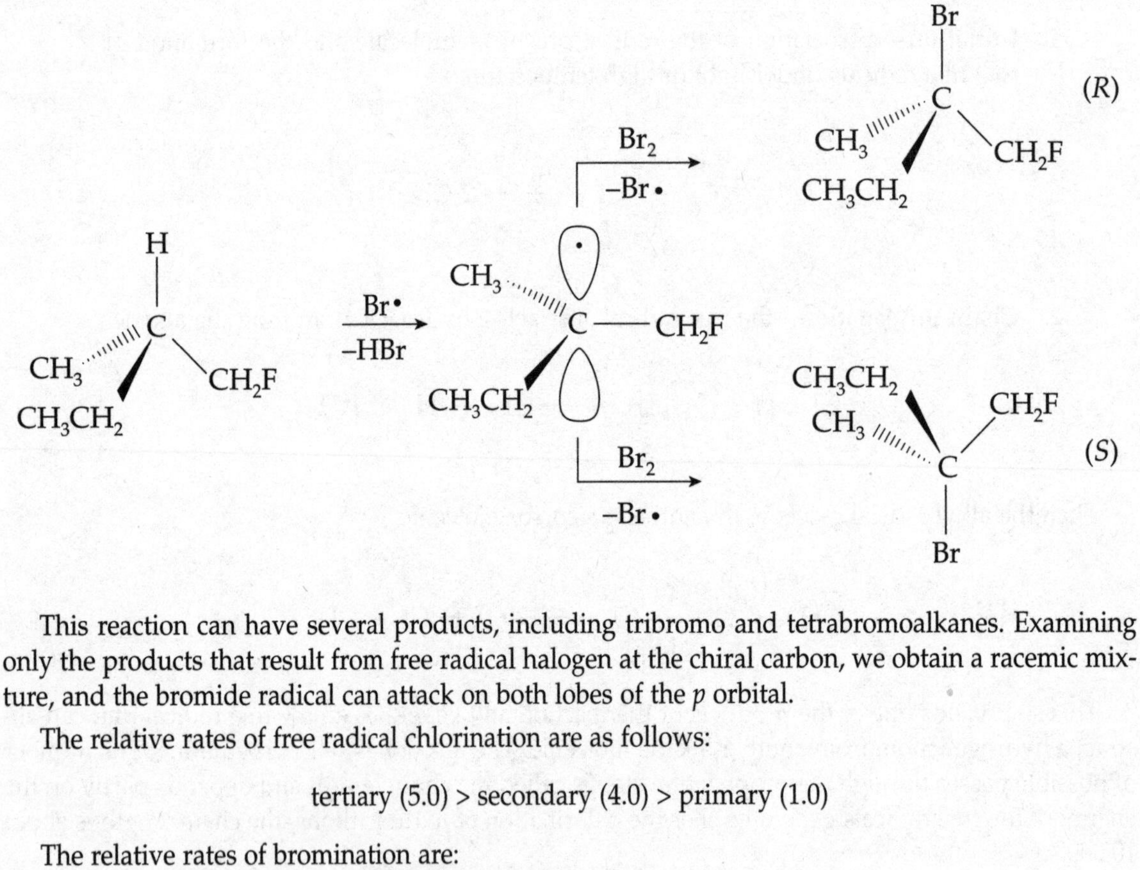

This reaction can have several products, including tribromo and tetrabromoalkanes. Examining only the products that result from free radical halogen at the chiral carbon, we obtain a racemic mixture, and the bromide radical can attack on both lobes of the p orbital.

The relative rates of free radical chlorination are as follows:

tertiary (5.0) > secondary (4.0) > primary (1.0)

The relative rates of bromination are:

tertiary (1,600) > secondary (80) > primary (1)

Therefore, bromine is more **regioselective** than chlorine in the substitution of tertiary hydrogens.

Example:

What is the structure of the main product formed by free-radical bromination of 2,2,4-trimethylpentane?

Solution:

Write the structure of the hydrocarbon and identify any tertiary hydrogen. The only tertiary hydrogen of 2,2,4-trimethylpentane is attached to C_4, and it is replaced by bromine:

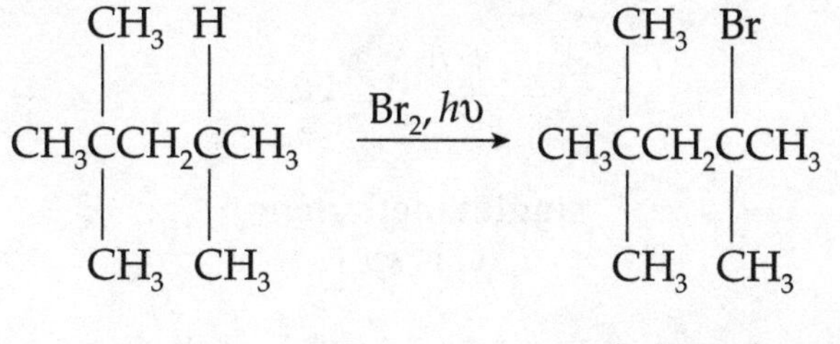
CH3 H
CH3CCH2CCH3
CH3 CH3
Br2, hυ
CH3 Br
CH3CCH2CCH3
CH3 CH3

major product

The tertiary hydrogens are abstracted more easily because of the lower bond dissociation energy of the C–H bond. BDE decreases from primary to tertiary carbons. The order of free-radical stability is similar to that of carbocation stability: It increases from methyl to tertiary. Free-radical intermediates can also be stabilized by hyperconjugation, and there is enhanced free-radical reactivity at the **allylic** (carbon next to a C=C double bond) and **benzylic** (carbon next to a benzene ring) positions, due to the resonance stabilization of the intermediate.

Example:

Write resonance structures for the $CH_2{=}CHCH_2\cdot$ and the Ph-$CH_2\cdot$ free radicals.

Solution:

Use half-arrows to show the movement of individual electrons between the carbon bearing the unpaired electron and the adjacent double bond:

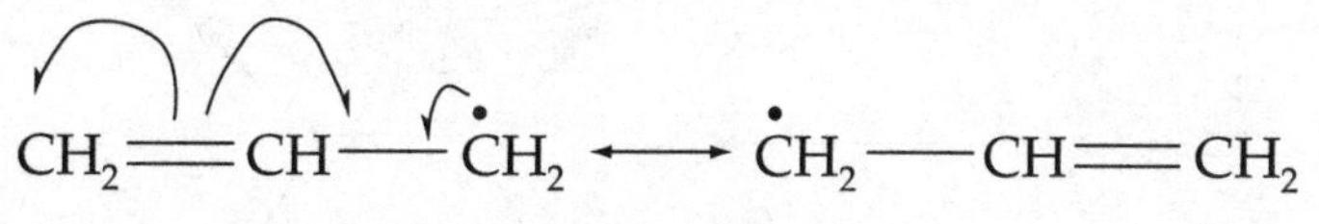
CH2=CH–CH2
CH2–CH=CH2

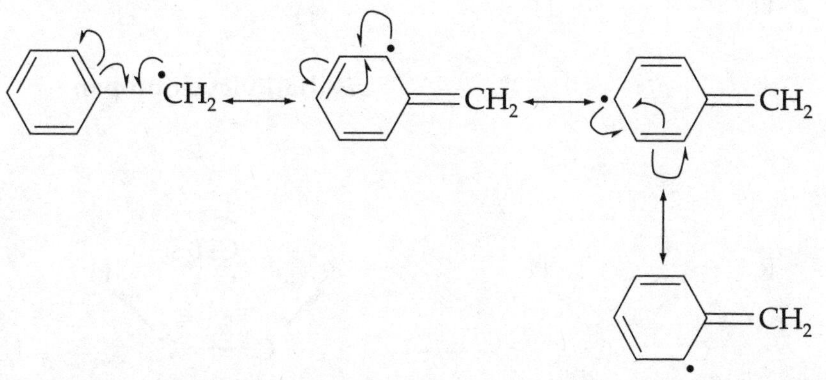
CH2
=CH2
=CH2
=CH2

Free radicals and carbocations are both planar and sp^2-hybridized. They also both undergo racemization at a chiral carbon, but unlike carbocations, free radicals do not tend to undergo rearrangement toward more stable species.

CARBENES

Carbenes are neutral molecules of general formula $R_2C:$ in which a carbon atom has two sigma bonds and two electrons.

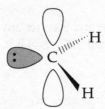

singlet methylene
(C is sp^2)

Carbenes are useful in organic synthesis. For instance, methylene is prepared by photolysis of diazomethane:

$$\left[:\overset{\cdot\cdot}{C}H_2 - \overset{\cdot\cdot}{N} = \overset{+}{N}: \longleftrightarrow CH_2 = \overset{+}{N} = \overset{-}{N}: \longleftrightarrow :\overset{-}{C}H_2 - \overset{+}{N} = N: \right] \xrightarrow{h\nu} :CH_2 + :N = N:$$

The carbon in methylene has only six electrons and is electrophilic. Carbenes can be used to convert alkenes to cyclopropanes. The reaction is stereospecific: *cis* alkenes yield *cis* cyclopropanes and *trans* alkenes yield *trans* cyclopropanes.

cis   *cis*-**dialkylcyclopropane**

trans   *trans*-**dialkylcyclopropane**
                         (racemic)

Dihalopropanes can also be prepared with dihalocarbenes, which are obtained by the reaction of a trihalomethane with a strong base such as $KOC(CH_3)_3$.

Example:

What are the products of the reaction of 1,2-dimethyl-1,4-cyclohexadiene with tribromomethane in the presence of sodium *tert*-butoxide? Which product predominates?

Solution:

First, write the equation for the generation of the carbene, then write the formula of the other reactant. Remember that the alkyl-substituted double bond is a better nucleophile than the nonsubstituted bond, and so it should yield the predominant product:

$$CHBr_3 + (CH_3)_3CO^- \longrightarrow :CBr_2 + (CH_3)_3COH + Br^-$$

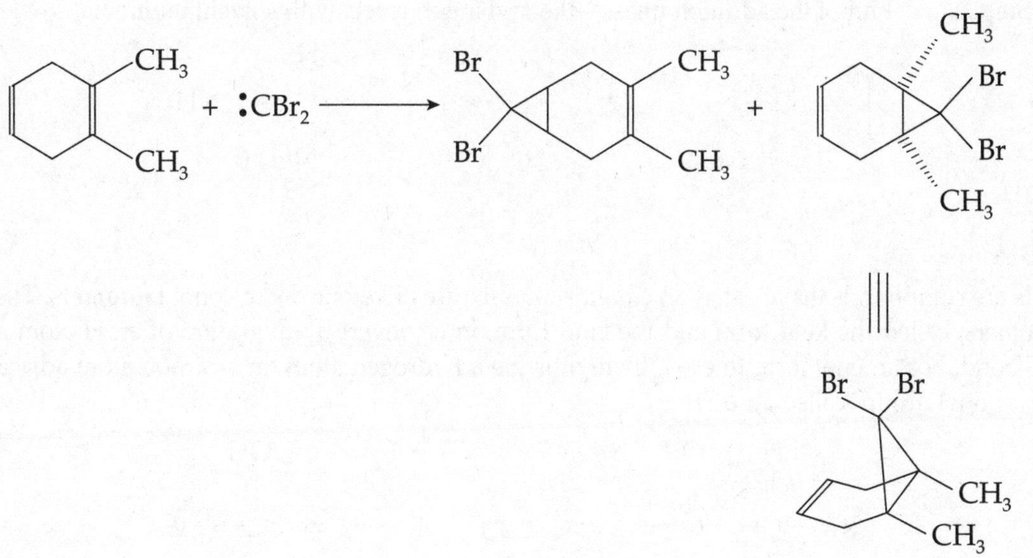

BENZYNES

Benzynes are compounds that are formed as reactive intermediates in the reaction of alkyl halides with strong bases (nucleophilic aromatic substitution). Their general structure is:

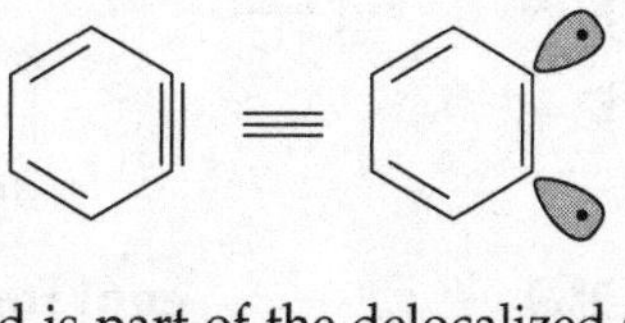

The first π bond of the triple bond is part of the delocalized π-electron system. The other π bond results from two overlapping *p* orbitals and lies in the plane of the ring. This bond is very weak because the *p* orbitals in the plane of the ring are not properly aligned for effective overlap. Also, the C–C≡C–C unit is not linear, so the structure is strained, and benzyne is highly reactive.

The elimination-addition mechanism illustrates the role of benzyne in nucleophilic aromatic substitution. This reaction proceeds in three steps.

Step 1:   Elimination stage—dihydrohalogenation of chlorobenzyne by the amide ion:

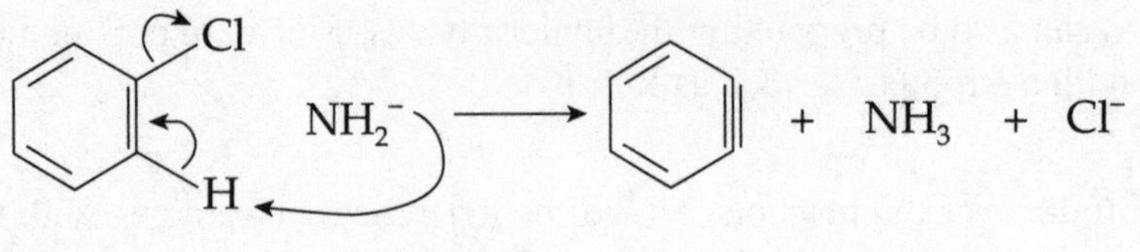

Step 2: Beginning of the addition phase—the amide ion reacts with benzyne to form a carbanion:

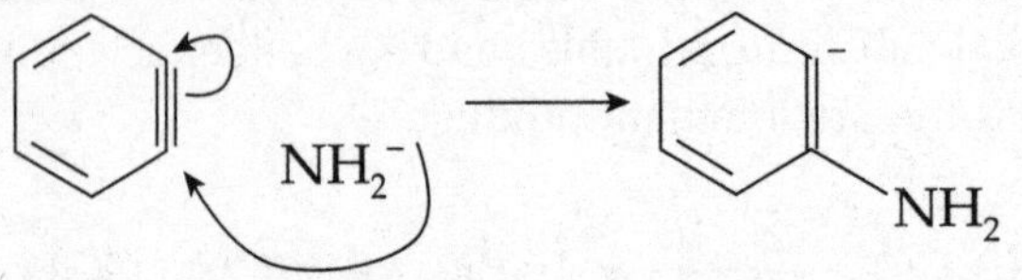

Step 3: End of the addition phase—the aryl anion reacts with solvent ammonia:

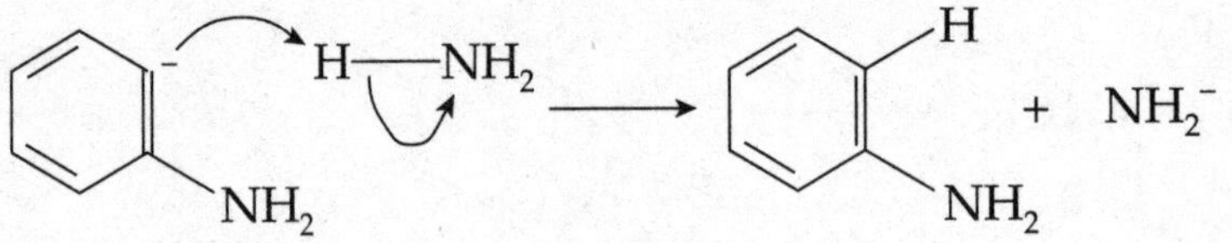

ENOLS

Enols are compounds that exist as an equilibrium mixture of ketone and alcohol **tautomers**. The two tautomers, called the **keto form** and the **enol form**, interconvert by migration of an H atom and a C=C bond. For an enol form to exist, there must be a hydrogen atom on a carbon atom adjacent to the carbonyl group (called an α H):

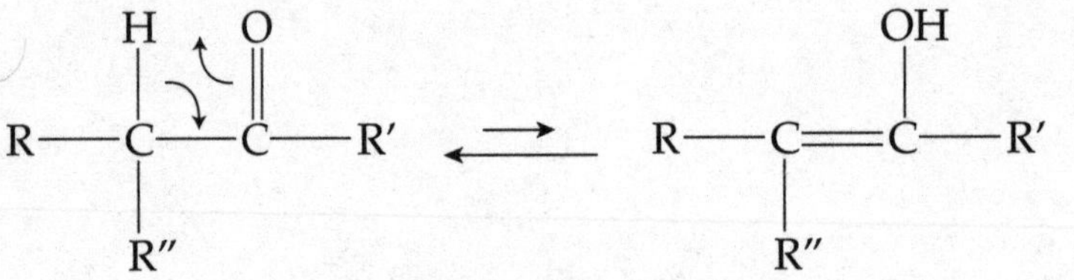

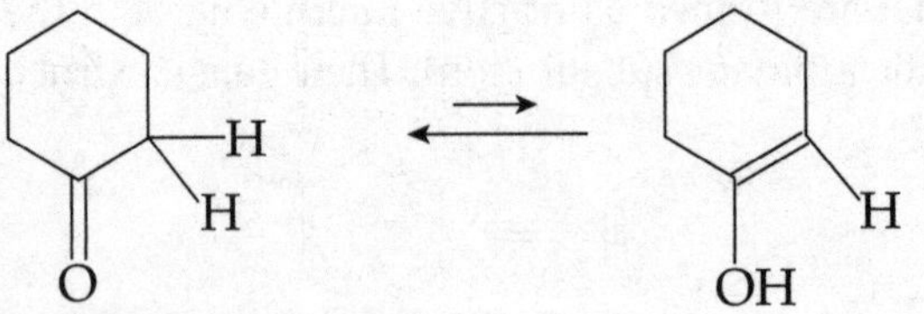

keto form (99.9%)   **enol form (0.10%)**

The keto form is more stable and predominates in simple ketones and aldehydes because the C–H and C=O bonds have greater bond energies than the C=C and O–H bonds. This is because the resonance energy of the carbonyl group is greater than that of the enol.

In a few cases, the enol form predominates. For example, in 2,4-pentanedione, the enol is stabilized by an intramolecular hydrogen bond and a conjugated system:

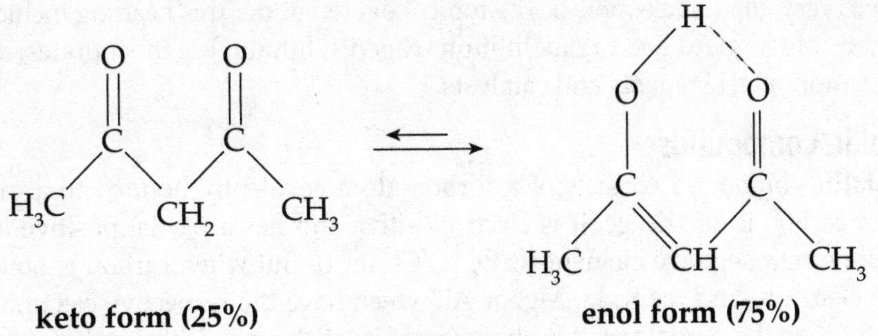

keto form (25%)　　　　　　　　　**enol form (75%)**

2,4-pentanedione

Keto and enol tautomers are real species, and it is possible to isolate them under the appropriate experimental conditions.

Example:

What are the keto and enol forms of C_6H_5OH, and which tautomer predominates?

Solution:

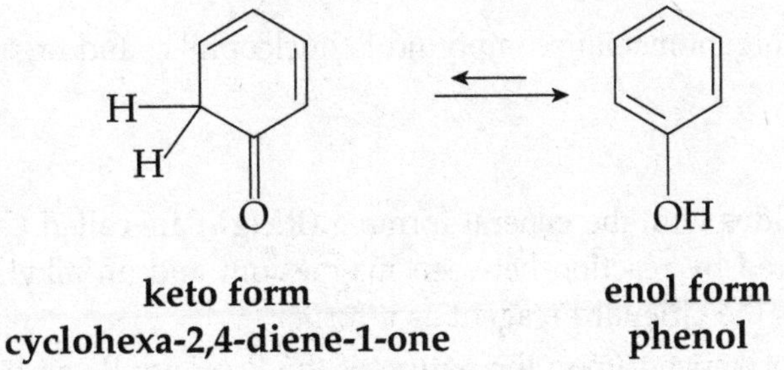

keto form　　　　　　　　　**enol form**
cyclohexa-2,4-diene-1-one　　　**phenol**

The enol form, phenol, predominates because it has a very stable aromatic ring.

Example:

2-Butanone exists in equilibrium in two enol forms. What are they, and which will predominate?

Solution:

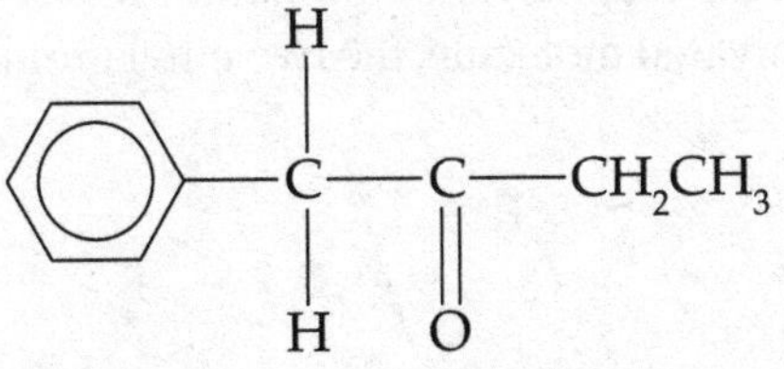

1-phenyl-2-butanone

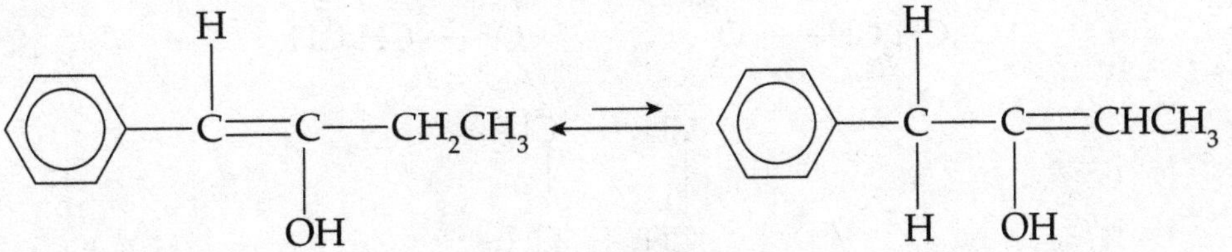

enol forms

The enol structure on the left will predominate because the C=C is conjugated with the aromatic ring.

ORGANOMETALLICS

Organometallic compounds are compounds in which a carbon is covalently bonded to a metal atom. This makes them very good nucleophiles. The topics covered under this heading include the preparation and reactions of Grignard and organolithium reagents, lithium organocuprates, and other main group and transition-metal reagents and catalysts.

Organometallic Compounds

An **organometallic** compound consists of a carbon atom covalently bonded to a metal. The electronegativity of carbon is 2.5; hence, it is electropositive and has a partial positive charge when it bonds to a more electronegative element (F, O, N, Cl, Br, I). But when carbon is bonded to a more electropositive element—such as K, Li, Mg, or Al, which have the respective electronegativities 0.8, 1.0, 1.3, and 1.6—then the partial positive charge resides on the metal, and carbon acquires a partial negative charge:

So the carbon of an organometallic compound is nucleophilic, and organometallics have a carbanionic character.

Grignard Reagents

Organomagnesium halides with the general formula **(RMgX)** are called **Grignard reagents**. A Grignard reagent is prepared by reaction between magnesium and an alkyl halide (RX) in an ether solvent, which stabilizes the Grignard reagent as it forms.

The reaction does not depend upon the nature of the R group; R can be a methyl or a primary, secondary, or tertiary alkyl; it may also be a cycloalkyl, vinyl, or aryl group. The order of halide reactivity is I > Br > Cl > F.

Alkyl halides are more reactive than vinyl or aryl halides. The most common solvent for use with Grignard reagents is diethylether, $(CH_3CH_2)_2O$. It stabilizes the reagent by donating unshared electrons to the empty orbitals of the magnesium atom, and its two ethyl groups solvate the alkyl fragments of the reagents. In the solvated molecule, the two ethyl groups, R and X, form a tetrahedron around the magnesium atom:

Example:

What is the product formed by reaction of p-chloroiodobenzene with 1 equivalent magnesium in diethylether?

Solution:

Since iodine reacts faster than chlorine, chlorine is unaffected and a carbon-magnesium bond replaces the carbon-iodine bond:

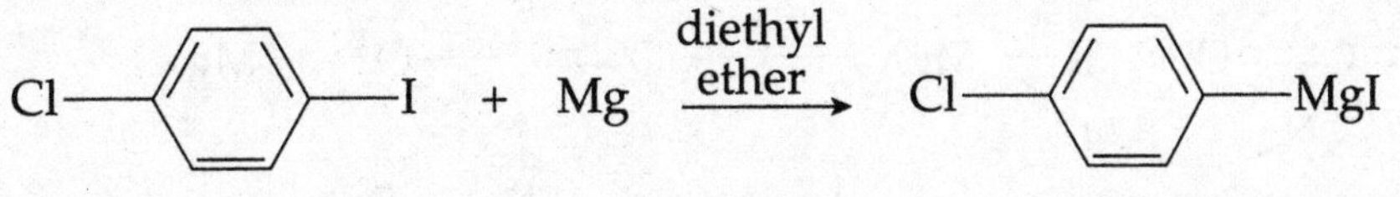

$$Cl-\!\!\!\bigcirc\!\!\!-I \ + \ Mg \ \xrightarrow{\substack{\text{diethyl} \\ \text{ether}}} \ Cl-\!\!\!\bigcirc\!\!\!-MgI$$

Grignard reagents have a carbanionic character, so they are very strong bases that react quickly with proton donors to form alkanes:

$$CH_3CH_2CH_2-\!\!\!MgBr \ + \ H-\!\!\!OCH_3 \longrightarrow CH_3CH_2CH_3 \ + \ CH_3OMgBr$$

Because they are such strong bases, Grignard reagents cannot be used with solvents or reactants that can act as proton donors (e.g., H_2O, alcohols, –NH, and –SH groups). Their alkyl or aryl groups act as nucleophiles in chemical reactions.

The most important reactions of Grignard reagents are reactions with carbonyl compounds. The carbon of the carbonyl group bears a partial positive charge, and it is readily attacked by the nucleophilic carbon of the Grignard:

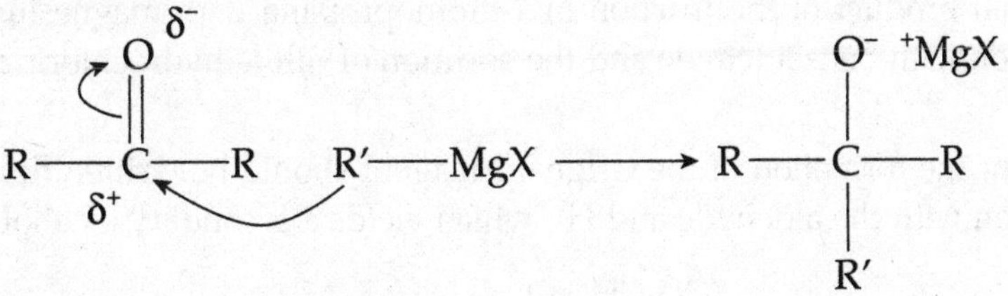

$$
\begin{array}{c}
\overset{\delta^-}{O} \\
\parallel \\
R-\underset{\delta^+}{C}-R \quad R'-MgX \longrightarrow R-\overset{O^- \ ^+MgX}{\underset{R'}{\overset{|}{C}}}-R
\end{array}
$$

The product is the magnesium salt of an alcohol. Treatment of the salt with water or aqueous acid yields the alcohol and a mixed inorganic magnesium salt:

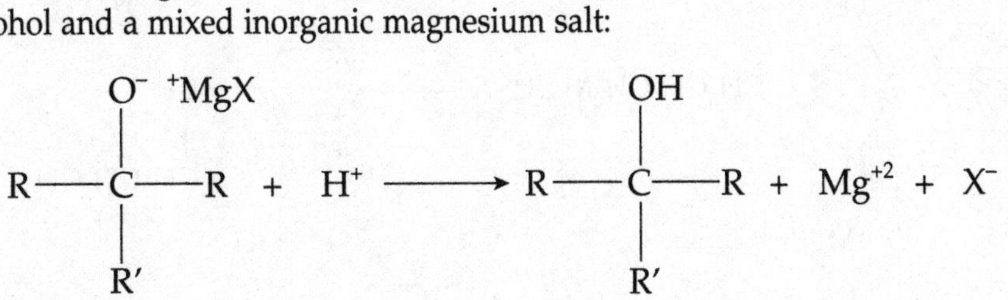

$$
R-\overset{O^- \ ^+MgX}{\underset{R'}{\overset{|}{C}}}-R \ + \ H^+ \longrightarrow R-\overset{OH}{\underset{R'}{\overset{|}{C}}}-R \ + \ Mg^{+2} \ + \ X^-
$$

The two steps of a Grignard reaction are usually combined into a single equation:

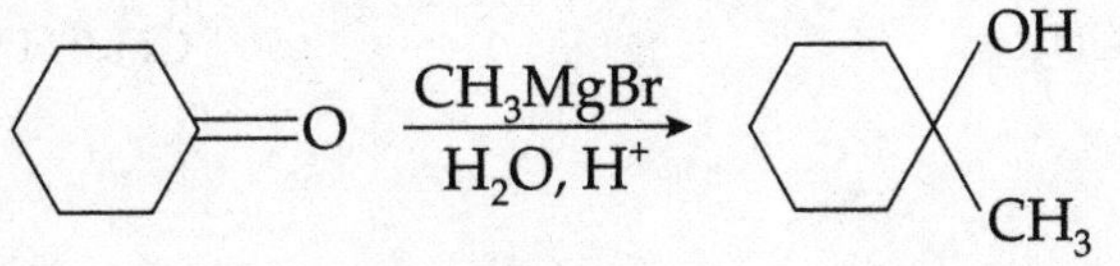

$$\bigcirc\!\!=\!O \ \xrightarrow{\substack{CH_3MgBr \\ H_2O, \ H^+}} \ \bigcirc\!\!\!\overset{OH}{\underset{CH_3}{}}$$

The reaction with carbon dioxide is slightly different; it yields a magnesium carboxylate salt that is insoluble in ether. This means that only one of the carbonyl groups reacts. Treatment of the salt with acid produces a carboxylic acid.

Some important products obtained with Grignard reagents are:

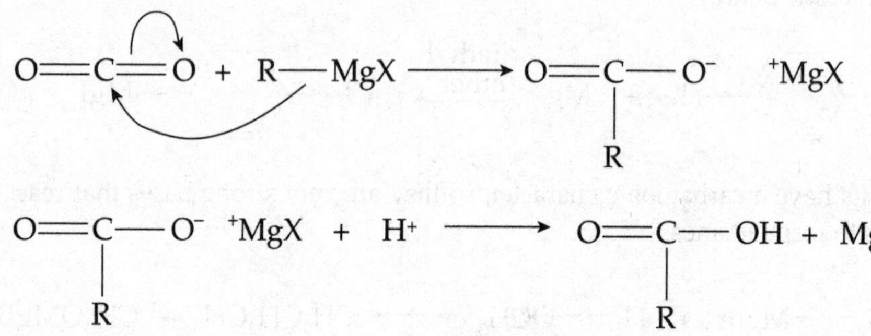

$$O=C=O + R-MgX \longrightarrow O=C-O^- \quad ^+MgX$$
$$\underset{R}{|}$$

$$O=C-O^- \; ^+MgX + H^+ \longrightarrow O=C-OH + Mg^{+2} + X^-$$

- Formaldehyde + RMgX → primary alcohol (RCH_2OH)
- Aldehyde (RCOH) + R'MgX → secondary alcohol (RCHOHR')
- Ketones (RCOR') + R''MgX → tertiary alcohol (RCOHR'R'')
- CO_2 + RMgX → carboxylic acid (RCOOH)

Example:

What is the final product of the reaction of 1-bromopropane with magnesium in diethyl ether, followed by reaction with benzaldehyde and the addition of dilute hydrochloric acid?

Solution:

The equation for the formation of the Grignard reagent should be written first, followed by that of Grignard reaction with the aldehyde and H$^+$, which yields a secondary alcohol:

$$CH_3CH_2CH_2Br + Mg \xrightarrow{(CH_3CH_2)_2O} CH_3CH_2CH_2MgBr$$

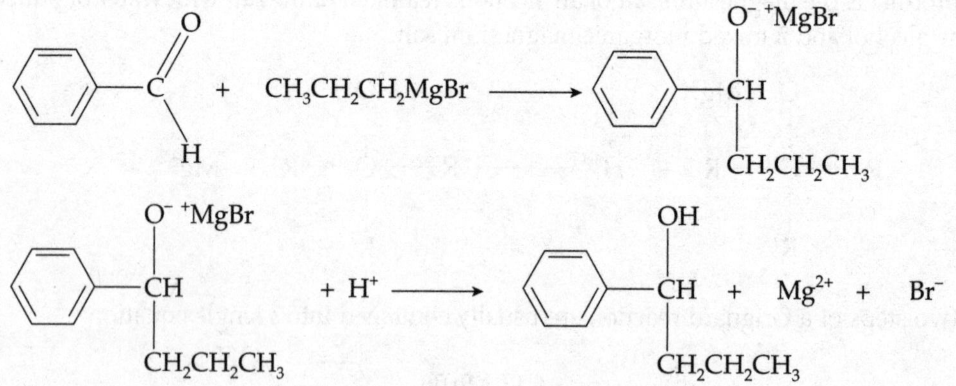

Example:

Show how you could prepare 2,3-dimethyl-2-butanol from 2-bromopropane.

Solution:

You must recognize that the product is a tertiary alcohol and thus must be obtained by reaction of a ketone with a Grignard. The Grignard formula is RMgX so 2-bromopropane is used to prepare RMgBr. The ketone required is acetone.

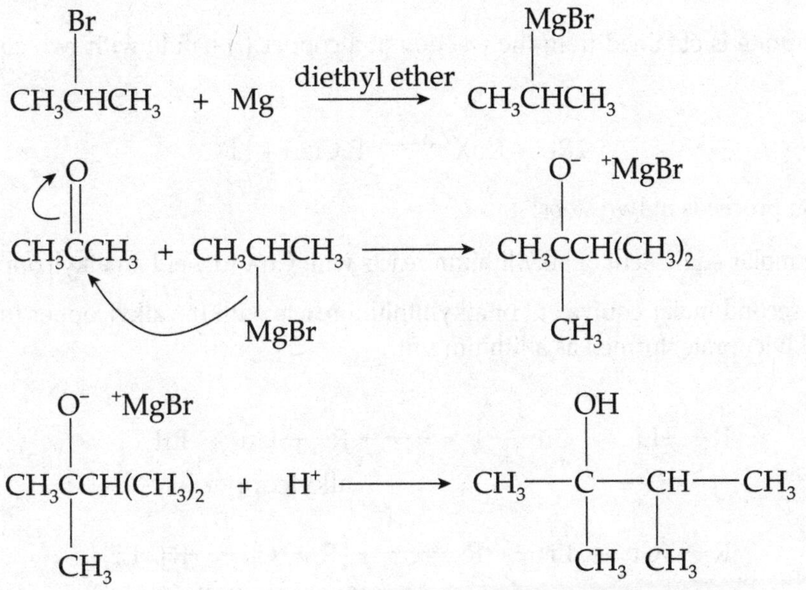

$$CH_3CHCH_3 \ (Br) \ + \ Mg \ \xrightarrow{\text{diethyl ether}} \ CH_3CHCH_3 \ (MgBr)$$

$$CH_3CCH_3 \ (O) \ + \ CH_3CHCH_3 \ (MgBr) \ \longrightarrow \ CH_3CCH(CH_3)_2 \ (O^-\ {}^+MgBr) \ (CH_3)$$

$$CH_3CCH(CH_3)_2 \ (O^-\ {}^+MgBr)(CH_3) \ + \ H^+ \ \longrightarrow \ CH_3-C-CH-CH_3 \ (OH)(CH_3)(CH_3)$$

2,3-dimethyl-2-butanone

ORGANOLITHIUM REAGENTS

Organolithium reagents and other Group I organometallics are prepared by the reaction of an alkyl halide (RX) with the desired metal in a wide variety of solvents. Unlike the preparation of RMgX, ether is not specifically required, although an aprotic solvent must be used:

$$RX \ + \ 2M \ (\text{Group I}) \ \longrightarrow \ RM \ + \ M^+X^-$$

$$CH_3CH_2CH_2Br \ + \ 2Li \ \longrightarrow \ CH_3CH_2CH_2Li \ + \ LiBr$$

Lithium is more electropositive than magnesium, so organolithium reagents are more reactive nucleophiles than Grignard reagents because the carbon atom carrying the lithium is more negative. Like Grignard reagents, they react with carbonyl compounds to form alcohols:

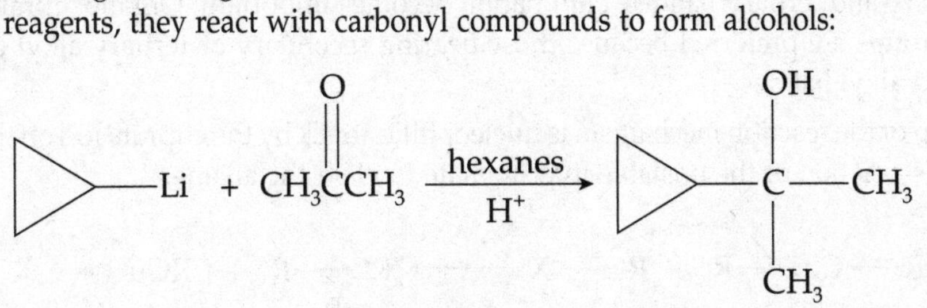

$$\triangle-Li \ + \ CH_3CCH_3 \ (O) \ \xrightarrow[H^+]{\text{hexanes}} \ \triangle-C-CH_3 \ (OH)(CH_3)$$

Lithium Organocuprates

Lithium organocuprates are particularly useful in coupling two alkyl fragments to produce a larger alkane in a synthesis called the **Corey-House reaction**.

Lithium dialkylcuprates (R_2–Cu–Li) are the preferred organometallic reagents for this reaction, and the most commonly used are:

- $(CH_3)_2$ Cu–Li, lithium dimethylcuprate
- $(H_2C=CH)_2$ Cu–Li, lithium divinylcuprate

A dialkylcuprate is obtained from the reaction of a copper (I) halide with two equivalents of an alkyl lithium:

$$2RLi + CuX \longrightarrow R_2CuLi + LiX$$

The reaction proceeds in two steps:

1. One molar equivalent of alkyllithium reacts with CuX to yield an alkylcopper (I).

2. The second molar equivalent of alkyllithium reacts with the alkylcopper to give a dialklylcuprate, formed as a lithium salt:

$$R{-}Li + Cu{-}I \longrightarrow R{-}Cu + LiI$$
$$\text{alkylcopper I}$$

$$R{-}Cu + Li{-}R \longrightarrow [R{-}Cu{-}R]^- Li^+$$
$$\text{lithium dialkylcuprate}$$

Lithium diarylcuprates are prepared in the same way. These reagents are useful for the synthesis of unsymmetrical alkanes of the type R–R', where R' (primary or secondary alkyl group, vinyl, or aryl group) comes from the alkyl halide:

$$R_2CuLi + R'X \longrightarrow RR'$$

$$(CH_3)_2CuLi + CH_3(CH_2)_8CH_2I \longrightarrow CH_3(CH_2)_8CH_2CH_3$$

| **lithium dimethylcuprate** | **1-iododecane** | **undecane** |

The reaction of cuprates with alkyl halides follows the S_N2 order of reactivity:

$$CH_3 > \text{primary} > \text{secondary} > \text{tertiary, and I} > Br > Cl > F$$

For secondary and tertiary halides, elimination becomes important. Organocuprates bearing primary halide groups are preferred because those bearing secondary or tertiary alkyl groups are less reactive toward alkyl halides.

The key step of the reaction mechanism is nucleophilic attack by the cuprate ion on the alkyl halide, followed by dissociation of the unstable intermediate to yield the alkane:

$$R{-}Cu^-{-}R + R'{-}X \longrightarrow R'{-}R + RCu + X^-$$

Example:

What combination of alkyl halide and cuprate reagent would you use for the preparation of 2-methylpentane? (There may be several correct answers.)

Solution:

Examine the structure of 2-methyl pentane and determine which C–C bonds can be formed. Remember that neither the alkyl halide nor the cuprate reagent should have secondary or tertiary alkyl groups. The C_3–C_4 or C_4–C_5 bonds could be formed in four different ways:

$$(CH_3)_2CuLi \ + \ BrCH_2CH_2CH(CH_3)_2 \longrightarrow CH_3 \text{——} CH_2CH_2CH(CH_3)_2$$

$$(CH_3CH_2)_2CuLi \ + \ BrCH_2CH(CH_3)_2 \longrightarrow CH_3CH_2 \text{——} CH_2CH(CH_3)_2$$

$$\Big[(CH_3)_2CHCH_2CH_2\Big]CuLi \ + \ CH_3Br \longrightarrow (CH_3)_2CHCH_2CH_2 \text{——} CH_3$$

$$\Big[(CH_3)_2CHCH_2\Big]CuLi \ + \ CH_3CH_2Br \longrightarrow (CH_3)_2CHCH_2 \text{——} CH_2CH_3$$

OTHER ORGANOMETALLIC REAGENTS

Organozinc reagents are prepared in the same way as other organometallic reagents:

$$RX + Zn \xrightarrow{\text{ether}} RZnX$$

They are not as reactive toward carbonyl compounds as organolithium or organomagnesium reagents.

They are often formed as reaction intermediates in reduction reactions between alkyl halides and zinc in acid media:

$$RX + \ Zn \longrightarrow \overset{\delta^-}{R} \text{——} \overset{\delta^+}{ZnX} + HX \longrightarrow RH + ZnX_2$$

1,2-Dihalides undergo dehalogenation by reaction with zinc. Here the C–Zn bond of the intermediate provides electrons for a β-elimination:

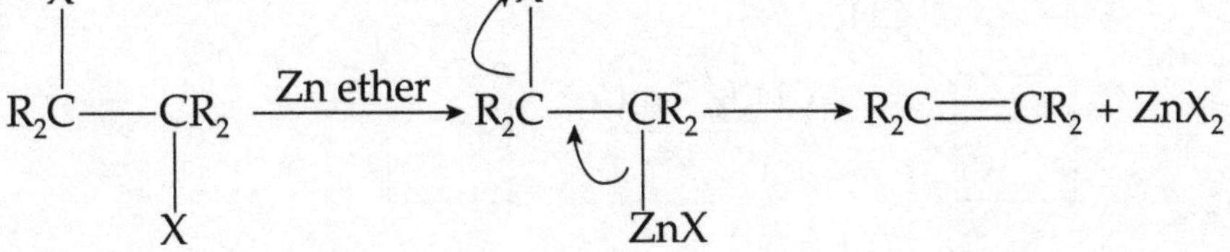

1,3-Dihalides are converted to cyclopropanes by treatment with zinc. The negative C–Zn bond acts as an internal nucleophile during cycloformation:

Cyclopropanes can be synthesized through another reaction involving organozinc: the **Simmons-Smith reaction**. The first step involves the generation of the iodomethylzinc iodide reactant. A zinc-copper couple (zinc covered with copper) is used with dimethylether as solvent:

$$ICH_2I + Zn \xrightarrow[Cu]{ether} ICH_2ZnI$$

The second step of the reaction is formation of the cyclopropane by reaction of the iodomethylzinc iodide with an alkene:

Example:

How could you use the Simmons-Smith reaction to synthesize:

Solution:

In the Simmons-Smith reaction, a CH_2 group is transferred from the organometallic compound to the alkene. Therefore, disconnect a CH_2 unit from the cyclopropene ring to identify the substrate:

The Simmons-Smith reaction is stereospecific, which means that the configuration around the double bond of the alkene is retained in the cycloalkane, as can be seen in *trans*-1,2-dimethylcyclopropane, obtained from *trans*-butene:

$$H_3C-C(H)=C(H)-CH_3 \xrightarrow[\text{ether}]{CH_2I_2, \text{ Zn(Cu)}}$$

The most useful **organomercury** compounds are formed when mercury (II) acetate, $Hg(O_2CCH_3)_2$, reacts with alkenes in a mixture of water and tetrahydrofuran (THF). This reaction is called **oxymercuration**, and the product formed is a β-hydroxyalkylmercury(II) acetate:

$$H_2C=CH_2 + Hg(O_2CCH_3)_2 + H_2O \longrightarrow HO-CH_2-CH_2-HgO_2CCH_3 + CH_3CO_2H$$

β-hydroxyalkyl-mercury(II) acetate

The product of an oxymercuration is not isolated; it's treated with a basic solution of sodium borohydride ($NaBH_4$) in a subsequent reaction called **demercuration**, which yields an alcohol.

Oxymercuration-demercuration gives better yields than the simple addition of water with H_2SO_4. The reaction sequence occurs according to Markovnikov's rule: the hydrogen atom introduced in step two attaches to the carbon that has the greater number of hydrogen substituents, and the hydroxyl group introduced in step one goes to the carbon atom that has the fewer hydrogen substituents:

$$HO-CH_2-CH_2-HgO_2CCH_3 \xrightarrow[\text{OH}^-]{NaBH_4} HO-CH_2-CH_2-H + Hg + CH_3CO_2^-$$

Example:

What is the oxymercuration-demercuration product of 1-pentene?

Solution:

Considering Markovnikov's rule, determine which carbon the hydrogen and hydroxyl groups will attach to. C_2 has fewer hydrogens and so will gain the –OH group:

$$CH_3CH_2CH_2CH = CH_2 \xrightarrow[\text{NaBH}_4,\ \text{OH}^-]{\text{Hg(OAc)}_2, \text{H}_2\text{O–THF}} CH_3CH_2CH_2\overset{\overset{\displaystyle OH}{|}}{CH} {-} CH_3$$

1-pentene   **2-pentanol**

Example:

What is the structure of the two alkenes that could produce 1-methylcyclopentanol by oxymercuration-demercuration?

Solution:

Examine the structure of the alcohol: The hydroxyl group is on a tertiary carbon. Therefore, an alkene with a double bond located either in the ring, between C_1 and C_2, or out of the ring at position C_1 could undergo reaction according to Markovnikov's rule:

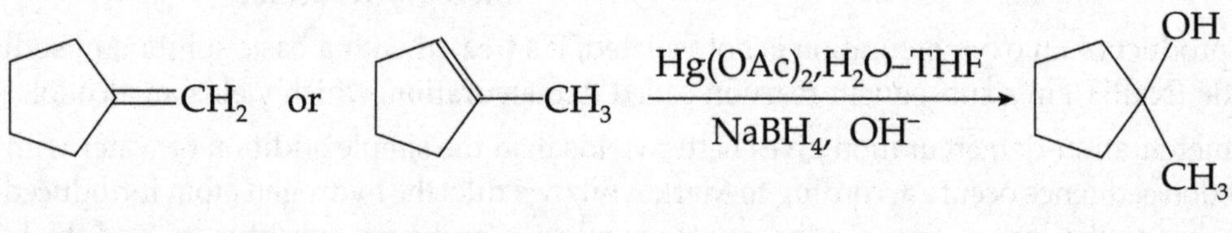

The oxymercuration-demercuration reaction has three steps. The first is the dissociation of mercury(II) acetate:

$$Hg(O_2CCH_3)_2 \rightleftharpoons {}^+HgO_2CCH_3 + {}^-O_2CCH_3$$

mercury(II) cation

The second step is the electrophilic attack of the π electrons of the C=C bond by the mercury cation, with formation of a bridged intermediate:

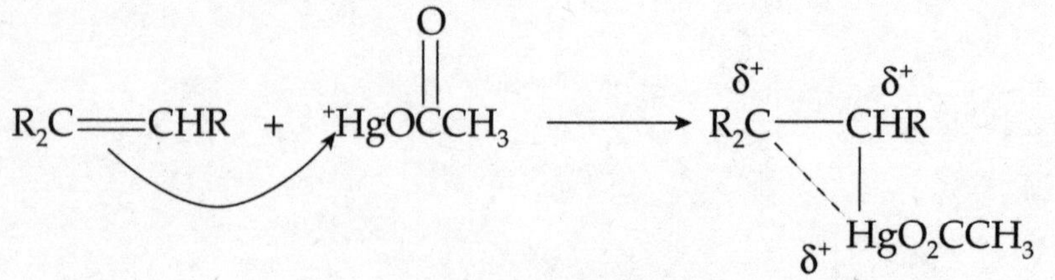

bridged carbocation intermediate

The final step is attack by H_2O and proton loss:

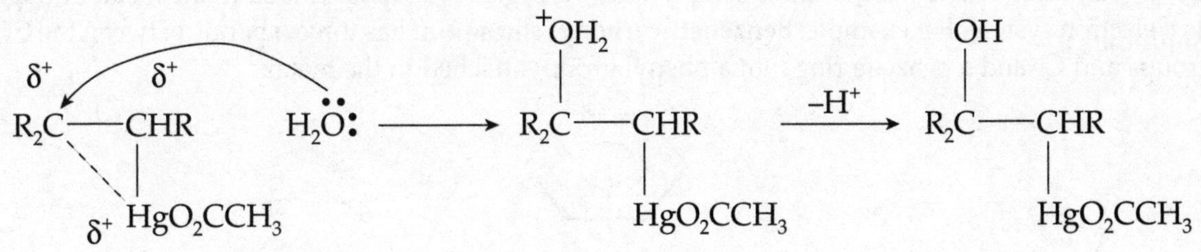

H_2O attacks the more substituted carbon of the bridge intermediate.

Oxymercuration-demercuration can be applied to the synthesis of ethers by substituting an alcohol for THF—the reaction is called **solvomercuration-demercuration**:

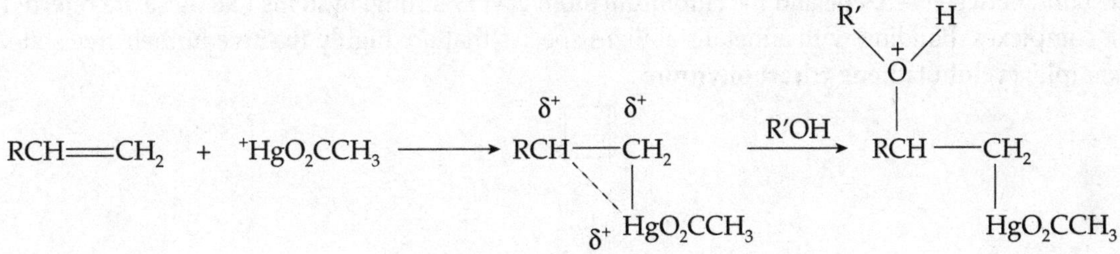

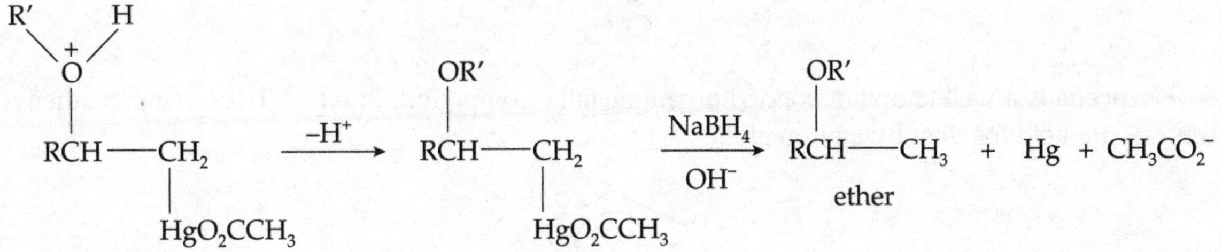

Example:

How would you prepare 2-methoxy-2-phenylpropane by solvomercuration?

Solution:

Examine the structure of this product. The methoxy group is on a tertiary carbon. According to Markovnikov's rule, ethers such as this are obtained only if the alkene substrate has its double bond between this carbon and an adjacent one. The solvent is methanol:

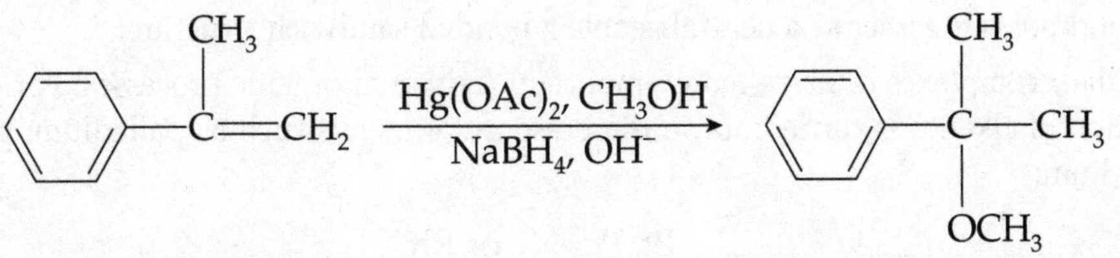

2-phenylpropene **2-methoxy-2-phenylpropane**

Many organometallic compounds are derived from transition metals such as iron, chromium, nickel, platinum, or rhodium. In these compounds, the organic group is bonded to the metal through its π electron system. For example, **benzenetricarbonyl chromium** has three σ bonds between the CO groups and Cr and a benzene ring (not a phenyl group) attached to the metal:

The bond between benzene and the chromium atom is very strong. Systems like these are referred to as π complexes. Bonding with a metal stabilizes species that are highly reactive in their free state. For example, **cyclobutadiene tricarbonyliron**:

Ferrocene is a well-known π bonded organometallic compound, in which two cyclopentadienyl radicals are held together by an iron atom.

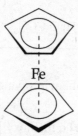

The iron atom donates two of its electrons to form a stable iron(II) ion, and the cyclopentadienyls become anions.

The compound holds together as a neutral, stable π bonded sandwich structure.

Metals and their complexes catalyze many important industrial organic processes. For example, the hydrogenation of alkenes is carried out in the presence of metals such as palladium, platinum, nickel, and rhodium:

$$H_2C = CH_2 \ + \ H_2 \ \xrightarrow{\text{Pt, Pd, Ni, or Rh}} \ CH_3 - CH_3$$

The first step involves the activation and binding of hydrogen atoms at reactive sites on the metal surface:

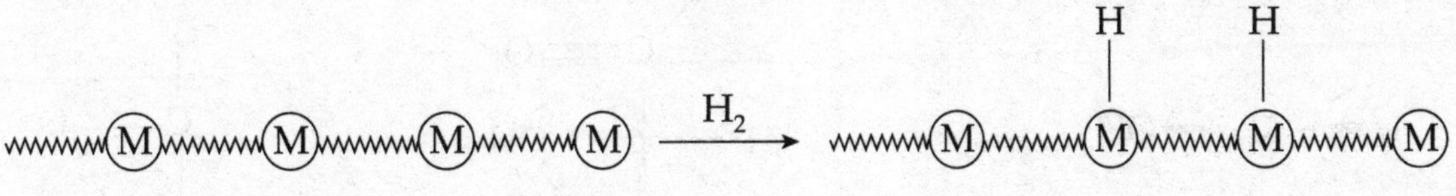

A second step transfers a hydrogen atom from the surface of the catalyst to one of the carbons of the alkene. The other carbon then binds to the metal:

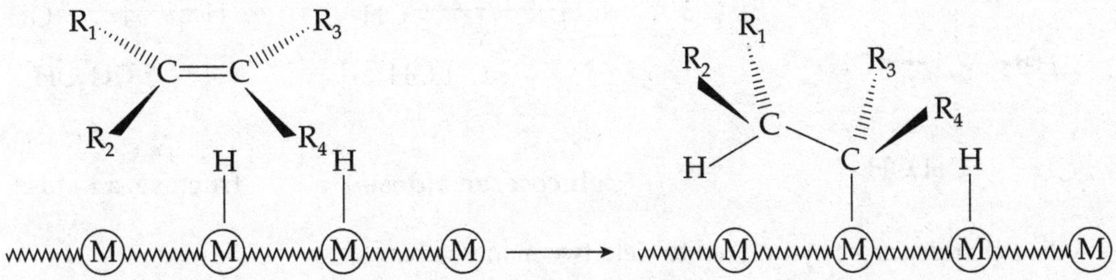

During the final reaction step, the second hydrogen is transferred. An alkane is obtained, and the catalyst is regenerated:

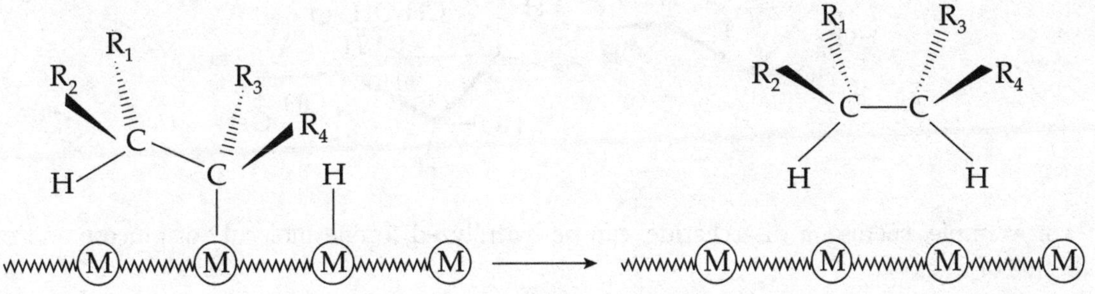

SPECIAL TOPICS

Organic compounds, by virtue of their covalent bonding, easily form macromolecular assemblies, of which the most important are proteins and nucleic acids, the building blocks of life. The topics covered under this heading include: *carbohydrates, nucleic acids, amino acids, peptides, proteins*, and *lipids*.

CARBOHYDRATES

Carbohydrates or **saccharides** have the general formula $C_n(H_2O)_m$. They include aliphatic polyhydroxaldehydes (**aldoses**), polyhydroxyketones (**ketoses**), and all compounds that yield them upon hydrolysis. The simpler carbohydrates are also called **sugars**. They are synthesized by almost all living organisms—plant and animals—as a source of metabolic energy. The oxidation of **glucose** to CO_2 and H_2O provides energy for all cells, and the conversion of glucose to **starch** is the main energy storage mechanism of plants.

Monosaccharides are saccharides that cannot be hydrolyzed to simpler structures.

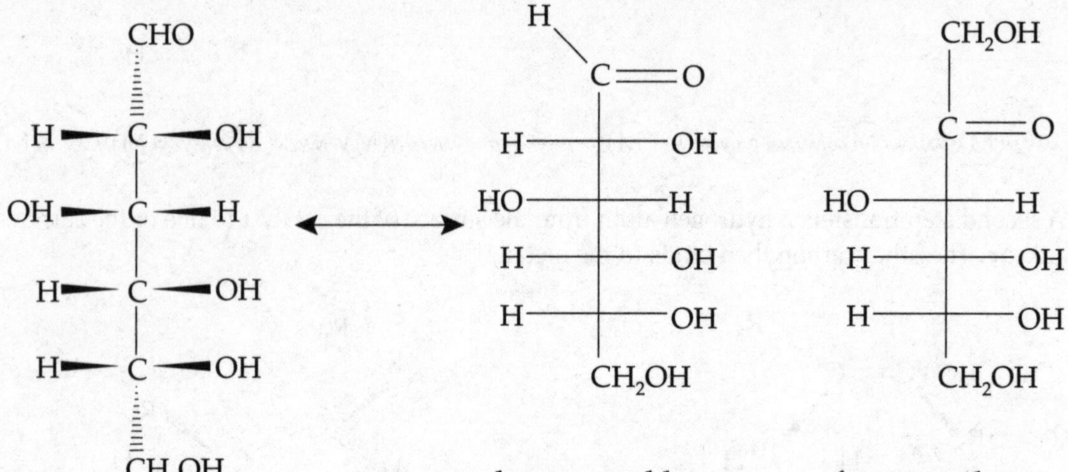

glucose, an aldose   fructose, a ketose

A **disaccharide** can be hydrolyzed to yield two monosaccharides.

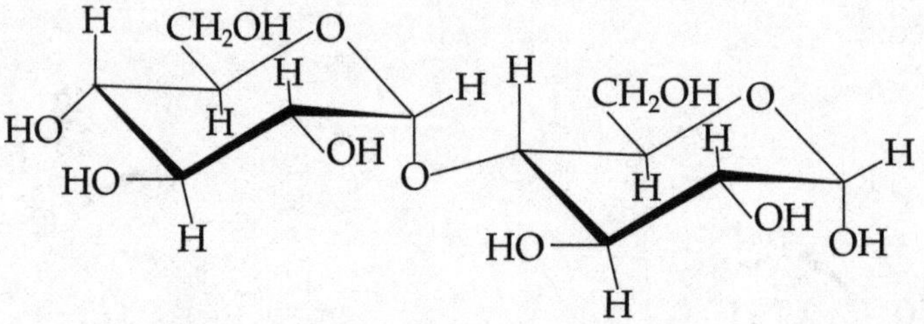

For example, sucrose, a disaccharide, can be hydrolyzed to one molecule of glucose and one molecule of fructose.

Carbohydrates are named as follows:

- **Aldoses** contain the aldehyde functional group, and **ketoses** contain the ketone group.

- The number of carbons in the chain determines the root name, and the names are followed by the suffix –*ose*.

Triose = 3 carbons

Tetrose = 4 carbons

Pentose = 5 carbons

Hexose = 6 carbons

Heptose = 7 carbons

- The configuration of the chiral carbon farthest from the CO group confers to the carbohydrate a stereochemical prefix, either D or L.

The D prefix refers to carbohydrates that degrade to (+) glyceraldehyde, and the L prefix designates those that degrade to (−) glyceraldehyde.

$$
\begin{array}{cc}
\text{CHO} & \text{CHO} \\
\text{H}\blacktriangleright\text{C}\blacktriangleleft\text{OH} & \text{HO}\blacktriangleright\text{C}\blacktriangleleft\text{H} \\
\text{CH}_2\text{OH} & \text{CH}_2\text{OH}
\end{array}
$$

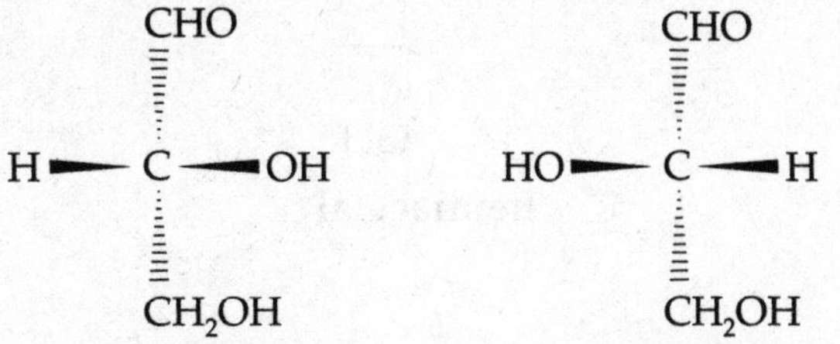

D-carbohydrates degrade to (+)-glyceraldehyde   **L-carbohydrates degrade to (−)-glyceraldehyde**

The D-carbohydrates have the −OH group in the bottom chiral carbon to the right in a Fisher projection.

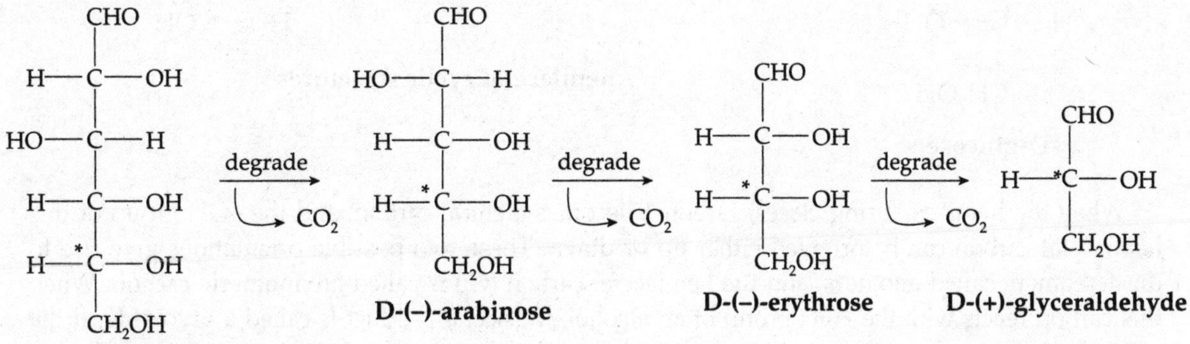

D-(+)-glucose   degrade → CO_2 **D-(−)-arabinose**   degrade → CO_2 **D-(−)-erythrose**   degrade → CO_2 **D-(+)-glyceraldehyde**

The D and L convention is not indicative of optical activity. The (+) and (−) convention is required to show which way a compound will rotate the plane of polarized light. So this means that a D-carbohydrate can rotate the plane of polarized light either clockwise or counterclockwise.

Carbohydrates form **epimers**, compounds whose stereochemistry differs at only one carbon:

C_2 epimers of aldohexose

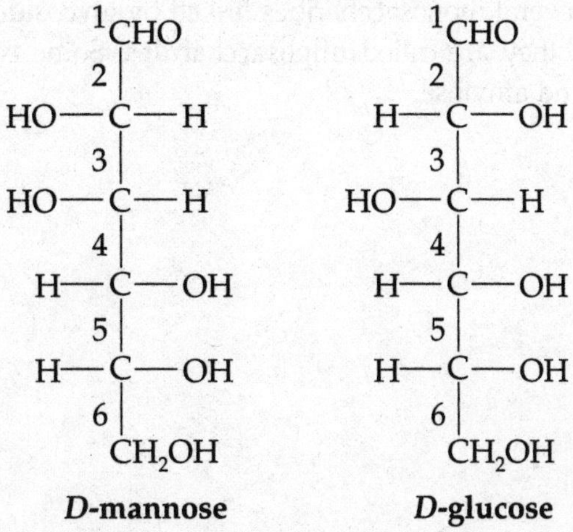

D-mannose   **D-glucose**

Cyclic Carbohydrates

In the solid state, aldoses exist as cyclic hemiacetals. In the liquid state, although they exist in both cyclic and open-chain forms, equilibrium generally favors the hemiacetal form.

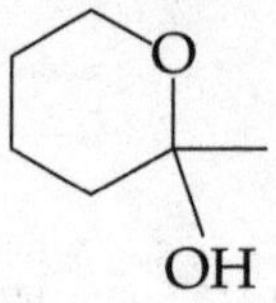

hemiacetal

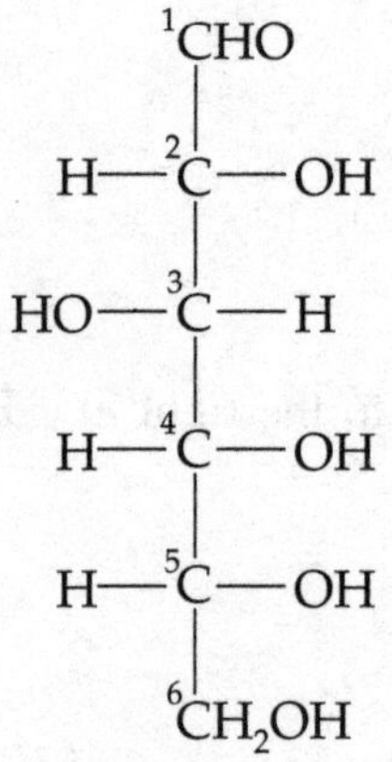

D-glucose

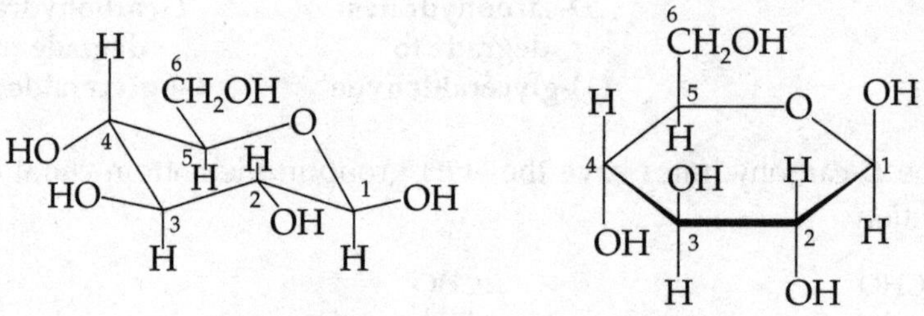

hemiacetal cyclic structures

When the hemiacetal ring closes, carbon 1 becomes a chiral carbon, and the –OH group of this hemiacetal carbon can be oriented either up or down. These two possible orientations give rise to diastereomers called **anomers**, and the hemiacetal carbon (C_1) is called an **anomeric carbon**. When this carbon reacts with the –OH group of an alcohol, the acetal product is called a **glycoside**. If the –OH group belongs to another carbohydrate molecule, the glycoside is a **disaccharide**. In disaccharide formation, anomeric carbons can adopt the following glycosidic bonding schemes:

1. The 1,1′ link: C_1 binds to the C_1 oxygen atom on the second carbohydrate.

2. The 1,4′ link: C_1 binds to the C_4 oxygen atom on the second carbohydrate.

3. The 1,6′ link: C_1 binds to the C_6 oxygen atom on the second carbohydrate.

Polysaccharides

Polysaccharides consist of several monosaccharides linked by glycosidic bonds. When they contain up to ten monosaccharides, they are called **oligosaccharides**. Some common polysaccharides are starch, glycogen, cellulose, and amylose.

NUCLEIC ACIDS

Nucleic acids are an important class of polysaccharides, and they consist of both **RNA** (ribonucleic acids) and **DNA** (deoxyribonucleic acids). These carbohydrate biopolymers consist of ribofuranose chains linked by phosphate ester groups. Illustrated below is DNA:

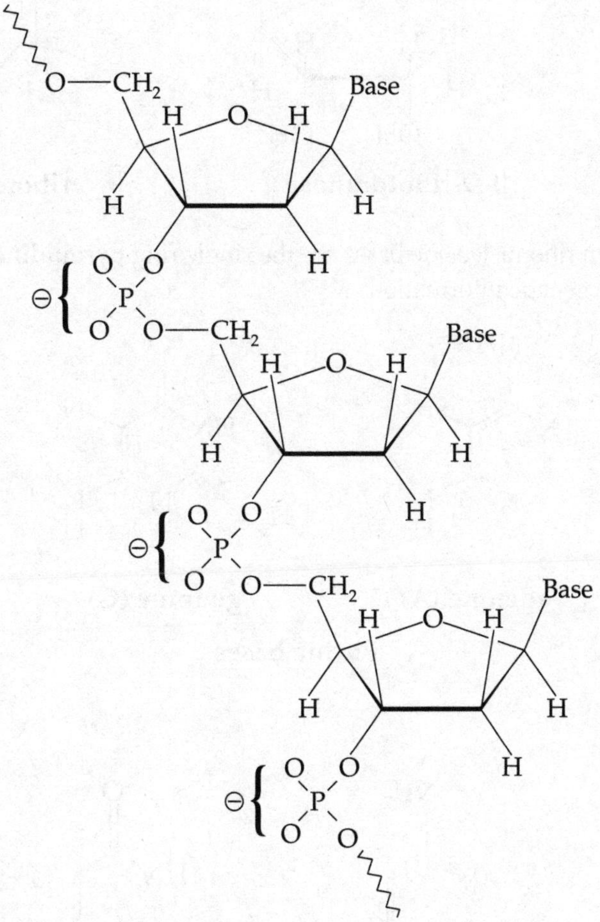

The building blocks of nucleic acids are **ribonucleosides**, which are glycosides of ribofuranose—or ribofuranosides β, derived from cyclic *D*-ribose:

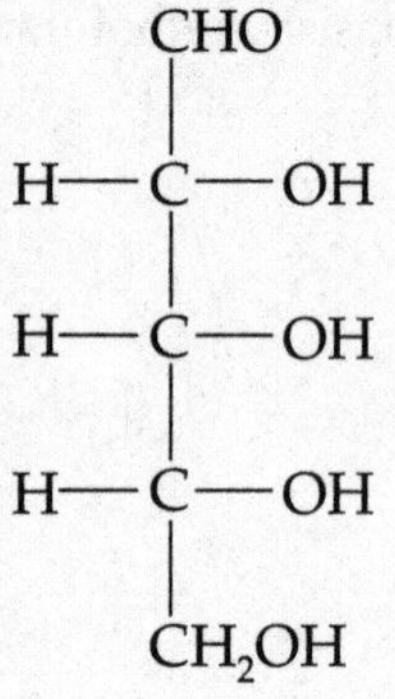

D-ribose 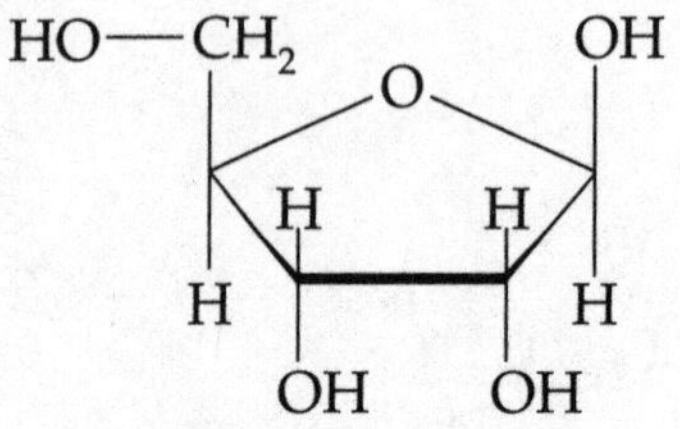   **β-D-ribofuranose** 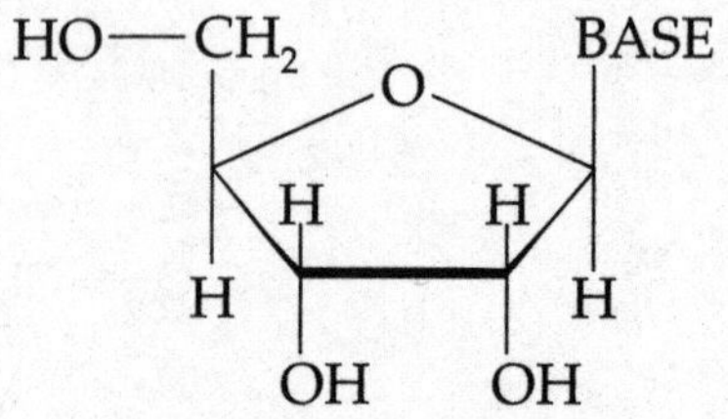   **ribonucleoside**

The most well-known ribonucleoside bases are the single ring **pyrimidine** bases and the two ring **purine**, which carry the genetic information:

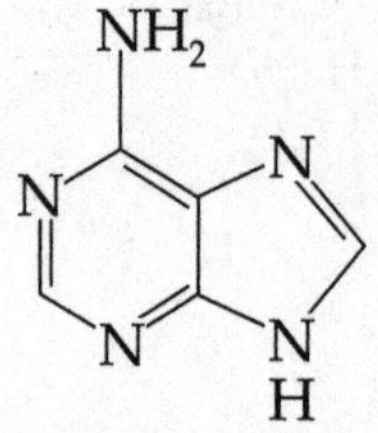

adenine (A) 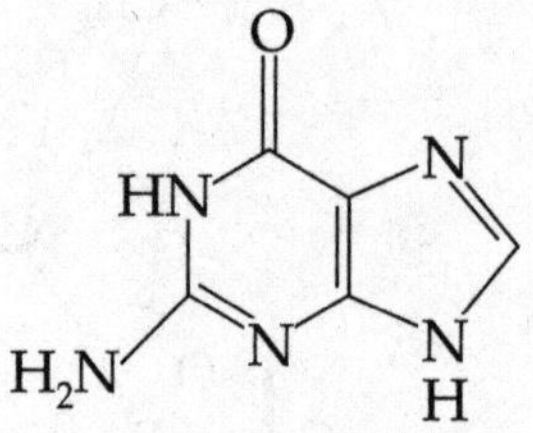   **guanine (G)**

Purine bases

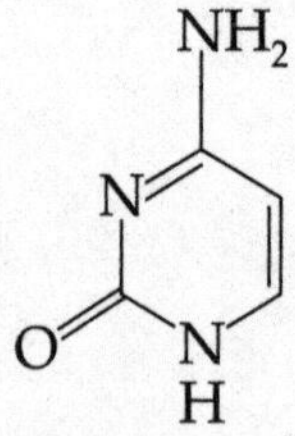

cytosine (C) 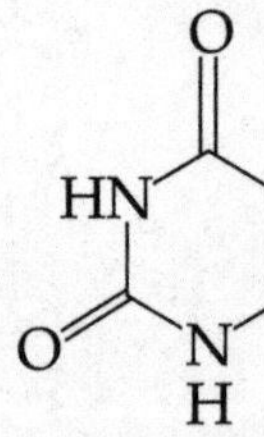   **uracil (U)**

Pyrimidine bases

When ribonucleosides are phosphorylated at their C_5 carbon, they are called **ribonucleotides**. The four common ribonucleotides of RNA are **cytidine monophosphate (CMP)**, **uridine monophosphate (UMP)**, **adenosine monophosphate (AMP)**, and **guanosine monophosphate (GMP)**.

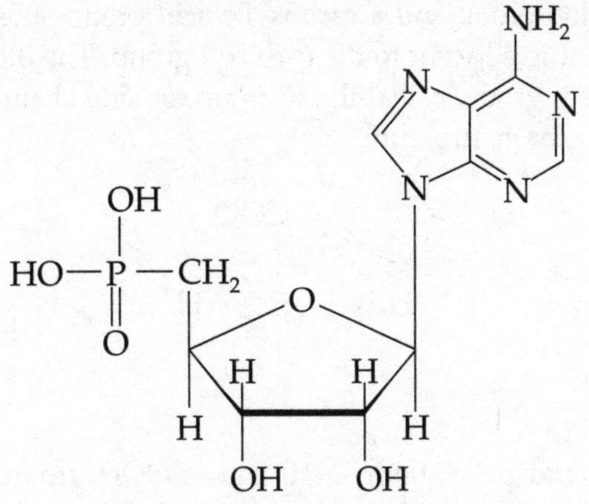

5′-adenylic acid (AMP)

The phosphate group on the 5′ carbon of a ribonucleotide can link with the –OH group of a 3′ carbon in another ribonucleotide. This bond is called a phosphoester linkage. When many ribonucleotide units are linked by these bonds, an RNA polymer is created. RNA polymers differ from one another only in the sequence of their constituent ribonucleotides.

The structure of **DNA** is similar to that of RNA. The deoxyribonucleosides are derived from **D-2-deoxyribose** and the bases are thymine (T) and three of the bases that are also found in ribonucleotides: cytosine, adenine, and guanine.

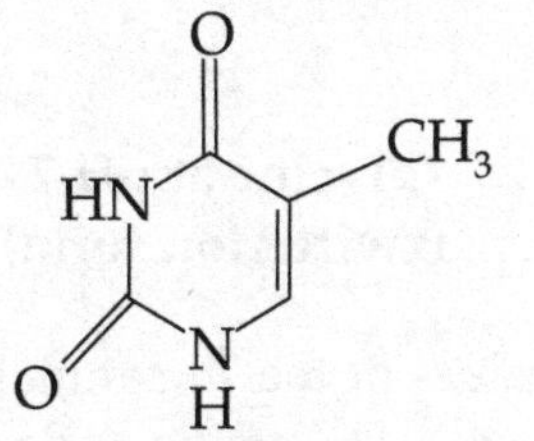

thymine (T)

The four corresponding deoxyribonucleosides are: **deoxycytidine, deoxythimidine, deoxyadenosine,** and **deoxyguanidine.** When phosphorylated, they, too, can link via phosphoester linkages to form the **primary structure** of a DNA strand. The bases can hydrogen bond with other bases in a process called **base pairing**. So cytosine and guanine can form one **base pair**, and thymine (uracil in RNA) and adenine can form another. The DNA molecule consists of a double chain of polynucleotides held together by hydrogen-bonded base pairs.

AMINO ACIDS

Amino acids bear charged groups of opposite polarity, which makes them dipolar **ions**, or **zwitterions**. Twenty common amino acids are found in all proteins and, with the exception of proline, they all consist of a primary amino group and a carboxylic acid group substituted to the same carbon, called the α-carbon because it is adjacent to the carboxyl group. The other two carbon bonds are to a hydrogen and a substitutent group, called the R group, or side chain. The 20 naturally occurring α-**amino acids** have the same basic structure:

$$
\begin{array}{c}
COO^- \\
| \\
H_3\overset{+}{N}\!-\!\underset{\alpha}{C}\!-\!H \\
| \\
R
\end{array}
$$

At physiological pH around pH 7, both $-NH_2$ and $-COOH$ groups are completely ionized in solution. The amino acid is both an acid and base, whereby the amino group can be protonated ($-NH_3^+$) and the carboxyl group is dissociated ($-COO^-$). They are accordingly referred to as **amphoteric** substances. Some amino acids have a third ionizable group in their R group. The ionization state of an amino acid is pH-dependent. At acidic pH (pH $\approx$ 1), the carboxyl group is protonated ($-COOH$), and the amino group is protonated ($-NH_3^+$). At alkaline pH (pH $\approx$ 10), the carboxyl group is deprotonated ($-COO^-$), and the amino group remains unchanged (NH_2).

$$
\begin{array}{c}
COOH \\
| \\
H_3\overset{+}{N}\!-\!C\!-\!H \\
| \\
H
\end{array}
\;\rightleftharpoons\;
\begin{array}{c}
COO^- \\
| \\
H_3\overset{+}{N}\!-\!C\!-\!H \\
| \\
H
\end{array}
\;\rightleftharpoons\;
\begin{array}{c}
COO^- \\
| \\
H_2N\!-\!C\!-\!H \\
| \\
H
\end{array}
$$

glycine at pH < 2.3   **glycine at pH 7**   **glycine at pH > 9**
(zwitterion form)

The following table lists the pK_a values of the 20 naturally occurring amino acids. All have pK_a values for the amino and carboxyl groups. The amino acids that have ionizable side chains show a third pK_a.

Amino Acid	R Group	pI	pK_a, α-COOH α-NH$_3^+$, R Group
Gly	–H	6.0	2.35, 9.78
Ala	–CH$_3$	6.0	2.35, 9.87
Val	–CH(CH$_3$)$_2$	6.0	2.29, 9.74
Leu	–CH$_2$CH(CH$_3$)$_2$	6.0	2.33, 9.74
Ile	–CHCH$_3$CH$_2$CH$_3$	6.0	2.32, 9.76
Phe	–CH$_2$Ar	5.5	2.16, 9.18
Tyr	–CH$_2$Ar–OH	5.7	2.20, 9.11, 10.13
Trp	–CH$_2$–indole	5.9	2.43, 9.44
Ser	–CH$_2$OH	5.7	2.19, 9.21
Thr	–CHOHCH$_3$	5.6	2.09, 9.11
Cys	–CH$_2$SH	5.0	1.92, 8.35, 10.46
Met	–CH$_2$CH$_2$SCH$_3$	5.7	2.13, 9.28
Asn	–CH$_2$CONH$_2$	5.4	2.11, 8.84
Gln	–(CH$_2$)$_2$CONH$_2$	5.7	1.99, 3.90, 9.90
Glu	–(CH$_2$)$_2$COOH	3.2	1.99, 3.90, 9.90
Asp	–CH$_2$COOH	2.8	2.10, 4.07, 9.46
Lys	–(CH$_2$)$_4$NH$_3^+$	9.7	2.16, 9.18, 10.79
His	–CH$_2$–imidazole	10.8	1.82, 8.99, 12.48
Arg	–(CH$_2$)$_3$NHC=NHNH$_2$	7.6	1.80, 6.04, 9.33

The pH at which the amino acid exists as an equilibrium mixture of anionic and cationic forms is called the **isoelectric point** (pI). The amino acids with nonionizable R groups have pI values close to 5. This is due to the fact that their –NH$_3^+$ group is somewhat more acidic than their –COO$^-$ group is basic. Asp and Glu both have R groups that contain an acidic carboxyl group; this lowers their pI values to ~ 3. Similarly, His, Lys, and Arg, respectively, have an imidazole, an amino group, and a guanidine in their R groups, and this is reflected in their high pI values.

glycine (Gly, G)   alanine (Ala, A)   valine (Val, V)   leucine (Leu, L)

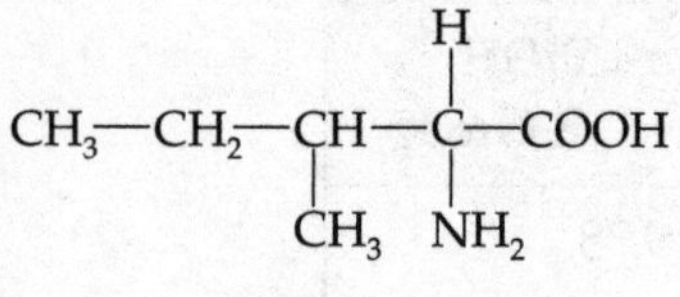

isoleucine (Ile, I)

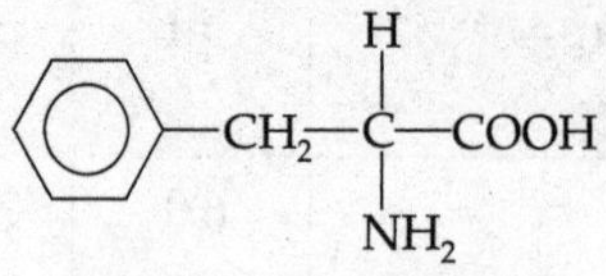

phenylalanine (Phe, F)

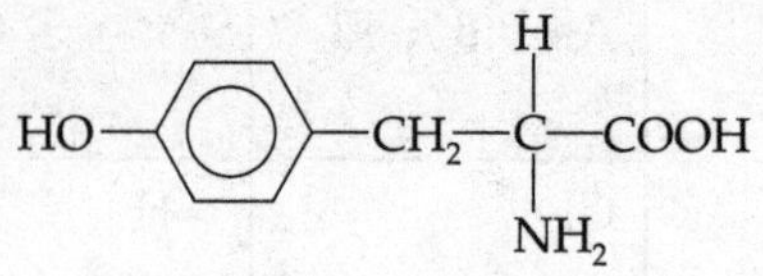

tyrosine (Tyr, Y)

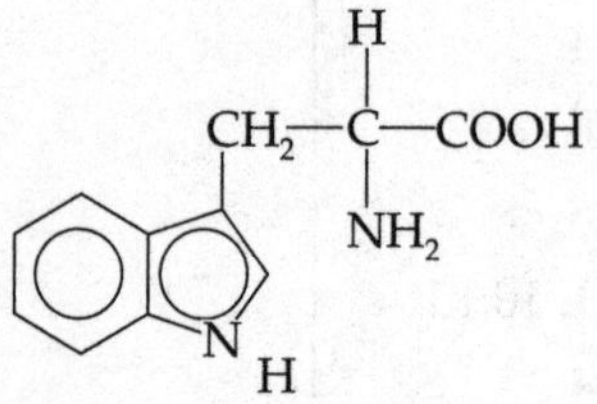

tryptophan (Trp, W)

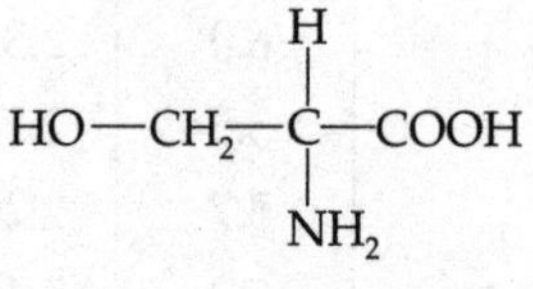

serine (Ser, S)

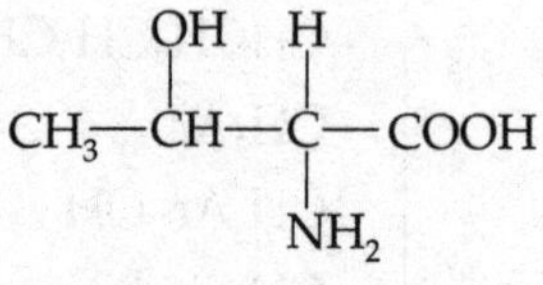

threonine (Thr, T)

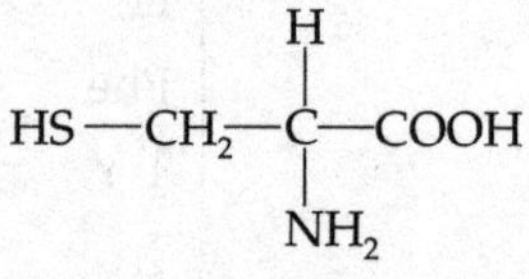

cysteine (Cys, C)

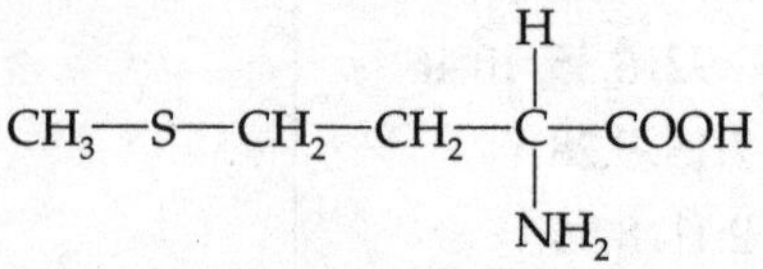

methionine (Met, M)

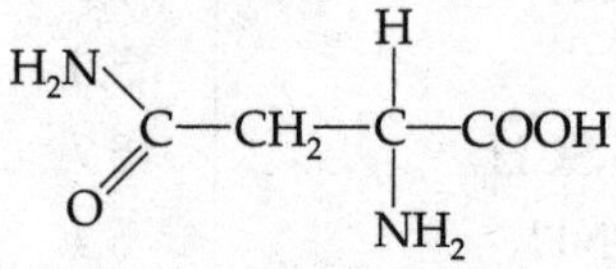

asparagine (Asn, N)

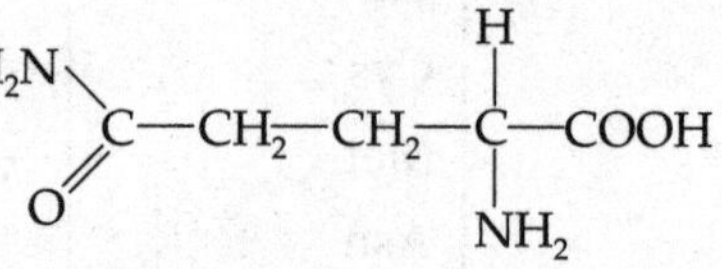

glutamine (Gln, Q)

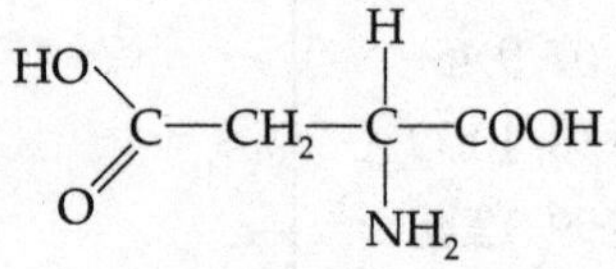

aspartic acid (Asp, D)

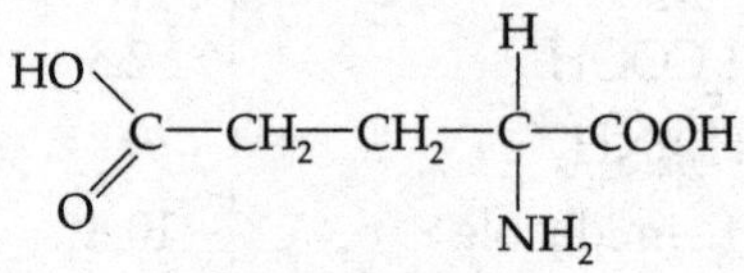

glutamic acid (Glu, E)

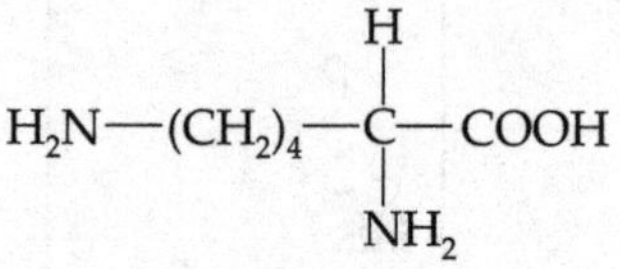

lysine (Lys, K)

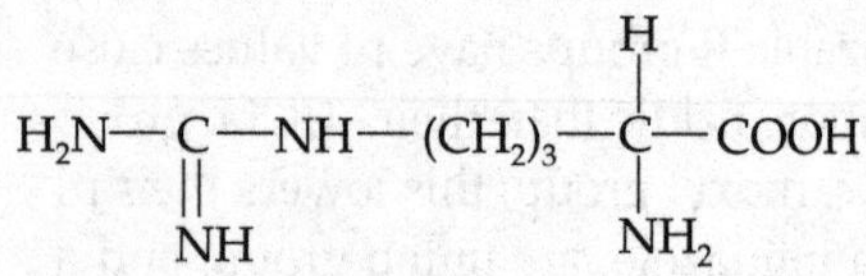

arginine (Arg, R)

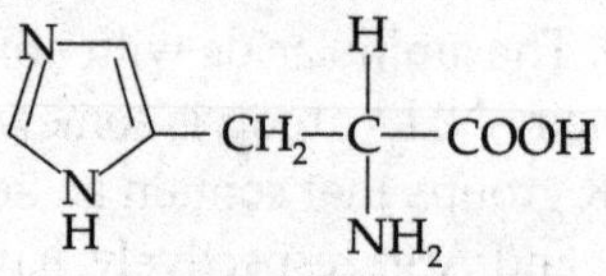

histidine (His, H)

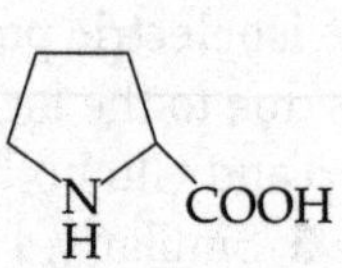

proline (Pro, P)

Peptides

Amino acids can link to form **peptides** via amide linkages called **peptide bonds** (also called amide bonds by organic chemists):

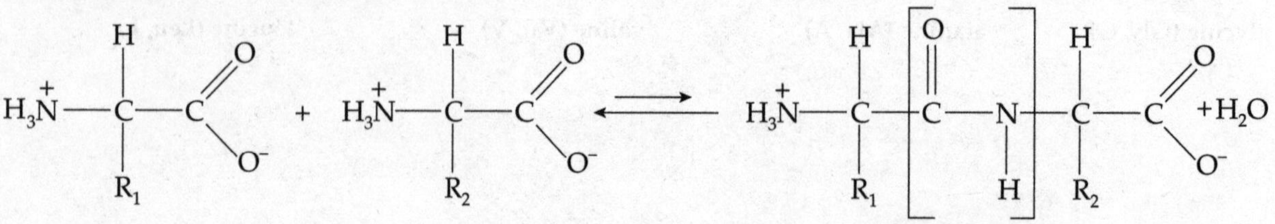

peptide bond

When several amino acids are joined by peptide bonds, a structure called a **polypeptide** is formed:

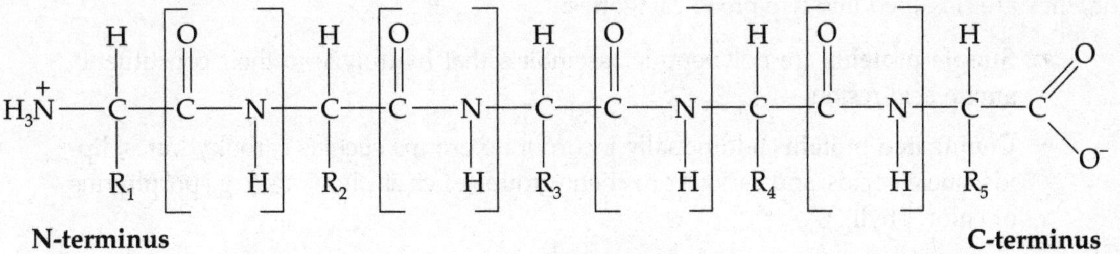

A pentapeptide

Polypeptide chains are oriented. By convention, the amino end is considered the starting point of the chain and is referred to as the "amino" or "N-terminus," and the end of the chain is called the "carboxyl" or "C-terminus." So a polypeptide consists of repeating amino acid units called the **backbone**, to which are attached distinctive **side chains** (R groups). The **sequence** of a polypeptide is given by using the abbreviations of its constituent amino acids. By convention, the first amino acid in the sequence is the N-terminus: Arg-Ala-Cys-Pro-Tyr-Glu-Asn. This heptapeptide starts with an arginine residue and terminates with an asparagine residue.

Besides the peptide bond, two polypeptide chains can be linked together by a covalent bond formed between two cysteine residues, called a **disulfide bridge**. This is a mild oxidation reaction, which converts two thiols to a disulfide. Two such cross-linked cysteines are called a **cystine**:

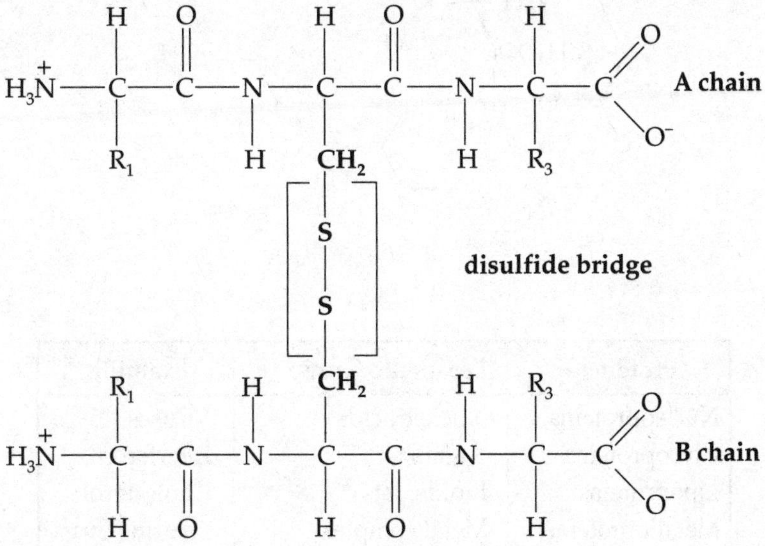

disulfide bridge

Proteins

Polypeptides have molecular weights that range between 5,000 and 200,000 daltons. The **dalton** is a unit of mass equal to the mass of one hydrogen atom. Thus, a polypeptide of molecular weight 10,000 has a mass of 10,000 daltons, or 10 kDa.

A kilodalton (kDa) is a unit of mass equal to 1,000 daltons.

Proteins are macromolecular assemblies with molecular weights in the millions. They are usually classified as a function of their biochemical function or shape. On the basis of their chemical composition, they are classified into two broad categories:

- **Simple proteins** are polypeptide assemblies that hydrolyze to their constituent amino acid residues.

- **Conjugated proteins** additionally incorporate groups such as carbohydrates, lipids, nucleic acids, and various prosthetic groups, such as pigments (e.g., porphyrins or chlorophyll).

Prosthetic groups are also called "active groups" because they are often the site of the main biochemical activity of the protein. Chlorophyll is an example of a prosthetic group:

Proteins	Prosthetic Group	Example
Nucleoproteins	Nucleic acids	Viruses
Glycoproteins	Sugars	Interferon
Lipoproteins	Lipids, fats	Cholesterol
Metalloproteins	Metal complex, metalloporphyrins	Azurin (Cu)
		Myoglobin
		Hemoglobin

The structure of proteins is organized at different levels:

- The **primary structure** refers to the covalent assembly; i.e., the amino acid sequence and the presence of disulfide bridges.

- The **secondary structure** refers to the arrangements adopted by the amino acid sequence. Three are possible: the **α-helix**, the **β-pleated sheet**, and the **random coil**, and they can coexist in the same protein.

*An **α-helix** is a polypeptide arrangement in which the carbonyl groups on one turn of the helix hydrogen bond to the hydrogens of the peptide N–H bond of the next turn. A **β-pleated sheet** is a polypeptide arrangement in which the chains line up side by side with the carbonyl groups of one chain hydrogen bonded to the hydrogens of the N–H bond of the adjacent chain. A **random coil** is any nonhelical or nonpleated sheet polypeptide arrangement.*

- The **tertiary structure** represents the complete three-dimensional conformation of the protein and the folding pattern of its secondary structure.

- The **quaternary structure** is the "sum total" of the protein assembly, including complexation with ligands, inhibitors, etc.

For example, hemoglobin is made up of four monomeric units that consist of the same amino acid sequence incorporating a heme prosthetic group (iron porphyrin complex). The amino acid sequence, or 1° structure, of hemoglobin, folds into several helices, each a 2° structure element, and these helices pack against one another to form a globular protein, the 3° structure. Four of these globular proteins associate to form the 4° structure of hemoglobin.

LIPIDS

Lipids are a major component of cells and animal tissues and can be extracted by nonpolar organic solvents. **Simple lipids** do not hydrolyze with acidic or basic solvents. They include **terpenes**—compounds with general formula $(C_5H_8)_n$—**steroids**, and **prostaglandins**.

general steroid structure

cholesterol

isoprene unit
contained in terpenes

vitamin A
a terpene with two isoprene units

Complex lipids are esters of carboxylic acids; they are easy to hydrolyze to acids and alcohols. They include **glycerides** and **waxes**.

Complex lipids are also called **fatty acids**; so glycerides are the fatty acid esters of glycerol. Triglycerides are called **fats** if they are solid at room temperature and **oils** if they are liquid.

Their carboxylic acids are straight chains that contain between 12 and 20 carbons, and they can be either saturated or unsaturated.

Saturated Fatty Acids

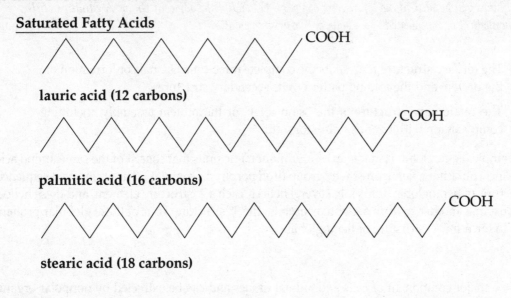

lauric acid (12 carbons)

palmitic acid (16 carbons)

stearic acid (18 carbons)

Unsaturated Fatty Acids

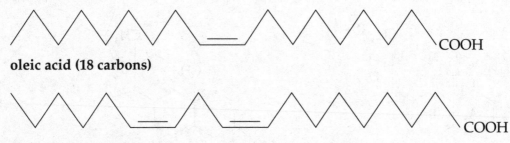

oleic acid (18 carbons)

linoleic acid (18 carbons)

PRACTICE PROBLEMS

1. 2, 3-Pentandiol has four possible stereoisomers. Which are enantiomers? Which are diastereomers?

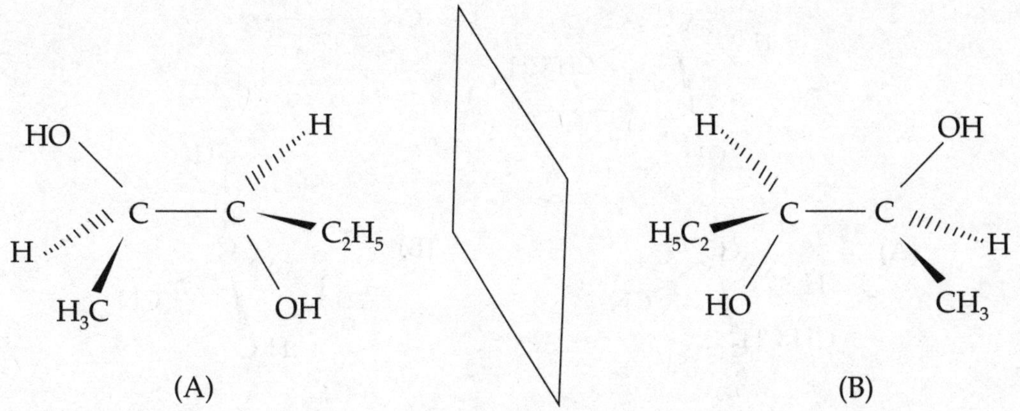

(A)

(B)

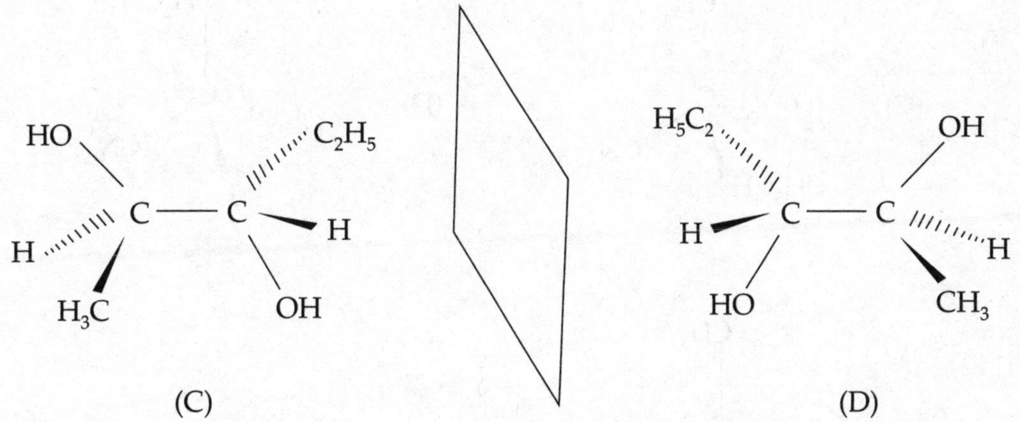

(C)

(D)

2. Which of the following sets of characteristics best describes an S_N2 reaction?

    (A) Homolytic cleavage, no carbocation intermediate, bimolecular process
    (B) Heterolytic cleavage, no carbocation intermediate, unimolecular process
    (C) Heterolytic cleavage, no carbocation intermediate, bimolecular process
    (D) Homolytic cleavage, carbocation intermediate, unimolecular process
    (E) Heterolytic cleavage, carbocation intermediate, unimolecular process

3. What is the structure of the S_N2 transition state and of the product of the following reaction?

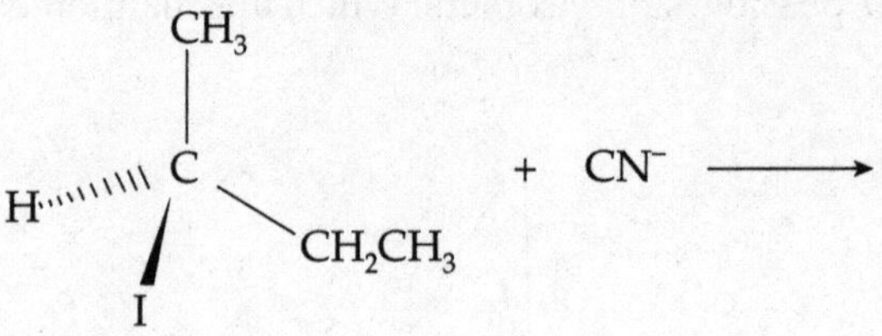

$$
\underset{\substack{\text{H}\cdots\text{C}\cdots\text{CH}_2\text{CH}_3 \\ |\!|\! \\ \text{I}}}{\overset{\text{CH}_3}{|}} \quad + \quad CN^- \longrightarrow
$$

(A)

$$
\underset{\substack{\text{H}\cdots\text{C}\cdots\text{CN} \\ \text{CH}_3\text{CH}_2}}{\overset{\text{CH}_3}{|}}
$$

(B)

$$
\underset{\substack{\text{I}\cdots\text{C}\cdots\text{CN} \\ \text{H}_3\text{C}}}{\overset{\text{CH}_3}{|}}
$$

(C)

$$
\underset{\substack{\text{I}\cdots\text{C}\cdots\text{CN} \\ \text{CH}_3\text{CH}_2}}{\overset{\text{CH}_3}{|}}
$$

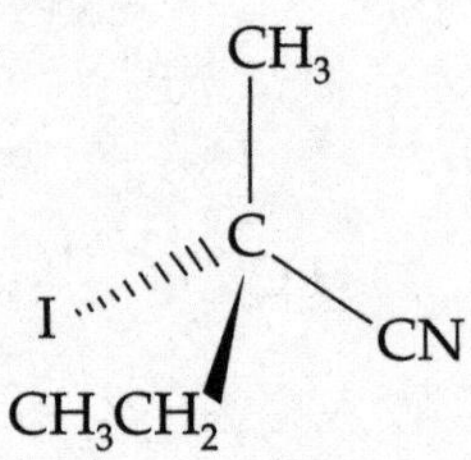

(D)

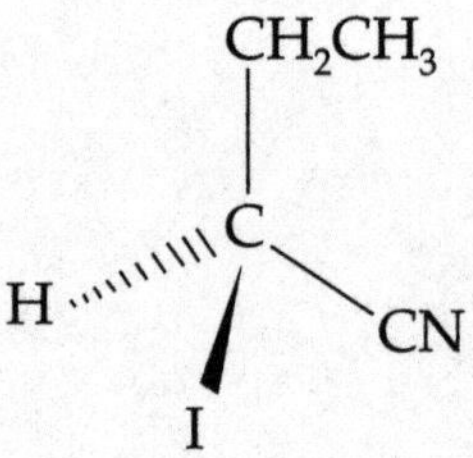

$$
\underset{\substack{\text{H}\cdots\text{C}\cdots\text{CN} \\ |\!|\! \\ \text{I}}}{\overset{\text{CH}_2\text{CH}_3}{|}}
$$

(E)

$$
\underset{\substack{\text{H}_3\text{C}\cdots\text{C}\cdots\text{CN} \\ \text{CH}_3\text{CH}_2}}{\overset{\text{CH}_3}{|}}
$$

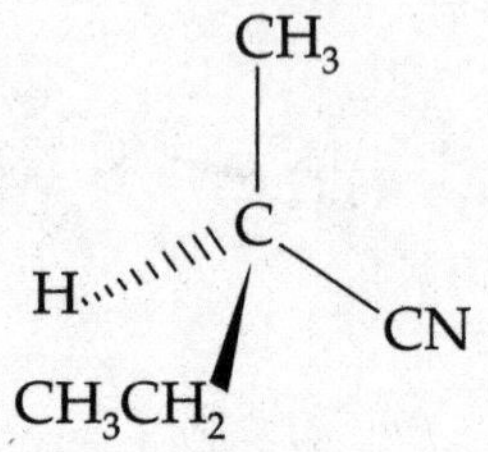

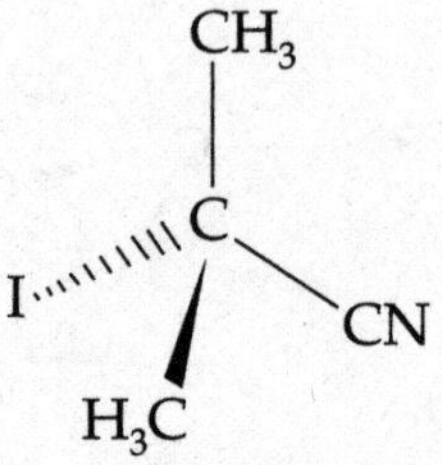

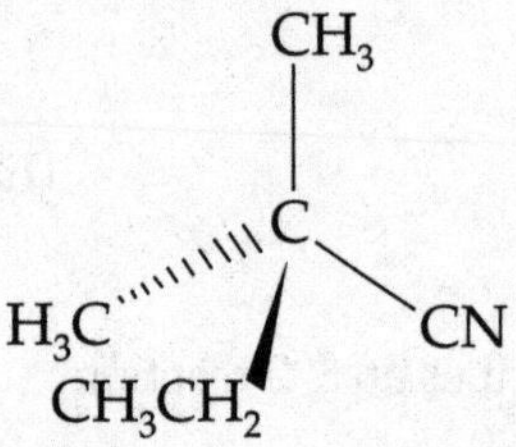

4. What is the order of increasing rate of S_N2 reaction for the following alkyl halides?

    (a) CH_3Br

    (b) $CH_3CHBrCH_3$

    (c) $CH_3CH_2CH_2Br$

    (d) CH_3CH_2Br

    (e) $(CH_3)_3CBr$

    (f) $CH_3CH_2CHBrCH_2CH_3$

(A) $a < f < b < c < d < e$

(B) $a < d < c < b < f < e$

(C) $f < b < e < c < d < a$

(D) $e < b < f < d < c < a$

(E) $e < f < b < c < d < a$

5. Which of the following best describes an S_N1 mechanism for the substitution of alkyl halides?

(A) Ionization reaction, first-order reaction, racemization, relative rate: 3° RX > 2° RX

(B) Ionization reaction, second-order reaction, racemization, relative rate: 3° RX > 2° RX

(C) Concerted back-side attack, first-order reaction, inversion of configuration, relative rate: CH_3X > 1° RX > 2° RX

(D) Concerted back-side attack, second-order reaction, racemization, relative rate: 3° RX > 2° RX

(E) Ionization reaction, first-order reaction, racemization, relative rate: CH_3X > 1° RX > 2° RX.

6. What is the correct order of S_N1 reactivity for the following compounds? Assume that there is no Wagner-Meerwein transposition.

    (a) 3-iodopentane

    (b) 2-iodo-2-methylbutane

    (c) 1-iodopentane

(A) $a < c < b$

(B) $b < c < a$

(C) $c < b < a$

(D) $c < a < b$

(E) $b < a < c$

7. Which of the following best describes an E2 mechanism for substitution in alkyl halides?

(A) Concerted and bimolecular reaction, antielimination of H and X, rate of reaction: 1° RX > 2° RX > 3° RX

(B) Ionization reaction, antielimination of H and X, rate of reaction: 3° RX > 2° RX > 1° RX

(C) Concerted and bimolecular reaction, no stereospecificity, rate of reaction: 3° RX > 2° RX > 1° RX

(D) Ionization reaction, no stereospecificity, rate of reaction: 3° RX > 2° RX

(E) Concerted and bimolecular reaction, antielimination of H and X, rate of reaction: 3° RX > 2° RX > 1° RX

8. What is the correct order of stability for the following alkenes?

(a) *trans*-C$_6$H$_5$CH=CHCH$_3$

(b) *trans*-CH$_3$CH$_2$CH=CHCH$_3$

(c) *cis*-CH$_3$CH$_2$CH=CHCH$_3$

(d) CH$_3$CH$_2$CH=CH$_2$

(A) d < b < c < a

(B) c < d < b < a

(C) d < c < b < a

(D) a < b < c < d

(E) d < c < a < b

9. What is the Hofmann product of the following elimination?

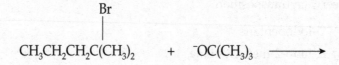

(A) CH$_3$CH$_2$CH$_2$C(CH$_3$)==CH$_2$

(B) CH$_3$CH$_2$CH==C(CH$_3$)$_2$

(C) CH$_2$==CHCH$_2$CH(CH$_3$)$_2$

(D) CH$_3$CH$_2$CH$_2$C(CH$_3$)$_2$OC(CH$_3$)$_3$

(E) None of the above

10. What would be the principle product of the following S_N1 reaction?

$$\underset{\underset{(CH_3)_2CHCHCH_2CH_2CH_3}{|}}{Br} + CH_3CH_2OH \longrightarrow$$

(A) $\underset{\underset{(CH_3)_2CHCHCH_2CH_2CH_3}{|}}{OCH_2CH_3}$

(B) $\underset{\underset{(CH_3)_2CCH_2CH_2CH_2CH_3}{|}}{OCH_2CH_3}$

(C) $\underset{\underset{(CH_3)_2CHCH_2CHCH_2CH_3}{|}}{OCH_2CH_3}$

(D) $\underset{\underset{(CH_3)_2CHCH_2CH_2CHCH_3}{|}}{OCH_2CH_3}$

(E) None of the above

11. Which of the following statements are true for the following Diels-Alder reaction?

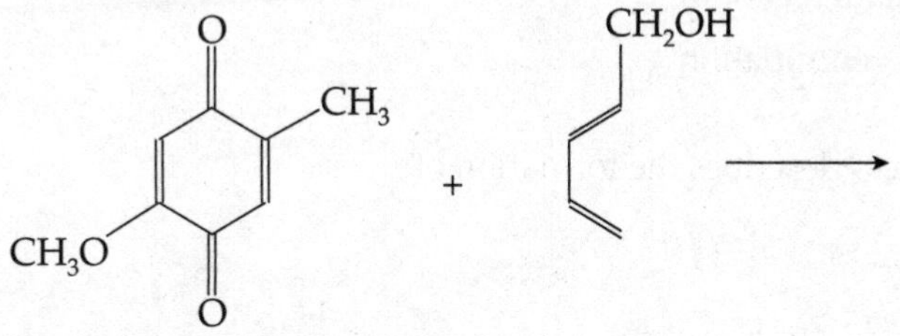

(a) The second reactant is the dienophile.

(b) The product of the reaction contains two rings.

(c) The product contains a cyclopentadiene ring.

(d) The reaction is stereospecific.

(A) a only
(B) b only
(C) d only
(D) b, c, and d
(E) b and d

12. Which of the following statements are true concerning nucleophilic aromatic substitution?

(a) Aryl halides undergo substitution in the presence of electron-withdrawing substituents on the ring.

(b) When an electron-withdrawing substituent is attached to the ring, a carbanion intermediate is observed.

(c) In the absence of electron-withdrawing substituents, a benzyne intermediate is observed.

(A) All of the above

(B) a and c

(C) b and c

(D) a and b

(E) None of the above

13. This reaction is an example of

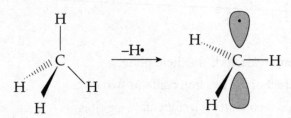

(A) Saytzeff's elimination

(B) Nucleophilic aromatic substitution

(C) Diels-Alder reaction

(D) Friedel-Crafts reaction

(E) Hofmann's elimination

14. The following process describes the formation of

(A) a carbocation

(B) a carbanion

(C) a free radical

(D) a carbene intermediate

(E) a heterolytic bond cleavage

15. To what species can the following set of characteristics be ascribed?

    (a) Heterolytic, or asymmetric, bond cleavage between a carbon atom and a less electronegative atom, such as a metal

    (b) Pyramidal, or sp^3-hybridized, ion

    (c) One sp^3 orbital contains a nonbonding pair of electrons

(A) Carbocation

(B) Carbanion

(C) Free radical

(D) Carbene intermediate

(E) A heterolytic bond rupture

16. What is the order of increasing stability for the following free radicals?

(a)

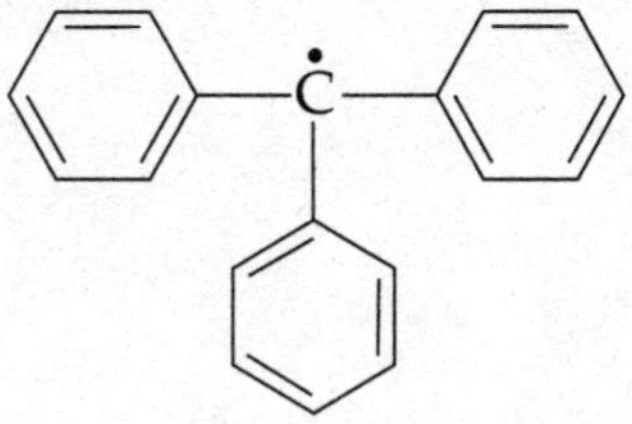

(b)

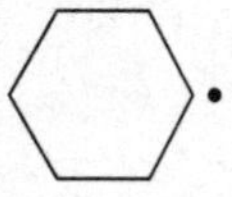

(c) 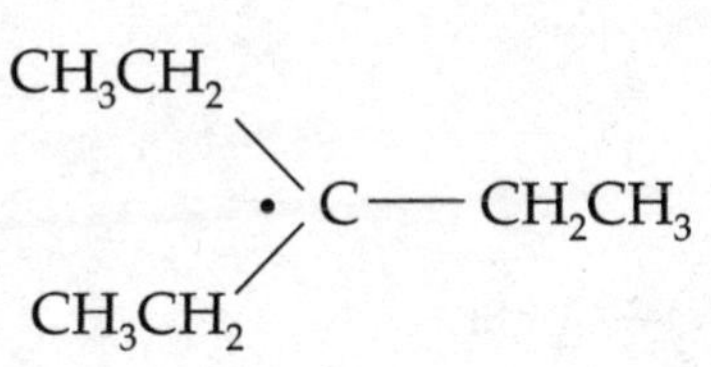 CH_3CH_2

        $\cdot C — CH_2CH_3$

    CH_3CH_2

(d)

    CH_3

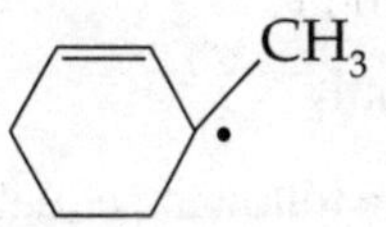

(A) c < b < d < a

(B) b < c < a < d

(C) b < a < d < c

(D) d < b < c < a

(E) b < c < d < a

17. Which of the following equations represents a propagation step?

(a) $Cl\cdot$ + $CH_2 = CH_2 \longrightarrow \cdot CH_2CH_2Cl$

(b)

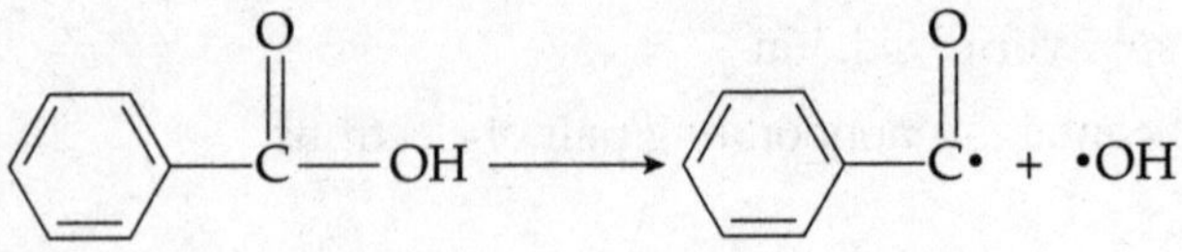

(c) $2CH_3\cdot \longrightarrow CH_3CH_3$

(d)

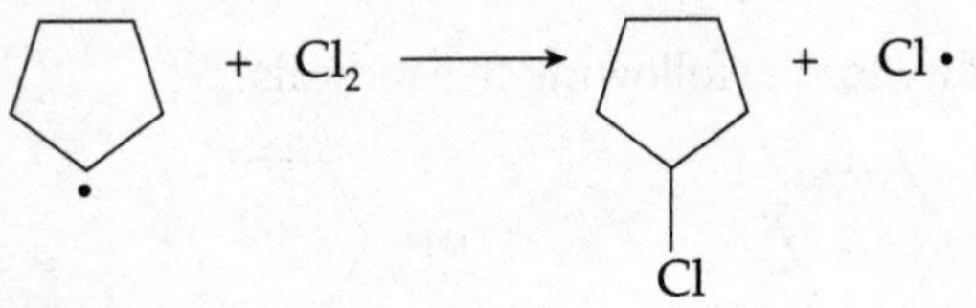

(A) a and d
(B) a only
(C) a and c
(D) b and c
(E) d only

18. Which of the following equations is not correct?

(A)

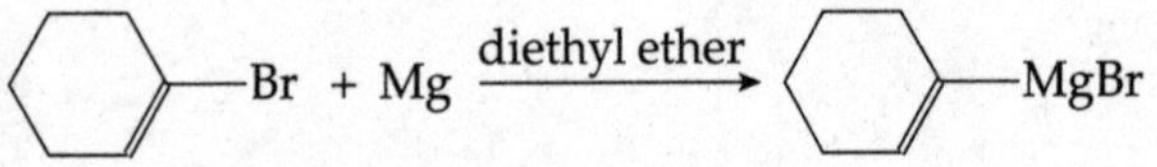

(B)

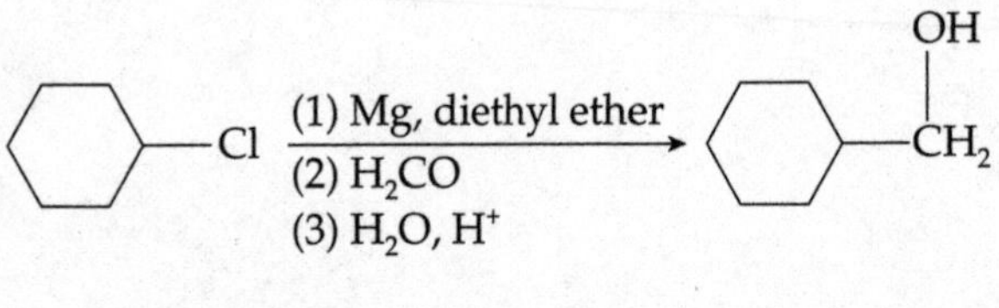

(C)

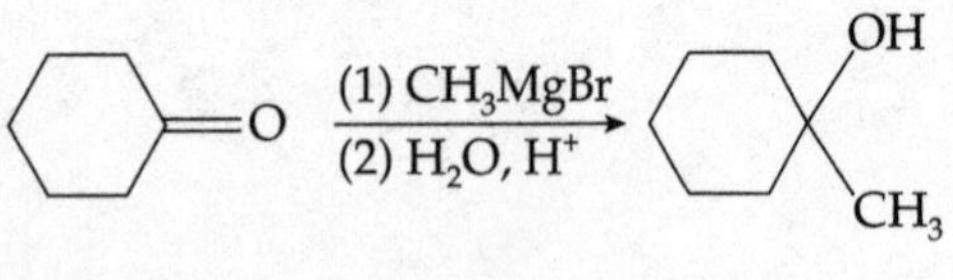

(D)

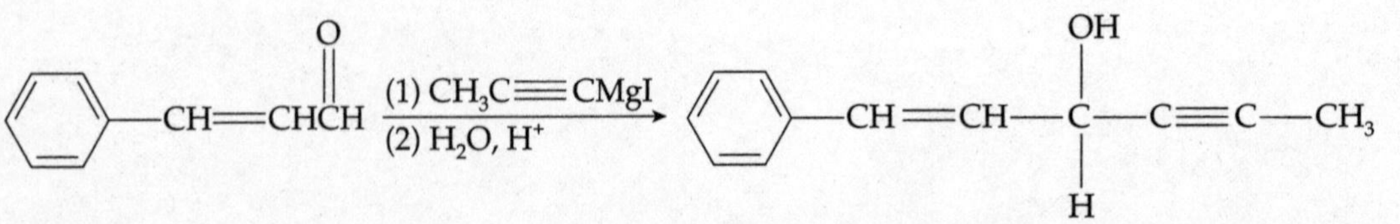

(E)

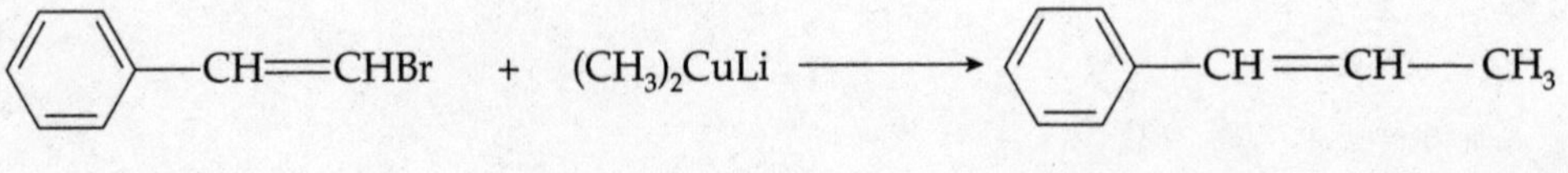

19. What is the formula of the carbonyl compound required for the following conversion?

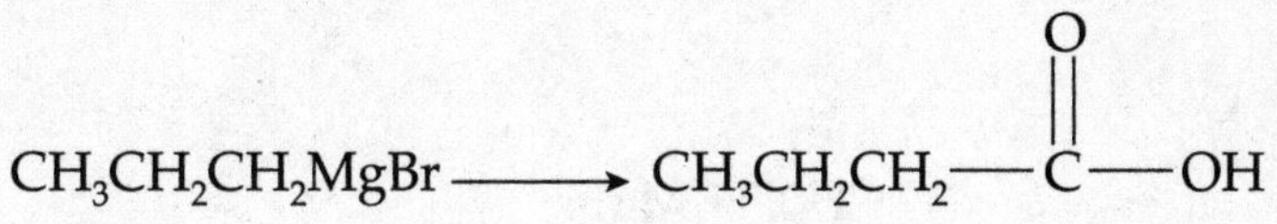

$$CH_3CH_2CH_2MgBr \longrightarrow CH_3CH_2CH_2-\overset{\displaystyle O}{\underset{\displaystyle }{C}}-OH$$

(A) CH_3COCl

(B) $HCOCH_3$

(C) $HCHO$

(D) CO_2

(E) None of the above

20. Which of the following compounds could yield a Grignard reagent?

(a) 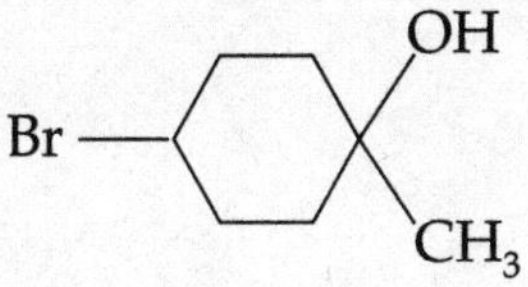 Br—[cyclohexane with OH and CH_3]

(b) 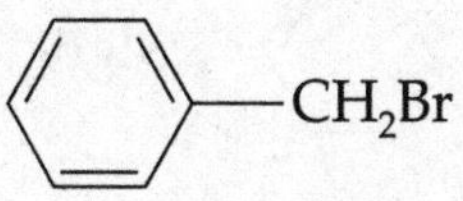 [benzene ring]—CH_2Br

(c) 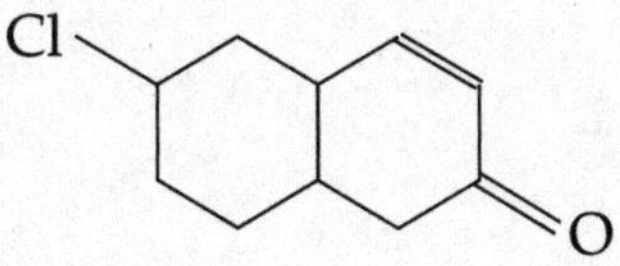 [Cl-substituted bicyclic ketone structure]

(d) $CH_3OCH_2CH_2I$

(e) 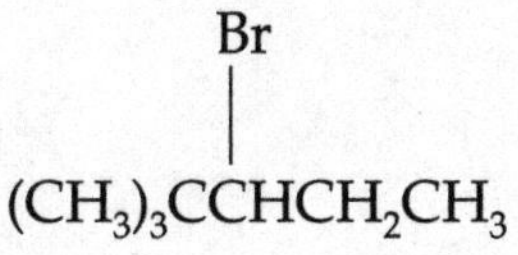 $(CH_3)_3CCHCH_2CH_3$ with Br

(f) 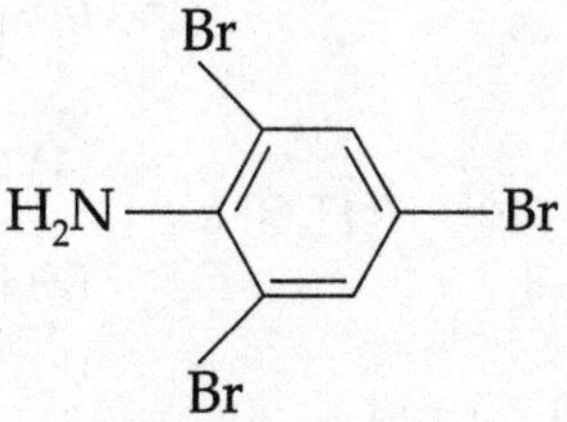 H_2N—[benzene ring with three Br]—Br

(A) b and e

(B) b, d, and e

(C) a, c, and f

(D) b, d, and f

(E) a, b, and f

21. Which of the following reactions would produce a tertiary alcohol?

(a) $CH_3C(=O)CH_2CH_3 \xrightarrow[(2)\ H_2O,\ H^+]{(1)\ CH_3CH_2MgBr}$

(b) $(CH_3)_3CMgBr \xrightarrow[(2)\ H_2O,\ H^+]{(1)\ CO_2}$

(c) 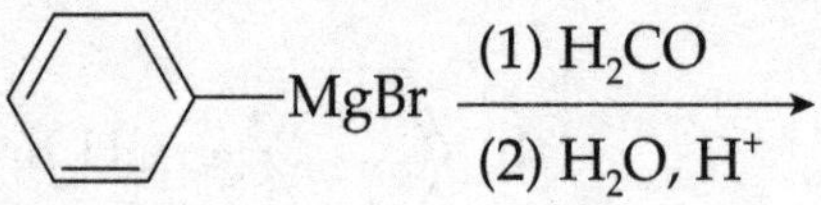

(d) 

(e) $CH_3CHO \xrightarrow[(2)\ H_2O,\ H^+]{(1)\ CH_3CH_2CH_2CH_2MgBr}$

(A) a and d
(B) c and e
(C) b only
(D) d only
(E) a only

ANSWERS TO PRACTICE PROBLEMS

1.

- (A) and (B) are enantiomers (mirror images that are not superimposable)
- (C) and (D) are also enantiomers
- (A) and (C) are diastereomers (stereoisomers that are not mirror images)
- (B) and (D) are diastereomers
- (A) and (D) are diastereomers
- (B) and (C) are diasteroemers

2. **C** The number 2 in S_N2 indicates that both the nucleophile and the substrate are involved in the transition state. The process is therefore bimolecular. In all substitution and elimination reactions, the bonds are broken heterolytically. Carbocation intermediates are involved only in S_N1 and E1 reactions.

3. **A** I is the leaving group. The nucleophile attacks the carbon atom on the opposite side of the leaving group, and the reaction proceeds with inversion of configuration. The transition state is shown below:

4. **E** Here you should consider the steric hindrance. As the number of substituents increases, the transition state becomes increasingly crowded, and the rate of reaction decreases. Therefore, the order of the increasing rate of the S_N2 reaction is $Me > 1° > 2° > 3°$.

5. **A** The rate-determining step in an S_N1 reaction is ionization of the tertiary or secondary halide to form a carbocation. The reaction is therefore unimolecular. The 1 means that the rate-determining step is first order.

6. **D** S_N1 reactivity follows the order of carbocation stability. The order of increasing stability is $3° > 2° > 1° > Me$.

7. **E** In the transition state of an E2 reaction, the attacking base and the leaving group want to be as far apart as possible. This *anti* positioning of H and X determines the stereochemistry of the alkene intermediate. Saytzeff's rule applies: The more highly substituted alkenes are more stable than less substituted ones.

8. **C** The stability of an alkene depends upon the number of substituents on the double bond; the most stable alkene is the most substituted. Alkene (c) is less stable than alkene (b) because of steric hindrance. Alkene (a) is the most stable because the double bond is conjugated with the benzene ring.

9. **A**   Hoffman's rule states that the less substituted alkene will predominate, and (A) represents the least substituted alkene. Here, the bulky *t*-butoxide ion preferentially attacks the least sterically hindered hydrogen atom.

10. **B**   One could expect this alkyl halide to form a secondary carbocation, which would yield product (A). However, this carbocation will undergo a 1,2-shift to form a more stable tertiary carbocation. So product (A) is the normal product, product (B) is the rearrangement product, and the rearrangement product predominates.

11. **E**   A Diels-Alder reaction occurs between a conjugated diene (the second reactant above) and a dienophile. The product always contains one more ring than was present in the reactants. The Diels-Alder reaction is stereospecific.

12. **A**   Aryl halides do not undergo substitution reactions as readily as alkyl halides do. Electron-withdrawing substituents such as nitro groups on the ring are required. When such groups are present, carbanions occur; when they are not present, benzyne intermediates result.

13. **D**   The Friedel-Crafts reaction is an example of electrophilic aromatic substitution. In the first step of the reaction, a carbocation is generated by reaction of the alkyl halide with aluminum trichloride. The second step is electrophilic attack on benzene to form the alkylbenzene.

14. **C**   The process illustrates a homolytic C–H bond cleavage, which results in the formation of a free radical. The intermediate is neutral and planar, and the unpaired electron in a *p* orbital is perpendicular to the plane of the atoms.

15. **B**   Carbanions are formed after heterolytic cleavage of a bond between a carbon and a less electronegative atom. The resulting carbon has one additional electron, and it is therefore negatively charged.

16. **E**   The order of stability of free radicals is methyl < primary < secondary < tertiary. Therefore, (b) is less stable than (c). Free radicals (a) and (d), though secondary, are stabilized by resonance and are more stable than (c).

17. **A**   (a) and (d) describe propagation steps of free-radical reactions, in which an alkyl free radical is generated.

18. **B**   In the first step of this reaction, a Grignard reagent is formed, and it should then react with formaldehyde to form a primary alcohol:

19. **D**   The reaction of a Grignard reagent with a ketone yields a tertiary alcohol, the reaction of a Grignard reagent with an aldehyde yields a secondary alcohol, and a Grignard reagent plus formaldehyde yields a primary alcohol, whereas a Grignard reagent plus CO_2 yields a carboxylic acid.

20. **B**   Compounds (a), (c), and (f) contain a functional group that would react with the Grignard reagent as soon as it is formed.

21. **A**   A Grignard reagent reacts with a ketone to produce a tertiary alcohol.

4

Physical Chemistry

Physical chemistry is the study of changes in energy and entropy and the rate of change of nonequilibrated systems. We will cover four topics under this heading: *Thermodynamics, Solution Dynamics, Kinetics*, and *Quantum Mechanics.*

THERMODYNAMICS

Thermodynamics deals with systems and their surroundings. It is the study of the transformations of various kinds of energies and the exchange of energy between systems and their surroundings. Nine topics are covered under this heading: *the first, second, and third laws of thermodynamics; ideal and real gases and solutions; thermochemistry; Gibbs and Helmholtz energies; chemical potential; chemical equilibria; phase equilibria; colligative properties;* and *statistical thermodynamics.*

SOME DEFINITIONS

Units and Constants

Pressure *(P):* $1 \text{ Pa} = 1 \text{ kg m}^{-1} \text{ s}^{-2}$
$1 \text{ atm} = 760 \text{ mmHg} = 101{,}325 \text{ Pa} = 1.01325 \text{ bars}$

Volume *(V):* $1 \text{ L} = 1{,}000 \text{ mL} = 10^3 \text{ mL}$
$1 \text{ m}^3 = 10^6 \text{ cc} = 1{,}000 \text{ L}$

Energy *(E, U):* $1 \text{ J} = 1 \text{ kg m}^2 \text{ s}^{-2} = 1 \text{ N m}$
$1 \text{ erg} = 10^{-7} \text{ J}$
$1 \text{ cal} = 4.184 \text{ J}$

Force *(F):* $1 \text{ N} = 1 \text{ kg m s}^{-2}$

Gas constant: $R = 1.987 \text{ cal K}^{-1} \text{ mol}^{-1} = 0.08206 \text{ L atm K}^{-1} \text{ mol}^{-1}$

System and Surroundings

- **System:** A system is any part of the universe, any object, and any quantity of matter. The systems of interest are *finite* and *macroscopic*, rather than microscopic: only *state properties*, i.e., measurable variables, are considered thermodynamic parameters. The detailed structure of matter is not taken into account.

- **Surroundings:** This includes everything around the system.

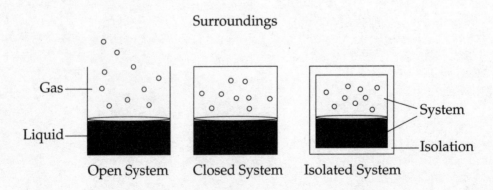

- **Boundary:** The boundary of a system is what encloses a system, setting it apart from its surroundings. This is an imaginary construct, which serves either to (a) completely isolate the system from its surroundings or (b) allow interactions between the system and its surroundings. Two types of transfer can occur between a system and its surroundings: (1) energy transfer and (2) matter transfer through the movement of particles (across the boundary between the system and its surroundings).

- **Types of systems:** Three types of systems can be defined on the basis of these two types of transfer: (1) **isolated systems**, in which no exchange of energy or matter occurs across boundaries; (2) **closed systems**, in which there is an exchange of energy, but not of matter; and (3) **open systems**, in which there is an exchange of both energy and matter.

State Properties

The state of a system in equilibrium is defined by a set of thermodynamic parameters called **state properties** or state variables. *A state property defines the state of the system.* These properties are interrelated; if one varies, at least one other property also varies. State properties are measurable; some include:

- Temperature *(T)*
- Volume *(V)*
- Pressure *(P)*
- Internal energy *(U)*
- Enthalpy *(H)*
- Entropy *(S)*

A state property does not depend on the path taken by a system as it changes states:

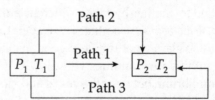

When thermodynamic quantities are path-dependent, as are heat *(Q)* and work *(W)*, they are not considered state properties. This is because the differentials of all state properties must be *exact*, such as dV in the case of volume, which remains the same for all processes occurring between the different states reached by a system. So a quantity whose differential is not exact is not a state property. Heat and work are then called *path functions*, because the quantities Q and W are different for different processes; i.e., dQ or dW are *inexact* differentials.

Intensive and Extensive Properties

Properties of a system can be either extensive or intensive.

Extensive properties—or capacity factors—depend on the amount of matter present in terms of mass. Examples are the total volume or the total energy of a system. They are equal to the sum of the parts; i.e., they are additive.

Intensive properties—or intensity factors—do not depend on the quantity of material present. Examples include temperature, molar volume, density, pressure, viscosity, refractive index, etc. At equilibrium, they are the same for every part of the system; i.e., they are not additive.

The equation that relates the thermodynamic properties of a system in a state of equilibrium is called an **equation of state**. The simplest equation of state is that for an ideal gas: $PV = nRT$, where n is the number of moles and R is the gas constant ($R = 8.3143 \text{ JK}^{-1}\text{mol}^{-1}$).

Equilibrium Systems and Thermodynamic Processes

A system is in a **state of equilibrium** when its properties do not vary with time. This implies the following conditions:

A Thermal equilibrium (T is the same everywhere in the system)

B Mechanical equilibrium (P is the same everywhere in the system)

C Chemical equilibrium (the chemical composition of the system does not vary)

When a closed system is displaced from equilibrium, it undergoes a process during which its properties change until a new state of equilibrium is reached. This process can be **isobaric** (occurring at constant pressure), **isochoric** (occurring at constant volume), **isothermal** (occurring at constant temperature), **adiabatic** (occurring with no exchange of heat between the system and its surroundings), or **cyclic** (initial state = final state).

> *Constant P = isobaric, constant T = isothermal, and constant V = isochoric. If no heat flows in or out of the system, $Q = 0$, and the conditions are adiabatic.*

In addition to this, a process is **reversible** if its direction can be reversed at any point by a change in external conditions, or **irreversible** if its direction cannot be reversed.

ADIABATIC PROCESSES

Systems can change from one state to another by many different processes. A process is **adiabatic** if the system is enclosed by an *adiabatic boundary* so that its temperature is independent from that of its surroundings. For example, thick glass wool is a very good insulator, and a vessel wrapped in it will reach thermal equilibrium with its surroundings very slowly. If glass wool totally prevents the exchange of heat (and thermal equilibrium between the vessel and its surroundings), it is an adiabatic boundary. A system enclosed in an adiabatic boundary remains at a temperature different from that of its surroundings; it never achieves thermal equilibrium with them. So an ideal adiabatic boundary is one across which the flow of heat is zero, even though there may be different temperatures on the two sides of the boundary.

The Ideal Gas

The simplest thermodynamic system is that of the **ideal gas**. Gases are composed of molecules in random motion. If the collisions between molecules are perfectly elastic and if the molecules don't attract each other, then the gas is said to be ideal. The collisions between the molecules and the walls of their container define the pressure P of the system (P = force per unit area). The temperature T of the system is directly related to the speed of the molecules and is also directly related to the average kinetic energy of any molecule in the system. The **internal energy (U)** of the system is the sum of the energies of the constituent molecules; it is a state property of the system. In an ideal gas, the internal energy depends only on the temperature and the number of particles; it does not depend on the volume occupied by the gas. The following equations describe the behavior of an ideal gas at all temperatures and pressures:

$$PV = nRT$$

$$U = U(T)$$

But no real gas *exactly* satisfies these equations.

The van der Waals Equation

Real gases have a more complicated equation of state because intermolecular interactions must be taken into account; molecules in a real gas attract each other. The equation for real gases is the modified ideal gas law, or the **van der Waals equation**:

$$\left(P + \frac{an^2}{V^2} \right)(V - nb) = nRT$$

where a is a constant that accounts for the force of interactions between gas particles and b is another constant, which accounts for the excluded volume.

Work and Heat

$$\Delta U = Q + W$$

expresses the relationship between heat and work, where ΔU is the change in internal energy, Q is heat, and W is work. We can come to an understanding of W from the following example:

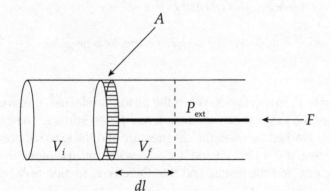

A = cross-sectional area of piston
dl = distance travelled by piston
P_{ext} = external pressure
F = force applied

$$\boxed{W = -P_{ext}(V_f - V_i)}$$

Given the piston in the above illustration, we can write:

$$W = F_{ext} \times dl$$

or

$$W = P_{ext} \times A \times dl = P_{ext} \times dV$$

Then the work done by this system as the piston moves from V_i to V_f is:

$$W = -\int P_{ext}\, dV$$

$$W = -P_{ext} \int dV$$

$$W = -P_{ext} \mid dV$$

$$W = -P_{ext}\,(V_f) - (-P_{ext}\,V_i)$$

and

$$W = -P_{ext}\,(V_f - V_i)$$

The exchange of energy can occur through heat or work. **Heat (Q)** is thermal energy that flows from a hot body to a cold one. When hot and cold bodies are in contact, a transfer of thermal energy takes place until a state of thermal equilibrium is achieved.

When energy is added as heat to a system, it is stored as kinetic and potential energy by the molecules of the system. The units of heat (a form of energy) are joules (*J*).

Work (W) involves the movement of matter from one place to another. Examples of work include pressure-volume *(PV)* work (which involves the expansion and compression of gases) and electrical or mechanical work. In thermodynamics, work always involves the exchange of energy between a system and its surroundings. **Mechanical work** occurs when a force, acting on a system, moves through a distance, as illustrated in the previous piston example.

If heat (Q) is added to a system, Q is positive. If heat (Q) is removed from a system, Q is negative.

If work (W) is done on a system, W is positive. If work (W) is done by a system, W is negative.

Example:

A gas is confined by a piston to a volume V_1 in a cylinder. When the piston is released, it moves outward because of the internal pressure of the gas that acts on the internal piston surface. The gas expands to a volume V_2 until equilibrium is reached between the gas pressure and the external pressure *P*. Calculate the work done by the system, if $P = 130$ kPa and if $V_2 - V_1 = 0.01$ m^3, assuming that the system is made up of the cylinder, the gas, and the piston, and that there is no friction between the cylinder and the piston.

Solution:

First, you should recognize that work is done *by* the system *on* the surroundings, which means that W is negative. Next, 1 kPa = 1 N • m^{-2} and 1 J = 1 N • m.

So $W = P\Delta V = (130$ kPa$)(0.01$ m$^3) = 1.30$ kN • m^{-2} • m^3 – 1.30 kJ. (Notice that work and energy have the same units.)

THE FIRST LAW OF THERMODYNAMICS

The first law of thermodynamics states that even though energy can be exchanged between a system and its surroundings, it remains constant.

> *The total energy of a system and its surroundings is always constant.*

Heat and work are both means by which the energy of a system can be changed. They are also measurable quantities. If a closed system is allowed to exchange only heat and work with its surroundings, the first law of thermodynamics can be written as follows:

$$U = Q - W$$

where U is the **total internal energy** of the system, Q is the heat added to the system, and W is the work done by the system. U is independent of the path taken by the system from its initial to its final state.

If the process is **adiabatic**—that is, if there is no exchange of heat between the system and its surroundings ($Q = 0$)—we can write $\Delta U = -W$.

Note that U is a system property, and its value depends on the state of the system. So a process that changes the system also changes U. Therefore, the integration of dU gives the difference between two values of the internal energy: $\int dU$ (from U_1 to U_2) $= \Delta U$. On the other hand, Q and W are *quantities* (i.e., not state properties of the system) and depend only on the path of the process. So dQ and dW denote infinitesimal quantities, and their integration gives a finite quantity:

$$\int dQ = Q \text{ and } \int dW = W$$

Therefore, $\int dU = \int dQ - \int dW$ leads to $\Delta U = Q - W$.

Enthalpy *(H)*

Enthalpy is expressed as follows:

$$H = U + PV$$

U, H, and PV have units of energy (joules). U, P, and V are also system properties, so it follows that H is also a system property.

For any process, the change in H is:

$$\Delta H = \Delta U + \Delta(PV) = \Delta U + P\Delta V + V\Delta P$$

For a constant pressure process, the last term is zero, and the equation becomes:

$$\Delta H = \Delta U + P\Delta V$$

Heat Capacity: C_p and C_v

The effect of temperature on the energy of chemical reactions is treated in terms of heat capacities.

Heat capacity is defined as the thermal energy that must be added to raise the temperature of a system by 1°C, under specified conditions. We can calculate the heat capacity of reversible processes, for which the path is fully specified.

Heat capacity measured at constant volume (C_V) is:

$$C_V = \left(\frac{\partial Q}{\partial T} \right)_V$$

In this equation, heat capacity is a measure of the amount of heat required to increase the temperature by ∂T, when the system is heated in a reversible process at constant volume. Under this restriction, no work can be done by the system. From the mathematical definition of the first law, $dU = dQ - dW = dQ - P\Delta V$ at constant volume, $\Delta V = 0$ and $dU = dQ$. So we can write

$$C_V = \left(\frac{\partial U}{\partial T} \right)_V$$

as an alternative definition of C_V. Since U, T, and V are system properties, so is C_V.

The heat capacity measured at constant pressure (C_p) is:

$$C_P = \left(\frac{\partial Q}{\partial T} \right)_P$$

As for C_p, this is a measure of the amount of heat required to increase the temperature by ∂T when the system is heated in a reversible process at constant pressure. We know that at constant pressure, $dH = dU + P\Delta V$. We also know that $dU = dQ - dW$ and that $dW = P\Delta V$ for a reversible process. Therefore, $dH = dQ$, and we can write another expression for C_p:

$$C_P = \left(\frac{\partial H}{\partial T} \right)_P$$

which shows that C_p is also a system property. The two equations above can also be written in the following form:

$$dU = C_V dT \text{ and } dH = C_P dT$$

These two equations are always valid for an ideal gas. Since real gases approach ideal-gas behavior at low pressure, these equations provide good approximations of real-gas behavior in the $P \rightarrow 0$ limit. It can also be shown that the following relationship exists between C_p and C_V for an ideal gas:

$$C_P - C_V = R$$

where R is the gas constant. The ratio of heat capacities is often given as $\gamma = \dfrac{C_p}{C_v}$ Combining this equation with $C_P - C_V = R$, we obtain an alternate expression:

$$\frac{R}{C_V} = \gamma - 1$$

At the zero-pressure limit, real gases approach ideal behavior. If a real gas is compressed to a finite pressure while retaining ideal gas behavior, the resulting state is then called an **ideal-gas state**. Ideal-gas heat capacities (^{ig}C) are used to describe a gas such as this. These ^{ig}C values are different for different gases and are a function only of temperature. For monoatomic gases such as helium and argon, the effect of temperature on molar heat capacity (heat capacity per mol of gas) in the ideal-gas state is negligible. The heat capacities are given by:

$$^{ig}C_V = \left(\frac{3}{2} \right)R \qquad ^{ig}C_P = \left(\frac{5}{2} \right)R \qquad \gamma = 1.67$$

For diatomic gases such as H_2, O_2, and N_2, heat capacities change very slowly with temperature.

Near 20°C, the values are:

$$^{ig}C_V = \left(\frac{5}{2}\right)R \qquad ^{ig}C_P = \left(\frac{7}{2}\right)R \qquad \gamma = 1.40$$

For polyatomic gases, such as CO_2 and CH_4, heat capacity varies significantly with temperature; γ is usually less than 1.3.

THE SECOND LAW OF THERMODYNAMICS

Entropy

Entropy is a measure of the disorder of a system and, like internal energy, it is an intrinsic property. It is also related to measurable quantities that characterize the system. For a reversible process, the change in entropy is given by the expression:

$$dS = \frac{dQ}{T}$$

The second law of thermodynamics states that the entropy change of any system and its surroundings, considered as a whole, is positive and approaches zero for any reversible process.

> *The entropy of the universe tends to increase.*

Perfectly reversible processes do not exist in nature, so all natural processes result in an increase in entropy. This is expressed as follows:

$$\Delta S_{total} \geq 0$$

where S_{total} refers to $S_{system} + S_{surroundings}$.

The idea of entropy can be summarized as follows:

- The total energy of the universe is constant, but the entropy of the universe is always increasing.

- All natural processes are spontaneous, which means that they must occur with an increase in entropy.

For example, the second law can be used to show that the flow of heat between two reservoirs at temperatures T_H and T_C (where the subscripts H and C mean hot and cold) must be from the hotter to the colder body. When heat is added to or extracted from a system, the system undergoes a finite entropy change at constant temperature, and $\Delta S = \frac{dQ}{T}$. The quantity Q is the same for both the hot and cold bodies, but Q_H and Q_C have opposite signs. Heat added to one body is considered positive, and heat extracted from a body is considered negative, so $Q_H = -Q_C$.

It follows that:

$$\Delta S_H = \frac{Q_H}{T_H} = -\frac{Q_C}{T_C}, \text{ and } \Delta S_C = \frac{Q_C}{T_C}, \text{ so}$$

$$\Delta S_{total} = \Delta S_H + \Delta S_C = \frac{-Q_C}{T_H} + \frac{Q_C}{T_C} = \left[\frac{Q_C(T_H - T_C)}{T_H T_C}\right]$$

According to the second law, ΔS_{total} must be positive, therefore, $Q_C(T_H - T_C) > 0$. So Q_C must be positive and represent the heat added to the cold body. Conclusion: Heat flows from a hot body to a cold body.

The process described above is spontaneous, and the **driving force** is the difference in temperature between the two bodies.

THE THIRD LAW OF THERMODYNAMICS

The first law of thermodynamics deals with the conservation of energy and the relationship between heat and work, and the second law deals with the spontaneous occurrence of chemical or physical processes. It defines only *changes* in entropy (ΔS), not entropy itself.

Absolute entropy values are the subject of the third law of thermodynamics, which deals primarily with the behavior of matter at very low (i.e., cryogenic) temperatures. Absolute zero (0 K) cannot be attained, and this is taken as evidence for the statement that the entropies of all crystalline materials are the same at absolute zero. This was first stated as the **Nernst heat theorem** but is widely known as the third law.

The entropy S of all perfect crystalline substances is the same at absolute zero.

At 0 K, the atoms in a pure, perfect crystal are perfectly aligned and do not move. There is no entropy of mixing because the crystal is pure (contains only one element). This means that if the entropy of each element in a crystalline state is taken as zero at the absolute zero of temperature, then every substance has a positive, finite entropy.

The third law allows us to obtain absolute values for the entropy of chemical compounds by calorimetric measurements. We can obtain the difference in entropy between 0 K and T using reversible additions of heat to a heat reservoir:

$$S_T - S_0 = \int \frac{dQ}{T}$$

The integration is performed from 0 to T. If a substance in a given phase is heated from T_1 to T_2, it gains entropy according to:

$$S_2 - S_1 = \int \frac{dH}{T} = \int C_P \frac{dT}{T} = \int C_P d(\ln T)$$

Again, integration is between T_1 and T_2 and graphed with a plot of $\dfrac{C_p}{T}$ versus T or C_p versus $\ln T$, if the required C_p values have been measured. However, C_p measurements are difficult below 15 K, so extrapolation to absolute zero is necessary. From 0 K to 25°C, the system undergoes a number of phase transitions. At each transition, C_p changes abruptly. The entropy change at the transition can be calculated using $\Delta S_{trans} = \dfrac{\Delta H_{trans}}{T_{trans}}$. By adding all of the contributions to entropy from 0 K to 25°C, we can get the standard entropy at 25°C, called $S°$.

Example:

The following C_p data were obtained for Na_2SO_4 (s):

T (K)	C_p (cal deg^{-1} mol^{-1})	C_p/T (cal deg^{-1} mol^{-1})
13.74	0.171	0.01244
16.25	0.286	0.01760
20.43	0.626	0.03064
27.73	1.615	0.05824
41.11	4.346	0.10571
52.72	7.032	0.13338
68.15	10.480	0.15377
82.96	13.280	0.160017

Calculate the absolute entropy of Na_2SO_4 (s) at 95.0 K.

Solution:

$$dS = n\frac{C_p}{T}\ dt \text{ at constant } P$$

Assume you have 1 mole of substance and integrate from 0 to 95 K:

$$\int dS = \int \frac{C_p}{T}\ dt \text{ integration from 0 to 95 K}$$

But we have no data from 0 to 13.74 K, so we must break up the integral into two parts:

$$\int \frac{C_p}{T}\ dt \text{ (from 0 to 13.74 K)} + \int \frac{C_p}{T}\ dt \text{ (from 13.74 to 95 K)}$$

A plot of $\dfrac{C_p}{T}$ versus T looks like this:

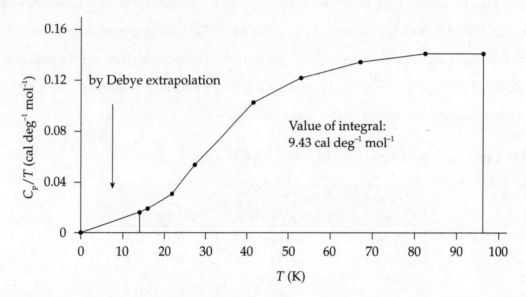

The value of the definite integral from 13.74 to 95 K corresponds to an entropy value of 9.43 cal K^{-1}. The first integral for which we have no data can be evaluated by **Debye extrapolation**:

For a solid at low T, $C_v = C_p = aT^3$.

And $\int \dfrac{C_p}{T}\, dt = \int \dfrac{aT^3}{T}\, dt = \int aT^2\, dt = \dfrac{aT^3}{3}$ from 0 to 13.74.

The lower limit is not used, so $\dfrac{a(13.74)^3}{3} = C_p$ at 13.74 K.

Using the graph, $\dfrac{a(13.74)^3}{3} = \dfrac{0.171}{3}$, since $C_p = aT^3$.

And $\dfrac{aT^3}{3}$ from 0 to 13.74 corresponds to an entropy value of 0.06 cal K^{-1}.

And $\int \dfrac{C_p}{T}\, dt$ (from 0 to 13.74 K) $+ \int \dfrac{C_p}{T}\, dt$ (from 13.74 to 95 K) equals

0.06 cal K^{-1} + 9.43 cal K^{-1} = 9.49 cal K^{-1}.

A perfect crystalline solid at 0 K has $S = 0$, so $S_0 = 0$ and $S_{95} = 9.49$ cal K^{-1} or 39.71 JK^{-1}.

Standard entropies, along with standard enthalpies, constitute the thermodynamic basis for the study of chemical equilibria and also define another important thermodynamic function, the standard Gibbs's free energy ($G°$).

IDEAL GASES AND SOLUTIONS

We saw that ideal gases were characterized by the absence of intermolecular forces and that the internal energy of an ideal gas does not depend on its volume:

$$\Delta U_T = 0 \quad \text{or} \quad \left(\frac{\partial U}{\partial V}\right)_T = 0$$

At constant temperature, a change in V also leads to a change in P; therefore $\left(\frac{\partial U}{\partial P}\right)_T = 0$. This is known as **Joule's law**, which is basically a statement that the internal energy of a perfect gas depends only on the temperature:

$$\left(\frac{\partial U}{\partial V}\right)_T = \left(\frac{\partial U}{\partial P}\right)_T = \frac{dU}{dT}$$

Ideal gases are also described by the following laws: **Gay-Lussac's law,** which states that *the volume of a given mass of gas is directly proportional to its temperature, if the pressure remains constant*. This law can be expressed as:

$$\left(\frac{V_2}{V_1}\right)_P = \left(\frac{T_2}{T_1}\right)_P$$

Boyle-Mariotte's law states that the volume of a given mass of gas varies inversely with the pressure, if the temperature remains constant:

$$\left(\frac{V_2}{V_1}\right)_T = \left(\frac{P_1}{P_2}\right)_T \quad \text{or} \quad PV = \text{constant}$$

It has been shown that for ideal gases, $C_P - C_V = R$. We know that $\gamma = \dfrac{C_P}{C_V}$; this is sometimes more conveniently expressed as $\gamma - 1 = \dfrac{R}{C_V}$. We have also shown that the adiabatic, reversible behavior of an ideal gas is expressed as $\left(\dfrac{T_2}{T_1}\right) = \left(\dfrac{V_1}{V_2}\right)^{\gamma-1}$.

Real gases show *PVT* relationships that deviate from ideal gas behavior. At high pressure, calculations performed with Clapeyron's equation *(PV = nRT)* deviate by 2–3%. Van der Waals attributed the failure of the *PV = nRT* relationship to the fact that it neglects (a) the volume occupied by the gas molecules and (b) the attractive forces among the molecules. The presence of molecules of a nonnegligible size means that a certain volume **(excluded volume)** is not available for molecules to move in. If *b* represents the excluded volume of a mole of a gas, then we can correct Clapeyron's equation to read *P(V – nb) = nRT*. Not surprisingly, the intermolecular attractions lower the mobility of each molecule. The pressure exerted by the gas is thus reduced, as if the number of molecules are effectively reduced. The second correction factor applies to pressure. Van der Waals' complete equation becomes

$\left(\dfrac{P-an^2}{V^2}\right)(V - nb) = nRT$, where a is a proportionality factor. The factors a and b are characteristic for each gas and temperature.

A solution is a homogeneous system that contains at least two constituents. It can be gaseous, liquid, or solid. The characteristics of an ideal solution are:

- $\Delta V_{mix} = 0$. An ideal solution is one in which the volume of the solution is equal to the volume of the unmixed components.

- $\Delta H_{mix} = 0$. There is no change of enthalpy in the system when the components are mixed to form a solution.

- The entropies of each component in an ideal solution are greater than the entropy of the pure, isolated materials.

A **real** solution is a solution in which the interactions between the molecules of the different components differ from the interactions between the molecules of the same components. Consider, for example, a solution of chloroform and acetone, in which dipole-dipole interactions occur: $Cl_3C–H\cdots O=C(CH_3)_2$. In this case, heat will be given off when the solution is formed, so $\Delta H_{mix} < 0$. The association between the molecules restricts their motion. This should give the system a less positive entropy than in an ideal solution.

THERMOCHEMISTRY

Thermochemistry is the application of the first law of thermodynamics to the study of chemical reactions. This subject deals with the measurement, or calculation, of the heat absorbed or released during a chemical reaction. Enthalpy is a state property. The enthalpy change of a reaction depends only on the enthalpies of the initial and final states, not on the path of the reaction. If a chemical reaction is represented by

$$\text{reactants} \rightarrow \text{products}$$

the changes in internal energy and enthalpy for the reaction are

$$\Delta U = U_{products} - U_{reactants}$$

and

$$\Delta H = H_{products} - H_{reactants}$$

If heat is absorbed during a reaction, ΔH and ΔU are positive, and the reaction is said to be endothermic. If heat is given off, ΔH and ΔU are negative, and the reaction is exothermic.

We have seen that $\Delta H = \Delta U + P\Delta V$. The difference between ΔH and ΔU is quite small if, at constant pressure, the change of volume during the reaction is slight, as is the case when solids and liquids are involved. If gases are involved, $P\Delta V$ can cause a significant difference between ΔU and ΔH. If the reaction produces a net change (Δn), the expression can be written as follows:

$$\Delta H = \Delta U + P\Delta V = \Delta U + \Delta(nRT) = \Delta U + RT\Delta n$$

Hess's Law

Hess's law states that if a reaction can be broken down into a number of steps, ΔH of the overall process is equal to the sum of the enthalpy changes of each step. This is true because H is a state property and is independent of the path.

Example:

The ΔH of the following reaction cannot be measured directly:

1. $C\ (s) + \dfrac{1}{2}O_2\ (g) \rightarrow CO\ (g)$

Use the following information to calculate ΔH of the reaction:

2. $C\ (s) + O_2\ (g) \rightarrow CO_2\ (g) + 393.5\ kJ$

3. $CO_2\ (g) + 283\ kJ \rightarrow CO\ (g) + \dfrac{1}{2}O_2\ (g)$

Solution:

Summing up equations 2 and 3 and canceling the identical terms gives:

$$C\ (s) + O_2\ (g) + CO_2(g) + 283\ kJ \rightarrow CO_2\ (g) + CO\ (g) + \dfrac{1}{2}O_2\ (g) + 393.5\ kJ$$

and

$$C\ (s) + \dfrac{1}{2}O_2\ (g) \rightarrow CO\ (g) + 103.5\ kJ$$

The result shows that heat has been released. For this reaction, we could write that $\Delta H = -103.5$ kJ.

Standard Enthalpy of Formation (ΔH°_f)

The enthalpy change of a reaction can be evaluated from the standard enthalpies of formation (ΔH°_f) of the reactants and products. The standard state is defined by 1 atm pressure and 25°C, and one in which the substance is in a stable physical state under these conditions. The enthalpy of formation of the elements in the standard state is zero. For example, $\Delta H^\circ_f\ (H_2(g)) = 0$ at 25°C. At higher temperatures, it becomes positive, and at lower temperatures it becomes negative. The standard enthalpy of formation of a compound is the enthalpy change that would occur if 1 mol of the compound were obtained directly from its elements at 1 atm and 25°C. For example, $C\ (graphite) + O_2\ (g) \rightarrow CO_2\ (g)$, $\Delta H^\circ\ (298\ K) = -393.5\ kJ$. Since the standard enthalpies of formation of C and O_2 are zero, $\Delta H^\circ_f\ (CO_2) = -393.5\ kJ$. The standard enthalpy of formation of compounds is often referred to as the **standard heat of formation**. The ΔH°_f of most compounds have been measured and recorded.

Standard Enthalpy of Reaction (ΔH°_{RX})

The standard enthalpy of a reaction, ΔH°_{RX}, is the difference in enthalpy between the products and the reactants, when both products and reactants are in their standard state at 298 K:

$$\Delta H^\circ_{RX} = \Sigma(\Delta H^\circ_f \text{ of products}) - \Sigma(\Delta H^\circ_f \text{ of reactants})$$

This equation is more useful than $\Delta H_{RX} = H_{products} - H_{reactants}$, because H cannot be measured. However, in accordance with Hess's law, we can evaluate ΔH°_{RX} through a succession of steps: first the determination of ΔH°_f of the reactants, then the determination of the ΔH°_f of the products, and finally, the determination of ΔH°_{RX}.

Example:

Calculate ΔH°_{RX} for the reaction: Fe_2O_3 (s) + 3 CO (g) $\rightarrow$ 2 Fe (s) + 3 CO_2 (g) using the following data: ΔH°_f (Fe_2O_3) = –822.2 kJ/mol, ΔH°_f (CO) = –110 kJ/mol, ΔH°_f (CO_2) = –394 kJ/mol.

Solution:

Remember that the ΔH°_f of a pure element is zero, so ΔH°_f (Fe) = 0. And using

$$\Delta H^\circ_{RX} = \Sigma(\Delta H^\circ_f \text{ of products}) - \Sigma(\Delta H^\circ_f \text{ of reactants})$$

gives us:

$$\Delta H^\circ_{RX} = 3\Delta H^\circ_f (CO_2) - [\Delta H^\circ_f (Fe_2O_3) + 3\Delta H^\circ_f (CO)] = 3(-394) - [-822.2 + (3)(110)] = 29.8 \text{ kJ/mol.}$$

Bond Dissociation Energy

Consider the reaction H–H + Cl–Cl $\rightarrow$ 2 H–Cl. The dissociation of the H–H and Cl–Cl bonds is an endothermic process that requires 436 and 242 kJ/mol, respectively. The formation of each H–Cl bond, however, is an exothermic process that releases 431 kJ/mol of energy. In this reaction, the reactants absorb 436 + 242 = 678 kJ/mol and are dissociated. When the atoms combine to form 2 HCl molecules, $2 \times 431 = 862$ kJ of energy is liberated. ΔH_R for this reaction is the difference between the energy absorbed by the reactants and the energy liberated by the formation of the products.

$$\Delta H_{RX} = \Sigma\Delta H(\text{bond enthalpies of reactants}) - \Delta H(\text{bond enthalpies of products})$$

Here, $\Delta H_{RX} = 678 - 862 = -184$ kJ for 2 mols of HCl, or $\Delta H_{RX} = -92$ kJ/mol. The bond enthalpy is the average energy required to break a particular bond in one mole of gaseous molecules. For example, Cl_2 (g) $\rightarrow$ 2 Cl (g), $\Delta H_{RX} = +242$ kJ/mol.

GIBBS AND HELMHOLTZ ENERGIES

Change in enthalpy and entropy are only two factors that affect the spontaneity of a chemical reaction. The Gibbs free energy or molar free enthalpy (G) combines these two thermodynamic factors:

$$G = H - TS$$

For a process that occurs at constant temperature, the variation in free energy is given by:

$$\Delta G = \Delta H - T\,\Delta S$$

Since H and S are state properties, G is also a state property. This fact allows us to study the influence of temperature on the spontaneity of a given process.

- If $\Delta G < 0$, then the reaction is spontaneous.
- If $\Delta G > 0$, then the reaction is not spontaneous.
- If $\Delta G = 0$, then the system is in a state of equilibrium.

Let's examine a reaction in which the entropy of the system decreases. This means that the final term, $-T\Delta S$, will be positive. The reaction is spontaneous only if ΔH is negative and large enough to overcome $-T\Delta S$. If we want to convert the energy of the reaction to work, enough energy must be left as ΔH to be delivered to the surroundings after $-T\Delta S$ has been accounted for. Only energy in excess of $-T\Delta S$ is available for work. The free energy is a measure of the work that can be done by the system after the entropy demand has been supplied by ΔH. This is the meaning of the word *free* in free energy. The effect of temperature on spontaneity can be summarized as follows:

- $\Delta S > 0$ and $\Delta H < 0$ spontaneous at all temperatures
- $\Delta S > 0$ and $\Delta H > 0$ spontaneous at high temperatures
- $\Delta S < 0$ and $\Delta H < 0$ spontaneous at low temperatures
- $\Delta S < 0$ and $\Delta H > 0$ nonspontaneous at any temperature

The Gibbs free energy applies to constant pressure processes. For constant volume processes, the **Helmholtz free energy (A)** is used:

$$A = U - TS$$

We can define the **standard free energy ($\Delta G°$)** as the ΔG of a process occurring under standard conditions (1 atm, 25°C, and 1 M concentration). If we define $\Delta G°_f$ as the $\Delta G°$ that occurs when 1 mol of a compound in its standard state is formed from its elements (also in their standard states), then we can write:

$$\Delta G°_{RX} = \Sigma \Delta G°_f(\text{products}) - \Sigma \Delta G°_f(\text{reactants})$$

CHEMICAL POTENTIAL

Consider a system that consists of one phase but has more than one component. The chemical potential of the ith component of this system is defined as

$$\mu_i = \frac{\partial G}{\partial n_i}$$

where n_i is the number of moles of component i. Then the chemical potential is the variation in free energy of the component during an increase in its quantity, and the **chemical energy** is μdn.

Each type of energy is the product of two factors, an intensity factor (an intensive property) and a capacity factor (an extensive property):

Type of Energy	Intensity Factor	Capacity Factor
Mechanical Fdl	Force F	Displacement dl
Volumetric PdV	Pressure P	Change of volume dV
Kinetic $\frac{1}{2}v^2dm$	$\frac{v^2}{2}$	Change of mass dm
Chemical μdn	Chemical potential μ	Change of quality dn

The intensity factors are potentials, the "tension," or "driving force" of the type of energy considered. For instance, temperature is the driving force of a heat transition. When two systems with different potentials interact, equalization of the potentials takes place at the expense of the corresponding capacity factors. The chemical potential is a driving force during mass transfer.

Consider, for example, a system that consists of two phases, a and b. The chemical potentials of component i in each phase are $(\mu_i)_a$ and $(\mu_i)_b$. At constant T and P, a certain amount of i is transferred from one phase into the other. If dn_i mols of i goes from a to b, then $\Delta G_b = (\mu_i)_b dn_i$ and $\Delta G_a = (-\mu_i)_a dn_i$ and the total change in free energy is $\Delta G_{total} = [(\mu_i)_b - (-\mu_i)_a]dn_i$.

Equilibrium between the two phases is achieved when $\Delta G_{total} = 0$ or when $(\mu_i)_b = (-\mu_i)_a$.

When phase equilibrium is achieved, the chemical potential of a component is the same in both phases.

PHASE EQUILIBRIA

A phase is defined as any part of a system that's homogeneous. **Gibbs's phase rule** provides a good tool for studying heterogeneous equilibria:

$$f = c - p + 2$$

where c is the number of components in the system, p is the number of phases present, and f is the number of degrees of freedom of a system.

The number of degrees of freedom of a system is defined by the number of independent variables, such as temperature, pressure, and concentration, that may be varied without altering the number of phases in the system.

To illustrate this concept, let us consider a one-component system. From the phase rule, we know that $c = 1$ and that $f = 3 - p$.

- If $p = 1$ (the system contains one phase), $f = 2$, and the system is bivariant.

- If $p = 2$ (the system has two phases), $f = 1$, and the system is univariant.

- If $p = 3$ (three phases), $f = 0$, and the system is invariant.

Pure water is a one-component system. Water can exist in three phases: ice, liquid, and steam. Because water is a one-component system, its maximum number of degrees of freedom is two. The water system, as with any one-component system, can be represented by a two-dimensional diagram. The most convenient variables to plot are P and T:

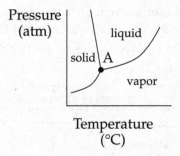

There are three areas, each of which represents a single phase. In these single-phase areas, the system is bivariant: P and T can be modified independently without altering the number of phases. The dividing lines between areas describe the conditions at which equilibrium exists. Along the lines, the system is univariant and has only one degree of freedom: For a given temperature, there is only one pressure at which two phases may coexist. The curves intersect at point A, a point at which all three phases are simultaneously at equilibrium called the **triple point**. At A, the system is invariant; there are no degrees of freedom, and neither P nor T can be altered without causing the disappearance of one of the phases.

COLLIGATIVE PROPERTIES

The presence of nonvolatile particles dissolved in a solvent can cause the physical properties of the solution, such as boiling point and freezing point, to differ from those of the solvent because the presence of a nonvolatile solute reduces the number of solvent particles per unit volume. The physical properties of dilute solutions that depend only on the number of molecules in solution, not on their chemical nature, are called **colligative properties**. The three most important colligative properties are freezing point depression, boiling point elevation, and osmotic pressure depression.

Raoult's law says that when a solute is added to a pure solvent, the vapor pressure above the solvent decreases. This is expressed as:

$$P_1 = i x_1 P_1^0$$

where P_1 = vapor pressure of the solvent with added solvent, x_2 = mole fraction of solvent, P_1^0 = vapor pressure of the pure solvent, and i = # of moles after the solution/#of moles before solution. This is a linear equation, so a graph of P_1 vs. x_1 gives a straight line with an elevation equivalent to $P^0_{solvent}$.

The presence of a solute modifies the freezing and boiling points of a solvent. The phase diagram of a solution when a nonvolatile solute is added looks like this:

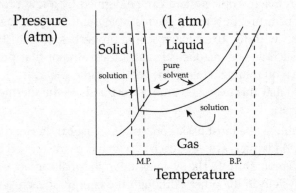

The phase diagram of the solution is generally displaced lower than that of the pure solvent.

The **freezing point depression (ΔT_f)** is given by:

$$\Delta T_f = K_f \times m_{solute} \times i$$

where K_f is a constant characteristic of the solvent, called the molal cryoscopic constant, and m_{solute} is the molality of the solute (mol solute/kg of solvent).

The ionizability factor, i, takes into account how many individual particles each solute molecule forms in solution. For example:

$$C_6H_{12}O_6(s) \xrightarrow{H_2O} C_6H_{12}O_6(aq) \quad i = 1$$
$$NaCl(s) \xrightarrow{H_2O} Na^+(aq) + Cl^-(aq) \quad i = 2$$
$$Ca(NO_3)_2(s) \xrightarrow{H_2O} Ca^{2+}(aq) + 2NO_3^- \quad i = 3$$

The **boiling point elevation (ΔT_b)** is given by:

$$\Delta T_b = K_b \times m_{solute} \times i$$

where K_b is a constant characteristic of the solvent, called the molal ebullioscopic constant, and m_{solute} is the molality of the solute.

The **osmotic pressure (π)**, defined as the pressure required to stop the migration of a solute across a semipermeable membrane, is the third colligative property:

$$\pi = CRT$$

where C is the concentration of the solution and T is the temperature in K. This equation shows that as C increases, so does osmotic pressure.

STATISTICAL THERMODYNAMICS

Statistical mechanics attempts to predict the probable behavior of a large collection (called an "ensemble") of molecules. Ensembles are characterized by specific macroscopic properties, such as volume, potential energy, pressure, and temperature. The individual molecules in an ensemble are distributed over a range of microscopic states, so they differ from each other. Instead of trying to precisely define the states of the constituent molecules of an ensemble, statistical mechanics describes their most probable states in an attempt to arrive at a good description of their macroscopic properties.

Statistical thermodynamics uses the distribution laws of statistical mechanics to calculate and predict the energies and molecular velocities of ensembles of molecules, as well as their most probable energies and velocities. A macroscopic system can be defined by a few properties, such as volume, pressure, density, or temperature. But from a microscopic point of view, there are a great number of quantum states consistent with the fixed macroscopic properties. In statistical thermodynamics, to calculate any property, such as energy, one calculates the value of that property in each quantum state. Supposing that each quantum state has the same weight, the average value of the property is taken. Then we postulate that this average value corresponds to the thermodynamic property from a macroscopic point of view.

The **canonical ensemble** is the most basic concept of statistical thermodynamics. A canonical ensemble is an assembly of A identical systems, each of which is characterized by its number of systems N, its volume V, and its temperature T. The systems are in thermal contact with each other, so energy can circulate from one system to the other. Although the energy of each system varies, the average energy is known. If we consider an ensemble of A systems in which A_i systems are distributed between macroscopic states (the states of the system defined by macroscopic quantities such as T, V, etc.) of energy E_i, then the probability of finding a system in a state of energy E_i is given by:

$$P_i = \frac{A_i}{A} = G_i \cdot \exp \frac{\left(\dfrac{-E_i}{KT}\right)}{\sum G_i} \cdot \exp\left(\frac{-E_i}{KT}\right)$$

where G_i is the degeneracy of the state E_i. The denominator of this equation is called the **canonical partition function (Z_c)** of the system:

$$Z_c(N, T, V) = \sum G_I \cdot \exp\left(\frac{-E_i}{KT}\right)$$

This distribution law can be compared with the **Boltzman distribution**: For an isolated system with N particles that can occupy various energy levels e_i with degeneracy g_i, the distribution is:

$$P_i = \frac{A_i}{A} = g_i \cdot \exp \frac{\left(\dfrac{-e_i}{KT}\right)}{\sum g_i} \cdot \exp\left(\frac{-e_i}{KT}\right)$$

The denominator of this equation is the **partition function (Z)** of the particle:

$$Z(T, V) = \sum g_i \cdot \exp\left(\frac{-e_i}{KT}\right)$$

The partition function is the bridge between the quantum mechanical energy states of a macroscopic state and the thermodynamic properties of the system. These properties can be expressed as a function of the partition function. For the canonical ensemble, examples include:

$$U = KT^2 \left(\frac{\partial \ln Z}{\partial T} \right)_{N,V}$$

$$P = KT \left(\frac{\partial \ln Z}{\partial V} \right)_{N,T}$$

$$S = KT \left(\frac{\partial \ln Z}{\partial T} \right)_{N,V} + K \ln Z$$

Since the Helmholtz energy is $A = U - TS$, we can also write:

$$A = -KT \ln Z(N, V, T)$$

Statistical thermodynamics also uses other ensembles, for example, the **microcanonical ensemble**, in which N, V, and U are fixed, and **the isothermal-isobaric ensemble**, in which N, T, and P are fixed. Each ensemble leads to a particular partition function, and each partition function leads to characteristic thermodynamic functions. In the isothermal-isobaric ensemble, the partition function is $\Delta(N, T, P)$, and a characteristic thermodynamic function is the Gibbs's free energy:

$$G = -KT \ln \Delta(N, T, P)$$

For the microcanonical ensemble (used to describe isolated systems) the partition function, called $\Omega(N, V, E)$, can be related to the entropy of the system:

$$S = K \ln \Omega(N, V, U)$$

The partition function is a summation over all possible quantum states. Therefore, this last equation shows that, for an isolated system, the entropy is proportional to the logarithm of the number of states available to the system.

SOLUTION DYNAMICS

We call those processes that bring a system out of equilibrium **transport processes**, because matter or energy is transported to the surroundings or to another part of the system. When unequilibrated forces exist in a liquid, they disrupt the state of mechanical equilibrium. **Fluid dynamics** is the study of the flow of liquids. Some aspects of fluid dynamics can be described by the study of **viscosity**, which is defined as the resistance offered by one part of a fluid to the flow of another part of the fluid. A fluid can be seen as an ensemble of superimposed layers of molecules. We can define the area of each layer as A and the distance between layers as dx. When the layers move between two plates with velocities v_1, v_2, etc., the process is called **laminar velocity**. At the boundary between the plates and the liquid, the velocity is zero. This is called the **no-slip condition**.

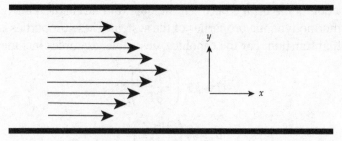

Motion of fluid between two plates

The velocities of the layers increase in the middle of the fluid and start decreasing from the middle toward the plates. Each layer velocity differs from the next one by dv. In laminar velocity, the force (F) required to maintain a constant velocity difference between two consecutive layers is directly proportional to A and inversely proportional to dx:

$$F = \eta A \left(\frac{dv}{dx} \right)$$

where η is the **viscosity coefficient**. The viscosity coefficient is the force per unit area required to move a layer of liquid with a velocity difference of 1 cm/s past a parallel layer that is 1 cm away. The viscosity coefficient is a physical quantity that is characteristic of each fluid. The viscosity of fluids is measured using either the **Poisseuille or Stokes equation**.

Poisseuille's Equation

$$\eta = \frac{\pi P t r^4}{8LV}$$

where V is the volume of the liquid; t is the time required for this volume to flow through a capillary tube of radius r, length L; and P is the pressure at the start of the process. The viscosity of a liquid is determined by comparison with a reference liquid, usually water. The ratio of the viscosity coefficients of the two liquids is:

$$\frac{\eta_1}{\eta_2} = \left(\frac{\pi P_1 r^4 t_1}{8LV} \right)\left(\frac{8LV}{\pi P_2 r^4 t_2} \right) = \frac{P_1 t_1}{P_2 t_2} = \frac{\rho_1 t_1}{\rho_2 t_2}$$

where P_1 and P_2 are proportional to ρ_1 and ρ_2, the densities of the liquids. When ρ_1, ρ_2, and η_2 are known, the viscosity coefficient η_1 of the liquid can be determined.

Stokes's Equation

Stokes's law describes the fall of a spherical body of radius r and density ρ, falling by gravity through a fluid of density ρ_1. Stokes's equation is:

$$F_1 = \left(\frac{4}{3} \right) \pi r^3 (\rho - \rho_1) g$$

where F_1 is the force acting on the spherical body and g is the acceleration due to gravity. This force F_1 is opposed by a frictional force due to the medium, which increases as the velocity of the falling sphere increases. When a uniform rate of fall is reached, the frictional force becomes equal to the gravitational force F_1. Stokes showed that F_2, the force due to friction, is

$$F_2 = 6\pi r \eta v$$

where v is the velocity of the falling sphere, once it has become constant. When the gravitational and frictional forces are equal, $6\pi r \eta v = \left(\dfrac{4}{3}\right) \pi r^3 (\rho - \rho_1) g$, and

$$\eta = \frac{\left[2r^2 \left(\rho - \rho_1\right) g\right]}{9v}$$

Stokes's equation is valid as long as the radius of the falling sphere is larger than the distance that separates the molecules of the fluid. **Fluidity** is a term often used in connection with viscosity. The fluidity of a substance ϕ is the reciprocal of the viscosity: $\phi = \dfrac{1}{\eta}$.

KINETICS

CHEMICAL DYNAMICS

Thermodynamics can be used to predict which processes will occur spontaneously, but it cannot predict the rate at which these processes occur. This is the subject of kinetics. Three topics are covered under this heading: experimental and theoretical chemical kinetics, fluid dynamics, and photochemistry.

EXPERIMENTAL AND THEORETICAL CHEMICAL KINETICS

Chemical kinetics is the study of the rates and mechanisms of chemical reactions. The hydrolysis of ATP to yield ADP and phosphate is a thermodynamically favorable reaction with $\Delta G^\circ = -30.5$ kJ mol^{-1} at 298 K and pH 7. But a solution of ATP at pH 7 and 298 K remains stable. How can this be explained?

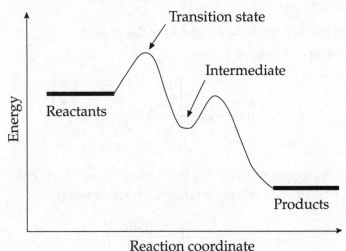

The energy profile shown above provides a clue. If we define the reaction coordinate (x-axis) as the length of the P–O bond that needs to be broken in ATP for the reaction to proceed, we know that the cleavage of this bond requires a lot of energy, and therefore that the reaction proceeds uphill to the transition state or, in other words, there is a high energy barrier, which accounts for the stability of ATP.

The maximum of the energy profile curve is called the **transition state**, and if a minimum occurs in the curve as the reaction proceeds to the reactants, it is called an **intermediate**. The **activation energy** is the difference between the energy of the reactants and that of the transition state (or activated complex).

The Reaction Rate

A **homogeneous** reaction occurs in one phase, and a **heterogenous** reaction occurs in more than one phase. Consider the following homogeneous reaction, which takes place in a closed system:

$$aA + bB \rightarrow cC + dD$$

A, B, C, and D represent different chemical substances, and a, b, c, and d are the stoichiometric coefficients of the balanced equation. The rate at which the reactants are consumed and the products are formed is proportional to these stoichiometric coefficients:

$$\frac{\left(\dfrac{dn_A}{dt}\right)}{\left(\dfrac{dn_B}{dt}\right)} = \frac{a}{b}$$

or

$$\frac{\left(\dfrac{1}{a}\right)}{\left(\dfrac{dn_A}{dt}\right)} = \frac{\left(\dfrac{1}{b}\right)}{\left(\dfrac{dn_B}{dt}\right)},$$

where t represents the time and n the number of moles present.

The **rate of conversion** (J) is defined as:

$$J = -\left(\frac{1}{a}\right)\left(\frac{dn_A}{dt}\right) = \frac{-\left(\dfrac{1}{b}\right)}{\left(\dfrac{dn_B}{dt}\right)} = \frac{\left(\dfrac{1}{c}\right)}{\left(\dfrac{dn_C}{dt}\right)} = \frac{\left(\dfrac{1}{d}\right)}{\left(\dfrac{dn_D}{dt}\right)}$$

and since A and B are disappearing and C and D are being formed, J is positive.

The rate of conversion per unit volume is called the **reaction rate (r)**:

$$r = \frac{J}{V} = -\left(\frac{1}{aV}\right)\left(\frac{dn_A}{dt}\right)$$

If V remains constant throughout the reaction,

$$\frac{-\left(\dfrac{1}{aV}\right)}{\left(\dfrac{dn_A}{dt}\right)} = \left(-\frac{1}{a}\right)\left[\frac{d\left(\dfrac{n_A}{V}\right)}{dt}\right] = \left(-\frac{1}{a}\right)\left(\frac{dC_A}{dt}\right) = -\left(\frac{1}{a}\right)\left(\frac{d[A]}{dt}\right)$$

where $[A]$ is the molar concentration of A.

Example:

What is r for the following reaction?

$$H_2 + Br_2 \rightarrow 2\ HBr$$

Solution:

$$-\left(\frac{d[H_2]}{dt}\right) = -\left(\frac{d[Br_2]}{dt}\right) = \frac{1}{2}\left(\frac{d[HBr]}{dt}\right)$$

The Order of Reactions

The order of a reaction is the power to which the concentration of a reactant is raised. In the reaction below, x moles of A react with y moles of B to form the product P:

$$xA + yB \rightarrow P$$

If the rate of formation of P is $\dfrac{d[P]}{dt}$, then an expression for r can be written as follows:

$$r = \frac{d[P]}{dt} = k[A]^a[B]^b$$

Such an expression is a **rate law** and is expressed as a function of the reactant concentrations, set in square brackets, at constant temperature. The exponents a and b are usually integers, and k is the **rate constant**. The above reaction is then of ath order in A, of bth order in B, and the overall order is $(a + b)$. The exponents a and b are the **partial orders**. The sum of the partial orders is the **total order** n. The exponents in the rate law can differ from the stoichiometric coefficients of the balanced equation. Therefore, rate laws cannot be derived from the stoichiometry of the overall reaction; they must be determined experimentally.

First-Order Reactions

For a first-order reaction of the type

$$aA \rightarrow products$$

the rate law expression is:

$$r = -\left(\frac{1}{a}\right)\left(\frac{d[A]}{dt}\right) = k[A]$$

If we define a rate constant for the rate of change of A, such that $k_A = a \times k$, then

$$\frac{d[A]}{dt} = -k_A[A]$$

or

$$\frac{d[A]}{[A]} = -k_A dt$$

To solve this differential equation, we integrate from state 1 to state 2 and get:

$$\frac{\int d[A]}{[A]} = -\int k_A\, dt$$

$$\ln\left(\frac{[A]_2}{[A]_1}\right) = -k_A(t_2 - t_1)$$

If state 1 is the initial state of the reaction (at $t = 0$) and if $[A] = [A]_0$, the equation becomes

$$\ln\left(\frac{[A]}{[A]_0}\right) = -k_A t$$

or

$$\ln[A] = -k_A t + \ln[A]_0$$

so,

$$[A] = [A]_0 \exp(-k_A t)$$

$[A]$ decreases exponentially for a first-order reaction, and a plot of $\ln\left(\dfrac{[A]}{[A]_0}\right)$ versus t gives a straight line with slope $-k_A$.

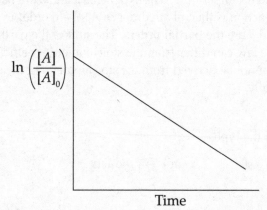

The **half-life** of the reaction is the time required for the initial concentration of the reactants to be reduced by half. So for $[A] = \dfrac{[A]_0}{2}$ and $t = t_{\frac{1}{2}}$, we get $t_{\frac{1}{2}} = \dfrac{\ln 2}{k_A}$.

Second-Order Reactions

There are two common forms of second-order rate laws:

1. For a reaction of the type aA → products, $r = k[A]^2$

   The rate law is $\dfrac{d[A]}{dt} = -k_A[A]^2$, and again $k_A = a \times K$

   It can be shown that $\left(\dfrac{1}{[A]}\right) - \left(\dfrac{1}{[A]_0}\right) = k_A t$ and that $t_{\frac{1}{2}} = \dfrac{1}{[A]_0 k_A}$.

A plot of $\dfrac{1}{[A]}$ versus t gives a straight line with slope k_A.

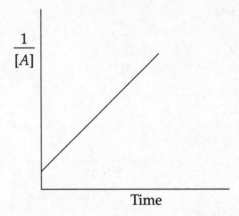

2. For a reaction of the type $aA + bB \rightarrow$ products, $r = k[A][B]$

    The rate law takes a more complicated form:

    $$\left\{\dfrac{1}{\left(a[B]_0 - b[A]_0\right)}\right\} \ln\left\{\dfrac{\left(\dfrac{[B]}{[B]_0}\right)}{\left(\dfrac{[A]}{[A]_0}\right)}\right\} = kt$$

Nth-Order Reactions

There are many nth-order rate laws. For those having the form $d[A]/dt = -kA[A]^n$, the rate law is as follows:

$$([A]/[A]_0)^{n-1} = 1 + [A]_0^{n-1}(n-1)k_A t \quad n \neq 1$$

$$t_{\frac{1}{2}} = (2^{n-1} - 1) / \{(n-1)[A]_0^{n-1} k_A\}$$

Zeroth-Order Reaction

The order of most reactions that involve only one reactant, $aA \rightarrow$ products, is either 1 or 2. A few reactions, however, are of order zero. In these cases:

$$r = -\left(\dfrac{1}{a}\right)\left(\dfrac{d[A]}{dt}\right) = k, \text{ or } \dfrac{d[A]}{dt} = -k_A$$

Integration gives the general expression:

$$[A] = -k_A t + [A]_0,$$

and

$$t_{\frac{1}{2}} = \dfrac{[A]_0}{2k_A}$$

For a zeroth-order reaction, a graph of $[A]$ versus t gives a straight line with slope $-k_A$.

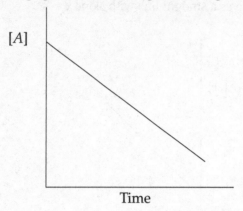

Reversible First-Order Reactions

The reaction $A \leftrightarrow B$ is first order in both the forward and reverse directions, so that $r_f = k_f[A]$ and $r_r = k_r[B]$, where the subscripts f and r mean *forward* and *reverse*, respectively. At equilibrium, the concentration of each species is constant. It can be show that:

$$k_r[B]_0 = k_f[A]_0 = (k_f + k_r)[A]_{eq}$$

This equation relates the equilibrium concentration of A to the initial concentrations of A and B. It can also be shown that the rate law equation for a reversible first-order reaction is given by:

$$[A] - [A]_{eq} = ([A]_0 - [A]_{eq})\exp\left(-\left(k_f + k_r\right)t\right)$$

Consecutive First-Order Reactions

Consider two consecutive irreversible reactions:

$$A \rightarrow B \rightarrow C$$

The rate constant of the first reaction ($A \rightarrow B$) is k_1, and that of the second reaction ($B \rightarrow C$) is k_2. So

$$[A] = [A]_0 \exp - k_1 t,$$

$$[B] = \frac{k_1}{\left(k_2 - k_1\right)}[A]_0[\exp(-k_1 t) - \exp(-k_2 t)]$$

$$[C] = [A]_0\left\{1 - \frac{k_2}{\left(k_2 - k_1\right)}\exp(-k_1 t) + \frac{k_1}{k_2 - k_1}\exp(-k_2 t)\right\}$$

Competing First-Order Reactions

Let's consider the simplest case:

$$A \rightarrow B \quad \text{and} \quad A \rightarrow C$$

with k_1 and k_2, respectively. The rate law is:

$$\frac{d[A]}{dt} = -k_1[A] - k_2[A] = -(k_1 + k_2)[A]$$

which leads to:

$$[B] = \frac{k_1}{(k_1 + k_2)}[A]_0[1 - \exp - (k_1 + k_2)t]$$

$$[C] = \frac{k_2}{(k_1 + k_2)}[A]_0[1 - \exp - (k_1 + k_2)t]$$

It is clear that $\frac{[B]}{[C]} = \frac{k_1}{k_2}$.

Reaction Mechanisms

The overall reaction stoichiometry does not necessarily yield information about the **reaction mechanism**, which is the process by which the reaction occurs.

For example, the reaction $2\,N_2O_5 \rightarrow 4\,NO_2 + O_2$ ($r = k\,[N_2O_5]$) occurs through a three-step mechanism:

Step 1:	$N_2O_5 \rightarrow NO_3 + NO_2$	$r_{step1} = k_{step1}[N_2O_5]$
Step 2:	$NO_3 + NO_2 \rightarrow NO + O_2 + NO_2$	$r_{step2} = k_{step2}[NO_3][NO_2]$
Step 3:	$NO + NO_3 \rightarrow 2\,NO_2$	$r_{step3} = k_{step3}[NO][NO_3]$

To be accepted as valid, a mechanism must satisfy two conditions:

(a) the sum of its elementary steps must be equal to the balanced equation of the overall reaction; and

(b) the mechanism must be consistent with the experimentally determined rate equation.

Here, NO_3 and NO are **reaction intermediates**: They are species that are formed in one step of the mechanism and consumed in a subsequent one. The NO produced in step 1 is consumed in step 3. For each occurrence of step 3, there must be one occurrence of step 2. However, steps 2 and 3 consume one NO_3 intermediate each. Therefore, there must be two occurrences of step 1 for each occurrence of steps 2 and 3. The overall reaction is the sum of two steps 1 + one step 2 + one step 3. The number of occurrences of a step is called the **stoichiometric number(s)** of the step; each step is called an **elementary reaction**. A **simple reaction** consists of only one elementary reaction. A **complex reaction** consists of more than one elementary reaction.

In the example above, the rate of each step can be expressed in terms of its **molecularity**, which is defined as the number of molecules that must collide for the reaction to proceed. So step 1 is unimolecular, and steps 2 and 3 are bimolecular. The individual rates of the different steps of the reaction may differ. Since the overall rate of the reaction cannot exceed the rate of the slowest step, we call the slowest step the **rate-limiting step**.

In the decomposition reaction of N_2O_5, we can determine that the limiting step is the first, because its rate equation, obtained directly from its molecularity, corresponds to the rate equation of the overall reaction, which is obtained experimentally.

Let's look at another set of reactions—this time, the decomposition of ozone. The reaction is

$$2\,O_{3\,(g)} \rightarrow 3O_{2\,(g)}, \text{ and } r = k\,[O_3]^2/[O_2]$$

and the suggested mechanism is

Step 1: $O_3 \leftrightarrow O_2 + O$ (fast), where $r_{forward} = k_1[O_3]$ and $r_{reverse} = k_{-1}[O_2][O]$

Step 2: $O + O_3 \rightarrow 2\,O_2$ (slow), where $r_2 = k_2[O][O_3]$

Step 2 is the rate-determining step, but its rate equation does not agree with the experimental rate equation for the overall reaction. Also, it contains [O], which is a reaction intermediate. But we can assume that $r_{forward} = r_{reverse}$, so

$$k_1[O_3] = k_{-1}[O_2][O]$$

and

$$[O] = \left(\frac{k_1}{k_{-1}}\right)\frac{[O_3]}{[O_2]}$$

Substituting the [O] thus obtained in the rate equation of step 2 gives us

$$r = \left(\frac{k_2 k_1}{k_{-1}}\right)\frac{[O_3]^2}{[O_2]} = \frac{k[O_3]^2}{[O_2]},$$

where $k = \dfrac{k_2 k_1}{k_{-1}}$.

Measurement of Reaction Rates

The most common method for determining rate laws is called the **initial-rate method**. In this method, the initial rate (r_0) is measured for several reaction trials of the reaction, and the initial concentration of one reactant at a time is varied. Consider for example the reaction

$$A + B \rightarrow C + D$$

Its rate law is in the form $r = k[A]^a[B]^b$, where a and b are the partial orders in A and B, respectively. We wish to determine a and b from the following data:

Experiment Trials	$[A]_{initial}$ (mol/L)	$[B]_{initial}$ (mol/L)	Initial Rate (mol/L · s)
1	0.100	0.005	1.40×10^{-6}
2	0.100	0.010	2.80×10^{-6}
3	0.200	0.010	5.60×10^{-6}

From trial 1 to trial 2, [A] is kept constant, but [B] is doubled, and as a consequence the initial rate doubles. This shows that the reaction is first order in B.

Mathematically, we obtain

$$\left(\frac{0.005}{0.010}\right)^b = \frac{1.}{2.}$$

where $\left(\frac{0.005}{0.010}\right)^b = \frac{1.40}{2.80}$, or $\left(\frac{1}{2}\right)^b = \left(\frac{1}{2}\right)^1$, and $b = 1$.

From trial 2 to trial 3, [B] is kept constant, but [A] is doubled. In this case, the initial rate of the reaction also doubles, which shows that the reaction is also first order in A:

$$\left(\frac{[A]_2}{[A]_3}\right)^a = \frac{r_2}{r_3},$$

where $\left(\frac{0.100}{0.200}\right)^a = \left(\frac{2.80}{5.60}\right)$, or $\left(\frac{1}{2}\right)^a = \left(\frac{1}{2}\right)^1$, and $a = 1$.

Therefore the order of the overall reaction is 2, and the experimental rate law is $r = k[A][B]$. The value of k can be obtained from the results of any experiment. From experiment 2,

$2.80 \cdot 10^{-6}$ mol $\cdot$ L^{-1}s^{-1} = k(0.100 mol $\cdot$ L^{-1})(0.010 mol $\cdot$ L^{-1}), where $k = 2.80 \cdot 10^{-3}$ l $\cdot$ mol^{-1} s^{-1}.

Example:

For the reaction 2 NO (g) + Cl$_2$ (g) → 2 NOCl (g), the following results were obtained:

$[NO]_0$ (mol/L)	$[Cl_2]_0$ (mol/L)	Initial Rate (mol/L $\cdot$ min)
0.20	0.20	0.35
0.20	0.40	0.70
0.40	0.40	2.80

Determine the rate equation and the value of k.

Solution:

When $[Cl_2]$ doubles and [NO] remains constant, the initial rate of the reaction doubles. So the partial rate is 1st order with respect to Cl$_2$. When [NO] doubles and [Cl$_2$] remains constant, the initial rate of reaction increases by a factor of 4. Then this partial rate is 2nd order with respect to NO.

Then the overall rate expression is $r = k[NO]^2[Cl_2]$. The value of k can be obtained from any of the four experiments; it is $k = 44$ L$^2 \cdot$ mol$^{-2} \cdot$ s^{-1}.

Collision Theory and Chemical Kinetics

The concentration dependence of a reaction rate is expressed by a rate law equation. Experiment also shows that most rate constants increase exponentially with temperature. Usually, k doubles for every 10°C temperature increase.

Collision theory states that reactants must collide to react. If temperature increases, so does the speed of the molecules and the frequency of collisions. However, the rate of a reaction is much slower than the calculated rate of collisions. This means that only a small collision percentage leads to an effective reaction. For every reaction, a threshold exists called **the activation energy**, which must be overcome for the reaction to occur. For example, in the reaction $2BrNO(g) \rightarrow 2NO(g) + Br_2(g)$, two Br–N bonds must be broken, and this requires energy. According to collision theory, this energy comes from the kinetic energy that the molecules have before colliding. This kinetic energy is transformed into potential energy, which is stored in a transition state called an **activated complex**. The Br–N bonds are broken in this activated complex and Br–Br bonds are formed. In our example, the reaction is exothermic. The rate of the reaction depends on the activation energy, not on the amount of energy liberated:

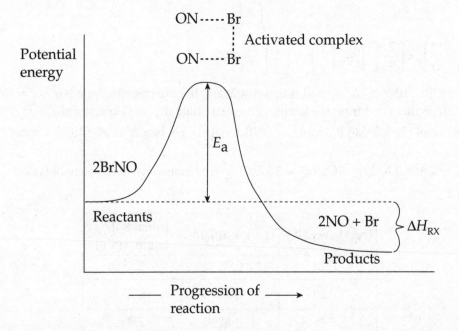

The above reaction energy profile shows that the colliding molecules must have an amount of kinetic energy at least equal to E_a. At a given temperature, only a fraction of the molecules have this required energy. The following graph shows the distribution of molecules as a function of the temperature:

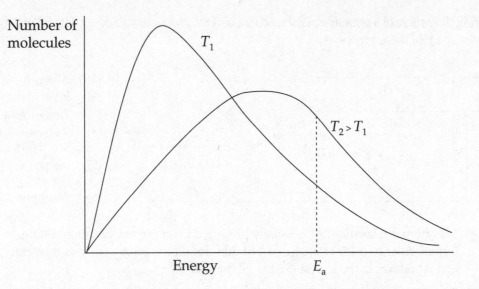

The number of molecules with energy greater than or equal to E_a at a temperature T_1 is given by the area under the curve. For $T_2 > T_1$, the area under the curve is clearly greater than for the T_1 area. Then the number of molecules that have energy greater than or equal to E_a is larger at $T_2 > T_1$ than at T_1. The number of effective collisions is also greater, and so is the reaction rate. Experiment also shows that not all collisions between molecules that have the required kinetic energy create new bonds. Only molecules that have a favorable orientation and with $E \geq E_a$ will actually lead to product formation. A favorable orientation is one that allows the new bonds to be formed.

Arrhenius's equation describes the relationship between k and E_a:

$$k = A \exp\left(\frac{-E_a}{RT}\right)$$

where k is the rate constant, R is the gas constant, T is the temperature in Kelvin, and A is a constant called the preexponential factor.

PHOTOCHEMISTRY

Photochemistry is the study of chemical reactions induced by light. In chemical or thermal reactions, the activation energy is supplied by intermolecular collisions. In photochemical reactions, energy is supplied by absorption of light. Usually, there are as many photons absorbed as there are molecules undergoing a transition to an excited state. This is known as the **Stark-Einstein law**. During a photochemical reaction, a photon may promote an electron to an excited electronic state where it is more likely to undergo a chemical reaction than in the ground state.

The absorption of energy by a molecule can be described as follows:

$$A + h\nu \rightarrow A^*$$

where A is the molecule in its ground state and A* is the molecule in an excited state. In most cases, all of the electrons of the ground state are paired. The total electronic spin (S) is zero and the multiplicity is $2S + 1 = 1$: the ground state is a singlet (S_0). In the excited states, if the unpaired electrons have opposite spins, S is also zero, and the excited states are also singlets $(S_1, S_2,$ etc.). If the unpaired electrons have identical spins, $S = 1$ and the multiplicity is 3. This is called a triplet state.

During the course of a photochemical reaction, several processes can occur. The following diagram illustrates some of these processes.

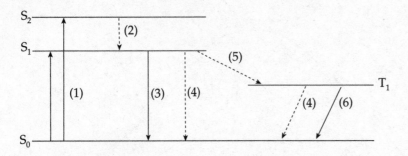

(1)	Absorption
(2)	Internal conversion
(3)	Fluorescence
(4)	Radiationless deactivation
(5)	Intersystem crossing
(6)	Phosphorescence

- **Vibrational relaxation:** A* is usually produced in an excited vibrational state. Intermolecular collisions transfer part of this vibrational energy to other molecules, and A* relaxes to the lowest excited vibrational level.

- **Internal conversion:** A molecule A* in its lowest vibrational state can make a radiationless transition to a different excited electronic state: $A^* \rightarrow A^{*'}$. For this process to occur, A* and $A^{*'}$ must have the same energy. The molecule $A^{*'}$ is generally in a lower electronic state, but in a higher vibrational state than A*:

$$A^*(v = 0) \longrightarrow A^{*'}(v = 5)$$

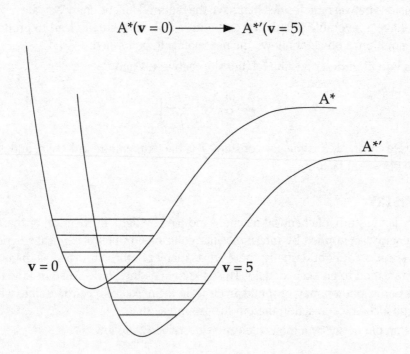

If A* and A*′ are both singlet or triplet states, the radiationless process is called **internal conversion**. If A* is a singlet electronic state and A*′ is a triplet electronic state, the radiationless process is called **intersystem crossing**.

- **Radiationless deactivation:** This occurs when A* transfers its electronic excited energy to another molecule and returns to its ground electronic state: A* + B → A + B*. The products A and B* can have additional translational, rotational, and vibrational energy.

- **Fluorescence:** Fluorescence occurs when light is emitted from an excited electronic state to a lower electronic state without spin change: $\Delta S = 0$. A* can lose its electronic energy by spontaneously emitting a photon, which brings it to the ground state:

$$A^* \rightarrow A + h\nu$$

If there are collisions between molecules, A* can lose its electronic excited energy and return to the ground state through internal conversion or intersystem crossing. In the absence of collisions, the typical lifetime of a singlet excited state is 10^{-8} s.

- **Phosphorescence:** This process is the emission of radiation from a triplet excited electronic state to a lower singlet state. This transition occurs with $\Delta S \neq 0$. Since the selection rule for electronic transitions is $\Delta S = 0$, phosphorescence has a very low probability. If there are intermolecular collisions, the excited electronic energy is lost to internal conversion and intersystem crossing. In the absence of collisions, however, the typical lifetime of an excited triplet state is 0.001 to 1 s.

A* is often formed in an excited vibrational level. If A* has enough vibrational energy, dissociation may occur:

$$A^* \rightarrow B + C$$

where the decomposition products may react further, especially if they are free radicals.

An example is that of an electronic transition in a diatomic molecule where A* has vibrational energy that exceeds the dissociation energy D_e:

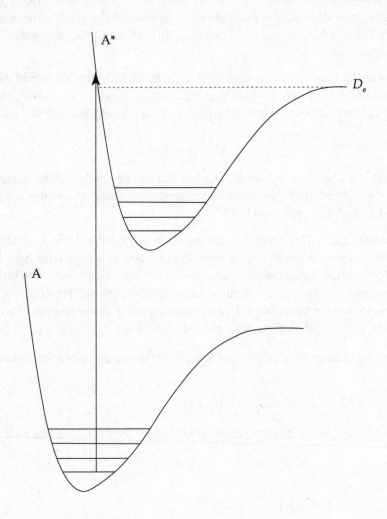

Excitation of a diatomic molecule to a repulsive electronic state (one in which there is no minimum in the potential energy curve) also leads to dissociation:

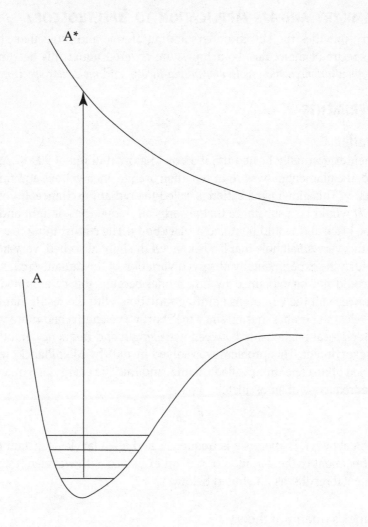

Quantum Yield

Consider the following decomposition reaction:

$$A_2 + h\nu \rightarrow 2A$$

The first step in this photochemical reaction is the absorption of a single photon by a molecule, A_2. As a result of this activation, the molecule dissociates. If the products react no further, the number of reacting molecules is equal to the number of photons absorbed. If, however, the photochemically activated molecule initiates a sequence of thermal reactions that deactivate the molecule, less than one molecule reacts per photon. The **quantum yield (Φ)** describes the relationship between the number of reacting molecules and the number of photons absorbed:

Φ = *(number of moles reacting per unit time) / (number of moles of light absorbed per unit time)*

QUANTUM MECHANICS

QUANTUM CHEMISTRY AND ITS APPLICATION TO SPECTROSCOPY

Quantum chemistry provides the key to understanding atomic and molecular structure, chemical bonding, and the spectra of molecules. Four topics are covered under this heading: *classical experiments, principles of quantum mechanics, molecular orbital theory,* and *molecular spectroscopy.*

CLASSICAL EXPERIMENTS

Blackbody Radiation

If a tungsten filament is gradually heated up, it starts to glow dull red at 900 K. As the temperature is further increased, the filament glows bright red, then orange, then yellow, and finally white, and at this point, *T* is 2,300 K. This glowing radiation is called the **radiant excitance**. If you were to think of a perfect absorber, it would be a substance that absorbs all frequencies of light and emits none. This substance would be black and would be called a **blackbody**. The closest thing to a true blackbody is a hollow cavity with a very small hole that leads to it: Of the light absorbed, very little can escape. At the turn of the century, the experimentally observed variation of the radiant excitance of a blackbody with wavelength could not be explained by any model because theory assumed that energy was divided equally between all the vibrations emitting radiation, with the result that the energy had to increase as the wavelength became shorter, since the short wavelengths had more vibrational modes. This is due to the reciprocal relationship between wavelength and frequency. In other words, theory could not explain experiment. This problem was solved in 1901 by Max Planck, who proposed that light energy consisted of discrete units, called **quanta**, and that the energy of a quantum was directly proportional to the frequency of an oscillator:

$$E = h\nu$$

In the expression above, E is energy, ν is frequency, and h is Planck's constant (6.626×10^{-34} Js^{-1}). This led to a new treatment of the variation of radiant excitance with wavelength in excellent agreement with experimental results, as illustrated below.

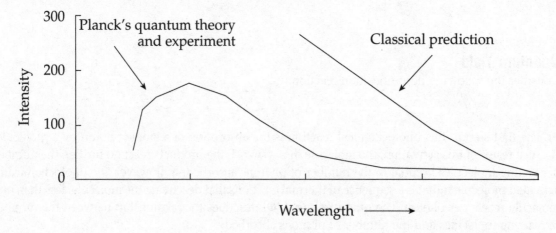

The Photoelectric Effect

In 1887, Hertz observed that electrons are emitted from a metal when the metal is irradiated with visible or ultraviolet radiation. He named this the **photoelectric effect**. It was quickly shown that (i) below a given cutoff frequency of incident radiation, no electrons were ejected from the metal surface, no matter how intense the radiation; (ii) above the cutoff frequency, the number of electrons emitted was directly proportional to the intensity of the radiation; and (iii) as the frequency of the incident radiation was increased, the maximum velocity of the ejected electrons increased. Classical theory could not explain these results, since it predicted that the emission of electrons should depend on the intensity of the radiation. This problem was solved by Einstein in 1905 with the help of Planck's quantum theory. He proposed that not only was the energy of an oscillator quantized, but that light itself consisted of particles—or **photons** with energy equal to $h\nu$. He explained the photoelectric effect by proposing that "work energy" (w) was required to remove an electron of given energy $h\nu$ from the surface of the metal according to

$$h\nu = \frac{1}{2} mv^2 + w$$

where $\frac{1}{2} mv^2$ is the kinetic energy of the emitted electron. If the energy of the electron $h\nu$ is less than w, the electron cannot be emitted, and if it is greater, the electron is emitted. There is also a frequency equal to $\frac{w}{h}$ that's just sufficient for the electron to be emitted. This clearly explained the frequency dependence of the photoelectric effect and the validity of the new quantum theory.

The Dual Nature of Light

Explaining blackbody radiation and the photoelectric effect required understanding that light had particle properties, that it consists of particles called photons. However, it was quickly realized that other properties of light, such as refraction, could be explained only by considering light as a wave. This led to the quantum mechanical theory on the **dual nature of radiation**, elaborated by de Broglie in 1924. He proposed that electrons could also behave as waves with wavelength λ given by

$$\lambda = \frac{h}{p} = \frac{h}{mv}$$

where p is the momentum of the electron, v its velocity, and m its mass, and h is Planck's constant.

The Uncertainty Principle

In 1926, Heisenberg realized that it was impossible to simultaneously measure the momentum and the position of a particle such as an electron, because performing one measurement would disturb the particle and prevent the accurate measurement of the second quantity. This is expressed in the **Heisenberg uncertainty principle**:

$$\Delta q \Delta p > \frac{h}{4\pi}$$

Or you could say that the product of the uncertainty of the position of the particle (Δq) and the uncertainty in its momentum (Δp) is greater than $\frac{h}{4\pi}$.

PRINCIPLES OF QUANTUM MECHANICS

The postulates of quantum mechanics:

- The physical state of a particle can be fully described by a wave function of the type ($\Psi_{x,y,z,t}$).

- The ($\Psi_{x,y,z,t}$) wave functions are obtained by solving the appropriate Schrödinger equation. For time-independent systems, this equation is:

$$\frac{h^2}{8\pi^2 m}\, \nabla^2\Psi + [E - V(r)]\Psi = 0$$

- Every dynamic variable that correlates with a physically observable property is expressed as a linear operator.

- Operators that represent physical properties are derived from the classical expressions for these properties.

- The eigenvalues obtained by solving the appropriate Schrödinger equation represent all possible values of an individual measurement of the quantity in question.

In quantum mechanical calculations, **operators** are represented with a circumflex accent over the symbol that represents the variable of interest. They are placed to the left of the function on which they are operating. For example, the classical variable for kinetic energy is E_k. The corresponding quantum mechanical operator is $\hat{E}_k$, and the operation that it performs on the function to which it is attached is $-\dfrac{h^2}{8\pi^2 m}\, \nabla^2$. So $\hat{E}_k\phi$ means that the operator $\hat{E}_k$ is operating on the function ϕ.

Schrödinger's Equation

Schrödinger's equation ($\Psi_{x,y,z,t}$) is a complex **wave function** used to describe the quantum mechanical state of a particle. It is a mathematical construct that cannot be experimentally verified. The wave function is used to describe the **probability density** of a particle; i.e., the probability of finding a particle (for instance, an electron) at time t at a given position $r = x, y, z$ in a volume dV. This probability (w) is proportional to the square of the wave function: $w_{x,y,z,t} = |\Psi|^2\, dV$

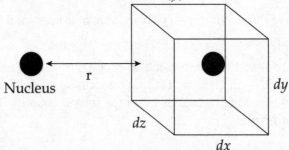

Electron "somewhere"
in a volume element dx, dy

The **time-dependent** wave function is used to describe the harmonic wave motion of a free particle:

$$\Psi(r, t) = (a)e^{i[wt - (\mathbf{k}\cdot\mathbf{r})]}$$

where: a = amplitude in units of $m^{-3/2}$

i = imaginary unit (= $\sqrt{-1}$)

w = frequency

k = wave number vector

r = radius vector describing the position of the particle in space

The wave function is also used to describe the motion of an electromagnetic wave traveling in a vacuum. The **time-independent Schrödinger equation** is:

$$\frac{h^2}{8\pi^2 m} \nabla^2 \Psi + [E - V(r)]\Psi = 0$$

where: ψ = wave function in units of $m^{-3/2}$

m = mass in kg

∇ = Laplace operator in units of m^{-2}

$V(r)$ = potential in units of J

E = energy in units of J

h = Planck's constant

Eigenfunctions are the solutions to this equation, and they exist only for specific **eigenvalues** of energy E. The totality of the eigenvalues for E yield the entire energy spectrum of the particle.

If $\lim (r \to \infty) V(r) = 0$, then the energy eigenvalues yield a **discrete** spectrum in the $E < 0$ range, and a **continuum** in the $E \geq 0$ range.

The Harmonic Oscillator

The harmonic oscillator is a particle that has mass m which, under the influence of a linearly applied force, will move in one or several directions with a frequency w_0. The Schrödinger equation for a **one-dimensional harmonic oscillator** is:

$$\frac{d^2\Psi}{dx^2} + \frac{8\pi^2 m}{h^2}\left[E - \left(\frac{m\omega_0^2}{2}\right)x^2\right]\Psi = 0$$

The eigenvalues of the harmonic oscillator are **quantized** and **equidistant**:

$$E_n = h\nu_0\left(\nu + \frac{1}{2}\right) \text{ with } \nu = 0, 1, 2, 3\ldots$$

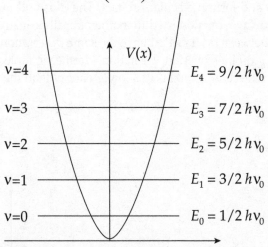

The **zero-point energy**, $E_0 = \frac{1}{2}h\nu_0$, is the lowest energy possible for the harmonic oscillator.

The harmonic oscillator is used to model:

- The vibrations of atoms and molecules
- The lattice vibrations of crystalline materials

MOLECULAR ORBITAL THEORY

Italic letters are used to describe molecular orbitals and Greek letters are used to describe the type of covalent bonding.

Example:

$H + H \rightarrow H_2$

When two H atoms approach one another, their respective $1s^1$ orbitals overlap, and energy is lost. As they overlap still more, they reach the lowest possible energy state, which dictates the bond length of the covalent s-s-σ bond. This creates a new orbital, which contains both electrons and belongs to both atoms.

Energy is required to break this bond in the hydrogen molecule—the same amount as was required to create the bond, 435 kJ/mol. This is the **binding energy**.

> *When atoms combine to form molecules, they attempt to achieve the lowest energy level.*
>
> *In covalent bonding, two single atomic orbitals combine to become a molecular orbital.*

p-p-σ bonding

p orbitals can also overlap and form molecular orbitals. The plus and minus signs are not charges; they refer to the sign of the wave function used to mathematically construct the orbitals. An overlap of orbitals is only possible between orbitals that have the same description or sign. When the positive or negative halves of two *p* orbitals overlap, a rotation-symmetric molecular orbital is formed: the *p- p-σ* bond. The resulting molecular orbital is at a lower energy than the single *p* orbitals:

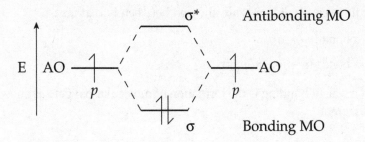

In the above representation, two atomic orbitals (AO), p orbitals, combine to form a p-p-σ orbital, the bonding MO, which contains the two p electrons, now shared by the molecule.

s-p-σ bonding

An atomic s-orbital and a p-orbital can also overlap to form a molecular s-p-σ orbital:

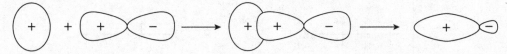

The wavefunction of the s-orbital can only be positive, so the overlap is always with the positive half of the p-orbital. The resulting rotation-symmetric molecular orbital is an s-p-σ orbital, which yields an s-p-σ-bond.

p-p-π-bonding

There are three p orbitals, designated p_x, p_y and p_z. When two atoms approach one another along an axis x, overlap can only occur with their respective p_x orbitals. This yields a p-p-σ bond. But when p_y and p_z orbitals approach one another along x, this yields a p-p-π orbital, which, unlike the s-p-σ orbital, is not rotation-symmetric. Rather, p-p-π orbitals are symmetric about a plane that contains the x-axis. This type of orbital overlap yields p-p-π bonding and the corresponding bond is called a π bond:

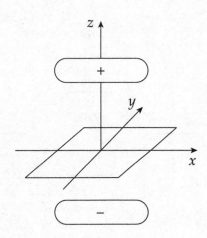

A maximum of three covalent bonds are allowed between two atoms:

- One p-p-σ bond (p_x-p_x-σ)

- Two p-p-π bonds (p_y-p_y-π; p_z-p_z-π)

One example of covalent bonding is the formation of molecular oxygen, as shown in the following molecular orbital diagram.

Example:

$O + O \rightarrow O_2$

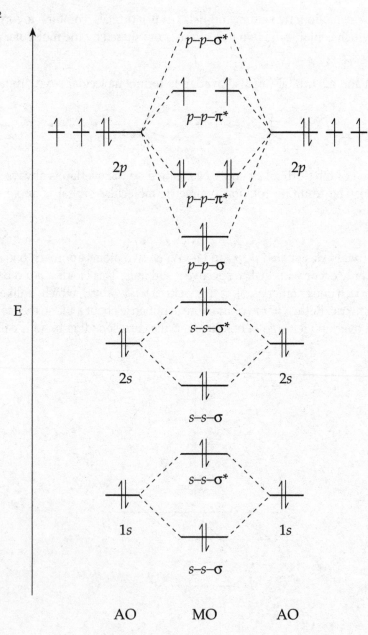

Molecular oxygen (O_2) consists of two oxygen atoms. Each oxygen atom has the following configuration: $1s^2\ 2s^2\ 2p^4$. In the diagram above, the corresponding atomic orbitals (AO) and molecular orbitals (MO) are represented by horizontal bars, and the electrons that they contain, by arrows. The diagram illustrates the bonding between the 8 electrons of one oxygen atom with the 8 electrons of another to form molecular oxygen with 16 electrons. The AO's are shown left and right of the central MO. The lower MO levels are filled first. Each oxygen atom has two electrons in its s orbitals ($1s$ and $2s$, for a total of 4 s electrons). These four electrons go into the bonding (s-s-σ) and antibonding (s-s-σ^*) molecular orbitals of O_2. Since both bonding and antibonding σ MO's are completely filled, $1s$ and $2s$ σ-bonding cancel out.

The next MO level (p-p-σ) can accommodate two electrons, and the next (p-p-π), accomodates four. The remaining two electrons go into the p-p-π^* antibonding orbital. There are a total of six electrons in the pi bonding orbitals, but two are in the p-p-π^* antibonding orbital, so two electrons cancel out in the bonding orbitals, and the *bond order* of molecular oxygen is $\dfrac{4}{2} = 2$.

$$\text{Bond order} = \frac{(\text{number of e's in bonding MO's})-(\text{number of e's in antibonding MO's})}{2}$$

Of the 16 electrons of molecular oxygen, 14 are paired, and two are unpaired in the p-p-π^* orbitals because of Hund's rule, which states that two electrons with the same spin must go in separate orbitals. Unlike molecules with paired electrons, which are diamagnetic and do not interact with a magnetic field, molecules with unpaired electrons have magnetic moments. They can interact with a magnetic field, and are said to be paramagnetic. From its MO diagram, molecular oxygen is predicted to have a magnetic moment, and this has been experimentally verified.

MOLECULAR SPECTROSCOPY

The Electromagnetic Spectrum

All types of electromagnetic radiation (gamma rays, x-rays, UV, visible, infrared, radio frequency) travel at the same velocity: 3.0×10^8 m/s. Electromagnetic radiation is characterized by two properties, **amplitude** and **periodicity**, and these properties are described using any of the following quantities: wavelength (λ), wave number ($\bar{v}$), or frequency (v):

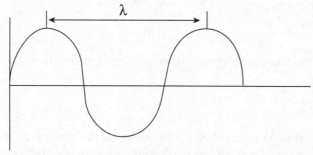

The wavelength (λ) is the distance from crest to crest on adjacent waves.

Radiation	Wavelength (nm)	Wave Number (cm^{-1})	Frequency ($Hz \times 10^{-12}$)
Extreme/far UV	10 to 200	10^6 to 50,000	30,000 to 15,000
Near UV	200 to 390	50,000 to 26,300	15,000 to 787
Visible	390 to 790	26,300 to 12,800	787 to 385
Near infrared	790 to 3,000	12,800 to 3,333	385 to 100
Infrared	3,000 to 30,000	3,333 to 333	100 to 10
Far infrared	30,000 to 300,000	333 to 33.3	10 to 1
Microwave	300,000 to 10^9	33.3 to 0.01	1 to 0.0003

Units

- **Wavelength** → 1μ (micron) = 1000 nm = 10,000 Å (angstroms) = 0.0001 cm = 10^{-6} m

- **Frequency** → Frequency (ν) is the number of waves that pass a given point in unit time. It is related to wavelength (λ) as follows:

$$\nu = \frac{c}{\lambda}$$

where c is the speed of light, $3.0 \times 10^8 \; \dfrac{m}{s}$.

For example, UV electromagnetic radiation at 3,000 Å corresponds to a frequency of

$$\nu = \frac{c}{\lambda} = \frac{3.00 \times 10^8 \, m \, s^{-1}}{3.0 \times 10^{-7} \, m} = 10^{15} \; s^{-1} \text{ or } 10^{15} \text{ Hz}$$

- **Wave number** → Wave number ($\bar{\nu}$) is the number of waves per unit distance, so it has the units of reciprocal distance (cm^{-1}).

$$\bar{\nu} = \frac{1}{\nu}$$

Optical Spectra

The energy of a photon (E_p) is given by:

$$E_p = h\nu$$

A molecule can absorb or emit this energy, thereby altering its rotational, vibrational, or electronic energy by an amount ΔE_m:

$$\Delta E_m = E_p = h\nu$$

If ΔE_m is positive, the photon is absorbed by the molecule in a process called **absorption**. If ΔE_m is negative, the photon is emitted by the molecule, and the process is called **emission**.

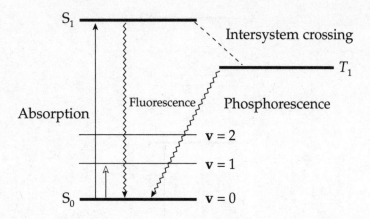

Electronic absorption takes place when the energy of the absorbed photon is in the UV or visible range. This is shown above by the S_0 to S_1 arrow. If the photon absorbed is in the infrared region, the absorption is vibrational and takes place between vibrational levels (labeled **v** above). Electronic absorption is allowed only between states of the same spin multiplicity (e.g., singlet to singlet) and is forbidden between states of different multiplicity (e.g., singlet to triplet). However, if two states of different multiplicity lie close to each other, the absorbed energy can be transferred between these states by a process called intersystem crossing. This is illustrated above by the dashed line.

Emission from the triplet state is called phosphorescence, and emission from the singlet state is called fluorescence.

A **spectrum** records the dependence of the absorption or emission intensity on wavelength or frequency.

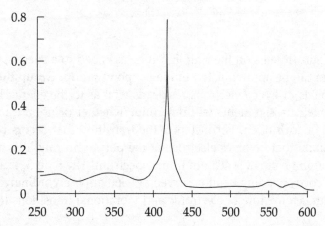

Above is the UV-Vis electronic absorption spectrum of a metalloporphyrin. Several factors affect the shape of its spectral bands; for instance, the **selection rules**, which determine whether or not a transition is allowed. This can be understood by taking a look at its (simplified) energy level diagram:

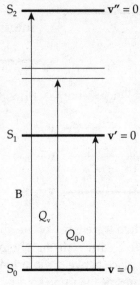

S_2 ———— $v'' = 0$

S_1 ———— $v' = 0$

B

Q_v

Q_{0-0}

S_0 ———— $v = 0$

Metalloporphyrin, D_{4h}

A metalloporphyrin has the following structure:

Depending on the substituents on the ring, it can be assigned to a specific point group. The one shown in our spectrum can be approximated in the D_{4h} point group. **Group theory** is used to assign symmetries to the orbitals in which electrons reside, as well as to the energy levels involved in the transition. These symmetry assignments will determine whether or not a transition can occur; i.e., whether it is **allowed** or **forbidden**. For instance, the transition that occurs between the S_0 and S_2 levels is a $\pi \rightarrow \pi^*$ transition that involves electrons of the porphyrin ring. It is allowed by symmetry and is observed as a strong band at ~ 408 nm in the spectrum. The S_0 to S_1 transition is not allowed by symmetry, and the corresponding band observed at ~560 nm is accordingly very weak. The other weak band at ~ 540 nm is a mixture of electronic and vibrational transitions (Q_v in the energy level diagram).

Another factor that will affect the band shape is the extent of **broadening**. Because of the Heisenberg uncertainty principle, the exact energy levels of a transition cannot be known. This is expressed as follows:

$$\Delta E \Delta t \approx \frac{h}{4\pi}$$

The extent of this "uncertainty" or **lifetime broadening** is inversely proportional to the lifetime Δt, and the broadening can be evaluated using:

$$\frac{\Delta v}{cm^{-1}} \approx \frac{2.7 \times 10^{-12}}{\Delta t}$$

Another broadening mechanism results from the **Doppler effect** due to the fact that molecules travel at high speeds in every possible direction. This causes Doppler shifts in the spectral lines, which broaden them. The effect is due to the fact that an object approaching an observer with speed v, while emitting radiation of wavelength λ, seems to be emitting from $\left[1-\left(\dfrac{v}{c}\right)\right]\lambda$ rather than from λ.

The environment in which the transition takes place will also affect the spectrum. For instance, the presence of a magnetic field will shift the energy levels between which the transition occurs, in what is called the **Zeeman effect**. Similarly, an electric field can shift spectral bands, and this is called the **Stark effect**:

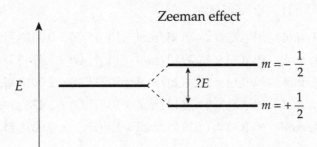

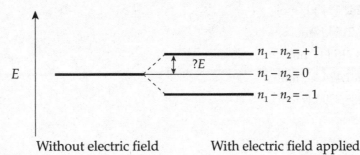

The Zeeman splitting is given by

$$\Delta E_Z = g \times m_j \times \mu_B \times B$$

where: g = Landé factor

m_j = magnetic quantum number

μ_B = Bohr magneton

B = magnetic field

The Stark splitting is given by

$$\Delta E_{Stark} = \left(\frac{3}{8\pi^2}\right)(hm_e eZ)(n_1 - n_2)\, n\, |\mathbf{E}|$$

where: h = Planck's constant

m_e = mass of the electron

Z = number of protons in nucleus

n_i = principal quantum number

$\mathbf{E}$ = electric field

PRACTICE PROBLEMS

Use the following data to answer questions 1 and 2.

At 25°C and 1 atm,

$$H_2\,(g) + \frac{1}{2}O_2\,(g) \rightarrow H_2O\,(l) \qquad\qquad \Delta H = -285.839 \text{ kJ/mol}$$

$R = 8.3143 \text{ JK}^{-1}\text{mol}^{-1}$
$1 \text{ atm·L} = 101.3 \text{ J}$
Molar volume of water: 18 mL/mol

1. Calculate the value of PV for H_2, O_2, and H_2O.

   (A) $PV(H_2) = 2.478$ kJ/mol $PV(O_2) = 2.478$ kJ/mol $PV(H_2O) = 0.0018$ kJ/mol
   (B) $PV(H_2) = 1.239$ kJ/mol $PV(O_2) = 1.239$ kJ/mol $PV(H_2O) = 2.478$ kJ/mol
   (C) $PV(H_2) = 1.478$ kJ/mol $PV(O_2) = 1.239$ kJ/mol $PV(H_2O) = 2.0018$ kJ/mol
   (D) $PV(H_2) = 1.239$ kJ/mol $PV(O_2) = 2.478$ kJ/mol $PV(H_2O) = 2.478$ kJ/mol
   (E) $PV(H_2) = 2.478$ kJ/mol $PV(O_2) = 1.239$ kJ/mol $PV(H_2O) = 0.0018$ kJ/mol

2. Calculate the change in internal energy, ΔU, for this reaction.

   (A) $\Delta U = +282.124$ kJ/mol
   (B) $\Delta U = -3.715$ kJ/mol
   (C) $\Delta U = +3.715$ kJ/mol
   (D) $\Delta U = -282.124$ kJ/mol
   (E) $\Delta U = -285.839$ kJ/mol

Use the following diagram and data to answer questions 3 and 4 :

$$H_2 \ (g \text{ at } 100°C) + \frac{1}{2} O_2 \ (g \text{ at } 100°C) \xrightarrow{\Delta H_{RX}} H_2O \text{ (liquid at } 100°C)$$

$$1 \quad \Delta H_1 \downarrow$$

$$H_2 \ (g \text{ at } 25°C) + \frac{1}{2} O_2 \ (g \text{ at } 100°C) \qquad\qquad 4 \quad \Delta H_4 \uparrow$$

$$2 \quad \Delta H_2 \downarrow$$

$$H_2 \ (g \text{ at } 25°C) + \frac{1}{2} O_2 \ (g \text{ at } 25°C) \xrightarrow[3]{\Delta H_3 = -285.839 \text{ kJ/mol}} H_2O \text{ (liquid at } 25°C)$$

$C_P \ (H_2)$ from 25°C to 100°C = 28.9 J deg^{-1}mol^{-1}.
$C_P \ (O_2)$ from 25°C to 100°C = 29.4 J deg^{-1}mol^{-1}.
$C_P \ (H_2O)$ from 25°C to 100°C = 75.5 J deg^{-1}mol^{-1}.

3. Calculate ΔH_1, ΔH_2, and ΔH_4.

     (A) $\Delta H_1 = -2.168$ kJ/mol $\Delta H_2 = -2.206$ kJ/mol $\Delta H_4 = +5.662$ kJ/mol

     (B) $\Delta H_1 = -2.168$ kJ/mol $\Delta H_2 = -1.103$ kJ/mol $\Delta H_4 = -5.662$ kJ/mol

     (C) $\Delta H_1 = -2.168$ kJ/mol $\Delta H_2 = -2.206$ kJ/mol $\Delta H_4 = -5.662$ kJ/mol

     (D) $\Delta H_1 = +2.168$ kJ/mol $\Delta H_2 = +1.103$ kJ/mol $\Delta H_4 = -5.662$ kJ/mol

     (E) $\Delta H_1 = -2.168$ kJ/mol $\Delta H_2 = -1.103$ kJ/mol $\Delta H_4 = +5.662$ kJ/mol

4. Calculate ΔH_{RX} for the reaction: $H_2 \ (g) + \frac{1}{2} O_2 \ (g) \rightarrow H_2O \ (l)$ at 1 atm and 100°C.

     (A) $\Delta H_{RX} = -283.448$ kJ/mol

     (B) $\Delta H_{RX} = +294.699$ kJ/mol

     (C) $\Delta H_{RX} = +283.448$ kJ/mol

     (D) $\Delta H_{RX} = -284.551$ kJ/mol

     (E) $\Delta H_{RX} = -294.699$ kJ/mol

5. Which of the following reactions shows the greatest decrease in entropy?

     (A) $C_3H_8 \ (l) + 5 \ O_2 \ (g) \rightarrow 3 \ CO_2 \ (g) + 4 \ H_2O \ (g)$

     (B) $C_3H_8 \ (g) + 4 \ O_2 \ (g) \rightarrow 3 \ CO_2 \ (g) + 4 \ H_2O \ (g)$

     (C) $C_3H_8 \ (g) + 5 \ O_2 \ (g) \rightarrow 3 \ CO_2 \ (g) + 4 \ H_2O \ (g)$

     (D) $C_3H_8 \ (g) + 5 \ O_2 \ (g) \rightarrow 3 \ CO_2 (g) + 4 \ H_2O \ (l)$

     (E) $C_3H_8 \ (l) + 5 \ O_2 \ (g) \rightarrow 3 \ CO_2 \ (g) + 4 \ H_2O \ (l)$

6. A process will be nonspontaneous when

    (A) $\Delta H°$ is positive and $\Delta S°$ is positive
    (B) $\Delta H°$ is negative and $\Delta S°$ is positive
    (C) $\Delta H°$ is negative and $\Delta S°$ is negative
    (D) $\Delta H°$ is positive and $\Delta S°$ is negative
    (E) none of the above

7. The condensation of any gas to a liquid is expected to have

    (A) a negative ΔH and a negative ΔS
    (B) a negative ΔH and a positive ΔS
    (C) a positive ΔH and a negative ΔS
    (D) a positive ΔH and a positive ΔS
    (E) none of the above

8. Which of the following equations are exothermic?

$$\text{I.} \quad \frac{1}{2}N_2 + O_2 \rightarrow NO_2 \qquad \Delta H_{RX} = +33.8 \text{ kJ}$$

$$\text{II.} \quad C + O_2 \rightarrow CO_2 + 395 \text{ kJ}$$

$$\text{III.} \quad H_2 + \frac{1}{2}O_2 \rightarrow H_2O \qquad \Delta H_{RX} = -241 \text{ kJ}$$

$$\text{IV.} \quad 2\,NaNO_3 + \text{heat} \rightarrow 2\,NaNO_2 + O_2$$

$$\text{V.} \quad N_2 + 3\,H_2 \rightarrow 2\,NH_3 + \text{energy}$$

    (A) I and IV
    (B) I, II, and V
    (C) II, III, and V
    (D) II, III, and IV
    (E) I, II, and III

9. Which of the following statements is false about the following reaction?

$$N_2\,(g) + 3\,H_2\,(g) \rightarrow 2\,NH_3\,(g) + 92 \text{ kJ}$$

    (A) The reaction is exothermic.
    (B) The energy content of the reactants is greater than that of the products.
    (C) If the system is cooled down, the equilibrium is displaced to the right.
    (D) If the pressure of the system is increased, the equilibrium is displaced to the left.
    (E) If some N_2 is taken from the system, the equilibrium is displaced to the left.

10. What reaction can be obtained from the following thermochemical data?

$$H_2SO_4\ (l) + 811\ kJ \rightarrow H_2\ (g) \rightarrow \frac{1}{8}\ S_8\ (s) + 2\ O_2\ (g)$$

$$H_2\ (g) + \frac{1}{2}\ O_2\ (g) \rightarrow H_2O\ (g) + 242\ kJ$$

$$\frac{1}{8}\ S_8\ (g) + O_2\ (g) \rightarrow SO_2\ (g) + 297\ kJ$$

(A) $H_2SO_4\ (l) \rightarrow H_2O\ (g) + SO_2\ (g) + \frac{1}{2}\ O_2\ (g)$ $\Delta H = -272\ kJ$

(B) $H_2SO_4\ (l) \rightarrow H_2O\ (g) + SO_2\ (g) + \frac{1}{2}\ O_2\ (g)$ $\Delta H = +272\ kJ$

(C) $H_2SO_4\ (l) + H_2\ (g) \rightarrow 2H_2O\ (g) + SO_2\ (g)$ $\Delta H = +272\ kJ$

(D) $H_2SO_4\ (l) \rightarrow H_2O\ (g) + SO_2\ (g) + \frac{1}{2}\ O_2(g) + 272\ kJ$

(E) $H_2SO_4\ (l) + H_2\ (g) \rightarrow H_2O\ (g) + SO_2\ (g) + 272\ kJ$

11. Which of the following statements applies to the following first-order reaction?

$$2\ N_2O_5\ (CCl_4) \rightarrow 4\ NO_2\ (CCl_4) + O_2\ (g)$$

    I. $v = k[N_2O_5]$

    II. $t_{\frac{1}{2}} = \dfrac{\ln 2}{k}$

    III. $[N_2O_5] = -kt + [N_2O_5]_0$

    IV. $v = k[N_2O_5]^2$

    V. $\ln[N_2O_5] = -kt + \ln[N_2O_5]_0$

    VI. $t_{\frac{1}{2}} = \dfrac{[N_2O_5]_0}{2k}$

(A) I, II, and V

(B) I, II, and VI

(C) II, V, and VI

(D) I, II, and III

(E) I, III, and VI

The reaction $I^- (aq) + OCl^- (aq) \rightarrow IO^- (aq) + Cl^- (aq)$ is believed to proceed through the following three-step mechanism:

Step 1: $\quad OCl^- + H_2O \underset{k_{-1}}{\overset{k_1}{\rightleftharpoons}} HOCl + OH \qquad$ fast equilibrium

Step 2: $\quad I^- + HOCl \overset{k_2}{\rightleftharpoons} HOI + Cl^- \qquad$ slow equilibrium

Step 3: $\quad HOI + OH^- \overset{k_3}{\rightleftharpoons} H_2O + IO^- \qquad$ fast equilibrium

Using this data, answer questions 12 and 13.

12. Identify the false statement.

   (A) The molecularity of each step is 2.
   (B) The limiting step is the second one.
   (C) HOCl is the only reaction intermediate.
   (D) The reaction is a complex reaction.
   (E) All the above statements are true.

13. What is the rate equation of the reaction?

   (A) $r = \left(\dfrac{k_2 k_1}{k_{-1}} \right) \dfrac{\left[I^- \right]\left[OCl^- \right]}{\left[OH^- \right]}$

   (B) $r = k_2[I^-][HOCl]$

   (C) $r = \left(\dfrac{k_2 k_{-1}}{k_1} \right) \dfrac{\left[I^- \right]\left[OCl^- \right]}{\left[OH^- \right]}$

   (D) $r = \left(\dfrac{k_2 k_1}{k_{-1}} \right) \dfrac{\left[I^- \right]\left[OH^- \right]}{\left[Cl^- \right]}$

   (E) $r = k_1 k_2[OCl^-][I^-]$

14. A solution contains 5.36×10^{-2} mol of a nonvolatile solute in 154 g of CCl_4 at 64°C. The vapor pressure of pure CCl_4 is 531 mmHg at 64°C. What is the vapor pressure of the solution?

   (A) 503 mmHg
   (B) 504 mmHg
   (C) 505 mmHg
   (D) 506 mmHg
   (E) 507 mmHg

15. The vapor pressure of water is 23.7 torr at 25°C. A solution of 5.00 g of a nonvolatile solute in 100 g of water has a vapor pressure of 23.3 torr at 25°C. What is the molar mass of the solute?

    (A) 54.6 g/mol

    (B) 46.8 g/mol

    (C) 58.4 g/mol

    (D) 52.5 g/mol

    (E) 56.0 g/mol

16. A solution of 0.40 g of a polypeptide in 1.0 L of aqueous solution has an osmotic pressure of 4.92 $\times 10^{-3}$ atm at 300 K. What is the molar mass of the polypeptide?
    ($R = 0.08206$ L $\cdot$ atm $\cdot$ K^{-1} $\cdot$ mol^{-1})

    (A) 2.0×10^6

    (B) 2.5×10^6

    (C) 2.0×10^2

    (D) 2.0×10^3

    (E) 2.0×10^4

17. The freezing point of a solution of 2.40 g of biphenyl (molar mass = 154 g/mol) in 75.0 g of benzene is 1.10°C lower than that of pure benzene. What is the value of the molal cryoscopic constant of benzene in °C/m?

    (A) –4.4

    (B) –5.4

    (C) –4.6

    (D) –5.0

    (E) –5.3

A catalyst increases the rate of a reaction by lowering its activation energy. Use this statement and the following diagram for the reversible catalyzed (B) and non-catalyzed reversible (A) reaction to answer questions 18–20.

$$A_2 + B_2 \rightleftharpoons 2\,AB$$

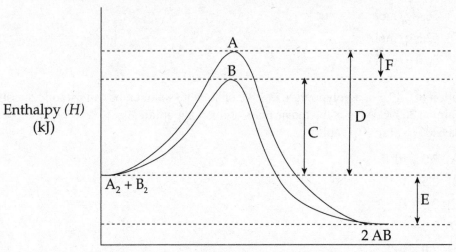

18. Use the average bond energies at 25°C to calculate the $\Delta H°_f$ of the hydrazine (H_2N-NH_2). $\Delta H°(N\equiv N)$ = 944 kJ/mol, $\Delta H°(N-N)$ = 163 kJ/mol, $\Delta H°(H-H)$ = 436 kJ/mol, $\Delta H°(N-H)$ = 388 kJ/mol.

19. The energy of activation of the reverse catalyzed reaction is

   (A) E
   (B) E + C
   (C) E + D
   (D) F
   (E) C + F

20. Which of the following statements are true?

   I.   The reverse catalyzed reaction is exothermic.
   II. The forward noncatalyzed reaction is spontaneous.
   III. ΔH_{RX} of the forward reaction = ΔH_{RX} of the reverse reaction.
   IV. The mechanism of this reaction consists of only one step.

   (A) I and II
   (B) III and IV
   (C) II and III
   (D) I and III
   (E) I and IV

ANSWERS TO PRACTICE PROBLEMS

1. **C** First examine the physical state of the reactants and the products, as well as the stoichiometric coefficients. The reactants are both in the gas phase. Since P and T are known, PV (H_2) = RT = (8.3143 JK^{-1}mol^{-1})(298 K) = 2.478 kJ/mol. Because of the stoichiometric coeficient, PV (O_2) = $\frac{1}{2}$ (2.478 kJ/mol) = 1.239 kJ/mol. H_2O is a liquid. And so PV (H_2O) = (1 atm)(18 × 10^{-3} L/mol) = 18 × 10^{-3} atmL/mol = 18 × 10^{-3} (101.3 J)/mol = 1.8 J/mol = 0.0018 kJ/mol.

2. **D** From the relationship $\Delta H = \Delta U + \Delta(PV)$, we obtain

   $\Delta U = \Delta H - \Delta(PV)$. $\Delta(PV)$ can be calculated from the values calculated in question 1.

   $\Delta(PV) = PV_{products} - PV_{reactants} = PV_{H_2O} - (PV_{H_2} + PV_{O_2}) = 0.0018 - (2.478 + 1.239) =$ −3.715 kJ/mol. Then, $\Delta U = \Delta H - \Delta(PV) = -285.839 - (-3.715) = -282.124$ kJ/mol.

3. **E** The heat contents of each step of the above process can be obtained from the relationship:

   $$\Delta H = C_p dT$$

   Integrating, we obtain $\Delta H = \int C_p dT$, from the initial to the final temperature. In the first step of the path, T goes from 100°C to 25°C. So

   $\Delta H_1 = \int C_p dT = C_p(T_{final} - T_{initial}) = 28.9 \text{ J} \cdot \text{deg}^{-1} \cdot \text{mol}^{-1} (25°C - 100°C) = -2.168$ kJ/mol.

   Similarly, we can also obtain ΔH_2 and ΔH_4: $\Delta H_2 = (\frac{1}{2})$ (29.4)(25 − 100) = −1.103 kJ/mol,

   and $\Delta H_4 = 75.5$ (100 − 25) = +5.662 kJ/mol.

4. **A** The diagram shows that there are two ways for the system to proceed from a state H_2 (g at 100°C), $\frac{1}{2} O_2$ (g at 100°C) to a state H_2O (l at 100°C). The change of enthalpy is determined by the state of the system and is independent of the path. In this case,

   $\Delta H_{RX} = \Delta H_1 + \Delta H_2 + \Delta H_3 + \Delta H_4 = -2.168 - 1.103 - 285.839 + 5.662 = -283.448$ kJ/mol.

5. **D** To answer this question, look for the greatest decrease in the number of moles of gas. Remember that the gas phase is more disordered than the liquid or solid phases. The answer is D because $\Delta n_g = 3 - (1 + 5) = -3$.

6. **D** A process is nonspontaneous when its $\Delta G°$ is positive. According to the Gibbs free-energy equation $\Delta G° = \Delta H° - T\Delta S°$, $\Delta G°$ is always positive when $\Delta H°$ is positive and $\Delta S°$ is negative.

7. **A** The condensation of a gas releases energy. Therefore the enthalpy change ΔH is negative. During condensation, the system goes from a state of great disorder (a gas) to a state of greater order (a liquid). The entropy decreases, and ΔS is negative.

8. **C** A reaction is exothermic when heat is released with product formation. This can be expressed in the equation itself or as a ΔH_{RX} with a negative value.

9. **D** The equation shows that 92 kJ of energy is released per mole of N_2. This means that the sum of the energies of the N_2 and H_2 molecules is greater than that of the NH_3 molecules formed and that the reaction is exothermic. If the system is cooled down, it will try to restore its thermal equilibrium by favoring the exothermic reaction. Therefore the equilibrium is to the right. If pressure is increased, the system will try to decrease it by reducing the number of particles: the equilibrium is displaced to the right. If N_2 is taken from the system, the equilibrium is displaced in the direction that allows the formation of N_2.

10. **B** This is an application of Hess's law. Summing up the enthalpies and all of the reactants and the products and canceling the identical terms yields equation B. Hess's law results from the fact that the enthalpy change of a reaction depends on the final and initial states of the system, not on the path taken to reach the final state.

11. **A** III and VI are characteristic of a zeroth-order reaction, and IV would be the rate equation if the reaction were second-order.

12. **C** The molecularity is the number of reactant molecules involved in a particular step. The reaction is complex because it involves more than one elementary step. The limiting step of a complex reaction is always the slowest. The reaction intermediates appear in one step and disappear in the next. HOCl is an intermediate because it appears in step 1 and disappears in step 2. HOI is also an intermediate because it appears in step 2 and disappears in step 3.

13. **A** The rate of this reaction should be the rate of its slowest step: $r = k_2[I^-][HOCl]$. HOCl is a reaction intermediate, and its concentration cannot be evaluated directly. However, we can replace it with an expression obtained from the equilibrium of step 1. For step 1, when a state of equilibrium is achieved, the rates of the forward and the reverse reactions are equal:

$$k_1[OCl^-] = k_{-1}[HOCl][OH^-]$$

We omit $[H_2O]$ because it remains constant throughout the reaction. Isolating [HOCl], we obtain

$$[HOCl] = \left(\frac{k_1}{k_{-1}}\right)\frac{[OCl]}{OH^-}$$

Finally,

$$r = k_2[I^-][HOCl] = k_2[I^-]\left(\frac{k_1}{k_{-1}}\right)\frac{[OCl]}{OH^-} = \left(\frac{k_2 k_1}{k_{-1}}\right)\frac{[I^-][OCl^-]}{[OH^-]}$$

14. **B** According to Raoult's law, $P_{solution} = x_{solvent}P^\circ_{solvent}$, where $x_{solvent}$ is the molar fraction of the solvent.

$$x_{solvent} = \frac{(\text{mole of solvent})}{(\text{mole of solvent} + \text{mole of solute})} = \frac{\dfrac{154\ g}{154\ g \bullet mol_{-1}}}{\dfrac{154\ g}{154\ g \bullet mol_{-1} + 5.36 \bullet 10_{-2}\ mol}} = 0.949.$$

Then $P_{solution} = x_{solvent}P^\circ_{solvent} = (0.949)(531\ mmHg) = 504\ mmHg$

15. **A** One of the most interesting aspects of Raoult's law is that it allows the determination of the molar masses of solutes. One can write:

$$x_{solvent} = \frac{P_{solution}}{P_{solvent}} = \frac{23.3}{23.7} = 0.983$$

Therefore, if x is the molar mass, then

$$x_{solvent} = \frac{\dfrac{100\ g}{18.0\ g \bullet mol_{-1}}}{\dfrac{100\ g}{18.0\ g \bullet mol_{-1} + 5.00\ g}} = 0.983$$

Solving this equation for x, one obtains $x = $ molar mass $= 54.6\ g/mol$.

16. **D** The osmotic pressure is one of the colligative properties: $\pi = CRT$. The molar mass can be evaluated in the following way:

$$\frac{\pi}{RT} = C = \frac{\dfrac{\text{mass of solute}}{\text{molar mass of solute}}}{V}. \text{ The molar mass is: molar mass} = \frac{m}{\pi} RT =$$

$$\frac{(0.40)(0.08206)(300)}{(0.00492)(1.00)} = \frac{2.0 \times 10^3\ g}{mol}$$

17. **E** The freezing point depression is another colligative property. It is given by:

$$\Delta T_f = -K_f m_{solute}$$

where m is the molality of the solute. The molal cryoscopic constant is

$$K_f = -\left(\frac{\Delta T_f}{m}\right) = \frac{-1.10^\circ\ C}{\dfrac{2.40\ g}{154\ g\,/\,mol}} = -\frac{5.3^\circ\ C}{m}.$$

Remember that the molality is defined as the number of moles of solute dissolved in 1 kg of solvent. The units mol/kg are abbreviated as the lower case letter m.

18.   The reaction of formation of hydrazine is given by $N_2 + 2 H_2 \rightleftarrows H_2N–NH_2$. The energy required to break the bonds of the reactants is $944 + 2(436) = 1,816$ kJ/mol. The energy liberated by the formation of the products is $163 + 4(388) = 1,715$ kJ/mol. So $\Delta H°_f$ = sum of the bond energies of the reactants – sum of the bond energies of the products = $1,816 – 1,715 = 101$ kJ/mol.

19. **B**   The energy of activation of the reverse catalyzed reaction is the difference between the energy of the activated complex (point B) and the energy of the reactants of the reverse reaction (AB). On the diagram, it is the sum E + C.

20. **B**   For the reverse reaction $\Delta H_{RX} (A_2 + B_2) > \Delta H_{RX} (2 AB)$. $\Delta H_{RX} > 0$, and the reaction is endothermic. The forward noncatalyzed reaction is not expected to be spontaneous because of its relatively large energy of activation. The catalyst modifies only the energy of activation of a reaction, not its ΔH_{RX}. Therefore III is true. Each elementary step of a reaction has its own energy of activation. This diagram clearly shows that the reaction has only one step.

5

Analytical Chemistry

Chemists employ a host of methods to separate, isolate, identify, and quantify chemical species. We will cover four topics under this heading: *Heterogeneous Solutions, Instrumental Methods, Applications,* and *Statistics and Standards.*

HETEROGENEOUS SOLUTIONS

Equilibrium systems that contain more than one phase are called **heterogeneous solutions**. We will cover five topics under this heading: *gravimetric analysis, solubility, precipitation titrations, chemical separations, and complexometry.*

GRAVIMETRIC ANALYSIS

In gravimetric methods, mass measurements of a **precipitate** are taken with a precise analytical balance.

Gravimetry involves the following steps:

1. Preparation of the analyte solution
2. Precipitation
3. Digestion of the precipitate
4. Filtration and washing of the precipitate
5. Drying and weighing of the precipitate
6. Determination of amount of analyte present

Here's an example of gravimetric analysis, the precipitation method used for determining the mass of calcium in water:

(i) An excess of oxalic acid ($H_2C_2O_4$) is added to a precisely known volume of natural water, and the subsequent addition of ammonia forms the oxalate ion:

$$H_2C_2O_4(aq) + 2NH_3(aq) \rightarrow C_2O_4^{2-}(aq) + 2NH_4^+(aq)$$

(ii) The oxalate ion then causes the precipitation of calcium oxalate:

$$Ca^{2+}(s) + C_2O_4^{2-}(aq) \rightarrow CaC_2O_4(s) \downarrow$$

(iii) The precipitate is collected in a crucible, weighed, dried, and then heated to 500°C to yield calcium oxide:

$$CaC_2O_4(s) + \Delta \rightarrow CaO(s) + CO(g) + CO_2(g)$$

(iv) The crucible and the calcium oxide are then cooled and the mass of CaO is determined by subtracting the known mass of the crucible. (The number of moles of CaO is equivalent to the number of moles of calcium.)

The following is a sample calculation.

Example:

A sample of 5.00 mL of water containing calcium is treated with an excess of oxalic acid in the presence of ammonia. The precipitate is filtered, dried, and then heated to 500°C. Its mass is determined to be 3.50 mg. Calculate the concentration of calcium in the sample in g/L.

Solution:

The solid obtained after heating is CaO (molar mass = 56.1 g/mol). The stoichiometry of the reaction is such that the number of moles of CaO obtained is equal to the number of moles of calcium initially present in the water sample. So

$$\text{Mass of Ca} = \left(\frac{\text{mass of CaO}}{\text{molar mass of CaO}}\right)\text{molar mass of Ca}$$

$$= \left(\frac{0.00350\text{ g}}{56.1\text{ g/mol}}\right)40.1\text{ g/mol}$$

$$= 2.5\text{ mg}$$

and

$$[Ca^{2+}] = \frac{2.5\text{ mg}}{5.00\text{ mL}} = \frac{0.5\text{ mg}}{\text{mL}} = 0.5\text{ g/L}$$

Gravimetric analysis can also involve **volatilization methods**. A volatile product can be collected and massed, or the mass of a volatile product can be determined by the mass loss of a certain sample.

For example, the gravimetric determination of the hydrogen carbonate content of antacid tablets is as follows:

$$2NaHCO_3(aq) + H_2SO_4(aq) \rightarrow 2CO_2(g) + 2H_2O(l) + Na_2SO_4(aq)$$

Carbon dioxide is collected in a tube containing an absorbent substance that retains it. The mass of CO_2 is then obtained by difference, and because the stoichiometry of reaction is one mole of $NaHCO_3$ per mole of CO_2, the amount of hydrogen carbonate can be determined.

Properties of Precipitates and Precipitants

- **Specificity and selectivity:** A good precipitant for gravimetric analysis should be *specific*—it should react with only one chemical species.

Dimethylglyoxime is highly specific; it precipitates only the Ni^{2+} ion. If not specific, a precipitating agent should at least be highly *selective* and react with a very limited number of species.

For example, silver nitrate is a selective reagent because the only common ions it precipitates out of acidic solutions are Cl^-, Br^-, I^-, SCN^-.

Some Important Points About Gravimetric Analysis

- **Ease of recovery of analyte:** A good reagent should also react with the analyte to form a precipitate that is easy to filter and wash, sparingly soluble so that there is no significant loss during the filtration and washing steps, unreactive with constituents of the atmosphere, and of known composition.

- **Particle size:** Precipitates made of large particles are easy to filter and are usually purer than those made up of small particles.

- **Colloidal and crystalline suspensions:** Colloidal suspensions are made of small particles (10^{-7} to 10^{-4} cm in diameter), that are invisible to the naked eye. These particles do not tend to settle to the bottom of the solution and can be difficult to filter. Crystalline suspensions are made of particles 0.1 mm or more in diameter. These particles tend to settle spontaneously and are easily filtered. It is preferential to choose reactions that produce a crystalline suspension.

- **Factors determining particle size:** These factors are experimental variables, such as precipitate solubility (S), reactant concentration, solute concentration (Q), and the rate at which the reactant is added. Particle size is related to a property of the system called **relative supersaturation**, which depends on the variables just mentioned.

$$\text{Relative supersaturation} = \frac{Q-S}{S}$$

Particle size varies inversely with supersaturation over the time period in which the reagent is added.

When $\dfrac{Q-S}{S}$ is large, the precipitate tends to be colloidal; when $\dfrac{Q-S}{S}$ is small, the precipitate tends to be crystalline.

- **Experimental conditions** should be chosen to minimize Q (by using dilute solutions and slowly adding the reagent) and to maximize S (run the reaction at elevated temperature). Note that colloidal solids can be precipitated from hot, well-stirred solutions that contain an electrolyte that ensures coagulation. In this context, an electrolyte is a solid upon whose surface colloidal particles are adsorbed.

- **Mechanism of precipitate formation:** Precipitates form in two ways: by nucleation or by particle growth. During **nucleation**, a small number of particles join together to produce a small solid. This nucleus may grow by the further accumulation of particles; this is particle growth.

  In precipitation, existing nuclei grow, and additional nucleation takes place. If nucleation predominates in the precipitation process, the precipitate is made of a large number of small nuclei and tends to be colloidal. If particle growth predominates, a fast-settling and easy-to-filter precipitate is obtained.

Treatment of Gravimetric Data

The results obtained from gravimetric analysis are usually obtained from two experimental measurements: the mass of the sample and the mass of a product of known composition.

SOLUBILITY

- The **solubility of a substance** is defined as the number of grams of solute necessary to form a saturated solution in one kilogram of water.

The fundamental rule of solubility: *Like dissolves like.*

A polar solvent can be used to dissolve a polar solute, and a nonpolar solvent can be used to dissolve a nonpolar solute.

- **Here are the steps of the dissolution process:**

1. The solute disperses in individual particles when its intermolecular forces are overcome. This process requires the input of energy $(\Delta H_1 > 0)$.

2. The intermolecular forces in the solvent also have to be overcome; this causes its expansion and allows greater accessibility to the solute particles. This process is also endothermic $(\Delta H_2 > 0)$.

3. Intermolecular forces are reformed as solute molecules that interact with solvent molecule forming solution. This step is usually exothermic $(\Delta H_3 < 0)$.

The change in enthalpy that accompanies the formation of a solution is called the **heat of dissociation**. It can be either positive or negative:

$$\Delta H_{diss} = \Delta H_1 + \Delta H_2 + \Delta H_3$$

Processes that require a lot of energy (i.e., they have a high ΔH_{diss}) do not tend to occur spontaneously.

Take a look at the solubility of NaCl in water. The first step in the dissociation of NaCl requires a lot of energy, because of the great strength of the ionic bond between Na^+ and Cl^-:

$$NaCl(s) \rightarrow Na^+(aq) + Cl^-(aq) \qquad \Delta H_1 = +790 \text{ kJ/mol}$$

The second step of the dissolution process (ΔH_2) is solvent expansion; it also requires a lot of energy because the hydrogen bonds of water must be broken. The third step (ΔH_3) describes solute-solvent interaction:

$$H_2O(l) + Na^+(aq) + Cl^-(aq) \rightleftharpoons Na^+(aq) + Cl^-(aq)$$

It is high and negative because the interaction between the ions and water is very strong. The combined second and third steps are then referred to as the heat of hydration:

$$\Delta H_{hydr} = \Delta H_2 + \Delta H_3 = -785 \text{ kJ/mol}$$

Overall,

$$H_{diss} = \Delta H_1 + \Delta H_{hydr} = 790 \text{ kJ/mole} - 785 \text{ kJ/mol}$$

$$\Delta H_{diss} = 5 \text{ kJ/mol}$$

The dissociation enthalpy is small, but positive. So why does salt dissolve so readily in water? Because entropy (disorder) strongly favors disssolution and outweighs small ΔH_{diss}.

Factors Influencing Dissolution

- **Structure:** Solubility increases if both the solute and the solvent have similar polarities (like dissolves like!).

  Because molecular structure determines the polarity of a compound, there is a clear relationship between structure and solubility.

Example:

  Vitamin A is liposoluble (fat-soluble). It is primarily composed of carbon and hydrogen and is nonpolar.

For this reason, it is soluble in body fat and not soluble in water. On the other hand, vitamin C contains several C–O and O–H bonds, which makes it polar and enables it to dissolve easily in water, but not in body fat.

- **Pressure:** Pressure exerts very little influence on the solubility of solids and liquids, but it has a remarkable effect on the solubility of gases. The influence of pressure on the solubility of gases is best expressed by **Henry's Law**: *In the absence of chemical reaction between the solute and the solvent, the quantity of gas dissolved in a solution is directly proportional to the pressure of the gas above the solution.*

- **Temperature:** The dissolution of solids occurs more rapidly at higher temperatures, but the quantity of solid that can be dissolved can either increase or decrease. Generally, the solubility of solids increases with temperature, but two notable exceptions to this rule are sodium sulfate and calcium carbonate. The solubility of gases in water always decreases with increasing temperature.

Solubility Product Constant

In a saturated solution of a slightly soluble ionic compound, an equilibrium exists between the solute and its ions:

$$PbI_2(s) \rightleftharpoons Pb^{2+}(aq) + 2I^-(aq)$$

Writing the equilibrium expression for the process gives K_{sp}, called the **solubility product constant**.

$$K_{sp} = [Pb^{2+}][I^-]^2$$

It is defined as the product of the concentrations of the ions of a salt in a saturated solution of that salt. The solubility product constant is related to the **solubility (s)**, which is defined as the mass of a substance that dissolves in 1 kg (or l) of water. Keep in mind that this equation shows that the equilibrium is independent of the amount of undissolved solute present.

Some Solubility Product Constants at $T = 25°C$

Substance	K_{sp}
Aluminum hydroxide, $Al(OH)_3$	2.0×10^{-32}
Barium carbonate, $BaCO_3$	8.1×10^{-9}
Calcium carbonate, $CaCO_3$	8.7×10^{-9}
Ferrous hydroxide, $Fe(OH)_2$	8.0×10^{-16}
Ferric hydroxide, $Fe(OH)_3$	4.1×10^{-38}
Lead sulfide, PbS	8.0×10^{-28}
Magnesium hydroxide, $Mg(OH)_2$	1.2×10^{-11}
Mercurous bromide, Hg_2Br_2	5.8×10^{-23}
Silver bromide, $AgBr$	4.0×10^{-13}
Zinc sulfide, ZnS	1.0×10^{-21}

Example:

Calculate the solubility of PbI_2 at 25°C. The K_{sp} of PbI_2 is 7.1×10^{-9}.

Solution:

When PbI_2 dissolves, one Pb^{2+} for every two moles of I^- are formed:

$$PbI_2 \rightarrow Pb^{2+} + 2I^- \text{ and } K_{sp} = [Pb^{2+}][I^-]^2$$

Let s represent the molar solubility of PbI_2. Since each mole of PbI_2 that dissolves yields one mole of Pb^{2+} and two moles of I^-, then $[Pb^{2+}] = s$ and $[I^-] = 2s$, and $[Pb^{2+}][I^-]^2 = 7.1 \times 10^{-9}$

or

$$(s)(2s)^2 = 7.1 \times 10^{-9} \text{ and}$$

$$s = \left(\frac{K_{sp}}{4}\right)^{\frac{1}{3}} = \left(\frac{7.1 \times 10^{-9}}{4}\right)^{\frac{1}{3}} = 1.2 \times 10^{-3} M$$

So the solubility in g/L is 1.2×10^{-3} moles/liter $\times$ 461.0 g/mole = 0.55 g/L.

PRECIPITATION TITRATIONS

The formation of a fairly insoluble compound occurs in precipitation reactions. Silver nitrate is one titrimetric agent that's widely used in precipitation reactions to determine the concentration of halides, certain divalent anions, and mercaptans, which precipitate as silver salts.

There are three stages in the titration curve for a precipitation reaction: preequivalence points, the equivalence point, and postequivalence points.

Example:

Consider the titration of an analyte C^- with the concentration M_{C^-}, with $AgNO_3$, with the concentration M_{AgNO3}.

The reaction is $C^-(aq) + Ag^+(aq) \rightarrow AgC(s)$, and $K_{sp} = [Ag^+][C^-]$

- **Preequivalence points:** Up to the equivalence point, C^- will be present in excess. Two steps are required to calculate the preequivalence point concentration of $[C^-]$.

  1. The concentration of analyte, M, after addition of a volume V_{AgNO_3}, is given by:

  $$[C^-] = \frac{(V_C \times M_{C^-}) - (V_{Ag^+} \times M_{Ag^+})}{V_{C^-} + V_{Ag^+}}$$

  2. A correction factor is then added to the preceding equation (because not all of the Ag^+ added will form a precipitate with the C^- in solution; AgC is only slightly soluble).

  $$[C^-] = \frac{(V_{C^-} \times M_{C^-}) - (V_{Ag^+} \times M_{Ag^+})}{V_{C^-} + V_{Ag^+}} + \frac{K_{sp}}{[C^-]}$$

The correction factor takes into account only the concentration of C^- ions that result from the dissociation of AgC(s).

$$\text{Correction factor} = [\text{C}^-]_{\text{diss}} = [\text{Ag}^+]_{\text{diss}} = \frac{K_{sp}}{\dfrac{[\text{AgC}]}{[\text{C}^-]}}$$

However, this correction term is necessary only when K_{sp} is relatively large, if the solutions are very dilute, or if the point considered is very near the equivalent point.

Having calculated $[\text{A}^-]$, we can then calculate the silver ion concentration using: $[\text{Ag}^+] = \dfrac{K_{sp}}{[\text{A}^-]}$ and then pAg, which is defined as:

$$\text{pAg} = -\log[\text{Ag}^+]$$

- **Equivalence point:** At the equivalence point, neither C^- nor Ag^+ is in excess. They exist in stoichiometric proportions: $[\text{Ag}^+] = [\text{C}^-] = \sqrt{K_{sp}}$.

- **Postequivalence points:** Now the titrant is in excess.

The concentration of silver ions is

$$\left[\text{Ag}^+\right] = \frac{\left(V_{\text{Ag}^+} \times M_{\text{Ag}^+}\right) - \left(V_{\text{A}^-} \times M_{\text{C}^-}\right)}{V_{\text{C}^-} + V_{\text{Ag}^+}} + \frac{K_{sp}}{\left[\text{Ag}^+\right]}$$

taking into account that $[\text{C}^-][\text{Ag}^+] = K_{sp}$.

The correction term also applies here, although it is usually negligible. The value of pAg can be obtained easily from the result of the calculation above.

Factors That Affect the Equivalence Point on a Graph

- Equivalent points, or end points, are sharp and easy to locate; small additions of titrants at these points cause large changes in the titration curve.

- End-point determination and precision also improve when the analytical reaction is nearer to completion. Therefore, the largest changes are observed for the reaction products that are the least soluble (small value of K_{sp}; these products form precipitates well and do not redissolve into solution).

CHEMICAL SEPARATIONS

Few analytical methods are so specific as to be completely free of interference.

In a chemical analysis, an **interference** is a species that behaves similarly to the analyte; this causes an error in the final analysis. Several procedures are available that overcome interferences, such as use of a **masking agent**, which reacts with an interference and prevents it from causing error in analysis or separating the analyte and the interference through separate phases with **solvent extraction**, **ion exchange**, or **electrolysis**.

Here's an example of this: The Fe^{3+} ion is an interference in the iodimetric determination of Cd^{2+}. The F^- ion is used as a masking agent because it complexes with Fe^{3+} and not Cd^{2+}.

Example:

The selective precipitation of metal sulfides can involve hydrogen sulfide as the precipitant. A saturated solution of H_2S is approximately 0.10 mol/liter. Hydrogen sulfide is a diprotic acid and it dissociates as follows:

$$H_2S(aq) \overset{K_2}{\rightleftharpoons} HS^-(aq) + H^+(aq)$$

$$HS^-(aq) \overset{K_2}{\rightleftharpoons} S^{2-}(aq) + H^+(aq)$$

with:

$$(K_1)(K_2) = \frac{[H^+]^2[S^{2-}]}{[H_2S]} = 6.8 \times 10^{-23}$$

The desired concentration of S^{2-} ion is achieved by controlling the pH of the solution.

If the pH = 1, then $[H^+] = 1 \times 10^{-22} M$ and $[S^{2-}] = 6.8 \times 10^{-22} M$.

The sulfide ion content of a saturated H_2S solution is inversely proportional to the square of the hydrogen concentration.

COMPLEXOMETRY

In compleximetric titrations, the titrant is a complexation agent; an organic agent that binds the analyte, usually a metal ion. Monodentate ligands and multidentate chelating ligands that bind metals more than once are Lewis bases that form coordinate covalent bonds with metal atoms/ions by donating pairs of electrons. Compleximetric titration is used to determine the concentration of metal ions in solution. A widely used chelating agent is ethylenediaminetetraacetic acid (EDTA), which has the structure:

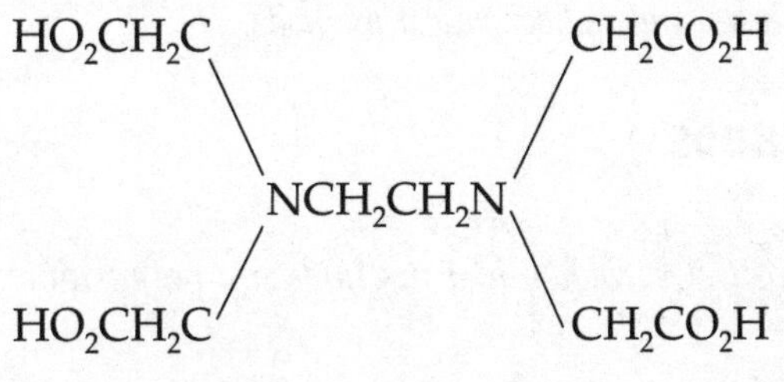

EDTA has six complexing groups—four R-COOH and two R_3 –N—that allow it to wrap around a metal ion. EDTA is an example of a **chelate**, which can take part in the following equilibrium:

$$\text{metal ion + ligands} \quad \rightleftharpoons \quad \text{Complex (chelate)}$$

Since the ligands of EDTA are within the same molecule, the equilibrium lies farther toward the formation of complex than a mixture of the unattached ligands.

Here's an example:

$$Ag^+(aq) + 2CN^-(aq) \Leftrightarrow [Ag(CN)_2]^-(aq)$$

This complex has an overall charge of –1.

Uncharged complexes also exist:

$$Ag^+(aq) + CN^-(aq) \Leftrightarrow [Ag(CN)](aq)$$

And here is a complex that has an overall positive charge:

$$Ag^+(aq) + 2NH_3(aq) \Leftrightarrow [Ag(NH_3)_2]^+(aq)$$

Formation Constants

Complexation reactions are often reversible and occur stepwise, and each step has a unique formation constant K_f.

For example, the formation of $[Ag(NH_3)_2]^+$ occurs in two steps:

$$Ag^+(aq) + NH_3(aq) \leftrightarrow [Ag(NH_3)]^+(aq) \qquad K_{f1} = \frac{[Ag(NH_3)]^+}{[Ag^+][NH_3]}$$

$$[Ag(NH_3)]^+(aq) + NH_3(aq) \leftrightarrow [Ag(NH_3)_2]^+(aq) \quad K_{f2} = \frac{[Ag(NH_3)_2]^+}{[Ag(NH_3)^+][NH_3]}$$

And the overall formation constant is the product of the formation constants of the two steps:

$$K_f = (K_{f1})(K_{f2})$$

INSTRUMENTAL METHODS

Ten topics are covered under this heading: *electrochemical methods, spectroscopic methods, chromatography, thermal methods, calibration of instruments, environmental applications, spectometric methods, electrochemical sensors, chemical methods, and radiochemical methods.*

ELECTROCHEMICAL METHODS

The two most important electrochemical methods are potentiometry and voltammetry.

Potentiometry

Potentiometry refers to a group of techniques that involves the measurement of EMF (electromotive force) compared to a standard zero current. The measurement of potential provides quantitative information about the compounds in a sample. There are two forms of potentiometry: **indicator electrode potentiometry** and **potentiometric titration**.

- **Indicator electrode potentiometry** uses an indicator electrode, the *ion-selective electrode*, that measures ion activity directly when it is immersed in an analyte solution, and is selectively sensitive to the element being determined. An ideal indicator electrode responds rapidly and accurately to changes in the concentration of the analyte ion. It is used in conjunction with a *reference electrode*, which is insensitive to the composition of the analyte and has a known and constant potential.

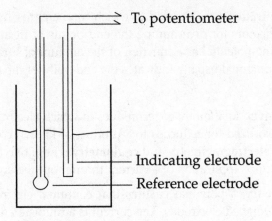

To potentiometer

Indicating electrode
Reference electrode

Setup for potentiometric measurement

There are two types of indicator electrodes: metal and membrane.

Metal electrodes function by sensing the transfer of electrons at the interface between electrode and solution.

Membrane electrodes function by sensing the transfer of ions from one side of a selectively permeable membrane to the other. These electrodes contain both a test solution and a reference electrode. The **glass electrode** used for pH measurements is an example of a membrane electrode, but glass electrodes that detect ions other than protons have been developed. Now Na^+, K^+, Rb^+, Cs^+, Li^+, Ag^+, and NH_4^+ can be potentiometrically measured by glass electrodes. Membrane electrodes can be either liquid or gas sensing. Like glass, crystals can also be used as membrane materials. An example of this is the solid-state fluoride electrode, in which the membrane consists of a single crystal of $LaCl_3$ doped with Eu(II) to increase its electrical conductivity. This electrode is $1{,}000 \times$ more selective toward fluoride than toward chloride, iodide, and bromide.

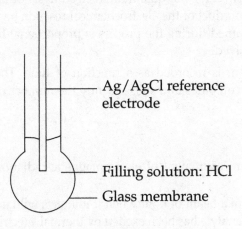

Ag/AgCl reference electrode

Filling solution: HCl
Glass membrane

The glass pH electrode

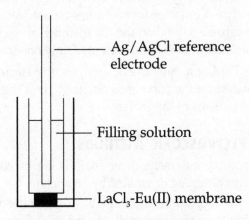

Ag/AgCl reference electrode

Filling solution

$LaCl_3$-Eu(II) membrane

An ion-selective electrode: The fluoride electrode

- **Potentiometric titration** uses electrodes, which can be either highly selective or universal, as indicators for determining the end points of titrations. These electrodes measure the potential as a function of the amount of titrant added, and a rapid change of potential usually indicates the end point of the titration.

Voltammetry

Voltammetry is the name given to a family of techniques in which electrolysis is carried out so that the analyte is completely oxidized (or reduced) to a product of known composition. The two main voltammetric methods are **electrogravimetry** and **coulometry**. These two techniques differ from potentiometry in that they require application of a current throughout the entire process.

- In **electrogravimetry**, a potential ensures that continual electrolysis is applied across carefully weighed electrodes. The current is administered and maintained at a high value, until the species is quantitatively deposited at one of the electrodes **(working electrode)**. Metals are reduced at the cathode to yield a metal deposit:

$$M^+(aq) + e^- \rightarrow M(s)$$

Unfortunately, the elements Ag, Pb, and Mn produce deposits of their oxides on the anode, so this method is not useful in solutions of these metal ions. The deposits may be impure if several reducible species are present in solution and if the applied potential is too high. This method is used for the quantitative determination of a small range of elements.

For example, the electrolysis of Cu^{2+} produces a deposit of Cu on a Pt cathode in an acidic solution, and the electrolysis of Br^- produces a deposit of AgBr on a silver anode.

In this case, the anode reaction is $Ag(s) + Br^- \rightarrow AgBr(s) + 1\ e^-$ where reduction occurs at the cathode.

- **Coulometric procedures**

Coulometry measures the quantity of electricity required for the quantitative electrolysis of an analyte. Coulometric procedures do not require that the product of the electrochemical reaction be a weighable solid, because the quantity of electricity consumed during the process is proportional to the amount of analyte present, if only one species is involved.

During a coulometric analysis, the electrolytic current is recorded as a function of time. The analysis of the curve thus obtained gives the number of coulombs and subsequently the number of equivalents of the analyte.

SPECTROSCOPIC METHODS

Spectroscopic methods of analysis are based upon the measurement of electromagnetic radiation that's absorbed or emitted by an analyte.

Absorption methods are based upon the attenuation of a beam of light when it interacts with an analyte. In **emission** methods, the light given off after an analyte has been excited by thermal, electrical, or radiant energy is analyzed.

Methods Based on the Absorption of Radiation

During absorption, the energy of the radiation is transferred to the analyte and, consequently, the energy of the incident radiation is decreased. Spectroscopic methods are often classified according to the region of the electromagnetic spectrum in which they work; for example, X-ray, ultraviolet, visible, or infrared spectroscopy.

Visible and Ultraviolet Spectrometry

In VIS or UV spectroscopy, the absorption (or emission) process results in an electronic rearrangement within atoms or molecules. The UV region of the spectrum ranges from the far UV (10–200 nm) to the near UV (200–400 nm). The VIS region extends from 400 to 750 nm. During the absorption process, the molecules are first in their ground electronic state. Upon absorbing incident radiation, they reach an excited state.

The emission process is the reverse of absorption; a molecule already in an excited state returns to a ground electronic state by the emission of a photon.

Terms used in absorption spectroscopy

- Transmittance *(T)* — the fraction of incident radiation transmitted by the sample. $T = \dfrac{I}{I_0}$, where I_0 and I represent the power of the beam before (I_0) and after passage (I) through the sample. It is a measure of the attenuation of a beam of radiation by an absorbing solution.

- Absorbance *(A)* — quantity defined by $A = -\log T = \varepsilon b c$, where ε is the molar absorptivity (which depends on the identity of the sample), b is the length of the measuring cell, and c is the molar concentration of the sample solution.

> This equation is referred to as the Beer-Lambert law:
>
> $$A = -\log T = 2 - \log\ (\%T) = \varepsilon b c$$

The value of ε is determined by various selection rules for each spectroscopy. Electronic transitions in absorption spectroscopy require (1) no change in spin multiplicity ($\Delta S = 0$) and (2) a change in parity (g-u or u-g) that leads to the selection rule $\Delta l = \pm 1$. For UV-visible spectroscopy, the value of ε is indicative of the type of electronic transition, as shown below:

Value of ε	Type of Electronic Transition
> 1000 M^{-1} cm^{-1}	Charge transfer (fully allowed)
1–1000 M^{-1} cm^{-1}	Laporte forbidden (no charge in parity), spin-allowed
< 1 M^{-1} cm^{-1}	Laporte forbidden and spin-forbidden

The absorbance is directly proportional to the amount of analyte present. The concentration of an analyte can be derived by comparing its absorbance to that of a standard of known concentration.

Infrared Spectroscopy (IR)

Many molecules absorb light in the IR region of the spectrum, which ranges from 30 to 3,000 cm^{-1}. The bands they produce in their IR spectra are due to vibrations of the molecule, which cause a change in dipole moment during absorption of IR radiation. The band shapes and positions depend on the symmetry of the molecule's vibrations, called **modes of vibration**. Illustrated below are different types of IR-active modes that are observed at different frequencies (ν) in the IR spectra:

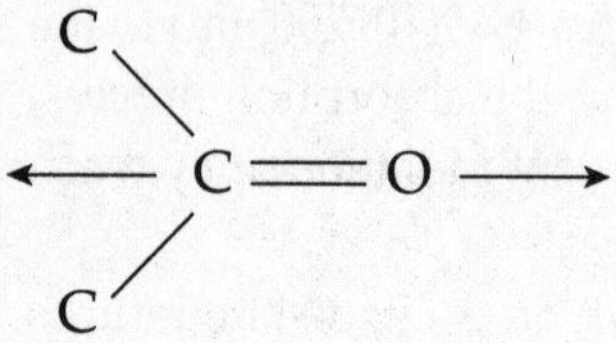

symmetric stretch 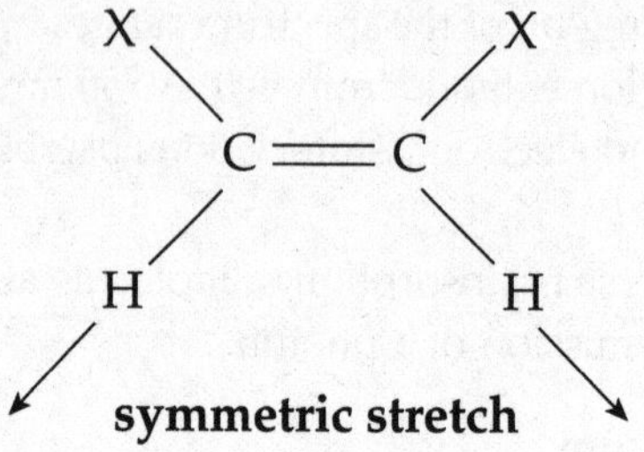   **symmetric stretch** 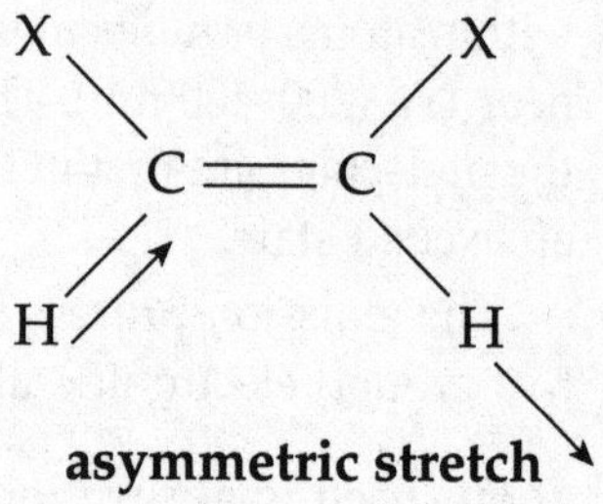   **asymmetric stretch**

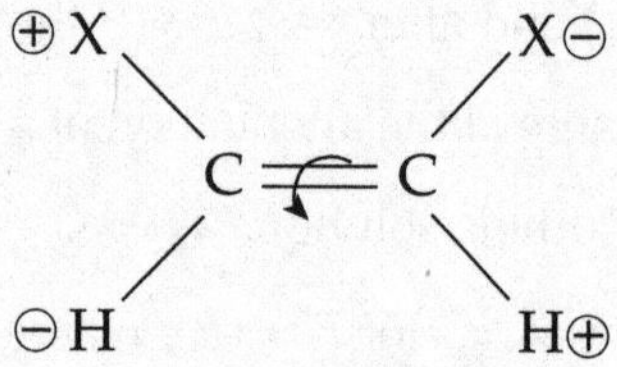

twist 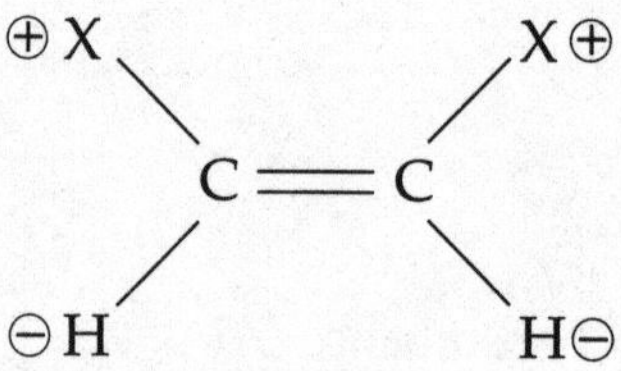   **wag**

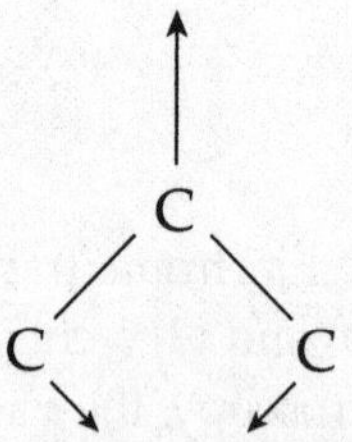

bending 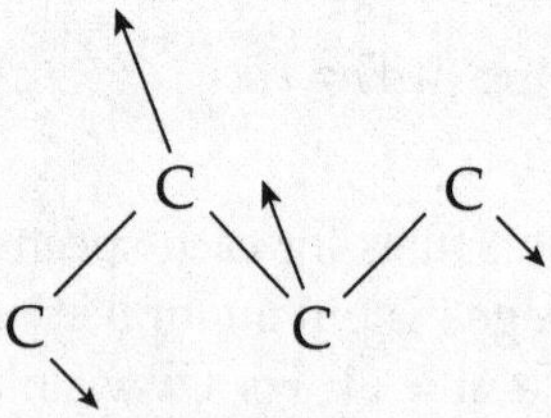   **bending** 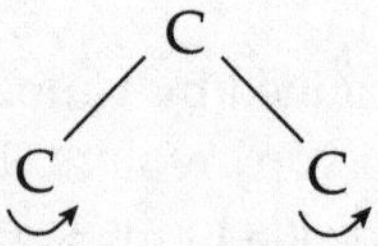   **rocking** 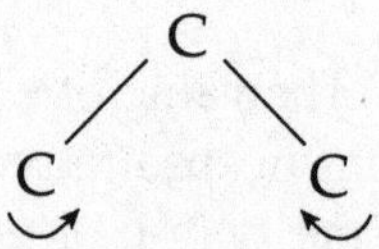   **scissoring**

The $\oplus$ and $\ominus$ symbols refer to motion out of the plane and into the plane of the paper, respectively. These modes appear in the IR spectrum at different frequencies, depending on the type of bond present, its strength, and on the nature of the bonded atoms. The following trends are generally observed and are used by chemists to characterize compounds:

- The higher the bond order, or the bond strength, the higher the IR frequency. So
  $\nu_{C\equiv C} > \nu_{C=C} > \nu_{C-C}$

- The greater the mass difference of the atoms involved in the vibrating bond, the higher the frequency.

In addition to specific modes of vibration that occur at specific IR frequencies, **group frequencies** are also observed. Group frequencies are associated with specific groups of atoms producing IR bands that are composite modes of vibration. Several of these groups of atoms consist of organic **functional groups**.

Group	IR $v(cm^{-1})$
OH, NH, CH	3,700–3,100
Aryl, olefinic CH	3,100–3,000
Aliphatic CH	3,000–2,700
Acidic COOH	3,100–2,400
C≡N	2,150–2,250
C=O	1,900–1,550
C=C and C=N	1,700–1,550
N=O	1,660–1,450
Aromatic N=O	1,330–1,530

The functional groups are very sensitive to their molecular environments. For example, it is possible to distinguish between a carbonyl or ester C=O group (stretch between 1,690 and 1,750 cm^{-1}), the C=O group of a carboxylic acid (stretch between 1,700 and 1,725 cm^{-1}), and that of an acid chloride (stretch between 1,770 and 1,820 cm^{-1}). Similarly, the C–H stretch is observed between 2,800 and 3,000 cm^{-1} in alkanes, but at ~ 3,300 cm^{-1} if the carbon is in acetylene, at ~ 3,050 cm^{-1} if it is in ethylene, and at ~3,000 cm^{-1} if it is attached to an aromatic ring.

Raman Spectrometry

Raman spectroscopy is another form of vibrational spectroscopy in the IR region of the EM spectrum; it complements IR. When monochromatic light is directed at a cell that contains a particular compound, the scattered, emergent light contains frequencies that differ from the original one. These differences correspond to changes in the vibrational and rotational states of the molecular species.

With small molecules, less-symmetric vibrations tend to yield intense infrared bands, whereas more-symmetric vibrations often lead to strong Raman bands. Raman spectrometry may be used for identification purposes, as well as for quantitative studies. As with IR, the intensities of the lines of interest are compared with the intensities of standard lines to determine quantities.

Microwave Spectrometry

The microwave region of the electromagnetic spectrum encompasses radiation that has wavelengths ranging from 1 mm to several centimeters. Absorption of this type of radiation causes changes in the rotational frequency levels of gaseous polar molecules. Microwave spectrometry is used to determine structural information.

^{1}H NMR

Chemists also use NMR (nuclear magnetic resonance) as a common spectroscopic technique for structural determination. In NMR, one of the useful quantities measured is the **chemical shift (δ)**, which allows for the identification of the bonding environment of specific hydrogen atoms. This chemical shift arises as follows: Atoms with an odd number of nucleons have magnetic moments. The hydrogen nucleus (1 proton) has two isoenergetic spin states, denoted +1/2 and –1/2. When placed in an external magnetic field, the nuclear spin states are split and no longer have the same energy. The higher energy state aligns its magnetic moment *against* the applied field and the lower energy state aligns *with* the field. The energy gap corresponds to the radio-frequency range, and radiation in that range can excite the nuclei, inducing spin flips between the higher and lower energy states. This is called **resonance**. NMR spectroscopy features a fixed radio frequency (usually 60 MHz) and a magnet that applies a varying magnetic field. When the resonance condition is met (when the spin flip occurs) a peak is recorded in the spectrum. The ability of the external magnetic field to affect the spin state of the hydrogen nuclei will depend on the extent to which the nuclei are shielded by surrounding electron clouds. The signals of more shielded protons will appear **upfield** in the spectrum, and the signals of less shielded protons will appear **downfield**. The chemical shift is usually expressed relative to a standard such as TMS, tetramethylsilane, $(CH_3)_4Si$, whose signal is assigned 0 ppm on the δ-scale.

> *The δ-scale chemical shift (ppm) is calculated as shift downfield from TMS (Hz)/total NMR spectrometer frequency (MHz).*

Common NMR spectrometer frequencies:

- 60 MHz ≡ 14,092 gauss
- 100 MHz ≡ 23,486 gauss
- 200 MHz ≡ 46,972 gauss

Shown below is the ^{1}H-NMR spectrum of ethanol (CH_3CH_2OH):

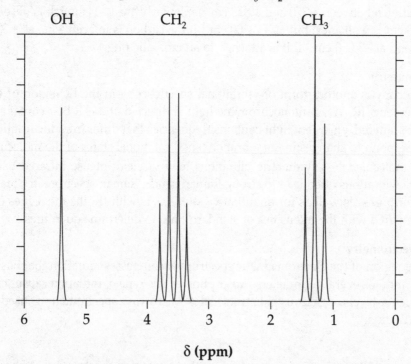

The signals from the protons reflect their differing magnetic environments: The signals of the more shielded protons appear first (upfield) to the right in the spectrum, followed by the signals of less shielded protons. This trend is also illustrated in the following table, which lists a few characteristic chemical shift values:

Type of H	Approximate δ (ppm)	Type of H	Approximate δ (ppm)
$R-CH_3$	0.9	$R_2C=CH_2$	5.5
R_2CH_2	1.2	$Ph-H$	7.5
R_3CH	1.4	$R-CHO$	9.5
$RC\equiv CH$	2.5	$RCOOH$	11
RCH_2X (X=halogen)	3.5		
ROH	4.5		

NMR chemical shifts generally depend on the following factors:

1. The proximity of electronegative atoms (F, O, N, Cl, Br, I) to the H in question decreases its shielding and results in a signal shift downfield; conversely, electropositive atoms increase H shielding.

2. The proximity of electron-withdrawing groups (C=O, aromatic carbons, C=C, C≡C...) also shift ^1H signals downfield.

3. The signals of hydrogens involved in H bonding are also shifted downfield.

4. The most shielded H's are found in alkanes.

Another feature of proton signals in high-resolution NMR spectra is that they are indicative of **spin-spin splitting**. In the example above, the signal for CH_3 is split into three peaks; that for CH_2, into four peaks. This is due to the coupling between the nuclear spins of the different protons; that is, each proton's magnetic environment is slightly different than that of its neighbor in a given group.

> *Spin-spin splitting is usually indicative of the magnetic nonequivalence of protons located on adjacent carbon atoms. N + 1 peaks are observed in the splitting of a given proton signal if N magnetically equivalent protons are found on the adjacent carbon.*

In the methyl group, the protons have four possible sets of spins, which will affect the magnetic environment of the two CH_2 protons, splitting their signal into four lines. Likewise, the CH_2 protons have three different sets of spins, so the CH_3 proton signal is split into three peaks.

Applying the splitting rule, CH_2 has two equivalent protons, so if its carbon is bonded to a methyl carbon, the CH_3 proton signal will be split into $N + 1$ peaks, or $2 + 1 = 3$. Similarly, CH_3 has three equivalent protons, so the signal for CH_2 will split into $N + 1$ peaks, or $3 + 1 = 4$ peaks. By convention, magnetically unequivalent hydrogens are assigned a and b subscripts.

¹³C NMR

The naturally occurring isotope of carbon, ^{12}C, is not NMR-active, since it has an even number of nucleons, but the ^{13}C isotope is. ^{13}C-NMR is a more intricate technique than ^1H-NMR because, in addition to ^{13}C spin-spin coupling, ^{13}C-^1H coupling also occurs. But techniques are available to obtain **proton-decoupled** spectra, which are then analyzed in terms of the ^{13}C chemical shifts. In this case, the information will be similar to that obtained from ^1H-NMR spectra; i.e., characteristic δ-values are associated with the different types of ^{13}C present in the molecule. The **proton-coupled** spectra will yield more information, because the number of protons bound to each ^{13}C present can also be determined.

Mass Spectrometry

Mass spectrometry concerns the determination of mass in the identification of compounds, specifically the mass to charge ratio (m/z) of gaseous ions.

The sample to be analyzed is first ionized, then bombarded with a beam of electrons. In this process, charged particles are formed, and these particles may be elemental, molecular, or fragmental in nature. The mass spectrometer then separates the ions according to their m/z ratio and determines the relative abundance of these ions. Structural information can be deduced from the observed ratios, and quantitative information can be derived from the relative abundance of each species.

Mass spectrometry is widely used in the structural determination of hydrocarbons. The ionization of the **parent molecules** (RS) in the vapor state by a beam of high-energy electrons can be described as follows:

$$R:S + e^- \rightarrow 2e^- + R \cdot S^+ \rightarrow R \cdot + S^+$$

In a first step, the parent molecule ionizes, yielding parent molecular ion, which then dissociates to yield other cations or neutral species. The resulting **mass spectrogram** will show peaks at the (m/z) values of the cations generated by ionization. The relative peak heights are proportional to the relative abundance of the cations.

Methods Based on the Emission of Radiation

Atomic Spectrometry

Atomic spectrometric techniques, for the most part, are based on the emission of radiation after absorption of energy by a sample. Because the electronic transitions are associated with large dipole changes, the techniques are very sensitive and are used primarily in the field of *elemental trace analysis*. The first step of an atomic spectrometric procedure is **atomization**. During this process, the sample is volatilized and decomposed to produce particles, which can either be atoms or ions. An example of the use of atomic spectrometry is in the determination of lead, tin, and zinc in brasses (copper alloys). The sample is first dissolved in acid and, after dilution of the solution, a known volume is injected into the spectrometer. Then volatilization separates the component ions or atoms for subsequent analysis.

Some of the techniques based on atomic spectrometry are: arc/spark emission spectrometry, in which electronic excitation is produced by electrical discharge and detection is accomplished by a photomultiplier; glow discharge atomic emission spectrometry; plasma emission spectrometry; flame emission spectrometry; atomic fluorescence spectrometry; and X-ray emission spectrometry.

Fluorimetry

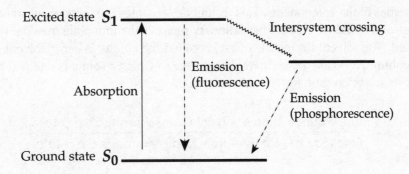

Fluorescence is caused by the absorption of radiant energy and reemission of some of this energy in the form of light. The light emitted is almost always of higher wavelength (i.e., lower energy) than the radiant energy initially absorbed. In true fluorescence, emission takes place in a short time (10^{-12} – 10^{-9} sec), because the radiation is emitted from the same excited state energy level in which absorption took place and the molecule has the same singlet spin multiplicity in both the ground state and in the excited state. But if intersystem crossing occurs to a state of different multiplicity (triplet), the light is emitted with a time delay (>10^{-8} sec), and the phenomenon is known as **phosphorescence**. Both of these phenomena are designated by the term **photoluminescence**.

Fluorescence has many practical uses in analytical chemistry. The electronic transitions involved are of the type $n \rightarrow \pi^*$ (an electron in a nonbonding orbital is promoted to a π-antibonding orbital, which leads to very weak fluorescence), and $\pi \rightarrow \pi^*$ (π-bonding to π-antibonding, which leads to very strong fluorescence).

The total fluorescence intensity F is given by:

$$F = I_0 \times 2.3\varepsilon c l\phi_f$$

where

I_0 is the intensity of the incident light

ε is the molar absorptivity

c is the concentration

l is the cell length

ϕ_f is the quantum yield of fluorescence

A fluorescence spectrum may be recorded as an emission or as an excitation spectrum. In an emission spectrum, the excitation wavelength is fixed and the spectrometer scans the fluorescence emission intensity as a function of wavelength. In an excitation spectrum, the detector remains fixed on an emission wavelength as the emission wavelength is scanned.

In absorbance (or UV-VIS) photometry, the sensitivity is limited by ε, and the minimum detectable concentration is 10^{-8} M. In fluorescence spectrometry, the sensitivity is limited only by the maximum intensity of the exciting light source; the limit of detection of this method is around 10^{-12} M.

CHROMATOGRAPHY

Chromatography is a method for physically separating mixtures based on the varying solubility and structural properties of the components. This technique separates mixtures of substances by using a **stationary** phase and a **mobile** phase. The stationary phase is the immobile material with which the column is packed. The solvent (or mobile phase) is called the **eluent**. When a solvent emerges from the end of the column, it is called the **eluate**. The degree to which a solute is retained by the column is measured by its retention ratio R:

$$R = \frac{\text{time required for the solvent to pass through the column}}{\text{time required for the solute to pass through the column}}$$

The denominator of this equation is the **retention time**. All chromatographic separations are based on differences in the speed at which solutes move through the column.

The equilibrium involved in the column can be described quantitatively by the partition coefficient K:

$$K = \frac{C_S}{C_M}$$

where C_S is the molar concentration of the solute in stationary phase and C_M is its concentration in the mobile phase.

In chromatography, it can be imagined that the column that contains the stationary phase is divided into N segments, in each of which one equilibrium occurs. Each of these imaginary segments is called a **theoretical plate**. If the total length of the column is L, the height equivalent of a theoretical plate (HETP) is:

$$\text{HETP} = \frac{L}{N} = A + \frac{B}{v} + C \cdot v$$

where A, B, and C are coefficients and v is the mobile phase velocity. This is called the *van Deemter* equation. A is related to eddy diffusion, B to longitudinal diffusion, and C to mass transfer. These coefficients can be evaluated using other equations. The smaller the HETP is, the better the separation.

Chromatographic results are presented in a **chromatogram**, which plots the elution profile of the separation achieved. The x-axis is the time and the y-axis is the detector response. In a typical chromatogram, the number of peaks indicates the number of components separated by the chromatographic procedure. The intensity of the peaks is proportional to the concentration of the separated substances, and their order of appearance will depend on the selected chromatographic principle. For example, in a size-exclusion chromatogram, the heavier components appear first.

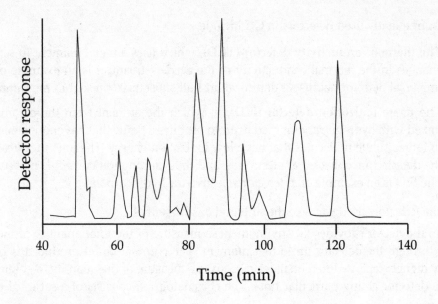

Gas Chromatography (GC)

In **gas chromatography**, a volatile liquid or gaseous solute is carried in a gaseous mobile phase called the **carrier gas**.

The stationary phase is usually a relatively nonvolatile liquid adsorbed on a solid support, and the moving phase is usually an inert gas. This most common form of GC is called **gas-liquid partition** chromatography.

When solid particles on which the solute can be adsorbed serve as the stationary phase, this is called **gas-solid adsorption** chromatography.

During a standard GC procedure, a volatile liquid sample is vaporized and swept into the column by the carrier gas. The solutes are separated from each other after passing through the column which contains the stationary phase. Finally, the gas stream flows through a detector, which sends a signal to a recorder. Although He and H_2 are the most common carrier gases in GC, N_2, CO_2, and Ar are also used. The lighter gases (H_2 and He) allow for more longitudinal diffusion (diffusion parallel to the direction of flow of the carrier gas) of solutes, which tends to decrease the column efficiency. The best carrier gases for difficult separations are heavier gases such as N_2 or CO_2, because they reduce the flow rate and increase column efficiency.

Detectors

The function of the detector is to sense and measure the small amounts of the separated components that are present in the carrier gas as it leaves the column. Some of the important properties of a detector in GC include:

- **Sensitivity** to the concentration of the analyte.

- **Linearity**, which refers to the concentration range over which the signal is directly proportional to the concentration of the analyte and not distorted.

- **Stability**, the extent to which the signal output remains constant with time.

- **Universal or selective response** to the components present in the mixture.

The most frequently used detectors in GC include:

1. **The thermal conductivity detector (TCD)**, which uses a metal filament to sense changes in the thermal conductivity of the carrier stream; it is an example of a universal detector because it detects almost all substances present in the sample.

2. **The flame ionization detector (FID)**, in which the effluent from the column is mixed with hydrogen and burned in air to produce a flame that has enough energy to ionize solute molecules that have low ionization energy. The ions produced in the detector are collected at electrodes, and the resulting ion current is measured. The FID is an example of a detector selective for hydrocarbons.

In GC, the detectors used can be either integral or differential.

An integral detector provides (at any moment) a measure of the total quantity of the solute that has passed through the detector up to that moment. The chromatogram produced is composed of successively higher steps. A differential detector gives a measure of the quantity of solute that passes through the detector at any particular time. The chromatogram consists of a series of peaks rather than steps.

Analysis of GC Chromatograms

For **qualitative analysis**, the peaks of a chromatogram can be identified by their retention times. For **quantitative analysis**, the area under each peak of interest is measured and correlated with the quantity of each component in the mixture.

It may happen that two solutes in a given sample have very similar retention times. Then the chromatogram will show overlapping peaks.

The resolution (R) of the peaks is determined by:

$$R = \frac{2\left(t_{R_2} - t_{R_1}\right)}{\left(W_{b_1} - W_{b_2}\right)}$$

where: t_{R_2} is the retention time for substance 2

t_{R_1} is the retention time for substance 1

W_{B_1} and W_{B_2} are the respective bandwidths of each peak

R indicates how effectively a given column separates two solutes. The separation factor S is equal to the ratio of the retention times and the ratio of the partition coefficients of the two solutes:

$$S = \frac{t_{R_2}}{t_{R_1}} = \frac{K_2}{K_1}$$

Liquid Chromatography

Classical liquid chromatography uses gravity-fed columns (in **size-exclusion** chromatography) and ionic resins (in **ion-exchange** chromatography). The first method separates the components of a mixture according to their molecular weights, whereas the second method separates them on the basis of their charge. **Molecular sieve gels** are used to pack size-exclusion columns, and the elution of the components proceeds with the heavier components eluting first, followed by the lighter ones. In ion-exchange separations, the column is packed with an **anionic** or a **cationic resin**, depending on the charge of the sample's components.

High-performance liquid chromatography (HPLC) uses a high pressure that forces the liquid through the column, which is packed with particles of very small diameter. HPLC is much more efficient than conventional liquid chromatography but cannot perform large-scale separations. The most common stationary phase contains nonpolar groups covalently bonded to 5- to 10-mm silicate particles. **Single-solvent elution** or **gradient elution** (in which solvents with decreasing polarity are used) is employed in liquid chromatography.

Detectors

The most frequently used detector in LC is the ultraviolet detector. UV-VIS absorption is monitored as the effluent from the column passes through the detector, which is held in a radiation beam. Changes in the light transmittance indicate that a solute is being eluted. The detector is highly sensitive, with detection limits of concentrations as low as 1×10^{-9} M for highly absorbing material. Other detectors include the fluorescence detector (for fluorescent solutes), the electrochemical detector, which measures the current associated with the oxidation or reduction of solutes, and the refractive index detector. This last detector can be used only for pure mobile phases (therefore it is not suitable for gradient elution) and has poor sensitivity.

THERMAL METHODS

Thermal methods of analysis study the effect of heat on a sample, the results of which provide qualitative and quantitative information about the sample.

Certain thermal events act as indicators for substances; these include phase transitions and glass transitions. Recording the change in the phase property as the temperature is varied results in a thermal analysis curve called a **thermogram**.

Thermogravimetry (TG)

Thermogravimetry is the study of the change in mass of a sample as its temperature is varied.

Many substances undergo weight changes that result in characteristic curves when they are heated over a certain temperature range. If the change can be linked to a particular event, the thermogram can be used for quantitative analysis, but this technique requires a **thermobalance**, which has a sample support inside a furnace so that its temperature can be easily controlled. This method is useful for inorganic substances and polymers but is limited to substances that undergo weight changes. Precision is usually around 1%.

Example:

When heated to 1,000°C, calcium oxalate monohydride undergoes three changes, all of which are accompanied by weight loss. Its thermogram plots sample weight vs. temperature, and it displays four plateaus, each lower than the previous one. The temperatures at which curve drops are observed are the transition temperatures. In the case of $CaC_2O_4 \cdot H_2O$, the thermogram reflects the following reactions:

1. Between 22°C and 200°C, loss of water:

$$CaC_2O_4 \cdot H_2O(s) \rightarrow CaC_2O_4(s) + H_2O(g)$$

2. Between 400°C and 500°C, loss of carbon monoxide and formation of calcium carbonate:

$$CaC_2O_4(s) \rightarrow CaCO_3(s) + CO(g)$$

3. Between 700°C and 800°C, loss of carbon dioxide and formation of carbon oxide:

$$CaCO_3(s) \rightarrow CaO(s) + CO_2(g)$$

Differential Thermal Analysis (DTA)

This method is based upon the measurement of the temperature difference between the sample and an inert reference material such as Al_2O_3, when they are both heated uniformly. The temperature of the reference sample rises steadily and linearly, and the same thing happens to the sample, except that a peak is observed when an exothermic process takes place and a depression is recorded when an endothermic process takes place. The deviation in temperature can be qualitatively and quantitatively analyzed, as displayed in the **differential themogram**, which is a diagram of ΔT vs. furnace temperature. The curve remains flat, as long as no endothermic or exothermic process occurs. When such processes take place, they are reflected in the thermogram as positive peaks (exotherms) or negative peaks (endotherms).

The instrumentation involves a single furnace containing both the sample and the reference. The temperature of the sample and the reference are measured separately by sensitive thermocouples. Precision is usually about 1%.

CALIBRATION OF INSTRUMENTS

In quantitative analysis, an analytical measurement must be accurately related to the composition of the sample. Only when the relationship between measurement and analyte obeys a strict and measurable proportionality can the amount of analyte be derived from the measurement. This proportionality must be established in **calibration procedures**.

For a simple calibration, a range of standards that contains varying amounts of the analyte is prepared. Then a calibration curve of signal against amount of analyte is plotted, and the results for samples of unknown concentration are interpolated from this calibration curve. An ideal calibration curve would be smooth over a wide range of analyte concentrations, but deviations must be expected at higher and lower ranges, and this means loss of precision.

ENVIRONMENTAL APPLICATIONS

Analysis of Atmospheric Samples

The atmosphere is primarily a mixture of N_2 (79%), O_2 (20%), and Ar (1%); together, these make up more than 99.9% of dry air. The atmosphere also contains variable amounts of water vapor and a number of minor and trace gaseous components, such as ozone, carbon monoxide, methane, nitric oxide, nitrogen dioxide, sulfur dioxide, and Freons, which are either naturally present or result from industrial activity. Chemical reactions occur and affect the composition of the atmosphere by changing the concentration of one or more of these components and generating new ones. Most analytical methods used to study atmospheric samples fall into one of three categories:

- Monitoring of components of ambient air

- Monitoring industrial emissions

- Measuring the specific toxicity of airborne substances

Many analytical methods are available for the analysis of atmospheric samples; listed below are the most common.

Gas Chromatography

Gas chromatography involves the separation of gaseous mixtures using the selective absorption of the components of interest on solids such as alumina, silica gel, molecular sieve, etc. Conventional detectors are used, including flame ionization detectors (FID) and electron capture detectors (ECD), but detectors that measure very low concentrations of specific contaminants may also be used.

SPECTROMETRIC METHODS

These methods are widely used in gas analysis. All gases that contain covalent bonds, except non-polar diatomic molecules (O_2, N_2, Cl_2), possess characteristic absorption spectra in the infrared-UV region. Their absorption depends on the concentration of the molecules and follows the Beer-Lambert law. Certain gas molecules fluoresce after they are stimulated to an excited state in a process called *chemiluminescence*. Analysis of atmospheric samples often involves measurements at very low concentrations, so that highly sensitive and selective analyzers such as the dual-beam nondispersive infrared (NDIR) or ultraviolet (NDUV) analyzer are necessary. Typically, for sample cells with path lengths of 100–200 mm, detection limits are at the ppm level.

Fourier Transform Spectrometry

Fourier transform spectrometry is a technique used for nondispersive measurement of spectra. It is usually applied in the infrared region (FTIR). In FTIR spectrometry, the entire frequency range is monitored simultaneously, so that several atmospheric components can be measured together. FTIR spectrometers are often used as GC detectors.

LIDAR (Light Detection and Ranging)

LIDAR operates similarly to radar. A pulse of light is emitted directly into the atmosphere by a high-power laser and is scattered by aerosols (aerosols are microscopic liquid or solid particles suspended in a gas). A proportion of the scattered light is absorbed and reemitted by the target analyte in the air and back-scattered along the transmission line. Then a detector receives the pulse, and information on the nature and position of the absorbing and scattering species can then be derived by measuring the time it takes for the pulse to return to the detector. Information on the chemical composition of the atmosphere is obtained by a LIDAR system, which operates in a differential mode (DIAL). Because the intensity of the scattered light is weak, LIDAR and DIAL are usually operated at UV or VIS lengths. These methods are currently used for monitoring NO, NO_2, O_3, and CO_2 and some organic molecules in air.

Photoacoustic Spectrometry (PAS)

In photoacoustic spectrometry, the sample is contained in a sealed chamber and irradiated with pulses of IR or UV light. Some of the energy is absorbed by the target molecule and released as heat, causing the temperature and pressure inside the chamber to rise, and microphones detect the pressure pulses thus produced. Specificity is achieved by selecting a radiation corresponding to a specific absorption band of the gas. The amplitude recorded by the microphone can be used in quantitative measurements of the target gases. PAS is applicable to a wide variety of gases and organic molecules (i.e., toluene) and is highly sensitive; the response is linear over a wide range of concentrations. Detection limits are very low; for instance, 150 ppb for carbon monoxide, 3 ppm for carbon dioxide, and 70 ppb for formaldehyde.

Other Spectrometric Methods

Correlation spectrometry is an analytical method in which the molecules to be analyzed are used to specify the analytical wavelength. **Tunable diode laser spectrometry** is similar to conventional IR absorption spectrometry, but the source is a diode laser with a very narrow line width, which enables the vibration lines of the target molecule to be resolved. This increases both the sensitivity and the selectivity of the technique.

ELECTROCHEMICAL SENSORS

When a gas is introduced in an electrochemical device that consists of a cell and two electrodes in contact with an electrolyte, a reaction may happen at one of the electrode-electrolyte interfaces. A current will be generated and correlated with the concentration of the gas. The sensing electrode may be made selective to a particular gas by enveloping the sensing electrodes in a suitable membrane through which the gas diffuses. Electrochemical sensors are available for the following gases: H_2, O_2, NO_2, NO, Cl_2, CO, SO_2, and HCN.

An example of an electrochemical sensor is the CO_2 sensor. Its design incorporates an indicating/reference electrode pair placed inside a tube that contains a solution of sodium hydrogen carbonate as internal electrolyte. The tube is sealed with a gas-permeable membrane. When the sensor is immersed in the sample solution that contains the CO_2 to be determined, diffusion of the carbon dioxide occurs through the membrane until equilibrium is reached, the point at which the concentration of CO_2 in the sample solution is equal to that of the internal electrolyte. Any change in the electrolyte's CO_2 concentration will also change its pH, and this pH change is detected by the electrode pair and converted to carbon dioxide concentration.

CHEMICAL METHODS

Most pollutant gases in the atmosphere are reactive and can be monitored by selective absorption from an air sample of known volume, followed by chemical analysis. For instance, SO_2 can be monitored by following its absorption into an H_2O_2 solution, and then its titration. Chemical methods often involve **gas detector tubes**, which are tubes packed with a reagent system suitable for analysis. After a gaseous sample is introduced into a gas detector tube, a reaction takes place (which can be redox, acid-base, etc.), and a color change occurs in the column packing. The concentration of the sample can be deduced from the length of the stain and comparison with calibration data. Gas detector tubes provide quick information, but they are not very specific.

Analysis of Water Samples

Because water has excellent solvent properties, it is recognized as the ultimate *sink* for pollutants. The common analytical tests performed on water samples include pH measurements and qualitative determinations, such as measurements for dissolved oxygen, total organic carbon, metals, salts, and trace organic substances.

pH, Acidity, and Alkalinity

pH is a measure of the acidity or basicity of a solution. Neutral water has a pH = 7.

Three common methods of pH measurement are: paper coated with an indicator dye (like litmus paper), indicator dyes (like phenolphthalein), and the pH electrode. Acidity measures the capacity of a solution to neutralize OH^- ions while basicity measures the capacity of a solution to neutralize

H^+ ions. Acidic solutions turn litmus paper red and basic solutions turn litmus paper blue. Indicator dyes change color at the pK_a of the dye, for instance, phenolphthalein turns a permanent pink color at a pH of 8.3. The pH of an acid solution can be obtained by titration with a strong base, sodium hydroxide, in the presence of an indicator dye. A pH electrode measures the voltage change in millivolts at a special composition glass electrode that senses H^+ ion concentration.

Determination of Dissolved Oxygen and Oxygen Demand

The amount of dissolved oxygen in water depends on the ambient temperature and pressure. Dissolved oxygen can be decreased or depleted by the biochemical breakdown of organic material in the water. These organic materials can be from animal, industrial, or agricultural sources. The **biochemical oxygen demand (BOD)** of certain organic processes can be determined by measuring the amount of O_2 present in water before and after the incubation of a sample for five days at 20°C. Dissolved oxygen is determined by using a dissolved oxygen electrode.

A titrimetric method called the Winkler method is also used, in which dissolved oxygen is used to oxidize Mn^{2+} to Mn^{4+}. The Mn^{4+} formed by this oxidation is then reduced in acidic solution in the presence of I^-, to form I_2, which is then titrated with sodium thiosulfate. The concentration of dissolved oxygen is obtained from the result of this titration. The sequence of reactions is:

$$MnO \cdot H_2O + \frac{1}{2} O_2 \rightarrow MnO_2 \cdot H_2O$$
$$MnO_2 \cdot H_2O + 2I^- + 4H^+ \rightarrow Mn^{2+} + I_2 + 3H_2O$$
$$I_2 + 2S_2O_3^{2-} \rightarrow S_4O_6^{2-} + 2I^-$$

One mole of $S_2O_3^{2-}$ is equivalent to 0.25 mole of O_2.

Total Organic Carbon

The BOD test described above gives us information on the oxidizability of the dissolved oxygen, but not on the total organic contents of the sample. To determine the total organic contain of a sample, a total organic carbon (TOC) test is performed. Several methods exist for this, but routine analysis is done by quantitative oxidation of the carbon to CO_2 with an ionization detector, such as those used in GC. The CO_2 can be formed from organic matter as follows:

- By quantitative oxidation of the organic carbon after acidification to remove interferences from carbonates and bicarbonates

- By oxidation of the organic carbon in a gas stream passed through a heated tube

- By oxidation of the organic carbon with potassium peroxydisulfate

Determination of Metals

Quantitative determination of metals is easily achieved by atomic spectroscopic methods such as flame emission spectrometry (FES), atomic absorption spectrometry (AAS), inductively coupled plasma-atomic emission spectrometry (ICP-ES), and inductively coupled plasma-mass spectrometry (ICP-MS).

Dissolved Salts

Water is an excellent solvent for ionic substances. The concentrations of dissolved substances in water can be determined with good sensitivity by electrical conductivity measurements. However, the determination of the concentrations of certain species may require individual reactions or chemical separation prior to these measurements. *Water hardness* refers to the properties of certain dissolved substances that lead to the formation of metal carbonate deposits in water, e.g., Ca^{+2}, Mg^{+2}, Fe^{2+}. Although all ionic species can be determined separately, total hardness is the quantity most regularly measured. This determination is performed by complexometric titration with EDTA at pH 10. Anionic species in water are measured and identified by chromatographic separation, followed by nonselective measurements such as conductivity. Ion-exchange chromatography is the method usually used for this.

RADIOCHEMICAL METHODS

There are three main reasons for which **radiotracers** are so useful in chemical analysis:

1. A chemical species can be labeled with a radioisotope, so that it becomes distinguishable from the unlabeled species. The radioisotope does not usually affect the chemical behavior of the labeled species. Tritium labels are an exception because of the significant mass difference between ^1_1H and ^3_1H.

2. Chemical environment does not influence the radioactive characteristics of an atom, so that a label can be detected wherever it appears.

3. During radioactive decay, particles and radiation are emitted with high energy and can be easily detected.

Instrumentation

In all radioactive methods, emissions are measured by a detector, which in turn emits a series of electrical pulses. Electrical pulses generated by the detector are amplified and sent to a recording device. When the detector is calibrated with standard sources, the proportionality between the activity of the source and the number of pulses generated by the detector within a given time (i.e., the count) can be determined; this gives a measure of the radioactivity of the source.

The three main types of detectors used in radiochemical methods are gas ionization detectors, semiconductors, and sodium iodide and liquid scintillation detectors.

Gas Ionization Detector

In this mode of detection, the ionizing radiation interacts with an ionizable gas, usually argon. The gas is maintained within a closed tube through which a thin wire anode courses. The anode is connected to a high voltage supply (300–3,000V), and when the ionizing radiation penetrates the tube, argon ions (Ar^+) and electrons are produced. The electrons are accelerated toward the anode, producing secondary ionization and an increase in the number of collisions between accelerated electrons and atoms. Electrical pulses are generated when electrons hit the anode.

Two types of gas ionization detectors exist:

1. The Geiger-Müller counter operates on high voltages, which leads to complete ionization of the filling gas; this saturates the detector. Under these conditions, the number of electrons produced is independent of the applied potential. Furthermore, the sizes of the pulses produced are all similar, irrespective of the nature and energy of the radiation.

2. The proportionality counter operates at lower voltages; here the size of the pulse is proportional to the energy of the radiation.

Semiconductor Detectors

With these detectors, the ionizing radiation hits the semiconductor atoms and lifts electrons into their conduction bands. The electrons can then travel very quickly toward the positive electrode. The positive species produced during the ionization cannot move freely, but the electrons (under the influence of high voltages, 3–5 kV), can move freely and are discharged at the anode to produce well-defined electrical pulses. There is a direct relationship between the energy of the radiation and the pulse size, which makes this detector an excellent choice for nuclear spectrometry.

Sodium Iodide Detector

In this type of detector, sodium iodide absorbs the radiation from the source and reemits it as UV light. Electrical pulses are then produced by a photocathode and a photomultiplier. The UV radiation exists at a strain center within the NaI crystal. To increase the efficiency of the detector, approximately 1% of the Na^+ ions is often replaced by the much larger Tl^+ ion; this creates more strain centers within the crystal.

Liquid Scintillation Counter

Some organic compounds can also absorb ionizing radiation and reemit it as UV light. The most common organic scintillators are conjugated aromatic compounds. They are frequently studied in solution; in these cases they are called **liquid scintillators**. The counting technique is used primarily with sources that are β-emitters with low particle energy. Some β⁻-emitters include ^3H, ^{14}C, and ^{35}S.

Liquid scintillation counting also requires the use of counting cocktails, which are made up of four components:

1. A solvent, which is usually toluene. Water is used with samples that are ionic.

2. An emulsifying agent that ensures good contact between the sample and the scintillator.

3. A primary scintillator that receives the energy (emitted by the source) and transfers it via its molecular orbitals to a secondary scintillator.

4. A secondary scintillator that reemits the absorbed energy at a longer wavelength in a region in which the photomultipliers are most efficient.

Interferences are often associated with liquid scintillation counting. Chemoluminescence arises when a chemical or biochemical reaction within the counting cocktail stimulates the emission of radiation. The sample can be refrigerated to slow down the process, heated to bring it to completion, or the interfering chemical can be removed—all of these procedures can attenuate the phenomenon. Chemical quenching arises when a chemical within the sample interacts with the scintillating radiation. Removal of the interfering chemical is the only solution for this. Color quenching occurs when a colored compound absorbs the scintillating radiation. Bleaching of the sample solution can solve this problem.

APPLICATIONS

STUDY OF CHEMICAL PATHWAYS

Chemical analyses frequently require separating an analyte from an interfering material, and specific quantitative procedures are used to achieve these separations. These procedures include solvent extraction, chromatography, and selective precipitation. The progress of these procedures is followed with radiotracers, which are very sensitive. So very small amounts of reactants are required to follow a chemical pathway. During the individual separation steps, the distribution of the species can be determined by simple measurements; the tracer indicates the efficiency or degree of completion of the procedure.

RADIOIMMUNOASSAY (RIA)

Immunogens are substances that have molecular masses of 6,000 or more and provoke an immunological response in animals. In RIA, a specific immunochemical reagent is used in sub-stochiometric amounts to determine the presence of a wide range of immunogens. This method relies on the specificity of immunochemical responses and the high sensitivities of radiotracer detectors. To design an RIA protocol, the appropriate antibody, or binding agent, must be obtained. This is achieved by forcing the immunogen to enter the bloodstream of an animal; this triggers the animal's natural defense system. Antibodies (binding agents) that are highly specific to the immunogen are produced by the animal, and these binding agents are sufficient for use in RIA. After an incubation period of 10 to 12 weeks (or until a sufficient amount of antibodies has been produced), blood is taken from the animal, and the serum containing the antibodies is separated. This serum is often called antiserum. The production of the antiserum is always the longest and most difficult step in the RIA procedure.

The rest of the procedure involves four main steps:

1. The binding agent must be mixed with measured amounts of the labeled analyte and the antiserum to analyze the sample.

2. This solution must be incubated at 2–4°C for one to two hours to allow a state of equilibrium to be established.

3. The bound and the free analyte must be separated; this is done by adsorption of the free analyte on activated charcoal or precipitation of the bound analyte with ammonium sulfate.

4. The activity ratio (A) between the bound and free analyte must be measured. The activity ratio is given by $A = \dfrac{Z}{X + Y - Z}$ where X is the amount of analyte in the sample (the quantity to be determined), Y is the amount of labeled analyte added, and Z is the amount of antiserum added. RIA is extremely useful in determining small amounts of organic compounds in complex matrices. RIA methods are not as complex as conventional procedures, because they use extremely specific binding agents and because analysis can be performed at the picogram level. RIA methods are extensively used in medicinal and forensic investigations, as well as in the determination of drugs (amphetamines, barbiturates, morphine, nicotine, penicillin, etc.), steroids (androgens, estrogens, progesterones, etc.), and hormones (growth

hormone, insulin, etc.). RIA methods are sensitive, specific, and simple to apply, but specific binding agents may be difficult to obtain, cross-reaction (interference) with molecules similar to the analyte can sometimes occur, and precision is generally about 1–3%.

REFERENCE: STATISTICS AND STANDARDS

STATISTICS USED IN CHEMISTRY
Statistics are used to check the accuracy of collected experimental data, to compare two experimental methods, to compress data, and to express the precision of a result.

Significant Figures
Significant figures are the *number of digits required to express a given quantity with precision*. When we say that a number is expressed to a given number of significant figures, this means that the last digit in the number always has an uncertainty of ±1. So a number expressed to four significant figures has an uncertainty of ±1 in its last digit.

The following numbers are all expressed to five significant figures (the uncertainty expressed in the last number is in boldtype):

0.1308**3**

1308.**3**

0.01308

Example of an addition:

310.**3**

8.418

<u>0.1609</u>

318.8789

Is this result correct, or is 318.**8** correct?

Neither. The correct answer is 318.**9**, because the first term of the addition, 310.**3**, which is expressed to 4 significant figures, has an uncertainty of one in its last digit; because of this, it invalidates the number of digits after the decimal in the other two terms. 318.**8** is also incorrect, because the 8 must be raised to 9, since the digit that follows the 8 (7) is > 5.

Rounding Off Numbers

210.04 = 210.0

210.06 = 210.1

210.05 = 210.0

210.15 = 210.2

The numbers above have been rounded off correctly: 210.04 is rounded off to 210.0 because the 4 is smaller than 5; similarly, 210.06 is rounded off to 210.1 because the 6 is greater than 5; 210.05 is rounded off to 210.0 because the 0 before the 5 is an even number; and 210.15 is rounded off to 210.2 because the 1 before the 5 is an odd number.

Percent Error

$$\% \text{ error} = \frac{\text{actual} - \text{measured}}{\text{actual} \times 100\%}$$

Consider the following expression: $\dfrac{(22.64 \times 0.3402 \times 0.06400)}{3.1433} \times 100\%$

The % error for each term is:

Term	% Error
22.64 ± 0.01	0.0442
0.3402 ± 0.0001	0.0294
0.06400 ± 0.00001	0.0156
3.1433 ± 0.0001	0.0032

Adding up the % errors: $0.0442 + 0.0294 + 0.0156 + 0.0032 = 0.0924\%$,

and

$$\frac{(22.64 \times 0.3402 \times 0.06400)}{3.1433} \times 100\% = 15.6821236$$

with 0.0924% error

or

$$\frac{15.6821236 \times 0.0924}{100} = 0.0145$$

, reported as 15.68 ± 0.01

We use the largest possible error (22.64 ± 0.01 or 1 in 2,264) seen in the lot above with respect to significant figures.

Two types of errors can affect the accuracy of a measured quantity. They are:

1. **Determinate errors:** These are errors that are instrumental, operative, and in methodology; these errors can be avoided or corrected.

2. **Indeterminate errors:** Accidental and random, these errors cannot be estimated or predicted except by mathematical probability theory, which states that indeterminate errors follow a Gaussian distribution. Statistics deals with this type of error.

Basic Statistics in Chemistry: Definitions

Some basic statistical definitions are illustrated below using the following series of numbers:

$$2, 4, 5, 6, 7, 7, 8, 9, 9, 9, 11, 11, 12$$

Mode	9 is the mode; i.e., the value that appears the most frequently in the group.
Arithmetic mean ($\bar{x}$)	The sum of the numbers (x_i), divided by their quantity N:

$$\bar{x} = \frac{\Sigma_{x_i}}{N} = \frac{100}{13} = 7.69$$

Median	The central value of the set (in this case, 8).
Geometric mean (m_g)	The product of the numbers, raised to the power $\dfrac{1}{N}$

or

$$m_g = (x_1 x_2 \ldots x_i)^{\frac{1}{N}}$$

$$(2 \bullet 4 \bullet 5 \bullet 6 \bullet 7 \bullet 7 \bullet 8 \bullet 9 \bullet 9 \bullet 9 \bullet 11 \bullet 11 \bullet 12)^{1/13} = 7.01$$

Mean deviation	The value of a measurement in a series minus the arithmetic mean of the series: $x - \bar{x}$
Absolute deviation	The absolute value of the mean deviation: $\lvert x - \bar{x} \rvert$
Standard deviation (S)	$S = \sqrt{\sum(x_i - \bar{x})^2 / N - 1}$

Example:

Given a series of data points (8, 11, 12, 13, 16), find the standard deviation.

Solution:

First, tabulate the data; start by calculating the statistical quantities you need to use the standard deviation equation $S = \sqrt{\sum(x_i - \bar{x})^2 / N - 1}$:

x	$x - \bar{x}$	$\lvert x - \bar{x} \rvert$	$(x - x)^2$
8	−4	4	16
11	−1	1	1
12	0	0	0
13	+1	1	1
16	+4	4	16
Total:	0	$\bullet / N = 10/5 = 2$	$(x - \bar{x})^2 = 34$

The arithmetic mean is:

$$\bar{x} = \frac{\sum x_i}{N} = \frac{1}{5}(60) = 12$$

And the standard deviation is:

$$S = \sqrt{\frac{\sum(x_i - \bar{x})^2}{N - 1}} = \sum = \sqrt{\frac{34}{5 - 1}} = 2.915$$

Standard deviation (S):

$$S = \sqrt{\frac{\sum x_i^2 - \dfrac{(\sum x_i)^2}{N}}{N - 1}}$$

This is an alternate standard deviation formula that does not require calculating of the mean. Using the values of the previous example with this formula, we see that

$$S = 2.915 \text{ since } N = 5, (\sum x_i)^2 = 3{,}600; \sum x_i^2 = 64 + 121 + 144 + 169 + 256 = 754$$

Variance:	The square of the standard deviation: S^2
Standard error of the mean:	$\dfrac{S}{\sqrt{N}}$
The confidence level:	$1 - \alpha$, where $\alpha = 0.05$ if a 95% level of confidence is desired, 0.01 for a 99% level, and 0.001 for a 99.9% level.

Chemists report their results at any one of these three confidence levels. At a confidence level of 95%, the measurement is referred to as "significant"; at 99%, it is "highly significant"; and at 99.9%, it is "very significant."

The confidence limit:	$\bar{x} \pm \dfrac{tS}{\sqrt{N}}$, where t is a statistical factor that is dependent on the desired confidence level and on the number of degrees of freedom.

Example:

A chemist makes 118 distinct measurements of the dielectric constant of ethanol. The mean value obtained is $x = 32.70$ debye and $S = 0.07$. At a 99% level of confidence, what is the true dielectric constant of ethanol?

t Values for Confidence Testing

Degrees of Freedom	Confidence Level 95% ($\alpha = 0.05$)	Confidence Level 99% ($\alpha = 0.01$)
1	12.706	63.657
2	4.303	9.925
3	3.182	5.841
4	2.776	4.604
5	2.571	4.032
6	2.447	3.707
7	2.365	3.500
8	2.306	3.355
9	2.262	3.250
10	2.228	3.169
25	2.060	2.787
∞	1.960	2.576

Solution:

Because the desired confidence level is 99%, $\alpha = 0.01$, and $N = 118$, so the number of degrees of freedom equals $N - 1 = 117$. Because $N - 1$ exceeds 25, the infinity value is used from the table of t values: for $N = \infty$, the t value is 2.576 at a confidence level of 99%. And the true dielectric constant of ethanol is equal to:

$$\bar{x} \pm \frac{tS}{\sqrt{N}} = 32.70 \pm \left[\frac{2.576 \times 0.07}{\sqrt{118}} \right] \text{debye} = 32.70 \pm 0.01659 \text{ debye}$$

$$= 32.70 \pm 0.02 \text{ debye}$$

Data Collection: The Method of Least Squares

When plotting data, we get a group of data points made up of x and y values. The x values are *independent* variables and the y values are *dependent* variables. The data do not usually plot in a straight line; more often *scatter* is present due to experimental error.

Since many chemical processes can be described by a straight line of the type $y = mx + b$, a method has been developed to obtain the best possible straight line from a series of experimental data points (which contain a degree of scatter).

This is called the **method of least squares**, which involves two equations. The first is used to calculate the slope m.

$$m = \frac{\sum x_i y_i - \left[\dfrac{\sum x_i \sum y_i}{N} \right]}{\sum x_i^2 - \left[\dfrac{\left(\sum x_i \right)^2}{N} \right]}$$

$$b = \bar{y} - m\bar{x}$$

where: n = number of data points

$$\bar{x} = \text{mean of } x \text{ values} = \frac{\sum x_i}{N}$$

$$\bar{y} = \text{mean of } y \text{ values} = \frac{\sum y_i}{N}$$

$\sum x_i$ = sum of x values

$\sum y_i$ = sum of y values

Example:

NADH has a strong absorbance at 340 nm; a calibration curve is prepared by recording the absorbance at that wavelength with samples of different concentrations. Get the best straight line from the experimental measurements using the method of least squares, and determine the concentration of a solution of NADH with absorbance at 340 nm, equal to 0.501, based on $y = mx + b$.

The values obtained for the different concentrations are as follows:

Concentration (mg/mL)	A_{340}
0.00	0.002
10.00	0.121
20.00	0.242
30.00	0.268
40.00	0.402
50.00	0.483
60.00	0.612
70.00	0.711
80.00	0.821
90.00	0.921
100.00	1.011

Rearranging:

x_i	y_i	x_i^2	x_iy_i
0.00	0.002	0.00	0.00
10.00	0.121	100.00	1.21
20.00	0.242	400.00	4.84
30.00	0.268	900.00	8.04
40.00	0.402	1,600.00	16.08
50.00	0.483	2,500.00	24.15
60.00	0.612	3,600.00	36.72
70.00	0.711	4,900.00	49.77
80.00	0.821	6,400.00	65.68
90.00	0.921	8,100.00	82.89
100.00	1.011	10,000.00	101.10

and

$$\left(\sum x_i\right)^2 x_i = 550.00$$

$$\frac{\sum x_i}{n} = \frac{550.00}{11} = 50 = x$$

$$\sum y_i = 5.594$$

$$\frac{\sum y_i}{n} = \frac{5.594}{11} = 0.508 = \overline{y}$$

$$\left(\sum x_i\right)^2 = 302,500.00$$

$$\sum (x_i)^2 = 38,500.00$$

$$\sum (x_iy_i) = 390.48$$

Then

$$m = \frac{\sum x_iy_i - \left[\dfrac{\sum x_i \sum y_i}{N}\right]}{\sum x_i^2 - \left[\dfrac{\left(\sum x_i\right)^2}{N}\right]}$$

$$= \frac{390.48 - \left[\dfrac{550.00 - 5.594}{11}\right]}{38,500.00 - \left[\dfrac{302,500.00}{11}\right]}$$

$$= \frac{110.78}{11,000} = 0.001$$

and

$$b = \bar{y} - m\bar{x}$$

$$= 0.508 - (0.01)(50)$$

$$= 0.008$$

The straight line is $y = mx + b$

$$y = 0.01x + 0.008$$

And the graph looks like this:

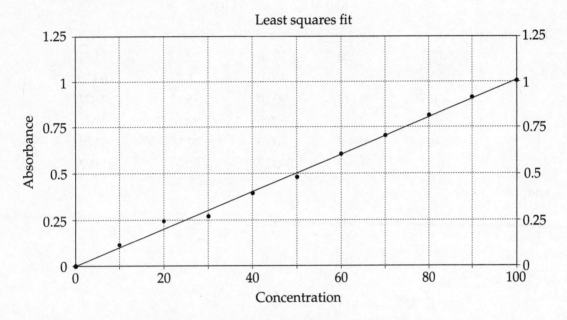

The concentration of the NADH sample can be extrapolated from the graph or by using Abs = mx + b, $0.501 = 0.01x + 0.008$, and x = concentration = 49.30 mg/mL.

The Correlation Coefficient

The correlation coefficient defines the correlation between two variables. It expresses a relationship between *observed* values and *probable* values. The higher the correlation between observed and probable values, the better the data.

The correlation coefficient r is calculated from two sets of data points as follows:

$$r = \frac{\sum x_i y_i - nxy}{\sqrt{(\sum x_i^2 - nx^2)(\sum y_i^2 - ny^2)}}$$

When r is between 0.90 and 0.95, the correlation is fair; when r is between 0.95 and 0.99, the correlation is good; and it's excellent when $r > 0.99$.

Example:

A calibration curve was prepared by plotting the concentration of benzhydroxamic acid versus its absorbance at 280 nm. Calculate the correlation coefficient.

[BHA] µM	A_{280}
10.0	0.203
20.0	0.412
30.0	0.614
40.0	0.819
50.0	0.957
60.0	1.001

Rearranging:

x_i	y_i	x_i^2	$x_i y_i$	y_i^2
10.0	0.203	100.0	2.03	0.041
20.0	0.412	400.0	8.24	0.170
30.0	0.614	900.0	18.42	0.377
40.0	0.819	1,600.0	32.76	0.671
50.0	0.957	2,500.0	47.85	0.908
60.0	1.001	3,600.0	60.06	1.002

and

$$n = 6$$

$$x = 35.0$$

$$y = 0.667$$

$$\sum y_i^2 = 3.169$$

$$\sum x_i^2 = 9,100.0$$

$$\sum x_i y_i = 169.36$$

and the correlation coefficient is:

$$r = \frac{\sum x_i y_i - nxy}{\sqrt{(\sum x_i^2 - nx^2)(\sum y_i^2 - ny^2)}}$$

$$r = \frac{169.36 - (6)(35.0)(0.667)}{\sqrt{\left[9,100.00 - (6)(35.0)^2\right]\left[3.169 - (6)(0.667)^2\right]}}$$

$$r = 0.99$$

The correlation is excellent.

SOLUTIONS AND STANDARDIZATION

General Terms

The following terms are found in expressions for concentration:

- **Molecular formula:** indicates the number and type of atoms present in a given molecule
- **Molecular weight:** the sum of the atomic weights of all of the atoms in a molecule
- **Mole:** a mole of a substance is the amount in grams of that substance that's numerically equal to its molecular weight in atomic mass units (amu)
- **Equivalent weight:** that weight required to react completely with one mole of another substance

One mole of any substance contains the same number of molecules or atoms: 6.02214×10^{23}. This is Avogadro's number.

The concentration of solutions is expressed as follows:

- **Molar concentration (M):** number of moles of substance in one liter of solution
- **Normal concentration (N):** number of equivalent weights of a substance in one liter of solution
- **Molality (m):** number of moles of substance per 1 kg of solvent
- **Percent by weight:** weight of solute/weight of solution $\times 100\%$

Dilutions are calculated using this formula:

$$Concentration_{final} \cdot Volume_{final} = Concentration_{initial} \cdot Volume_{initial}$$

Example:

Calculate the volume of 0.1 M HCl needed to prepare 50 ml of 0.05 M HCl.

Solution:

$$M_f V_f = M_i V_i$$

$$V_i = \frac{M_f V_f}{M_i}$$

$$V_i = \frac{0.05\ M \times 50\ ml}{0.1\ M}$$

$$V_i = 25\ ml$$

So 25 ml of 0.1 M HCl should be diluted to 50 ml; i.e., 25 ml of 0.1 M HCl + 25 ml H_2O.

Standard Solutions

Standard solutions are prepared by dissolving an accurately massed amount of a primary standard in a known volume of solution, using volumetric glassware. A **primary standard** is a chemical of very high purity (> 99.99%). Potassium acid phthalate is a primary acid standard that is commonly used to standardize base solutions. Na_2CO_3 is a standard base used to standardize acid solutions.

If the chemical substance is not pure enough, it can be reacted with a primary standard. For example, NaOH is not a primary standard because it absorbs water easily; i.e., it is hygroscopic. But its reaction with potassium acid phthalate—itself a primary standard—turns it into a standard solution that can be used as a titrant:

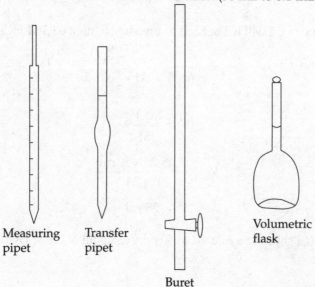

Standardized solution
used to titrate

Now the concentration of the NaOH solution can be determined with a high degree of accuracy. Similarly, Na_2CO_3 (primary standard) is used to standardize sulfuric acid.

Measurement of Volume

Volume is measured using volumetric glassware (pipets, beakers, graduated cylinders).

The most accurate glassware are:

Volumetric flasks: calibrated to contain a known volume of solution at a given temperature (20 or 25° C)

Burets: calibrated to deliver a known volume of solution (50 mL to 0.1 mL)

Measuring pipet

Transfer pipet

Buret

Volumetric flask

Chemical Equations

$$Na_2SO_4 + BaCl_2 \rightarrow BaSO_4 + 2NaCl$$

This equation shows the quantities of reagents that react in this chemical reaction. For example, by the law of conservation of mass, 142 g (1 mole) of Na_2SO_4 will react with 208 g (1 mole) of $BaCl_2$ to yield 233 g of $BaSO_4$ (1 mole) and 117 g of NaCl (2 moles). Notice that 142 g + 208 g = 233g + 117 g.

Molar Calculation

$$\textit{For any substance, number of moles} = \frac{weight \ (in \ grams)}{molecular \ weight}$$

Example:
How can the mass of SO_3 be determined in solution?

Solution:

1. SO_3 exists in solution as a part of the following equilibrium:

$$SO_3(g) + H_2O(l) \leftrightarrow H_2SO_4 \ (aq)$$

2. Adding NaOH will cause all of the $SO_3(g)$ to be converted first to H_2SO_4 *(aq)* and then, via this neutralization, into the soluble sodium sulfate salt:

$$NaOH + H_2SO_4 \rightarrow Na_2SO_4 \ (soluble) + H_2O$$

3. The amount of SO_3 is determined by calculating the mass of SO_4^{2-}, since there is a 1:1 molar ratio of SO_3 to SO_4^{2-} in **Solution:**

So the mass of $SO_3 = \dfrac{\text{mass of precipitate} \times \text{molecular weight } SO_3}{\text{molecular weight } BaSO_4}$

PRACTICE PROBLEMS

1. Write the dissolution equilibrium established between the following ionic compounds and their ions. Then, for each, write the solubility product, K_{sp}.

   (A) CuI

   (B) $Ba(IO_3)_2$

   (C) $Pb_3(PO_4)_2$

   (D) $La(IO_3)_3$

   (E) $La_2(C_2O_4)_3$

2. Given the following standard electrode potentials, which will be the strongest reducing agent?

   $$Mg^{2+} + 2e^- \leftrightarrow Mg \qquad E^o = -2.37 \text{ V}$$

   $$Fe^{2+} + 2e^- \leftrightarrow Fe \qquad E^o = -0.44 \text{ V}$$

   $$Cr^{3+} + e^- \leftrightarrow Cr^{2+} \qquad E^o = -0.41 \text{ V}$$

3. Given the solubility product constant of barium iodate, $Ba(IO_3)_2$, calculate the solubility in g/L and the molar concentration of the ions at equilibrium.

   $$K_{sp} = 1.6 \times 10^{-9}; \text{ molar mass} = 487 \text{ g/mol}$$

   $$Ba(IO_3)_2(s) \leftrightarrow Ba^{2+}(aq) + 2IO_3^-$$

4. Calculate the solubility product constant of bismuth (III) sulfide. The solubility is 9.9×10^{-16} mol/L.

   $$Bi_2S_3(s) \leftrightarrow 2Bi^{3+}(aq) + 3S^{2-}(aq)$$

ANSWERS TO PRACTICE PROBLEMS

1. (A) $CuI(s) \leftrightarrow Cu^+(aq) + I^-(aq)$

    $K_{sp} = [Cu^+][I^-]$

    (B) $Ba(IO_3)_2(s) \leftrightarrow Ba^{2+}(aq) + 2IO_3^-$

    $K_{sp} = [Ba^{2+}][IO_3^-]^2$

    (C) $Pb_3(PO_4)_2(s) \leftrightarrow 3Pb^{2+}(aq) + 2PO_4^{3-}(aq)$

    $K_{sp} = [Pb^{2+}]^3[PO_4^{3-}]^2$

    (D) $La(IO_3)_3(s) \leftrightarrow La^{3+}(aq) + 3IO_3^-(aq)$

    $K_{sp} = [La^{3+}][IO_3^-]^3$

    (E) $La_2(C_2O_4)_3(s) \leftrightarrow 2La^{3+}(aq) + 3C_2O_4^{2-}(aq)$

    $K_{sp} = [La^{3+}]^2[C_2O_4^{2-}]^3$

2. The answer is magnesium, because its standard reduction potential is the most negative. The more negative the standard reduction potential, the greater the tendency the reduction to be oxidized.

3. $K_{sp} = [Ba^{2+}][IO_3^-]^2 = s(2s)^2 = 4s^3$

    $$s = \left(\frac{K_{sp}}{4}\right)^{\frac{1}{3}} = \left(\frac{1.6 \times 10^{-9}}{4}\right)^{\frac{1}{3}} = 7.4 \times 10^{-4} \text{ mol/L}$$

    $s = (7.4 \times 10^{-4} \text{ mol/L})(487 \text{ g/mol}) = 0.36 \text{ g/L}$

    $[Pb^{2+}] = s = 7.4 \times 10^{-4} \text{ mol/L}$

    $[IO_3^-] = 2s = 1.5 \times 10^{-3} \text{ mol/L}$

4. $K_{sp} = [Bi^{3+}]^2[S^{2-}]^3 = (2s)^2(3s)^3 = 108s^5$

    $K_{sp} = 108s^5 = 108(9.9 \times 10^{-16})^5 = 1.0 \times 10^{-73}$

6

GRE Chemistry
Practice Test

Material in the tables on pages 330 and 331 may be useful in answering the questions in this examination.

PERIODIC TABLE OF THE ELEMENTS

1 **H** 1.0																		2 **He** 4.0
3 **Li** 6.9	4 **Be** 9.0											5 **B** 10.8	6 **C** 12.0	7 **N** 14.0	8 **O** 16.0	9 **F** 19.0	10 **Ne** 20.2
11 **Na** 23.0	12 **Mg** 24.3											13 **Al** 27.0	14 **Si** 28.1	15 **P** 31.0	16 **S** 32.1	17 **Cl** 35.5	18 **Ar** 39.9
19 **K** 39.1	20 **Ca** 40.1	21 **Sc** 45.0	22 **Ti** 47.9	23 **V** 50.9	24 **Cr** 52.0	25 **Mn** 54.9	26 **Fe** 55.8	27 **Co** 58.9	28 **Ni** 58.7	29 **Cu** 63.5	30 **Zn** 65.4	31 **Ga** 69.7	32 **Ge** 72.6	33 **As** 74.9	34 **Se** 79.0	35 **Br** 79.9	36 **Kr** 83.8
37 **Rb** 85.5	38 **Sr** 87.6	39 **Y** 88.9	40 **Zr** 91.2	41 **Nb** 92.9	42 **Mo** 95.9	43 **Tc** (98)	44 **Ru** 101.1	45 **Rh** 102.9	46 **Pd** 106.4	47 **Ag** 107.9	48 **Cd** 112.4	49 **In** 114.8	50 **Sn** 118.7	51 **Sb** 121.8	52 **Te** 127.6	53 **I** 126.9	54 **Xe** 131.3
55 **Cs** 132.9	56 **Ba** 137.3	57 ***La** 138.9	72 **Hf** 178.5	73 **Ta** 180.9	74 **W** 183.9	75 **Re** 186.2	76 **Os** 190.2	77 **Ir** 192.2	78 **Pt** 195.1	79 **Au** 197.0	80 **Hg** 200.6	81 **Tl** 204.4	82 **Pb** 207.2	83 **Bi** 209.0	84 **Po** (209)	85 **At** (210)	86 **Rn** (222)
87 **Fr** (223)	88 **Ra** 226.0	89 †**Ac** 227.0	104 **Rf** 261.0	105 **Db** 262.0	106 **Sg** 263.0	107 **Bh** 262.0	108 **Hs** 265.0	109 **Mt** 266.0	110 § 269.0	111 § 272.0	112 § 277.0						

§Not yet named

*Lanthanum Series

58 **Ce** 140.1	59 **Pr** 140.9	60 **Nd** 144.2	61 **Pm** (145)	62 **Sm** 150.4	63 **Eu** 152.0	64 **Gd** 157.3	65 **Tb** 158.9	66 **Dy** 162.5	67 **Ho** 164.9	68 **Er** 167.3	69 **Tm** 168.9	70 **Yb** 173.0	71 **Lu** 175.0

†Actinium Series

90 **Th** 232.0	91 **Pa** 231.0	92 **U** 238.0	93 **Np** 237.0	94 **Pu** (244)	95 **Am** (243)	96 **Cm** (247)	97 **Bk** (247)	98 **Cf** (251)	99 **Es** (252)	100 **Fm** (258)	101 **Md** (258)	102 **No** (259)	103 **Lr** (260)

TABLE OF INFORMATION

Electron rest mass	$m_e = 9.11 \times 10^{-31}$ kilogram
Proton rest mass	$m_p = 1.672 \times 10^{-27}$ kilogram
Neutron rest mass	$m_n = 1.675 \times 10^{-27}$ kilogram
Magnitude of the electron charge	$e = 1.60 \times 10^{-19}$ coulomb
Bohr radius	$a_0 = 5.29 \times 10^{-11}$ meter
Avogadro number	$N_A = 6.02 \times 10^{-23}$ per mole
Universal gas constant	$R = 8.314$ joules/(mole · K) = 0.0821 L · atm/(mole · K) = 0.08314 L · bar/(mole · K)
Boltzmann constant	$k = 1.38 \times 10^{-23}$ joule/K
Planck constant	$h = 6.63 \times 10^{-34}$ joule·second
Speed of light	$c = 3.00 \times 10^8$ m/s $= 3.00 \times 10^{10}$ cm/s
1 atmosphere pressure	1 atm $= 1.0 \times 10^5$ newtons/meter2 = 1.0×10^5 pascals (Pa)
Faraday constant	$\mathscr{F} = 9.65 \times 10^4$ coulombs/mole
1 atomic mass unit (amu)	1 amu $= 1.66 \times 10^{-27}$ kilogram
1 electron volt (eV)	1 eV $= 1.602 \times 10^{-19}$ joule
Volume of 1 mole of ideal gas at 0°C, 1 atmosphere	$= 22.4$ liters

GO ON TO THE NEXT PAGE.

NO TEST MATERIAL ON THIS PAGE

CHEMISTRY TEST
Time—170 Minutes
141 Questions

Directions: Each of the questions or incomplete statements below is followed by five suggested answers or completions. Select the one that is best in each case and then fill in the corresponding space on the answer sheet.

Note: Solutions are aqueous unless otherwise specified.

Throughout the test the following symbols have the specified definitions unless otherwise noted.

T = temperature M = molar
P = pressure m = molal
V = volume   L = milliliter(s)
S = entropy   g = gram(s)
H = enthalpy   m = nanometer(s)
U = internal energy   L = liter(s)
R = molar gas constant   kg = kilogram(s)
n = number of moles   atm = atmosphere(s)

---

1. Choose the answer below that accurately describes the hybridization of the central atom and the molecular geometry of BF_3.

   (A) sd^2, trigonal planar
   (B) sp^2, pyramidal
   (C) sp^2, trigonal planar
   (D) sd^2, pyramidal
   (E) spd, trigonal planar

2. Of the following, which acid doesn't completely dissociate in solution?

   (A) HF
   (B) HBr
   (C) HCl
   (D) HNO_3
   (E) $HClO_4$

3. How many unpaired electrons are there in a ground-state chromium atom?

   (A) One
   (B) Two
   (C) Three
   (D) Four
   (E) Six

GO ON TO THE NEXT PAGE.

4. Which of the following substances is a good reducing agent?

   (A) NaCl
   (B) $LiAlH_4$
   (C) N_2
   (D) $KMnO_4$
   (E) O_3

5. Identify the element with the greatest first ionization energy.

   (A) Ce
   (B) C
   (C) Cl
   (D) Ca
   (E) Cs

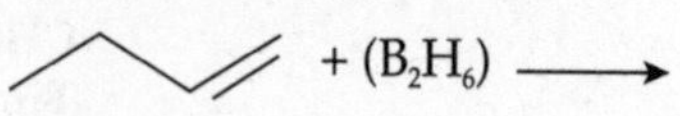

$+ (B_2H_6) \longrightarrow$

6. After treatment of the reaction mixture above with hydrogen peroxide, sodium hydroxide, and water, what is the product of the reaction?

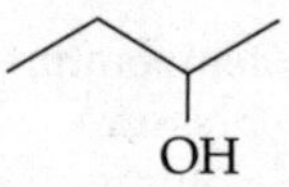

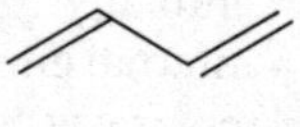

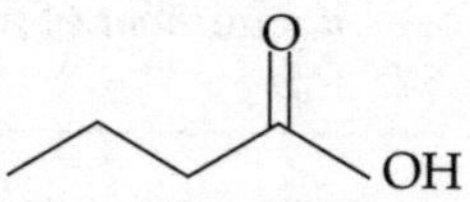

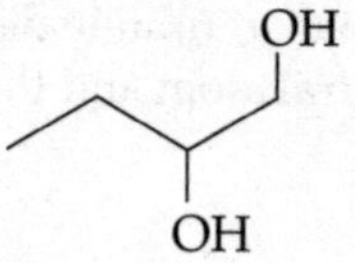

GO ON TO THE NEXT PAGE.

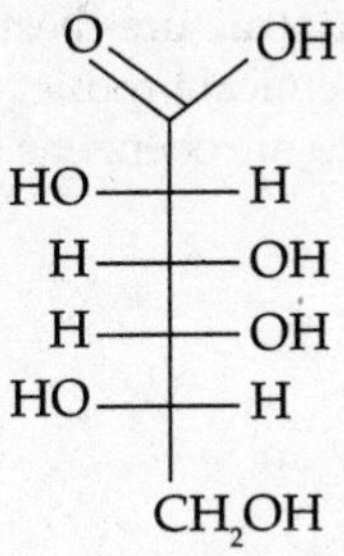

O=C—OH

HO——H

H——OH

H——OH

HO——H

CH_2OH

7. Which of the following compounds is an epimer of the molecule above?

(A)

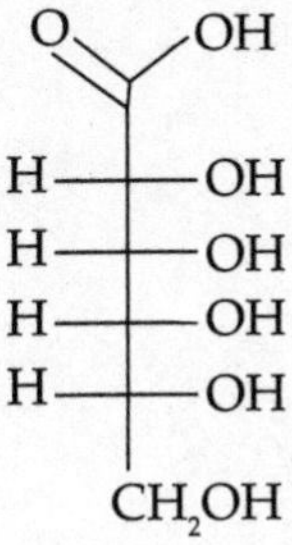

O=C—OH

H——OH

H——OH

H——OH

H——OH

CH_2OH

(E)

O=C—OH

H——OH

HO——H

HO——H

H——OH

CH_2OH

(B)

O=C—OH

HO——H

HO——H

HO——H

HO——H

CH_2OH

(C)

HO—C=O

HO——H

H——OH

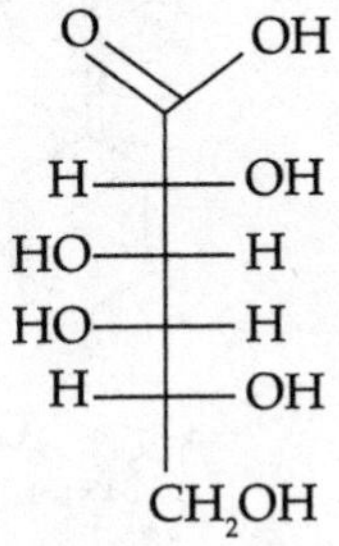

H——OH

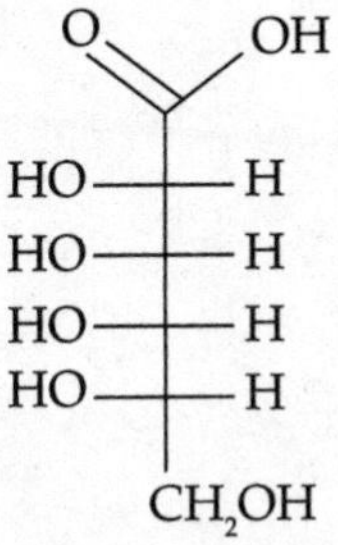

HO——H

CH_2OH

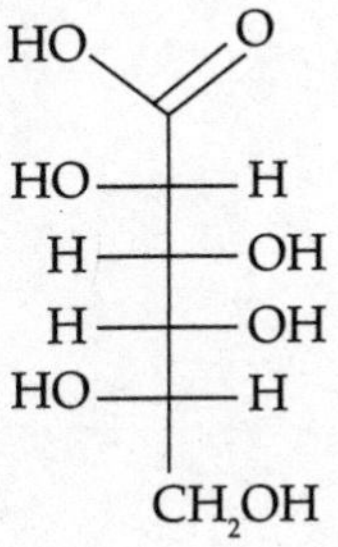

(D)

O=C—OH

HO——H

H——OH

H——OH

H——OH

CH_2OH

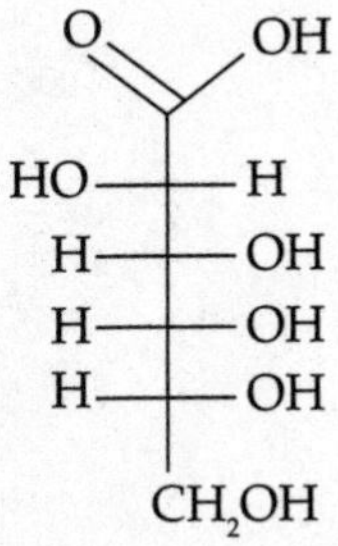

GO ON TO THE NEXT PAGE.

8. Which of the following molecules contains the aldehyde functionality of exo stereochemistry?

(A)

CHO

(B)

CHO

(C)

CHO

(D)

CHO

(E)

CHO

9. Which of the following resonance structures best illustrates why the major regiochemical product of the electrophilic addition of BR_2 to nitrobenzene is NOT p-bromonitrobenzene?

(A)

(B)

(C)

(D)

(E)

GO ON TO THE NEXT PAGE.

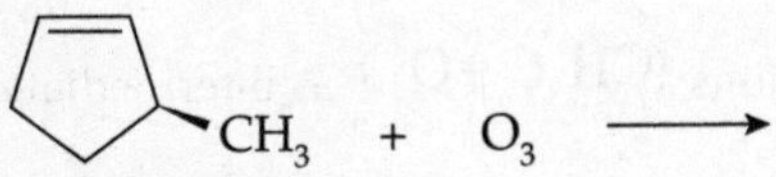

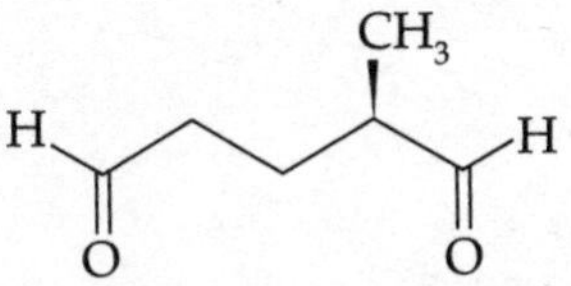

$$Ph(Et)_2N \; + \; CH_3CH_2I \; \rightarrow \; PhN(Et)_3N^+I^-$$

10. After treatment with Zn/H_2O, what is the product of the reaction above?

(A)

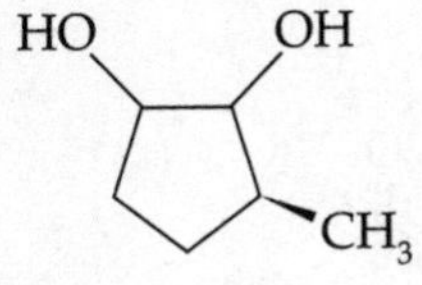

(B)

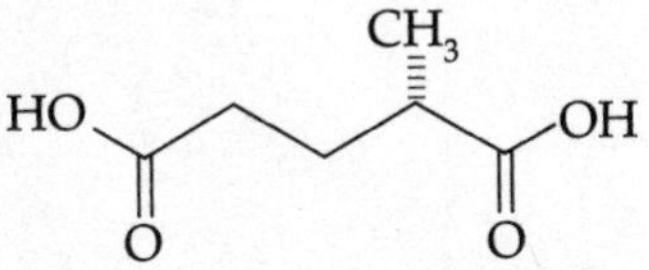

(C)

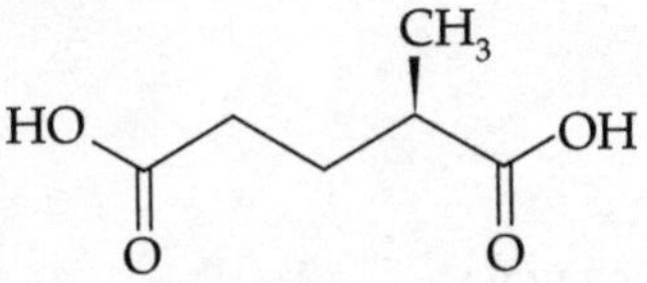

(D)

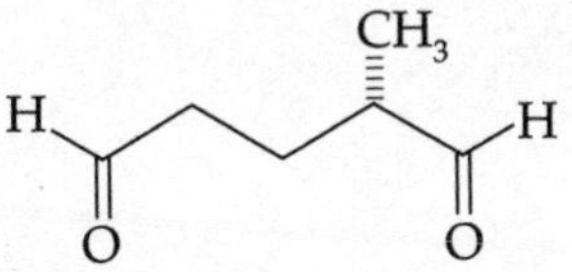

(E)

11. The reaction above is an example of which of the following?

(A) Nucleophilic substitution
(B) Electrophilic addition
(C) Radical chain reaction
(D) Elimination
(E) Electrophilic aromatic substitution

GO ON TO THE NEXT PAGE.

12. Which of the following reactions would be most likely to produce acylium ions $(CH_3C \equiv O^+)$ as intermediates in the reaction mechanism?

(A)

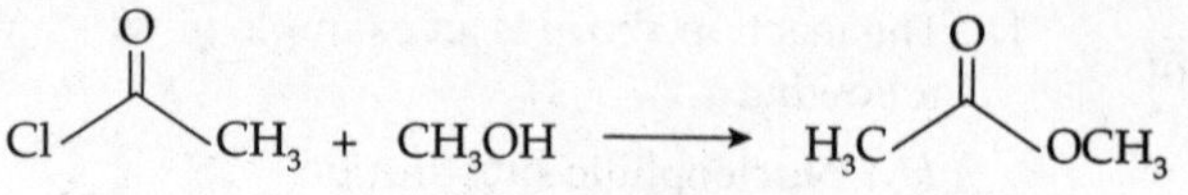

(B)

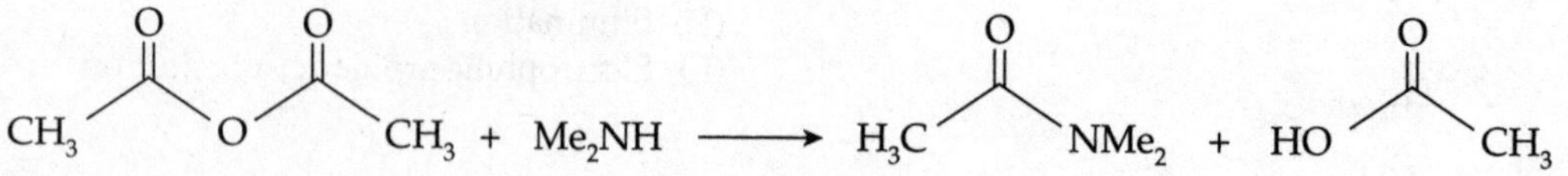

(C)

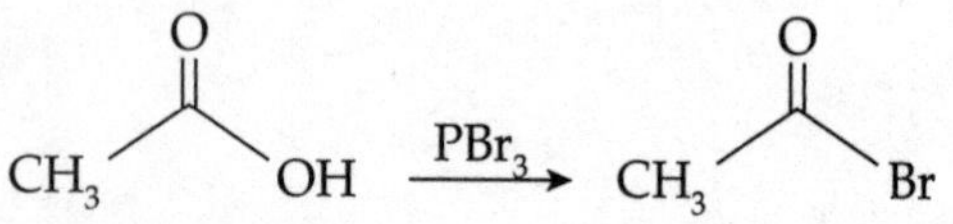

(D)

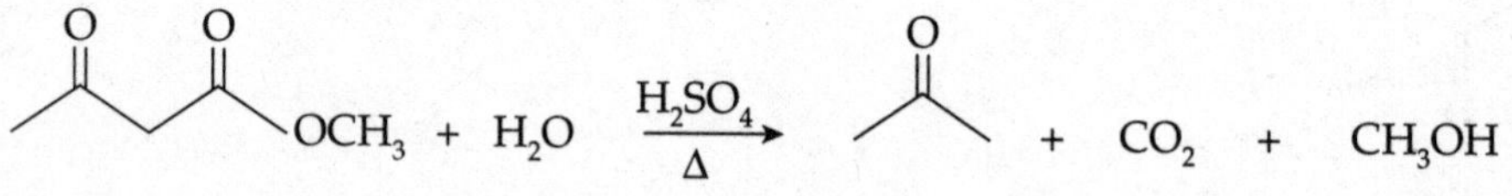

(E)

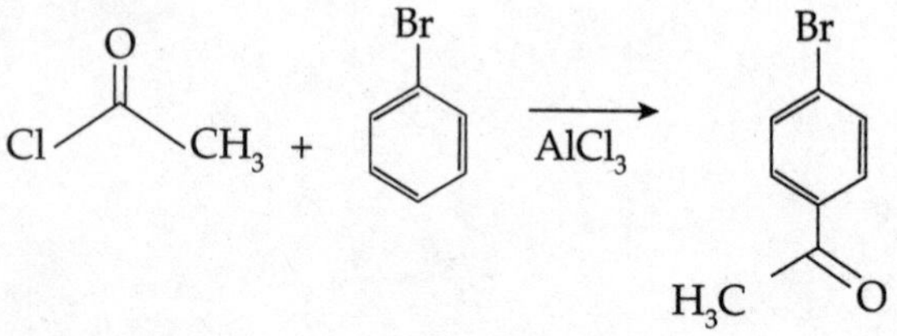

---

13. Which of the following is not commonly used as a primary standard for acid/base titrations?

(A) Potassium bicarbonate
(B) Potassium hydrogen phthalate
(C) Potassium hydroxide
(D) Borax ($Na_2B_4O_7$)
(E) HCl

GO ON TO THE NEXT PAGE.

14. Which of the following graphs accurately represents the potential applied to the working electrode in a typical cyclic voltammetry experiment?

(A)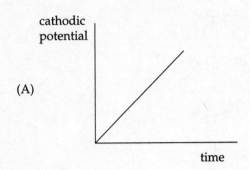

(B)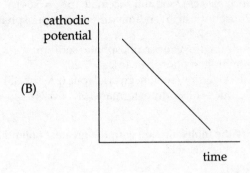

(C)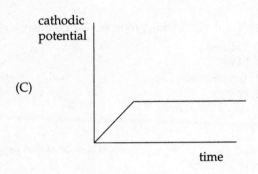

(D)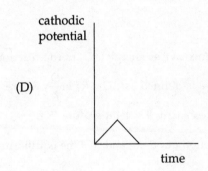

(E)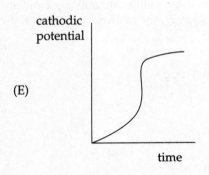

GO ON TO THE NEXT PAGE.

15. Which of the following conjugate acid/base pairs should be used to prepare a buffer with pH near 7.15?

    (A) Succinic acid/sodium succinate (pK_a = 5.64)
    (B) Phosphoric acid/sodium dihydrogen phosphate (pK_{a1} = 2.15)
    (C) Sodium dihydrogen phosphate/sodium hydrogen phosphate (pK_{a2} = 7.20)
    (D) Glycylglycine/sodium glycylglycate (pK_a = 8.35)
    (E) Formic acid/sodium formate (pK_a = 3.74)

16. Identify the molecule/ion with the greatest potential to act as a Lewis acid.

    (A) $^+CH_3$
    (B) ^-CN
    (C) NH_3
    (D) BF_4^-
    (E) CO_2

17. $A \leftrightarrow B$

    The instantaneous free energy (ΔG) of the reaction shown above is defined as $\Delta G = RT \ln \frac{Q}{K}$, where

    R = the gas constant, T = temperature (K),

    Q = the reaction quotient, and K = the equilibrium

    constant. Under what conditions does $\Delta G = \Delta G°$,

    the standard reaction free energy?

    (A) When [B] >> [A]
    (B) When $Q = K$
    (C) When Q is negative
    (D) When [B] = [A]
    (E) When [A] = 0

18. Which of the following is an appropriate rate constant for a very fast bimolecular reaction?

    (A) Infinite
    (B) 10^{-13} s^{-1}
    (C) 10^{-13} $m^{-2}s^{-1}$
    (D) 10^{-9} ms^{-1}
    (E) 10^9 $m^{-1}s^{-1}$

19. The kinetic energy *(KE)* of a revolving particle is described by

    (A) $KE = \frac{1}{2}ml^2$

    (B) $KE = \frac{1}{2}I\omega$

    (C) $KE = \sqrt{\frac{1}{2}mv^2}$

    (D) $KE = \frac{1}{2}I\omega^2$

    (E) $KE = \sqrt{\frac{1}{2}I\omega^2}$

20. Which of the following properties is/are intensive?

    (A) Volume
    (B) Mass
    (C) Temperature
    (D) Energy
    (E) All of the above

21. $\Delta E_{univ.} = \Delta E_{sys.} + \Delta E_{surr.} = 0$ can also be stated as:

    (A) $H = E + PV$
    (B) $\Delta H = NC_p\Delta T$
    (C) $\Delta S_{total} < 0$
    (D) $\Delta G = \Delta H - T\Delta S$
    (E) $\Delta E = q + w$

22. For a given reaction with a rate constant k and an activation energy E_a, the Arrhenius equation is given by

    (A) $\ln k = \ln A - \frac{E_a}{RT}$

    (B) $k = Ae^{-RT/E_a}$

    (C) $k = Ae^{E_a/RT}$

    (D) $\ln k = \ln A + \frac{E_a}{RT}$

    (E) $k = E_a e^{-A/RT}$

GO ON TO THE NEXT PAGE.

23. Which of the following expressions accurately describes the radii of electron orbits allowed within the Bohr model of the hydrogen atom?

(A) $r = \dfrac{\mathcal{E}_0 \hbar^2 n^2}{4\pi m e^2}$, $n = 1, 2...$

(B) $r = \dfrac{4\pi \mathcal{E} \hbar^2 n^2}{m e^2}$, $n = 1, 2...$

(C) $r = \dfrac{4\pi m e^2}{\mathcal{E} \hbar^2 n^2}$, $n = 1, 2...$

(D) $r = a_0$

(E) $a_0 = \dfrac{4\pi \mathcal{E}_0 \hbar^2 n^2}{m e}$, $n = 1, 2, 3...$

24. The Frank-Condon principle provides an estimate of which of the following values?

(A) Force constant of a bond
(B) Bond strength
(C) Intensity of vibronic transitions
(D) Extent of internal conversion
(E) Dipole moment

25. The exact solution of the Schrödinger equation for He cannot be obtained due to

(A) the size of the atom
(B) intersystem crossing
(C) internal vibrations
(D) interelectronic repulsion
(E) j–j coupling

26. Which process is spontaneous at constant temperature and pressure?

(A) $\Delta G_{sys} < 0$
(B) $\Delta G_{sys} = 0$
(C) $\Delta G_{sys} > 0$
(D) Both A and B
(E) Both B and C

27. Which labels are correct for the following phase diagram of H_2O?

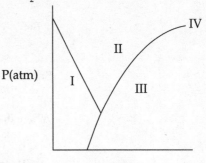

(A) I solid; II liquid; III gas; IV triple point; V critical point
(B) I liquid; II solid; III gas; IV triple point; V critical point
(C) I gas; II liquid; III solid; IV critical point; V triple point
(D) I gas; II liquid; III solid; IV triple point; V critical point
(E) I critical point; II liquid; III solid; IV gas; V triple point

28. Identify the instrumental method that doesn't rely on irradiation of a sample with electromagnetic radiation.

(A) NMR
(B) IR
(C) UV–Vis
(D) GC
(E) X-ray diffraction

GO ON TO THE NEXT PAGE.

29. Coulometric titration relies on detecting of the number of electrons generated in a chemical reaction. For example, hexene can be titrated with Br_2 generated by the electrolytic oxidation of Br^-:

$$2\,Br^{\ominus} \longrightarrow Br_2 + 2e^- \qquad\qquad (1)$$

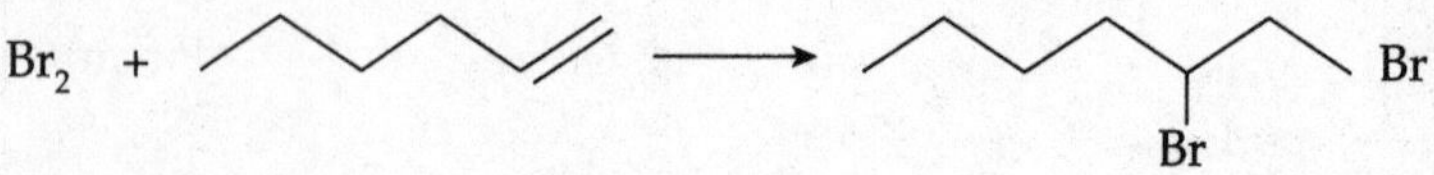

$$(2)$$

Where does reaction (1) occur?
I. Cathode
II. Anode
III. In the vapor phase above the solution

(A) I
(B) II
(C) III
(D) I and III
(E) II and III

---

30. Calculate the work done by a system of 1.00 mol of ideal gas as it expands irreversibly at constant $T = 100$ K from a P of 100 atm to 10 atm. The external pressure is held constant at 1 atm. [$R = 0.08206$ L $\cdot$ atm/mol $\cdot$ K].

(A) 0.739 L $\cdot$ atm
(B) 0.0739 L $\cdot$ atm
(C) 7.39 L $\cdot$ atm
(D) –0.739 L $\cdot$ atm
(E) –0.0739 L $\cdot$ atm

31. If the signal-to-noise ratio for a one-scan NMR spectrum is 3, what is the signal-to-noise ratio for an average of 36 scans for the same sample?

(A) 3
(B) 6
(C) 9
(D) 12
(E) 18

GO ON TO THE NEXT PAGE.

32. Which of the following numbers balances the stoichiometry of this reaction?

$$2Ca_3(PO_4)_2 \ (s) + 6SiO_2 \ (s) + 10C \ (s) \rightarrow$$
$$P_4 \ (s) + \_CaSiO_3 \ (s) + 10CO \ (g)$$

(A) 2
(B) 6
(C) 8
(D) 4
(E) 5

33. In which of the following titrations does pH = 7.0 at the equivalence point?

   I.   Strong acid/strong base
   II. Weak acid/strong base
   III. Strong acid/weak base

(A) I only
(B) II only
(C) III only
(D) II and III only
(E) I, II, and III

34. Which of the following describes the amino group as a substituent in electrophilic aromatic substitution?

(A) Weakly activating, ortho-para directing
(B) Strongly activating, ortho-para directing
(C) Weakly deactivating, meta directing
(D) Strongly activating, meta directing
(E) Strongly deactivating, ortho-para directing

35. Which of the following classes of compounds is most prone to decarboxylation following hydrolysis?

(A) β–keto esters
(B) δ–keto esters
(C) α–halo amides
(D) α–halo esters
(E) β–hydroxy acids

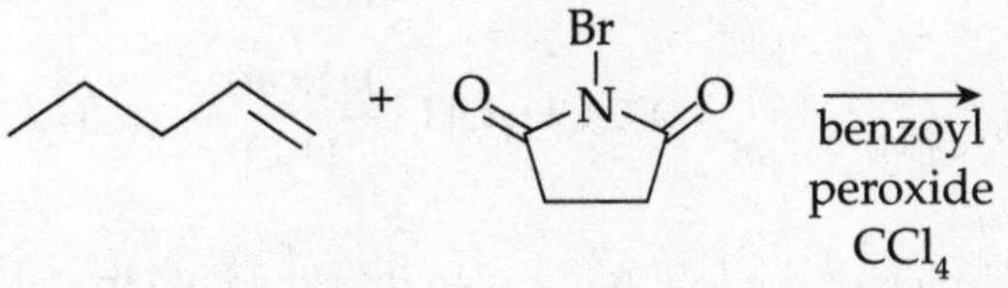

36. Predict the product of the reaction shown above.

(A)

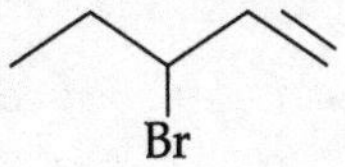

(B)

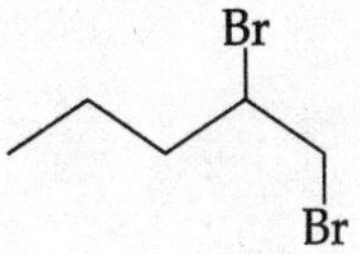

(C)

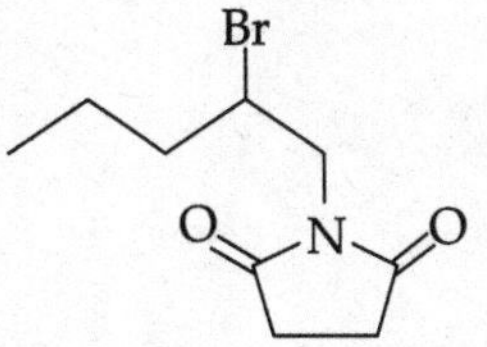

(D)

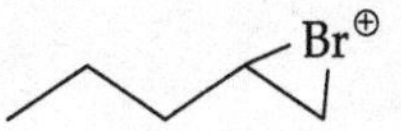

(E)

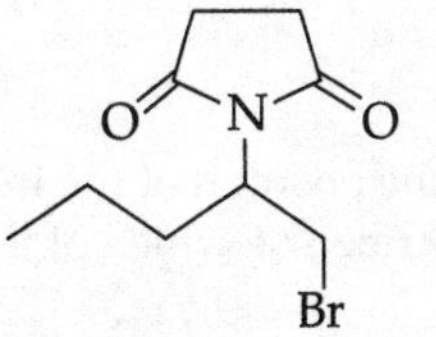

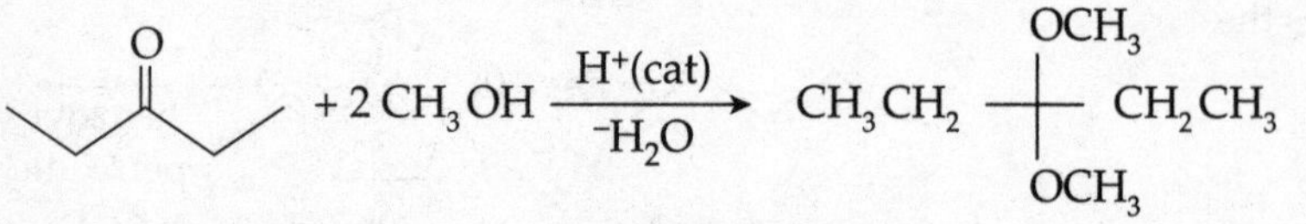

37. Which of the following is an intermediate in the ketal-forming reaction shown above?

(A)

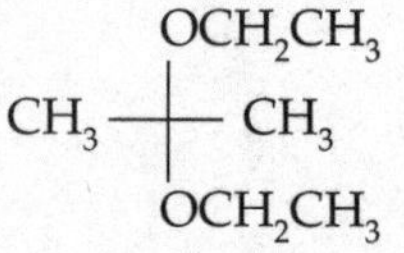

(B)

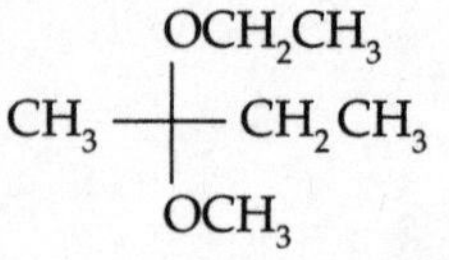

(C) + OH

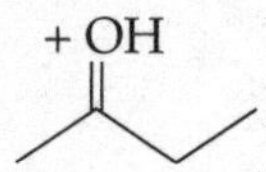

(D)

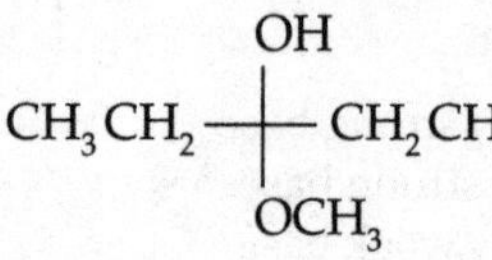

(E) $CH_3 \overset{\oplus}{O}$

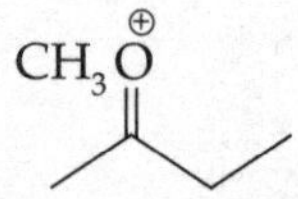

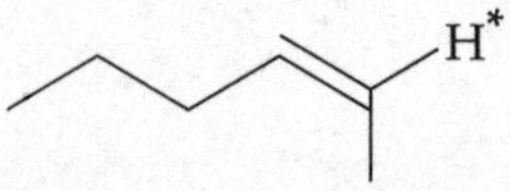

38. In the structure above, the position of the indicated (*) hydrogen is best described as which of the following?

(A) Geminalic
(B) Vicinylic
(C) Vinylic
(D) Allylic
(E) Acetylinic

39. Rank the following radicals in order of increasing stability.

   I. $\cdot CH_3$

   II. $\cdot C(CH_3)_3$

   III. $\cdot CH(CH_3)$

(A) I < II < III
(B) I < III < II
(C) II < I < III
(D) II < III < I
(E) III < II < I

40. In the mass spectrum of 2-hexanone, which of the following is LEAST likely to be an observed species?

(A) 85 m/z
(B) 37 m/z
(C) 100 m/z
(D) 57 m/z
(E) 43 m/z

41. In which of the following molecules is the bonding most ionic?

(A) $NiCl_2$
(B) CsF
(C) BCl_3
(D) Br_2
(E) PH_3

GO ON TO THE NEXT PAGE.

42. Rank the following ligands in order of increasing field strength.

$$H_2O \quad\quad CO \quad\quad I^- \quad\quad {}^-OH$$
$$I \quad\quad\quad\quad II \quad\quad\quad III \quad\quad\quad IV$$

(A) II < I < IV < III
(B) II < I < III < IV
(C) III < IV < I < II
(D) III < IV < II < I
(E) IV < III < I < II

43. Which of the following mixed metal oxides has a spinel structure in the solid state?

(A) $MgTiO_3$
(B) RuO_2
(C) $FeCr_2O_4$
(D) Cr_2O_3
(E) $KNbO_3$

44. According to the 18-electron rule, which of the following compounds would be expected to be most reactive? (Atomic numbers: Fe = 26, Os = 76, Co = 27, Ir = 77, W = 74, Cp = cyclopentadienide.)

(A) $H_2Fe(CO)_4$
(B) Cp_2Os
(C) $(PMe_3)_3Co(Me)_2Br$
(D) $(PPh_3)_2Ir(CO)Cl$
(E) $W(CO)_3(PEt_3)_2Cl_2$

45. A 100-mL solution containing $AgNO_3$ was treated with excess NaCl to completely precipitate the silver as AgCl. If 5.70 g AgCl was obtained, what was the concentration of Ag^+ in the original solution?

(A) 0.03 M
(B) 0.05 M
(C) 0.12 M
(D) 0.30 M
(E) 0.40 M

46. The ionic strength of an aqueous solution containing 0.05 M NaCl and 0.02 M Na_2SO_4 is

(A) 0.11 M
(B) 0 M
(C) 0.09 M
(D) 0.19 M
(E) 0.15 M

47. Polarography is performed with the exclusion of atmospheric oxygen. Why is this?

 I. Oxygen has no dipole moment.
 II. Oxygen can be easily reduced to H_2O.
 III. Oxygen is in equilibrium with O_3^-, a highly polar molecule.

(A) I, II, and III
(B) I and II only
(C) I only
(D) II only
(E) III only

48. Which of the following detectors is not commonly paired with a gas chromatograph?

(A) Flame ionization detector
(B) Electron capture detector
(C) Interferometer
(D) Thermal conductivity detector
(E) Mass spectrometer

49. Which of the following instruments is used for the measurement of magnetic susceptibilities?

(A) NMR spectrometer
(B) Microwave spectrometer
(C) IR spectrometer
(D) Raman spectrometer
(E) Gouy balance

50. Which of the following homoleptic carbonyl complexes would be expected to be the most reactive?

(A) $Cr(CO)_6$
(B) $Fe(CO)_5$
(C) $Mn_2(CO)_{10}$
(D) $Co_2(CO)_8$
(E) $V(CO)_6$

51. Which of the following point groups contains an inversion center (i) as one of its symmetry elements?

(A) C_{4v}
(B) C_s
(C) T_d
(D) D_{2d}
(E) C_{6h}

GO ON TO THE NEXT PAGE.

52. How many resonances in the ^{31}P NMR spectrum (^{31}P is 100% abundant with a nuclear spin of $\frac{1}{2}$) would you expect for *trans*-(P(Ph$_3$))$_4$RuH$_2$?

    (A) 0
    (B) 1
    (C) 2
    (D) 3
    (E) 4

53. Which of the following equations accurately describes electron affinity (EA)?

    (A) $\text{ion}^-_{(g)} \rightarrow \text{ion}_{(g)} + e^-$ $\Delta E = \text{EA}$
    (B) $\text{atom}_{(g)} \rightarrow \text{ion}^{\oplus}_{(g)} + e^-$ $\Delta E = \text{EA}$
    (C) $\text{atom}_{(g)} + e^- \rightarrow \text{ion}^-_{(g)}$ $\Delta E = \text{EA}$
    (D) $\text{ion}^{2-}_{(g)} \rightarrow \text{ion}^-_{(g)} + e^-$ $\Delta E = \text{EA}$
    (E) $\text{ion}^{2-}_{(g)} \rightarrow \text{ion}^-_{(g)} + e^-$ $\Delta E = \text{EA}$

54. Which of the following molecules is NOT subject to Jahn-Teller distortion?

    (A) VCl$_4$
    (B) ReF$_6$
    (C) Ti(H$_2$O)$_6$$^{3+}$
    (D) Cu(NH$_3$)$_6$$^{2+}$
    (E) Ni(CO)$_4$

55. Identify which of the following statements is FALSE.

    (A) The vapor pressure of a liquid decreases with increasing atmospheric pressure.
    (B) The value of an equilibrium constant is dependent on temperature.
    (C) The rate of a spontaneous reaction cannot be determined solely by its Gibbs free energy.
    (D) During a phase transition, the temperature of a substance must be constant.
    (E) The addition of a catalyst to a reaction at equilibrium has no net effect on the system.

56. Which of the following accurately describes the Lux-Flood definition of acidity?

    (A) $\text{HCl} + \text{NaOH} \rightarrow \text{NaCl} + \text{H}_2\text{O}$
    (B) $\text{CaO} + \text{SiO}_2 \rightarrow \text{CaSiO}_3$
    (C) $\text{BH}_3 + \text{NH}_3 \rightarrow \text{H}_3\text{N}-\text{BH}_3$
    (D) $2\text{H}_2\text{O} \Leftrightarrow \text{H}_3\text{O}^+ + \text{OH}^-$
    (E) $\text{Ni} + 4\text{CO} \rightarrow \text{Ni(CO)}_4$

57. Which of the following does not describe structure-types of polyhedral polyboron-hydride cage compounds?

    (A) Quadro-
    (B) Nido-
    (C) Arachno-
    (D) Closo-
    (E) Klado-

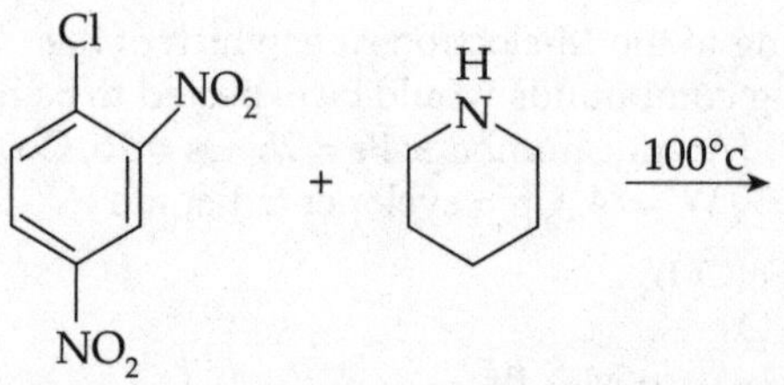

58. In the nucleophilic aromatic substitution reaction undergone by the reagents shown above, the piperidine attacks which position of the aromatic ring?

    (A) Ortho to the chlorine position
    (B) Meta to the chlorine position
    (C) Para to the chlorine position
    (D) At the chlorine position
    (E) None of the positions

GO ON TO THE NEXT PAGE.

59. Which of the following compounds is NOT aromatic?

(A)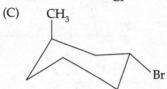

(B)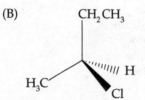

(C)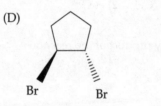

(D)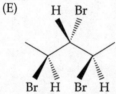

(E)

60. An S_N2 reaction on a chiral center with configuration R must result in a product with a configuration that is

(A) exclusively S
(B) exclusively S or achiral
(C) racemic
(D) exclusively R or achiral
(E) exclusively S, or R, or achiral

61. Which of the following compounds is achiral?

(A)

(B)

(C)

(D)

(E)

62. All of the following are powerful electrophiles except

(A) BF_3
(B) Br^+
(C) NO^+
(D) PH_3
(E) $AlCl_3$

GO ON TO THE NEXT PAGE.

63. For the synthesis of dioxin shown below, the first step of the reaction mechanism is best described as

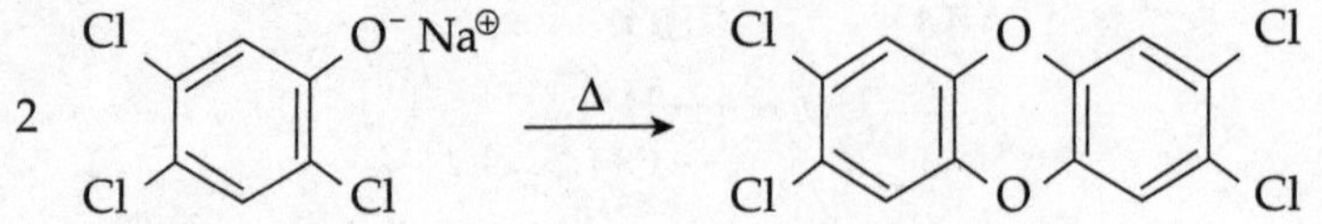

dioxin

(A) radical cyclization
(B) electrophilic substitution
(C) free radical addition
(D) nucleophilic addition
(E) chloride elimination

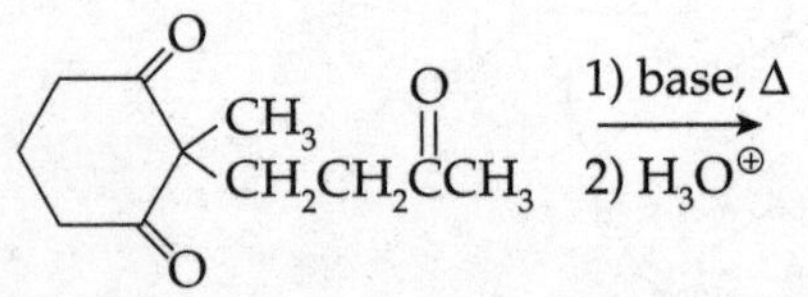

64. Predict the primary product of the reaction conditions above.

(A)

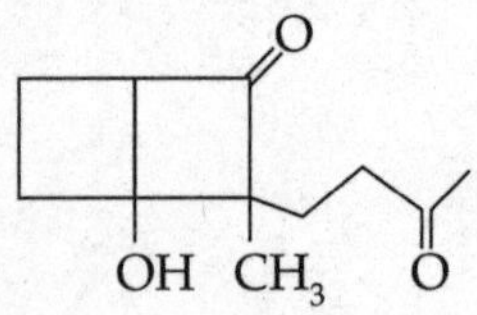

(B)

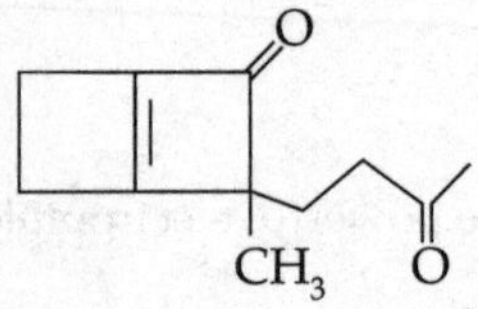

(C)

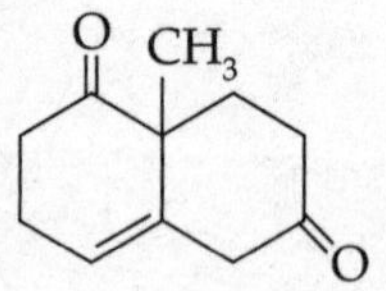

(D)

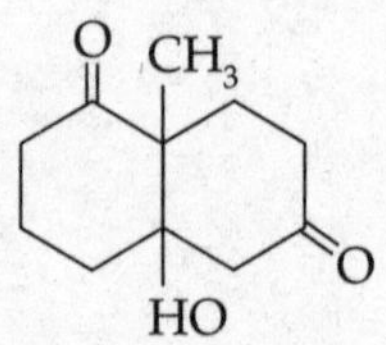

(E)

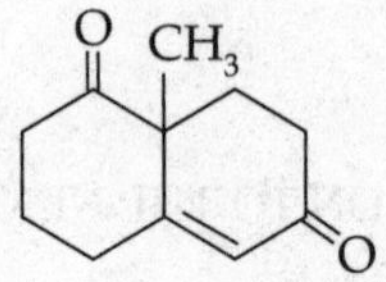

65. What is the bond order of He_2^+?

(A) 0

(B) $\frac{1}{2}$

(C) 1

(D) $1\frac{1}{2}$

(E) 2

66. Which of the following statements is a valid derivative of the steady-state approximation?

(A) A viable kinetic model can be generated if the concentrations of all reactants are assumed to be constant.
(B) A system at equilibrium tends to stay at equilibrium.
(C) In a two-step reaction where only the first step is reversible, the concentration of the intermediate is negligibly small.
(D) In a two-step reaction where the first step is irreversible and the second step is reversible, the concentration of the intermediate is negligibly small.
(E) None of the above.

GO ON TO THE NEXT PAGE.

67. A Hermitian operator ($\hat{A}$) can be generally defined by which of the following? (Assume f and g are well-behaved functions.)

(A) $\int_{-\infty}^{\infty} g^* \hat{A} f \, dx = \int_{-\infty}^{\infty} f \hat{A}^* g^* dx$

(B) $\int_{-\infty}^{\infty} f^* f \, dx = \int_{-\infty}^{\infty} g^* g \, dx$

(C) $\int_{-\infty}^{\infty} g^* \hat{A} \, dx = \int_{-\infty}^{\infty} f^* \hat{A} \, dx$

(D) $\int_{-\infty}^{\infty} g^* \hat{A} \, dx = \int_{-\infty}^{\infty} f^* \hat{A} \, dx$

(E) $\int_{-\infty}^{\infty} \hat{A} f \, g^* dx = \int_{-\infty}^{\infty} \hat{A} \, g^* f \, dx$

68. Orbital energies obtained from Hartree-Fock calculations can be used to approximate which of the following values?

(A) Rotational energy levels
(B) Ionization energy of an atom
(C) Vibrational energy levels
(D) Bond dissociation energies
(E) Potential energies

69. Which expression describes the force between the proton and electron (ε_0 = permittivity of free space)?

(A) $\dfrac{\varepsilon_0 e^2}{\pi r^2}$

(B) $\dfrac{4\pi e^2}{\varepsilon_0 r^2}$

(C) $\dfrac{4\pi \varepsilon_0}{r^2 e^2}$

(D) $\dfrac{r^2}{4\pi \varepsilon_0 e^2}$

(E) $\dfrac{e^2}{4\pi \varepsilon_0 r^2}$

70. The Born-Oppenheimer approximation neglects

(A) spin
(B) coupling
(C) nuclear motion
(D) interelectronic repulsion
(E) molecular vibrations

71. The Stern-Gerlach experiment demonstrated the existence of

(A) mass
(B) charge
(C) spin
(D) waves
(E) particles

72. A harmonic oscillator is used as a model for

(A) molecular rotation
(B) the hydrogen atom
(C) a particle in a box
(D) electronic transitions
(E) molecular vibration

73. What is the slope of the following line?

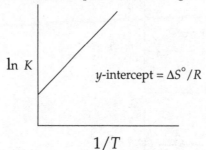

(A) $\dfrac{1}{T \ln K}$

(B) $\dfrac{-\Delta H^\circ}{R}$

(C) $\dfrac{\Delta S^\circ T}{R}$

(D) $\dfrac{\ln K}{T}$

(E) $\dfrac{-\Delta H^\circ R}{T}$

GO ON TO THE NEXT PAGE.

74. When will a spontaneous process in an isolated system have $\Delta S_{sys} < 0$?

(A) Always
(B) For reversible processes
(C) For very negative ΔH
(D) At high T
(E) Never

75. What is the eigenvalue of the momentum operator, $\hat{P}_x = -i\,\hbar\frac{\partial}{\partial x}$ with eigenfunction e^{ikx} ?

(A) ik
(B) $-i\hbar k$
(C) $\hbar k$
(D) ikx
(E) e^{ikx}

76. Which diagram illustrates the probability density for a particle in a one-dimensional box?

(A)

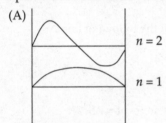

$n = 2$

$n = 1$

(B)

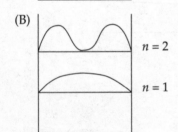

$n = 2$

$n = 1$

(C)

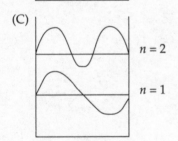

$n = 2$

$n = 1$

(D) Both B and C

(E) Both A and B

77. Which of the following procedures will increase the retention time of an analyte on a GC column?

  I. Increasing the column length
  II. Raising the % of the stationary phase
  III. Increasing the column temperature

(A) I only
(B) III only
(C) I, II, and III
(D) I and II only
(E) II and III only

78. The "common ion effect" addresses the solubility of salts in polar solvents. Which of the following statements encapsulates the "common ion effect"?

(A) Polar solvents dissolve polar solutes. Likewise, nonpolar solvents dissolve nonpolar solvents.
(B) A salt will be more soluble if one of its constituent ions is already present in solution.
(C) In a polar solvent, salts with the same anion will have similar solubilities.
(D) A salt will be less soluble if one of its constituent ions is already present in solution.
(E) Increasing the ionic strength of a solution increases the solubility of salts in it.

79. The intermolecular forces in benzene at room temperature can be described as

(A) only covalent
(B) only electrostatic
(C) both covalent and electrostatic
(D) gravitational
(E) repulsive

GO ON TO THE NEXT PAGE.

80. For citric acid ($C_6O_7H_8$), $pK_{a1} = 3.13$, $pK_{a2} = 4.76$, $pK_{a3} = 6.40$. Which of the following statements about the relative concentrations of the listed species at pH = 2.0 is true?

      I. $C_6O_7H_5^{3-}$
     II. $C_6O_7H_6^{2-}$
    III. $C_6O_7H_7^{1-}$
    IV. $C_6O_7H_8$

(A) I > II > III > IV
(B) II > III > IV > I
(C) IV > III > I > II
(D) III > IV > II > I
(E) IV > III > II > I

81. The reaction of benzoic acid with phosphorus tribromide yields which of the following?

(A)

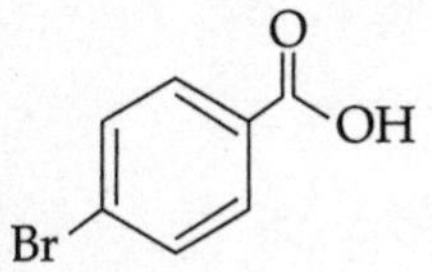

(B)

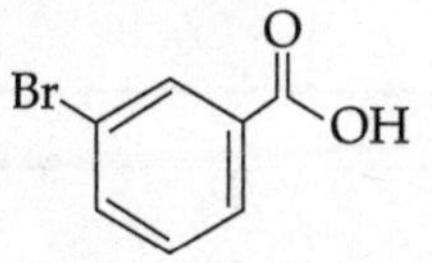

(C)

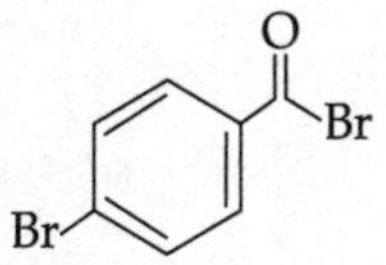

(D)

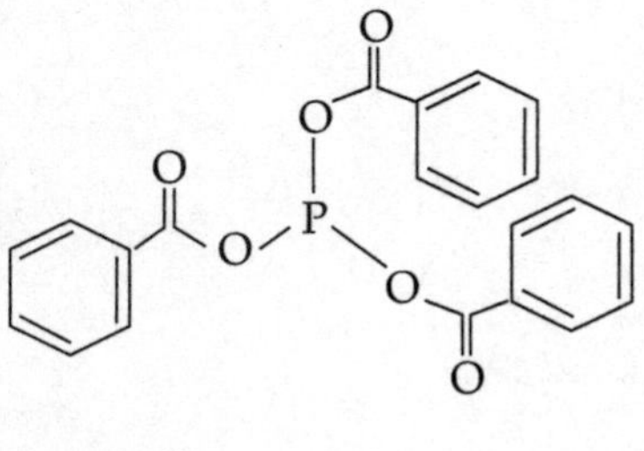

(E)

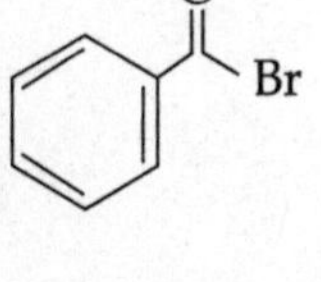

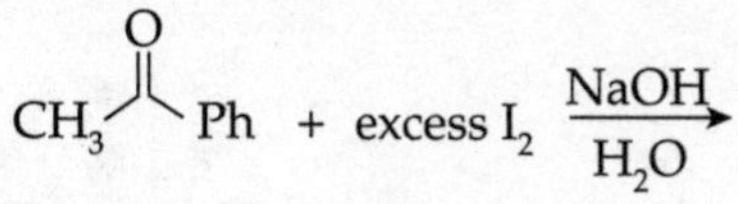

82. The iodoform reaction shown above gives which of the following as products/byproducts?

(A)

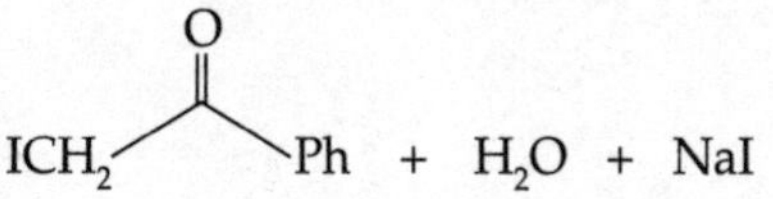

ICH_2 Ph   + H_2O +   NaI

(B)

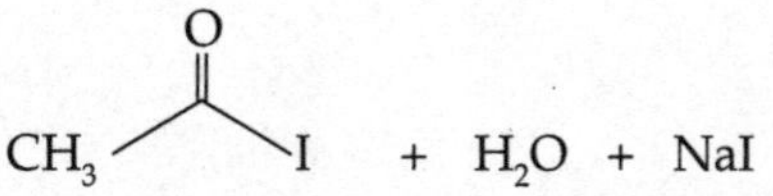

CH_3 I   + H_2O +   NaI

(C)

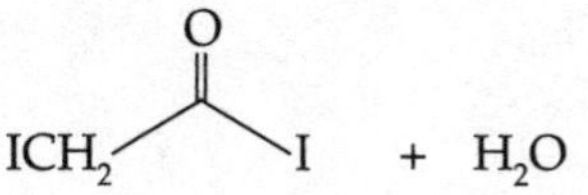

ICH_2 I   + H_2O

(D)

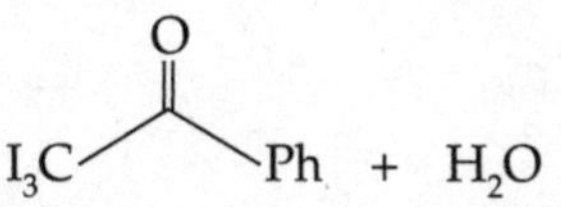

I_3C Ph   + H_2O

(E)

$Na^{\oplus}{}^{\ominus}O$ Ph   + CHI_3 + H_2O

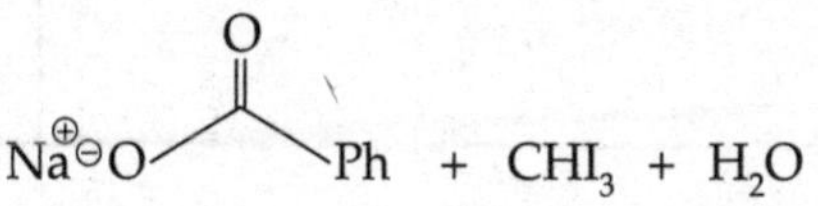

GO ON TO THE NEXT PAGE.

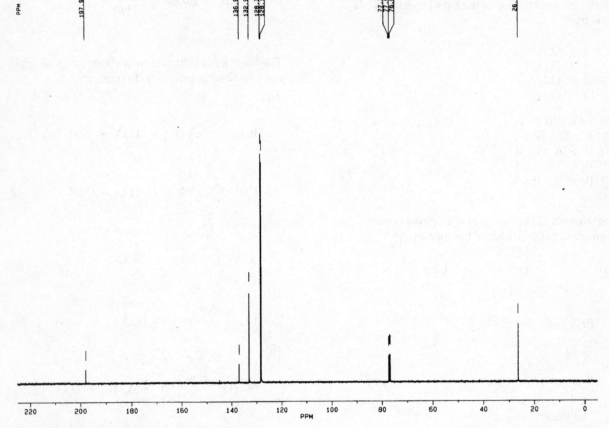

PPM 197.901 136.951 132.910 128.389 128.115 77.321 76.684 75.684 26.383

| 220 | 200 | 180 | 160 | 140 | 120 | 100 | 80 | 60 | 40 | 20 | 0 |

PPM

83. The 100-megahertz carbon nuclear magnetic resonance (proton decoupled) shown above is consistent with which of the following structures? (Ignore the 3 resonances at ~ 77ppm as they belong to the solvent, not the analyte.)

(A)
Ph—CH(OH)—CH₃

(B)
Ph—C(=O)—H

(C)
Ph—O—CH₂CH₃

(D)
Ph—C(=O)—CH₃

(E)
4-Br—C₆H₄—C(=O)—OH

GO ON TO THE NEXT PAGE.

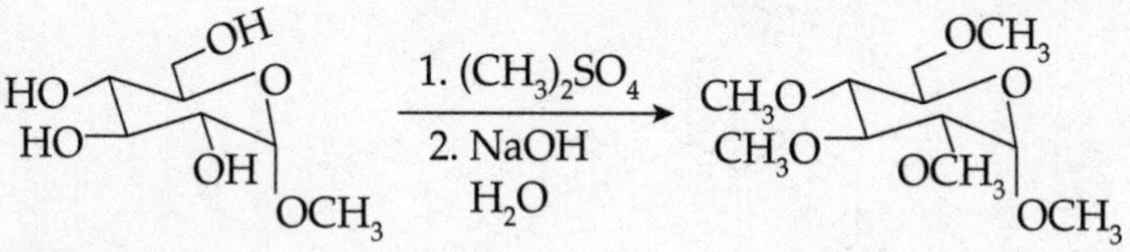

84. In the reaction shown above, the dimethyl sulfate behaves as a source of

A) $^-CH_3$
B) $\cdot CH_3$
C) $^+CH_3$
D) $^+OCH_3$
E) $^-OCH_3$

I.

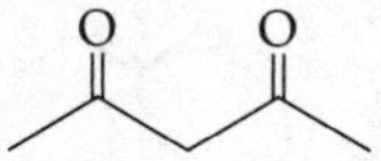

II.

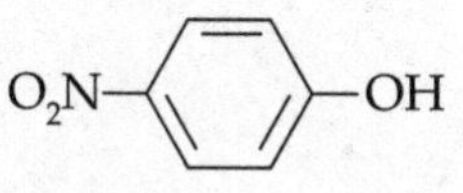

III.

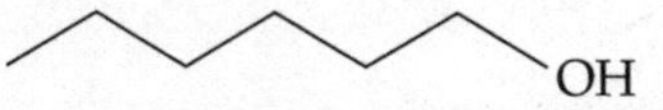

IV.

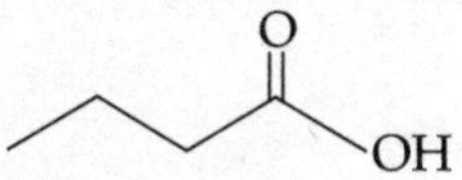

85. Which of the following indicates the order of decreasing acidity of the four molecules shown above?

(A) III > I > II > IV
(B) III > I > IV > II
(C) III > II > I > IV
(D) IV > I > II > III
(E) IV > II > I > III

GO ON TO THE NEXT PAGE.

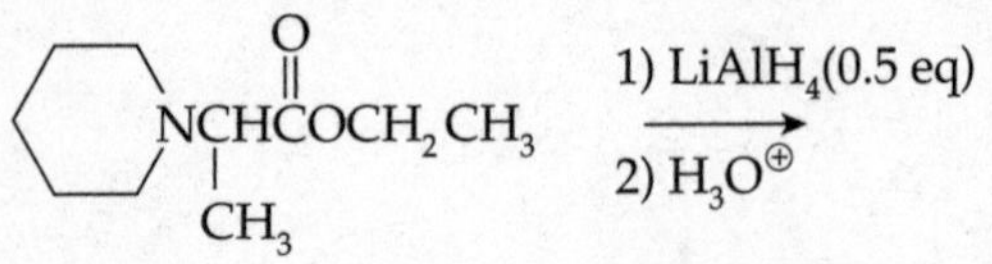

1) LiAlH$_4$(0.5 eq)

2) H$_3$O$^{\oplus}$

86. Which of the compounds below is obtained by the reaction shown above?

(A)

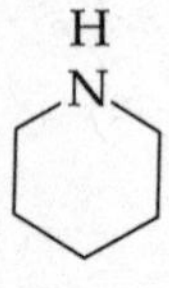

(B)

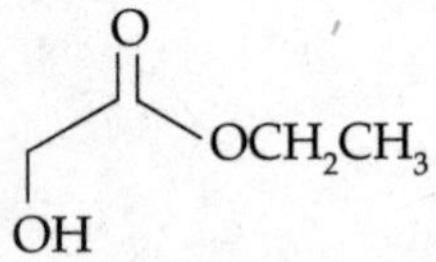

(C)

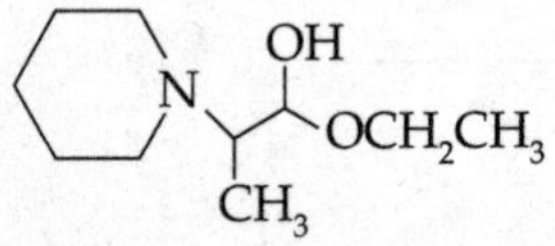

(D)

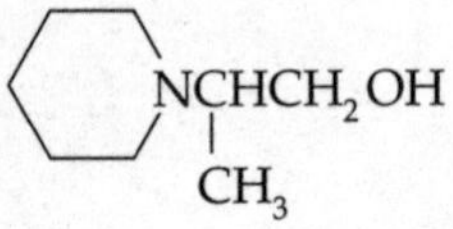

(E)

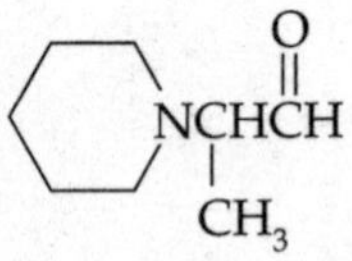

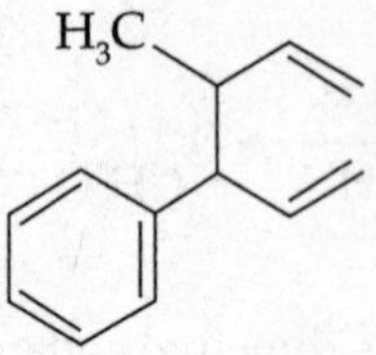

88. If the molecule above were to undergo a [3,3] sigmatropic rearrangement, which of the following would be the product?

(A)

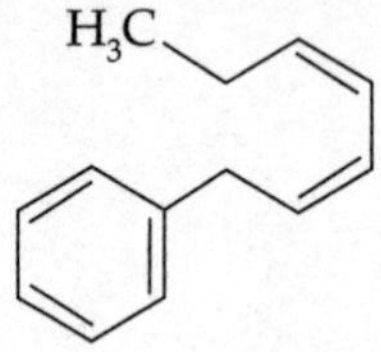

(B)

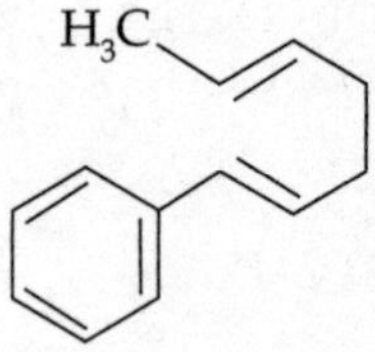

(C)

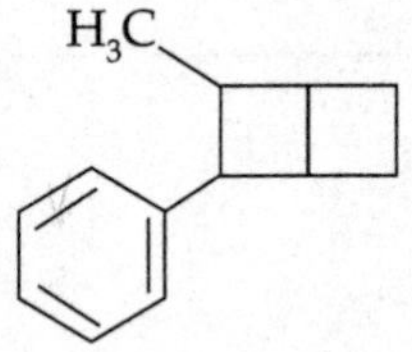

(D)

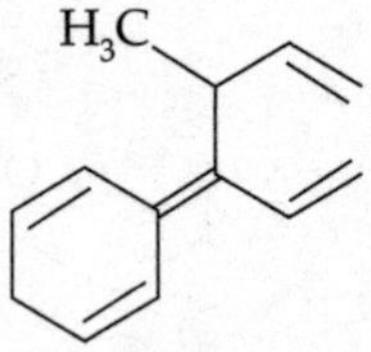

(E)

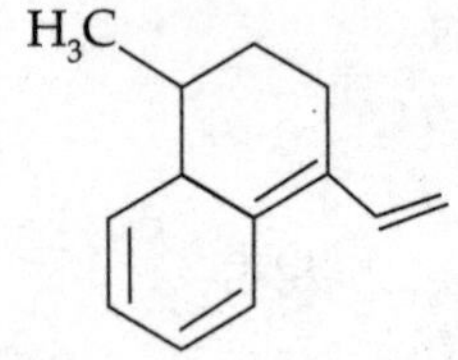

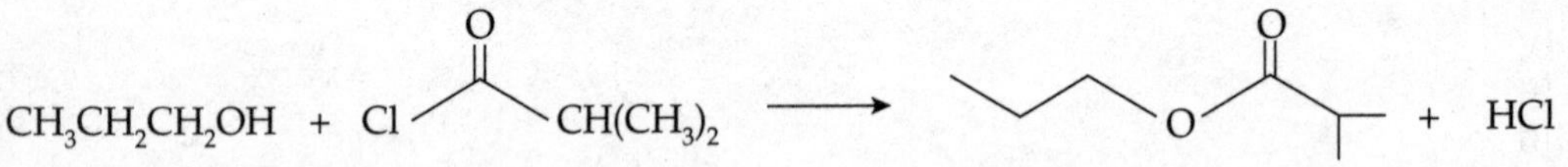

CH$_3$CH$_2$CH$_2$OH + $\longrightarrow$ + HCl

87. Which of the following reaction categories best describes the reaction shown above?

(A) Amination
(B) Alkylation
(C) Acylation
(D) Oxidation
(E) Reduction

GO ON TO THE NEXT PAGE.

89. Which of the following atoms has the greatest atomic radius?

(A) Al
(B) Li
(C) O
(D) K
(E) Br

90. Which of the following is the ground-state term symbol for a neon atom?

(A) $^1P_0$
(B) $^1S_0$
(C) $^2S_{1/2}$
(D) $^2D_{1/2}$
(E) $^1S_{3/2}$

91. Which of the following compounds would be expected to have the greatest lattice binding energy?

(A) LiBr
(B) $LiNO_3$
(C) LiCl
(D) LiF
(E) LiI

92. Which of the molecules below displays facial stereochemistry?

(A)
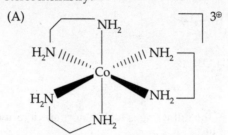

(B)
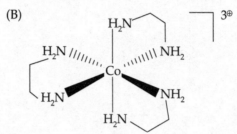

(C)
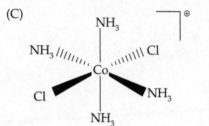

(D)
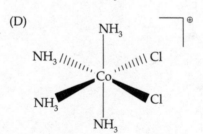

(E)

GO ON TO THE NEXT PAGE.

93. According to the solvent system definition, which of the following is the strongest base?

(A) CH_3CO_2H
(B) NH_3
(C) H_2SO_4
(D) C_2H_5OH
(E) H_2O

94. Which of the following is NOT a normal vibrational mode of BCl_3?

(A)

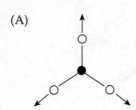

(B)

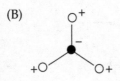

(C)

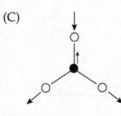

(D)

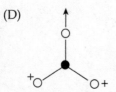

(E)

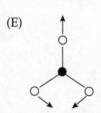

95. Of the following molecular properties, isotope effects are LEAST likely to be observed in

(A) electronic transitions
(B) covalent bond strength
(C) effusion rate
(D) vibrational transitions
(E) nuclear magnetic spin

96. The lines in a rotational spectrum are not equally spaced due to

(A) anharmonicity
(B) antifugal repulsion
(C) interelectronic repulsion
(D) reduced mass
(E) mass defect

97. The daughter nuclei formed when ^{18}F undergo positron emission are

(A) ^{14}N
(B) ^{16}O
(C) ^{18}O
(D) ^{19}F
(E) ^{20}Ne

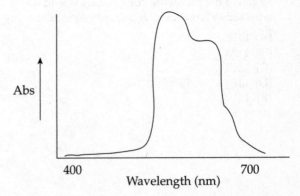

98. What is the most likely color of the substance whose UV-Vis spectrum is shown above?

(A) Red
(B) Black
(C) Blue
(D) Orange
(E) Colorless

GO ON TO THE NEXT PAGE.

99. Identify the gas for which the *Ideal Gas Law, PV=nRT*, provides an exact description.

   (A) He
   (B) H_2
   (C) SF_6
   (D) All of the above
   (E) None of the above

100. Which of the following reaction sequences offers the best combination of reagents to give the highest yield of methylamine, CH_3NH_2?

   (A) NH_3 + $ClMgCH_3$

   (B) NH_2-NH_2 +

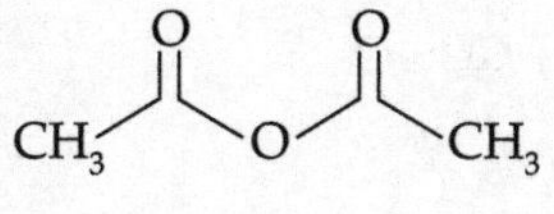

   (C) 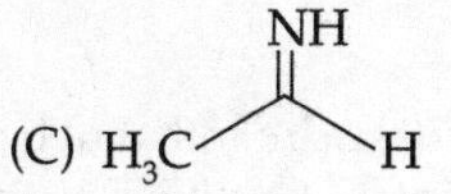 + $NaBH_4$

   (D) NH_3 + CH_3I

   (E) H_3CN_3 + $LiAlH_4$

101. Which of the following compounds contains a $Zn(s)|$ triple bond?

   (A) Benzylcyclopentylamine
   (B) Benzonitrile
   (C) Phenyl azide
   (D) Trimethylammonium chloride
   (E) Benzaldehyde

102. The Dieckmann condensation of diethyl hexanedioate, $CH_3CH_2OC(O)CH_2CH_2CH_2CH_2C(O)OCH_2CH_3$, in the presence of sodium ethoxide leads to formation of which of the following products?

   (A)

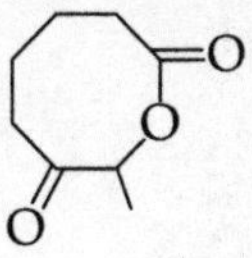

   (B)

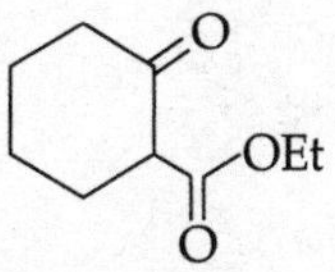

   (C)

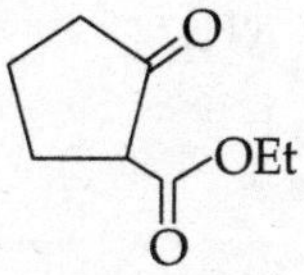

   (D)

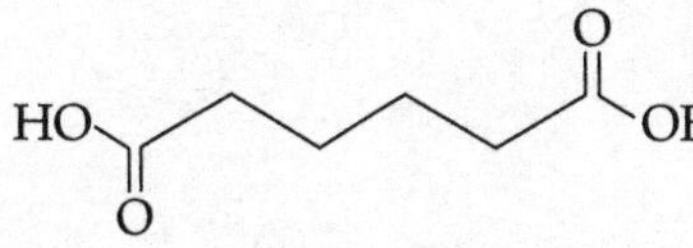

   (E)

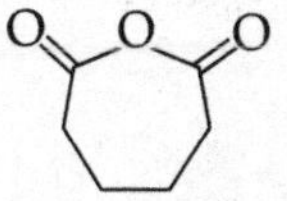

GO ON TO THE NEXT PAGE.

103. Which of the following represents the correct structure of the dipeptide valylvaline (val-val)?

(A)

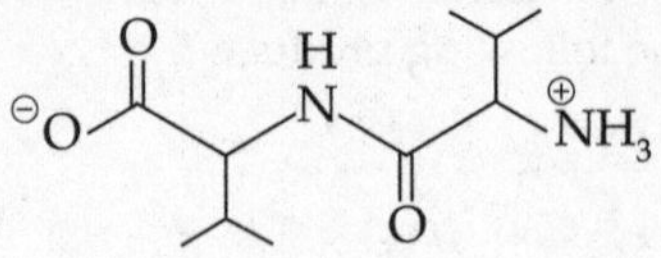

(B)

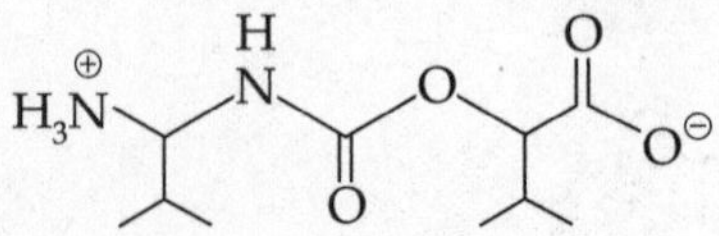

(C)

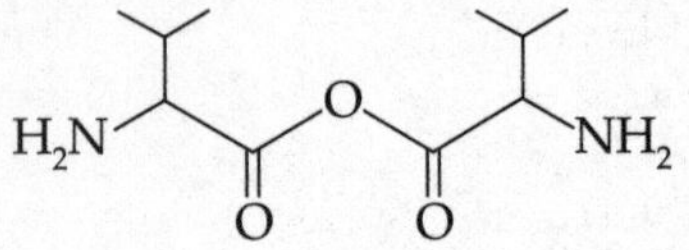

(D)

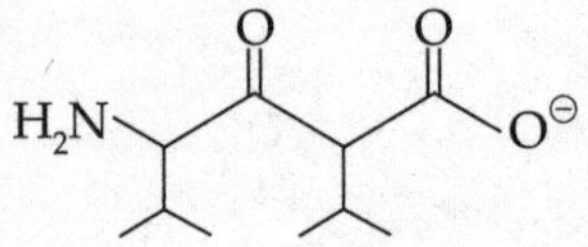

(E)

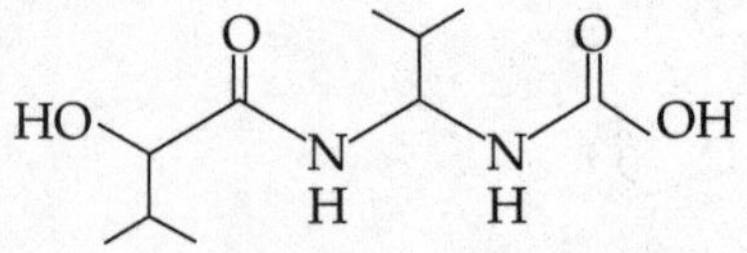

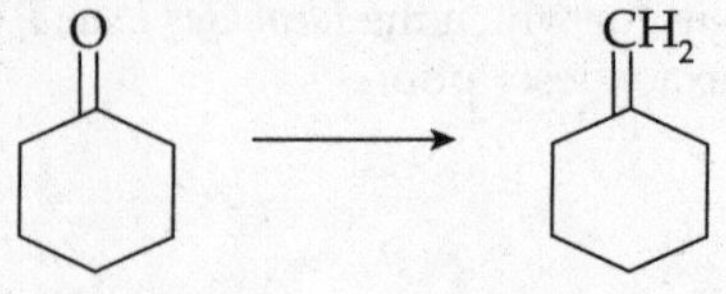

104. The reaction shown above could successfully be performed using which of the following reagents?

(A) Ph_3PCH_2

(B)

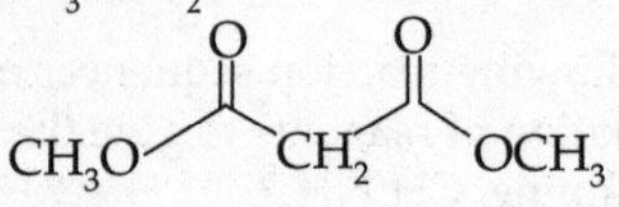

(C) CH_2Br_2

(D) $CH_2=O$

(E) PCC

105. A 5 g sample of menthol in 100 mL of ethanol has an optical rotation of +2.46° at 20°C using a 10-cm sample tube and a sodium lamp (D line, $\lambda = 589.3$ nm). What is the specific rotation of menthol?

(A) –49.2°
(B) +49.2°
(C)   +2.46°
(D) –2.46°
(E)   +4.92°

GO ON TO THE NEXT PAGE.

106. Which of the following functional groups is LEAST likely to be found in the interior of a mammalian cell?

(A) Amide
(B) Ester
(C) Carboxylic acid
(D) Carboxylate salt
(E) Acid chloride

107. Given that the reaction below is at equilibrium at 1 atm, what effect would the sudden, isothermal addition of 0.5 atm Ar have on this system?

$$NO_2(g) + NO_3(g) \leftrightarrow N_2O_5(g)$$

(A) No effect
(B) Shift the system to the left
(C) Shift the system to the right
(D) Shift the system, but in a direction that cannot be predicted
(E) Cause N_2O_5 to precipitate as N_2O_5Ar

108. Which of the following forms an acidic solution upon dissolving in water?

(A) N_2
(B) Ar
(C) O_2
(D) CO
(E) CO_2

109. Which of the following is the best description of the geometry of PCl_5?

(A) Tetrahedral
(B) Trigonal pyramid
(C) Trigonal bipyramid
(D) Square pyramid
(E) Octahedral

110. If there are five d electrons in Mn^{2+} and the d orbitals are split by a tetrahedral ligand field, one could expect to find

(A) one unpaired electron in the presence of a strong ligand field
(B) one unpaired electron in the presence of a weak ligand field
(C) three unpaired electrons in the presence of a strong ligand field
(D) three unpaired electrons in the presence of a weak ligand field
(E) five unpaired electrons in the presence of a strong ligand field

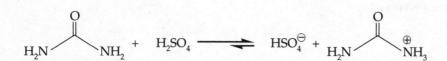

111. In the equilibrium shown above, hydrogen sulfate ion acts as

(A) a catalyst
(B) an acid
(C) a base
(D) a spectator ion
(E) an oxidizing agent

GO ON TO THE NEXT PAGE.

112. Which of the following is the most common oxidation state of the lanthanide elements?

(A) +1
(B) −1
(C) +2
(D) −2
(E) +3

113. In the electrochemical cell described by the following cell diagram, what reaction occurs at the anode?

$$Zn(s)\big|ZnCl_2\,(aq)\big|Cl^-(aq)\big|Cl_2(g)\big|C(s)$$

(A) $Zn^\circ \rightarrow Zn^{2+} + 2e^-$
(B) $Zn^{2+} + 2e^- \rightarrow Zn^\circ$
(C) $Cl_2 + 2e^- \rightarrow 2Cl^-$
(D) $2Cl^- \rightarrow Cl_2 + 2e^-$
(E) $Zn + Cl_2 \rightarrow ZnCl_2$

why is cl not allowed at anode side?

114. Vessel A (volume = 300 mL) is charged with 150 torr of ethylene at room temperature. Using liquid N_2 as a refrigerant, the gas is quantitatively condensed into vessel B (volume = 5 mL). What is the pressure inside vessel B if it is sealed and warmed to room temperature?

(A) 1,500 torr
(B) 3,000 torr
(C) 6,000 torr
(D) 9,000 torr
(E) 45,000 torr

115. A 10.0 ± 0.1 mL sample of trimethyl aluminum was found to have a mass of 7.52 ± 0.08g. What is the percent uncertainty in the density calculated from these values?

(A) 14%
(B) 7.2%
(C) 1.4%
(D) 0.14%
(E) 0.72%

116. The concentration of mercury in a coastal stream was tested over five years. During this time, 260 measurements were taken and the average concentration of mercury was found to be 20 ppb. At the 95% confidence level, the error in this measurement is 4 ppb. What is the relationship between the confidence level and experimental uncertainty?

(A) 95% of the measurements were between 16 and 24 ppb.
(B) There is a 95% chance that the true concentration is between 16 and 24 ppb.
(C) The true mean must be between 22.8 and 15.2 ppb.
(D) The experimenters are 95% sure that the error is 4 ppb.
(E) None of the above.

117. Solute A has a partition coefficient of 4 between diethyl ether and H_2O. If 100 mL of a 0.1 M aqueous solution of solute A is extracted twice with 100 mL of diethyl ether, what is the molarity of A in the aqueous layer?

(A) $1.7 \times 10^{-3}\,M$
(B) $4.0 \times 10^{-3}\,M$
(C) $5.6 \times 10^{-2}\,M$
(D) $6.3 \times 10^{-2}\,M$
(E) $5.6 \times 10^{-3}\,M$

GO ON TO THE NEXT PAGE.

118. If $K_1 < K_2$, which of the following rate laws is consistent with the mechanism proposed for the conversion $NO_3 + NO \longrightarrow 2NO_2$?

Proposed mechanism:
$$NO_2 + NO_3 \xrightarrow{k_1} N_2O_5$$
$$NO + N_2O_5 \xrightarrow{k_2} 3NO_2$$

(A) $\dfrac{d[NO_3]}{dt} = k_1k_2[NO_2][NO_3]$

(B) $\dfrac{d[NO_3]}{dt} = -k_1k_2[NO_2][NO_3]$

(C) $\dfrac{d[NO_3]}{dt} = -k_1k_2[NO_3][NO]$

(D) $\dfrac{d[NO_3]}{dt} = -k_1[NO_2][NO_3]$

(E) $\dfrac{d[NO_3]}{dt} = k_1[NO_2][NO_3]$

119. The classical wave equation is defined by which of the following [$u(x,t)$ is the amplitude, v is the speed]?

(A) $\dfrac{\partial^2 u}{\partial x^2} = \dfrac{1}{v}\dfrac{\partial^2 u}{\partial t^2}$

(B) $\dfrac{\partial^2 u}{\partial t^2} = \dfrac{1}{v}\dfrac{\partial^2 u}{\partial t^2}$

(C) $\dfrac{\partial^2 u}{\partial x^2} = v\dfrac{\partial^2 u}{\partial t^2}$

(D) $\dfrac{\partial^2 u}{\partial t^2} = v\dfrac{\partial^2 u}{\partial t^2}$

(E) $\dfrac{\partial^2 u}{\partial t^2} = t\dfrac{\partial^2 v}{\partial t^2}$

120. Given the reaction $A \rightarrow B + C$, where $\Delta H_{rx}n$ is negative, what effect would increasing the temperature (at constant pressure) have on the system at equilibrium?

(A) No change
(B) Cannot be determined
(C) Shift to the right
(D) Shift to the left for K < 1, and to the right for K > 1
(E) Shift to the left

121. Which reaction best illustrates a redox reaction?

(A) $H_2S(aq) \rightarrow H^+(aq) + SH^-(aq)$
(B) $H_2(g) + Cl_2(g) \rightarrow 2HCl(g)$
(C) $CaCO_3(s) \rightarrow CaO(s) + CO_2(g)$
(D) $K_2O(s) + CO_2(g) \rightarrow K_2CO_3(s)$
(E) $MgO(s) + SO_3(g) \rightarrow MgSO_4(s)$

122. Calculate the change in entropy when 1.00 mol of H_2O is vaporized under ambient conditions.

$$[\Delta H_{vap} = 40.66 \text{ kJ/mol}]$$

(A)   109 J / K • mol
(B)   52 J / K • mol
(C)   520 J / K • mol
(D) 1,090 J / K • mol
(E) 5.20 J / K • mol

123. The number of mictrostates (Ω) available to a system of N particles confined to a volume (V) can be expressed by the equation, $\Omega = (cV)^N$, where c is a constant. This is best explained by the fact that

(A) entropy is an extensive property
(B) entropy is an intrusive property
(C) the number of states scales linearly with particle number
(D) the number of states is independent of particle number
(E) enthalpy is an intensive property

GO ON TO THE NEXT PAGE.

124. Atomic absorption spectroscopy (AA) was used to analyze the calcium content of milk. Solution 1 was prepared by mixing 10.00 mL of milk with 5.00 mL of a 0.1 molar solution of Ca^{2+}, then diluting to a total volume of 100.0 mL. Solution 1 gave an absorbance of 3.0 units. Solution 2 was prepared by diluting 10.00 mL of milk to 100.0 mL and gave an absorbance of 2.0 units. What was the concentration of Ca^{2+} in the original milk sample?

(A) $1.0 \times 10^{-4} M$
(B) $5.0 \times 10^{-5} M$
(C) $2.0 \times 10^{-4} M$
(D) $1.0 \times 10^{-3} M$
(E) $1.5 \times 10^{-4} M$

125. An unknown acid solution was presumed to be either HCl or H_2SO_4. Which one of the following salt solutions would produce a precipitate in the presence of H_2SO_4 but not HCl?

(A) $LiNO_3$
(B) NH_4NO_3
(C) $CsNO_3$
(D) $Ba(NO_3)_2$
(E) $AgNO_3$

126. *Wavenumber*, cm^{-1}, the unit used on the *x*-axis of an IR spectrum, is a direct measurement of photon

(A) heat
(B) absorption
(C) transmission
(D) wavelength
(E) frequency

127. Which of the following solids is most ionic?

(A) C_{60}
(B) Mn
(C) SiO_2
(D) BN
(E) $NaBH_4$

128. The concentration of ions in solution can be described by the solubility product (K_{sp}) for the salt and the activities (δ) of the ions. Which of the following expressions describes the concentration of Cr^{3+} in a solution of $Cr(IO_3)_3$?

(A) $\left[Cr^{3+}\right] = \dfrac{K_{sp}\left[IO_3^{-}\right]^3}{\delta Cr^{3+}\delta IO_3^{-}}$

(B) $\left[Cr^{3+}\right] = \dfrac{K_{sp}}{\delta Cr^{3+}\left[IO_3^{-}\right]^3 \delta IO_3^{-}}$

(C) $\left[Cr^{3+}\right] = \dfrac{K_{sp}\delta Cr^{3+}\left(\delta IO_3^{-}\right)^3}{\left[IO_3^{-}\right]^3}$

(D) $\left[Cr^{3+}\right] = \dfrac{K_{sp}}{\delta Cr^{3+}\left[IO_3^{-}\right]^3\left(\delta IO_3^{-}\right)^3}$

(E) $\left[Cr^{3+}\right] = \dfrac{K_{sp}\delta Cr^{3+}\delta IO_3^{-}}{\left[IO_3^{-}\right]^3}$

GO ON TO THE NEXT PAGE.

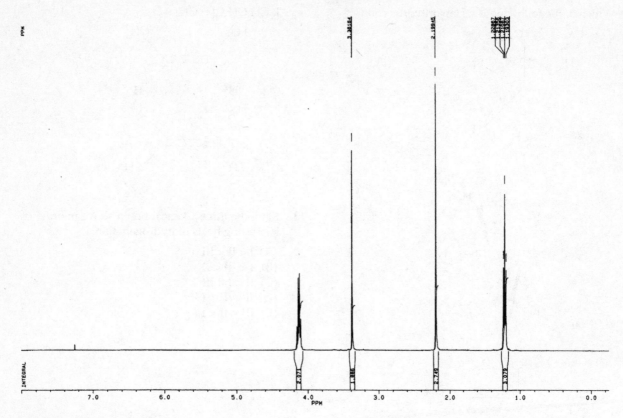

129. The 400-megahertz proton nuclear magnetic resonance spectrum above is consistent with which of the following structures?

(A)

(B)

(C)

(D)

(E)

GO ON TO THE NEXT PAGE.

130. Which of the following is a Haworth projection?

(A)

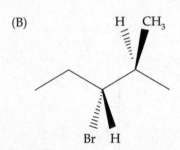

(B)

H   CH₃

Br   H

(C)

CH₂OH

HO

H   H   H

O   H

H

OH

OH   OH

(D)

CHO

H——OH

HO——H

HO——H

HO——H

——OH

(E)

OH

HO

O

H

OH

OH

OH

I. $CH_3CH_2CH=CH_2$

H_3C CH_3

II.   H   H

H_3C H

III.   H CH_3

131. Rank the three alkenes shown above in order of increasing heats of hydrogenation.

(A) I < II < III
(B) I < III < II
(C) II < I < III
(D) II < III < I
(E) III < II < I

GO ON TO THE NEXT PAGE.

132. Which of the following represents the product of an aldol condensation between benzaldehyde and 3,3-dimethylbutan-2-one?

(A) 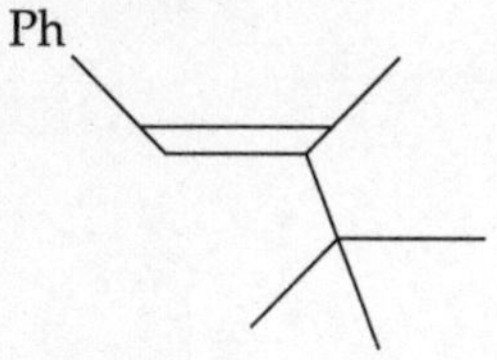 Ph

(B)

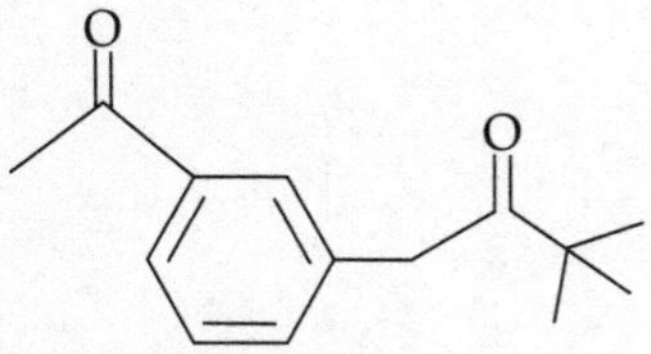

(C)

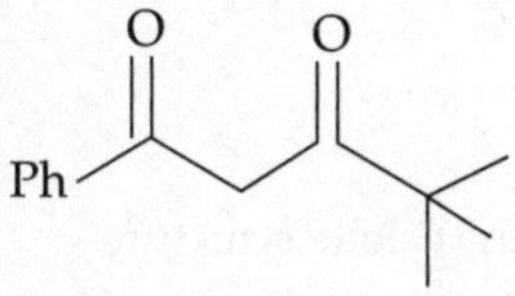

Ph

(D)

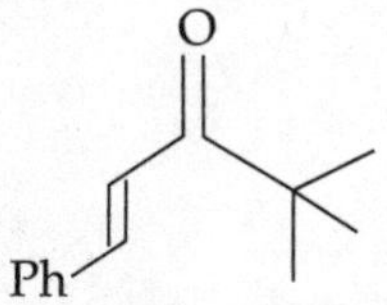

Ph

(E)

Ph

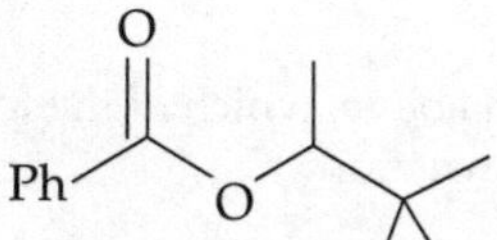

133. Which of the following reactions is known for being regioselective?

(A)

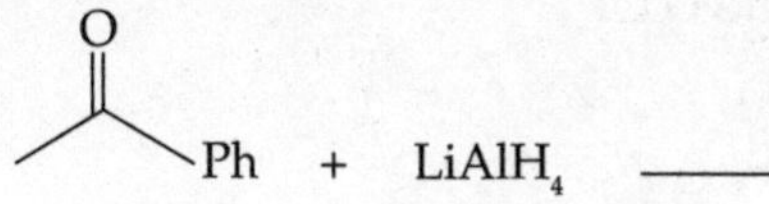

Ph + LiAlH$_4$ ⟶

(B)

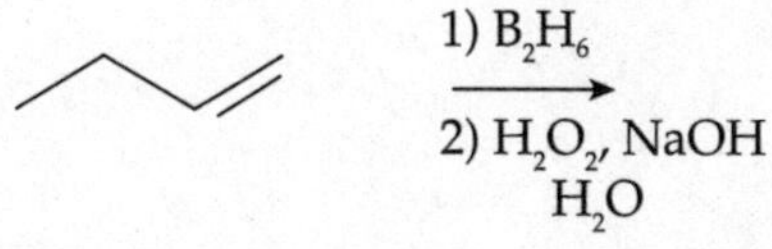

1) B$_2$H$_6$
⟶
2) H$_2$O$_2$, NaOH
H$_2$O

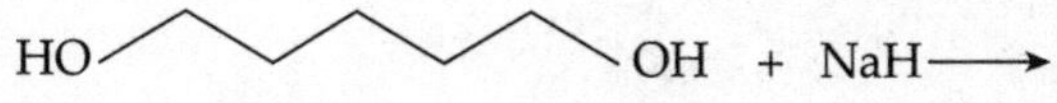

(C) HO ⟍⟍⟍⟍ OH + NaH ⟶

(D)

Br

H$_3$C ⟍⟍⟍⟍ D + NaN$_3$ ⟶

H

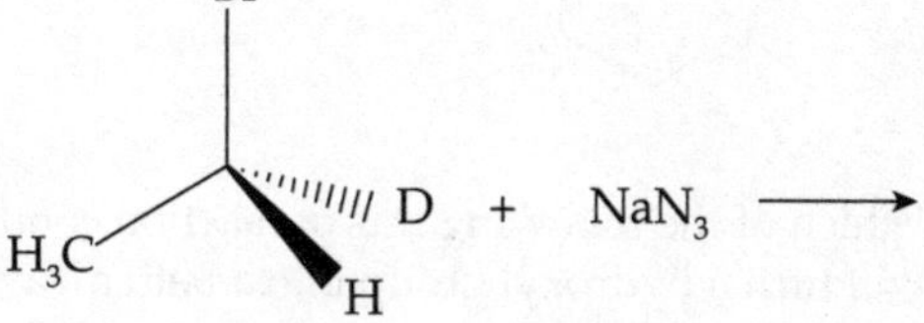

(E)

+ ⟶

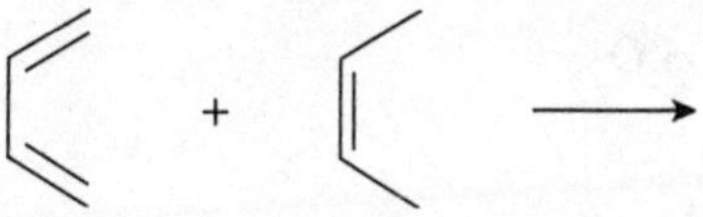

BrCH$_2$CH$_3$ + Mg → MgBrCH$_2$CH$_3$

134. Of the following choices, which would be the best choice of solvents in which to conduct the reaction shown above?

(A) Acetone
(B) Acetonitrile
(C) Diethyl ether
(D) Methanol
(E) Ethyl acetate

GO ON TO THE NEXT PAGE.

135. Which of the following compounds would NOT become partially deuterated upon treatment with NaOD and D_2O?

(A)

(B) $EtNH_2$

(C) Ph–O–Me

(D) ~~~SH

(E) ~~~CO_2H

136. Which of the following sets of reaction conditions will turn a hydroxyl group into a better leaving group?

(A) KOH, H_2O_2

(B) Cl–$SiMe_3$

(C)

Cl—C(=O)—CH_3

(D)

—S(=O)(=O)—Cl , [pyridine]

(E) HS~~~SH, NaOH

137. Predict the shape of the molecule ClF_3 based on VSEPR theory.

(A) Trigonal planar
(B) Pyramidal
(C) Seesaw
(D) T-shaped
(E) Linear

138. Which of the following does NOT describe an atomic orbital where $l = 2$?

(A) d_{z^2}
(B) d_{xy}
(C) d_{zy}
(D) d_{yz}
(E) d_{x^2}

139. What is the bond order for the species Cl_2^+?

(A) 0

(B) $\frac{1}{2}$

(C) 1

(D) $1\frac{1}{2}$

(E) 2

140. Lithium nitrate has the calcite structure (rhombohedral $R\bar{3}c$). What is the coordination number of the metal atom?

(A) 2
(B) 4
(C) 5
(D) 6
(E) 8

$$^2_1H + ^1_1H \rightarrow\ ^3_2He + ?$$

141. In the reaction shown above, which of the following is a byproduct of the reaction?

(A) Gamma ray
(B) Proton
(C) Electron
(D) Neutron
(E) Positron

STOP

IF YOU FINISH BEFORE TIME IS CALLED,
YOU MAY CHECK YOUR WORK
ON THIS TEST.

7

GRE Chemistry Practice Test Answers and Explanations

1. **C** To determine hybridization, count the number of groups of electrons around B in BF_3. Recall that every nonbonding pair, single bond, double bond, and triple bond count as just 1 group each. Therefore, the boron atom is surrounded by three groups—i.e., three single bonds and no nonbonding electrons. Since each group of electrons requires an orbital to house them, boron must use up one s-orbital and two p-orbitals in BF_3. Therefore the hybridization of the boron is sp^2, which always leads to trigonal planar geometry.

2. **A** The six strong acids that completely dissociate are HCl, HBr, HI, HNO_3, $HClO_4$, and H_2SO_4 (only the first H in H_2SO_4 is *strong*).

3. **E** At first, the ground-state electron configuration for Cr appears to be [Ar] $4s^2 3d^4$. However, recall that Cr and Cu (and most of the other elements in their families) gain additional stability by promoting a valence s electron to half fill or completely fill their d subshell. So the actual ground state configuration for Cr is [Ar] $4s^1 3d^5$, where each d electron is in its own orbital (Hund's rule). This results in 6 unpaired electrons (choice E).

4. **B** Reducing agents readily lose electrons. Reducing agents are identifiable because they tend to consist entirely of elements with low electronegativities. $LiAlH_4$, also abbreviated *LAH*, is the best choice and happens to be one of the best reducing agents known (choice B).

5. **C** Ionization energy is a periodic trend that increases "up and to the right" on the periodic table. The element closest to the top right is Cl (choice C).

6. **A** Hydroboration/oxidation of an alkene results in the formation of the anti-Markovnikov (less substituted) alcohol.

7. **D** Epimers are stereoisomers that differ at one and only one stereocenter.

8. **C** The term "exo" is used for bicyclic systems to denote whether a substituent on a bridge is on the side of the smaller bridge. "Endo" refers to a substituent on a bridge that is on the side of the larger bridge.

9. **B** First of all, potential resonance structures must have the correct overall charge. Since nitrobenzene has an overall charge of 0, we can eliminate choices D (overall –1) and E (overall –1). Information in the question reminds us that electrophilic addition at the *para* position is unfavorable for nitrobenzene. Keeping in mind that by definition, electrophilic addition involves the addition of an atom or a group of atoms that have some positive charge character, the resonance structure for choice B leads to highly unfavorable positive-positive charge repulsion at the para position. Therefore choice B is the best choice.

10. **D** Ozonolysis cleaves double bonds and oxidizes the carbons that were participating in double bonds into aldehydes/ketones. We can eliminate choices A, B, and C. During ozonolysis, stereochemistry is preserved in the rest of the molecule. Therefore, if the absolution configuration of the chiral center in the original molecule is S, then it must also be S in the ozonolysis product (choice D).

11. **A** In this reaction, the nucleophilic (having some negative charge) nitrogen atom attacks the first carbon in ethyl iodide and displaces the iodide. We can eliminate choices B and E because this N is not an electrophile (having some positive charge); it's a nucleophile. There are no radicals (unpaired electrons) present anywhere in this reaction, so we can also eliminate choice C. Choice D, elimination, requires

the loss of at least two atoms and the formation of a new pi bond—and that didn't happen (eliminate choice D). This reaction is just a S_N2 reaction, where the N is the nucleophile and iodide is the leaving group. Note that in the end, N carries a +1 formal charge because it becomes a quaternary amine after forming the new bond with the ethyl group. Choice A is the correct choice.

12. **E** Acylium ions are formed when one of the two single bonds of a carbonyl is heterolytically cleaved. This is observed most often when an acid halide is dehalogenated with a Lewis acid, such as AlX_3 or FeX_3. Choice E is the answer. We can eliminate choices A, B, and C because they are carboxylic acid derivative reactions that all proceed through an sp^3 hybridized tetrahedral intermediate, not via the sp hybridized acylium intermediate. Choice E is decarboxylation, which proceeds via a concerted intramolecular proton/electron transfer.

13. **C** Potassium hydroxide is very hygroscopic, and its weight is difficult to determine accurately. This is why KOH solutions for weak acid/strong base titrations are always "standardized."

14. **D** The key to this answer is the cyclic nature of the experiment. A linear voltage ramp is applied between t_0 and t_1. Between t_1 and t_2 the potential is brought back to the starting value. None of the other graphs show a cyclic potential.

15. **C** According to the Henderson-Hasselbalch equation, when pH = pK_a, [HA] = [A^-]. Hence, a buffer is best able to resist changes in pH ranges near its pK_a.

16. **A** Lewis Acids are molecules/ions that can accept a pair of nonbonding electrons to form a covalent bond. Not surprisingly, molecules/ions that contain an atom without an octet are good Lewis acids. The only choice that has an atom without an octet (or bitet in the case of H) is the carbocation in choice A.

17. **D** Recall that ΔG and $\Delta G°$ are related by the expression $\Delta G = \Delta G° + RT\ln Q$. When Q is 1, ΔG equals $\Delta G°$ (because ln 1 = 0 and the right side of the equation drops out). Here, since $Q = [B]/[A]$, the condition where [B] = [A] gives $\Delta G = \Delta G°$ (choice D).

18. **E** Ignore "very fast"—it has nothing to do with getting the answer. Rate law is defined as rate = k[reactants]x. For a bimolecular, or second-order, reaction, the rate law takes the form rate = k[reactants]2. Keeping in mind that all rates must have units of "concentration over time," the only rate constant, k, that would give this is choice E. Note that choices B, C, and D would be rate constants for first order, third order, and zeroeth order reactions, respectively.

19. **D** Starting with the familiar form for kinetic energy, $K = \frac{1}{2}mv^2$ (where m = mass and v = linear velocity), we can make a few simple substitutions to arrive at the expression for a rigid rotator. The velocity of a rotating particle has units of radians/second and is called angular velocity (ω). This is related to linear velocity by the following expression: $v = r\omega_{rot}$ (where r is the radius of rotation). The moment of inertia (I) is given by $I = mr^2$. Using simple algebraic substitution, we arrive at $K = \frac{1}{2}I\omega^2$.

20. **C** An intensive property is one which is independent of the sample size. Of the properties listed, mass (b) and volume (a) are clearly not intensive because they are measures of size. Energy (d) is proportional to size, so it is also not intensive. Hence, of the properties listed, only temperature is intensive.

21. **E** Both are statements of the first law of thermodynamics.

22. **A** The expression $\ln k = \ln A - \dfrac{E_a}{RT}$ can easily be rearranged to the more familiar $k = Ae^{\frac{-E_a}{RT}}$. Both expressions give a linear plot of $\ln k$ versus $\dfrac{1}{T}$, which is the empirical observation that underlies the Arrhenius equation.

23. **B** The Bohr model relies on two assumptions: First, the force holding the electron in a circular orbit around the nucleus is supplied by the electrostatic attraction between the proton and the electron: $\dfrac{e^2}{4\pi\varepsilon_0 r^2} = \dfrac{mv^2}{r}$. Second, angular momentum is quantized: $mvr = n\hbar$, $n = 1, 2, 3 \dots$ Combining these assumptions gives B.

24. **C** Like the Born-Oppenheimer approximation, the Frank-Condon principle states that because nuclei are so much more massive than electrons, electronic motion is almost instantaneous relative to nuclear motion. This allows us to calculate the probabilities (and hence, intensities) of vibronic transitions from the individual electronic and vibrational transitions.

25. **D** The complete Schrodinger equation for the He atom includes three terms, two of which are hydrogenic Hamiltonians and one of which accounts for the interaction of the two electrons with each other. It is this third term that makes an exact solution impossible.

26. **A** By definition, when ΔG is less than zero (or negative), that process is spontaneous. Therefore, choice A is the correct choice. ΔG greater than zero (or positive) indicates that the forward process is nonspontaneous, and that the reverse process would be spontaneous. $\Delta G = 0$ indicates the system is at equilibrium.

27. **A** P (atm)

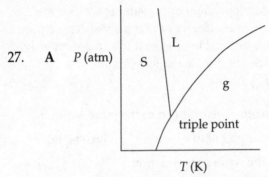

This is easiest by reasoning that the solid is favored at high pressure and low temperature, the liquid is intermediate, and the gas is favored at low pressure and high temperature.

28. **D** Spectroscopic methods always use light (electromagnetic radiation) to elucidate information about the structure of a molecule. Therefore we can eliminate NMR (radio waves), IR (infrared), UV-Vis (UV and visible), and X-ray diffraction (X-rays), leaving gas chromatography (choice D).

29. **B** For any electrochemical or electrolytic cell, <u>o</u>xidation occurs at the <u>a</u>node and <u>r</u>eduction occurs at the <u>c</u>athode (vowels and consonants stay together). So reaction (1), which is an oxidation, must occur at the anode. We can eliminate choices A, C, and D. It is very unlikely that this process occurs in the vapor phase because ions have an incredibly low vapor pressure at standard conditions; thus choice E is unlikely.

30. **A** Since the question indicates that the gas is expanding (i.e., pressure is decreasing during this process), the gas must be doing work on the surroundings. Therefore, the answer must be a positive number. We can eliminate choices D and E. The exact solution is:

$$V_1 = \frac{nRT}{P_1} = \frac{(1 \text{ mol})\left(0.08206 \dfrac{\text{L} \cdot \text{atm}}{\text{mol} \cdot \text{K}}\right)(100\,\text{K})}{100 \text{ atm}} = 0.0821 \text{ L}$$

$$V_2 = 10V_1 = (0.0821 \text{ L})(10) = 0.821 \text{ L}$$

$$\text{Work} = W = -P_{\text{ext}}\Delta V = -(1.0 \text{ atm})(0.821 - 0.0821)$$

$$= 0.739 \text{ L} \bullet \text{atm}$$

31. **E** A single scan gave a signal-to-noise ratio of 3. Averaging n scans increases the ratio by a factor of the square root of n. In this case, $n = 36$, the square root of 36 is 6, and 6 times 3 = 18, the signal-to-noise ratio of one scan, so the answer is E.

32. **B** Looking at the reaction, 6 Ca atoms are present in the reactants. Therefore, 6 $CaSiO_3$ must present as products (choice B).

33. **A** At the equivalence point, exactly the right amount of titrant has been added to the sample to completely neutralize both compounds into their respective conjugates. Recall the conjugate rules: 1) the conjugates of *strong* acids and bases are neutral, 2) the conjugate acid of a *weak* base is acidic, and 3) the conjugate base of a weak acid is basic. Therefore, at the equivalence point, only a tritation between a strong acid and a strong base will have pH = 7 (choice A).

34. **B** The amino group directs to the ortho and para positions due to resonance and makes the aromatic ring much more electron-rich, which is strongly activating.

35. **A** β-Keto esters decarboxylate upon hydrolysis by loss of CO_2 from the carboxylic acid intermediate.

36. **A** *N*-Bromosuccinimide is a good source of Br• and monobrominates the allylic position of alkenes. It does not add across alkenes.

37. **D** In the formation of a ketal (the aldehyde version is called an *acetal*) two equivalents of alcohol are added to the carbonyl, one after another. No carbon-carbon bonds are formed or broken. So we can eliminate choices A, B, C, and E because they indicate alteration to the carbon skeleton. Choice D is correct because an intermediate of ketals is the hemiketal (meaning half-ketal) which is a functional group recognized by a carbon having both an -OH and -OR group.

38. **C** Two substituents are said to be geminal if they are on the same carbon atom; this eliminates choice A. Two substituents are said to be vicinal if they are on adjacent carbon atoms, which eliminates choice B. The allylic position is one carbon removed from an alkene, and the acetylenic position is that of the carbon atom of a $C \equiv C$ triple bond. The indicated H atom, which is attached to the carbon atom of a $C = C$ double bond is in the vinylic position.

39. **B** Radicals, like carbocations, are electron deficient. Inductive effects involving neighboring carbon atoms can stabilize electron deficient carbons. Therefore, the more carbon substituents that are directly bonded to the radical carbon, the more stable that radical will be (choice B).

40. **B** The radical cation of 2-hexanone is likely to fragment in a mass spectrometer as illustrated below:

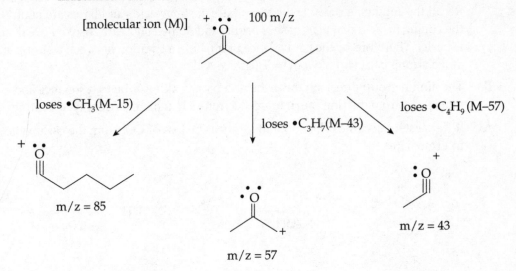

41. **B** The bonding is most ionic in CsF since the difference in electronegativity between Cs and F is greatest.

42. **C** Ligands are ranked in the spectrochemical series according to how much they tend to increase the splitting of orbitals, D. Since CO is a very strong field (low spin) ligand relative to the others, we can eliminate choices A and B. Since iodide is a very weak field (high spin) ligand, the correct choice is C.

43. **C** Spinel structures are usually adopted by compounds with the formula $M^{II}M_2^{III}O_4$.

44. **D** The electron count for each complex is given below, using the covalent method.

$H_2 Fe(CO)_4$		Cp_2Os		$(PMe_3)_3 Co(Me)_2Br$	
2H	$2e^-$	2Cp	$10e^-$	$3PMe_3$	$6e^-$
Fe	$8e^-$	Os	$8e^-$	Co	$9e^-$
4CO	$8e^-$		$18e^-$	2Me	$2e^-$
	$18e^-$			Br	$1e^-$
					$18e^-$

$(PPh_3)_2 Ir(CO)Cl$		$W(CO)_3(PEt_3)_2Cl_2$	
2 PPh$_3$	$4e^-$	W	$6e^-$
Ir	$9e^-$	3 CO	$6e^-$
CO	$2e^-$	2PEt$_3$	$4e^-$
Cl	$1e^-$	2Cl	$2e^-$
	$16e^-$		$18e^-$

45.   E   Given that the MW of AgCl is 143.4 g/mol, the number of moles of AgCl precipitated is:

$$\text{Moles AgCl} = \frac{5.70g}{143.4g/mol}$$

$$= 0.040 \text{ moles}$$

Since the molar ratio of Ag^+ in AgCl is 1, the number of moles of Ag^+ in the original solution was also 0.040. Therefore the concentration of the original solution was:

$$\text{Molarity } Ag^+ = \frac{\text{moles } Ag^+}{\text{Volume (L)}}$$

$$= \frac{\text{moles } Ag^+}{\text{Volume (L)}}$$

$$= 0.40 \ M \text{ (choice E)}$$

46.   A   The ionic strength of a solution is given by $\mu = \frac{1}{2}\left(c_1 z_1^{\ 2} + c_2 z_2^{\ 2} + ...c_n z_n^{\ 2}\right)$, where c_i is the concentration of the ith species and z_i is the charge on that species. For this solution,

$$c_{Na} = 0.05 + 0.04 = 0.09M$$
$$\left(z_{Na^+}\right)^2 = \left(1\right)^2 = 1$$

$$c_{Cl} = 0.05M \qquad\qquad c_{SO_4^{2-}} = 0.02M$$
$$\left(z_{Cl^-}\right)^2 = \left(-1\right)^2 = 1 \qquad \left(z_{SO_4^{2-}}\right)^2 = \left(-2\right)^2 = 4$$

Plugging in, we get

$$\mu = \frac{1}{2}\left(0.09 + 0.05 + 0.08\right)M$$
$$\mu = 0.11 \ M$$

47.   D   In polarography, the current is measured as a function of the potential of the working electrode. For example, cyclic voltammetry is a polarographic technique. Redox chemistry is relevant here, whereas polarity of the molecule (answers I and III) is not.

48.   **C**   Interferometers are used for Fourier transform techniques. Gas chromatography never gives data that can be interpreted by an interferometer. The other detectors are commonly used with GCs.

49.   **E**   Of the choices listed, only a Gouy balance may be used to measure magnetic susceptibilities. The other common means is the Faraday method.

50.   **E**   The electron counts for all of the choices are given below. $V(CO)_6$ is predicted to be the most reactive of these compounds since it has only 17 electrons.

$Cr(CO)_6$	
Cr	$6e^-$
6 CO	$12e^-$
	$18e^-$

$Fe(CO)_5$	
Fe	$8e^-$
5 CO	$10e^-$
	$18e^-$

$Mn_2(CO)_{10}$	
2 Mn	$14e^-$
10 CO	$20e^-$
Mn–Mn	$2e^-$
	$36e^-$

(or $18e^-$/Mn)

$Co_2(CO)_8$	
2 Co	$18e^-$
8 CO	$16e^-$
Co–Co	$2e^-$
	$36e^-$

(or $18e^-$/Co)

$V(CO)_6$	
V	$5e^-$
6 CO	$12e^-$
	$17e^-$

51.   **E**   Only C_{6h} contains an inversion center (i). Listed below are all the symmetry elements present in each of the point groups listed.

C_{4v}: E, $2C_4$, C_z, $2\sigma_v$, $2\sigma_d$

C_s: E, σ_h

T_d: E, $8C_3$, $3C_2$, $6C_4$, $6\sigma_d$

D_{2d}: E, $2S_4$, C_z, $2C_z^1$, $2\sigma_d$

C_{6h}: E, C_6, C_3, C_2, C_3^2, C_6^5, i, S_3^5, S_6^5, σ_n, S_6, S_3

52. **B** *trans*-$(PPh_3)_4RuH_2$ will have only one ^{31}P NMR resonance since all four PPh_3 groups are equivalent.

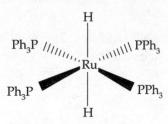

53. **C** Electron affinity is the energy released when an atom gains one additional electron. Therefore, choice C is the correct answer.

54. **E** Molecules are subject to Jahn-Teller distortions if they are nonlinear molecules in an electronically degenerate state. Distortion occurs to lower symmetry and remove the degeneracy and hence lower the energy. Since Ni^0 is d^{10}, it cannot undergo a Jahn-Teller distortion.

55. **A** Choices B, C, D, and E are all true statements. Choice A is a false statement—i.e., the vapor pressure of a substance only depends upon: 1) that substance's temperature, and 2) mole fraction when in solution (see the colligative property of VP depression and Raoult's Law).

56. **B** Choices A and D are best thought of in Brönsted-Lowry acidity terms. Choices C and E are best thought of in Lewis acidity terms. Choice B, in which oxide transfer occurs, is best thought of according to the Lux-Flood definition.

57. **A** Choices B, C, D, and E describe polyhedral polyboron-hydride cage compounds. The prefix *quadro*- describes four atoms bound in a quadrangle (e.g., a square).

58. **D** In nucleophilic aromatic substitution, the incoming nucleophile always attacks an aromatic carbon atom that is substituted with a good leaving group. This is in sharp contrast to electrophilic aromatic substitution, where the incoming electrophile attacks an unsubstituted carbon atom of the aromatic framework.

59. **B** Hückels' rule tells us that an aromatic compounds must have a cyclic array of *p* orbitals and $4n + 2$ π electrons. All of the choices except B fit these qualifications.

60. **E** S_N2 reactions are stereospecific, always proceeding via backside attack. Therefore, only one stereospecific product will be obtained (we can eliminate choice C). Although it is often overlooked, it is possible for the attacking nucleophile to be identical to a group already present on the chiral center, thus rendering that carbon achiral. Choice A neglects this possibility; eliminate it. Finally, while it is true that S_N2 involves inversion at the point of substitution, this DOES NOT mean that R automatically becomes S, and S automatically becomes R. Recall that absolution configurations are based upon group prioritization, and since one group leaves and a new group arrives, it is possible for the prioritization to change in a way that R stays R or S stays S. Therefore, choice E is the best choice.

61. **E** Choice E is achiral since it has an internal plane of symmetry (meso).

62. **D** PH_3 is not an electrophile since, like ammonia, it has a lone pair (on P). The other choices are all electron-deficient.

63. **D** The first step is nucleophilic addition. This reaction is an example of a double-nucleophilic aromatic substitution.

64. **E**

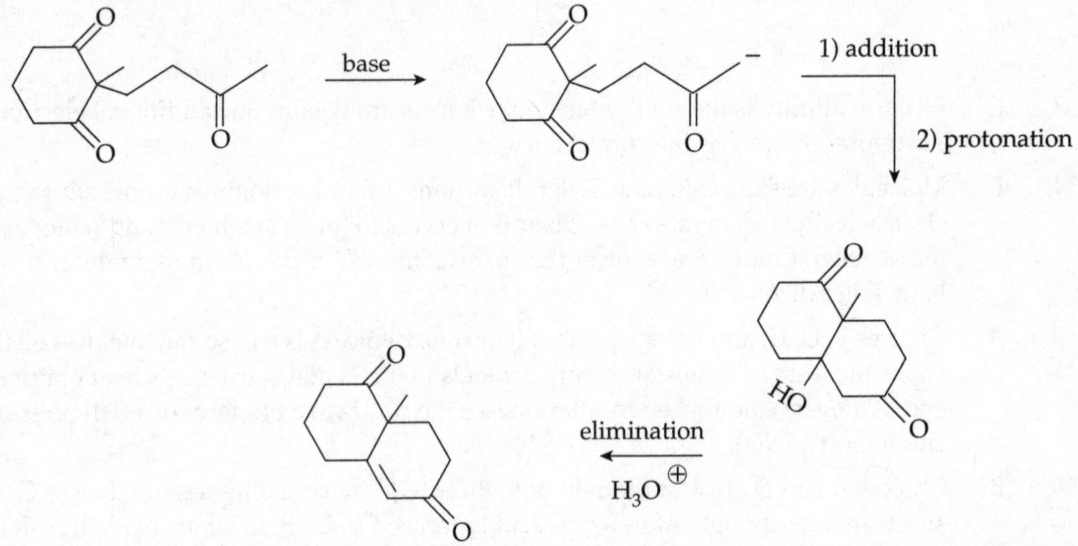

base → 1) addition 2) protonation

elimination $H_3O^{\oplus}$

This reaction condition drives an intramolecular aldol condensation resulting in a new ring, a process called a Robinson Annulation. In cases where many α-hydrogens and carbonyls are present in the same molecule, such as here, Robinson Annulations favor formation of the least strained ring systems. Therefore, we can eliminate choices A and B because of their high ring strain. The most likely course of events is:

1. Abstraction of a α-hydrogen from the side chain methyl group.

2. Attack by the resulting carbanion on one of the carbonyl carbons in the ring (they're identical), forming a new six-membered ring and an OH functional group.

3. Dehydration/elimination of the OH forming a double bond that is conjugated to a carbonyl for additional stability.

65. **B** The ground-state electronic configuration of He_2^+ is given by $\left(1\sigma_{1s}\right)^2\left(1\sigma_{1s}^*\right)^1$. There are two bonding electrons and one antibonding electron. Bond order is defined as $BO = \frac{1}{2}$ (# of bonding electrons – # of antibonding electrons). For He_2^+, this is $BO = \frac{1}{2}(2-1) = \frac{1}{2}$.

66. **C** Answer A can be eliminated because no reaction would occur if concentrations of reactants were constant. Answer B can be eliminated because the steady-state approximation applies to kinetics, not thermodynamics. Answer D can be eliminated because the intermediate can build up in the situation described. Answer C is correct because if the concentration of the intermediate is close to zero, it can be assumed to be constant—simplifying the algebra of the corresponding rate equation.

67. **A** This is the definition of a Hermitian operator.

68. **B** Koopman's theorem allows us to use the same orbitals to calculate the energies of both the neutral atom and the ion. The ionization energy is calculated by subtracting the HF energy of the atom from the exact energy of the ion.

69. **E** The coulombic force between two charged particles is defined as $\text{Force} = \dfrac{e^2}{4\pi_0 r^2}$.

70. **C** The Born-Oppenheimer approximation was first used to solve the Schröedinger equation for H_2. For this two-nucleus, two-electron system, the equation can be simplified by noting that electrons move much more quickly than the nuclei can respond. Hence, it was assumed that nuclear motion can be neglected.

71. **C** A beam of silver atoms passed through a nonhomogeneous magnetic field was split into two components corresponding to $2l + 1 = 2$, $l = \dfrac{1}{2}$. This proved the existence of spin.

72. **E** Analysis of molecular vibration assumes that a chemical bond is analogous to two weights connected by a spring. The classical approximation is termed "the harmonic oscillator," and its differential equations can be applied to the molecular situation.

73. **B** This is a van Hoff plot, which is used to determine ΔH° and ΔS° from thermodynamic data. Starting with $\Delta G^\circ = RT \ln K = \Delta H^\circ - T\Delta S^\circ$, we can easily rearrange to $\ln K = \dfrac{-\Delta H^\circ}{RT} + \dfrac{\Delta S^\circ}{R}$.

    If $\ln K$ is plotted vs. $\dfrac{1}{T}$, the slope will be $\dfrac{-\Delta H^\circ}{R}$.

74. **C** According to the relation $\Delta G = \Delta H - T\Delta S$, ΔG can be negative (spontaneous) for negative ΔS only if ΔH has a larger negative value (choice C).

75. **C** To operate on the eigenfunction e^{ikx} with the operator $P_x = -i\hbar\dfrac{\partial}{\partial x}$, first take the partial derivative of the eigenfunction with respect to x. This gives $\dfrac{\partial}{\partial x}\left(e^{ikx}\right) = ike^{ikx}$.

Multiplying by $-i\hbar$ (as dictated by the operator) gives

$$(-i\hbar)(ik)e^{ikx} = -i^2\hbar k e^{ikx}$$
$$= (-1)(-1)\hbar k e^{ikx}$$
$$= \hbar k e^{ikx}$$

Hence the eigenvalue is $\hbar k$.

76. **B** The general wave function for a particle in a one-dimensional box is given by:
$\lambda(x) = B\sin\left(\dfrac{n\pi x}{a}\right)$, where B is a constant, a is the length of the box, and n is the energy level. The probability density is given by $\lambda^2(x)$, which looks like the graphs in B. Furthermore, choices A and C are erroneous because there is no such thing as a negative probability.

77. **D** Retention time in GC is governed by the equilibrium of the analyte between the solid and gas phases of the column. Increasing the column length (I) and percent stationary phase (II) both increase the amount of solid phase and concomitantly the amount of time the analyte can spend interacting with the solid (i.e., not moving down the column). Increasing the column temperature makes the analyte more volatile; hence it spends more time in the vapor phase. This means that the analyte will have a smaller retention time.

78. **D** Although A and E are both true, neither is the "common ion effect." The common ion effect is a direct extention of LeChatelier's principle. Hence, the answer is D.

79. **B** Intermolecular forces are forces between molecules, not within molecules. (If the question had been asked about intramolecular forces, C would have been correct.) To answer this question, you have to know that benzene is a liquid at room temperature. Clearly, the forces cannot be repulsive (eliminating E), or the liquid would not have any cohesive properties. In general, the three main classes of intermolecular forces are: 1) ionic forces (commonly called ionic bonds, even though no appreciable electron sharing is occurring), 2) dipole forces (which include hydrogen bonding), and 3) London dispersion forces. Benzene primarily experiences London dispersion forces.

80. **E** At pH = 3.13, pH = pK_a, and H_3A should be roughly the same concentration as H_2A^-. Since pH 2.0 is roughly 1 unit lower than 3.13, H_3A:H_2A^- should be about 10:1. Hence, H_3A is the dominant species in solution.

81. **E** PBr_3 reacts with alcohols and carboxylic acids to make bromoalkanes and acid bromides, respectively. It does not undergo electrophilic aromatic substitution reactions.

82. **E** In basic aqueous solution, excess halogens react with methyl ketones in a process called a *haloform reaction*. The organic products are a carboxylate salt and haloform molecule having the molecular formula CHX_3. In particular, iodoform reactions are used as quick diagnostic tests for the presence of methyl ketones because iodoform itself, CHI_3, is a yellow solid and its formation is easily recognizable.

83. **D** The spectrum indicates six signals; in other words, the presence of six types of equivalent carbons. Examination of the answer choices reveals that choices B and E only have five kinds of carbons, therefore we can eliminate them. Of the remaining choices, choice D is the best possibility because of the presence of the down-field signal at about 200ppm, which is indicative of a carbonyl carbon.

84. **C** The reactions of R–OH groups with dimethyl sulfate is a simple substitution reaction where oxygen acts as the nucleophile, and Me_2SO_4 is a source of $^+CH_3$.

85. **E** Carboxylic acids are the most acidic organic functional group. Therefore, choices A, B, and C can be eliminated. Phenols are also weak acids, so choice E is the answer.

86. **D** $LiAlH_4$ is a strong source of 4 equivalents of H^- (hydride). Therefore, 0.5 equivalents will provide two equivalents of hydride, which will reduce the ester to an alcohol via an aldehyde.

87. **C** *Amination* is the addition/formation of an amine group, and since there are no Ns anywhere in this reaction, we can eliminate choice A. *Alkylation* is the addition of a new carbon fragment via carbon-carbon bond formation. No new C–C bonds were formed here, so we can eliminate choice B. The oxidation numbers of all atoms remain unchanged during the reaction, therefore we can eliminate choices D and E. In *acylation*, a carbonyl with an R group is added to a molecule (in this case, an alcohol).

88. **B** This reaction, called a Cope rearrangement, involves redistribution of six electrons (4π and 2σ) as shown below.

89. **D** In a row (period), atomic radius decreases going left to right. In a column (group), atomic radius increases going down. Therefore choice D is the largest.

90. **B** For neon, L = 0, S = 0, and J = 0. Therefore, the ground-state term symbol is $^1S_0$.

91. **D** Since these are all ionic compounds, electrostatic forces can be assumed to be entirely responsible for the cohesive forces on the lattice. According to Coulomb's Law:

$$F = Kq_1q_2/r^2 \text{ where Energy} = Kq_1q_2/r$$

Since the charges for all of the ion pairs, q_1 and q_2, given in the choices are ± 1, it is the internuclear distant, r, of each ion pair that is the determinant factor. According to the equations above, the smaller the r, the greater the energy. So using the periodic trend in atomic/ion size, LiF (choice D) is the ion pair with the smallest internuclear distance.

92. **E** Facial (fac) stereochemistry is used to denote three ligands that share a face of an octahedron.

93. **B** NH_3 is the strongest base among the choices by any of the common definitions. According to the solvent system definition, a base is a species that increases the concentration of the characteristic anion.

94. **D** Only choice D is not a normal vibrational mode, since it does not preserve the center of mass of the molecule.

95. **A** Foremost, isotope substitution will affect all molecular properties that are mass dependent. Because reduced mass by definition is mass dependent, choices B and D would be affected. According to Graham's Law, the rate of effusion of a gas is inversely proportional to the square root of the MW (choice C is affected). And because of differing numbers of nucleons, isotopes often have different nuclear magnetic spins. Finally, because nuclear masses are always massive compared to an electron, differences in isotopic nuclear mass generally have a nondetectable effect on electronic transitions.

96. **B** As rotation increases, the centrifugal force causes the bond to stretch. This results in the uneven spacing between lines of a rotational spectrum.

97. **C** Positron emission is a type of beta decay. During beta decay, nuclear mass remains approximately constant. Therefore, choice C is the only possible answer. The rigorous solution is:

$$^{18}_{9}F \rightarrow \, ^{18}_{8}O + \, ^{0}_{+1}e$$

Conserving mass (superscript) and charge (subscript) gives choice C.

98. **C** The sample absorbs in the orange-red region, so the sample transmits blue.

99. **E** No real gas is ideal. All real gases have fractional molecular volumes and experience intermolecular forces—violations of the basic assumptions that go into the ideal gas law. Therefore, while the ideal gas law can provide numbers that aren't too far off for many gases under many conditions, it never provides an exact description (choice E).

100. **E** Choice A can be ruled out since both reagents are strong nucleophiles and bases. In choice B, the electrophile is an acylation agent, not a methylation agent. Choice C would produce ethylamine, not methylamine. Choice D would produce a mixture of $MeNH_2$, Me_2NH, Me_3N, and Me_4N^+I. Only choice E, reduction of methyl azide, will give a good yield of $MeNH_2$.

101. **B** The $C \equiv N$ functional group is referred to either with the prefix *cyan* or suffix *nitrile* (choice B).

102. **C**   The Dieckmann condensation is an intramolecular version of the Claisen condensation. Choice C correctly depicts the product.

103. **A**   Valine $\left(\text{HO} \overset{\overset{\text{O}}{\|}}{} \text{NH}_2\right)$ can form a peptide (amide) bond with another valine to form val-val, choice A.

104. **A**   Direct conversion of an aldehyde or ketone into an alkene can be accomplished via a Wittig reaction. The key reagent in a Wittig reaction is an organophosphorus *y* reagent given in choice A.

105. **B**   Specific rotation is determined by the following equation: $\left[\alpha\right]_D^{20} = \dfrac{\alpha}{l \cdot c}$

where $\left[\alpha\right]_D^{20}$ is the specific rotation, α is the observed optical rotation (°), l is the sample path length (dm), and c is the concentration (g/mL).

106. **E**   The key to the question is recognizing which functional group is NOT stable in aqueous solution. Choices A and B are stable in water and the key functional groups in proteins and fats, respectively. Choices C and D are also stable in water—i.e., they are the functional groups for the C-terminus in polypeptides, fatty acids, and a host of important metabolites such as acetate, acetic acid, citrate/citric acid, and lactate/lactic acid. However, acid chlorides, like acid anhydrides, immediately react with water, often explosively (choice E).

107.   **A**   This is a bit of a trick question. Le Châtelier's principle states increasing pressure shifts an equilibrated system to the side with fewer gas molecules (fewer is based upon stoichiometry). So choice C looks attractive, but it is wrong because Le Châtelier's principle does not apply when pressure is increased by the addition of an inert gas—only changing pressure due to changing volume applies. For this special case, the equilibrium is not disturbed in any way (choice A).

108.   **E** CO_2 dissolves in water to form carbonic acid, H_2CO_3.

109.   **C** PCl_5 has a phosphorus atom surrounded by five Cl atoms and no nonbonding pairs of electrons. Therefore, P's hybridization must be sp^3d (one orbital is required per group of electrons), and sp^3d hybridization always gives trigonal bipyramid geometry (choice C).

110.   **A**   The strong field (Td) and weak field (Td) splittings are shown below with five electrons.

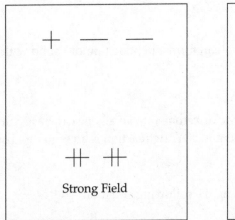

Strong Field

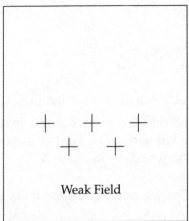

Weak Field

111.   **C**   According to the reverse reaction, HSO_4^- is accepting an H^+. Therefore, it is acting as a Lowry-Bronsted base (choice C).

112.   **E**   The *lanthanide* or *rare earth* elements are metals, and therefore will not be found with negative charges or negative oxidation numbers. Eliminate choices B and D. These metals are most commonly found in the +3 oxidation state (choice E).

113.   **A**   Cell diagrams are read as:

Anode | Anodic Solution | Cathodic Solution | Cathode

For any electrochemical or electrolytic cell, **o**xidation occurs at the **a**node and **r**eduction occurs at the **c**athode (vowels and consonants stay together). Therefore, the correct choice must be an oxidation. We can eliminate choices B and C. We can also eliminate choices D and E because Cl is never allowed to enter the anodic side of the cell. Therefore, choice A is the correct answer.

114. **D** This is a simple application of the ideal gas law: $PV = nRT$. If P_1 is 150 torr and $V_1 = 300$ mL, $T_1 = T_2$, $n_1 = n_2$, and R is constant, $\dfrac{P_2}{P_1} = \dfrac{V_2}{V_1}$. $\therefore P_2 = \left(\dfrac{V_2}{V_1}\right)(P_1)$.

115. **C** For division, all absolute uncertainties are first converted into relative uncertainties (percents). Then these are analyzed using

$$\left(\frac{\Delta d}{d}\right)^2 = \left(\frac{\Delta m}{m}\right)^2 + \left(\frac{\Delta V}{V}\right)^2$$

$$\frac{\Delta d}{d} = \sqrt{\left(\frac{\Delta m}{m}\right)^2 + \left(\frac{\Delta V}{V}\right)^2} \quad \frac{\Delta d}{d} = \sqrt{\left(\frac{0.1}{10}\right)^2 + \left(\frac{0.08}{8}\right)^2}$$

$$\frac{\Delta d}{d} = \sqrt{(0.01)^2 + (0.01)^2} \quad \frac{\Delta d}{d} = \sqrt{2 \times 10^{-4}}$$

$$\frac{\Delta d}{d} = 1.4 \times 10^{-2}$$

and the percent uncertainty is 1.4%.

116. **B** This answer encapsulates the definition of a confidence interval.

117. **B** The *partition coefficient* is defined as the ratio $[A]_{solvent\ \#1}/[A]_{solvent\ \#2}$ at equilibrium. In this case, the partition coefficient would be written as $[A]_{Et2O}\ /\ [A]_{aqueous} = 4$. Considering that the volumes of both solvents are identical, the ratio of concentrations and numbers of moles are the same. So the key to this problem is recognizing that if the number of A in ET_2O is 4 times greater than in H_2O, then one-fifth, or only 20% (not 25%), of the A remains in the H_2O in each extraction. Therefore,

$$[A]_{Final\ H_2O} = 0.1\ M_{Initial\ H_2O} \times \frac{1}{5}_{first\ extraction} \times \frac{1}{5}_{second\ extraction}$$

$$= 0.004\ (choice\ B)$$

118. **D** In principle, there are two ways of expressing the rate of a chemical reaction:

1. *The Normalized Empirical Rate Expression:*

$$\text{Rate} = -(1/\text{coefficient})(d[\text{reactant}]/dt)$$
$$= +(1/\text{coefficients})(d[\text{product}]/dt)$$

2. *The Rate Law:*

$$\text{Rate} = k[\text{reactant 'n'}]^{(\text{n's coefficient in the rate determining step})}$$

For this reaction, the *Normalized Empirical Rate Expression* with respect to NO_3 can be written as

$$\text{Rate} = -(1/1)dNO_3/dt = -dNO_3/dt$$

For the *Rate Law*, only the rate determining—i.e., slowest—step matters, so step 2 and k_2 can be ignored completely. So the Rate Law here is

$$\text{Rate} = k_1[NO_2]^1[NO_3]^1$$

Setting these two rate equations equal to one another and moving the negative sign to the right side gives choice D. Note that choices A and E could have been eliminated in the first place because $[NO_3]$ should decrease as a reactant. Choices A and E lack the negative sign that indicates a decrease with time.

119. **A** $\dfrac{\partial^2 u}{\partial x^2} = \dfrac{1}{v}\dfrac{\partial^2 u}{\partial t^2}$ is the definition of the classical wave equation.

120. **E** According to Le Châtelier's principle, the direction in which an equilibrium is disturbed can be predicted if ΔH_{rx} is known (eliminate choice B). A straightforward way of solving this is to write "HEAT" into the reaction either as a reactant for endothermic reactions or as a product for exothermic reactions. Here, the reaction is exothermic, so

$$A \rightarrow B + C + \text{"HEAT"}$$

Then, since temperature is a measure of "HEAT," we would expect increasing T, or "HEAT" to shift the system to the left. Choice E is the answer.

121. **B** Choice A is an acid-base reaction. Choices C, D, and E show no change in oxidation number. For the reaction shown in answer choice B, the hydrogens in H_2 have an oxidation state of 0, and the chlorine atoms in Cl_2 also have an oxidation state of 0. However, in the product HCl, the hydrogen is +1 and chlorine is –1.

122. **A** The following equation applies: $\Delta S_{vap} = \dfrac{\Delta H_{vap}}{T_b}$, where T_b is the temperature of vaporization in Kelvin. Since the boiling point of H_2O is 373 K, the calculation is:

$$\frac{40.66\ \text{kJ/mol}}{373\ \text{K}} = 109\ \text{J/K}\cdot\text{mol}$$

123. **A** The number of particles N must be an exponent in the equation since entropy is an extensive property and it scales with the number of particles according to the Boltzmann equation, $S = K\ln\Omega$.

124. **A** This is an example of standard addition. The relevant equation is:

$$\frac{[\text{analyte}] \text{ in solution 1}}{[\text{analyte}] \text{ in solution 2}} = \frac{\text{Absorbance of solution 1}}{\text{Absorbance of solution 2}}$$

For solution 1, $\left[Ca^{2+}\right] = \dfrac{(10.00)([Ca^{2+}\text{in milk}]) + (5.00)(1.0 \times 10^{-4} M)}{100}$

$$\left[Ca^{2+}\right] = \frac{10x + 5 \times 10^{-4}}{100} M$$

For solution 2, $\left[Ca^{2+}\right] = \dfrac{(10.00)([Ca^{2+}\text{in milk}])}{100} M$

$$\therefore \frac{10x + 5 \times 10^{-4}}{10x} = \frac{3}{2}$$

$$30x = 20x + 1 \times 10^{-3} M$$

$$10x = 1 \times 10^{-3} M$$

$$x = 1 \times 10^{-3} M$$

125. **D** Recall some fundamental solubility rules:

1. All Group I metal salts and NH_4^+ salts are *soluble*.

2. All NO_3^- salts are *soluble*.

3. All silver, lead, and mercury salts are *insoluble*.

Therefore, addition of Li^+, NH_4^+, or Cs^+ would not produce a precipitate with either acid (eliminate choices A, B, and C). Silver, Ag^+, would form precipitates with both acids (choice E is out). Ba^{2+} is somewhat unique, even among other Group II elements, because $BaCl_2$ is soluble while $BaSO_4$ is not (choice D).

126. **E** Absorption and transmission are always on the *y*-axis in an IR spectrum (eliminate choices B and C). Imagine for a second that *wavenumber* had units of cm; the correct answer would clearly be wavelength. However, in reality, *wavenumber* has units of 1/cm, or 1/wavelength. Remembering that the inverse of wavelength is frequency, choice E must be the best choice.

127. **E** Choices A and B cannot be ionic because they are composed of only one element each. BN (choice D) has a graphite-like structure with covalent bonding between B and N atoms. Although the Si–O bonds in SiO_2 are polar, the $Na^+BH_4^-$ interaction is a purely ionic interaction because BH_4^- has eight valence electrons and cannot accept another covalent bond.

128. **D** Including activities, K_{sp} is defined as $K_{sp} = \left(\delta Cr^{3+}\right)\left[Cr^{3+}\right] \times \left(\delta IO_3^-\right)^3 [IO_3^-]^3$. This is easily arranged to give D.

129. **B** The spectrum indicates 4 signals; in other words, the correct answer must have 4 types of equivalent hydrogens. Examination of the answer choices reveals that choices C, D, and E can be eliminated because they have 2, 5, and 2 types of equivalent hydrogens respectively. Of the remaining choices, the presence of two singlets, a triplet, and a quartet is only consistent with choice B. Note that choice A's spectrum would have two triplets and two quartets.

130. **C** Choice A is a Newman projection.

Choice B is a dashed-wedged-line notation.

Choice C is a Haworth projection.

Choice D is a Fischer projection.

Choice E is a chair notation.

131. **E** Since these are all isomers of one another, the heats of hydrogenation will track with the degree of substitution. The monosubstituted alkene (I) will be the greatest. The *cis*-disubstituted will be greater than the *trans* compound.

132. **D**

Since there is only one site (the alpha methyl group) for tautomerization, the enol/enolate can only form in one place. This makes D the only possible choice.

133. **B** A reaction is regioselective when there are two (or more) possible sites (regions) for reactivity, but one is preferred over the other. Hydroboration is regioselective since it prefers to give the less substituted (not the more substituted) alcohol.

134. **C** Since the product of this reaction is a Grignard reagent, which is a powerful base/nucleophile, an inert solvent of choice must be: 1) aprotic—i.e., have no OH or NH groups, and 2) not susceptible to nucleophilic attack—i.e., have no C's with partial positive charge. Given that the structures of the choices are

$$CH_3CCH_3 \quad\quad CH_3C{\equiv}N \quad\quad (CH_3CH_2)_2O \quad\quad CH_3OH \quad\quad CH_3COCH_2CH_3,$$

(A)   (B)   (C)   (D)   (E)

only diethyl ether, choice C, meets these requirements.

135. **C** Protic hydrogens—i.e., H's bonded to O, S, and/or N—readily exchange with one another. Recall that D, deuterium, is an isotope of H and exchanges just like H. Therefore, this question is just asking which molecule is aprotic. Choice C is the only aprotic molecule given.

136. **D** The usual method for making an –OH group into a better leaving group is to form a tosylate (OTs) group by reacting the alcohol with tosyl chloride (TsCl) and pyridine.

137. **D** ClF_3 will be T-shaped since it has three substituents and two lone pairs.

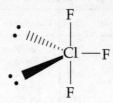

138. **E**   The *d*-orbitals ($l = 2$) are d_{z^2}, d_{xy}, d_{xz}, d_{yz}, and $d_{x^2-y^2}$.

139. **D**   Below are the molecular orbital diagrams for Cl_2 and Cl_2^+.

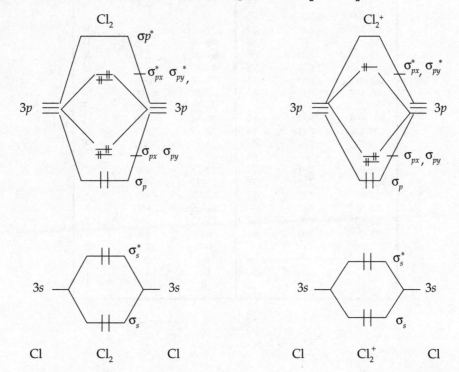

140. **D**   The calcite structure of CO_3^{2-} (carbonate ion) is adopted by many other species, including $MgCO_3$, $FeCO_3$, $LiNO_3$, $NaNO_3$, and YBO_3. The coordination number of the metal ion is 6.

141. **A**   Conserving mass (the superscripts) and charge (the subscripts), we find that helium-3 already accounts for all of the mass and charge of hydrogen-2 and hydrogen-1. Therefore, any additional products must have a mass and charge of 0. Choice A, a photon of light, is the only possibility.

TOTAL SCORE

Raw Score	Scaled Score	%	Raw Score	Scaled Score	%
141	950	99	76–78	690	62
139–140	940	99	73–75	680	60
137–138	930	98	71–72	670	58
135–136	920	97	68–70	660	54
133–134	910	96	65–67	650	52
131–132	900	95	63–64	640	49
			60–62	630	46
129–130	890	94	57–59	620	43
127–128	880	93	54–56	610	40
124–126	870	92	52–53	600	38
121–123	860	90			
119–120	850	89	49–51	590	34
116–118	840	88	46–48	580	31
113–115	830	86	44–45	570	28
111–112	820	85	41–43	560	25
108–110	810	84	38–40	550	22
105–107	800	82	36–37	540	19
			33–35	530	17
103–104	790	80	30–32	520	14
100–102	780	79	28–29	510	12
97–99	770	78	25–27	500	9
95–96	760	76			
92–94	750	74	22–24	490	7
89–91	740	73	20–21	480	6
87–88	730	71	17–19	470	4
84–86	720	69	14–16	460	3
81–83	710	67	12–13	450	2
79–80	700	64	9–11	440	1
			6–8	430	1
			4–5	420	1
			1–3	410	1
			0	400	1

More expert advice from The Princeton Review

Increase your chances of getting into the graduate school of your choice with The Princeton Review. We can help you get higher test scores, make the most informed choices, and make the most of your experience once you get there. We can also help you make the career move that will let you use your skills and education to their best advantage.

Need More?

If you're looking to learn more about how to raise your GRE Chemistry score, you're in the right place. We have helped countless students get into their top-choice grad schools.

One way to increase the number of acceptance letters you get is to raise your test scores. So if you're experiencing some trepidation, consider all your options.

We consistently improve prospective grad school students' scores through our books, classroom courses, private tutoring, and online courses. Call 800-2Review or visit *PrincetonReview.com* for details.

Check out all the ways you can raise your GRE score:
• GRE Classroom Courses
• GRE Online Courses
• GRE Private Tutoring
• *Math Workout for the GRE*
• *Verbal Workout for the GRE*